D0087304

Black Psychology
Third Edition

Black Psychology

Third Edition

Edited by
Reginald L. Jones
Hampton University

Cobb & Henry • Publishers
Berkeley, California

ATS Library
Nyack. NY 10960

Black Psychology, Third Edition

Copyright © 1991 by Reginald L. Jones

All rights reserved. No portion of this book may be reproduced in any form without the written permission of the publisher.

Cobb and Henry Publishers
P. O. Box 4900
Berkeley, California 94704-4900

Cover design by Mark van Bronkhorst

Book design and typesetting by Cragmont Publications

Manufactured in the United States of America

Na'im Akbar. Mental Disorder Among African Americans. *Black Books Bulletin*. Volume 7, 1981. Reprinted by permission of the author and publisher.

Arthur C. Jones. Psychological Functioning in African Americans: A Conceptual Guide for Use in Psychotherapy. *Psychotherapy*, Volume 22, 1985. Reprinted by permission of the author and publisher.

James M. Jones. The Concept of Race in Social Psychology. In *Review of Personality and Social Psychology*, Volume 4, 1983. Copyright 1983 by Sage Publications, Inc. Reprinted by permission of the author and Sage Publications, Inc.

James M. Jones. Racism: A Cultural Analysis of the Problem. In *Prejudice, Discrimination and Racism*, edited by J. F, Dividio and S. L. Gaertner. Copyright 1986 by Academic Press. Reprinted by permission of the author and Academic Press.

Barbara J. Shade. African American Patterns of Cognition. In Barbara J. Shade *Culture Style and the Educative Process*. Copyright 1989 by Charles C Thomas, Publishers. Reprinted by permission of the author and Charles C Thomas, Publishers.

Library of Congress Cataloging-in-Publication Data

Black psychology / edited by Reginald L. Jones. — 3rd ed.
     p.   cm.
   Includes bibliographical references and index.
   ISBN 0-943539-05-6 : $39.95
   1. Afro-Americans—Psychology. I. Jones, Reginald Lanier, 1931- .
E185.625.B58   1991
155.8'496073-dc20   91-18010
                                          CIP

Contents

III. Deconstruction

IV. Reconstruction

V. Applications of Black Perspectives

Fields of Psychology

Counseling and Psychotherapy

Preface

In the preface to the Second Edition of *Black Psychology* (1980) I wrote the following:

> Writings in the first edition pointed to the need to develop a black perspective in our conceptualization, research, and practice. Only rarely was such a perspective actually adopted, and the examples that were given represented only a beginning specification of what the shape of a psychology of black Americans—informed by a black perspective—might look like. There was the feeling, articulated or hinted at in virtually every first edition paper, that there was sufficient uniqueness to the black experience to suggest the development of a black psychology. As an extension of this viewpoint, it was suggested, for example, that education for blacks ought somehow to have objectives and content which more nearly approximated the black experience, and that to be effective in their work, teachers, counselors, and psychotherapists needed to proceed from theoretical perspectives that were more Afrocentric than Eurocentric. Many of the above objectives were accomplished. For example, doctoral dissertations and masters theses are now conducted on topics in black psychology that would have been unthinkable a decade ago, and a generation of black social scientists is being trained with knowledge of black perspectives which supplant or complement conventional viewpoints.

> Given such developments, the content of the second edition of *Black Psychology* will be somewhat different from the first. However, the same structure will be retained, along with several papers, most of which have been updated. To produce an entirely new volume would be to suggest that there was no core of writing and thinking around which the subject matter of black psychology is organized. But there is a core.

> While the structure of the volume has been retained, the treatment has broadened and deepened. Moreover, we are witnessing actual application of concepts that were identified earlier. Thus, while we were content earlier to indicate that white counselors and teachers needed to be sensitive to black lifestyle, language, and behavior, or that tests were discriminatory, we are now able to indicate what is to be learned, what is to be changed, and how. In a number of instances, specific guidelines are provided.

> Little of the current psychological literature on issues of importance to black people has been approached from an articulated

theory-based black perspective. It may be some time before such perspectives are developed and articulated but, in the meantime, some assessment is needed to guide present understanding, action and research. Consequently, a number of critical reviews of important topics in education, counseling, personality, and mental health have been included in the second edition. These reviews should do much to apprise us of where we are, and where we need to go in our theory, intervention, and research activities.

The second edition also gives greater attention to historical perspectives. For example, Guthrie gives an excellent historical perspective of psychology and black Americans, while Franklin presents important information on early black responses to the intelligence testing movement. Significant historical perspectives on counseling are presented by Banks and Jackson. Attention to problems in their historical context has been an area of significant activity since publication of the first edition.

The organization and, to a significant degree, the content, of the third edition are remarkably different from that of the previous editions. Of the forty-one papers in the present edition, twenty-four are entirely new while the remaining papers have been revised, some substantially so.

Because this work is expected to be a resource for advanced students and professionals (in addition to those having their first introduction to the subject), I have opted for inclusiveness in subject matter coverage. That is, authors were encouraged to report their ideas, studies and research in detail rather than cursorily or illustratively. This was done with the idea that the text may be used selectively, so readers can expect solid coverage in any chapter read. But even though the coverage is meant to be comprehensive, there is a point of view represented, usually one that is alternative to many extant notions about psychological dimensions of African American behavior; the reader should be aware, therefore, that this is not a value-free text.

The earlier editions focused on traditional areas of concern,—i.e., personality, education, psychological assessment, and racism, among other topics. These concerns have been retained in the present edition, but they are configured differently. While racism has been retained as a separate topic of concern, as have sections on psychologists and psychology in the community, and perspectives, the present volume is more generic in its organization. Thus the large subheadings are: I. Overview; II. Perspectives; III. Deconstruction; IV. Reconstruction; and V. Applications of Black Perspectives. The latter section (V), gives specific attention to Fields of Psychology, Counseling and Psychotherapy, Psychologists and Psychology in the Community, Racism, and Research.

The Overview, Section I, retains the classic article by Joseph White, "Toward a Black Psychology" and also includes Linda James Myers' article on world view. This article is placed to emphasize the significance of the Afrocentric perspective in the current edition and is intended to inform the readings that follow.

The Perspectives section (II) has been broadened to include the Afrocentric perspective (Akbar), to introduce the humanistic perspective (Jenkins), and to communicate that black psychologists are not a mind on the perspective(s) that should inform and direct African or (Black) psychology (Baldwin). Previous papers on historical (Guthrie), philosophical (Nobles), and behaviorist (Hayes) perspectives are retained.

Section III (Deconstruction) critiques and evaluates the literature and practice in areas of critical importance to African American personality and psychological testing. The first three papers by, respectively, Baldwin, Brown and Hopkins on black self-hatred; by Ward, Banks, and Wilson on delayed gratification; and by Banks, Ward, McQuater and DeBritto on locus of control, critique key constructs that continue to be used to account for the behavior of African Americans in a wide variety of contexts: academic, economic, and employment, to name a few. The evaluation and understanding of this literature, therefore, is critical for students of the African American experience, as is our understanding of the impact of psychological testing on African Americans (paper by Williams and Mitchell).

Section IV is titled Reconstruction. The purpose of the decontruction section was to disassemble a flawed literature on certain constructs that have been applied, perjoratively, to African Americans, while the reconstruction section reassembles the literature by discarding what appears inappropriate and retaining that which is not. But not all of this writing is simply a critique of work and thinking judged to be inappropriate. Instead, the papers in this section introduce novel and sound alternative ideas, interpretations, and constructs. The African American is the frame of reference and the point of departure and the purpose of the section is to present, from African American perspectives, descriptions of cognitive and noncognitive attributes of African Americans.

In section V the perspective of black psychologists are applied to a number of areas, some of which, heretofore, have not received systematic attention. Thus, in the section devoted to the application of black perspectives to fields of psychology, papers are included on applications to psychophysiology (Harrell, Clark, and Allen), organizational psychology (Bowman), and experimental psychology (Boykin), in addition to papers on topics that have received somewhat more attention in past writings (educational psychology, White; developmental psychology, McLoyd;and social psychology, Jones). Other parts of Section V present papers on Psychologists and Psychology in the Community; Racism; Counseling and Psychotherapy; and Research.

Karenga, in his text *Introduction to Black Studies* (1982), identified three schools of black psychology: the traditional school, the reformist school, and the radical school. While this tripartite scheme does not represent the only categorization of the thinking of black psychologists (Jones and Jackson have suggested similar categories, for example), they do provide a useful framework for discussing some of the work to be included in the present volume.

The Traditional school, Karenga notes, "is defined by: 1) its defensive and/or reactive posture; 2) its lack of concern for the development of a Black Psychology and its continued support of the Eurocentric model with minor changes; 3) its concern with changing white attitudes, and 4) its being essentially critical without substantial correctives" (p. 325).

The Reformist school, Karenga suggests, is concerned about white attitudes and behaviors, "but focuses more on change in public policy than on simply attitudinal change," and furthermore, "begins to advocate an Afro-centric psychology, but combined with a traditional focus on change that would, ostensibly, benefit both blacks and whites."

The Radical school, according to Karenga, makes no appeal to whites and directs its attention "to Black people in terms of analysis, treatment and transformation." Radical school members "insist on and are developing a psychology that has its roots in the African worldview (Jackson, 1982; King et al., 1976). Moreover, the practitioners of this school are socially conscious theorists and practitioners who advocate self-conscious participation of Black psychologists and Black people in the transformation of social reality through cultural and political struggle" (p. 325).

The third edition of *Black Psychology* retains some contributions that Karenga would probably label as reformist, but many papers would be classified as radical. Included in this new edition, therefore, are contributions by Myers ("The Psychology of Knowledge: The Importance of World View"), Akbar ("The Evolution of Human Psychology for African Americans"; "Mental Disorder Among African Americans"; and "Paradigms of African American Research"), and Baldwin ("African [Black] Psychology: Issues and Synthesis"; and "The Black Self-Hatred Paradigm Revisited: An Afrocentric Analysis"). Introduction of the thinking of these Afrocentrically oriented scholars constitutes a substantial body of the new material that complements the work of like-minded colleagues who are also included in the present edition.

Whether or not Black psychology is ready to adopt, wholesale, Afrocentricity as its cornerstone remains a matter of debate. It may eventually achieve this status as several important new writings make a strong case for this orientation (Asante's, *Afrocentricity*; and Myers', *Understanding an Afrocentric Worldview*). In the meantime, the purpose of the present edition is to expose the reader to the range of extant ideas about black psychology. The relative merits of the various orientations and perspectives are likely to be a subject of continuing debate.

As in previous editions of *Black Psychology*, I am most indebted to a number of individuals for their contributions and assistance. First and foremost are the authors. They responded to deadlines, revisions and publication delays with uncommon grace and forbearance. Authors, I thank you. Without your creative scholarship, no *Black Psychology* would be possible.

I am also grateful to Carol Brooks, Sharon Caesar and Amber Gray at the University of California at Berkeley for assistance in preparing the manuscript, to Mark van Bronkhorst for graphic design work, and to Fred Felder of Cragmont Publications for book design and typesetting. The physical attributes of this volume are a direct result of the high quality of their work. Of course, I accept full responsibility, not only for the content, but for any flaws that remain.

Finally, it is with deep love and appreciation that I express gratitude to my wife, Michele, for her love, caring and support, as always, as I completed this work.

Reginald L. Jones

Contributors

Na'im Akbar, Ph.D.
Research Assistant in Clinical Psychology, Department of Psychology, Florida State University and Executive Director, Mind Productions (a private consulting company), Tallahassee, Florida

Brenda A. Allen, Ph.D.
Assistant Professor, Department of Psychology, Smith College, Northampton, Massachusetts

Joseph A. Baldwin, Ph.D.
Professor of Psychology and Chairman, Department of Psychology, Florida A&M University, Tallahassee, Florida

W. Curtis Banks, Ph.D.
Professor, Department of Psychology, Howard University, Washington, D.C.

Edward J. Barnes, Ph.D.
Deceased, was Associate Dean, College of Arts and Sciences and Director of University-Community Educational Programs at the University of Pittsburgh

A. Wade Boykin, Ph.D.
Professor, Department of Psychology, Howard University, Washington, D.C.

Phillip J. Bowman, Ph.D.
Associate Professor in the Departments of Afro-American Studies, Psychology, and Educational Policy Studies, University of Illinois at Urbana-Champaign, Urbana, Illinois

Raeford Brown, Ph.D.
Associate Professor, Department of Psychology, Florida A&M University, Tallahassee, Florida

Vernessa R. Clark, Ph.D.
Assistant Professor, Department of Psychology, Morehouse College, Atlanta, Georgia

James P. Comer, M.D.
Maurice Falk Professor of Child Psychiatry, Director, Yale-New Haven School Development Program, Yale Child Study Center, New Haven, Connecticut

William E. Cross, Jr., Ph.D.
Associate Professor, Africana Studies and Research Center and Graduate Departments of Psychology, and Human Development and Family Studies, Cornell University, Ithaca, New York

Anne Marie DeBritto, Ph.D.
Senior Associate Research Scientist, Educational Testing Service, Princeton, New Jersey

Lloyd T. Delaney, Ph.D.
Deceased, was a clinical psychologist and certified psychoanalyst in private practice in New York City; and Associate Professor at Queens University

V.P. Franklin, Ph.D.
Professor of History, Department of History and Politics, Drexel University, Philadelphia, Pennsylvania

Lawrence E. Gary, Ph.D.
Director and Professor, Institute of Urban Affairs & Research, Howard University, Washington, D.C.

Robert V. Guthrie, Ph.D.
Clinical Psychologist in Private Practice, San Diego, California

Jules P. Harrell, Ph.D.
Professor, Department of Psychology, Howard University, Washington, D.C.

William A. Hayes, Ph.D.
Project Director, Oakland Cancer Control Program of the Northern California Cancer Center, Oakland, California

V. Robert Hayles, Jr., Ph.D.
Director, Human Resources, Pillsbury Technology Center, Grand Metropolitan Food Sector, Minneapolis, Minnesota

Janet E. Helms, Ph.D.
Professor, Department of Psychology, University of Maryland, College Park, Maryland

Thomas A. Hilliard, Ph.D.
Deceased, was a Visiting Lecturer at the University of California at Berkeley and a Community Clinical Psychologist at the Westside Community Mental Health Center, San Francisco

Reginald Hopkins, M.S.
Ph.D. Candidate in Social Psychology, Department of Psychology, Howard University, Washington, D.C.

Gerald G. Jackson, M.S.
President, New Arena Consulting (a mental health consulting firm), Somerset, New Jersey

Adelbert H. Jenkins, Ph.D.
Associate Professor of Psychology and Director, Undergraduate Studies in Psychology, Faculty of Arts and Science, New York University, New York, New York

James A. Johnson, Jr., Ph.D.
School Administrator, Austin, Texas

Arthur C. Jones, Ph.D.
Clinical Psychologist in Private Practice, Clinical Associate Professor of Psychiatry at the University of Colorado Health Sciences Center, and Teaching Affiliate in the School of Professional Psychology, University of Denver, Denver, Colorado

Ferdinand Jones, Ph.D.
Director, Psychological Services, and Professor of Psychology, Brown University, Providence, Rhode Island

James M. Jones, Ph.D.
Professor of Psychology, University of Delaware (Dover, Delaware) and Executive Director of Public Interest, American Psychological Association, Washington, D.C.

Reginald L. Jones, Ph.D.
Distinguished Professor of Psychology and Special Education and Chair, Department of Psychology, Hampton University, Hampton, Virginia

Courtland Lee, Ph.D.
Director, Counselor Education Program, Department of Human Services, University of Virginia, Charlottesville, Virginia

Richard Majors, Ph.D.
Clinical Fellow in Psychology, Harvard Medical School, Cambridge, Massachusetts

Vonnie C. McLloyd, Ph.D.
Professor, Department of Psychology, Research Scientist, Center for Human Growth and Development, and Faculty Associate, Center for Afro-American and African Studies, University of Michigan, Ann Arbor, Michigan

Gregory V. McQuater, Ph.D.
Manager, Management Development, Pepsico Company, Purchase, New York

Horace Mitchell, Ph.D.
Vice Chancellor of Student Affairs, University of California, Irvine, Irvine, California

Linda James Myers, Ph.D.
Associate Professor in the Departments of Black Studies, Psychology and Psychiatry, Ohio State University, Columbus, Ohio

Wade W. Nobles, Ph.D.
Director, Institute for the Advanced Study of Black Family Life and Culture, Inc. (Oakland, California) and Professor, School of Ethnic Studies, Department of Black Studies, San Francisco State University, San Francisco, California

Thomas A. Parham, Ph.D.
Counseling Psychologist and Director of Career Planning and Placement Center, and Director, Counseling, University of California, Irvine, Irvine, California

Howard P. Ramseur, Ph.D.
Psychologist, Psychiatry Service of the Medical Department, Massachusetts Institute of Technology and Private Practitioner, Cambridge, Massachusetts

Barbara J. Shade, Ph.D.
Dean, School of Education, University of Wisconsin-Parkside, Parkside, Wisconsin

Geneva Smitherman, Ph.D.
Professor and Director, African American Language and Literacy Program, Department of English, Michigan State University, East Lansing, Michigan

Wanda E. Ward, Ph.D.
Associate Professor of Psychology & Director, Center for Research on Minority Education, University of Oklahoma, Norman, Oklahoma

Gayle D. Weaver, Ph.D.
Research Associate, Institute for Urban Affairs and Research, Howard University, Washington, D.C.

Joseph L. White, Ph.D.
Professor of Psychology, Psychiatry and Comparative Culture, University of California, Irvine, Irvine, California

Robert L. Williams, Ph.D.
Professor, Departments of Psychology and Afro-American Studies, Washington University at St. Louis, St. Louis, Missouri

Sheri Wilson, M.S.
Ph.D. Student in Developmental Psychology, Department of Psychology, Howard University, Washington, D.C.

Overview

I. Overview

Two papers are included in this section. The first is the watershed paper on modern black psychology written by Joseph White ("Toward A Black Psychology"). The second paper is seminal work by Linda James Myers on world view. These papers provide a perspective on the rest of the work in this volume.

White's paper is a classic. Written in 1970, it gives the compelling reasons for developing a Black psychology: traditional principles and theories simply have not had sufficient explanatory power to account for the behavior of blacks. White presents alternative conceptions of black family life, black dialect, black paranoia, and black lifestyles which provide the meat of black psychology. And while these conceptions could only be introduced in the 1970s, as will be apparent in writings included in the present edition, considerable research and writing has been amassed on the topics White addressed.

While White's paper has given a contemporary ring to the need for development of a black psychology, it should by no means be believed that his insights, or the insights of other contributors to the present volume, are new. As Guthrie ("The Psychology of African Americans: An Historical Perspective") indicates in the section following, there has been a persistent response by African American scholars to issues related to the psychological dimensions of black life in this country.

Myers' paper is entitled ("The Psychology of Knowledge: The Importance of World View"). Sue (1978) defined world view as

> ... the way in which people perceive their relationship to nature, institutions, other people, and things. World view constitutes our psychological orientation in life and can determine how we think, behave, make decisions, and define events. Our cultural upbringing and life experiences frequently determine and influence our world views. For minorities in the United States, however, a strong determinant of world views is very much related to racism and the subordinate position assigned minorties in society ... (p. 458).

In her paper, Myers highlights the importance of the subjective and self-knowledge in the generation of knowledge and reminds us that the psychogenesis of knowledge occurs in a social context. Myers also introduces the notion of an Afrocentric world view—as contrasted with a Eurocentric world view—as the key to understanding the behavior of African Americans. She concludes by reminding us that relationships among one's conceptual system, world view, and behavior (including how science is done) are internally consistent.

The concept of an Afrocentric world view is highlighted in the

3

present volume in Nobles' writings on African Philosophy, Akbar's discussions of the evolution of human psychology for African Americans, Baldwin, Brown and Hopkins' evaluation of the black self-hatred literature, Nobles' writings on the black self-concept, Jackson's treatment of the emergence of the black perspective in counseling, Arthur Jones conceptual guide for psychotherapy with black patients, and Akbar's paradigms of African American research. The notion of an Afrocentric world view is an integral part of the present volume.

Reference

Sue, D.W. (1978). World views and counseling. *Personnel and Guidance Journal* 56(7), 458-462.

Toward a Black Psychology

Joseph L. White

Regardless of what black people ultimately decide about the questions of separation, integration, segregation, revolution, or reform, it is vitally important that we develop, out of the authentic experience of black people in this country, an accurate workable theory of black psychology. It is very difficult, if not impossible, to understand the lifestyles of black people using traditional theories developed by white psychologists to explain white people. Moreover, when these traditional theories are applied to the lives of black folks many incorrect, weakness-dominated, and inferiority-oriented conclusions come about.

In all fairness it should be said that only a few white psychologists publicly accept the idea advanced by Dr. Jensen that black people, according to his research findings, are at birth genetically inferior to whites in intellectual potential. Most psychologists and social scientists take the more liberal point of view which in essence states that black people are culturally deprived and psychologically maladjusted because the environment in which they were reared as children and in which they continue to rear their own children lacks the necessary early experiences to prepare them for excellence in school, appropriate sex role behavior, and, generally speaking, achievement within an Anglo middle-class frame of reference. In short, we are culturally and psychologically deprived because our experiential background provides us with inferior preparation to move effectively within the dominant white culture.

A simple journey with the white researcher into the black home may provide us with some insight into how such important, but somewhat erroneous, conclusions are reached. During this visit to the black home the researcher may not find familiar aspects of the white culture such as Book-of-the-Month selections, records of Broadway plays, classics, magazines such as *Harpers*, the *Atlantic Monthly*, or the *New York Review of Books*. He also might observe a high noise level, continuously reinforced by inputs from blues-and-rhythm radio stations, TV programs, and several sets of conversations going on at once. This type of observation leads him to assume that the homes of black children are very weak in intellectual content, uninteresting, and generally confusing places to grow up. Somehow he fails to see the intellectual stimulation that might be provided by local black newspapers, informative rapping, *Jet, Ebony, Sepia*, and the Motown sound. Black children in these same homes who supposedly can't read (even preschoolers) can sing several rock and blues tunes from memory and correctly identify the songs of popular entertainers. These same researchers or educational psychologists listening to black speech assume that our use of nonstandard oral English is an example of bad grammar without recognizing the possibility that we have a valid, legitimate, alternate dialect. As the white educational psychologist continues with what for him has become a standard analysis, the next step becomes one of setting up programs which provide black children with the kind of enrichment he feels is needed to overcome and compensate for their cultural deprivation. As a consequence of this type of thinking, in recent years from Head Start and New Horizons to Upward Bound, we have repeatedly witnessed the failure of compensatory and enrichment educational programs. Possibly, if social scientists, psychologists, and educators would stop trying to compensate for the so-called weaknesses of the black child and try to develop a theory that capitalizes on his strengths, programs could be designed which from the get-go might be more productive and successful.

Many of these same so-called culturally deprived youngsters have developed the kind of mental toughness and survival skills, in terms of coping with life, which make them in many ways superior to their white age-mates who are growing up in the material affluence of Little League suburbias. These black youngsters know how to deal effectively with bill collectors, building superintendents, corner grocery stores, hypes, pimps, whores, sickness, and death. They know how to jive school counselors, principals, teachers, welfare workers, juvenile authorities, and, in doing so, display a lot of psychological cleverness and originality. They recognize very early that they exist in an environment which is sometimes both complicated and hostile. They may not be able to verbalize it, but they have already mastered what existential psychologists state to be the basic human condition; namely that in this life, pain and struggle are unavoidable and that a complete sense of one's identity can only be achieved by both recognizing and directly confronting an unkind and alien existence.

The black family represents another arena in which the use of traditional white psychological models leads us to an essentially inappropriate and unsound analysis. When the black family is viewed from a middle-class frame of reference, which assumes that the psychologically healthy family contains two parents, one male and one female, who remain with the child until he or she becomes a young adult, the fact that the same black male is not consistently visible to the white observer of the black family leads to a conclusion that the black family unit has a matriarchal structure. Once the idea of the matriarchal family is accepted, it is very tempting to use Freudian psychological theories to explain why black children, especially black males, who are reared in this type of one-parent family with an absent father develop psychosexual and identity hang-ups. Even more damaging, the male and female offspring of the matriarchal family carry their own hang-ups into the next generation, only to have the matriarchal cycle repeat itself. Indeed, one white social scientist in making the black family a case for national action took the view that the major problem confronting black people had to do with reorganizing our family into a two-parent unit.

A closer look at the black family might show that the matriarchal or one-parent view fails to take into consideration the extended nature of the black family. Looking at the number of uncles, aunties, big mamas, boyfriends, older brothers and sisters, deacons, preachers, and others who operate in and out of the black home, a more valid observation might be that a variety of adults and older children participate in the rearing of any one black child. Furthermore, in the process of childrearing, these several adults plus older brothers and sisters make up a kind of extended family who interchange roles, jobs, and family functions in such a way that the child does not learn an extremely rigid distinction of male and female roles. A case comes to mind of a young white social worker, who, after observing a teen-age black male going about the business of cooking, cleaning house, washing clothes, and obviously helping his mother care for the younger children in his family, wrote in her report that his masculine development might be harmed by such obviously feminine activities. What the social worker failed to see was that this particular black male teenager did not rigidly separate these male and female roles in his own mind, and more importantly he also helped out his mother with a part-time job, was a member of the track team at a local high school, an able student, had a very healthy sex life with some of the younger women in the neighborhood, and was respected by the street brothers of the gang culture when it came down to his abilities to "throw hands" when such activities were necessary.

If the extended family model proves to be more accurate than the matriarchal conception describing the black family, this means that we can turn our attention away from continuous description of the unhealthy psychosexual and social role conflicts in black children and young adults and move toward ways of strengthening the extended family, as opposed to some basic reorganization of the black family. Furthermore, if the concept of the extended family is accurate, our teenagers and young adults may have potentially fewer identity conflicts than those who come from families who expose them to extremely rigid distinctions between male and female roles and duties. Maybe people who want to make the black family a case for national action should stop talking about making the black family into a white family and instead devote their energies into removing the obvious oppression of the black community which is responsible for us catchin' so much hell.

These examples of the cultural-deprivation hypothesis and the matriarchal family model were used to illustrate the need for a psychological explanation and analysis of black life styles which emerges from the framework of the black experience. Not only will the understanding of the black frame of reference enable us to come up with more accurate and comprehensive explanations, but will also enable us to build the kinds of programs within the black world which capitalize on the strengths of black people. This is especially critical in the field of education because the most successful educational models tend to capitalize on the experiences which the child brings to the classroom, as opposed to constantly reminding the child of his weaknesses. Not all traditional white psychological theory is useless. It has already been implied that the views of the existential psychologists, with their recognition of pain and struggle as an unavoidable condition, apply to the lives of black people. The views commonly advanced by a group of psychologists called self-theorists may be helpful because the self-theorists take the view that in order to understand what a person is and the way he views the world, you must have some awareness of his experiential background, especially as it might include experiences with the institutions such as the home, family, immediate neighborhood, and the agencies of both cultures which directly affect the person's life.

To continue our discussion, rather than argue that black people are totally psychologically unique, it would seem that our experience with—and management of—key psychological concepts, as they pertain to the handling of contradictions, role of the hero, language systems, the meaning of work, and a healthy sense of suspiciousness, differ profoundly as we compare the black experience with the white Anglo experience.

In a feeling-oriented culture, apparent—and when examined closely, superficial—logical contradictions do not have the same meaning as they might have in the Anglo culture. A white psychology student became thoroughly confused when he was provided with the opportunity to observe a particular brother one Sunday in what the student thought to be three very different and contradictory sets. The student by prior arrangement was allowed to watch the brother interact within the context of a 1968-type black nationalist rally. The brother in question was a very active participant in the audience. He seemed to enjoy the anti-honky rhetoric, shouted and clapped at appropriate moments, and gave the speakers repeated replies of "Right on." Immediately following the rally this same brother walked across the street to a black, storefront church-type revival, grabbed a tambourine, rocked with the sisters, called on the Holy Ghost, and sang an unsolicited solo entitled *Where Shall I Be When the First Trumpet Sounds?* Next, the brother walked to a bar a block away, drank more than a little gin, and began to hum and keep time with the lyrics of *Chain of Fools* by Aretha Franklin. During the interview which occurred in the bar, the white psychologist opened by asking, "Don't you see any basic contradiction between participation in a black nationalist rally, a storefront revival, and sitting in this bar drinking gin?" (and I might add popping his fingers). The brother replied to the question by stating that not only did he not see any contradiction but that he looked forward to all three sets every Sunday because he basically just "dug on it." What might have represented a contradiction to the white psychologist meant nothing to the brother in the sense that all three sets were part of the same experience for him at a feeling level. As part of the same experience pool, with unimportant surface differences, the brother felt equally at home during all three activities. Within the black experience, the church can be seen as an arena of strength or as an escapist movement. What is important is that these two views do not negate each other and can exist within the same person side by side. Closely related to the easy style of handling contradictions, it can also be stated that black people have a greater tolerance for conflict, stress, ambiguity, and ambivalence. White psychologists fail to take this into consideration when they assume that because we have a lower-class background, black people are therefore more impulsive, emotionally immature, and have less tolerance for stress.

In terms of the role of the hero, the dominant white culture is steeped in the tradition of a hero who is infallible, scores his triumphs with godlike skill, follows all the rules, and finally retires undefeated. The whole psychology of the hero in black and white cultures is different. In the black culture the hero is by and large the brother who messes with the system and gets away with it. Black people on the whole could care less about a few political figures partying it up in the West Indies at The Man's expense. They can dig it and can identify with it. Whereas this same hero, according to the white psychologists, is interpreted as the villain. In literature the two hero themes come together in John O. Killen's novel *And Then We Heard the Thunder*. Solly Saunders, as the noble savage, is a black college graduate serving as an officer in the Army during World War II. He runs into a brother in his outfit who, as the villain, talks back to the officers, ignores the rules, and follows his own self-determination-oriented mind. Because of this bad brother, Solly goes through some changes and at the end of the book the "bad nigger" emerges as the hero. Nowadays the bad nigger is very much in the vogue as the hero in the black community, yet white people continue to perceive this person as the villain and cannot understand why black folks currently reject white people's favorite Uncle Toms. As a people we have to trust our own kinds of perceptions and not absorb white expectations of superheroes and villains.

Black people have a genuine understanding of brothers like Eldridge Cleaver. Eldridge became kind of a cultural hero in the United States. A lot of white people, including white radicals, were disappointed because he didn't stand trial. They said that he had let down his responsibility to his people and wasn't a credit to his race." But anybody who had heard Eldridge, read his books, or knew anything about his life and where he had been, knew that he was not going to go back there again.

Heroes are also important because they serve as role models for children, and in children's books produced by white publishers the black role model is often notoriously absent. Black children in the process of growing up need to see themselves realistically reflected in books, movies, radio, TV, and the like. By seeing themselves reflected it confirms that they exist and provides them with identification figures and images. After a righteously profound rebuking by black educators, a few white publishers of children's literature and TV producers are slowly trying to correct the situation. Let us take a brief look at their efforts. A typical children's story might start out with some white boys playing baseball. At about the middle of the game a white boy's mama makes him come home for lunch; the white players talk it over and finally invite the black youngster to join the ball game. The brother proceeds to strike out six people in a row, hits four home runs, picks a runner off at second base, and later wins the game by setting up the double play. Psychologically, what this story does is to project the image of a "supernigger" and implies that they are okay in ones and twos. On the other hand, one does not have to be a super white boy to gain membership on the team or a respectable position in life. The average everyday white boy sees himself reflected throughout the white culture in pictures, books, films, radio and TV during the process of growing up. Whereas the black child has to settle for distorted images— recently the supernigger image and prior to that images projecting the noble savage, beast, Bojangles, and other clowns. From a black psychological standpoint we have to work to make the kind of breakthrough that puts black children in typical situations rather than into distorted unreal worlds.

With respect to the use of language, the oral tradition with its heavy rap, folk tales, blues, spirituals, and down-home sermons has a vital impact within the black experience. Historically speaking, any discussion of the black experience with language is further complicated by the fact that words were used to express and conceal at the same time.

Certain ideas had to be conveyed to the brothers and the same ideas had to be hidden from the white man. The slavemaster in the antebellum South listening to the field "nigras" singing "Steal away, steal away to Jesus, steal away home" were deceived into believing that the brothers and sisters were thinking only about Heaven. The real message was about stealing away and splitting up North. Black language is also very deep in hidden meanings, intuition, and nuances. A poem like "The Signifying Monkey" confuses even the most hip revolutionary ofay, yet brothers who cannot read or write know exactly what the poem means—it is foolish, if not suicidal, to fight a powerful enemy on its own ground and to neutralize obvious advantages, the monkey engages in effective trickery, deceit, and a black form of psychological warfare known as "signifying." These same so-called illiterate brothers also intuitively know when the white power structure is being dishonest, jiving, and otherwise engaging in tricknology. As part of our oral tradition, the dozens, as a game of one-upmanship in which clever remarks are exchanged about the mamas, aunties, and grandmamas of the contestants, causes white psychologists and linguists nothing but confusion. Assuming the dozens to be part of our matriarchal bag, they literally think we want to have destructive sexual encounters with our mamas. An alternate historical explanation from the black experience might be that the brothers and sisters use the dozens as a game to teach them how to keep cool and think fast under pressure, without saying what was really on their minds. In translating black language forms into standard oral English, we should remember that some of the meaning will automatically be lost because these words and idioms are accompanied by a very rich background of gestures, body motions, and voice changes. Despite the loss in translation, black educators should continue with their efforts to write black language programs with standard English equivalents. Since black children are exposed to two cultures they should be able to express themselves in more than one dialect of the English language.

The folklore of white American culture repeatedly emphasizes the value and virtues of hard work. Work is supposed to cleanse us, move us ahead economically, and allow us to advance to positions of higher prestige and authority. In a sense, hard work pays off, and generations of Americans were reared to believe in the idea that through personal effort one could go from rags to riches. Stokely Carmichael has repeatedly stated that if hard work was the key to advancement "Black people would be the richest people in the country." We have worked in the fields from sunup to sundown, laid rails, picked cotton, scrubbed floors, messed with chain gangs, reared other people's children and at the end of three centuries have very little to show for this monumental effort at hard work. Since hard work has not dramatically altered the future of black people, we have evidence to believe that what happens to a person is more related to luck or chance than it is to hard work. To plan with the belief in the future is to plan for disappointment and heartbreak. Hence black folk have done their best to deal with the concrete realities and needs of the present. This does not mean that black people are present oriented in the sense that they are impulse ridden or incapable of delayed gratification. What it means is that the benefits of the white dream of hard work have not paid off for us. That being the case, as a group, our management of time is not bound or guided by a future orientation and time is not measured in the work-unit values of the dominant white culture.

Part of the objective condition of black people in this society is that of a paranoid condition. There is, and has been, unwarranted, systematic persecution and exploitation of black people as a group. A black person who is not suspicious of the white culture is pathologically denying certain objective and basic realities of the black experience. The late sociologist E. Franklin Frazier touched on this very well in *Black Bourgeoisie*, and the authors of *Black Rage* discuss the value of healthy black paranoia. White psychiatrists and psychologists often have considerable difficulty working constructively with the hostility and suspiciousness of black patients. This is because their frame of reference tells them that excessive suspiciousness is psychologically unhealthy. If a white dude were to tell a white psychiatrist that people have been systematically picking on him from his front door clear to the White House, the psychiatrist would diagnose him as in a psychotic, paranoid state and hospitalize him. Using a black frame of reference with a black patient should not result in the same diagnosis, and possibly white psychiatrists should stop diagnosing us and spend some of their time working to change the system which persecutes black people.

A comprehensive theory of black psychology will have to explain in much greater detail the dynamics of the black home, family, hero, role models, language systems, work and time management, and the nature of suspiciousness. Many other areas will have to be included, and hopefully the challenge of excellence will be met by a younger generation of black students who are deeply committed to the development of a true psychological picture of the black experience.

One of the primary reasons why interracial group sensitivity encounters often fail to make adequate progress may be due to the fact that black people and white people have different priorities, expectations, ways of viewing the world, and life styles. When black people confront white people, what they primarily want is a legitimate acknowledgment of their point of view and a follow-up with appropriate actions. But when a white person is pushed up against a wall, the worst thing he can do is admit that the party who pushed him up there has a valid point of view. In a group encounter when black people escalate the verbal fireworks the white reaction is to feel angry, threatened, alienated, or guilty. Were whites to drop their defensiveness and acknowledge the legitimacy of the black point of view, they might be able to move from there to a more cooperative relationship. But the white culture is so deeply entrenched in the whole concept of face-saving, sin, and repayment for past wrongs-doings, that it expects an Old Testament eye-for-an-eye type of retaliation.

On TV NET showed a black/white encounter in which each group was forced to take the roles of the others. White masks were put on black people, and black masks were put on white people. While this was a short encounter, perhaps in the future for training people in the black experience we should have them try to be black for a longer time with some of their experiences taking place outside the protective setting of the group.

In closing, one further comment on group encounters might be considered. While white people in their group encounters with other white people may need to deal with the questions of sex, aggression, affection, tenderness, shame, and guilt, black people, especially black change agents, have a completely different set of priorities. In moving from one pattern to another and more rapidly from one crisis situation to another, if one is not careful, it is easy to slip into a state of psychological fatigue with the accompanying symptoms of depression and angry despair. In this state of mind, without realizing it, we begin to use words like revolution, liberation, Tomming, imperialism, agent-provocateur, and many others in very general, undefined global ways—sometimes more for self-affirmation than for real communication. Furthermore, in such a psychological state of fatigue it is very difficult to see clearly both the goals one is striving for and the relevance of the tactic to the immediate situation. We mix up rhetoric about change with the process of change itself. Rhetoric properly applied can make us psychologically conscious of what it means to be black. But we must not equate the imagery of this black consciousness with the actualities of concrete social progress. A carefully developed psychological group encounter conducted with change agents, coordinated by a black person with psychological training in the black experience, might facilitate the process of regeneration, self-renewal, and meaningful communication. Like any human endeavor, in order to continue to be creative and productive, the black struggle must construct models which will take care of the process of internal cleansing and meaningful reflection and as such serve as self-corrective guides.

Expanding the Psychology of Knowledge Optimally: The Importance of World View Revisited

Linda James Myers

For several years I have pondered the question, "What is the nature of knowledge and its relationship to conceptual systems (the particular set of assumptions on which we rely to give structure to our reality), and the subsequent truths which therein emerge?" The purpose of this paper is to describe what I have learned about the nature of knowledge and its relationship to conceptual systems and "truth" as I have sought to examine two conceptual systems, one dominant and the other non-dominant in Western culture. While in the past special emphasis has been placed on the need to consider the validity of an alternative set of assumptions or conceptual system within the Western academy (Myers, 1984), current focus will be on exploring a fundamental need to test those assumptions that too often go unobserved as we engage in "scientific" endeavors. Also, the consequences of adhering to the two very different sets of assumptions in the pursuit of knowledge will be examined, as well as the importance of the emergence of a holistic, optimal conceptual system for the preservation of humankind.

> Mental bondage is invisible violence . . . Creators and beneficiaries of belief systems develop a vested interest in the system . . . Priests or professors are ordained or certified as purveyors of the system, sometimes with the belief that they are objective or scientific. The general public usually accepts and comes to depend upon the doctrine or "knowledge."
> Asa Hilliard, Introduction to Stolen *Legacy*

> My people are destroyed for lack of knowledge.
> *Hosea 4:6.*
> *The Holy Bible*

Within the domain of academe we claim the pursuit of knowledge as our objective. But exactly what is the nature of this we pursue? For socially conscious psychologists aware of the plethora of problems confronting the world, this question is particularly pertinent in light of the responsibility we have been given to find solutions and introduce viable alternatives to the dominant cultural frame of reference that is not working because of the pervasive influence of racism on all aspects of functioning in the dominant society. The mentality that would be racist or sexist is seeing the world based upon a particular set of assumptions. In a racist/sexist society, these assumptions or this less optimal conceptual system has become so hegemonous and pervasive that this lens used to view the world is often considered the only one valid or existent. The nature of one's perception, cognition, the social context of the psychogenesis of knowledge and truth will emerge from these assumptions.

What have we learned about the racist/sexist mentality so dominant in this culture and the conceptual system that fosters it? Is this conceptual system different from the one which is used to do "science"? While we suggest that it is not, we will also suggest that the nature of the conceptual system will likely lead its adherents to act as if the assumptions used in doing "science" are somehow different from those used daily and are "objective." So with considerable evidence, much of which I will discuss later, the segmented nature of world view created by this sub-optimal conceptual system proves self-alienating and prevents those embracing its assumptions from fully acknowledging their humanness and thus that of others in a different way. Being disconnected from conscious awareness of their inability to truly disengage from their role in creating reality and at the same time fearing to trust it, adherents of the world view persist in denial tactics which consist of attempting to count and measure what they think (infer) others think, to determine what is. Knowledge is not fully integrated or synthesized. In contrast, Myers (1988) describes an alternative conceptual system, which fully integrates awareness of one's humanness into the pursuit of knowledge, and in fact capitalizes on that factor recognizing knowledge of self as the essential feature of the nature of truth. Where before unachieveable, synthesis is made possible. Let us explore these ideas in greater detail.

Perception, Cognition, and Knowledge

Synthesis of knowledge in Western psychology has proven extraordinarily difficult, primarily because of the segmented nature of the world view dominant in the West. So while cognitive psychology teaches that perception is not a passive act in which the individual is simply an observer, but an active process where the perceiver can, to a degree, be said to construct his/her perception, in our daily functioning we tend to forget that. The world discerned by the senses is not an external world, but our own projected perception of what our mind is programmed to give meaning to or label. If we ignore this fact our perspective may become rigid and we discount the views of others. In our minds, much like a computer, information that is not in the expected or acceptable format is ignored or misinterpreted (Neisser, 1976). Consequently those coming from an alternative view based on another set of assumptions are misunderstood.

Genetic psychology (genetic epistemology) warns against the acceptance of the "reality" of an object and of immediate "evidence," otherwise known as data, yet we rely on these heavily in "scientific" enterprise. How and what we see in the world is influenced by structural biases in our perceptual systems (Mahoney, 1976), likely at the level of conceptual systems. We know that our cognitive apparatus structures the field of perception, but do not use this information to influence how we do business in any meaningful way.

The relationship of our perception to an external world is at best symbolic, yet this knowledge is not factored into the set of philosophical assumptions and principles upon which we rely— our conceptual system. The evidence of the senses can only be accepted as evidence of the nature and role of our participation in its creation. We speak of our senses as guides, but they have only the capacity to function as servants. The mind sees, hears, smells, tastes, and feels. Nature has been said to be a dull affair, soundless, scentless, and colorless. It is the mind which gives things their quality, their foundation, and their being. The stuff of the world is the mind stuff according to Eddington (1931, p. 44), a modern theoretical physicist. But the conceptual system of dominant socialization in this culture emphasizes an external, "objective," material reality.

Neuropsychologist Kenneth Pelletier (1978) describes the structures of perception within the brain as dependent upon the programming and distribution of holograms (i.e., stores of pieces of information from which the whole can be recounted). Out of an infinity of possible perceptions, certain outcomes are preselected by the specific hologram of the brain. Only the most frequently occurring events which become consistent overtime, reinforce themselves to become subjectively and socially institutionalized as the average state of consciousness. If the conceptual system grounding our world view allowed for the synthesis of this knowledge into meaningful praxis, concerns over cultural pluralism would be obliterated.

Even though we should be able to see the same principle quite readily in language, we tend to miss it. Out of infinite sensory experience, language is created by selecting those things which are repetitive in experience and believed useful to attend. Experiences which are unlabeled at the sensory input level, do not become part of the language and typically do not intrude into consciousness, thus the nature of the experience of culture and language often hold more meaning and the potential basis for understanding others than frequently considered.

Social Context and the Psychogenesis of Knowledge

The importance of the subjective in cognitive processes must be stressed, but the psychogenesis of knowledge cannot be attributed to the isolated individual. The psychogenesis of knowledge in the individual occurs in a social context. Therefore the role of dominant culture with its particular conceptual system of socialization becomes critical. Coldman (1971, cited in Preiswerk and Perrot, 1978) describes the process as intraindividual (within the individual) with interaction between the conscious and unconscious and interindividual (between individuals) on conscious and nonconscious levels.

Intraindividually, the unconscious refers to the Freudian notion of the comparmentalization in affective and cognitive life between what one knows consciously and that which one has never managed to raise to the level of consciousness or which one has repressed. Between individuals, nonconsciousness refers to lack of awareness of that which is under social view. In other words, an individual integrates into his/her "knowledge" these aspects of experience common to a society based not only on manifest expressions of social thought but also on those aspects underlying and implicit in social interaction (i.e., the philosophical assumptions and principles structuring the world view or the conceptual system).

For example, society may espouse a value for cultural pluralism, but at the same time perpetuate institutional structures that prevent it and insure assimilation (Myers, 1981). On a conscious level an individual in that society may say "I support the right of every ethnic group to participate." Unconsciously they may mean, "as long as they do it my way, like me." The same individual may be unconscious of feelings of insecurity, inferiority, and/or inadequacy surrounding what would happen to his/her own sense of self, if the ethnically different were to be accepted for their difference. Between individuals, continuing the same example, we might find that the nonacceptance of "true" cultural *difference* is totally outside of the awareness of the dominant cultural group (nonconscious). On a conscious level members of the dominant group are likely not to really know what the "other" culture is like except on a superficial level (i.e., based on the perception and understanding their own culture's conceptual system allows). Therefore, it will be easy for the dominant group in seeking additional members to make itself more heterogeneous to select those potentially (superficially appearing) different candidates with essential characteristics (i.e., beliefs, world view, conceptual systems) most like themselves. As a consequence, the status quo is reinforced, and no substantive change takes place. Although we may now have added blacks or women to our group, we chose only those blacks or women who think and see the world as we do.

Thus, we see that the social context of the psychogenesis of knowledge has to be examined in light of a cultural world view in terms of the particular conceptual system being utilized. A conceptual system consists of those philosophical constructs one adheres to, forming the lens through which one sees the world or structures reality. Let us contrast the world views dominant in European/European American culture with African/African American culture as the historical point of generation, following the philosophical aspects of cultural differences outlined by Nichols (1976) at the meeting of the World Psychiatric Association.

In terms of ontology, the Eurocentric view assumes predominantly a material (five-sense) reality, with highest values placed on the acquisition of objects (axiology). External knowledge is assumed to be the basis of all knowledge (epistemology) and one knows through counting and measuring. The logic of this conceptual system is dichotomous (either/or) and the process (means which we will achieve our goals) is technology (all sets are repeatable and reproducible). The consequent basis for identity/self worth in this system is external criteria (e.g., how one looks, what one owns, prestige and status symbols).

These assumptions and principles are at the roots of racism and other societal "isms" and are thus sub-optimal—less than the best to achieve harmonious interpersonal relationships. To the extent one internalizes the conceptual system, security and well-being is external to the individual and one is perceptually looking outside oneself to find someone to be "better than." This realization does not mean that all people acknowledging European descent are racist, but rather anyone buying into the conceptual system is at risk of its natural consequences, which are the segmentation and self-alienation fostered by the separation of the material and spiritual.

The Afrocentric ontology assumes reality is both spiritual and material at once (spiritual/material, extrasensory as can be known through five senses) with highest value on positive interpersonal relationships between women/men (axiology); self knowledge is assumed to be the basis of all knowledge (epistemology), and one knows through symbolic imagery and rhythm. The logic of this conceptual system is diunital (union of opposites) and the process is ntulogy (all sets are interrelated through human and spiritual networks). The consequent basis for identity/self worth is intrinsic in being. This conceptual system is structured to yield the achievement of everlasting peace and happiness, and if one values this aim, it is optimal. Not all people acknowledging African descent buy into this view, rather it has been identified as a generalized historically characteristic cultural ethos.

Conceptual systems as divergent as the sub-optimal and optimal just identified will yield very different perceptions, cognitions, and experiences for their adherents. We need only examine history to see what happens when people holding the two views come into contact. The sub-optimal has the propensity to try to control and dominate, although it is time limited. The optimal tends to accept and harmonize, yet go beyond the limits of time and space to re-emerge as triumphant. Although we can trace the historical points of generation of each view, these references become meaningless in light of the fact that individuals have the power to define reality for themselves and that what really differentiates people is not how they appear, but their mentality. From an optimal view, all people are African people if they go far enough back into their ancestry, holistically back to the beginnings of human culture and civilization. Optimal theory brings to forefront the realization that we are all one people.

Research has shown that individuals holding divergent assumptions and expectations about the world may draw contrary inferences from the same set of experiential events (Brunner & Goodman, 1947,; Brunner & Postman, 1947; McGuinnies, 1949; Postman & Brunner, 1949; Black & Vanderplas, 1950). Both Kuhn (1962) and Weimer (1976) have asserted that the phenomenon of factual relativism makes untenable the popular belief that science grows by sequential accumulation of more and more facts. If it is true that facts acquire their meaning only in conceptual perspective, then it is not reasonable to claim that the empirical foundations of science are immutable. Even within a system solely concerned with purely natural, observable phenomena, reality becomes less and less knowable as observations become more refined (LeShan, 1969). Einstein (Schilpp, 1949) contends that pure logical thinking of a count and measure, five-sense variety cannot yield us any knowledge of the empirical world; all knowledge of reality starts from experience and ends in it, and is subsequently subjective. Observation, the fruit of perception, is thus embedded in and inseparable from interpretation, even at the level of common sense (Harris, 1967).

Though extant within Western science, the pieces of knowledge that would lead to a more holistic world view remain fragmented due to the shortcomings of the dominant conceptual system, as illustrated by many philosophers of science. The method of science is misconceived by those who persist in the view that both the knowledge in general and the natural sciences in particular, sense observation is primary and self-contained, and must somehow be used as an independent check upon the accuracy of theories (Popper, 1959).

A scientific theory is a more or less organized and coherent interpretation of what is observed, without which the observed facts lose their character and significance. Observation is saturated with interpretation, of which theory is no more than the development. Theory and observation form the single whole of knowledge. The aim of science is to improve the "more or less" coherently organized system so that it becomes more comprehensive and self-consistent. Verification, therefore, always consists in the assembling of mutually corroborative evidence the interconnections of which make the denial of the theory impossible without a breakdown of the entire conceptual scheme (Harris, 1967). The field of knowledge that attempts to organize comprehensively the deliverances of the sciences into a single world view by means of a universal conceptual scheme in which all sciences can be integrated is called metaphysics. An optimal conceptual system provides the rational framework for such comprehensive and cohesive scheme.

Knowledge is directly related to human interest. We do not build up knowledge through objective perceptions, nor do we scientifically cognize an object before entering into other, more primary relationships with it. One knows "things" to the extent one engages in subjective relationships with them. The notion of and way of the "other" exists in one's being as a subject. Rather than eliminating subjectivity, which is anyway impossible, one must deepen it according to Davis (1981). In "the human sciences" involvement is our primary way of knowing and every involvement is pre-determined by our involvement in our attunement to ourselves. For the most part, we don't know our "objects" because we don't know ourselves. Objectivity is best conceived as a decentration process whereby the "mental distance between subject and object is reduced. (Devereaux, 1967). These are implicit in the assumption of an optimal conceptual system.

Despite the abundance of information cautioning us against "bad science," unacknowledged personal biases continually find their way into scientific research when a sub-optimal conceptual system is used, particularly in the social science. For example, sexism has been shown to pervade all phases of research in formulation of concept and theories (Bart, 1971; Broverman, et al, 1971; Chesler, 1972; Weisstein, 1969); choice of problem to be investigated (Millman, 1971); test construction (Johannson & Harmon, 1972; Milton, 1959; Munley, Fretz & Mills, 1972); selection of subjects (Carlson, 1971; Schultz, 1969; Schwabaker, 1972); and the overgeneralization of findings from males to all people (Dan & Beekman, 1972; Bowen, 1971).

Hempel (1966) notes that scientific research occurs in a given time period (Zeitgeist), geographic location, cultural context, and social milieu of which the investigation is a product. The pursuit of knowledge presupposes some set of values concerning what is worthwhile (Kaplan,

1964; Nobles, 1974; Staples, 1976). Kaplan (1964) and Rudner (1966) argue that an explicit statement of values reduces bias resulting from them. Fine (1982), in reviewing research on the black family also found that values affected virtually every stage of the investigatory process. We can with the articulation of the conceptual system from which we are working, reduce bias tremendously.

Self Knowledge as the Basis of all Knowledge

In light of what we have discussed thus far, "good science" not only acknowledges the subjective, but explores its exact nature in detail in order to reveal "true" knowledge. Ancient Africans built their science on the realization of the value of the subjective. This fact is made evident in their epistemological assumption that self-knowledge is the basis of all knowledge and that one knows through symbolic imagery and rhythm (Nichols, 1976). These ideas, extant thousands of years before Western historians pinpoint the beginning of their civilization, are now resurging in optimal theory and in Western science in what Fritzj of Capra (1982) has deemed a paradigm shift. The movement away from the materialist, mechanistic conception of the universe in modern physics is slowly being replicated in the "human sciences." Many scholars would applaud such a shift, being aware of the negative consequence of the fragmented, materialist world view. The more holistic, integrated, spiritual/material conception proves valid according to scientific method of the West, Eastern philosophies of the Orient, and the common sense of Africa. The fragmented, mechanistic world view was initially propagated by only a minority of the world's cultures, the European/European-American, and even the height of their "science" we see has now converged with the beliefs predominant in the rest of the world of knowledge. Eddington (1931) states that by recognizing that the physical world is entirely abstract and without "actuality" apart from its linkages to consciousness, we restore consciousness to the fundamental position instead of representing it as an inessential complication occasionally found in the midst of inorganic nature at a late stage of evolutionary history.

Because the conceptual system forms the basis for defining reality and "seeing" the world, that the fragmented, materialistic world view is still widely held in this society, may be said to be evidence of a serious incidence of cultural lag. Capra (1975) characterizes the entire Western world view as fragmented and on the road to destruction with its penchant for resource depletion, environmental pollution, and human alienation and conflict. Burgest (1981) identifies the same traits and shows how they indeed account for the oppression of African people. Contrasting what he calls the Eurolinear with the Afrocircular world view, we see the fragmented, material versus the holistic, spiritual/material respectively. Clark (1972) goes as far as specifying the relationships between the two views and approaches to science: he cites the European/Western scientific aims of prediction and control versus the African/Eastern aim of understanding and unification. He states that the origins of the European/Western view reside in the intellectual separation of mind and matter. Richards (1979) also identifies the externalized, non-reflexive approach of Western science as a basic tool of oppression and intellectual imperialism.

Based upon these perceptions we might conclude that the relationships between one's conceptual system, world view, and behavior (even how one does science), are internally consistent. In addition, to the extent one is willing to truly pursue knowledge and acknowledge his/her conceptual system, that pursuit will likely converge with the perceptions of others who have done the same.

Knowledge and Truth

Truth has been defined in many ways, to name a few, as fidelity, constancy, honesty, state of being the case or fact, a transcendent fundamental or spiritual reality, fidelity to an original, or to a standard, and God (Webster, 1969). Most scholars would hope that their pursuit of knowledge would lead them to the "truth," however they define it. Akbar (1976) argues that rather than leading to truth, the conceptual system that we have characterized as sub-optimal, fragmented and materialist, leads to false knowledge. Based upon an optimal conceptual system which assumes a holistic spiritual/material ontology, this would be the case.

Naturally, an antithetical conceptual system that separates spirit and matter, assumes no natural order, seeks to control nature, and operates as if experience were an accumulation of discrete events, would be seen as yielding false knowledge to the holist. To the adherents of the segmented world view, the holistic conceptual system would likely be perceived as incomprehensible, yielding false knowledge. Within the segmented view, intelligence will be measured by how well one can count and measure and recall information. The evidence of a great scholar within this system will be the number of publications produced without regard to the impact on humankind. Because truth is believed unknown, consensual, or relative in this system and one must act as if one is objective in "testing" things empirically, empiricism is assigned special value, as if there were some non-empirical way to function.

From the optimal perspective, true knowledge must prove consistent with nature (empirically verifiable) and harmonize with the natural order of the universe; high value is placed on being in harmony with nature. In this way, truth becomes a unifying principle. The conceptual system functions such that moment by moment we are perceiving infinite and unique varieties of the same extrasensory essence, spirit manifest. Self is extended in time and space to include the venerated ancestors, the yet unborn, the entire community, and all of nature (Nobles, 1978).

The optimal view posits human consciousness as the undisputable fact of the universe which is known to us by direct and immediate self-knowledge. To know oneself is to realize one's identity and role in the totality of consciousness. The segmented system's way of knowing by counting and measuring will often appear to be an elaborate research method for discovering the obvious or common sense to the holistic. Many have noted such differences in cognitive style (Boykin, 1978; Cooper, 1981; Horton, 1967; Levi-Strauss, 1967; Morgan, 1980; Myers, 1981). Additional evidence of this mentality functioning can be seen in the African conceptions of time and existence. After so-called physical death, a person is considered to exist in the Sasa (immediacy) as long as he/she is remembered or recognized by name (Nobles, 1972). The emerging paradigmatic shift in the Western view needs these kinds of Afrocentric constructs, particularly if interpreted based on optimal theory, in order to make some of the discoveries in modern physics and other areas salient for daily functioning. My bias toward the optimal conceptual system has been made quite apparent. Differing philosophical tenets yield differing conceptual systems and subsequently different experiences and knowledge for their adherents. All world views are valid in the sense that how one sees the world is how one sees the world, or whatever one believes is, is for them at the time believed. However, careful examination of systems of belief make evident that some systems are more holistic and comprehensive, depending on the limitations set by definition (e.g., a material conception of reality is by definition finite and limited, a spiritual/material is infinite and unlimited). As we examine and understand the psychology of knowledge and realize that the choice of conceptual systems is ours, power becomes the ability to define reality. How we define reality will be the key to our liberation or our entrapment toward oppression. If we remember our ancient African ancestors built their educational system utilizing the assumptions of an optimal conceptual system, and understand that it was a deification process through which man/woman could achieve everlasting peace and happiness (James, 1954), we can realize the fullness of our inheritance. This conceptual system fostered the first scripts, the first number system, iron-ore technology, the pyramids, and so on.

Cruse (1967) cautioned that the special function of the Negro intellectual is a cultural function, redeeming American cultural depravity stemming from the segmented, sub-optimal conceptual system/world view. Optimal theory emerging from the adoption of an optimal conceptual system used to examine life can bring us back to conscious realization of the supremely good (divine) order which exists outside the consciousness of most of us because we are conceptually incarcerated (Myers, 1986).

Conclusion

In summary, the nature of knowledge is quite subjective. Good "science" and "knowing" in general not only acknowledge the subjective, but also explore its exact nature in detail in an effort to reveal "true" knowledge. Part of the exploration must include examination of the conceptual system being utilized at every stage of the process of "knowing" and doing science. A conceptual system refers to those philosophical constructs we use to define and structure reality, and is, therefore, basic to the way in which we perceive and interpret. It is the basis of our world view. The validity of any particular conceptual system must be measured in terms of its self-consistency and long-term consequences for the experience of its adherents. All people have a conceptual system, usually shaped for the most part by the culture with which they identify. People interested in the pursuit of knowledge must be forthright in their declaration and honest in their evaluation of the conceptual system used in their work. Many of the problems of bias in "scientific" research can be ameliorated and our knowledge expanded by examining the nature and role of our conceptual system in experience. Known to have studied the teachings of our ancient African ancestors, Aristotle made the following report:

> He who thus considers things in their first growth and origin, whether a state or anything else, will obtain the clearest view of them.

> Aristotle

References

Akbar, N. (1976). *Natural psychology and human transformation.* Chicago: World Community of Islam in the West.

Bart, P. (1971). Sexism and social science: From the gilded cage to the iron cage, or, the perils of Pauline. *Journal of Marriage and the Family, 33,* 734-747.

Blake, R., & J. Vanderplas, J. (1950). The effect of pre-recognition hypotheses on vertical recognition thresholds in auditory perception. *Journal of Personality, 19,* 95-115.

Bowen, D.D. (1971). Reported patterns in TAT measures of needs for achievement, affiliation and power. *Journal of Personality Assessment, 37,* 424-430.

Boykin, W. (1978). Psychological/behavioral verse in academic/task performance: Pretheoretical considerations. *Journal of Negro Education, 47.*

Broverman, I.K., Vogel, S.R., Broverman, D.M., Clarkson, F.E., Rosenkrantz, P.S. (1972). Sex-roles stereotypes: A current appraisal. *Journal of Social Issues, 28,* 58-78.

Brunner, J., & Goodman, C. (1947). Value and need as organizing factors in perception. *Journal of Abnormal and Social Psychology, 42,* 33-44.

Brunner, J., & Postman, L. (1947). Tension and tension release as ongoing factors in perception, *Journal of Personality, 15,* 300-308.

Burgest, D.R. (1981). Theory on white supremacy and black oppression. *Black Books Bulletin, 7*(2), 26-31.

Capra, F. (1982). *The turning point: Science, society, and the rising culture.* New York: Simon & Schuster.

Capra, F. (1975). *The Tao of physics.* New York: Bantam Books.

Carlson, R. (1971). Where is the person in personality research? *Psychological Bulletin, 75,* 203-219.

Chesler, P. (1971). *Women and madness.* Garden City, NY: Doubleday.

Clark, C. (1972). Black studies or the study of black people. In R. Jones (Ed.), *Black psychology,* (1st ed). New York: Harper & Row.

Cooper, G. (1981). Black language and holistic cognitive style. *The Western Journal of Black Studies, 5*(3), 201-207.

Crewsaw, C. (1980). *Children of two cultures: A holistic approach to learning and teaching.* Unpublished manuscript.

Cruse, H. (1967). *The crisis of the Negro intellectual.* New York: William Morrow.

Dan, A.J., & Beekman, S. (1972). Male versus female representation in psychological research. *American Psychologist, 27,* 1078.

Davis, W. (1981). Toward a hermeneutics of subjectivity. *Papers in Comparative Studies.* Columbus, OH: The Ohio State University.

Devereaux, G. (1967). *From anxiety to method in the behavioral sciences.* Paris: Mouton.

Eddington, A. (1931). *The nature of the physical world.* New York: MacMillian.

Fine, M. (1982). *Social science research into the nature of the black family.* Unpublished manuscript.

Harris, E. (1967). *Science and metaphysics: Method and explanation in metaphysics* (pp. 125-131). Proceedings of the American Catholic Philosphical Association, Washington, DC.

Hempel, G.G. (1966). *Philosophy of natural science*. Englewood Cliffs, NJ: Prentice-Hall, Inc.

Horton, R. (1967). African traditional thought and Western science. *Africa, 37*(1), 50-71; 155-187.

James, G. (1954). *Stolen legacy*. New York: Philosophical Library.

Johansson, C.B., & Harmon, L.W. (1972) Strong vocational interest blank: One form or two. *Journal of Counseling Psychology, 19*, 404-410.

Jones, W.T. (1982). World views: Their nature and their function. *Current Anthropology, 13*, 86.

Kaplan, A. (1964). *The conduct of inquiry*, New York: Chandler Publishing Company.

Kuhn, T. (1962). *The structure of scientific revolutions*. Chicago: University of Chicago Press.

LeShan, L. (1969). Physicists and mystics: Similarities in world view. *Journal of Transpersonal Psychology, 1*(2), 20-40.

Levi-Strauss, C. (1967). *Structural anthropology*. New York: Anchor Books.

Mahoney, M.J. (1976). *Scientist as subject: The psychological imperative*. Cambridge, MA: Ballinger.

McGuinnies, E. (1949). Emotional and perceptual defense. *Psychological Review, 56*, 244-251.

Millman, N. (1971). Observations on sex-role research. *Journal of Marriage and the Family, 33*, 772-776.

Milton, G.A. (1959). Sex differences in problem solving as a function of appropriateness of the problem content. *Psychological Reports, 5*, 705-708.

Morgan, H. (January/February, 1980). How schools fail black children. *Social Policy*.

Munley, P., Fretz, B.R., & Mills, D. (1973). Female college students' scores on the men's and women's strong vocational interest blanks. *Journal of Counseling Psychology, 20*, 285-289.

Myers, L. (1981). The nature of pluralism and the African American case. *Theory into Practice, 20,*(1), 3-6.

Myers, L. (1984). The psychology of knowledge: The importance of world view. *New England Journal of Black Studies, 4*, 1-12.

Myers, L. (1986). A therapeutic model for transcending oppression: A black feminist perspective. *Women and Therapy, 5*, (4), 39-49.

Myers, L. (1988). *Understanding an Afrocentric world view: Introduction to an optimal psychology*. Dubuque, Iowa: Kendall/Hunt Publishers.

Neisser, U. (1976). *Cognition and reality*. San Francisco: Freeman.

Nichols, E. (November, 1976). *The philosophical aspects of cultural differences*. World Psychiatric Association, Ibadan, Nigeria.

Nobles, W. (1972). African philosophy: Foundation for black psychology. In R. Jones (Ed.), *Black psychology* (1st ed.). New York: Harper & Row.

Nobles, W. (1974). Africanity: Its role in black families. *The Black Scholar, 5*, 10-17.

Pelletier, K.R. (1978). *Towards a science of consciousness*. New York: Delacorte Press.

Popper, K. (1959). *The logic of scientific discovery*. New York: Harper & Row.

Postman, L., & Brunner, J. (1949). Multiplicity of set as a determinant of perceptual organization. *Journal of Experimental Psychology, 39*, 369-377.

Preiswerk, R., & Perrot, D. (1978). *Ethnocentrism and history: Africa, Asia, and Indian American in Western textbooks*. New York: NOK Publishers.

Richards, D. (1979). The ideology of European dominance. *The Western Journal of Black Studies, 3*(4), 244-248.

Rudner, R.S. (1966). *Philosophy of social science*. Englewood Cliffs, NJ: Prentice-Hall.

Schilpp, P.A. (Ed.), (1949). *Albert Einstein: Philosopher-scientist*. Evanston, IL: The Library of Living Philosophers.

Schultz, D.P. (1969). The human subject in psychological research. *Psychological Bulletin, 72*, 214, 228.

Schwabacker, S. (1970). Male vs. female representation in psychological research: An examination of the *Journal of Personality and Social Psychology*. *Catalogue of Selected Documents in Psychology*, 20-21.

Staples, R. (1976). *Introduction to black sociology*. New York: McGraw Hill.

Webster's Seventh New Collegiate Dictionary. (1969). Springfield, MA: G.C. Merriam Company.

Weimer, W. (1976). *Psychology and the conceptual foundation of science*. Hillsdale, NJ: Lawrence Erlbaum Associates.

Weisstein, N. (1969). Kinder, Kuche, Kirche as scientific law: Psychology constructs the female. *Motive, 29*, 6-7.

Woodson, C. (1933). *The Mis-education of the Negro*. Washington, DC: The Associated Publishers.

Perspectives

II. Perspectives

Diverse views of black social and behavioral scientists on the nature of black psychological reality, on the possibilities of developing a black psychology, and of the potential contributions of such an activity are presented in Part II. In the present, as in the previous editions, there is agreement that explanations of African American behavior which are alternative to European perspectives must be developed. And as was also the case in the earlier editions, a variety of approaches to the accomplishment of this goal are presented.

Most articles in the previous editions, especially the first, were devoted to establishing the validity of our concerns, for example, that there were indeed alternative ways of looking at black behavior, that African philosophy was indeed potentially useful in helping us understand the behavior of African Americans, and that African American social behavioral scientists must be in the vanguard of this enterprise. Many important, indeed some classic, contributions were introduced in the two previous editions, including papers by Nobles, Guthrie, and Hayes. They are retained here and several quite different points of view are added to them.

We begin with Guthrie's paper ("The Psychology of African Americans: An Historical Perspective") which informs us that the insights and points of view introduced in this volume are not new. As Guthrie indicates, there has been a persistent response by African American scholars to issues related to the psychological dimensions of black existence. Guthrie addresses four historical events (Darwin's Origins of the Species, Sir Francis Galton's Eugenics, William McDougall's Theory of Instincts, and Mendelian Genetics) that have influenced research and thinking on the psychology of African Americans. Guthrie gives an historical perspective on the academic origins of black psychology as well, and he concludes with a discussion of the goals and objectives of the psychology of African Americans, with directions for study and research in this area.

Any discipline that seeks to understand the nature of black behavior must take into account the experiences which shaped that behavior. It is not surprising, then, that we should turn to Africa in our attempts to account for the values, customs, attitudes and culture of African Americans. The need for such an orientation is the thesis of Nobles' paper ("African Philosophy: Foundations of Black Psychology"). Nobles believes the task of Black psychology should be to understand the behavioral definition of African philosophy, and the documentation of its modification over time. Nobles outlines various elements of African philosophy he believes have relevance for African Americans (unity, kinship, death, and immortality) and documents their presence in contemporary African

American life. There should be no mistaking that the present volume, like the previous ones, has not been developed to articulate a unified point of view with respect to "Black psychology" but rather to present a range of perspectives on psychology as related to African Americans. There has not been sufficient work by African Americans scholars across the various fields to develop a completely workable Black psychology, a task that will probably take many years. At the present time the work of Nobles holds promise as a cornerstone in the development of a distinctive Black psychology. The influence of his thinking will be seen in a number of papers in the present volume.

Hayes ("Radical Black Behaviorism") and Jenkins ("A Humanistic Approach to Black Psychology") present points of view that are quite literally at opposite ends of the spectrum. A central tenet of Hayes view is that the behavior of African Americans is controlled by forces outside the individual, while Jenkins makes a compelling case for individual agency (power, control). Hayes urges that a discipline of Radical Black Behaviorism be established. Such a discipline would be limited to the study of behaviors that can be observed, measured, and reproduced. Explanations are those that produce and maintain the behavior to be explained.

Jenkins reminds us that ". . . more and more . . . psychology is coming to see that something important is left out when one relies on external stimulus factors as the sole constructs for trying to understand behavior." He stresses the importance of "individual agency, independent of the external givens of the situation, as a necessary component of all human action." Thus, a person's intentions and goals are important motivating factors in the person's behavior. Finally, Jenkins applies this (humanistic) orientation to issues related to the concept of self, intellectual performance, and mental health.

Akbar ("The Evolution of Human Psychology for African Americans") and Baldwin ("African [Black] Psychology: Issues and Synthesis") provide sound critiques of European American and Black psychological perspectives and make the case for African psychology. Akbar introduces the Afrocentric perspective, critiques the notion of the black norm and ghetto-centric perspectives, and shows how European American, Black, and African psychology each deal with conceptions of self, time orientation, human goals, and epistemology (how we know, what we know). Also supporting an African (Black) psychology, in a penetrating analysis Baldwin calls our attention to such issues as inconsistencies among scholars in the definition and parameters of African (Black) psychology and the range of African people to be included under the Black psychology rubric. Baldwin reminds us that African (Black) Psychology needs no justification since it derives from a longstanding world view that, in fact, precedes European civilization.

The Psychology of African Americans: An Historical Perspective

Robert V. Guthrie

We live in a labeling and measuring society. Whatever exists or is thought to exist in any quantity must be weighed, named, and otherwise measured. Our technologically advanced society which has created a continuing and demanding need for the understanding and measurement of physical entities has also created an incredible obsession for the attempted quantification of intangible human attributes. This quantophrenic obsession found among a wide continuum of behavioral scientists has resulted in and, unfortunately, created more difficulties and biases than it has produced usefulness and fairness. This is not because statistics, research methodologies, and paradigms do not work, quite to the contrary, but rather because of inherent problems found in predicting and interpreting human behavior. Human behaviors are not static conditions. For the most part they are learned and maintained because of their consequences. (1) Human behavior is affected by an infinite number of social and environmental variables; (2) behavioral consequences are derived from social and environmental circumstances and these circumstances strongly influence behavior; (3) isolating human behaviors cannot be accomplished with the exactitude as we do with physical quantities; (4) human behavior is subject to elusive and varying definitions, and interpretations are strongly influenced by socioeconomic status and cultural predispositions of the interpreter. Among the most captivating and engrossing aspects of the psychological labeling and measuring processes have been these attempts to measure and qualify human traits and abilities in respect to some model of normalcy (Guthrie, 1970). For example, psychological diagnosis is in itself often misleading and tells us little about the client; however, it reveals much more about the environment in which the observer finds the individual (Murphy, 1976). Anthropological, sociological and psychological data suggest that behaviors labeled as bizarre in one culture might be considered acceptable in another cluture even when these cultures are contiguous rather than separated by continents or great distances. Over 25 years ago, Frantz Fanon succinctly dealt with the cultural model of normalcy in *Black Skins, White Masks* when he explored the concept that "A normal Negro child, having grown up within a normal family, will become abnormal on the slightest contact with the white world. (Suggestive here is an expression of societal reaction theory which holds that normalcy categorization and labeling follows the needs of the power holders in a given society.) Complicating this problematic matrix of labeling, measuring, and the resulting cultural biases, is the belief that *authenticity* exists when findings are published or otherwise uttered by experts from the psychological, sociological, and educational fields who, more often than not, have not experienced any significant degrees of interactions, sensitivities, and/or rapport with the populations being studied. Along this line, there is a disturbing tendency voiced by traditional academicians in which the importance of identification, sensitivity, and rapport, for example, race of the psychometric examiner, has been devalued and replaced by other emphases. (This view frequently is expressed in those academic departments in which little or no minority representation is witnessed.) Now this raises several points of interest: Can one be labeled an expert or be knowledgeable in the uncertain science of human behavior merely because one completes a set of traditional courses taught in traditional academic settings? It is ludicrous and sheer nonsense to believe that expertise or competency can be acquired by this route; however, with the phenomenal numerical growth of psychologists since 1940, an interesting form of consensual and circular validations has occurred which reinforces and lends credence to the proposition that academic traditionalism produces competency.

Traditional academic psychology has strongly defended and literally brainwashed its students as to what a psychologist is, what psychology is about, its subject matter, and its direction. All of this has occurred through years of less than successful attempts at solving the riddles of human behavior. And as a result, traditional academic psychology has evolved into a sterile, pedestrian science which leans heavily upon statistical analyses to the point where calculating, cold, unemotional robots who can perform mathematical manipulations have become our authorities. This is especially tragic when one stops to realize that the black life cycle, from conception to death, is strongly influenced by an interplay of environmental and physical factors which create a need for a psychology of African Americans.

These kinds of problems have created many difficulties in past interpretations of what African Americans are reported to be all about. When I began to write this paper on the topic of *Psychology of African Americans,* my most difficult task, beyond trying to select which aspect of this broad subject to discuss, was to decide how to come to grips with these historical problems of what has been said, studied, and taught to millions of Americans under the label of scientific facts. Realizing that I could not possibly sidestep these issues and effectively deal with the task at hand, I recalled the last few sentences in my book, *Even The Rat Was White; A Historical View of Psychology*.

At present there exists a scientific community of black scholars whose daily lives are affected by racism. This has brought about unified concerns on a number of issues within the discipline of psychology. Concern over inappropriate research stances (deficit modeling) and applied problems (urban and community psychology) are among the major priorities of black psychologists. And then this sentence, "While at present it is difficult to justify the existence of a black psychology, there is a theoretical basis for its creation." After writing approximately ten pages of this paper, a rhetorical syllogism stopped everything. That is, to assume that there is a psychology of African Americans is to assume that there is a body of information that is relevant to a specific group of people that can be formed out of existing scientific knowledge or, can yet be developed for this purpose. Then the question with the obvious answer comes about, "Is there a need for a body of knowledge directed specifically to African Americans that traditional psychology has failed to provide in order to meet the needs of this population?" It is hardly debatable that the science of psychology has failed not only in the provision of adequate knowledge for black people, but has contributed immensely in constructing barriers to the proper mental sets and processes needed to provide and/or construct such data. It goes without saying that there exists a wealth of data that indicates that psychology's time honored psychometric tools are not only biased against black people but fall short of providing any useful data in predicting talents, capabilities, or skills for the majority of black youngsters.

Considering these introspections, I have decided to present and briefly discuss the following questions:

1. What are the intellectual predispositions that must be understood in order to clear the way for a psychology of African Americans?
2. Just what is the psychology of African Americans?
3. What directions are needed to properly advance the study of the psychology of African Americans?

Historical Barriers in the Study of African Americans

The academic profession of psychology has been faced with many obstacles in grasping objective truth in the psychological study of African Americans. Among these barriers have been submission to faulty and in many cases unworthy authority, influence of custom, and racial prejudices. During the late nineteenth century, the emerging discipline of psychology cut a wide swath through the ivy halls of academia at a time when the Western environmental atmosphere was infected by overt racism and social Darwinism. (Black people were scarcely out of the bonds of "legalized slavery.") The profession of psychology, most importantly academic psychology, was strongly influenced by four events which not only affected philosophical biases and research stances concerning African Americans, but in addition provided a *gestalt* impacting upon attempts to objectively study the psychology of African Americans. These events reinforced what can be referred to as nativistic themes by declaring that *human differences resulted from causes within people rather than environmental forces in society.* Therefore the "plight" of blackness, including the so-called culture and cycle of poverty, were blamed on inherent inadequacies of blacks themselves. This concept can still be strongly observed in the public education system that seems to say "the schools are all right only the wrong children show up." So minor changes occur in the system. Schools seem to be the place where cultural biases are finally riveted on the minds of the young. There is a growing body of evidence that many of the so-called learning disabilities seem to result from forcing left-hemispheric functioning on children with a natural bent for apprehending the world in visual rather than verbal forms (Behavior Today, 1977).

Probably more than any other single force, psychology's reliance on the principles of psychoanalysis stimulated and encouraged the belief of inherent inadequacies within individuals. Most certainly, the belief in the Oedipus complex as the basis of culture and society points to the strong acceptance of intrapsychic bases of personal and group inadequacies. Freud's *Totem and Taboo* (1912) underscored the belief that the behaviors of "primitive" man were similar to that of the psychoneurotic because the system of taboos used by people of color were thought to be the same as the obsessive-compulsive actions of the neurotic found in European society. Coupled with the hypothesis of sexual repression as a critical factor in the etiology of European neurosis, the connection was, and is still frequently used to describe and explain the behavior of blacks and has led to unfortunate interpretations for and by African Americans. Take for example the psychometric projective techniques such as the Rorschach and Thematic Apperception Tests, and the Minnesota Multiphasic Personality Inventory which depend heavily upon psychoanalytical theoretical underpinnings for their interpretations. Although there is much doubt regarding the validity of these tests, psychologists have and continue to use and view them as valid. I have discussed at considerable length in my writings, the problems of (1) culturally biased psychologists who administer and interpret culturally biased psychological tests and (2) the general background and training of most clinicians. I will not belabor these points here, but I do refer you to the chapter "Psychometric Scientism" in *Even the Rat Was White.*

Darwin's Origin of the Species by Means of Natural Selection

Darwin's theory of evolution influenced the development of modern psychology as much as any other single event in the nineteenth century. It would be impossible to understand what psychologists today are trying to accomplish or why they go about it as they do unless one first understood something of the importance of evolutionary theory. The *survival of the fittest* shibboleth maintained that only the strongest and most intelligent individuals would survive in the struggle between individual and individual and between individual and environment. It was Darwin who underscored the appeal for recognizing the importance of individual differences by placing the onus of an individuals' plight on the individual. This line of reasoning has led many psychologists to focus their research stances on sensory and intellectual differences between individuals in order to solve the puzzle of which people succeed and which do not succeed. Therefore, emphasis upon deficit modeling in research, that is, psychopathology, cognitive dissonance, and gaming theories can be traced to this origin. Deficit theories have been used to explain much of the behavior of blacks as individuals and as a group. For example, the belief expressed and popularized during the 1960s which certainly has Darwinian origins, proclaimed that "deep-seated structural distortions" in the life of African Americans existed and resulted in a "tangle of pathology" which was convincing to many Americans, both black and white. Deficit modeling, which interpreted the absenteeism of the black male as a crime rather than emphasizing the inequities of the environment can also be traced to Darwinian thinking. Interpretations viewing the female-dominated black family as pathological misled many academicians because the white middle-class yardstick failed to recognize that the fatherless, "broken homes" were an adaptation with intrinsic strengths of its own.

The black family, as we all know, is often an extended one, including grandparents, aunts, and uncles as well as children. This is more correctly viewed as a source of social cohesion rather than disintegration. The principal sources of the view that the scholastic failure of black children stemmed not from the schools but rather from the student's home environment and family background can be traced to nativistic lines of reasoning.

Sir Frances Galton's Eugenics

Galton provided the linkage between scientific naturalism and psychology. Galton's *Hereditary Genius: Its Laws and Consequences* (1869) attempted to illustrate that genius and greatness followed family lines; *English Men of Science* (1874) and *Natural Inheritance* (1899) were similar efforts which supported his genetic biases. Galton's strong belief in the importance of inheritance led him to propose a science of heredity, *eugenics*, which promoted the idea of racial improvement through selected mating and sterilization of the "unfit." This belief and support of eugenics has extended itself into several facets of contemporary psychological philosophies. The statistical properties emanating from intelligence quotients, etc., are frequently used to support the need for eugenics. William Schockley, an avowed eugenicist extended the eugenic notion to explain that many of the "large improvident families with social problems have constitutional deficiencies in those parts of the brain which enable a person to plan and carry out plans" (Guthrie, 1976). (He localizes this deficiency in the brain's frontal lobes). In order to halt the dysgenic trend, he called for a bonus plan in which cash payments would be made to black people with IQs below 100 who voluntarily submitted to sterilization operations. To support his genetic attribution theory of intelligence and social problems, Schockley drew upon studies comparing the intelligence quotients of identical white twins separated at birth and subsequently reared in different environments. These studies reported that the measured IQs were similar in identical twins regardless of environmental differences. Schockley interprets this data as conclusive evidence of the importance of heredity. The baseline for Schockley's eugenic reasoning is Cyril Burt's famous survey of separated identical twins. Burt contended that there was a high correlation between the IQs of identical twins even when they were reared completely separately and in disparate socioeconomic backgrounds. It is now fairly evident that Burt concocted his data including the writings of his so-called "phantom graduate students." The fact that Burt's research went unchallenged until after his death in 1971 says much for the authenticity factor in behavioral research. Incidentally a recent examination of the intelligence issue, "IQ Test Performance of Black Children" (Scarr and Weinberg, 1976), clearly illustrates the malleability for IQs under rearing conditions relevant to the tests and schools. But beyond these debates is the fact that millions of dollars and much human effort have been poured into the psychometric business making it difficult for those directly or indirectly involved in the industry to agree that the IQ concept is null and void. Just as the Binet test was legally challenged in 1916 and in 1977, it will take many similar challenges to achieve limits on the use of IQ tests and their results to perpetuate the eugenicist's hereditary-environment debate.

William McDougall: Theory of Instincts

McDougall, who has been called the "Father of Social Psychology," promulgated, among other very strong racist concepts, the dogma of instrincts in humans, for example, that inborn and unlearned response tendencies determined social behavior. Widespread stereotyping that categorized African Americans as easy-going, happy, and lazy resulted from this concept. This line of reasoning, in psychological thought, stems back nearly 76 years. In 1899, the Cambridge Anthropological Society sent an expedition to the Torres Straits to study the "mental life" of the inhabitants.

For the first time trained experimental psychologists investigated, by means of an adequate laboratory experiment, a people in a low state of culture under their ordinary conditions of life (Wade, 1976). This study was made in the best tradition of Wundtian psychophysics. Hearing, vision, taste, tactile acuity, pain, and motor speed were all performed on the unsuspecting, cooperative sepia-skinned villagers. Unsurprisingly, these studies concluded that the "wild natives" were inferior to Western man and out of this view and similar theories, the instinct theory flourished. A series of similar studies conducted on black Americans during the early 1900's supported previous predispositions of racial stereotyping. Most notable of these studies is Ferguson, *The Psychology of the Negro* (1916). While the instinct theory is one of historical interest and has been debunked by most contemporary psychologists, much of the vestiges of this concept can still be seen in hereditarian arguments.

Mendelian Genetics

The last of the four nativistic themes involves the impact of Mendelian genetics. Though the Austrian monk Gregor Mendel published his scientific inquiry on the genetic differences of garden peas in 1866, it was not until 1900 that the dust was blown off his research and the disturbing parallel was made between agricultural and human inheritance. Mendel's discovery was of major importance because it helped to establish the fact that genetic traits come to the individual in unites rather than through a blending of qualities from one's ancestors. While Mendel's work was valid for *physical* differences, it led many researchers to make quick, unsubstantiated parallels to psychological and other nonphysical aspects of human behavior, without regard for environmental conditions. It was within this genetic framework that the belief that genetic differences in black people, vis-a-vis white, existed. For example, G. Stanley Hall, the founding father of the American Psychological Association maintained that:

> No two races in history, taken as a whole, differ so much in their traits, both physical and psychic, as the Caucasian and the African. The color of the skin and the crookedness of the hair are only the outward signs of the many far deeper differences, including cranial and thoracic capacity, proportions of the body, nervous system, glands, and secretions, vita sexualis, food, temperament, disposition, character, longevity, instincts, customs, emotional traits, and diseases. All of these differences as they are coming to be better understood, are seen to be so great as to qualify if not imperil every inference from one race to another, whether theoretical or practical so that what is true and good for one is often false and bad for the other (Guthrie, 1976).

In this connection, early anthropomorphic research additionally contributed biases to the psychology of black Americans by correlating such physical factors as skin color differences, hair texture, and the size of lips to psychological conditions.

The historical factors of genetics, eugenics, psychometrics, and early philosophies that I have briefly mentioned not only influenced early behavioral scientists who were studying and reporting on the psychology of black Americans but, as you can surmise, strongly biased present-day interpretations. These historical barriers, consequently, have created the need to establish and maintain academic courses to provide accurate and useful information for black Americans. The applied subject matter for the psychology of black Americans must grow from strong theoretical investigations; hence, the need for a Black psychology is called for.

Black Psychology and the Psychology of African Americans

Black psychology is an outgrowth of "Third World" philosophies which are not committed to the authenticity of traditional European and American psychology, but are born out of a need promulgated through neglect rather than traditional theoretical stances. Its American academic origins extend back nearly 40 years when Herman Canady, then a professor of psychology at West Virginia State College (Institute, West VA.) drew attention to the need for establishing courses concerned with the psychology of African Americans. After surveying nearly every black college during the 1930s, Canady concluded "that no institution offers a course in race psychology and that no institution offers a course with the distinct title of *The Psychology of the Negro.*" He decried this absence of such subject matter and called for the creation of such courses. Along with Francis Cecil Sumner, the Father of African American Psychology, he convened the first conference of black psychologists in July 1938 at Tuskegee Institute (Alabama). The convention's theme, "The Negro Youth Looks at Occupations in America," included eminent black psychologists: Drs. Oran Eagleson (Spelman College, Atlanta, Ga.), Martin Jenkins (Cheyney Teachers College, Cheyney, Pa.), Howard Long (District of Columbia Public Schools), Bertram Doyle (CME Church, Nashvill, Tenn.), Charles Cooper (A & T College, Greensboro, N.C.), and J. Otis Smith (Alcorn A & M college, Lorman, Miss.) Topics concerning the home, church, community, and cultural awareness were discussed. Similar to our present colloquium series on the Black Life Cycle, this 1938 meeting of black psychologists was also concerned with the gestalt of black experiences.

While most young people are primarily interested in the more applied aspects of psychological findings, it is extremely important that the foundation for Black psychology emanate from a strong empirical base. I envision Black psychology as a scientific study of behavior attempting to understand life as it is lived. Black psychology should be involved in a most interesting, interwoven kind of investigation concerned with the struggles, pleasures, interests, desires, habits, aims, drives, motivations, feelings, actions, and wants . . . all those bits of behavior that have molded black people into complex, unique, living beings. Due to the urgency of our mission, Black psychology should not only attempt to *understand* behavior, it should strive to disseminate its scientific findings directly to the community as soon as possible, in a manner that lends itself to application. In this sense, it is a systems approach to psychological science.

Black psychology finds itself akin to various fields: psychiatry, sociology, linguistics, biology, anthropology, and political science. In emphasizing the fusion of this psychology with others, Black psychology will thrive on a polygamy with kindred disciplines and it is hoped that the marriage between traditional psychology, anthropology, sociology, and political science will produce the goals for significant knowledge.

What Is the Psychology of African Americans?

There is a disturbing tendency, in many quarters, to speak of the African American as if there was some monolithic social group involved. We cannot fall into this logic for there is as much diversity in the black community as there is in any other community. The common bond of blackness and its resulting strengths have brought about unified concerns across many dimensions, yet differences occur. A panoramic view of our versatility and variances can be seen in the writings of early African American sociologists who vividly described the world from a black perspective. Their articles and books are among the most outstanding classics of this century. Sociologists Allison Davis and John Dollard wrote *Children of Bondage* (1940) which examined and illustrated a multiracial community with all its caste and class lines. Involved were the many attitudinal and value distinctions of black people. Du Bois' *The Souls of Black Folk* (1903) pointed to the double life that every black person must live in order to survive the racism in this country. E. Franklin Fraziers's series of studies, *The Negro Family in the United States* (1939); *The Negro in the United States* (1940); and *Black Bourgeoisie* (1957) examined both negative and positive attributes of black communities during the 1940s. His discussions of the "world of make believe" that the black middle class had created to compensate for feelings of inferiority in a white world dominated by business enterprises became the center of debate among blacks as well as whites.

With migrations to northern, eastern, and western urban areas, a number of unfortunate behavioral consequences have occurred from existing in densely populated areas, living on marginal incomes or with marginal expenditures for homemaking or childbearing, living in clusters isolated from one another by barriers of ethnicity, and living in proximity to high crime areas. One behavioral aspect of such environmental conditions can be viewed in the parallel drawn by Pierce (1974) between oppressive, stressful urban conditions and exotic environments where humans live under great duress, such as during a space expedition. He feels that the inner-city youngster experiences far greater psychological stress than an adult on a space vehicle. (It should be noted that much of this present discussion would apply to any human, regardless of race, who lives under such conditions. In this country, however, this means we are speaking of a disproportionately large number of people who have other than white skin.) Nevertheless, it follows that the inner-city resident has more positive attributes, both in quality and quantity, because of the situations. That they survive is a tribute to their psychological strengths; to remain invulnerable to unspeakable distress and hardship, all compounded by racial discrimination and injustice bespeaks of courage. The fact that much current data show blacks with strong self-images is indicative of how hopelessness has been tamed. By any definition, these are impressive monuments and belie any too ready categorization that blacks have a negative self-image.

Suggestions to Advance the Study of the Psychology of African Americans

It has been said that there are four types of research efforts, three of which need to be avoided in our efforts to advance the study of black Americans.

1. Useless and False. (The earlier discussion of Cyril Burt's research findings is especially relevant here.)
2. Useless and True. (Examples of this category can be located in many professional journals.)
3. Useful and False. (Overzealous researchers in an attempt to alleviate social inequities are vulnerable to violate research findings.)
4. Useful and True. (It is in this category where major attention should be focused.)

In order to assist in comprehending the many factors involved in the psychology of African Americans and to increase the probability of producing useful and true results, a need to focus upon a systems analysis to provide an understanding and a theoretical base for individual and group behavior is suggested. Systems analysis does not simply mean a multiplicity of diagrams showing flows and uncontrolled behaviors in an environment. There are two distinct advantages to a systems analysis for the study of Black psychology: (1) the notion of such an analysis will be applicable to the many kinds of behavioral occurrences found in black communities and (2) generalizations developed from observing one kind of behavioral occurrence can be discovered to be valid for other, sometimes discrepant, kinds of events. In each case, the advantage lies in having a concept or generalization that applies to multiple situations and hence that requires a smaller conceptual set than if each situation had to be dealt with independently. An interesting and valid case in point is the analysis of the black family, as discussed by Billingsley (1968), which illustrates the interactions and interdependence within a large context (Kuhn, 1974).

While all environments can be analyzed by a systemic evaluation, the urban black milieu is of particular complexity and needs our close attention. Along this line, we will find that at every point and interaction in the systems loop, specialized needs will become apparent. The cultivation of skills and knowledge for analysis and management of social systems for the psychological study of black people must be developed through existing courses and seminars taught in academic departments, for example, Afro-American Studies and/or Black Studies.

Conclusion

In this paper I have attempted to briefly discuss and outline the following three points.
1. The historical predispositions that must be understood in order to clear the way for a psychology of African Americans.
2. A discussion on the goals and objectives of the psychology of African Americans.
3. Directions needed to properly advance the study of the psychology of African Americans.

The intellectual brainpower of African Americans is infinite and the future of African Americans rests with our youth. It is commendable that in this nuclear era when humankind is exploring the mysteries of intergalactic space travel and the unknown secrets of the ocean's floors that African Americans have not lost contact with themselves.

References

Behavior Today (1977). *The Professional Newsletter*, Vol. 8, No. 4.

Fanon, F. (1952). *Black skin, white masks*. New York: Grove Press.

Guthrie, R. (1970). *Being black: Psychological and sociological dilemmas*. San Francisco: Canfield Press.

Guthrie, R. (1976). *Even the rat was white: A historical view of psychology*. New York: Harper & Row.

Kuhn, A. (1974). *The logic of social systems*. San Francisco: Jossey-Bass.

Murphy, J. (1976, March). Psychiatric labeling in cross-cultural perspective. *Science,,* Vol. 19.

Pierce, C.M. (1974, June). *The mundane extreme environment and its effects on learning.* Paper presented at the National Institute of Education. Navy, Office of Research, Washington, D.C.

Wade, N. (1976, November). News and comment. *Science*, Vol.20.

African Philosophy: Foundations for Black Psychology

Wade W. Nobles

African Americans derive their most fundamental self-definition from several cultural and philosophical premises which we share with most West African "tribes" (See Note 1). In exploring the character of these premises, which are basic conceptions of the nature of man and his relation to other men and his environment, we hope to establish a foundation upon which a black psychology can be constructed. Thus, it will be contended that black psychology is something more than the psychology of so-called underprivileged peoples, more than the experience of living in ghettoes or of having been forced into the dehumanizing condition of slavery. It is more than the "darker" dimension of general psychology. Its unique status is from the positive features of basic African philosophy which dictate the values, customs, attitudes, and behavior of Africans in Africa and the New World.

The notion of common experience or common ethos seems almost fictional if one accepts uncritically the research finding of many so-called Africanists who argue that the territory of the Western region of Africa held and still does hold within its boundaries many different "tribes," each having its own language, religion, and customs. However, one must note the orientation of these many Africanists whose incidental whiteness colors much of what they have to say. One must, therefore, be conscious of the inherent social dialectic. That is to say, while most foreign students of Africa have maintained that the Western "tribes" have little shared experience because each has a distinct language and religion and many unique customs, they have overlooked "the similarities of the forest for the differences *between* the trees." In this view, it is suggested that the overemphasis given tribal differences by white investigators is the anthropological or scientific version of the imperialist strategy of "divide and conquer." Hence, it is likely that many white ethnographers are predisposed by conscious or unconscious racist assumptions to focus upon superficial differences and are thus "blinded" to underlying similarities in the experiential communality of African peoples. Fortunately, however, this anthropological analog of the "divide and conquer" strategy has been redressed by black (and even by a few white) scholars (Mbiti, 1970; Herskovits, 1958). These scholars maintain that "tribal" differences in Africa were minor compared to the binding quality of their communality. This author suggests that what supported this regional communality was a set of guiding beliefs—an ethos. Closer examination of the region indicates that the ethos determined two operational orders. The first is the notion that the people were part of the natural rhythm of nature: They were one with nature. The second order is the notion of the survival of one's people—that is, the "tribe." Hence, the African experience defines man's place (role) in nature's scheme.

However, unlike a written constitution, the ethos is more akin to a spiritual disposition and probably could best be described a collective unconsciousness. Although the ethos cannot be scientifically (i.e., empirically) examined with current methodology, it is believed that one way to understand the essential and pervasive nature of the African (black) ethos is to explore and understand African philosophy (Note 2). It follows therefore that insofar as the African (black) ethos is distinct from that of the prevailing white ethos (upon which traditional psychology was founded) then a black psychology based upon the black ethos must also be uniquely different from white psychology. It is this principle that allows African philosophy to take its place as the foundation for black psychology.

African Philosophy

Religion and Philosophy

John Mbiti (1970) defines African philosophy as "the understanding, attitude of mind, logic, and perception behind the manner in which African peoples think, act, or speak in different situations of life." What is central to Brother Mbiti's definition is the "spiritual disposition," the "collective consciousness,"—in a word, the ethos. At this point, it should be made very explicit that when talking about the ethos one is talking about it in the context of African philosophy. In a sense, the ethos can be considered the operational definition of African philosophy. More specifically, this "collective consciousness" can be described as a *vita attitude*. That is to say, a kind of faith in a transcendental force and a sense of vital solidarity.

Examination of preslavery Africa suggests that there were hundreds of African peoples, or tribes, and some would suggest that each had its own philosophical system. More sophisticated scholarship indicates that for West Africa in general, philosophy was the essence of the people's existence, and that the many tribes shared one overriding philosophical system. It was through religion, however, that this philosophical system was expressed. In this sense religion and philosophy are the same phenomenon. Hence, to understand the essence of these peoples' existence one must examine their religion, proverbs, oral traditions, ethics, and morals—keeping clearly in mind that underlying the differences in detail is a general philosophical system which prevailed in Africa. Religion, however, is the more observable phenomenon and as such it permeated every aspect of the African's life. It was, in a very real sense, not something for the betterment of the individual, but rather something for the community of which the individual was an integral part. For the traditional African, to be human was to belong to the whole community (Mbiti, 1970, p. 5). Curiously enough, many African languages did not have a word for religion as such. Religion was such an integral part of man's existence that it and he were inseparable. Religion accompanied the individual from conception to long after his physical death. As most scholars of African religion will attest, one of the greatest difficulties in studying African religion and philosophy is that there are no sacred scriptures or texts. A great number of beliefs and practices were and can be found in African society. However, these beliefs and/or traditions were handed down from father to son for generation upon generation. As such, and in accordance with the prevailing *oral tradition*, the beliefs were corporate and the acts were communal. Traditional religion in Africa was not proselytized. The people were their religion. Thus, individuals could not "preach" their religion to "others." As was noted above, religion was the observable phenomenon and, for the most part, the tribes seemingly were observably different. For instance, the Dogon conception of the universe is based, on the one hand, on the principle of vibrations of matter, and on the other hand, on a general movement of the universe as a whole (Forde, 1954, p. 84). For the Dogon, proliferation of life was directed by a perpetual alternation of opposites—right-left, high-low, odd-even, male-female—all reflecting the principle of twinness (no mention of right-wrong). Like all creatures, these twin beings, living images of the fundamental principle of twinness in creation, were each (i.e., both opposites) equipped with two spiritual principles of opposites. That is, each of them was himself a pair. This notion of man's unity with the universe is reflected in the Dogon belief that "man is the seed of the universe" (Forde, 1954). Hence, the organization of the earth's system is reproduced in every individual. The Fon of Dahomey believed that at the beginning of the present world there were the pair (twins) Mawu-Lisa—Mawu the female, Lisa the male. They were "regarded as twins and their union was the basis of the organization of the world" (Forde, 1954, p. 219). The Mende, also of West Africa, believed that each parent gave to their offspring some aspect of its (the child's) unified constitution. For instance, the Mende believed that the physical part of an individual (i.e., bones, flesh, etc.) is provided by the father through the semen he puts into the mother. The child's spirit (Ngafa) is contributed by its mother. The Ashanti believed that the human being is formed from the blood (Mogya) of the mother and the spirit (Ntoro) of the father (Forde, 1954, p. 196). Both peoples nevertheless believed that the spirit and the physical body and blood unite as one in making the new human being. In this sense each tribe had its own religious (life) system, and for one to have propagated his religion would have involved propagating the entire life of the people concerned. However, the substance of each tribal life system was not different.

Traditional Africans made no distinction between the act and the belief. "What people do is motivated by what they believe, and what they believe springs from what they do and experience" (Mbiti, 1970, p. 5). Action and belief in traditional West African society were not separated. They belonged to a single whole. Accordingly, traditional beliefs made no concrete distinction between the spiritual and the physical. Note that the Mende perceived physical and spiritual components as uniting to make the human. Life after death is found in all African societies. However, belief in the continuation of life after death did not represent a hope for the future or possibly a better life when one dies. For the African, once dead, there was neither Heaven to be hoped for nor Hell to be feared. Again, this reflects the idea of vital force.

The whole of one's existence was an ontological religious phenomenon. The African was a deeply religious being living in a religious universe (Mbiti, 1970). For him to live was to be involved in, to be part of, a religious drama. As noted, traditional African religion was a religious ontology. As such, the ontology was characteristically very anthropocentric—everything was seen in terms of its relation to man.

Notion of Unity

The anthropocentric ontology was a complete unity which nothing could break up or destroy. Everything was functionally connected; to destroy one category completely would cause the destruction of the whole of existence, including the Creator. God was viewed as the originator and sustainer of man. The spirits explained man's destiny. Man was the center of the ontology. The animals, plants, and natural phenomena constituted the environment in which man lived. In addition to the five categories, *there existed a force, a power, or energy which permeated the whole universe.* In this kind of natural order (i.e., unity), God was the source and ultimate controller of the energy, but the spirits also had access to it. A few human beings—the Shaman (i.e., medicine men, priest, and rainmakers)—possessed the knowledge and ability to tap, manipulate, and use to a limited degree this energy. For the Dogon the social order was projected in the individual. An indivisible cell which, on the one hand, is a microcosm of the whole, and on the other hand has a circumscribed function. Not only was a person the product of his institutions, he also was their motive power. Lacking, however, any special power in himself, he was the representative of the whole. The individual affected the cosmic order which he also displayed (Forde, 1954). As stated earlier, a prevailing belief (Dogon) was that the organization (unity) of the earth's system was reproduced in every individual. This notion of the unity of things was so ingrained that the Mende, for instance, had developed a sense of collective responsibility. Also ingrained in the notion of unity is a particular conception of time.

Concept of Time

African philosophy concerned itself with two dimensions of time—the past and the present; and this conception of time helped to explain the general life system of traditional Africans (Note 3). The direction of one's life system was from the present dimension backward to the past dimension. For the people, time itself was simply a composition of past events. Very little concern was given to time in and of itself. It existed, but the African time concept was (is) very elastic. It encompassed events that had already occurred, those that are taking place, and those that will occur immediately (Mbiti, 1970). What had no possibility of occurring immediately or had not taken place fell into the category of "no time" (Mbiti, 1970). Time as reckoned by phenomena. "Actual time" was what (events) was present or past and, because time essentially moved backward rather than forward, the traditional African set his mind not on future things but chiefly on what had taken place. Thus, the West African's understanding of all things—that is, the individual, the tribe (community), and the five characters of the universe—was governed or dominated by these two dimensions (past and present) of time. In order to make sense, or be real, to the West African, time had to be experienced; and the way in which one experienced time was partly through one's own individual life and partly through the life of the tribe which went back many generations before one's birth. Because time was reckoned by phenomena, "instead of numerical calendars, there were what one would call phenomenon calendars, in which the events or phenomena which constituted time were reckoned or considered in their relation with one another as they take place" (Mbiti, 1970). The Mandingo for instance had (have) a distinct "seasonal" calendar which reflected the changing of the seasons. Hence, the phenomenal changes of the environment constituted time. For most Africans, time was meaningful at the point of the event and not at the mathematical moment. Thus, in traditional life, any period of time was reckoned according to its significant events.

Recognizing the associations and connotations that the English words *past, present*, and *future* have, Brother Mbiti uses two Swahili words (Sasa and Zamani) to represent present and past. Sasa has the sense of immediacy, nearness, nowness (Mbiti, 1970). It is the period of immediate concern for the people because that is *where* or *when* they exist. The Sasa period is not mathematically or numerically constant. Each member of the tribe has his own and, hence, the older the person, the longer his Sasa period. Each tribe (society, nation) also has its own Sasa period.

The Zamani period is not limited to what Europeans call the past. It overlaps or encompasses the Sasa and the two are not separable. The Sasa feels or disappears into the Zamani. However, before events become incorporated into the Zamani, they have to be realized or actualized within the Sasa dimension. Thus, events (people) move backward from the Sasa dimension to the Zamani dimension. In a sense, Zamani is the graveyard of time (Mbiti, 1970). The Sasa dimension binds individuals and their immediate environment together. As such, it determines the experiential communality, encompassing the conscious limits of the tribe. The Zamani dimension, however, encompasses the Sasa dimension in a sort of spiritual medium and thus gives a common foundation to the universal reality and binds together all created things. All is embraced within the Zamani.

Everything has its center of gravity in the Zamani period, with nothing ever ending. West African peoples expect human history to continue forever, because it is part of the natural rhythm moving from Sasa to Zamani. The Mende apparently have a belief in rebirth or reincarnation. Children are sometimes named after a particular ancestor, especially when they bear resemblance to him. This behavior inevitably seems to suggest that the Mende, like other West African peoples, have a notion that the life cycle is renewable. Human life is part of the rhythm of nature, and just as the days, months, seasons, and years have no end, there is no end to the rhythm of birth, puberty, initiation, marriage, procreation, old age, death, entry in the community of the departed (the living dead), and entry into the company of the spirits. Life is an ontological rhythm, and abnormality or the unusual is what disrupts the ontological harmony.

Death and Immortality

In many African tribes, a person was not considered a full human being until he had gone through the whole rhythmic process of physical birth, naming ceremony, puberty, initiation rites (sometimes in the form of ceremonial rebirth), and finally marriage and procreation. Then, and only then, was one fully "born"—a complete person. Similarly, death initiated the systematic rhythmic process through which the person gradually was removed from the Sasa to the Zamani period. Hence, death and immortality have especial significance in West African traditions. After physical death, as long as a person was remembered and recognized (by name) by relatives and friends who knew him (i.e., remembered his personality, character, and words and incidents of his life), he would continue to exist in the Sasa period. When, however, the last person who knew him also died, then the former passed out of the horizon of the Sasa period and, in effect, became completely dead. He no longer had any claims to family ties. He entered the Zamani period; that is, he became a member in the company of spirits.

The departed person who was remembered (recognized) by name was what Brother Mbiti calls the living-dead. He was considered to be in a state of personal immortality. The Mende believed that a person survives after death and that his surviving personality goes to the land of the dead (Forde, 1954). Those in personal immortality were treated symbolically like the living. The cycle of an individual ancestor, the Mende believed, lasted as long as the dead person was remembered in prayers and sacrifices (Forde, 1954). Hence, they were respected, given food and drink in the form of libations, and listened to and obeyed. Being remembered (recognized) and respected while in personal immortality was important for the traditional African, a fact which helps one to understand the religious significance and importance of marriage and procreation in West African societies. Procreation was the surest way to insure that one would not be cut off from personal immortality. In a kind of multiplicative fashion, polygamy reinforced one's insurance.

Inevitably, as stated earlier, the point was reached when there was no longer anyone alive who would recognize and give respect to the (living-dead) person. At this point, the process of dying was completed. However, he did not vanish out of existence. He now entered into the state of collective immortality. Now in the company of the spirits, he had at last entered the Zamani period. From this point on, the departed became nameless spirits who had no personal communication or ties with human families.

In terms of the ontology, entrance into the company of the spirits is man's final destiny. Paradoxically, death lies "in front" of the individual; it is a "future" event of sorts. But, when one dies, one enters the state of personal immortality and gradually "goes back" into the Zamani period. It should be emphasized that the African ontology was endless; such a view of man's destiny should not be construed to mean the end. Nothing ever ends.

Kinship: Collective Unity

Before concluding this brief and cursory review of African philosophy, a few words should be devoted to West African kinship, especially because kinship tied together the personal life system. Before they had carved up and colonized West Africa, Europeans could not say where one tribe ended and another tribe began. The number of people who made up what might be considered a tribe varied greatly. Depending upon the enumerator or ethnographer, many tribes were classified as unique and distinctly separate or simply as one.

Studies of African religious beliefs and practices demonstrate that among the many so-called distinct tribes there were more similarities (communalities) than differences (Mbiti, 1970). This author contends that all tribes shared basic beliefs—in the "survival of the tribe" and in the fact that the tribe was an integral and indispensable part of nature. Belief in tribal survival, was reflected in and sustained by a deep sense of kinship—probably one of the strongest cohesive devices in traditional life. Kinship controlled all relationships in the community (Mbiti, 1970). It included animals, plants, and nonliving objects. In effect, kinship bound together the entire life system of the tribe.

The kinship system stretched laterally (horizontally) in every direction as well as vertically. Hence, each member of the tribe was related not only to the tribal ancestors (both living-dead and spirits) but also to all those still unborn. In addition, each was a brother or sister, father or mother, grandmother or grandfather, cousin or brother-in-law, uncle or aunt, or some relation to everybody else. Africans still have many kinship terms which define the precise relationship binding any two people. Knowledge of one's tribal genealogy, vertical and horizontal, was extremely important. It imparted a sense of sacred obligation to extend the genealogical line. Through genealogies, persons (individuals) in the Sasa period were firmly linked to those who had entered the Zamani period.

To summarize: "In traditional life, the individual did not and could not exist alone" (Mbiti, 1970). The individual owed his very existence to other members of the "tribe," not only those who conceived and nourished him but also those long dead and still unborn. The individual did not exist unless he was corporate or communal; he was simply an integral part of the collective unity. Africans believed that the community (tribe) made, created, or produced the individual; thus, the existence of the community was not imagined to be dependent on individual ingression.

Unlike Western philosophical systems, the African philosophical tradition does not place heavy emphasis on the "individual." Indeed one might say that in a sense it does not allow for individuals. It recognizes that "only in terms of other people does the individual become conscious of his own being" (Mbiti, 1970). Only through others does one learn his duties and responsibilities toward himself and others. Most initiation rites were designed to instill a sense of corporate responsibility and collective destiny. Thus, when one member of the tribe suffered, the entire tribe suffered; when one member of the tribe rejoiced, all of his kinsmen—living, dead, and still unborn—rejoiced with him. When one man got married, he was not alone, nor did his wife "belong" to him alone. The children from all unions belonged to the collective body.

Whatever happened to the individual happened to the corporate body, the tribe, and whatever happened to the tribe, happened to the individual. A concept the Ashanti share with all other Akan peoples is that "the dead, the living, and those still to be born of the 'tribe' are all members of one family." A cardinal point in understanding the traditional African's view of himself; his self-concept, is that he believes: "I am because we are; and because we are, therefore, I am" (Mbiti, 1970).

Experiential Communality

Cultural Configuration

Any basic cultural anthropology text will give one a general feeling about why and how man began to live in groups. However, what is not discussed in most texts is the interaction between man—in the group—and man's particular environment. The notion of particular environment is an important one for this presentation because it determines the common elements of the group's living experiences. For instance, primitive people living in the Sahara Desert respond differently to their environment than inhabitants of the frigid zones or polar regions (Note 4). And those living in the tropic regions of the Congo would respond still another way to the elements in their environment. A more pointed example is provided by the differences between people living in postindustrial and preindustrial environments. It can be said that the uniqueness of one's environment determines the parameters of one's experience.

Experiential communality is defined here as the sharing of a particular experience by a group of people. It helps to determine what the people will ultimately be like, and, congruently, what ethos, or set of guiding beliefs, a people will follow. These guiding beliefs, in turn, dictate the creation and adoption of the values and customs which in the final analysis determine what social behavior a people will express in *common*—their cultural configuration. Thus, experiential communality is important in determining society's fundamental principles—its beliefs about the nature of man and what kind of society man should create for himself.

The peoples of Africa have traditionally lived in units or clusters commonly referred to as "tribes." For centuries West Africa has characteristically consisted of rolling stretches of tall grassy plains with intermittent bush country and scattered tropical rain forest (Bohannan, 1964). Within this region, the traditional peoples (tribes) were closely related to each other, yet distinct. Each tribe had its own distinct language which was related to the languages of all the other tribes in the region. African languages have been classified as of the Sudanic family (Werner, 1930) and the Niger-Congo stock (Bohannan, 1964). The closely related Bantu languages, the most well known of the Niger-Congo group, ranged from the west coast to most of central and southern Africa (Bohannan, 1964). Clearly, just as there was a common geographical flavor to the region, so, too, did its inhabitants develop and maintain common behaviors (Note 5).

The physical nature of the experiential communality is important mainly in that the more unique or distinct it is, the higher the probability that the physical boundaries hinder the influx of neighboring cultural elements. Likewise, it also allows for the development and protective maintenance of indigenous cultural elements. Just as important, however, is the interaction of communal man with his unique environment. The quintessence of this phenomenon is that it results in a set of guiding beliefs which dictate the values and customs the people adopt. Ultimately, this set (or sets) of values determines man's social behavior.

As noted earlier, close examination of the African ethos suggests two operational orders—survival of the tribe and oneness with nature. It was also suggested then that the ethos is probably the focal point of black psychology. The remainder of this paper will be devoted to offering evidence pointing to the continuing functioning of an African ethos.

African Reality and Psychological Assumptions

Black psychology is more than general psychology's "darker" dimension. African (Black) psychology is rooted in the nature of black culture which is based on particular indigenous (originally indigenous to Africa) philosophical assumptions. To make black psychology the dreaded darker dimension of general psychology would amount to distorting African reality so that it will fit Western psychological theories and/or assumptions. For example, a study of the history of general psychology reveals that the controversial mind-body problem stems from the set of early Greek myths known as the Orphic Mysteries. One myth recounts how Dionysus was killed by the *evil* Titans and Zeus saved Dionysus' heart and killed the Titans. Zeus then created man from the "evil" Titan ashes and Dionysus' heart. Hence, man has a dual nature: He is both *evil* and *divine.* However, the assumptions arising from these early myths caused a problem. There had to be an evaluation of what was "good" and what was "bad." Assuming a dichotomy of the mind and the body, the early philosophers suggested that the body was the "bad" and the mind was the "good"—beliefs accepted unquestionably during the early period of general psychology's emergence as a "science." Not surprisingly, psychology chose the mind (good) as the domain of its inquiry.

The African concept of man is fundamentally different. Dogon, Mende, and Ashanti all assume man's dual nature but do not attempt to *divide* "mind" from "body" or refer to or imply an inherent good or evil in either aspect of the duality. The propositions of "the notion of unity," "one with nature," and "survival of the people" deny the possibility of such an artificial and arbitrary dichotomy. What is seemingly dualistic is the concept of "twinness." However, as stated earlier, the twin components unite to make the unified man. For Africans, who believed that man, like the universe, is a complicated, *integrated,* unified whole, concerns such as the mind-body controversy would never arise and theoretical developments and/or analysis based solely on the explication of the "mind" or the "body" as separate entities would be useless.

Although the mind-body issue is a single example, it is believed sufficient to demonstrate how philosophical assumptions determined the scientific investigation of psychology. Certainly particular people cannot be meaningfully investigated and understood if *their* philosophical assumptions are not taken into account.

Toward Black Psychology

This brings us closer to black psychology's evolution from African philosophy. The remaining question is how does one know or how can one "prove" that Africans living in the Western world, and in contemporary times, still have or maintain an African philosophical definition. Black psychology's development is contingent first upon analysis of the linkages between distinct experiential periods in the lives of Africans, and second upon the demonstration of the particular ways in which African philosophy, interacting with alien (particularly Euro-American) philosophies, has determined contemporary African (black) people's perception of reality.

On the Question of Proof

> History is an endeavor toward better understanding, and, consequently, a thing in movement. To limit oneself to "describing science as it is," will always be to betray it . . . . (Bloch, 1953)

For black psychology—and the many other social science areas which are attempting to "blackenize" themselves in order to "explain" contemporary African peoples—the question of proof centers around more than determining whether a particular cultural element (e.g., an artifact) has been retained. The focus must be on the philosophical-psychological linkages between Africans and African Americans (or Americanized Africans).

To determine whether—and to what extent—African orientation has persisted, one must ask "How could it have been maintained?" "What mechanism or circumstances allowed it to be maintained?" An orientation stemming from a particular indigenous African philosophy could only be maintained when its cultural carriers were isolated (and/or insulated) from alien cultural interaction and if their behavioral expression of the orientation did not openly conflict with the cultural-behavioral elements of the "host" society. If the circumstances of the transplantation of New World blacks met one or both of these conditions, then it is highly probable that the African orientation was retained. This writer maintains that a factor that often facilitated the retention of the African orientation was the particular region's physical features. And the slaves' accessibility to Western indoctrination was probably directly related to the degree of the retention of the African orientation. The rigidly enforced isolation of blacks allowed New World Africans to retain their definition (orientation). Thus, the oppressive system of slavery indirectly encouraged the retention, rather than the destruction, of the African philosophical orientation.

Throughout the New World, large numbers of Africans lived, segregated in given areas. Lorenzo Turner (1958) notes that "wherever Negroes were in the United States, the policy of racial segregation must have often aided in keeping alive the African influence. It is proposed here that a comparative historical analysis of such areas as Brazil, Jamaica, Dutch Guiana, the rural South, and the northern ghetto would reveal a striking and direct correlation between (1) ecological and geographic factors and accessibility of interaction with Westerners and (2) maintenance of the African orientation. Not until the television "explosion" of the early 1950s did the African orientation come fully into contact with Western (Euro-American) styles of behavior and the American way of life.

Expressive behavior and cultural modalities are determined by philosophical definition. One can observe "Africanisms" throughout the New World because the orientation that allows a people to develop or continue to utilize particular cultural elements was not interfered with. Thus, the statement "We are an African people" is valued because, for the most part, New World conditions did not permit the enculturation of the African orientation.

Considerations for Black Psychology

The experiential communality of African peoples can be subdivided into periods. For Africans living in the Western world, particularly in North America, the breakdown used here is (1) the African experience (prior to 1600), (2) the slavery experience (1600 to 1865), and (3) contemporary black America (1865 to present).

However, rather than treat a few specific behavioral transitions, the discussion will focus on several major philosophical positions and correlative behavioral modalities. The first is survival of the people. From this philosophical position an extended definition of self evolved. That is to say, the self was by philosophical definition the "we" instead of the "I." Tribal membership became the most important identity. One's identity was thus rooted in being an Ashanti, or an Ibo rather than the person, Lodagaa Nyakyusi, who just happened to be an Igbira. Thrust into an alien culture, the "we" notion seemingly came under severe attack. Many scholars note, for example, the prevalent practice during slavery (second distinct experiential communality period) of purposely separating members of the same tribe in order to break down the collective reinforcement of a common definition. However, additional information suggests that in North America the system of slavery was extremely unstructured in its beginning. Nevertheless, the system eventually came to define itself in terms of black people. During this same period, the notion of tribe or peoplehood which is crucial to the "we" notion underwent a particular modification. Clearly, Africans recognized and respected the distinctions of the tribe. The understanding that one was an Igbira or an Ibo suggested many things. However, the philosophical position within each tribe was the set of guiding beliefs which prescribed the survival of the tribe as a first order. As the system of American slavery began to define slavery in terms of Africans, tribe was more broadly defined in the minds of the Africans. Hence, one sees Africans no longer giving the Ibo or Igbira distinction its former level of importance but rather adopting broader categories. Thus, as slavery was moving closer and closer to its final definition, the slaves themselves were moving closer to African or black as the final definition of tribe. Thus, the notion of survival of the tribe was not changed or modified during the slavery experience. In fact, one could suggest that the slavery experience allowed the underlying communality of West Africa to surface and define itself as African. Hence, in slavery, the cardinal point, "I am because we are; and because we are, therefore, I am," was not destroyed. In contemporary times, one can note the prevalence of benevolent societies and the role of the Negro church as expressing clear concern for the survival of the tribe.

The second philosophical position that has survived the effects of different experiential periods is the idea of man being an integral part of the "natural rhythm of nature," or, one with nature. Clearly, this can be seen within the African experience in terms of the anthropocentric ontology. The expression of this natural rhythm in the initiation rites gave definition to many of the periods within a person's Sasa dimension. This notion of rhythm also was expressed in the "talking drums."

In traditional African society, the living setting was the community and the emphasis was placed on living in the community not living in a particular household. Even in contemporary times, the "community" seems to manifest this same perception. One could propose that seeing oneself as an integral part of a community is the contemporary definition of man being an integral part of the natural rhythm of nature.

The oral tradition has clearly been transmitted throughout the three experiential periods. As indicated earlier, beliefs and traditions were handed down from father to son for generations upon generations. This tradition gave tremendous importance to the mind or the memory (Note 6). Remembering phenomenal events in one's Sasa period was very important if not crucial. The slavery tradition seemingly allowed this tradition to continue. That is, because oral communication was the only acceptable system—laws prohibited slaves from being taught to read and write—slavery unknowingly permitted the cultural transmission of the African traditional emphasis on oration and its consequent effects on the mind or memory to remain pretty much in tact. Brother Dr. Joseph White (1970) suggests that playing the "dozens" as part of the oral tradition is a game used by black youngsters to teach themselves to keep cool, think fast under pressure, and not say what is really on their minds. Things like rapping and the dozens could also be viewed as *initiation rites* or possibly instances where the "power" of the word is used to make the "individual" psychologically feel better. For example, the Avogan and the Lobi Singi (Herskovits, 1966) are ritualized orations and dance ceremonies where the offended is afforded release of suppressed emotions by ridiculing another. The Dogon have a very interesting circumstance in which certain relations are characterized by exchanges of often obscene insults and gestures (Forde, 1954). Is this the dozens in African form, or better yet are the dozens an African tribalism that has been maintained throughout the different experiential communalities? Another aspect of the oral tradition is the naming ritual. In traditional times, a child was named after an ancestor to symbolize his (the ancestor's) return (Forde, 1954). Often the name typifies a special event in the child's life. Hence, because a person acquired names as he associated with different special experiences, one person may have many names. One need only examine the names of black people to reveal historical tenacity in this orientation—for example, Bojangles, Brown Bomber, Stepin Fetchit, Wilt-the-Stilt, Muddy Waters, Iceberg Slim.

With certain modifications, tribalisms have been transmitted in the form of Africanisms throughout the New World experiential periods. Cooperative effort (tribalism) was expressed in the slavery experience. The "Knights of Wise" symbolize that notion and the notion of the survival of the tribe. Funerals in contemporary black America are very symbolic of the custom of reaffirming the bonds of kinship. Distinct motor habits also have been maintained up to the present. Photographic analysis of a particular dance in the Ashanti Kwaside rite illustrates a perfect example of the Charleston. Morality was taught in traditional times via the use of animal tales. Parables were widely prevalent during slavery—the most notable being the "Brer Fox, Brer Rabbit Tales." In contemporary times, one simply notes the use of animal names to denote certain qualities. In the black communities (villages) throughout this country, women and men are referred to a "foxes," "cows," "bears," "buzzards," "dogs," and so forth. The style of talking (dramatic pauses, intonation, and the like), are all reminiscent of a people in tune with the natural rhythm of nature—in tune with the oneness of nature.

The concept of time clearly is illustrative. The attitude that time is phenomenal rather than mathematical can be demonstrated to persist throughout the suggested experiential periods. The notion of CPT (colored people's time) has been translated to mean thirty minutes to an hour later than the scheduled meeting time. However, in the minds of Africans (blacks), time is flexible and the event begins when one gets there. This author thus suggests that a more appropriate enunciation of CPT is "communal potential time."

Black psychology must concern itself with the question of "rhythm." It must discuss, at some great length, "the oral tradition." It must unfold the mysteries of the spiritual energy now known as "soul." It must explain the notion of "extended self" and the "natural" orientation of African peoples to insure the "survival of the tribe." Briefly, it must examine the elements and dimensions of the experiential communalities of African peoples.

It is my contention, therefore, that black psychology must concern itself with the mechanism by which our African definition has been maintained and what values its maintenance has offered black people. Hence, the task of black psychology is to offer an understanding of the behavioral definition of African philosophy and to document what, if any, modifications it has undergone during particular experiential periods.

Notes

1. Like most words that refer to things African, the English usage of the word "tribe" has mixed connotations. In addition, one must recognize that the defining characteristic for a tribe was completely alien and arbitrary. As British and American anthropologists changed their definitions of what constituted a tribe, so changed the physical size of a tribe's membership.

   Although Africa can be considered a cultural entity, most African Americans came from West Africa. While there is diversity, the author assumes that there are unifying cultural themes. For a rather different point, however, see R.A. Lavine, Personality and Change in J.N. Padden and E.W. Soja, *The African Experience, Vol. 1.* (Evanston, Ill.: Northwestern University Press, 1970). For present purposes, West African is seen as extending from Senegal to Angola.

2. Note that given African philosophy is for the most part unwritten and has no conceptual terms as we know them. The understanding of African philosophy is accomplished by analyzing the traditional structures reflected in tales, proverbs,

myths, and such. It is these which in turn reflect the structural concepts of the philosophy.

3. African is a very large continent and there are some differences in the concept of time in different areas. For example, hunters have a different conception of time than those in farming communities. In the present paper, the author is making certain simplifying assumptions for purposes of exposition.

4. Primitive is used here in the original sense (without negative connotations)—that is, primary, first, early.

5. In this case, behavioral tools—that is, languages.

6. Not in the mind—body dichotomy tradition.

References

Abraham, W.W. (1962). *The mind of Africa*. Chicago: University of Chicago Press.

Bloch, M. (1953). *Historians craft*. New York: Knopf. (Translated by Peter Putnam).

Bohannan, P. (1964). *Africa and Africans*. New York: American Museum of Science Books.

Forde, D. (1954). *African worlds*. London: Oxford University.

Gamble, D.P. (1957). *The Wolof of Senegambia*. New York: International Publication Service.

Herskovits, M.J. (1958). *The myth of the Negro past*. Boston: Beacon Press.

Jahn, J. (1961). *Muntu*. New York: Grove Press.

Kenyatta, J. (1938). *Facing Mr. Kenya*. London: Vintage Books.

Mbiti, J.S. (1970). *African religions and philosophies*. Garden City, NY: Anchor Books, Doubleday.

McCall, D.F. (1969). *Africa in time-perspective*. New York: Oxford University Press.

Murdock, G.P. (1959). *Africa: Its peoples and their cultural history*. New York: McGraw-Jill.

Oliver, R., & Fage, J.D. (1962). *A short history of Africa*. Baltimore: Penguin.

Parrinder, G. (1969). *Religion in Africa*. Baltimore: Penguin.

Radcliff-Brown, A., & Forde, D. (Eds.). (1967). *African systems of kinship and marriage*. New York: Oxford University Press.

Taylor, J.V. (1963). *The primal vision*. Philadelphia: Fortress Press.

Temples, P. (1959). *Bantu Philosophy*. Paris: Presence Africaine.

Turner, L. (1958). African survivals in the New World with special emphasis on the arts. *Africans Seen by American Negroes. Paris: Presence Africaine.*

Werner, A. (1925). *Structure and relationship of African languages*. London: Kegan Paul.

White, J. (1970). Guidelines for black psychologists. *The Black Scholar, 1*(5), 52-57.

White, J. (1970a, August). Toward a black psychology. *Ebony*, pp. 25, 44-45, 48-50, 52.

Radical Black Behaviorism

William A. Hayes

The development of a black psychology has advanced through two overlapping phases. The first phase questioned the conclusions of white psychologists whose research and theories inevitably specified some deficit, deficiency and/or distortion in the psychological makeup of black people as compared to whites. The second phase questioned the assumptions upon which white psychologists based their theories and research while indicating that their biased results were partially a function of these assumptions. Among other things, the third phase must initiate a critical examination of the rules of science adopted by Western psychology. The present paper introduces the thesis that psychology adopted a definition of science that would allow the inclusion of psychology among the scientific disciplines. It adopted rules of science which would at once allow psychologists to find expression for their cultural and racial biases while presenting themselves as scientific investigators of human behavior. Their rules of science not only allow for such contradictions, but the profession dispenses rewards to those psychologists whose theories or research conclusions more closely approximate that which is most intuitively satisfying to the masses of a racist society. After a brief review of the development of a self-serving science, Radical Black Behaviorism is offered as the basis for a true science of behavior which will lead to a better understanding of black people.

Science and Psychology

Psychology has always been sensitive to its image as a science. Students of psychology are taught that psychology was once a part of philosophy, but became a science when is separated from philosophy, largely through the work of Gustav Fechner. Fechner's psychology was an experimental psychology whose methods closely approximated the methods of physics. In 1908, William McDougall defined psychology as a "science of behavior." Subsequently, introductory textbooks in psychology have devoted pages to the justification of psychology as a science. While most psychologists view psychology as a science, people trained in the traditional natural sciences (mathematics, physics, biology, etc.) often view psychology as a nonscience. These differences in perception suggest differences in the definition of science.

Like "psychology," the word "science" means different things to different people. Brown and Ghiselli (1955) explicated several frequently used interpretations of the word "science":

1. Science is used to refer to certain subject-matter fields such as physics, geology, mathematics, etc. This interpretation excludes the subject matter of psychology as a science (p. 3).
2. Science also is used to refer to those activities which made use of instruments like microscopes, electric meters, and other gadgets considered too difficult for most people to understand and use (p. 3).
3. Sets of theories and/or laws used to explain natural phenomena is another interpretation of science. The laws of gravity and relativity are viewed as examples of this interpretation (p. 4).
4. Science is often viewed as a set of scientific procedures all subsumed under the general term "scientific point of view." This term also means several things to several people (p. 4).
5. Science as a technical method of solving problems is the most widely held meaning. This view holds that science is a general method on a conceptual level and a variety of specific methods which can be adapted to the specifics of the problem-solving endeavor (p. 4).

Psychology adopted the last definition of science. Thus, psychology is considered a science because it uses the scientific method of inquiry. It had adapted the general scientific method to achieve the maximum utility for studying the specific problems of psychology. The adaptation of the general scientific method results in a set of rules of science which govern theory construction and research for psychologists. It is this set of rules of the psychologist as a scientist that must be critically scrutinized by black psychologists.

Myth of the Scientist

The myth of the scientist in psychology as an objective, emotionally detached researcher whose only interest is in the advancement of knowledge is an extension of the myth that psychology is a science. In their explication of psychology as a science, Brown and Ghiselli (1955) define a scientist as one "who rigorously applies the scientific method" (p. 10). Given this definition, one could be a scientist if they rigorously apply the scientific method of a scientist in spite of the content of the discipline they are studying. The importance of the discipline's content (subject matter) lies in the types of modification of the general scientific method necessary to apply the method to the content. An understanding of how psychology supports scientific racism requires that one examine the modifications to the general scientific method made by psychology.

The myth further suggests that the scientist has certain characteristics which mitigate against careless mistakes and biases. Consider the following quotes from Brown and Ghiselli:

> One of the chief characteristics of the scientist is his flexibility. His purpose is to improve his beliefs rather than defend them. He is suspicious of his generalizations. He is forever questioning their validity and deliberately seeking further facts in order to test them . . . of all people he is the most expert in changing his mind, that is, he is continuously vigilant to bring his findings up to date in terms of trustworthy evidence (p. 12).

> The scientist thrives on change. He is progressive because he is never too certain of his facts. He encourages systematic doubt (p. 13).

While Brown and Ghiselli realize that the hypothesis the scientist chooses to investigate is partially determined by his interest, knowledge, training, and motivation, they stop short of including biases, prejudices, and racism as effective determinants.

Rules of Science

Psychology's adoption of the definition of science as a general method of inquiry required it to modify the general method to fit the content of psychology. Although psychology has been defined as the science of behavior, the modifications made resulted in the acceptance of mentalism as a legitimate aspect of a science of behavior. The specific mechanism by which this contradiction was affected was the invention and propagation of concepts like intervening variables and hypothetical constructs.

William James, who considered himself a tough-minded scientist, raised the issue of how psychology was to account for the manner in which mental life intervened between external stimuli ("impressions made from without upon the body") and behavior ("reactions of the body upon the outer world"). The concept of an intervening variable was introduced by E. C. Tolman (1936) as a means of accounting for mental processes in the analysis of behavior. The concept was later modified to include imaginary neural processes in addition to psychic ones. Kantor (1964) suggested that the use of intervening variables became a technique for "loading the organism with internal principles and powers" (p. 183).

During the next decade, the functions and use of intervening variables became so confused that MacCorquodale and Meehl (1948) felt the need to distinguish between intervening variables and hypothetical constructs. The definition of intervening variables was to be restricted to the original use implied by Tolman's original definition—pure summary of shorthand devices with no meaning beyond that transmitted by its stimulus and response referents. Examples of intervening variables were Skinner's *reserve*, Hull's *habit strength*, Lewin's *valence*, and Tolman's *demand*. Hypothetical constructs were defined as processes or entitles which are not directly observable and were not capable of being reduced to empirical terms. Examples of hypothetical constructs included Guthrie's *M.P.S.'s*, Hull's *anticipatory goal responses*, Allport's *biophysical traits, anxiety* as used by Mowrer, Dollard, and Miller, and most theoretical constructs used in psychoanalytical theory.

While the introduction, criticism, and debate on the value of intervening variables and hypothetical constructs took place largely within the field of learning, their eventual acceptance had important implications for theory construction in all of psychology. Not only did it lead to the "scientific" use of a wide variety of unobservable, intraorganismic constructs like needs, tension, anxiety, and ego strength, but to the postulation of intraorganismic dynamic systems such as personality, intelligence, and motivation. The systems, in turn, required the development of more abstract concepts like *nomological nets* and psychological tests, the validation of which requires the use of *construct validity*.

Pseudoscientific Analysis of Black Behavior

Psychology's definition of science, the myth of the psychologist as a scientist, and the modification of the rules of science have created a scientific posture for psychology that is significant to the development of black psychology for several reasons. The scientific posture assumed by psychology has lead to a selectivity among white psychologists characterized by the unwillingness or inability to hear and process points of view contrary to their own intellectual and cultural biases, except those conclusions of psychological research that are consistent with their biases. On the other hand, the same psychologists examine, reexamine, and critically reanalyze data which lead to conclusions contrary to their position. Students of the sociology of knowledge have previously noted this differential receptivity among researchers, without pointing out the potential for this differential receptivity to become a vested interest.

Psychology's scientific posture has also lead to a scientific elitism which is quick to label black psychologists' contributions as emotional, subjective reactions lacking in the scientific rigor which characterizes the work of true scientists. Scientific elitism places a higher value on research activities which subscribe to the rules of science adopted by psychology, while devaluing the contributions of black psychologists whose conclusions are contrary to those who subscribe to the widely held biases.

The most damaging consequence of the scientific posture is that it gives scientific sanction to the use of pre-and nonscientific concepts as a means of explaining the behavior of black people. It provides white psychologists with a license to give scientific credence to their *autistic creations.*

It is interesting to note that psychology does not include as part of its scientific posture the notion of scientific progress. The discerning student of science understands that progress in science is defined as movement from the subjective to the objective, from the unobservable to the observable, from the unmanipulatable to the manipulatable. Psychology has made little scientific progress in the past. Its attempt to explain behavior has moved from the use of such concepts as demonology to ids, ego, and superegos to a variety of constructs including various forms of personality, intelligence, and motivation. These explanatory constructs are no more observable, objective, or manipulatable than the prescientific construct of demons. They do, however, create the need for a multibillion dollar industry to develop tests to measure these unobservable constructs. To object to the specific set of assumptions that led to the development of specific tests is also an important function of black psychology. Black psychologists' greatest task is to destroy the illusion of science under which Western psychology presently hides its biases. Its terminal goal must be to develop a science of human behavior which objectively explains the behavior of all people without bias.

Introduction to Radical Black Behaviorism

Radical Black Behaviorism is an approach to studying and understanding the behavior of black people without subscribing to the definition and rules of science which permit and encourage mentalistic and reductionistic explanations. It subscribes to the principles of radical behaviorism as espoused within the context of The Experimental Analysis of Behavior (Sidman, 1960; Skinner, 196). Radical Black Behaviorism follows

the traditions of empiricism, operationism, and logical positivism in philosophy and the increasingly sophisticated behaviorism of John Watson,
Clark Hull, B.F. Skinner, and others. The approach is radical in that it *elects*
to explain as much of behavior as possible by demonstrating functional
relationships between observable and quantifiable environmental events
on the one hand and behavior which is also observable and quantifiable
on the other.

Any approach to the study of human behavior short of a science
leaves room for biased and racist orientations and interpretations
which are not in the best interest of black people. Radical Black Behaviorism represents the most scientific approach to the study of human
behavior. As such, it stands as the antithesis of the most damaging and
oppressive components of American psychology. Among other things,
Radical Black Behaviorism insists upon explanations rather then conceptualizations; it is intolerant of mentalistic interpretations and theories which often serve as the pseudoscientific justification of personal
and institutional racism; and it focuses upon consequences of behavior
rather than causes and motives underlying the behavior. More importantly, it has a utility for black people which seems to have gone unrecognized.

Explanations Versus Conceptualizations

The so-called explanations of black behavior in the American psychological literature stand as the greatest monument to the need for an
alternative. Psychological literature is replete with attempts to explain
black behavior or "psychological phenomena" by resorting to hypothetical mental structures, presumed needs, attitudes, and the like. Because these so-called explanations go beyond observable events, they
are conceptualizations of behavior rather than explanations of behavior. Conceptualizations are based more on one's theoretical orientation
and/or implicit theories of people and behavior being explained. The
practice of conceptualizing rather than explaining behavior is often
combined with case studies or anecdotes. An example is provided by
Erikson (1950):

> Consider, for example, the chances of a continuity of identity in the
> American Negro child. I know a colored boy who, like our boys,
> listens every night to Red Rider. Then he sits up in bed, imagining
> that he is Red Rider. But the moment comes when he sees himself
> galloping after some masked offenders and suddenly notices that
> in his fancy Red Rider is a colored man. He stops his fantasy. While
> a small child, this boy was extremely expressive, both in his plea-

sure and his sorrows. Today he is calm and always smiles; his language is soft and blurred; nobody can hurry him or worry him—or
please him. White people like him (p. 241).

In the same book Erikson further "explains" the problems of black
identity:

Tired of his own caricature, the colored individual often retires in
hypochondriac invalidism as a condition which represents an analogy to the dependence and relative safety of defined restriction in
the South; a neurotic regression to the ego identity of the slave (p.
242).

The above explanations may serve to illustrate three points. First,
as late as the 1950s, anecdotal evidence was still very much a part of
contemporary American psychology. It is interesting to note that Lloyd
Morgan's canon in 1891 led to the elimination of the use of anecdotal
evidence and mentalistic concepts in psychology as explanations of the
behavior of black people. While anecdotal evidence has taken the form
of case studies and mentalistic explanations have donned the pseudo-
scientific cloak on intervening variables and hypothetical constructs,
they are still unacceptable as explanations to a science of human behavior. Seldom is the reader informed of the number of cases the writer has
encountered which did not conform to the particular theoretical position he is espousing. Without this information, one suspects that the
writer entertains a conceptual position and is attentive only to behaviors and situations that support his position in fact or through elaborate
interpretations. We can only conclude that such writers are more committed to their theoretical formulations than to a realistic understanding of black behavior.

Mentalistic explanations such as "neurotic regression to the identity of the slave" defy any attempt for observable support; thus, they
are not explanations. The use of such conceptualizations maximizes
the probability that personal biases will be included. Given the same
set of behaviors, different observers may arrive at very different, erroneous explanations of behavior. This is illustrated in a clever study by
Haughton and Ayllon (1965). These investigators shaped the repetitive
response of holding a broom using reinforcement techniques and a
female patient in a psychiatric hospital. Baseline observations taken in
an obtrusive manner indicated that the patient spent 60 percent of her
waking time lying in bed, approximately 20 percent sitting and walking, and the remainder in activities associated with meals, grooming,
and elimination. Broom holding was shaped by reinforcing the patient
with cigarettes while she held the broom. The broom-holding behavior was quickly developed to the point that the patient resisted having
the broom taken away. Two psychiatrists were asked to observe and

evaluate the patient from behind a one-way mirror. One psychiatrist gave the following evaluation:

> Her constant and compulsive pacing holding a broom in the manner she does could be seen as a ritualistic procedure, a magical action. When regression conquers the association process, primitive and archaic forms of thinking control the behavior. Symbolism is a predominant mode of expressing deep-seated unfulfilled desires and instinctual impulses. By magic, she controls others, cosmic powers are at her disposal, and inanimate objects become living creatures.
>
> Her broom could be then:
>
> 1. a child that gives her life and she gives him in return her devotion
> 2. a phallic symbol
> 3. the scepter of an omnipotent queen (Haughton and Ayllon, 1965, p. 98).

The second psychiatrist gave a different evaluation; he saw the broom as "some essential perceptual element in her field of consciousness" and the behavior as a "stereotyped form of behavior such as is commonly seen in rather regressed schizophrenics" and "analogous to the way small children or infants refuse to be parted from some favorite toy, piece of rag, etc." (Haughton and Ayllon, 1965).

One wonders how many mentalistic explanations or evaluations have been given to the detriment of black people. In spite of the fact that such evaluations have no scientific merit, they are continuously used.

It is unfair to suggest that mentalistic explanations are only espoused by white psychologists and psychiatrists. Black psychologists and psychiatrists adopt the methods and orientations of their white mentors; therefore, their explanations tend to be of the same kind, but seasoned by the black experience. Grier and Cobbs, two black psychiatrists, provided illustrations in *Black Rage* (1968). Black mentalistic explanations of black behavior are no more acceptable than white mentalistic explanations.

Radical Black Behaviorism is limited to the study of behaviors that can be observed, measured, and reproduced. Similarly, its explanations of behavior are also in terms of events that can be observed, measured, and reproduced. Thus, Radical Black Behaviorism is never in the position of explaining behavior, an observable event, by the postulation of an unobservable event. Any explanation based upon hypothetical mental structures, dynamics, or presumed needs is considered invalid. Valid explanations are ones that specify the actual conditions that reliably produce and maintain the behavior to be explained (Reynolds, 1968). Consistent use of definitions governed by this requirement negates the possibility of confounding explanation and bias.

Consequences Versus Cause

The guiding principle of Radical Black Behaviorism states that people act upon the environment in such a way that the environment changes. The environmental change is the consequence of behavior. The nature of the consequence determines the probability that the same class of responses will occur given smaller environmental conditions.

Two important implications are inherent in this principle. First, it implies that the consequence of behavior is vital to its explanation. The focus on the consequence of behavior allows explanations based upon an individual's present environment rather than specifying causes in terms of events occurring prior to the behavior being explained. Attempts to specify causes inevitably lead to inward, unobservable characteristics of the individual, which mediate between the environment and behavior. Because events occurring at any time in the person's past history can be specified as a cause, it is highly probable that different psychologists will specify different causes of the behavior. Again, biased interpretations and assumptions can play a major role in the explanation. Moreover, if a previous event can be specified as a cause of the behavior, the knowledge contributes little to the potential for changing behavior.

Knowledge of the consequence of behavior that controls the behavior leads immediately to the suggestion that behavior can be changed through manipulation of the consequences. Because consequences are observable, this focus is potentially more scientific and therefore more acceptable to a science of human behavior.

Clearly, black people have been the victims of explanations whose major focus was on cause rather than consequence. Blacks have high absenteeism rates in industry *because* they are lazy and unmotivated; blacks do not perform well on achievement tests *because* they are intellectually inferior. Seldom are the differences in consequences (salaries, job offers, etc.) in working or academic behavior related to different rates of performance between whites and blacks in work and academic settings. Radical Black Behaviorism rejects the specification of previous life events as causing behavior as unscientific and harmful to the well-being of black people.

Focus on Individual

Black people in America are seen as a rather homogenous group by the lay public and professionals. While giving cursory recognition to individual differences, behavioral scientist continuously attribute group characteristics to blacks. Howard Odum (1910), in a work described as "an effort to contribute something toward the scientific knowledge of the Negro," described the social and mental traits of blacks. Among other things, Odum's study found blacks to be expressive in their abuse of others, liars, exaggerators, and lovers of music; gregarious in their sexual morality, sociality, and conformity to law and the group; and, responsive to forceful circumstances and to emotions (pp. 272-273).

Conclusions from the above and other pseudoscientific investigations (Garrett, 1945; Jensen, 1969) have become a part of white America's perception of black people and result in white people's reacting to individual blacks as if they were unintelligent, immoral, and so on. Often these perceptions work to the detriment of blacks, as is suggested by the studies of Rosenthal and Jacobson (1968).

The focus on blacks as a group is given credibility by the use of the normal curve and sophisticated statistical analyses. True statistical tests demonstrate functional relationships, but the functional relationships are between selected variables or events and groups of people, not between events and individuals. Thus, statistics have contributed more to making psychology a study of the behavior of groups than to understanding individual behavior. Psychology perpetuates the myth that its principles founded on group data are applicable to the individual. Consequently, decisions which affect the future and well-being of individuals in major ways are based upon tests and scales whose validity has been established and can *only* be established through the statistical analysis of scores from groups of subjects. For example, the validity of intelligence tests for a single individual has never been established, but the same tests are used as the basis upon which a child is placed in a special rather than a regular classroom in school. When questioned about the validity of the decision for the individual, the validity indexes, based upon so-called representative groups, are inevitably given as justification. Radical Black Behaviorism rejects not only such use of statistics, but also the concepts of intelligence and intelligence measurement.

Alternatives to statistical analyses of group data and statistical control have been established by contributors to The Experimental Analysis of Behavior (EAB) (Skinner, 1966; Sidman, 1960). Experimental control and research paradigms based upon replications have been used to demonstrate functional relationships between individual behavior and its controlling conditions. It is the demonstration of functional relationships through manipulation of controlling conditions that differentiates the EAB's study with an N of 1 from traditional psychology's case study. Unlike traditional psychology, the methods and principles established in basic research laboratories are directly applicable to programs designed to change behavior in clinical, educational, or other settings.

Practical Utility of Radical Black Behaviorism

One of the most important criteria by which any alternative to contemporary American psychology must be judged is its practical utility to blacks in the struggle for equality. The black movement has been characterized in various ways. Some have called it an economic struggle, others call it a political struggle, while still others feel that morality plays the most important role. The elements common to all these perceptions are people and their behavior. A science of human behavior should have a lot to say about the nature of the problem, but it should also lead to concrete suggestions for the solution of the problem.

The focus on behavior as the primary element of the black struggle and white resistance is not an original contribution of Radical Black Behaviorism. Such a focus is implied in the popular conception of the problem as "colonization of the mind." The implication is that the minds of blacks have been colonized to the extent that they respond in a manner that is highly predictable and consistent with the wishes of the "colonizer." Familiar statements such as "His head is in the wrong place" and "You've got to get your head together" indicate the popularity of this conception among blacks. While the focus is on behavior, the behavior is controlled by the mind. Any changes in behavior must be preceded by changes in the mind.

This conceptualization has the same disadvantage as the use of mentalistic concepts in psychology. It suggests that the first task of blacks in the movement is to initiate and/or facilitate the necessary mental changes in themselves. The procedures to be used and the criteria for sufficient change or its measurement are not clear. Thus, this conception does not predict behaviors that are useful to the struggle. Perhaps this is why so much time and energy are spent developing "black pride."

Without rejecting the need for or the utility of developing black pride, Radical Black Behaviorism supports a different perception of the struggle. The control of black people's behavior is seen as the bone of contention over which blacks and whites struggle. White America struggles to maintain its control of black people's behavior, while blacks struggle to control their own behavior. Freedom, then, is seen as true interdependence between races or equal amounts of control by both races over the other's behavior.

During slavery, whites maintained virtually complete control over the behavior of blacks through the use of aversive control. Slaves worked to avoid punishment. Whites were reinforced for maintaining the system, as goods were produced with minimal expense and profits were high. With the abolition of slavery, new methods of control were developed. In addition to continued aversive control by so-called hate groups, mechanisms of economic control were instituted. Blacks began to be paid for their work, but only under the reinforcement schedules defined by whites. Thus, meager pay was made contingent upon high rates of behavior in an environment almost completely controlled by whites. This system of economic dependence still serves as the basic mechanism by which the behavior of contemporary blacks is controlled. One can argue that the history of blacks in America supports the contention that the basis of the whites' struggle was to maintain economic superiority as much as it supports the contention that the control of blacks' behavior was the fundamental issue. The issue is placed in proper perspective when one realizes that the economic superiority of whites is contingent upon their ability to maintain control over black behavior.

Behavioral control is far from the sinister control over mind and body often projected by the entertainment media. Behavioral control refers to the systematic manipulation of certain environmental events in such a way that the observed effect occurs in a predictable manner. The resulting effect may be to accelerate, decelerate, or maintain the behavior upon which the event is made contingent. Behavioral control requires two conditions to be maximally effective. First, the controller must have significant control over the environment in which the controlled behaves. The greater the control the former has over the latter's environment, the greater the potential for realizing the desired effect. Second, the controlled must be experiencing a state of deprivation; otherwise, aversive control mechanisms must be used.

The implications of the first condition for black people are clear. To maintain economic superiority, whites in America must maintain control over the behavior of blacks by any means necessary. The major institutions of the society, job sources, and regulating and enforcement bodies must remain in control of white people. Community control and separatism cannot be tolerated unless there is some supramechanism by which whites can control the larger unit which results from such black unifications.

The second requirement mitigates against whites' giving equality to blacks out of the goodness of their hearts. To be economically superior, whites must control blacks; to control blacks in a manner that is reasonably consistent with the rhetoric of democracy, blacks must be kept in a state of deprivation. Because money is the chief reinforcer in our society, it is reasonable to expect blacks to remain economically deprived. From this perspective, the racial differences in income, which hold when amount of education is controlled, take on a new meaning. Economic deprivation of blacks must be maintained to maintain behavioral control over blacks, while maintaining the myth of democracy. It is clear that as blacks increasingly gain control over their own behavior and therefore, contribute proportionally less to maintaining white economic superiority, one can expect increasing amounts of overt, aversive control.

Radical Black Behaviorism must address the issue of behavioral control directly. It recognizes that humans' ability to control other humans' behavior via a variety of mechanisms is a reality. It must participate in the ongoing development of methods and principles of behavioral control, both in and outside the experimental laboratory. It is only through knowledge of the principles of behavioral control that blacks will be able to resist white control and develop effective means of countercontrol.

Radical Black Behaviorism is offered as an alternative to the more diffuse black psychology currently being proposed. Radical Black Behaviorism embraces radical behaviorism (Skinner, 1964; Day, 1969) and the experimental analysis of behavior as the basis upon which a radically objective science of human behavior can be developed. As a potential science, it rejects the mentalistic concepts of contemporary psychology, is individualistic in its approach, and has immediate utility for meeting the needs of black people.

References

Brown, C.W., & Ghiselli, E.E. (1955). *Scientific method in psychology*. New York: McGraw-Hill.

Day, W.F. (1969). Radical behaviorism in reconciliation with phenomenology. *Journal of the Experimental Analysis of Behavior, 12*, 315-328.

Erikson, E.H. (1950). *Childhood and society*. New York: Norton.

Garrett, H.E. (1945). A note on the intelligence scores of Negroes and whites in 1918. *Journal of Abnormal and Social Psychology, 40*, 344-346.

Grier, W.H., & Cobbs, P.M. (1968). *Black rage*. New York: Basic Books.

Haughton, E., & Ayllon, T. (1965). Production and elimination of symptomatic behavior. In L.P. Ullman, & L. Krasner (Eds.), *Case studies in behavior modification*, (pp. 94-98). New York: Holt, Rinehart and Winston.

James, W. (1950). *The principles of psychology*. New York: Dover Publications. (reprinted by special arrangement with Holt, Rinehart and Winston).

Jensen, A.R. (1969). How much can we boost IQ and scholastic achievement? *Harvard Educational Review, 39*, 1-23.

Kantor, J.R. (1963). Events and constructs in psychology. In M.H. Marx (Ed.), *Theories in contemporary psychology*. New York: Macmillan.

MacCorquodale, K., & Meehl, P.E. (1948). On a distinction between hypothetical constructs and intervening variables. *Psychological Review, 55*, 95-107.

Odum, H.W. (1910). *Social and mental traits of the Negro*. New York: Columbia University Press.

Reynolds, G.S. (1968). *A primer of operant conditioning*. Glenview, Ill.: Scott, Foresman.

Rosenthal, R., & Jacobson, K.F. (1968). *Pygmalion in the classroom: Teacher expectation and pupils' intellectual development*. New York: Holt, Rinehart and Winston.

Sidman, M. *Tactics of scientific research*. New York: Basic Books.

Skinner, B.F. (1964). Behaviorism at fifty. In T.W. Wann (Ed.), *Behaviorism and phenomenology* (pp. 79-97). Chicago: University of Chicago Press.

Skinner, B.F. (1966). What is an experimental analysis of behavior? *Journal of the Experimental Analysis of Behavior, 9*, 213-218.

Tolman, E.C. (1951). Operational behaviorism and current trends in psychology. In M.H. Marx (Ed.), *Psychological theory*. New York: Macmillan.

A Humanistic Approach to Black Psychology

Adelbert H. Jenkins

Introduction

In the last two decades a new generation of African American psychologists has questioned the ways in which psychological theories have been used to describe the situation of African Americans (see various writers in this volume). Studies based on traditional psychological theory have focused on the ways in which African Americans have developed ineffective modes of personal and social adaptation. At the same time they have neglected to show how African Americans have surmounted the daunting circumstances of their history here. Indeed, it is true that African Americans have responded as if "shaped" by the "contingencies" imposed upon them by the racist society (Hayes, 1980). In many instances this has led to features in the African American personality which could be called "adaptive inferiority" (Pugh, 1972). But we know, too, from a closer reading of history and from personal observation that this has not been all there is to the psychological story of African Americans. It has taken something more for African Americans to get to the level of psychological growth that they have achieved against such odds.

Often novelists and poets have been more successful than social scientists in capturing other aspects of African Americans' functioning. Thus, Ralph Ellison noted that he set himself the goal as a writer:

> to commemorate in fiction . . . that which I believe to be enduring and abiding in our situation, especially those human qualities which the American Negro has developed despite and in rejection of the obstacles and meannesses imposed upon us (1964, p. 39).

Langston Hughes also captures this spirit of the perseverance of African Americans in his poem "Mother to Son" where he portrays a mother urging her son not to turn back in his struggle for accomplishment, reminding him that she has kept "a-climbin' on" in spite of the fact that "Life for me ain't been no crystal stair" (1926, p. 187).

As I have suggested elsewhere (Jenkins, 1982) the failure of western social scientists to be interested in such qualities is not only a func-

tion of racist trends in American institutions, including its social science. The problem is also that the dominant model in western psychology has been a "mechanistic" one, a model that sees the human
individual as the relatively passive object of internal drive states and/or
environmental "contingencies". From this point of view the human
being is portrayed as primarily a *re-actor*, only a responder to the givens
that are presented by something or someone else. When emphasis is
placed on the forces acting on people as a general rule in psychology, it
is understandable that with respect to blacks one would stress the formidable forces that seem to have controlled their destinies and shaped
their lives against their will. More and more, however, psychology is
coming to see that something important is left out when one relies on
external stimulus factors as the sole constructs for trying to understand
behavior. There is a growing recognition of the degree to which the
human individual is "an active responsible agent, not simply a helpless
powerless reagent" in life and that we must include in our science a
view of the human being as one "who insists on injecting himself into
the causal process of the world around him" (Chein, 1972, p. 6). This
kind of emphasis, which complements the more familiar description of
human functioning in general, is necessary for a fuller understanding of
the psychology of the African American. Thus, throughout history
blacks have not only been reactive, they have also taken a *pro-active*
stance to events. Where they could they nurtured and promoted a sense
of themselves designed to have a shaping influence on their lives different from what their oppressors intended.

The perspective that best portrays this needed additional side of
human functioning is one that we will begin by calling a "humanistic"
approach to psychology. Although this approach acknowledges that
behavior is affected by forces acting on the individual, it does not stop
there. It goes on to stress the importance of individual agency, independent of the external givens of the situation, as a necessary component
of all human action. Now, first let's clarify the use of the term "humanistic" as it is being used here. This word has been applied to the work of
a number of psychologists such as Abraham Maslow, Carl Rogers, and
writers from an existential psychological position, among others (see
Rychlak's (1981) discussion of this movement). In my use of the term
here I do not intend to explore this humanistic "school" as such but
rather to emphasize points which characterize the term humanism in a
more overarching way. The basic humanistic themes I shall discuss can
be seen in a number of theorists not primarily associated with the humanistic school more narrowly defined (Rychlak, 1981). One essential
aspect of the perspective on humanism that I shall develop here is the
"assumption that the individual 'makes a difference' or contributes to
the flow of events" (Rychlak, 1976, p. 128).

In addition, humanism, as I will use it, is to be distinguished from the term "humanitarianism." The latter term refers to having the goal of contributing to an ever-increasing level of social well-being and personal development for all humankind. This is a goal shared by many mechanistic and humanistic theorists alike. The critical point here is that these two positions differ in the way they portray the human being whose condition they seek to better.

Humanism in Psychology

In this section of the paper I will bring the humanistic conception into clearer focus by looking at the alternative approaches taken by mechanistic and humanistic perspectives on certain fundamental aspects of human functioning. The topics of causation, meaning, and the action of mentality will be briefly considered.

Intentions as Causes

Much of psychology has been cast in a scientific worldview that uses a third-person, or what one might call an "extraspective" point of view, as the proper way of looking at the situations in which people are involved. This is characteristic of the methods that the natural sciences have used successfully in describing and predicting non-human events. From this vantage point the primary job is to identify the "causes" acting *on* the individual framed in language appropriate to the postulated force. So we have had "hydraulic" models and information theory models and computer models of human behavior. While such paradigms have been useful to some extent, in typically mechanistic fashion they tend to view the human individual almost totally from the *observer's* point of view. They assume that the subject's behavior can be accounted for solely in terms of what happens to him or her. From an Aristotelian perspective this would be seen as an "efficient cause" characterization of events because it focuses on the impetus or force that impels behavior. This is the typical definition of the notion of causation in scientific parlance.

The humanistic view requires in addition that when considering *human* behavior we take an *introspective* view of events, from the subjective frame of reference of the actor. It requires that we take into account how the actor sees things, because what a person *intends* to do, what purposes and goals (s)he holds in mind, for the sake of which (s)he strives, represent powerful motivating factors in that person's behavior as well. To include such a perspective into our explanatory framework is to add the Aristotelian notion of a "final cause," which is a "teleological" or "telic" perspective on human behavior. Such a view emphasizes that human behavior is always governed in part by the end *(telos)* the actor has in mind.

While telic concepts have been considered inappropriate to analysis in the natural sciences, humanists consider them perfectly fitting as a part of the scientific investigation of human behavior (Chein, 1972; Rychlak, 1988). The theoretical framework in this paper is actually a "telic-humanistic" psychological perspective. This term is meant to emphasize the idea that the human individual is an important causal agent in his/her life by seeking to carry out intentions which (s)he sets. So, for example, a student's intention to become a doctor, a plan about the future held in mind in the present, can be a powerful motivating factor influencing the kinds of behaviors that she carries out in the ensuing years and the ways in which she overcomes obstacles placed in her path.

In considering the behavior of African Americans the usefulness of a telic approach is reflected in Powdermaker's observations (1943) that in interracial situations, historically blacks often acted in submissive ways with the intent to mock whites; or at times they acted meekly in the face of outrageous provocations by whites, but with the intent to carry out a personally meaningful sense of Christian dignity and moral superiority. Their behavior outwardly examined often gave little hint of what they had in mind, but their capacity to endure can sometimes only be explained by including this introspective view.

In my formulation of these issues (Jenkins, 1982) I have also highlighted Robert White's discussion of "competence" motivation as an important example of intentionality which begins to develop in early infancy and gradually takes self-conscious shape in later life (1963). White suggests that many of the young infant's early interactions with the world are not drive-dominated, but reflect its effort to reach out and have a satisfying effect on the world and, in essence, be *effective*. This tendency develops into a life-long striving to become ever more *competent* in one's transactions with the physical and social world. This is an example of a powerfully motivating intention that governs all people's lives, including, of course, the lives of black persons.

Dialectical Mentality

A second important point in this humanistic perspective also derives from ancient Greek philosophy and contrasts two approaches to establishing meaning. On the one hand, people search for meanings which are singular, "unipolar," clear in their significance and free of alternative or ambiguous connotations. Science is concerned with investigating the world in ways that lead to such descriptions of reality. This is a "demonstrative" approach to the world and it is the single perspective in meaning valued by mechanistic theorists.

On the other hand, people have the capacity to take a "dialectical" or "bipolar" approach to meaning (Rychlak, 1979). From this point of view many concepts of interest to people cannot be fixed with singular certainty. The meaning of such concepts or events must be "framed" by the opposite or alternative implications of the concept. For example, the notion of "up" is defined with reference to a notion of "down"; "truth" implies a notion of "mendacity"; fixing an object along the dimensions of "beauty" requires an accompanying notion of "ugliness." It is true of course that physical or social events in a given culture can be seen to have a singularly defined and seemingly compelling character, but it is important to understand that we have the capacity to conceive of those events differently from how they seem to be. So to take an example, I see a bird sitting in a tree and although the bird really is there I can imagine alternatives, even while looking at the bird, which I have never seen before. For example, I can imagine that bird sitting on a telephone pole at the moment or I could think of a dog sitting on that limb where the bird is now. That is to say, human mentality has the capacity to transcend conceptually the "actualities" of a given reality and imagine different views about the ways things *could* be.

The telic-humanistic theorist does not deny that human beings function usefully in demonstrative modes. (S)he simply posits that the dialectic mode is a necessary addition to capture a significant aspect of human mentality. More to the point of our discussion here, white society told African Americans they were inferior as human beings and incapable of accomplishment. This was an idea that society tried to establish demonstratively as a "fact" about African American people. Enforced by brute strength this had a telling effect on many African Americans. However, at the same time there was the capacity within the thinking of African Americans, more or less strong in different people and usually supported by group or family experiences, to resist this point of view (Lester, 1968) and to sustain alternative perspectives of competence and self-worth in the face of such adversity. This human capacity to envision dialectic alternatives allowing the expression of competence strivings has been a major factor in the psychological survival of African Americans.

Active Mentality

A third important aspect of the theoretical framework being advanced here has to do with the nature of mentality. It contrasts the philosophic perspectives of the British empiricists such as John Locke, with the continental European philosophers such as Immanuel Kant. The mechanistic approach sees individual mentality basically as being developed by the stimuli impinging upon it; that is the image of a relatively passive mentality shaped by the forces acting on it. By contrast, the humanistic theorist sees the individual as mentally active and conceptually structuring the things going on around him or her. From this (Kantian) view people actively structure and construe their reality and then respond to the world as they conceive it.

This is true of human mentality from birth. People are not simply blank slates waiting for the imprint of experience, as the Lockean view would have it, although of course such input is very important in determining the course of development. The organization that the individual finds in reality is to an essential degree created by the individual's mental activity. In this sense mentality is like a pair of spectacles shaping what we know. We are always on "this side" of the spectacles; reality as such is always on the "other side" of the categories created by our conceptual spectacles. There is always:

> a myriad of possibilities in the continually arising experience of life
> ... mentation works within this flux of possibility and seeks to stabilize it in conceptual regularities ... There is always more in sensory experience than meets the conceptual eye (Rychlak & Williams, 1983, p. 16). Thus, mentation is always selective. What mentality "conceptualizes" or stabilizes is only one of the many possible ways of structuring an experience. From this view a person's reality is a construction made about the sensory data available. Variants of such a "constructionist" view of knowledge are gaining considerable prominence in psychology (Scarr, 1985). The strong statement of the (Lockean) mechanist position, philosophical "realism," sees the observer as being outside reality seeking to accurately describe the material order that is seen to be there. The Kantian theorist recognizes that (s)he creates the order (s)he finds in nature. In failing to recognize its inevitable contribution to what it "knows" the mechanistic view runs the danger of failing to recognize its biases. From a black psychological perspective Western psychology has committed just such errors (Thomas & Sillen, 1972).

To sum up, from the telic-humanistic perspective behavior is governed partly by the subjectively derived intentions that people set from among the dialectical alternatives presented to them. We come to the world with an active mentality which gradually structures our conception of reality and it is this conception to which we respond. This point of view which emphasizes the person's contribution as a causal factor in his/her life is meant to enrich our view of the human being by supplementing the typical psychological depictions of the individual which characterize him or her as being only a respondent to stimuli. Of course thoughts and actions do partly reflect internal drive and environmental contingency factors not of our own making. But a full picture of human beings includes the view of people as also making important contributions to their experience and their destiny independent of such factors. With respect to the African American the point is that blacks have survived objectively oppressive circumstances by calling on universal aspects of human psychological capacity such as those I have been describing. In many instances they have actively and intentionally brought to their lives conceptions of their competence that have been at variance with the judgments made of them by the majority society. Now let's look briefly at some of the psychological topics to which this approach to the African American can be applied. We will touch on issues related to the concept of self, intellectual performance, and mental health.

The Concept of "Self"

An emphasis in this paper so far has been the way in which African Americans as people have been active in their manner of addressing their life circumstances. This has not just been a kind of aimless flailing about or a mere emphasis on doing rather than thinking about things. African Americans have often acted with a purposiveness and as much as possible with a sense of direction and identity, i.e., a sense of self.

Self-Concept

The term self which is a critical one for the telic-humanistic view is frequently used with regard to the notion of self-concept, that image we get as we direct our gaze at what we consider to be "me" and "mine," as William James put it. This is a picture of ourselves as the object of our consideration, the sense of "what I am" (Keen, 1970). The image of the self is multi-faceted. There are many components we hold as a part of our concept of ourselves, some carried at a more conscious level than others and some held with more of a sense of pride and self-acceptance than others.

This multifaceted notion of self has been usefully applied to understanding literature on self-esteem among African American children. Reviews of that literature have seemed to lead to conflicting conclusions. Some studies even when well-designed seemed to show that black children had low self-esteem; other studies have shown high self-esteem among black children (Jenkins, 1982, Chap. 2). Cross (1985) noted that of those studies showing low self-esteem, most seemed to be tapping feelings about racial group orientation. Studies showing high self-esteem among African Americans tended to be those reflecting feelings about self without reference to their racial self-evaluation. This suggested to Cross a "multiple reference point" basis for self-evaluation among blacks. Thus, the data have reflected:

> the complexity of self-esteem and the fact that black children have used more than one set of reference points to evaluate themselves depending partly on what they were being asked to do. If the reference point was self-esteem from the vantage point of racial group membership, it might contain some negative feelings, while at the very same moment they might feel quite positive about other parts of themselves (Jenkins, 1982, p. 30-31). This conception is quite consistent with a view of the sense of self as multifaceted.

Self as Agent

There is clearly a dialectic quality to the idea of self. Although it refers to the differentiated view we have of our being, the term is also meant to refer to a feeling of psychological unity that we have about ourselves. Thus, there is a stable sense of personhood that subsumes the various aspects of "me." This sense of personal unity is perhaps more easily seen in that aspect of self reflected in the sense of *agency* that we have. This dimension of the sense of self is the sense "that I am" (Keen, 1970). This conception of self grows as we recognize ourselves as beings who take initiative and make decisions. This sense of self is a way of describing our ability to come to a situation full of possibilities (as most situations are) and make choices. As we do this we gain a sense of orientation and identity which gives a kind of "logical thrust" to the perspectives we develop in life (Rychlak, 1988).

Furthermore, as we do this we shape the course of our lives. One of the implications of this notion is that we bear responsibility, in one sense of the word, for what we become. Based on the intentions we are trying to advance we choose one set of alternatives, when we could conceivably have chosen others. This idea is captured in Frost's poem "The Road Not Taken" (1964) in which a traveler, a metaphor for the self as conceived here, pauses at a point where the path in a wood diverges. Taking one of the paths, the one less worn by travel, the voyager comes to realize that that choice "has made all the difference." The main point here is that all humans, as seen in the light of the choices they make, are to an important degree self-creating beings. I believe that African Americans have made use of this principle in promoting their survival. With a kind of native wisdom many black people have been about the business of self-creation. Whatever their actions may have seemed to an observer—sharply resistant in one case, unusually passive in another—such actions were frequently guided by the intention to sustain some feeling of self-worth and dignity that would promote their survival and growth.

Cognition and Intellectual Performance

Turning to our next area of consideration we come to a topic that has been pointed out as a particular challenge to a conception that seeks to emphasize competent capacities in African Americans as a group, namely, the area of intellectual performance. The lagging school achievement of inner-city black children has been chronicled in the daily newspapers for years and remains a major social and educational problem. The telic-humanistic position does not have a unique perspective on intellectual performance as such, but the thrust of this orientation does lead to a particular way of looking at these issues. The humanistic position does not take the lower performance of large numbers of black children as a true measure of their ability. Rather the telic position is fully supportive of the statement made by the sociologist Jane Mercer that "All ethnic groups have equal potential for acquiring any human culture" (1979, p. 53). Other social scientists take similar positions (Heath, 1986; Kagan, 1976).

This idea can be spelled out in the terms of the telic-humanistic point of view. As we have indicated in the above discussion about mentality all human beings are seen to "come at" the world not only with the capacity to register and take in information but also with an active tendency to meet experience "at the level of sensation (input) with a creative capacity to *order* it via patterns that constitute meaning and meaningfulness" (Rychlak, 1988, p. 326). This activity is called "conceptualizing": "To *conceptualize* is to put a frame (order, organization, etc.) onto experience . . ." (Rychlak, 1988, p. 294). Thus, all infants are mentally active beings in relation to the world within a few hours of birth, albeit in a very rudimentary way. Over time, of course, this activity becomes more sophisticated as the child's abilities mature. The earlier activity provides a framework within which later encounters with the world are interpreted. The person participates actively in the process of learning about the world.

> Learning (which is an important aspect of intelligence) does not simply result from something falling into our mental storage bin, as it were. It involves actively extending the meaning framework that we have developed to new situations in order to make sense of them. When we have made sense of them, that is, imposed an order on them, we have learned something. (Jenkins, 1982, p. 55).

Thus, learning involves actively "bringing forward" prior conceptualizations and the associated intentions to apply to a new situation. This view of the learning process reflects Rychlak's "logical learning theory" (LLT) point of view (Rychlak, 1988). This term refers to the fact that a conceptual pattern (a logos) provides the framework through which one encounters the world. We understand and act in a situation according to how we conceive it not just because of its objectively "real" features. The LLT perspective maintains that all groups of people bring these active conceptualizing processes to experience and such processes are basic to intellectual ability. Intelligence is not some special capacity that only certain groups have, although of course individual people may differ for a variety of reasons in the efficiency with which they use this capacity.

If this is so how are we to account for the poorer performance by African American children on aptitude and achievement tests? Discussion of this issue has been influenced by differing conceptions regarding the nature of intelligence. Can it be represented as primarily a single general ability or are there important multiple facets to intellectual performance? The former notion has been more influential and from the beginnings of the mental testing movement in the United States it has been contended that blacks were inferior in native ability to whites (Kamin, 1974). This argument reached one of its most sophisticated formulations in the recent presentation by Jensen (1969) regarding Level I and Level II abilities. The former set presumably govern learning by rather simple processes of association which depend more on recency and frequency of contact with a stimulus. The latter set involve learning by grasping the underlying similarities, the less evident "deep structure" as it were, in a stimulus array. Level II skills include the ability to reason and to develop concepts and these are the skills emphasized in school. According to this conception, African American and lower-class children's relatively poorer performance in school is because they are genetically lacking in these abilities.

As we know there has been much controversy over Jensen's views. McKenzie's recent discussion of these issues (1984) is an important and thoughtful one. One of the tragic outcomes of this debate is that whatever the contribution that inherited abilities make to intellectual performance the way this issue has been raised has deflected attention away from what might be done to develop the full potential of minority and lower-class children.

For one thing the traditional point of view puts considerable emphasis on standard I.Q. test performance as the sufficient indicator of who possesses higher level intellectual capacity. The standard tests of conceptual ability are reasonably good at indicating what a child can do in school *now*. However, as they are typically scored, they do not necessarily indicate what a child could do in the future if special remedial interventions were to be made or if the learning situation were to be changed. The position which sees intellectual performance as based on a fixed general ability heavily influenced by genetic factors argues that the results of paper and pencil "intelligence tests" give a valid indication of whether the child "has it" or not. If not, then presumably (s)he should be tracked into a less demanding curriculum. In fact there can be a variety of reasons, different for different children, why a child does not perform as well as (s)he might. Even if one were to take the more popular position that intelligence is primarily a single general ability, intellectual performance could probably be enhanced by taking into account the influence of prior developmental experience, cognitive style, test format and the motivational setting of the test situation (Jenkins, 1982, Chap. 3).

For example, with respect to prior learning experience Feuerstein (1979) has suggested that the kind of functioning that seems to limit some children to inadequate performance on more abstract (Level II) materials stems from having learned a *style* of responding to intellectual situations which is too limited to be useful on complex cognitive tasks. In discussing such children, he argues that they are limited to a "reproductive modality" of dealing with stimuli because they see themselves as "passive recipient(s) of information rather than as active generator(s) of new information and ideas . . ." (Feuerstein, 1979, p. 81). Thus intellectual performance from this perspective is a function of the way the child has come to conceptualize or frame the learning activity; it is not primarily the effect of inborn characteristics.

Feuerstein (1979) goes on to discuss his strategies for teaching presumably "retarded" performers how to use more active approaches to cognitive tasks. Other research suggests that some children who do poorly on intellectual tests already have skills which they do not recognize as being applicable to a given task situation either because their prior experience has not made the usefulness of such skills salient for them (Golden et al., 1974; Scrofani et al., 1973) or because they feel somewhat alienated by the test format (Franklin & Fulani, 1979). Children learn according to a given external expectation, for example a school lesson plan, when the conceptualizations they have developed and that which they are being asked to learn seem meaningfully and pleasingly connected.

> If the learning situation is framed in unfamiliar ways or if the situation is associated with negative affective (evaluations) and seems strange and forbidding, then learning and intellectual performance are likely to be hampered (Jenkins, 1982, p. 57).

When the test situation is changed without altering the difficulty of the cognitive task, performance of lower-class children can be shown to be comparable to that of middle-class children. In addressing the value of using other than the standard I.Q. tests to investigate intellectual problem solving ability in children from varying social class and ethnic groups, Yando et al. note: ". . . a better understanding of children in our society who are not middle-class white children can be gained only if we attempt to devise measures and define situations that allow their competencies to emerge" (1979, p. 107). Reflected in this quote is support for the idea that African American children have active competencies; it is up to educational professionals to elicit and help develop these skills.

Alternative to the idea that intellectual ability is a general factor is the notion that intelligence represents an aggregate of distinct and identifiable abilities. This idea which also has a long history in research has recently been given new consideration. Sternberg (Trotter, 1986) in a recent discussion of his "triarchic" theory of intelligence proposes that there are "componential," "experiential," and "contextual" aspects of problem-solving activity involved in intelligent behavior. His perspective includes in intellectual skill the capacity to use analytic cognitive abilities in both creative and practically meaningful ways. Gardner (1985) takes a more expansive view of the issue. He postulates seven basic "frames of mind" which fit his definition of intelligence: "the ability to solve problems, or create products, that are valued within one or more cultural settings" (1985, p. x). His theory based on a careful review of the research literature tries to take into account neuropsychological and psychometric as well psychological and cultural factors. Although his perspective is not yet empirically substantiated, he provides a cogent framework for criticizing the traditional implication that "intelligence" is confined to what we in the western industrial culture value, namely the logico-mathematical and linguistic abilities, which are only *two* of Gardner's intelligences. He also questions a conception that confines intelligence to that which can be measured by paper and pencil tests alone. This is a critique similar to that of Yando et al. (1979). These lines of criticism support the idea that all people come into the world with active problem-solving abilities and that we have much to learn to frame human intelligence in ways that enable us to demonstrate that.

Mental Health and Psychotherapy

The issue of mental health and the black community is too large to be dealt with comprehensively here. In trying to bring a teleologic psychological perspective to these issues we can return to the concept of self and self activity which is so central to this humanistic point of view. For all people the effort to sustain healthy and realistic self-esteem is a primary goal. The teleologic view suggests that this involves the individual's confronting the uncertainty of experience, affirming a set of goals (values) and working to carry them out. In so doing the person develops his/her sense of agency or self activity. Within my abbreviated treatment of the topic here, one way of characterizing mental disorder is to see it as disturbed self activity. Jerome Frank notes that when people come to a mental health professional for assistance they are often in a state of "demoralization," feeling as if they have "failed to meet their own expectations or those of others . . . unable to cope with some pressing problem (and feeling) powerless to change the situation or themselves" (1973, p. 314). By contrast one characteristic of the psychological situation for an individual who is feeling relatively positive about himself is the sense of having behavioral options for sustaining that sense of self-esteem. Demoralization represents a state in which the individual feels (s)he has exhausted such options for self activity.

This way of characterizing emotional disorder is not just applicable to black people, of course, but for blacks from day to day there is the added problem of coping with personal and institutional racism. Racism is a continuing assault on the effort of African Americans to maintain a sturdy sense of self. Most African Americans are able to muster sufficient defensive and adaptive resources based on a solid enough sense of competence to put aside some of the negative feelings stirred by such encounters with society. However, if a person's history is sufficiently troubled or events become too crushing the individual may develop clear symptomatology (see Jenkins, 1982, Chap. 6, for a further discussion of these issues from this humanistic point of view).

Psychological Treatment

As a result of their experiences in the United States African Americans have learned to be cautious and to shield their sense of self in various ways, hence it is likely that when African Americans come to psychotherapy, they come with suspicions about how fairly they will be dealt with by the mental health establishment (Block, 1981). Although coming for help in order to get themselves back on track, they also are concerned about protecting their sense of self-esteem. The literature has suggested that African Americans tend to drop out of therapy early as compared to white persons (Gibbs, 1985; Sue, 1977). This is not because African Americans are not suitable for psychotherapy. Psychotherapy allows the patient to symbolize and reflect on the experience of self in the world. African American people of varying socioeconomic circumstances are certainly able to do that and are inclined to do so if given the opportunity. Lerner in her study of short-term psychodynamically oriented therapy in an inner-city setting noted that persons in her clinic sample while not discounting quite harrowing external circumstances still often had a "sense that something inside themselves prevented them from struggling effectively to realize their full psychosocial potential" (1972, p. 33). The issue then is not so much the African American patient's suitability for therapy but rather the therapist's skill in conducting it. (The telic theoretical perspective subsumes a variety of approaches to psychotherapy including psychodynamic and cognitive-behavioral ones [Rychlak, 1979, Chap. 8]. We shall be more concerned with the psychodynamic perspective here.)

Managing the Early Sessions

Some writers suggest that it is particularly important to work actively in early phases of the treatment to engage the African American client or (s)he may leave (Griffith and Jones, 1979). The telic-humanistic theory speaks to this observation by noting that we are all persons who bring the tendency to evaluate affectively the situations of which we are a part. The extent that a situation is meaningful to us includes our "affective assessment" of it as being something we like or something we dislike. Such judgments affect whether we approach and participate more in a given situation or whether we retreat from the event. Based on a considerable amount of empirical research regarding the importance of such processes to people in confronting unfamiliar circumstances (Rychlak, 1988) it is likely that minorities bring such active assessing processes into the therapy situation. I suggest that this process might well operate with particular force for African Americans in the early stages of psychotherapy (Jenkins, 1985).

Gibbs (1985) provides a good analysis of the dynamics of the beginning phase of a therapy relationship with many African American clients. She notes that black clients in a consulting or therapeutic relationship tend to take an "interpersonal" rather than an "instrumental" orientation to the encounter initially. That is, they are especially tuned in to the interaction process between therapist and client rather than on getting immediately to the task-related aspects of the problem that brought them to therapy. She suggests that one can see this in several "micro-stages" in the first two or three sessions of the treatment process. These micro-stages which she spells out in some detail reflect the therapist's capacity to be attuned to the patient's sensitivity about status and/or ethnic differences between client and therapist. If satisfied with the therapist's ability to equalize such differences and show acceptance of the client's cultural concerns and style as well as the personal problems tentatively posed, the client begins to become more self-disclosing. As this "interpersonal" phase evolves further with the therapist's tactful guidance, the client becomes able to commit him/herself to the task-centered aspects of the treatment.

For our considerations the point of Gibbs' discussion is that the initial somewhat guarded and aloof manner that many black clients seem to present may not just be defensiveness. From the humanistic perspective what seems to happen in the early phase of a therapy is that African American clients make active use of the broad human capacities for affective assessment that they tend to rely on more in their everyday interaction in this society. Such responses reflect the agency of an actively assessing mentality deciding on what seems to be the best way of understanding what is going on and how to proceed consistent with principles of self-enhancement. Thus, even when African American clients seem relatively passive in the opening moments of an interpersonal phase of therapy, they are actively involved in an evaluation of the therapist. This process reflects the operation of self activity and has an impact on whether therapy will get off the ground.

Relationship Dynamics

Gibbs' discussion of relationship issues early in therapy is consistent with a clear trend in current approaches to psychodynamic therapy generally (Gill, 1983; Luborsky, 1984; Strupp & Binder, 1984). Luborsky writing about his "supportive-expressive" approach to psychoanalytic therapy notes, "It is the relationship problems that are the most accessible and therapeutically usable expression of (the patient's) conflicts; they tend to be directly involved in the patient's suffering and therefore to require change" (1984, p. 17). This emphasis on relationship issues in some of the clinical literature has application to minorities. In a recent discussion of issues pertaining to psychotherapy with black patients, Enrico Jones (1985) suggests that "empathy," the therapist's capacity to share and understand affectively the experience of the other, and "countertransference," the nature of the therapist's personal reactions to the patient, are two key terms for psychotherapy with African Americans. Regarding countertransference reactions Jones notes that while any patient may evoke such attitudes:

> Black patients may evoke [them] more frequently. The reason for this seems to be that social images of blacks still make them easier targets for therapists' projections and that the culturally different client provides more opportunities for empathic failures (1985, p. 178).

Jones maintains that self-knowledge and the continuing effort to remain aware of one's ongoing psychological processes are the best ways of preventing dysfunctional intrusions of personal reactions into the therapy.

With respect to empathy, Schwaber's considerations of this topic in broader patient contexts have relevance both to the humanistic view and to our consideration of minority clients. She stresses that empathy refers to a way of perceiving—an "experiencing from *within* the patient's experience" (1980, p. 216). Empathic observation attempts to look through the patient's eyes, as it were, taking an introspective view. One of Schwaber's particular concerns is the patient's reaction to the therapist in the treatment setting. She suggests that the participants in therapy are best seen as making up a "contextual unit." Each one's experience of "reality" in that unit comes from how each views the other's participation, as well as from what each brings to it in terms of personality dispositions. In this view the therapist does not necessarily have the only viable perspective on the reality between them. In such a therapeutic stance Schwaber notes that her listening "is characterized by my sustained effort to seek out my place in the patient's experience, as part of the context that is perceived or felt" (1983, p. 523).

With these ideas in mind there are a number of points which are relevant to our topic here. First, Schwaber's emphasis on heightening our imaginative capacities empathically to see the work and ourselves more clearly through the client's eyes is an especially important perspective for the black client. It is these perceptions of us that are so important to the establishment and progress of the relationship with this client (Gibbs, 1985). Secondly, her "contextual unit" conception highlights the idea that there are alternative ways of conceiving reality. The more one has a sense that one is looking at the world not so much the way it "is," but rather viewing it through one's construction of it, influenced by one's own social and personal vantage point, the more open one is to recognizing the partialness of one's own truth and the possibility of other useful truths. A therapist who takes a stance which holds philosophically that there are valid alternative perspectives on reality is likely to be able to be more open to cultural difference and allow the minority client more room for growth.

One of the hallmarks of American racism has been the assumption that the Euro-American cultural vision represented *the* "reality." Other cultural perspectives were seen as distortions. Minorities coming to mental health institutions have expected to be greeted from this perspective. Contact with an "authority" who believes that (s)he is not the arbiter of reality should be especially liberating for the black patient. I think this is one implication of some research on the impact of therapist attitudes on treatment outcome. Lerner(1972) found that low income patients showed more improvement in therapy when seen by therapists holding "egalitarian" attitudes toward low-income people in general than did clients not seen by therapists holding such attitudes. Ross (1983) using the same measure of therapist attitude found that low-income African American patients remained in therapy longer when seen by therapists with egalitarian attitudes.

Conclusion

In conclusion, I have suggested that a systematic teleologic approach in psychology provides a needed complement for understanding African Americans. Such an approach recognizes the active independent mentality inherent in all human beings. In the course of this paper I have briefly examined the applicability of this approach to three topics pertinent to black psychology. I have suggested that though heir to the range of human failings most African Americans have persevered to create and sustain as viable a sense of self as their personal and social circumstances would allow. In addition I have maintained that African Americans have active intellectual capacities which can be nurtured by an educational system that is sensitive to the diverse forms of human potential. Finally, I have suggested that when the African American individual is experiencing a pervasive sense of demoralization with respect to self-efficacy, psychotherapy governed by principles which seek to clarify and ally the therapist with the patient's point of view can be useful.

References

Block, C. B. (1981). Black Americans and the cross-cultural counseling and psychotherapy experience. In A. J. Marsella, & P. B. Pedersen (Eds.), *Cross-cultural and psychotherapy*, pp. 177-194. Elmsford, N.Y.: Pergamon Press

Chein, I. (1972). *The science of behavior and the image of man*. New York: Basic Books.

Cross, W.E. Jr. (1985). Black identity: Rediscovering the distinction between personal identity and reference group orientation. In M.B. Spencer, G.K. Brookins, & W.R. Allen (Eds.), *Beginnings: The social and affective development of black children*, pp. 155-171. Hillsdale, N.J.: Erlbaum.

Ellison, R. (1964). That same pain, that same pleasure: An interview. In R. Ellison (Ed.), *Shadow and act*. New York: Signet Books.

Feuerstein, R. (1979). *The dynamic assessment of retarded performers: The learning potential assessment device, theory, instruments, and techniques*. Baltimore: University Park Press.

Frank, J. D. (1973). *Persuasion and healing: A comparative study of psychotherapy* (2nd ed.) Baltimore: Johns Hopkins Press.

Franklin, A. J., & Fulani, L. (1979). Cultural content of materials and ethnic group performance in categorized recall. In A. W. Boykin, A. J. Franklin, & J. F. Yates (Eds.), *Research directions of black psychologists*. New York: Russell Sage Foundation.

Frost, R. (1964). The road not taken. In *Complete Poems of Robert Frost*. New York: Holt.

Gardner, H. (1985). *Frames of mind: The theory of multiple intelligences*. New York: Basic Books.

Gibbs, J. T. (1985). Establishing a treatment relationship with black clients: Interpersonal vs. instrumental strategies. In C. Germain (Ed.), *Advances in clinical social work practice*. Silver Spring, Md.: National Association of Social Work, Inc.

Gill, M. (1983). The interpersonal paradigm and the degree of the therapist's involvement. *Contemporary Psychoanalysis, 19*, 200-237.

Golden, M., Bridger, W.H., & Montare, A. (1974). Social class differences in the ability of young children to use verbal information to facilitate learning. *American Journal of Orthopsychiatry, 44*, 86-91.

Griffith, M. S., & Jones, E. E. (1979). Race and psychotherapy: Changing perspectives. In J. H. Masserman (Ed.), *Current psychiatric therapies, 18*, pp. 225-235. New York: Grune & Stratton.

Hayes, W. A. (1980). Radical black behaviorism. In R. Jones (Ed.), *Black psychology* (2nd ed.). New York: Harper & Row.

Heath, S. B. (1986). Sociocultural contexts of language development. In D. D. Holt (Ed.), *Beyond language: Social and cultural factors in schooling language minority students*, pp. 143-186. Los Angeles: Evaluation, Dissemination and Assessment Center, Calif. State University.

Hughes, L. (1926). Mother to son. In *Selected poems of Langston Hughes*. New York: Alfred A. Knopf.

Jenkins, A. H. (1982). *The psychology of the Afro-American: A humanistic approach*. Elmsford, N.Y.: Pergamon.

Jenkins, A. H. (1985). Attending to self-activity in the Afro-American client. *Psychotherapy*, *22*, 335-341.

Jensen, A. R. (1969). How much can we boost I.Q. and scholastic achievement? *Harvard Educational Review*, *39*, 1-123.

Jones, E. E. (1985). Psychotherapy and counseling with black clients. In P. Pedersen (Ed.), *Handbook of cross-cultural counseling and therapy*, pp. 173-179. Westport, CT: Greenwood.

Kagan, J. (1976). Cognitive development. *JSAS Catalog of Selected Documents in Psychology*, *6*, 96. (Ms. No. 1338, 36 pgs.)

Kamin, L. J. (1974). *The science and politics of I.Q.* Potomac, Md.: Lawrence Erlbaum.

Keen, E. (1970). *Three faces of being: Toward an existential clinical psychology.* New York: Appleton-Century-Crofts.

Korchin, S. J. (1976). *Modern clinical psychology.* New York: Basic Books.

Lerner, B. (1972). *Therapy in the ghetto: Political impotence and personal disintegration.* Baltimore: Johns Hopkins University Press.

Lester, J. (1968). *Look out whitey! Black power's gon' get your mama!* New York: Grove.

Luborsky, L. (1984). *Principles of psychoanalytic psychotherapy: A manual for supportive-expressive treatment.* New York: Basic Books.

McKenzie, B. (1984). Explaining race differences in I.Q.: The logic, the methodology and the evidence. *American Psychologist*, *39*, 1214-1233.

Mercer, J. R. (1979). *SOMPA: System of multicultural pluralistic assessment.* (Technical Manual) New York: The Psychological Corporation.

Powdermaker, H. (1943). The channeling of Negro aggression by the cultural process. *American Journal of Sociology*, *48*, 750-758.

Pugh, R. W. (1972). *Psychology and the black experience.* Monterey, CA: Brooks/Cole.

Ross, S. (1983). Variables associated with dropping out of therapy. *Dissertation Abstracts International*, *44*, 616B (University Microfilms No. DA830785).

Rychlak, J. F. (1976). Is a concept of "self" necessary in psychological theory, and if so why?: A humanistic perspective. In A. Wandersman, P. J. Poppen, & D. F. Ricks (Eds.), *Humanism and behaviorism: Dialogue and growth*, pp. 121-143. Elmsford, Ill.: Pergamon Press.

Rychlak, J. F. (1979). *Discovering free will and personal responsibility.* New York: Oxford University Press.

Rychlak, J. F. (1981). *Introduction to personality and psychotherapy: A theory-construction approach* (2nd ed.). Boston: Houghton Mifflin.

Rychlak, J. F. (1988). *The psychology of rigorous humanism* (2nd ed). New York: Wiley.

Rychlak, J. F., & Williams, R. N. (1983). *Dialectical human reasoning: Theoretical justification and supporting evidence drawn from the method of triassociation.* Manuscript submitted for publication.

Scarr, S. (1985). Constructing psychology: Making facts and fables for our times. *American Psychologist*, *40*, 499-512.

Schwaber, E. (1980). Self psychology and the concept of psychopathology: A case presentation. In A. Goldberg (Ed.), *Advances in self psychology*, pp. 215-242. New York: International Universities Press.

Schwaber, E. (1983). A particular perspective on analytic listening. *Psychoanalytic Study of the Child*, *38*, 519-546.

Scrofani, P. J., Suziedelis, A., & Shore, M. F. (1973). Conceptual ability in black and white children of different social classes: An experimental test of Jensen's hypothesis. *American Journal of Orthopsychiatry, 43*, 541-553.

Strupp, H. H., & Binder, J. L. (1984). *Psychotherapy in a new key: A guide to time-limited dynamic psychotherapy.* New York: Basic Books.

Sue, S. (1977). Community mental health services to minority groups: Some optimism, some pessimism. *American Psychologist, 32*, 616-624.

Thomas, A., & Sillen, S. (1972). *Racism and psychiatry.* New York: Brunner/Mazel.

Trotter, R. J. (1986, August). Three heads are better than one. *Psychology Today,* pp. 56-62.

White, R. W. (1963). Ego and reality in psychoanalytic theory. *Psychological Issues, 3*, Serial No. 11.

Yando, R., Seitz, V., & Zigler, E. (1979). *Intellectual and personality characteristics of children: Social-class and ethnic-group differences.* Hillsdale, N.J.: Lawrence Erlbaum.

The Evolution of Human Psychology for African Americans

Na'im Akbar

There has been a rapid evolution in the thinking about the psychology of African Americans since 1970. That evolution has progressed from a self-negating perspective which viewed the model human being as necessarily nonblack to a self-affirmative perspective which sees the African as a model of universal man. In a relatively brief time, scholars have dissected the youthful psychology which has grown-up in Europe and America over the last 100 years and has sought to salvage human psychology from the precipice of mechanized, human destruction. This discussion is a brief review of the evolution of that thinking about the psychology of African Americans.

Several scholars have presented extensive comparisons regarding the philosophical basis of conceptualizing the world from European vs. African perspectives (Akbar, 1976; Clark, 1972; Clark (X), et al. 1975 and Dixon, 1976). The differences in these philosophical perspectives have been cited as the basis of the differences in European and African behavior as well as differences in the methods of observation of those behaviors (Baldwin, 1976; Jackson, 1976, 1979 and Nobles, 1974, 1976). Jackson (1979) in a provocative study reviewed the origin and development of "Black Psychology" and some of the key issues regarding the development of that field of inquiry. This discussion draws upon the valuable discussion of Jackson and perhaps extends his observations a step further into analyzing the conceptual development which has occurred in the thinking of, particularly, Afro-American psychologists over the last 15 years.

We shall characterize the three major developments in the conceptualization of Afro-American psychologists as "Euro-American," "Black," and "African" perspectives. These three orientations have certain characteristics which define their methodology, and by implication structure the definitions and ontology which emerge from these perspectives.

These three stages of conceptual growth have first evolved in terms of their orientation. An orientation determines one's reference point for assessing normality. Throughout most of the history of observations of Afro-American behavior in the West, that reference point has clearly been Euro-centric. Baldwin (1976) observes that the standards of observation which have led to persistent conclusions of the "social pathology" of black behavior has resulted from the Euro-centric assumptions in the use of measures of black behavior. Baldwin (1976) continues:

> The traditional social pathology view of black behaviors is therefore based on a European conception or definition of reality, or more precisely, a European distortion of the reality of black people. Its rise to prominence in the psychological literature, naturally then, merely reflects the vested social power of Euro-American psychology (and white people generally in European American culture) to legitimate European definitions of reality rather than the necessary objective credibility appeal of its presumed validity (p. 8).

From this Eurocentric reference point, normality is established on a model of the middle class, Caucasian, male of European descent. The more one approximates this model in appearance, values and behavior, the more "normal" a person is considered to be. The major problem with such normative assumptions for non-European people is the inevitable conclusion of deviance on the part of anyone, unlike this model. In fact, the more distinct or distant you are from this model the more pathological one is considered to be. The obvious advantage for Europeans is that such norms confirm their reality as the reality and flaunts statements of their supremacy as scientifically based "fact."

Even a casual observation of the history of psychology will well-demonstrate that the volumes of psychological literature from the last 100 years have been based on observations primarily on Europeans, exclusively Caucasian, predominantly male and overwhelmingly middle class. Thomas and Sillen (1972) have well-demonstrated this fact in their extensive review of *Racism and Psychiatry*. The formulations of such notable thinkers who have shaped the thought of Euro-American psychology such as Sigmund Freud (1953), G. Stanley Hall (1904), Carl Jung (1953), William McDougall (1908) and B. F. Skinner (1971) have all directly or indirectly asserted the superiority of European races over non-European races. Despite the diversity of the so-called "Schools" of Western psychology, they seem to merge unequivocally in their assumption of the Euro-centric point of view and the superiority of people of European descent. It is not surprising that the conclusions reached from the application of their concepts and methods have concluded the invariable inferiority of non-Caucasian peoples.

The use of this Eurocentric reference point by non-European (Caucasian) observers has resulted in many non-Caucasian observers having become advocates of their own inferiority. It is for this reason that many so-called "black psychologists" have been identified with the same racist tradition which has characterized the majority of Western psychology and its research findings. Such findings have obsessively dealt with the alleged self-rejection, inferior intellect, defective families and contorted motivations of African Americans. These conclusions are not unlike the typical conclusions of the European American psychologist. As I have observed elsewhere (Weems, 1973):

> The logical fallacy in this inappropriate attribution of normative statements about non-white people is the assumption that to be intelligent (or for that matter, psychologically healthy in general) is to act like a European rather than as an agent of your own culture.

The orientation of "Black Psychology" is "ghetto-centric." Jackson (1979) has accurately portrayed the early development of Black Psychology as "reactive." He further observes:

> (Black Psychology) can be readily traced to the 1920's when Afro-American psychologists first published research studies to dispel the notion of Afro-American inferiority and sought to increase the psychological services rendered to the Afro-American community. These heuristic works and pioneering efforts were, for the most part a reaction to the existence of institutional racism and individual acts of discrimination, and, therefore, merely constituted a racist perspective (p. 271). This reactive aspect of "Black Psychology" was necessary and served a vital purpose in the evolution of thought about the psychology of African Americans. It was probably one of the initial insights of the African American scholars that one of the primary shortcomings of traditional psychology was its fallacious normative definitions. It was clearly perceived by writers such as Clark (1965)—who has condemned the Black Psychology movement since its inception—that the insistence upon viewing African American behavior in the light of European American norms was clearly conceptually faulty. The response was to decry the Caucasian, middle class norm and to assert the necessity of analyzing African American behavior in the context of its own norms. These norms were assumed to be the behaviors of southern-born, working class, African American ghettos-dwellers. Such a norm, though introducing bias against large numbers of African Americans was certainly more valid than the traditional norms which had been applied.

Joseph White (1972) in his landmark piece "Toward a Black Psychology" asserted the need for this new norm. He states:

> . . . it is vitally important that we develop, out of the authentic experience of black people in this country, an accurate workable theory of Black Psychology. It is very difficult, if not impossible to understand the life styles of black people using traditional theories developed by white psychologists to explain white people. Moreover, when these traditional theories are applied to the lives of black folks many incorrect, weakness-dominated, and inferiority-oriented conclusions come about (p. 43).

White (1972) asserts quite correctly that the effort to use the norm of middle class is European American behavior. An example which he offers is of the designation of "culturally deprived" to a group of black youngsters who he describes as having developed the kind of "mental toughness and survival skills, in terms of coping with life, which make them in many ways superior to their white age-mates." He continues:

> These black youngsters know how to deal effectively with bill collectors, building superintendents, corner grocery stores, hippies, pimps, whores and sickness and death. They know how to jive school counselors, principals, teachers, welfare workers, juvenile authorities, and in doing so, display a lot of psychological cleverness and originality. They recognize very early that they exist in an environment which is sometimes both complicated and hostile (p. 44).

The irony of this black norm assertion is that it invariably validates itself in comparison with whites. White's assertion that such a perspective actually makes "them superior to their white age-mates" is the consistent conclusion from the black norm. Ultimately, the norm remains the same since African American behavior is still being compared with the rejected norm. The statement of what it meant to be "black" was never considered an adequate statement unless that condition was in some way compared with whites. The consequence is an inevitable entrapment in the same circle.

The other limitation of the "black norm" as adopted in the Black Psychology movement is the conclusion that the adaptation to the conditions of America by African Americans constitutes a reasonable normative statement about African American behavior. The problem with such an assumption is the acceptance of many adaptive but ultimately self-destructive behaviors as legitimate. For example, the pimp becomes glorified as a cultural hero because of his material attainment. For very much the same reason, the drug pusher can become a hero because he, in White's words, "is the black culture hero who messes with the system and gets away with it." As a consequence, such destructive adaptations emerge as new cultural norms for the African American community.

Utilization of the ghetto-centric norms rendered "Black Psychology" irrelevant to a large middle class of African Americans who were, ironically, the authors of Black Psychology. A classic example of this irony was the robust condemnation of the Moynihan conclusions about the African American family. Based on the Euro-centric norm and models of Freudian psychology, Moynihan concluded that the "Black Family" as essentially pathogenic or responsible for the origin of many psychological and social problems of African Americans. The outcry was intense and extreme from black and "liberal" white psychologists, sociologists, and other social scientists. Typical of this outcry was the statement by psychologist Joseph White (1972):

When the black family is viewed from a middle-class frame of reference, which assumes that the psychologically healthy family contains two parents, one male and one female, who remain with the child until he or she becomes a young adult, the fact that the same black male is not consistently visible to the white observer of the black family leads to a conclusion that the black family unit has a matriarchal structure ... A closer look at the black family might show that the matriarchal or one parent view fails to take into consideration the extended nature of the black family (pp. 44-45). Though the description of an extended family is true from a point of view, it inadvertently establishes a new and equally biased norm based upon the ghetto-centric perspective. The large number of intact African American families are then suspect in regard to the "black norm." Though the extended family concept is valid as a structure of African American families, it is important to realize that the nuclear family can also have validity for African Americans. The assumption that one must choose one or the other due to majority participation raised serious questions about the validity of the norm being applied. As we shall see below, the application of a more universal norm could legitimize either pattern.

The weakness of the Euro-centric and ghetto-centric perspectives is their reliance on a statistical norm as the model of human order. Implicit in both perspectives is an assumption that a majority in a particular context can effectively determine what is natural for human beings. In fact, throughout European American psychology, there is a serious fallacy which confuses normative (or normal) with natural. We have seriously criticized this tendency which we call "democratic sanity," elsewhere (Akbar, 1979).

The orientation of African Psychology is nature-centric. It takes as its norm, the nature of the human being and the functioning of nature in general. It is important to note at this juncture that we use the term "African" advisedly. In fact, we might more appropriately describe this approach as "natural psychology" (Akbar, 1976). This reservation is crucial because of the numerous distorted images which can be observed in post-colonial, modern Africa. A misapplication of the concepts of African Psychology has come from the effort to document or disprove the African Psychology model by conducting field surveys or studies of contemporary urban African behavior. The assumption of the African Psychology theoreticians has been since its inception that the philosophical foundations of African Psychology (Nobles, 1972) represent a pure model of the African person in particular and universal man in general. "African Psychology" has gained growing popular usage over the last several years, so we use it here, but with the aforementioned reservations.

The writer is aware that the use of vague language like "human nature" is a harping back to the "pre-scientific" assertions of 19th century European philosophy. Precisely because of the false security in such pseudo-objective notions as "behavior" and "statistical norms," we reassert the validity of concepts such as "human nature." The use of a nature-centric perspective maintains that there are absolute standards and principles guiding human behaviors.

For example, one of the principles of African Psychology is "survival of the Tribe" or the principle of collective survival. Under the influence of this principle, one can observe a wide variety of behaviors geared towards that end. Many behaviors can fit this standard of human nature. The critical point is that the norm is not a statistical majority, but a life concept of collective survival. From this point of view, we can more fully appreciate Nobles' (1978) description of the African American family structure as "elastic." Such a family can be as effectively nuclear as extended, depending upon what kinds of circumstances were necessary for survival of the family (tribe). The same point is true of functions within the family. According to Nobles (1978):

> Functionally, or the performance of its (family) functions, would be
> fluid or elastic. That is, the performance of a particular function
> does or can "expand" into many other functions.

The whole notion of fixed and inflexible role definitions does not become a criterion of effective family functioning. As a consequence, arguments for the presence or absence of a physical father is a moot question regarding family effectiveness. Instead, the issue becomes adequacy of function rather than the presence of a particular role occupant. The concept of a matriarchy or a patriarchy is a meaningless analysis. Equally useless, is the argument of a nuclear as opposed to an extended family, for the same reasons.

There are other absolute norms about the nature of man which are drawn from both historical, philosophical, religious and esoteric descriptions of man and his nature. Assumptions about the perfectibility of man, his capacities for self-mastery, consciousness and conscience as well as man's inseparability from man, are viewed as preeminent influences in human nature form the African Psychological perspective.

Axiology (Values)

Issues of values are seldom discussed in scientific enterprises. This is in part due to a pervasive denial of the role of values in guiding so-called "scientific" activity. In fact, it is the erroneous claim that values are absent in the "objectivity" of science which rather systematically excludes values as an issue in the discussion of science. Dr. Jacob Carruthers (1972) observes rather astutely:

> ... the science or (experimental) methodology is neutral or objective, it is the science of control through intervention and/or the unnatural alteration (if possible) of all objects (p. 3). So, what is assumed to be value-free is itself a value. The choice of values or the values guiding ones pursuit constitutes one of the critical distinctions between approaches to the study of man.

The essential axiological (or axiomatic, if you will) position taken by the European American psychological perspective is the value of objectivity. It starts as Carruthers (1972) continues by assuming:

> a theory about harnessing certain forces and subduing certain oppositions to the deserved change. Western science assumes that any desirable modification of nature is dictated .... Thus not only is it right to modify nature to supply needs, but it is also right to conform nature to all other tastes, in keeping with the doctrine of enlightened self-interest. (pp. 3-4). In other words, the value of objectivity adopts a point of view of the essential relationship in nature to be man-over-object. Man is viewed as the instrument of control and all other things (and occasionally people of lesser power) are objects subject to that control. The individual self is viewed as the center of reality and all else is object. So if self is male, then all that is female is object; if self is Caucasian, then all that is non-Caucasian is object and is therefore subject to male, Caucasian, etc., control or unnatural alteration.

Social science is replete with examples of this tendency to objectify by ordinal or nominal classification. Again, Dr. Carruthers (1972) observes:

> ... modern methodology is based upon ordinal classifications. The various phenomena are ranked according to imagined or imposed objective values such as magnitude or complexity or natural arrangements derived from so-called systematic comparisons (p. 4). Classifications which are frequently encountered in social science literature of the European American variety frequently reduce people to categories like "the aged," "the schizophrenic subjects," "the culturally deprived," etc. Such categories which are initially nominal are invariably treated in some qualitative fashion resulting in an ordinal classification based on superordinate-subordinate arrangement. The necessity to refer to people involved in psychological studies as "subjects" is clearly instructive about the goal of such studies to the subject. This is the value of the "valueless" European American experimental methodology.

A final value implication of the European American methodology is the assumption that the observer is not a participant in what he observes. This arbitrary suspension of universal interconnection is an astounding feat of logical fallacy. By altering the classification or depersonalizing the personalities into an (E)xperimenter and a (S)ubject, there is an assumption that the E is free to peek without detection or intrusion. Such an assumption perpetuates the platonic notion that man and nature are two different realms of being. This assumption frees man to run amok in his role as master over nature. In fact, Carruthers (1972) goes on to point out:

> The assumptions are based on the so-called self-evident notion that nature is uneven in supplying the needs of man; thus, the maximization of individual survival can be achieved by modification of natural supply (p. 3).

The axiological position of Black Psychology is racialism. This value assumes race to be the critical human issue in the study of African American behavior. As the European American operates effectively from his position of man-to-object, the Black Psychologist views the critical relationship of black-to-white as the paradigmatic relationship. The condition of white oppression of blacks is accepted as a given and the essential value of Black Psychology is mastery over oppression and the oppressor. In fact, psychiatrist Frances Welsing (1974) defines "Black Psychiatry" as "counter racism."

The works of eminent black scholars such as Clark (1965), Fanon (1967), Grier and Cobbs (1968) and non-black scholars such as Kardiner and Ovesey (1951), Karon (1958) and many others have well-illustrated this position. The assumption that black personality is a cumulative by-product of sustained oppression is one of the major positions of these writers. Furthermore, it is assumed that the only meaningful approach to the study of black persons is from the perspective of oppression and in terms of the black experience with whites in America. In fact, the idea is that African Americans would be just like European Americans or perhaps, more appropriately would be European Americans if it were not for oppression. There is also an assumption of commonality among those who have experienced oppression. It is not unusual for some African American social scientists to adopt a Marxist position which uncritically equates the racial oppression of people of African descent with other economically and/or socially oppressed peoples.

The extension of this value perspective asserts that essentially whatever is black is of positive value and what is white is of negative value. This is in direct contrast to the Caucasian domination and exploitative use of "objective" methodology which has objectively concluded everything "white" to be positive and everything "black" negative. The reactive quality of Black Psychology is reflected in this mirror image of European American psychology. The "Black Psychologist" involves himself with the process of delineating those "black" positive characteristics and those white negative ones. In other words, it follows the tradition of Dr. Welsing's "counter-racist Psychiatry."

The essential value of the African psychological system is the centrality of man. In the African Cosmology, man is the center (Nobles, 1980). "The animals, plants, and natural phenomena constitute the environment in which man lives" (Nobles, 1980). Nobles (1980) continues: "everything was functionally connected; to destroy one category completely would cause the destruction of the whole of existence, including the Creator." Man and his world are clearly interdependent and the objective approach which completely excludes subjectivity is logically fallacious. The African approach identifies the relevance of psycho-historical traumata such as slavery and the cultural barbarism of certain people but these considerations are not reactive. Though the experiences of oppression are critical in terms of assessing the contemporary African experience, this cosmology evolved long before the coming of the European and it would be self-effacing to reduce its perspective to "racialism" or experiences with the European. The Axiology of African Psychology identities a Divine Creator as the originator and sustainer of man. Nature is in harmony with herself and the desirable state is a harmonious relationship with nature. Consequently, mastery over environment is not the essential value of African Psychology. Neither is mastery over oppression viewed as a preeminent concern because without oppression man would find himself in a teleological vacuum. However, the preeminent value is self-mastery which presupposes the active elimination of oppressive yokes in order to realize this value. Man is conceived as a microcosm of the universe, therefore, in mastering self one has mastered the essential processes of nature.

Those things which facilitate effective human development are valued. Human values are paramount and objects are evaluated as they impact upon the human situation. Objects are never evaluated as having greater prominence than people.

Conceptions of Self

The three approaches also differ in terms of how they define self. The definition of self or "person" in psychology is critical because such a definition determines both the approach to description, assessment and ultimately reconstruction, if such should become necessary. In other words, ones conception of consciousness is at the foundation of ones approach to method in the study of the human mind.

European American Psychology takes as its arena of study the individual ego, behavior and consciousness. The commonality in the European American approach to personality is its emphasis on individuality. From Adler's "creative self" through Maslow's "actualized self" and Mead's "looking glass self," the conception is consistent that self is an individual phenomenon. All of these approaches give the highest credibility to the individual and his unique experiences. So from Skinnerian to Freudian psychology, we can observe that there is a common emphasis on individual differences as being the best description of human experience.

Black Psychology describes the arena of study as being the collective experience of oppression. What must be studied to understand the human experience is the shared experience of oppression of the shared phenomenon of being an oppressor. The degree to which one is conscious of shared oppression is assumed to be a measure of "black awareness" or "black personality." Therefore, we get models of black personality such as the Cross (1971) model which describes development of black personality as growing from Negro (or unawareness of oppressive realities) to black (hyperawareness of oppression and the oppressor) to transcendence (where blackness is integrated). Semaj (1980) introduces an excellent critique of the limitations of this analysis, which would take this discussion somewhat afield to fully review. However, the essential issue is that personality for African Americans is conceptualized as the emergence of consciousness of oppression. This approach which begins to see personality as a collective phenomenon is a critical contribution of "Black Psychology." It makes a radical departure from the European American preoccupation with the individual and his isolated experience. There is a "quantum leap" in this conceptualization though the intention was to merely address the shared reality of oppression.

African psychology conceptualizes self as an unqualified collective phenomenon while respecting the uniqueness of the individual self as a component of the collectivity. Nobles' (1980) description of the African ethos as a "collective consciousness" typifies this notion. The African conception of personality is captured in the formula given by Mbiti (1970): "I am because we are; and because we are therefore I am." Whatever happened to the individual impacted on the corporate body, the tribe and whatever happened to the tribe reverberated into the individual. This conception identified the appropriate arena of study as being the collective consciousness or again, what Nobles (1980) refers to as the "experiential communality" or the sharing of particular experience by a group of people. Nobles (1980) argues that the experiential communality is important in determining society's fundamental principles—its beliefs about the nature of man and what kind of society man should create for himself. In other words, description, assessment and even reconstruction is assumed to be a collective rather than an individual phenomenon. This is critical not only in terms of how people define their psychology, but also in terms of the kind of society which people give their energies to. To the extent that this self-conception of African people is alien to that of the European American society, one would expect many Africans well-adjusted to their "experiential communality" to be quite deviant in such an alien society (see, Akbar, 1979).

Time Orientations

Another distinction in the approaches is in terms of how time is conceptualized. Time conceptions are critical in that they determine which events are most significant. Most importantly time becomes that which maintains the cadence of people's lives. It determines their rate and intensity of activity as well as their priorities about life. Their motivations and orientations are determined through the cadence established by their time orientation. Time is such a powerfully subjective factor that people seldom consider that their time orientation is actually idiosyncratic. They rather automatically assume that everyone else is out of order if they are not moving consistent with their rhythm. This is particularly true when there is a strong investment in objective measures of time.

Certainly, the most extreme of these objective time-measuring cultures is the European American culture. Their approach or orientation to time is predominantly futuristic. Their rhythm as a consequence is exceedingly urgent and pressured since it is essentially impossible to ever catch-up with the future.

This futuristic orientation is played-out in their study of human psychology. The objectives of their study are focused on the goal of prediction and control. The concepts, instruments and methods of European American psychology are ones that are geared towards future outcomes as opposed to enhancement of the present or elaboration of the past. For example, there is often greater credibility given to predictive assessment devices than is given to the actual here-and-now performance of people or the history of their prior performance. Child-rearing practices, learning methods and even psychotherapy are future-oriented. Non-Europeans have often been described as deficient because of an inadequate future-orientation. This is another example of the attribution which emanates from the ethnocentrism. As we commented above, ethnocentric time is probably the most notorious of the projections which comes from ethnocentrism. Time is as idiosyncratic as is the heartbeat responding directly to ones own life (cultural) experience and reality.

Time in the European American system is a concrete commodity: it is brought and sold as is any other product. In many systems of psychotherapy, for instance, the time is viewed as a critical dimension of the psychotherapy. The "clock time" is strictly adhered to regardless of the emotional state of the client. Scheduled meeting times are viewed as sacred and clients are routinely charged for their appointment times whether they keep them or not. Though elaborate theoretical justifications are given for such actions, this is still a graphic illustration of the concrete conception of time in the European American's orientation.

The mathematical reality of the clock has the same tyrannical hold on European American's conception of reality as does quantification throughout their science. The symbolic numbers that are associated with the rhythm of time are assumed to literally be the abstraction of time. With the projection towards the future working with this concretizing of time, human conduct actually becomes a servant to time and behavior is judged by its adequacy in responding to time.

The Black Psychology time focus is on the recent past of the African American experience and the present conditions of oppression and its multifarious manifestations. The future is not considered as relevant. There is actually no consideration of prediction since racism is considered a constant and the experiences and behaviors of African Americans is determined by racism. The African American rhythm is assumed to actually be determined by its reaction to racist oppression.

The time orientation is primarily past and present in this system of thought. The assumption is that to understand current behaviors, one need only understand the history of racism and to be conscious of contemporary expressions of oppression. Time is actually reckoned by the pain of oppression. This condition and when it has been manifest is the focus of the rhythm of time. So one is a victim of time because time itself actually becomes a part of the oppressive process in an oppressive environment. In the African system, time is viewed as cyclical rather than linear. Consequently, "now" is the past and the future since those dimensions are immersed in the present. The past was focused upon as the source of instruction because "the direction of one's life system was from the present dimension backward to the past dimension" (Nobles, 1980). Nobles (1980) goes on to describe the African conception of time thus:

> For the people, time itself was simply a composition of past events. Very little concern was given to time in and of itself. It existed, but the African time concept was (is) very elastic ... Time was reckoned by phenomena ... In order to make sense, or be real, to the

West African, time had to be experienced; and the way in which one experienced time was partly through one's own individual life and partly through the life of the tribe which went back many generations before one's birth. We see in this description a very distinct orientation to time from the European American perspective which we described above. There is first of all, a basic acceptance of the notion that time is a subjective phenomenon, so the likelihood that one feels compelled to impose his time perspective on others is reduced in the African system. This might in part account for the absence of colonizing and proselytizing activities historically on the part of Africans. Many of the differences in motivations and behaviors among people of African descent and people of European descent can be seen to be attributable to their differences in conceptualizing the rhythm of life, which we call time. Jackson (1979) makes a compelling argument for the African American's treatment of time as growing out of this African conception of time. It is important to observe however that though the future orientation does not predominate in the African system, there is a consideration of the future. History informs us that the first clocks and calendars were established by Ancient African people. The ability to plan and develop for crops, migrations, etc., was well entrenched in the African lifestyle. Certainly, much of the metaphysical life of African people was relegated by a future orientation, but the future was understood to be contained in the present. The future is conceptualized as a repetition of the infinite cycles of being which all meet in the powerful experience of the present. The future is actually viewed as a reenactment of the past and progress is the application of the best lessons of the past and the avoidance of repeating disastrous errors from the past.

Human Goals

The next area of difference in the approaches to human psychology is in terms of the conceptualized goal of the human being. The conceptualization of goals determines the basis for effectiveness of the human being. Therefore, mental health and mental disorder are determined by effectiveness in achieving the goals of the self or personality. So, the theoretical import of hypothesized goals is critical in terms of evaluating the adequacy, effectiveness, i.e., sanity of the person. Variation in perception of goals can lead to serious discrepancies in the assessment of mental health as well as the prioritizing of energies for groups of people.

The European American approach sees the person as essentially directed towards pleasurable gratification. The Behaviorists assume that, all behavior hinges on rewards and punishments. Freud assumes the primal need of immediate gratification of either sexual or aggressive drives and Maslow assumes a hierarchy of needs for gratification at various levels. Again, the diversity of the schools merge in the shared assumption that the critical goal of human personality is the desire for gratification.

The emphasis of Black Psychology is that the essential goal of human behavior is survival. The emphasis on survival skills character- ized the majority of the literature in this area: Grier and Cobbs (1968), White (1978) and other similar writers have emphasized the survival skills of African Americans as being the primary goal and accomplish- ment of personality. The constant confrontation with racism and op- pression is viewed as the consistent reality and strategies to out-maneuver threats to survival by African Americans is the goal of personality. Staples (1974) for example, builds his theory of the black family on a survival-adaptation basis. His assumption is that confronta- tion with slavery and subsequent oppression shaped the African Amer- ican family through its struggles to survive. The essential goal of the Black Psychology orientation was formulated as in this example as: "how do we overcome the oppression of European Americans?"

Though survival, no doubt represents a basic goal of human exis- tence as it is a goal of all life forms, the limitation of the Black Psychol- ogy orientation is that it views the goal of survival only vis-à-vis the oppressive European American. It does not address the goal of personal- ity in the absence of oppression. The goal of African American existence again takes its form in reaction to the conditions of oppression.

African Psychology offers the goal of self-affirmation and self-per- petuation as the objective of human personality. It advocates that the affirmation of ones unique history and the perpetuation of ones collec- tive self and cultural reality is the goal of human personality. The human being is focused on the full manifestation and perpetuation of who he is as a collective phenomenon. This clearly is not oppositional to the Black Psychology perspective of "survival against oppression." African Psychology sees oppression as an incidental but disturbing ob- stacle to human self-affirmation which is not unlike many similar issues.

Epistemology

Epistemology defines "how we know, what we know." What is the legitimate form of acquiring knowledge and how do we identify that knowledge has been acquired? The latter part of this question has, of course, become a major objective of the psychologist and educator. The way that the psychologist defines what's actually knowledge and how it is acquired becomes paramount in his determination of who has adequate knowledge facility. The degree to which measurement of intelligence has permeated the concern of psychology throughout its history is an indication of how critical this question is. The fact that alleged discrepancies in intellectual faculties has served as the justification for the discriminatory treatment of African Americans also indicates why this issue of epistemology is so important for conceptualizing human functioning.

In European American psychology, knowledge of the outer environment particularly as it is experienced by the European American person is considered as the basis of legitimate knowledge. The concept of IQ is rooted in the idea that the greater is ones store of information about the typical middle class, Caucasian American environment, its attitudes, values and techniques, the greater is ones IQ=Intelligence=Knowledge. The issue of self-mastery, the applicability or even the validity (Truth) of the acquired knowledge is not an issue. The European American epistemology identifies knowledge as essentially recall or recognition of essential objects, processes, or experiences within the typical European American experience. The key element of this epistemology is that what is to be known is external to the person and ones knowledge pool is assessed by what is known of his external world.

The reactive quality of Black Psychology is again reflected in its epistemology. The assumption of Black Psychology is that intelligence for African Americans is the knowledge which he has of the working class, traditional African American environment. This is well-demonstrated in Robert Williams' (Wright and Isenstein, 1975) approach of culture-specific testing which he bases on a principle of cultural match or mismatch:

> Learning one activity either facilitates or hampers the learning of another, contingent upon the similarity or dissimilarity between the learner's cultural background and the material to be learned (p. 9). On this basis, Williams established the Black Intelligence Test of Cultural Homogeneity (BITCH). He devised the test by drawing from a glossary compiled of African American slang, "his personal experiences and that of his friends who had lived in the African American community" (Wright and Isenstein, 1975). Dr. Williams' approach is not unlike that of Drs. Wechsler, Binet and others (in this regard) who have developed European American instruments for measuring "intelligence." The difference, of course, is the cultural experience being called upon as exemplary of knowledge. The limitation in both approaches is its epistemological conclusion that what is knowable is external and the inevitable bias which comes from variations in experience of the external. Williams did not

advocate the innate intellectual inferiority of European Americans due to their consistently lower performance on the BITCH, as do his Caucasian counterparts.

African Psychology assumes a universal knowledge rooted in knowledge of the make-up of the human being himself. The most direct experience of the self is through emotion or affect. Vernon Dixon (1976) observes:

> Homeland and overseas African persons know reality predominantly through the interaction of affect and symbolic imagery, i.e., the synthesis of these two factors produce knowledge. In the "pure" Africanized world view of the unity of man and the phenomenal world, there is no empty perceptual space between the self and phenomena. Affect refers to the feeling self, the emotive self engaged in experiencing phenomena holistically (p. 70). Dixon (1976) makes another important distinction in this regard, relating to African epistemology. He says:

> Affect, however, is not intuition, for the latter term means direct or immediate knowledge (instinctive knowledge) without recourse to inference from or reasoning about evidence. Affect does interact with evidence, evidence in the form of symbolic imagery (p. 70).

This knowledge via "self" or holistic knowledge is critical in terms of understanding African Psychology. The relationship to reality inferred by African Psychology is one which relegates as doubtful any of the measures of knowledge which identify only external reality. The measure of intelligence in psychology would be observed in "effective living and development." Effective living would not be demonstrated on a typical European American IQ measure. Instead, one would need a more dynamic evaluation of a person's experience of himself as well as an evaluation of the socio-cultural environment surrounding the person. In other words knowledge would be reflected in the degree to which a person is capable of maneuvering an environment offering obstacles to his development. So, intelligence would entail (1) knowledge of the collective reality of self, (2) knowledge of environmental obstacles to effective (collective) self-development, (3) actions initiated to remove or master such obstacles and ultimately (4) knowledge of the Divine and universal laws which guide human development into ultimate knowledge of the Creator. These components of knowledge are most directly "known" through the "affect-symbolic imagery" as described by Dixon above. Dixon (1976) notes: symbolic imagery is the use of phenomena (words, gestures, tones, rhythms, objects, etc.) to convey meaning." Consequently, an adequate inference of intelligence would require effectively tapping the full-range of a people's symbolic imagery as well as ascertaining which are the most effective forms of such imagery which are used. One could not evaluate a person's "knowledge" without knowing how effectively that person conducts his full being. Therefore, the possibility of a man being adjudged a genius on the basis of his external knowledge yet proving to be morally inept would be impossible in African Psychology. Genius, by definition, would identify not only what you knew, but the kinds of judgments and prudent uses made of what you know. The four (4) dimensions must be understood as interdependent in terms of assessment of knowledge.

Another example would be that knowledge can only be adjudged or assessed as adequate if it is used in the service of the collective self. Cognition is not presumed to exist independent of self-liberating action. Unlike the European American and Black Psychology approaches which assess both knowledge (cognition) and achievement independent of self-affirming activity, the holistic reality of African Psychology could not hypothesize such an inconsistency. The most "intelligent" among those assessed through African Psychology would in the extreme show the greatest self-knowledge and higher knowledge of the Creator and his mission for man as understood through universal wisdom. In the light of such an approach, it is not surprising that the leaders perceived as most intelligent by the majority of African Americans (looking at their experience from this perspective) would be people such as Nat Turner, Harriet Tubman, Martin Luther King, Malcolm (X) Shabazz, Elijah Muhammad, Marcus Garvey, and others. All of these models invariably came equipped with Universal wisdom as well as secular knowledge of the external world. The kind of response to such leadership (knowledge) as well as the expression of such knowledge is done via the affect-symbolic imagery defined above. The ideas are communicated and received, not by words alone, but from the full range of affective and symbolic imagery.

The intelligent being from the perspective of African Psychology is a moral being. Morality represents the imperative of ordered life functioning for the purpose of effective human development. Knowledge of such principles and, of course, the implementation of them is as much a measure of intelligence as is the shrewd and facile manipulation of principles of material creation. The holistic conception of human life requires attention to and progressive understanding of laws which regulate the outer life "and" the inner life. The degree to which the person understands and utilizes these laws for the purpose of collective self-liberation is the supreme measure of intelligence and well-adjusted functioning. In the light of such an approach to intelligence, the assessment of intelligence is not a quantitative phenomenon. It is seen in the quality of life which a person gives himself to. Such an approach makes moot the issue of racial superiority/inferiority and nature/nurture controversies as they relate to intelligence. The assessment of superiority and inferiority is done on the basis of the quality of life chosen and the utilization of human growth potential. Again, the assertion is that material accouterments constitute only a limited portion of life quality, and such achievements must be evaluated in the light of humane and just usage of such resources. Ultimately, the intelligent man finds peace for himself and helps to bring it to others. Such is viewed as the nature of the harmonious universe and is therefore within the natural potential of all human beings.

Another aspect of epistemology which directly proceeds from the above discussion is the assumption made about the essence of things. Particularly, in attempting to understand the human being, ones definition of the human essence is crucial. The definition of essence merely represents the conception of the lowest possible form to which the human being can be reduced. European American psychology views this essence as material. It is this materialism which has devolved psychology from the study of the psyche (or soul) to its current status as the study of behavior. The European American preoccupation with mind=brain formulations, hypothesizing that the totality of human life can be understood from brain-functioning represents the epitome of the European American concept of essence as material. The pervasive conviction that what can be observed by the senses represents the essence of human life defines this epistemology. The direct inference, epistemologically is: what can be observed and is material is real and therefore knowable. What is unobservable and not material represents the unknowable or nonreality. Therefore, the equation of external or outer technology with human superiority and even reality becomes understandable in the light of their epistemology. It is not surprising how people with less opulent outer appearance are adjudged inferior, uncivilized, undeveloped, unintelligent or savage, even when such people may far-surpass European Americans in justice, charitableness, compassion, contentment and peacefulness. Black Psychology followed a similar course because of its emphasis on the physical exploitation of oppression. The tendency to view the essence of human life as the outcome of struggle and oppression results in a material conception of the human being. The view that blackness is sacrosanct is the obverse of the view that whiteness is supreme. Frances Welsing's "counter-racist psychiatry" epitomizes such an approach. As the European American has justified his exploitation of non-Caucasians on the basis of his superior material (i.e., white skin color), Welsing (1979) argues that the basis of such exploitation is due to their inferior material (i.e., color inadequacy) and their fear of the superior material (i.e., significant skin pigment) of black, brown, red and yellow peoples. The goal of "counter-racism" according to Dr. Welsing (1974) is to "efficiently and effectively checkmate the behavioral system of racism (white suprem-acy)." The essence of this conceptualization of the human being is ma-terial.

As we have suggested throughout this discussion, there is consid-erable justification for the spokespersons of "Black Psychology" to focus on the exploitation of African people by Europeans as a central issue in conceptualizing the psychology of African Americans. As Baldwin (1986) concludes in his analysis: "(Black) Psychology is therefore proac-tive as well as reactive, and it is most certainly political. Notwithstand-ing its reactive aspects, however, its thrust is clearly toward proactivity, that is self-definition and self-determination" (p. 246). The urgency of the historical oppression of African people by Europeans demands ur-gent and unprecedented attention. However, it is ultimately debilitat-ing to ones conceptual development if a battle strategy becomes ones "Weltanschauung." Fanon (1968) insightfully notes:

> But, if nationalism is not made explicit, if it is not enriched and
> deepened by a very rapid transformation into a consciousness of
> social and political needs, in other words into humanism, it leads
> up a blind alley (p. 204).

There are some who would argue that such a position is accomodationist and advocates a transcendence beyond the persisting realities of racism and oppression. Such is clearly, not the position of this discussion. What is described as an evolution is that which has become increasingly more expansive in addressing the total needs of human beings, particularly the historically exploited and excluded from conceptualizations of humanity. It also recognizes the real limita-tions of field weaponry when the struggle has moved into the halls of scholarship addressing the control of minds rather than bodies. African Psychology affirms itself and in so doing counteracts whatever is de-structively alien. African Psychology maintains that the essence of the human being is spiritual. This means that man reduced to his lowest terms is invisible and of a universal substance. This writer (Akbar, 1976) has discussed elsewhere that the African conception of personality is fundamentally built on the notion of a force which defines the man's continuity with all things within the world. This implies that man is ultimately reducible to the universe itself which gives man universal potential. This assumption of the ultimate spiritual nature of the human being hypothesizes the potential harmony of people with each other and the remainder of the universe. There is no assumption of essential conflict in an interdependent cosmos. Material by its very na-ture is fragmented and in conflict. The material world operates on prin-ciples of polarity and conflict and if ones system of thought remains at this level, conflict becomes inevitable. The Freudian conclusion of the essence of man being a conflict between life force (libido) and death force (thanatos) is not surprising. The Skinnerian notion of the essence of man's development centering around the conflict of avoidance of punishment and the acquisition of rewards is also consistent with this view. We can even understand the vital relationship of black/white conflict being the essential element in the materially based Black Psychology epistemology.

African Psychology sees the man reducible ultimately to a universal substance which affirms his oneness with the essence of the universe. Man's worth is adjudged potentially as compatible as are the relationships between all of the mutually facilitating components of nature itself. The human being is considered as potentially harmonious and vast as the universe itself. With such a definition of the essence of the human being, we can better understand the conceptions of intelligence which were discussed above. As a final aspect of "epistemology," the issue of "how" we know becomes a point of significant departure among the various approaches to human psychology which we have identified in this discussion. The conceptualizations of intelligence and essence identify what is knowable within an epistemological framework. How what is knowable becomes known is highly significant in conceptualizing the workings of human psychology.

European American psychology identifies this process as rational thought or cognition. Cognition or thinking is considered to be a rather mechanical process which follows certain systematic rules of logic. Logic, objectivity and rationality automatically preclude affect in terms of Western thought. Thinking is considered to be effective only when it is free of subjectivity (i.e. emotion or affect). The only things that are validly known are known by this process. As we discussed above, objectivity is a prime value in European American axiology, because it is presumed to be the only appropriate and reliable way to obtain knowledge. Feeling is identified as a contaminant to "good and pure" thought.

Syed Khatib (aka Cedric Clark, 1972) observes that:

> Our philosophical heritage—that is, what is taught in our public schools—is firmly grounded in European conceptions of reality. The dualistic conception of Descartes, as defined by the British Empiricist thinkers, particularly Hume, Locke, and Mill, still stands as the scientific foundation of contemporary psychology. The only "truth" that matters according to these thinkers, is that which is given to us by our sensory experience with things. The mind may exist, but it is totally independent of matter, and what "matters" (i.e. is important) is the reality of the matter. Matter is sense; the mind is non-sense, or would result in nonsense if one philosophized on it too long (p. 12).

This observation well-characterizes the modality of European American epistemology. From such an orientation we can see how psychology has reduced human intelligence to a score on an IQ test or human misery to a score over 70 on the MMPI. We can also see why a psychotherapist who "feels" with a suffering client is described as experiencing "counter-transference" rather than sharing with another human being. Khatib (Clark, 1972) quotes the historian of psychology, Boring, as claiming that the science of psychology "first lost its soul, then its consciousness." He goes on to observe that, "at least one contemporary writer has since added that psychology threatens to go out of its mind completely." (Clark, 1972). Even human identity is characterized through rational experience: "cogito ergo sum (I think therefore I am)" which comes from Descartes captures this cognitive orientation of European American psychology. It is a brief step to conclude that one who is not adequately cognitive (i.e., with a low IQ score) is an inferior human being.

Black Psychology takes a completely opposite point of view. The assumption in Black Psychology is that the best way to know what we know is through affect or feeling. Joseph White describes the culture of African Americans as a feeling-oriented culture." White (1972) says: "In a feeling-oriented culture, apparent and when examined closely, superficial, logical contradictions do not have the same meaning as they might have in the Anglo culture." White (1972) continues:

> Closely related to the easy style of handling contradictions, it can also be stated that black people have a greater tolerance for conflict, stress, ambiguity, and ambivalence. White psychologists fail to take this into consideration when they assume that because we have a lower class background, black people are therefore more impulsive, emotionally immature and have less tolerance for stress. (pp. 46-47).

Such an approach to characterizing "black culture" is appropriate in the light of the negative characterizations of African American affectivity which have grown out of the Anglo approach to psychology. The black psychologist reacted in self-defense in declaring black culture as a feeling culture and therefore appropriate in many of its responses viewed as pathological by European American Psychology.

Again, because of the focus of Black Psychology on oppression as the critical human experience, there is a focusing on the hatred or negative feeling of the racist and the suffering and pain (feelings) experienced by the victims of oppression. One is tempted to conclude from the analysis of Black Psychology that the predominant human feeling modality is pain or suffering. African Psychology assumes a rhythmic balance between affect and cognition. As we quoted Dixon (1976) above: "Affect does interact with evidence, evidence in the form of symbolic imagery." This process of synthesis is essential to the African Psychological perspective because it gives a balanced perspective on feeling and cognition. There is a recognition that knowledge is acquired from sensory experience as well as the subjective experience of affect. African Psychology assumes that the perimeters of knowledge are rational, affectional and moral boundaries. Rationality represents the order of exoteric or outer principles of reality and morality represents the order of principles of esoteric or inner reality. Feeling is the mediating process between these dimensions. Such an approach provides a guide and a context for the often ungrounded nature of rational knowledge. The classic example is the kind of human suffering that has emerged from the exclusively rational approach to nuclear weapons in contrast to the potentially great human contribution which could come from a morally guided use of the knowledge of nuclear energy.

As we observed previously in this discussion, balance is considered critical in African Psychology. Moral or affective dimensions unchecked by rational or cognitive dimensions results in an human imbalance which ultimately lays the conceptual foundation for human destruction.

Summary

Black Psychology emerged from the kinds of negative statements about African Americans which have characterized the vast majority of the European American psychological literature. Black Psychology was a reaction. It remains the political or militant arm of the study of African Americans within the European American context. Black Psychology is self-affirmative, particularly in its denial of the self-denigration conceptualizations of European American psychology.

African Psychology attempts to look at some of the basic philosophical assumptions about the nature of man and the universe as it emerges out of classical African Philosophy and world view. It attempts to identify the characteristics of the human being in the light of Divine revelation as well as modern science.

This discussion has looked at the basic philosophical assumptions of the three basic approaches to the study of human (primarily African American) behavior as stages in the evolution of our thought about the psychology of African Americans. The conclusion that we draw shows a growth in our concept which gives us an ever-expanding horizon for study. European American concepts are appropriate for a time and a context, i.e. the time and context which views the African American as a deviant from the Anglo world for those observers who maintain the insignificance of race and cultural plurality may still find such an approach appropriate and valuable. Black Psychology represents an effort to come to grips with the overwhelming ethnocentrism of European American psychology with a counter-ethnocentrism. The approach is emphatically reactive and predicates its existence on the postulates of European American Psychology. African Psychology may more properly be characterized as natural psychology, in that it attempts to identify the natural laws of the universal human experience. It does not deny the necessity of the often militant stance of Black Psychology, nor does it deny the considerable distance of Europeans from this model of natural human form. It asserts, however, that the principles of African Psychology represent the Creator's model whereby a people most in accord with the original and natural laws of human nature are likely to find compatibility with these principles. In order to do so, the human being must be liberated from the contaminants of materialism, individualism, dualism and hedonism which obscure universal vision and proper human evolution.

References

Akbar, N. (1980). Mental disorder among African Americans. *Black Caucus Journal*, *2,1*, 1-7.

Akbar, N. (1976). *Natural psychology and human transformation*. Chicago: World Community of Islam in the West.

Akbar, N. (1976). Rhythmic patterns in African personality. In L. King (Ed.), *African philosophy: Assumptions and paradigms for research on black persons*.

Baldwin, J. (1976). Black psychology and black personality. *Black Books Bulletin*, *4,3*, 6-11, 65.

Baldwin, J. (1986). African (Black) psychology: Issues and synthesis. *Journal of Black Studies, 16, 3*, 235-249.

Carruthers, J. (1972). *Science and oppression*. Chicago: Center for Inner City Studies. Northeastern Illinois University.

Clark, K. (1965). *Dark ghetto*. New York: Harper & Row.

Clark, C. (1972). Black studies or the study of black people? In R. Jones (Ed.), *Black psychology*. New York: Harper & Row.

Clark, C. X. (1976). *Voodoo or IQ: An introduction to African psychology*. Chicago: Institute of Positive Education Black Pages (People???).

Cross, W.E. (1971). Negro to black conversion experience: Toward a psychology of black liberation. *Black World, 20, 9*, 13-27.

Dixon, V. (1976). Worldviews and research methodology. In L. King (Ed.), *African philosophy: Assumptions and paradigms for research on black persons*. Los Angeles, CA: Fanon R & D Center.

Fanon, F. (1968). *The wretched of the earth*. New York: Grove Press.

Freud, S. (1953-74). *The standard edition of the complete psychological works*. J. Strachey (Ed.). London: Hogarth Press.

Grier, W., & Cobbs, P. (1968). *Black rage*. New York: Basic Books.

Hall, G. (1904). *Adolescence*. New York: Appleton.

Jackson, G.G. (1976). Cultural seedbeds of the black backlash in mental health. *Journal of Afro-American Issues, 4,1,* 70-91.

Jackson, G.G. (1979). The origin and development of black psychology: Implications for black studies and human behavior. *Studia Africana, 1, 3,* 270-293.

Jung, C.G. (1953-78). *Collected works*. H. Read, M. Fordham, & G. Adler (Eds.). Princeton: Princeton University Press.

Kardiner, A., & Ovesey, L. (1962). *The mark of oppression*. Cleveland: World Publishing Company.

Karenga, M. (1982). *Introduction to black studies*. Inglewood, CA: Kawaida Publications.

Mbiti, J. (1970). *African religions and philosophy*. Garden City, NY: Anchor Books.

McDougall, W. (1908). *Social psychology*. New York: Luce.

Mosby, D. (1972). Toward a new specialty of black psychology. In R. Jones (Ed.), *Black psychology*. New York: Harper & Row.

Nobles, W. (1974). Africanity: Its role in black families. *The Black Scholar. 5, 9,* 10-17.

Nobles, W. (1976). African science: The consciousness of self. In L. King, V. Dixon, & W. Nobles (Eds.), *African philosophy: Assumptions and paradigms for research on black persons*. Los Angeles, CA: Fanon Research & Development Center.

Nobles, W. (1978). The black family and its children: The survival of humaness. *Black Books Bulletin, 6, 2,* 6-14.

Nobles, W. (1980). African philosophy: Foundations for black psychology. In R. Jones (Ed.), *Black psychology*. New York: Harper & Row.

Semaj, L. (1980). *Models for an Africentric psychology*. Presented at the Community Clinical Psychology Conference, Southern Regional Education Board, Atlanta.

Skinner, B. F. (1971). *Beyond freedom and dignity*. New York: Knopf.

Staples, R. (1974). The black family in evolutionary perspective. *Black Scholar, 5, 9,* 2-9.

Thomas, A., & Sillen, S. (1972). *Racism and psychiatry*. New York: Bruner/Mazel Publishers.

(Weems) X, L. (1973). *Guidelines for African humanism*. Presented at the meeting of the International Association for Cross-Cultural Psychology. Ibadan, Nigeria.

Welsing, F. (1974). *Definitions in counter-racist psychiatry*. Unpublished manuscript. Washington, D. C.

Welsing, F. (1974). *The cress color confrontation theory*. (Private printing). Washington, DC.

White, J. (1972). Toward a black psychology. In R. Jones (Ed.), *Black psychology*. New York: Harper and Row.

Wright, B.J., & Isenstein, V. (1975). *Psychological tests and minorities*. Mental Health Studies and Reports Branch, NIMH.

African (Black) Psychology: Issues and Synthesis

Joseph A. Baldwin

During the past two decades, many of our progressive black psychologists and social scientists have devoted a great deal of attention to formulating a conceptual and operational framework for the study of psychological phenomena as they bear on the cultural-survival condition of African American people (Akbar, 1975, 1976b; Baldwin, 1976, 1985; X(Clark), McGee, Nobles & Akbar, 1975; Jackson, 1982; R. Jones, 1972, 1980; King, Dixon & Nobles, 1976; Nobles, 1972; Plumpp, 1973; Smith, Burlew, Whitney & Mosley, 1970; Thomas, 1971; Welsing, 1970; White, 1970; Williams, 1978; Williams, 1981; Wright, 1974). Much of this activity has come to define the conceptual parameters of what we now regard as African (Black) Psychology. However, as I have previously noted (Baldwin, 1976), there are basic disagreements among black psychologists concerning the definition and parameters of African and/or Black psychology. Some have questioned whether it should exist in the first place. Thus, in our thrust toward formalizing this general body of knowledge, it is appropriate that we attempt to bring clarity to the concept *African (Black) Psychology*.

Issues in Conceptualizing African (Black) Psychology

It is important to note, first of all, that while some black psychologists have found it difficult to justify the existence of Black psychology (e.g., Guthrie, 1976; Hayes, 1972), most appear to recognize basic problems in the applicability of Western (white-European) psychology to the experiences of black or African people. Nevertheless, it is peculiar to observe that a substantial number of black psychologists, while accepting the existence of or need for African (Black) psychology, do not conceptualize it as an independent enterprise separate from Western Psychology (see Cross, 1971; Evans, 1971; Guthrie, 1976; Hayes, 1972; Jones 1972; Mosby, 1972; Pugh, 1972; White, 1972; Williams, 1978).

It appears therefore that these issues represent very real problems for many black psychologists. I submit that the problem results from the

intellectual-conceptual dependency (or incarceration) and Western op-
pression-education (indoctrination) of many of our black scholars (Baldwin, 1979, 1980b; Hare, 1969; Nobles, 1976b, 1982; Woodson, 1969).
It should be clear that given the basic fact of *cultural relativity* across
African and European populations (Akbar, 1975, 1976b; Baldwin, 1976,
1985; Carruthers, 1981; X(Clark), 1972; X(Clark), et al., 1975; Jackson,
1979, 1982; J. Jones, 1972; King, et al., 1976), African (Black) psychology
needs no more justification of its existence than does Western psychology. Even though modern-day African psychology, often referred to
rather exclusively as Black psychology, *formally* expressed itself as a *reaction* to Western Psychology (Akbar, 1976b; Jackson, 1979), such an obscure mode of development does not represent its natural state of
evolution. Because African people existed, in fact preexisted Europeans
as a distinct and independent cultural entity apart from European people, it follows that a distinctive African (Black) psychology existed, irrespective of when and how black social scientists actually formalized the
concept in Western society. African (Black) psychology from this perspective thus derives naturally from the "worldview" or philosophical
premises underlying African culture itself (as does Western psychology
relative to the worldview of European culture). Clearly then, the justification for African (Black) psychology's existence as well as its independence from Western psychology inheres in the fundamental
distinctness between and independence of African and European-Cos-
mologies (Baldwin, 1980b; Carruthers, 1972, 1979, 1984; X(Clark),
1972; Dixon, 1976; Nobles, 1980; Williams, 1974).

Beyond these obvious and fundamental problems among black
psychologists, there is disagreement about substantive definitions of
African (Black) psychology as well. For example, Joseph White (1970,
1972), one of the first African American psychologists to employ the
concept Black psychology, and others (e.g., Mosby, 1972; Pugh, 1972;
Williams, 1978), the term Black psychology refers to an accurate workable theory of black behavior drawn from the authentic experience of
black people in American society. Building upon White's conception,
Louis Williams (1978) proposes that:

> Black psychology is the psychological consequence of being
> black. In this work, problems and issues of psychology have
> been presented from a variety of operational viewpoints, in-
> cluding those of Eastern, African, Western, and Afro-American
> experience. While the approach to psychology adopted in this
> treatment owes very little to each of these and other view-
> points, it centers on a general principle of the uniqueness of the
> black experience . . . The general principle, black experience,
> has been taken from Joseph White's article . . . out of the au-
> thentic experience of black people we must build a viable Black

psychology . . . this notion is central in the definition of Black psychology. (p. 3)

Wade Nobles (1980), on the other hand, another African American psychologist employing this concept, and others (e.g., Akbar, 1975; Baldwin, 1976; X(Clark), 1972; X(Clark), et al., 1975) find it applicable to African experience in general (including the African American experience). According to Nobles (1980), "African (Black) Psychology is rooted in the nature of black culture which is based on particular indigenous (originally indigenous to African) philosophical assumptions." (p. 31) Nobles further states that:

> Black psychology must concern itself with the question of "rhythm." It must discuss, at some great length, "the oral tradition." It must unfold the mysteries of the spiritual energy known as "soul." It must explain the notion of "extended self and the "natural" orientation of African peoples to insure the "survival of the tribe." Briefly, it must examine the elements and dimensions of the experiential communalities of African people . . . Black psychology must concern itself with the mechanism by which our African definition has been maintained and what value its maintenance has offered black people. Hence, the task of Black psychology is to offer an understanding of the behavioral definition of African philosophy and to document what, if any, modifications it has undergone during particular experiential periods. (p. 35)

From these relatively extreme conceptions of African (Black) psychology (Williams and Nobles), we can see that another basic point of disagreement among African American psychologists concerns not only whether or not the concept of African (Black) psychology should necessarily encompass the totality of African experience (or merely myopically encompass only the African American experience), but some question the meaning of the concept itself. While one may very well question how such an obscure distinction was forged, much of the problem derives from the influence of our Western training in psychology. Such training imposes an obscure kind of "uniqueness" on African American experience apart from African experience, thus creating a pseudo phenomenon called African American subculture, presumably distinct in basic ways from its parent African culture. Also, many African American psychologists and social scientists use the concepts African and black (Afro-American, African American, race *vs.* culture, etc.) quite differently. (I shall return to this problem momentarily). Some African American psychologists therefore have (peculiarly) found it necessary and tenable to conceptualize some form of basic distinction between these traditionally interchangeable concepts.

A related and fundamental point of disagreement among African

American psychologists concerns whether the concept of African (Black) psychology encompasses the study of *all* psychological phenomena in the universe, including African as well as the Western (European) experience (Baldwin, 1976, 1980b; X(Clark), 1972; X(Clark), et al., 1975; Jackson, 1979), or merely that characterizing black or African people alone (Cross, 1971; Mosby, 1972; Pugh, 1972; White, 1970, 1972; Williams, 1978). The critical question is whether or not African (Black) psychology is fundamentally relevant to the survival and proactive thrust of African people. If the answer is no, then we have obviously chosen to ignore a most vital fact of black experience by relegating it to the status of irrelevance to the black or African scientific enterprise. I suggest that such a choice would be fatalistic and reduce the meaning and value of African (Black) psychology for the black world to blatant and irresponsible worthlessness. On the other hand, however, if the answer is yes, and surely most of us recognize this logical necessity, it seems clear that a psychology which focuses exclusively on African (Black) experience would contribute little toward enhancing the survival of African people since many impediments to black survival reside in the social universe outside the boundaries of the African experience. Hopefully as we move toward greater clarity in the meaning of African (Black) psychology, we will achieve greater clarity with respect to its scope.

The Locus of Problems in Definition

Notwithstanding these very basic controversies and no doubt deriving from and contributing to them, I noted earlier there also exists a basic tendency among black psychologists toward disagreement over whether the terms black and African have the same meaning, hence the concepts Black psychology and African psychology (and this I believe is the hub of most of the issues raised thus far). For example, some black psychologists suggest a basic distinction between the two concepts (Akbar, 1976b; Mosby, 1972; White, 1970, 1972; Williams, 1978), while others seem to use both concepts more or less synonymously (Akbar, 1975; Baldwin, 1976; Khatib (Cedric X), 1972, 1980; X(Clark), et al., 1975; Nobles, 1976b, 1980).

While I suspect that much of the problem is subtle in its occurrence, it is a fundamental one, nevertheless. For example, in the earlier discussion, it was indicated that some black psychologists who use the term Black psychology rather exclusively also confine their focus to the African American population. In such cases, they tend to anchor Black psychology in an obscure "reactive-type" of American or Western-created phenomenon called black culture or "subculture." I also observed that others who use the term "Black Psychology" apply it to African (Black) people generally (including African Americans). In these cases, they tend to anchor African (Black) psychology in the African Cosmological framework which is relatively independent of Western culture.

In an article relevant to this general problem, Gerald Jackson (1979) proposes that African psychology represents, more or less, the "innovative-inventive" component of Black psychology, which suggests that the former is subsumed under the latter (i.e., African psychology as a component of Black psychology). From his survey of the definitional controversy among black psychologists, Jackson observed that:

> The appellate "Black psychology" is basically a generic designation for an emerging perspective in the field of psychology. Its embryonic stage of development is clearly illustrated in its range of definitions. At one extreme, Black psychology has been pictured not so much as a distinct academic discipline but as a reaction to an interpretation of psychology as a "white" or Euro-centric endeavor . . . . At the other end of the continuum, some have hailed Black psychology as the "third great psychological-philosophical tradition with characteristic strengths and weaknesses" . . . . Much more reflective of the contemporary application of Black psychology, Sims (1977) stated that it is "concerned with redefining existing psychological principles and concepts, and developing additional models that will reveal the strengths of black people . . . (it will) offer behavioral guidelines that have been examined in terms of their applicability to the specific needs and problems of black people" . . . . At the present time, it will be seen Black psychology is a composite of reactive, inventive and innovative components and extends . . . "to the total behavior in all situations of black people throughout the world" . . . (Jackson, 1979, p. 271).

While this type of problem and obscurity appears to characterize the work of many African American psychologists, certainly most of us would agree that to speak of black people and black experience outside of the context of African culture and African experience is meaningless. Relative to his notion of the inventive component of Black psychology, Jackson (1975) has further noted:

> A more germinal line of investigation, Black psychology proposed, is to view the behaviors attributed to Afro- Americans in terms of their African cultural and philosophical antecedents . . . . An African referent also provides insight into contemporary conflicts between Afro and Euro-Americans by showing their origin in the basic differences between an African and European ethos . . . Black psychology, it will be seen, not only provides a rationale for why

certain cultural factors continued in the United States . . . . Moreover, full comprehension of the meaning and significance of the papers by (Joseph) White had to await . . . the ascendancy of African psychology or the inventive component of Black psychology . . . prior to the contemporary expression of an African perspective in psychology . . . . Black psychology was clearly defensive in posture . . . . African psychology, then, facilitated the conceptual advancement . . . (pp. 274-276).

Thus, while much of the controversy remains, it is clear that regardless of the term chosen (Black psychology or African psychology), the reference ultimately, must be to African phenomena. Whatever distortions that continue to exist in these kinds of conceptions (i.e., the seemingly unnecessary black/African distinction) undoubtedly derives from the obscure psychological consequences of our oppression in Western society (Baldwin, 1979, 1980b, 1985; Hare, 1969; Nobles, 1976b, Note 2). Hopefully, as African Americans (including black psychologists) continue to shed more and more of the psychological obscurities of Western oppression, the concept African (Black) psychology will achieve popular usage among black psychologists as the umbrella concept under which all other psychological concerns and issues are subsumed. This approach seems to be more functionally relevant to the survival of black people given the clearer cultural-philosophical meaning (land-base, history, language, etc.) of African (Black) psychology over that of Black psychology (as I have described its confused and distorted usage to date). In view of this perspective, in the interest of clarity, and given the fact that these concepts are in effect interchangeable/synonymous, we should recognize that African psychology is what we are about here.

A Functionally Relevant Definition of African (Black) Psychology

In an earlier article (Baldwin, 1976), I tried to isolate and organize what then existed of these various issues and develop from them a formal definition of African (Black) psychology. I also tried to distinguish the definition from that of African (Black) personality. It is my firm belief that while the phenomenon of black personality is inherently a major substantive area of African (Black) psychology, it is not the only substantive area subsumed thereunder. This perspective obviously finds it necessary and important to emphasize such a distinction (between the concepts psychology and personality). Succinctly, this position is as follows:

African psychology is defined as a system of knowledge (philosophy, definitions, concepts, models, procedures and practice) concerning the nature of the social universe from the perspective of African Cosmology. "African Cosmology" thus provides the conceptual-philosophical framework for African (Black) psychology (Baldwin, 1980a, p. 23)

This definition means that African (Black) psychology is nothing more or less than the uncovering, articulation, operationalization and application of the principles of the African reality structure relative to psychological phenomena. Hence, an understanding of African Cosmology—the African worldview—is essential to an understanding of African (Black) psychology (Baldwin, 1976, 1980a; X(Clark), 1972; X(Clark), et al., 1975; Nobles, 1980).

The Nature of African Cosmology

Essentially, African Cosmology is governed by the overriding theme or ontological principle of Human-Nature Unity, or Oneness with Nature, or Harmony with Nature (Carruthers, 1981; Mbiti, 1970; Nobles, 1976a, 976b, 1976c, 1980). This means that humanity (consciousness) forms an integral-inseparable part of Nature (Dixon, 1976), a Oneness of Being. All aspects of Nature, then, including consciousness, are interrelated and interdependent, forming one phenomenal reality—a communal phenomenology (Nobles, 1980). A number of supporting principles derive from the basic theme of African Cosmology. Among them are emphases on Groupness (survival of the group), Sameness and Commonality; Corporateness, Cooperation, Collective Responsibility, and Interdependence. Taken together, this body of principles comprising African Cosmology defines the African Survival Thrust (or worldview). It is Africentric because it derives from, centers on and thereby reflects-reinforces the basic nature of African people. It is indeed the center of the universe. African (Black) psychology therefore is about the interpretation, articulation, institutionalization and perpetuation of the African Survival Thrust as it relates to psychological phenomena in particular, and the universe in general (Baldwin, 1976, 1980a, 1980b; Khatib, 1972, 1980; Nobles, 1976a, 1980). This rather general conception of African (Black) psychology thus attempts to address all of the critical issues raised in the earlier discussions. For example, it should be clear from this conception that African (Black) psychology, in deriving (naturally) from the framework of the African worldview, is therefore independent of Western psychology. It should also be clear that this conception of African (Black) psychology encompasses not only the phenomenon of black or African personality, but also European and Asian personality, and any other phenomenal aspects of the social universe. Of course, as I noted earlier, this framework suggests that Western psychology can be similarly defined relative to European Cosmology (albeit highly questionable as to its status within the Natural Order). Beyond this, however, I further argue that African (Black) psychology is indeed Human Psychology or Natural Psychology (Akbar, 1976a, 1976b, Note 1), since African people (including those in the diaspora) in their natural essence (being in accord with the Natural Order) seem to represent the only true model of humanity (i.e., Natural Order or Natural Process). African people also represent the historical referent point for humanity as well. (Diop, 1974).

Where the meanings of African and Black psychology are concerned, perhaps the most critical aspect of this problem in definition lies in the fact that, unfortunately, anytime black psychologists set out to analyze and explain some so-called "black phenomena," the black community far too quickly and erroneously ascribes the label of Black or African psychology to such work, irrespective of the worldview or philosophical framework undergirding and directing these endeavors (Baldwin, 1976, 1979; Khatib, 1972; Nobles, 1976a, Note 2). Upon closer examination, we almost invariably find much of this obscure activity by black psychologists to be merely *Western psychology in blackface*. African (Black) psychology, therefore, means much more than black psychologists focussing on black phenomena. Thus, black psychologists, social scientists, and the black community at large need to recognize this fundamental fact before misrepresentations of Black psychology get totally out of hand, if this hasn't occurred already (consult issues of *The Journal of Black Psychology* for illustrations of this problem).

Conclusion

I have argued that Black psychology is indeed African psychology if correctly defined and understood, irrespective of the fact that many misguided or uninformed black psychologists erroneously apply the label of Black psychology to their apparently obscure and misrepresenting activities. Unfortunately most of those who have rallied around an exclusive use of the concept Black psychology have contributed greatly to (and generally continue to contribute to) the marked confusion and ambiguity in its definition, forging an unnatural separation between the terms black and African. While we may not be able to immediately achieve agreement over these vital definitions between the conceptually liberated (Africentric) and incarcerated (Eurocentric) camps of black psychologists, we must not allow the conceptually incarcerated thinkers among us to legitimate their obscure and often potentially mentacidal activities by misrepresenting them as African (Black) psychology.

We may conclude, based on this analysis, that African (Black) psychology is therefore "proactive" as well as "reactive," and it is most certainly "political." Notwithstanding its reactive aspects, however, its thrust is clearly toward proactivity, i.e., self-definition and self- determination. African (Black) psychology seeks to reaffirm the human essence of Africanity, and in so doing will affirm its centrality in the Natural Order.

Reference Notes

1. Akbar, N. The evolution and development of human psychology for African Americans. Unpublished manuscript.
2. Nobles, W.W. African consciousness and liberation struggles: Implications for the development and construction of scientific paradigms. Unpublished manuscript.

References

Akbar, N. (1976a) *Natural psychology*. Chicago: World Community of Islam in the West.

Akbar, N. (1976b). BBB Interviews Na'im Akbar. *Black Books Bulletin, 4(3)*, 34-39.

Akbar, N. (1975). The rhythm of black personality. *Southern Exposure, 3*, 14-19.

Baldwin, J.A. (1985). Psychological aspects of European cosmology in American society. *The Western Journal of Black Studies, 9* (4), 216-223.

Baldwin, J.A. (1980a). An Africentric model of black personality. *In Proceedings of the Fourteenth Annual Convention of the Association of Black Psychologists.* Washington, D.C.: ABPsi.

Baldwin, J.A. (1980b). The psychology of oppression. In M.K. Asante & A. Vandi (Eds.), *Contemporary Black Thought*, Beverly Hills: Sage Publications.

Baldwin, J.A. (1979). Education and oppression in the American context. *Journal of Inner City Studies, 1, 62-83.*

Baldwin, J.A. (1976). Black psychology and black personality. *Black Books Bulletin, 4(3)*, 6-11, 65.

Carruthers, J.H. (1984). *Essays in ancient Egyptian studies.* Los Angeles: Timbuktu Publications.

Carruthers, J.H. (1981). Reflections on the history of the Afrocentric worldview. *Black Books Bulletin, 7(1),* 4-7, 25.

Carruthers, J.H. (1972). *Science and oppression.* Chicago: Center for Inner City Studies, Northeastern Illinois University.

Cross, W. (1971). Negro-to-black conversion experience: Toward a psychology of black liberation. *Black World, 20(9),* 13-27.

Diop, C.A. (1974). The African origin of civilization. Westport, Conn.: Lawrence Hill Publishers.

Evans, R.A. (1971). The relevance of academic psychology to the black experience. In H.J. Richards (Ed.), *Topic in Afro- American studies.* Buffalo: Black Academy Press.

Guthrie, R.V. (1976). *Even the rat was white: A historical view of psychology.* New York: Harper & Row.

Hare, N. (1969). The challenge of a black scholar. *The Black Scholar,* (December issue), 58-63.

Hayes, W.A. (1980). Radical black behaviorism. In R.L. Jones (Ed.) *Black psychology.* New York: Harper & Row.

Jackson, G.G. (1982). Black psychology: An avenue to the study of Afro-Americans. *Journal of Black Studies, 12(3),* 241-260.

Jackson, G.G. (1979). The origin and development of black psychology: Implications for black studies and human behavior. *Studia Africana, 1(3),* 270-293.

Jones, J.M. (1972). *Prejudice and racism.* Reading, Mass.: Addison-Wesley.

Jones, R.L. (1972, 1980). (Ed.) *Black psychology.* (First and Second Editions). New York: Harper & Row.

Jones, R.L. (1970). (Ed.) *Sourcebooks on the teaching of black psychology,* Volumes I and II. Washington, D.C.: The Association of Black Psychologists.

Khatib, S. (1980). Black studies and the study of black people: Reflections on the distinctive characteristics of black psychology. In R.L. Jones (Ed.), *Black psychology.* New York: Harper & Row.

Khatib, S. (Cedric Clark), (1972). Black studies or the study of black people? In R.L.Jones (Ed.), *Black psychology.* New York: Harper & Row.

Khatib, S. (Cedric X), McGee, D.P., Nobles, W., & Akbar, N. (Luther X), (1975). Voodoo or IQ: An introduction to African psychology. *Journal of Black Psychology, 1(2),* 9-29.

King, L.M., Dixon, v.J., & Nobles, W.W. (1976). (Eds.), *African philosophy: Assumptions and paradigms for research on black persons.* Los Angeles: Fanon R & D Center.

Mbiti, J.S. (1970). *African religions and philosophy.* New York: Anchor Books.

Mosby, D.P. (1972). Toward a new specialty of black psychology. In R.L. Jones (Ed.) *Black psychology.* New York: Harper & Row.

Nobles, W.W. (1980). African philosophy: Foundations for black psychology. In R.L. Jones (Ed.) *Black psychology.* New York: Harper & Row.

Nobles, W.W. (1976a). African science: The consciousness of self. In L.M. King, et al. (Eds). *African philosophy: Assumptions and paradigms for research on black persons.* Los Angeles: Fanon R & D Center.

Nobles, W.W. (1976b). Black people in white insanity: An issue for black community mental health. *Journal of Afro-American Issues, 4,* 21-27.

Nobles, W.W. (1976c). Extended self: Rethinking the so-called Negro self-concept. *Journal of Black Psychology, 2*(2), 15- 24.

Plumpp, S. (1973). *Black Rituals.* Chicago: Third World Press.

Pugh, R.W. (1972). (Ed.), *Psychology and the black experience.* Belmont, CA: Wadsworth Publishing Company.

Smith, W.d., et al. (1979). (Eds.), *Reflections on black psychology.* Washington, D.C.: University Press of America.

Thomas, C. (1971). (Ed.), *Boys no more: A black psychologists view of community.* Beverly Hills: Glencoe.

Welsing, F. (1970). *The Cress theory of color confrontation and racism.* Washington, D.C.: Private Printing.

White, J. (1972). Toward a black psychology. In R.L. Jones (Ed.), *Black psychology.* New York: Harper & Row.

White, J. (1970). Guidelines for black psychologists. *The Black Scholar. 1*(5).

Williams, C. (1974). *The destruction of black civilization.* Chicago: Third World Press.

Williams, L. (1978). *Black psychology: Compelling issues and views.* (Second edition). Washington, D.C.: University Press of America.

Williams, R.L. (1981). *The collective black mind: An Afro-centric theory of black personality.* St. Louis: Williams & Associates, Inc.

Woodson, C.G. (1933, 1969). *The miseducation of the Negro.* Washington, D.C.: Associated Publishers.

Wright, B. (1974). The psychopathic racial personality. *Black Books Bulletin, 2*(2), 25-31.

Deconstruction

III. Deconstruction

The papers in this section have been written to provide a critical evaluation of several constructs (*black self-hatred*, "The Black Self-Hatred Paradigm Revisited: An Africentric Analysis" by Baldwin, Brown and Hopkins; *delay of gratification*, "Delayed Gratification in Blacks," by Ward Banks, and Wilson; and *locus of control*, "Are Blacks External: On the Status of Locus of Control in Black Populations," by Banks, Ward, McQuater, and DeBritto) and activities (ability and aptitude testing) that have occupied an important role in mainstream explanations of the behavior of African Americans ("The Testing Game" by Williams and Mitchell). The significance of these papers resides in the fact that they critically evaluate constructs that are often used to predict or explain virtually all aspects of African American behavior, including academic performance, economic functioning, political behavior, psychopathology, moral behavior, interpersonal relationships, social deviance, civil rights activism, future orientation, performance in sports, and inability to succeed in psychotherapy, to name a few.

As will soon become apparent, authors of papers in this section have undertaken penetrating methodological analyses of a wide ranging literature and have provided incontestable support for their conclusions that research studies suggesting that African Americans are deficient in the areas addressed (i.e. black self-hatred, locus of control, and delay of gratification) are seriously flawed. Even a casual reading of these papers will reveal something of the egregious errors that are made in interpreting the research literature.

For several important reasons, African American social and behavioral scientists have shown a continuing interest in matters related to aptitude, ability, and the psychological assessment of African Americans. There is, first, the very unbalanced coverage of the literature, particularly with respect to reporting studies of black-white comparability, or studies of African American superiority. Second, there is the misapplication of tests with African Americans. Third, there is concern with the frame of reference against which test results are interpreted. Fourth, African American scholars have been concerned about the failure to look at test construction and use in their political, economic, and cultural contexts.

It is not surprising, therefore, that black scholars are concerned about the misapplication of psychological tests with African Americans. Those who use tests should know for example, (1) that tests should be applied only to groups and subclasses included in the standardization population; (2) that many instruments having sufficient reliability for group predictions may be inappropriate for individual prediction; and

(3) that validity data should be developed for the situations and on the groups on whom the tests would be used. These axioms, and others, are repeatedly violated in testing African Americans. Guilford (1967) and Cronbach (1970) have unequivocably stated limitations of tests when used with racial and cultural groups:

> That there are differences in means of test scores among racial groups, no one can deny. The meaning of these differences is not easy to determine. It can be stated as a general principle, from all that we have considered with respect to conditions and their effects upon test scores, that difference among means reflect differences in needs and opportunities for the development of various kinds of abilities within the culture in which the individuals have their existence (Guilford, 1967, p. 408).

In a related vein, Cronbach (1970) notes:

> We must accept Liverant's . . . conclusion that to decide "what is or is not intelligent behavior involves a cultural value judgement" and that a person's variation in efficiency from task to task must be explained by examining his expectations and the rewards available (p.248).

Williams and Mitchell, in a novel treatment of the subject, give an overview of testing problems as viewed by game producers (test publishers), game advocates (schools, colleges, universities, and employers), game dealers (counselors, psychologists, teachers, etc.), and game pawns (students, employees), and apply these concepts to testing in higher education (Scholastic Aptitude Test [SAT], American College Testing Program [ACT], Graduate Record Exam [GRE], Law School Aptitude Test [LSAT], Medical College Aptitude Test [MCAT], and so on).

We should not think, however, that concerns about race and abilities are unique to the current generation of African American scholars. Far from it. As Franklin indicates in the final paper in this section ("Black Social Scientists and the Mental Testing Movement, 1920-1940"), there has been a rich tradition of study and rebuttal of ideas about African American ability by African American social and behavioral scientists—from writings as early as the late 1800's, including heavy activity in the period between 1920 and 1940. The issues captured the attention of some of our most outstanding African American scholars (e.g., W.E.B. Dubois, Martin Jenkins, and Horace Mann Bond) and serve to remind us of our continuing concern with these matters.

The Black Self-Hatred Paradigm Revisited: An Africentric Analysis

Joseph A. Baldwin,
Raeford Brown and Reginald Hopkins

Introduction

During the late 1970s, the senior author (Baldwin, 1979) pre-sented an extensive and incisive analysis of the abundant accumulation of theories and research findings that had been generated in Western psychology and social science up to that point, which converged around the thesis of a pathogenic self-conception in African Americans beginning in early childhood. This pathogenic self-conception among African Americans was ultimately reducible to the vicious Euro-centric construct of "black self-hatred". The 1979 analysis also explored some of the counter-claims, contradictions, refutations and general contro-versies characterizing this notorious literature. One major conclusion drawn from that analysis was that this literature germinated in white racism or Eurocentric supremacy, and therefore began as an enterprise of distortion and blatant falsification rather than as an objective scien-tific analysis. It was therefore designed and fashioned to serve the needs of white or European-American supremacy from its very inception. Thus a related major conclusion was that even if African Americans do harbor feelings of self-rejection (whether at a personal or an extended level), the Western psychological literature cited was clearly unable to and incapable of conceptualizing, assessing, explaining or predicting it accurately, nor generate the appropriate intervention strategies to ad-dress this misdefined and distorted phenomenon. Why? Because West-ern psychology, it was convincingly argued, (whether practiced by Euro-American psychologists or by their black proteges) effectively de-nied the existence of a distinct African American culture as the only valid conceptual framework for defining, understanding and explain-ing black behavior.

The "original" (pre-publication) draft of the 1979 manuscript (al-though Editorial review deleted it) actually pointed out that a detailed discussion of the nature of the "African self-concept" and its relatedness to the issue of the African American self-conception was beyond the scope of that work. However, the significance of this relationship for a thorough treatment of the black self-concept was implicit in the 1979 analysis. The general problem being raised in that manuscript was not so much the actual nature of the relationship between African and African American self-orientation, but rather the fact that in the black self-hatred literature, little or no consideration was even given to the possible existence of such a relationship and its significance to our understanding and explaining the phenomenon called the black self-concept.

The present paper will "revisit" this literature, but not for the purpose of simply restating or improving upon the already well-stated and decisive 1979 analysis. What we intend here is to elaborate further upon and follow through to its logical conclusion the 1979 analysis, in hope of finally dispensing with this (in our view) irrelevant, insidiously racist and "conceptually incarcerated" (Nobles, 1976a) literature (for black psychological scholars in particular, and black social scientists in general). In this work, we will briefly review the 1979 analysis, examine more recent activities and trends in this area since the 1979 publication, and most importantly, expand all of this discussion with an extensive elaboration on the significant role of culture (Euro-American culture and African American culture) in clarifying the true nature of the problem under consideration herein. We will conclude by proposing the appropriate research directions that germinate from the Africentric paradigm.

The Significance of Culture in the Study of African American Behavior

The present analysis will attempt to detail the role of culture and cultural oppression in the examination of African American behavior in general, and that of the black self-concept in particular. Culture, as we define it herein, refers to the operationalization of a people's cosmology or worldview in the everyday approach to life of the people. That is, culture represents the institutionalized expressions, practices and products of a people's cosmology. Therefore an understanding of the concept of "cosmology" or "worldview" is necessary to an understanding of culture. These concepts refer to the distinct way in which a people construe. (i.e., define, organize, etc.) reality; their particular approach to life, existence, the universe or cosmos; their system of guiding beliefs or basic assumptions about life (The African Psychology Institute, 1982; Baldwin, 1980, 1985; Dixon, 1976; Nobles, forthcoming). We commonly used concepts such as ontology, ethos and philosophy to represent this phenomenon or some important components of it. In short then, cosmology or worldview constitutes the ideological and philosophical underpinnings or foundation of culture.

In the multicultural American society, we naturally find operating more than one cultural reality or worldview. Where African Americans are concerned, we find operating in American society the formally institutionalized European-American worldview, as well as the indigenous (and oftentimes "suppressed") African American worldview (Baldwin, 1980, 1985; Dixon, 1976; Nobles, 1976a, 1976b). The implications of this multicultural framework for the study of African American behavior should be clear. As Baldwin (1979) has noted:

> . . . given the multicultural nature of American society we must be extremely cautious in interpreting the experiences of black people in this country. Such a perspective recognizes that American society encompasses a variety of systems of cultural definitions (or sociocultural orientations), some of which are fundamentally different in nature. Within this sociocultural context, then, one must be cautious not to use the framework of one racial-cultural group's experiences to interpret and explain the experience of another. Thus, it may very well depend upon which racial-cultural system of definitions is operative as to what kinds of observations are made and the types of explanations and interpretations ultimately derived (p.52).

Where the issues of the African American self-concept and personality are concerned, there are two basic (so-called) cross-cultural approaches that can be taken in this general area of study. One approach emphasizes the traditional Western/Eurocentric (Euro-American) psychological paradigm (the mythological cross-cultural paradigm), while the other approach emphasizes a true cultural relativistic paradigmatic perspective, the fundamental distinction between the two being that in operating from the framework of Western psychology's (pseudo) cross-cultural paradigm, we inherently assume Eurocentric cultural monism. This monistic perspective imposes an erroneous cultural homogeneity between the African American and Euro-American communities. This approach leads one to assume that only the experiences of American slavery and racial oppression have forged basic differences in experience between black and white people in this country. The factor of race, in the sociogenetic sense (i.e., racial inferiority), may often be given consideration in this regard also (see Guthrie, 1976). At any rate, it follows from such a framework that where differences in behavior are found to exist between blacks and whites, an explanation of such differences is to be pursued (all other factors presumably being equal) in terms of these basic sources of variability in experience between the two racial groups. Within the framework of Western psychology's so-called cross-cultural paradigm, then, blacks are treated rather erroneously as if they were more or less "dark skinned Europeans", separated in social experience only in terms of American slavery, American racism and inferior genetic condition. This paradigm therefore obscures not only the actual nature of the African American self-orientation as substantially derived from the African cultural experience (Akbar, 1979; Baldwin, 1976, 1981; Dixon, 1976; Nobles, 1973, 1976a, 1980), but also the fundamental integrity of African culture itself.

On the other hand, when operating within the framework of a genuine cultural relativistic perspective, one does not assume European cultural monism or that cultural homogeneity exists between African American and European-American peoples. To the contrary, one assumes that fundamental differences in social reality and cultural experiences do indeed exist between blacks and whites in America beyond the very narrow criteria noted in the foregoing. This perspective assumes that the cultural orientation of black people in this country is very much African in its basic nature (Akbar, 1976, 1979, 1984; Baldwin, 1981; Khatib et al., 1979; King et al., 1976; Nobles, 1974, 1976a, 1980), notwithstanding some degree of distortion that may have resulted from over three centuries of victimization by Euro-American cultural oppression (Akbar, 1981; Baldwin, 1980, 1984, 1985; Nobles, 1976c). Therefore, differences in behaviors between African Americans and European-Americans are always examined and interpreted within the context of this total perspective (Akbar, 1980; Khatib et al., 1979; King et al., 1976). Thus the true cultural relativistic approach assumes the existence of fundamental differences between African American culture and European-American culture and their corresponding psychological functioning and behavioral manifestations.

Recalling the earlier cited warning from the 1979 analysis, we social scientists must exercise extreme caution when considering theory and research concerning black people in the multicultural and racist social context of Western society, lest we run the risk of distorting and misrepresenting the phenomenon under examination. Of course, it is our contention here that the Western psychological approach to the study of the black self-concept has ignored such a warning and thereby has generated a basic misrepresentation of this phenomenon.

This analysis will examine the black self-hatred literature from the vantage point of the true cultural relativistic approach as it is employed in Black Psychology. The Africentric paradigm which we will explicate later in our discussion, naturally fits appropriately within the framework of the true cultural relativism approach. A major thesis of this paper, of course, is that the Africentric paradigm represents the only pardigmatic posture that should be viewed as having any meaningful validity in the examination and explanation of African American behavior (Baldwin, 1986). Let us now turn our attention to an examination of the Eurocentric paradigm that (we believe) has so severely distorted our approach to understanding the African American (so-called) self-concept through, among other things, the introduction and promulgation of the nefarious construct of "black self-hatred."

The Eurocentric Paradigm and the Concept of Self

The essential nature of the concept of self as defined by Western psychological thought is a derivative of the European worldview (Baldwin, 1985; Dixon, 1976; Nobles, 1976a). This philosophical orientation is undergirded by the guiding principles of (a) "control over nature" and (b) "survival of the fittest." The assumption that the process of thought (i.e., cognition, consciousness) distinguishes human beings from their surroundings (nature) no doubt accounts for the Eurocentric adherence to the principle of "control or mastery over nature." Since human beings are capable of complex mental function, the European internalized the belief that man was also destined to rule over all of that which he could contemplate (Dixon, 1976). Thus the principle of control over nature represents the relentless propensity of the European self or the corporate European personality toward achieving mastery and domination over the universe. The European self is therefore separate from and in conflict with nature. This principle is operationalized through such major themes as oppression, suppression, repression, and the unnatural alteration or reordering of all objects that are inconsistent with its value framework. The corollary principle of survival of the fittest is best evidenced in the scientific theory of social Darwinism in which the focus of the self is based on a value for the individual over the collective. Emphasis is placed on the individual's "uniqueness," distinctiveness and difference. This concept of self germinates from the axiomatic position which purports that; "I think, therefore I am" (Dixon, 1976). Again, inherent value is placed on the individual as separate and distinct from his environment and world of experience.

This emphasis on the individual also highlights a dualistic notion of the individual as separate and independent from the social group or collective. This notion purports that the individual's identity can be forged independently of the group identity which is primarily responsible for the individual's existence. This value for and belief in an individual or personal identity that supersedes collective identity can be seen in such European values as "Doing your own thing" and the excessive emphasis on "Me, Myself, and I" (Dixon, 1976).

It follows from these principles, then, that the European values which come to define the essential nature of the concept of self are

those that emphasize "individualism, uniqueness, difference, independence, material-physical characteristics and individual rights. These Eurocentric values for the self are translated into psycho-behavioral
modalities that are best expressed in terms of the self as competitor,
aggressor, initiator, influencer, and controller (Baldwin, 1985; Dixon,
1976; Ogletree, 1976; Welsing, 1981). According to Nobles (1974), these
"European-based psycho-behavioral modalities (are) traceable to values
and customs characteristic of that community and the guiding principles reflected in it."

Thus, it would logically follow that the self as defined from the
European perspective reflects an external, physical, and materialistic
orientation to reality, rather than a spiritual or metaphysical orientation. The concern for controlling nature thrust European culture into
external and material-based criteria for assessing the quality of the self.
A healthy/successful self-concept is usually assumed to be shared by
those who are striving for self-worth through competition for control
over objects in terms of material criteria such as money, property and
physical dimensions of status. It is not surprising then that those individuals in this society who purportedly have the lowest sense of self-
worth are typically the poor and those most culturally and physically
distant from European culture.

This emphasis on an external and physical definition of the self
can be readily observed in the Western psychological research on self-
concept, which invariably seeks to define the essential quality of self in
terms of the physical dimension of race/color. The variety and consistency of the self-concept research in Western psychology that invariably employs physical characteristics such as skin color, hair texture,
facial features, etc., as the elemental quality of the self clearly evidence
this phenomenon. This clearly illustrates that not only is the European
definition of the self essentially a physically/materially-based phenomenon, but the value for specific physical characteristics are entirely
grounded in the European social reality. According to the Euro-centric
perspective, the negative implications for the self-worth of people of
African descent, within this Eurocentric social reality, provides the basis
for the so-called psychological phenomenon that has come to be
known as black self-hatred (Baldwin, 1979).

Now turning to the notion of the black self-concept, and the consequent notion of black self-hatred, we find that even in the absence of
definitive corroborative data, the Eurocentric paradigm would logically
demand the mythification of such concepts. Employing the principal
of survival of the fittest, the African, in comparison to Europe-
ans/whites, has historically been assumed to be intellectually, culturally
and psychologically inferior by Western science. This assumption of
inferiority, by definition, relegates the assessment of the black self-

concept as unhealthy and deficient in comparison to that of his/her white counterpart.

The mythification of the notion of black self-hatred emanates from the parenthetical projection on the part of European-American social scientists. This mythification erroneously assumes that African Americans operate from the same cultural reality as that of European-Americans and thereby share the cultural motives that derive from the ethos of control over nature and survival of the fittest. Given white supremacist ideology that germinates from the Euro-centric paradigm, the assumption of black self-hatred would no doubt have surfaced irrespective of any evidence to the contrary. This analysis suggests that the notion of black self-hatred constitutes a myth designed to substantiate the motive of European racial supremacy that characterizes the Eurocentric scientific paradigm. A brief review of this literature in Western psychology will, we believe, firmly substantiate our position.

Evolution of the Black Self-Hatred Paradigm

Early theoretical models and research focusing on the black self-concept grew out of the social looking glass and generalized significant others models of Charles Cooley (1902) and George Mead (1934) respectively. These models supported the idea that the individual's conception of him/herself arises through his interaction with other members of his society making up his/her "significant" social circle. "Social Looking Glass" theory proposes that one's self-conception is primarily determined by the way in which it is reflected or mirrored through the eyes of significant others (how others react toward him/her). While these early Western models both stressed the more or less *indigenous properties* of the surrounding social ecology of the individual (i.e., family, peers, neighborhood, community) in self-concept formation, this important consideration underwent a major extension in later formulations of black self-hatred theories based on these earlier notions.

Euro-American social scientists generally concluded that this type of model was appropriate to assess the nature of the interaction between the African American and European-American communities (Baldwin, 1979; Smith, 1980). Hence, European-American racism and racist practices are construed to represent the African American community's social looking glass (i.e., their generalized significant others) reflecting derogatory images of blacks. Through African American's *internalization* of and/or identification with the (generalized) European-American racist attitude toward blacks, or through so-called objective comparisons (housing, employment, income, etc.), blacks come to view themselves (cognitively and affectively) as whites view them. This black self-hatred may also take the disguised form of a defensive/displaced (outward) aggression.

Empirical Support for Black Self-Hatred

As was noted in the 1979 analysis, the popular evidence used to support the black self-hatred thesis comprised the following:

(1) The Racial Preference Studies consisting of; (a) the various racial stimuli presentation studies (i.e., racial dolls, pictures and other stimulus objects) with children subjects; and (b) the various color preference and self-report (including reference group) surveys: (2) The Clinical Case Studies consisting of racially focused and/or interpreted interviews with mentally disturbed clients while in treatment: (3) The Field observations and anecdotal approach consisting of rather unstructured observations and the examinations of various documents and materials having supposedly racial connotations. The so-called racial preference studies represent the most extensive and widely cited area of evidence in the black self-hatred literature. These studies have been focused on black children, from 3 years old up to mid-adolescence. In this type of research, a variety of fantasy-like projective measures are used, typically employing (so-called) racial dolls, pictures or some other presumed racially connotated stimulus objects, and they all occur in the general context of a contrasting or forced-choice identification procedure (Baldwin, 1979). The children are generally assessed in three areas: (1) appropriate racial identification, (2) appropriate self-racial identification, and (3) presumed racial evaluation (self and/or reference group focus may be used depending on the study).

Early studies in this area claimed to have generated evidence that black children tend to choose white dolls over brown dolls as self-representations, and/or in terms of associating them with some presumed value. Similarly, some of these studies have shown that some black children also tend to choose pictures of whites over blacks in the same fashion as their doll selections. In addition, some black children in these studies have been reported to have chosen white or lighter colors over darker ones in coloring either drawings which they had made of themselves, or simply a drawing which they were asked to color the same as their own skin color. Finally, some studies have been reported which show that some black children tend to draw pictures of either themselves, or some other black person in a form that the investigator views as a disfiguration, or as having a psychologically demeaning

Table 1

Sample of Studies Claiming White Preference in Blacks

Studies	Mode of Stimulus	Mode of Response	Systematic Inquiry into Nature of Response	Cross-Cultural Consideration	Race of Experimenter	Race of Sample
Asher & Allen (1969)	Dolls Test	Color of Doll Chosen	No	No	Mixed	Mixed
Clark & Clark (1939, 1940)	Line Drawings	Racial Choice in Drawing	No	No	Black	Black
Clark & Clark (1947, 1950)	Dolls Test	Color of Doll Chosen	No	No	Black	Black
Frisch & Handler (1967)	Draw-a-Person	Racial Features in Drawing	No	No	Not specified	Mixed
Goodman (1952)	Dolls Test	Color of Doll Chosen	No	No	White	Mixed
Greenwald & Oppenheim (1968)	Dolls Test	Color of Doll Chosen	No	No	White	Mixed
Helgerson (1943)	Pictures Test	Racial Choice in Picture	No	No	White	Mixed
Horowitz (1939)	Line Drawings	Racial Choice in Drawing	No	No	White	Mixed
Landreth & Johnson (1953)	Pictures Test	Racial Choice in Picture	No	No	White	Mixed
Morland (1966)	Pictures Test	Racial Choice in Picture	No	No	Mixed	Mixed
Radke et al. (1950)	Pictures Test	Racial Choice in Picture	No	No	White	Mixed
Radke & Trager (1950)	Pictures Test	Racial Choice in Picture	No	No	White	Mixed
Stevenson & Stewart (1958)	Dolls Test	Color of Doll Chosen	No	No	Mixed	Mixed

Reprinted from Baldwin, 1979

significance. Table 1 summarizes some essential features of a representative sample of these earlier studies.

Numerous other studies beyond those listed in Table 1 have also claimed to have generated more or less similar findings using one or more of the popular methodologies in this area. Following the early 1960s, a smaller pool of so-called racial preference findings began to accumulate showing many black children making more black preference choices than white preference choices (see Baldwin, 1979; Clark, 1982; Farrell & Olson, 1983; Jordan, 1981; Porter & Washington, 1979). This more recent pro-black trend in the racial preference literature is explained (in Western oriented scholarly circles) as the social-psychological consequences of the 1960s "black consciousness movement." While many of these studies appear to have been designed to refute the earlier (pre 1965) studies claiming support for black self-hatred, some of the contemporary preference research, however, also show many black children continuing to make white preference or anti-black racial evaluations (Banks, 1984; Clark, 1982; H. McAdoo, 1985; Semaj, 1980; Spencer, 1984). Much of the contemporary preference research seems to have adopted a multiple measure and multi-dimensional approach to the study of racial identification and evaluation (McAdoo, 1985; Semaj, 1980; Spencer, 1984) to apparently off-set or reduce some of the confounding effects of the racist milieu of American society, and the research "demand" and "expectations" it has obviously imposed on earlier methodologies. Some of these recent studies have also tried to integrate social and developmental theories into this area to apparently provide for a more comprehensive (multi-dimensional), valid and reliable assessment of this phenomenon beyond mere race/color theory.

An interesting aspect of these recent multi-dimensional approach studies tend to show black children exhibiting positive self-concepts or personal self-esteem and moderate to strong white preferences on generally most of the measures used, i.e., dolls, pictures, other projectiles, direct preference questions, etc. These studies argue, therefore, that black children's personal self-esteem is independent of or compartmentalized from their racial self-esteem (Jordan, 1981).

Illustratively, Semaj (1980) hypothesized that racial preference (personal and reference group preferences) is developmentally dependent on the ability to perceive racial constancy, which in turn is developmentally dependent on conservation (object permanence-constancy) ability. In his study, 80 black children from 4 to 11 years old, 56% males and 44% females, were administered a battery of cognitive, perceptual and attitudinal measures, including play dough and wooden blocks, picture cards and colored photographs of black and white children and adults as stimulus objects. Construction tasks and perceptual tasks, as well as identification, categorization and evaluation preference tasks in response to verbal cues, comprised the bases for assessing impersonal and social cognitive abilities, racial constancy ability, and social affect behavior. His findings revealed that: (a) virtually all (95%) of the older subjects (10-11 year olds) demonstrated conservation or the appropriate impersonal cognitive ability, while only a small percentage (30%) of the youngest subjects displayed this skill; (b) the minority of both 4-5 year olds and 10-11 year olds (20% and 40% respectively) showed racial constancy ability; (c) the majority of the subjects (69%) chose the black pictures as appropriate to their own racial identity and category (regardless of age groups); (d) the youngest and oldest groups (4-5 and 10-11 year olds) showed equivalent black/white preferences, while the middle-age groups (6-7 and 8-9 year olds) displayed black preference trends. His data also showed that the children's racial preferences were independent of their self-evaluations. Semaj concluded that his hypothesis was partially supported, in that impersonal cognition or conservation ability appeared to developmentally precede social cognition or racial constancy perceptual ability, but were not developmentally related to racial preference behaviors. He further concluded that black children apparently develop a "bicultural" identity by age 11.

In another study, Spencer (1984) tested 130 black children, ages 4-6.5 years old and approximately half of each sex, to assess the relationships between self-concept, race awareness and racial attitudes (including racial preferences). Using racial picture cards and paper doll cut-outs, a prominent self-concept values test and a vocabulary measure, she found that 80% of the children obtained positive self-concept scores and at the same time showed an anti-black/white preference in their racial attitudes. Spencer concluded that black preschoolers effectively compartmentalize their personal identity or self-concept from their reference group evaluations or racial preferences. McAdoo (1985) reported similar findings in her multiple-measures, longitudinal study of three different samples of black children, ages 5-10.8 years old, over a five-year period, notwithstanding some inconsistencies relative to regional variations.

Banks (1984), another researcher in this area, reported similar findings on a sample of 98 black suburban children up through their mid-teens from racially integrated neighborhoods and schools. Banks found that black children from predominantly white communities and schools tended to have positive-self-concepts and to be anti-black/pro-white in their attitudes and preferences. He referred to this phenomenon as a "bi-racial" orientation. Banks also found the anti-black/white preference tendency to become stronger with age among these black children from integrated settings.

Clinical-Field Observations and Anecdotal Evidence

The clinical case studies and the field observations, as noted previously (Baldwin, 1979), have generally been used as a supplementary data pool to the more systematic racial preference findings on black children. Supposedly, the and field studies have broadened the application and implications of the racial preference evidence to wider segments of the African American community. Such issues as skin-color conflicts and conflicts over other physical features among blacks, the presence of anger and hostility toward whites as well as toward self and other blacks, among a host of other social artifacts and presumed behavioral indicators of black self-hatred, have been the focus of other studies in this area. From the early research of Bevis (1921), Dollard and his associates (Dollard, 1937; Davis & Dollard, 1940), through Grier & Cobbs (1965, 1971) and into the present era (Wilkinson, 1974, 1980) this mostly unstructured, unsystematic and certainly dubious pool of data has accumulated and has been used as definitive evidence in the racial preference literature (see Baldwin, 1979).

A Critical Analysis of the Black Self-Hatred Literature

As was observed earlier, and as was noted in Baldwin's 1979 critique, most of the traditional research concerning black self-hatred has used as its conceptual framework the European worldview. This worldview is projected in the theoretical models of the social looking glass theory, psychoanalytic conflict and defense mechanism theory and symbolic interactionism theory as well as the other similarly oriented models (see Baldwin, 1979). The proponents of these theoretical models have attempted to explain the phenomenon of black self-hatred essentially as the net result of racial oppression. They propose that black people, especially children, acquire their self-conception from their interaction with the Euro-American community rather than from the African American community.

The illogical basis of such an assertion has been effectively demonstrated by many black social scientists and some white social scientists as well (Baldwin, 1979; Nobles, 1973, 1976a; Porter & Washington, 1979). The most definitive studies in this regard have been the self-report research. Such studies have consistently shown black respondents to exhibit high levels of self-esteem and positive attitudes toward themselves (Baldwin, 1979). In an attempt to explain this consistent and obvious contradictory trend in the literature, recent theories, as previously noted, have drawn a distinction between self-orientation/esteem and reference group orientation/esteem. The so-called clarifying argument therefore emerged proposing that black self-hatred is more correctly conceptualized as a negative "reference group" orientation, not a negative "self"-orientation (H. McAdoo, 1985; J. McAdoo, 1985; Semaj, 1980; Spencer, 1982a; 1982b; 1984). None of the various attempts to explain (or to refute) the so called black self-hatred phenomenon, including both early and contemporary attempts, have varied substantially in terms of their implicit or explicit Eurocentric conceptual framework. This is a very important consideration given that most of the presumed "black oriented" contemporary research and theorizing in this area (carried out by black investigators) have seemingly set out to clarify and no doubt refute the black self-hatred conclusion. Thus even in the case of the more recent studies conducted by primarily black researchers, methodological and conceptual flaws continue to dominate this literature.

Methodological Critique

Following the 1979 analysis, we will briefly concentrate on four related areas of concern: the nature of the stimuli, the nature of the responses, the instrumentation/measures used, and the failure to employ a true cultural relativistic approach. An analysis of the methodologies employed in this literature raises serious questions regarding the validity and reliability of the proported findings representing this research. As was noted in Baldwin's (1979) critique, there is little doubt that the nature of the stimuli used in these studies had a substantial effect on obscuring the responses of the subjects. The commercial exposure of black dolls and black pictorial presentations (as well as "black" toys in general) portrayed in realistic and positive forms (see Wilkinson, 1974, 1980) was virtually non-existent prior to the early-to mid 1960's. There have been many findings which have revealed that familiarity with the stimulus and other confounding stimulus characteristics and contextual factors influence these outcomes (Baldwin, 1979). Such confounding factors as facial expression and sex of the stimulus, whether the stimulus is presented on the right or left side of the subject, the cleanliness of the character constituting the stimulus, the race and sex of the experimenter/interviewer, demographics, linguistics, etc. have all been shown to determine the responses of subjects in these studies beyond the factor of color or racial characteristics of the stimulus (Baldwin, 1979; Sattler, 1973; Wilkinson, 1974). In addition, it has been shown that the capricious nature of most children's responses to such stimuli also consistently challenge the interpretive competency of these researchers. From the early racial preference studies of Clark & Clark (1939, 1950) to the more recent work of Semaj (1980) and others

(H. McAdoo, 1985; Spencer, 1984), black children's rationales for their so-called racial preference choices have defied the presumed (Eurocentric) logic of the black self-hatred prediction models. Black children's reports of why they chose "white" objects have varied widely, with very few directly indicating a white racial preference conclusion (Baldwin, 1979).

Beyond these methodological problems, one of the more fundamental errors made in this literature had been the use of inappropriate measures to assess the racial attitudes and self-orientation of African American people. In spite of the fact that the historical, anthropological and social science research literatures are replete with evidence supporting basic cultural differences between blacks and whites in this country (Billingsley, 1968; Delaney, 1956; Dixon, 1976; DuBois, 1902, 1946; Karenga, 1982; Khatib et al., 1979; Nobles, 1972, 1974; White, 1984; Williams, 1976), most of the black self-hatred researchers have rather arrogantly (whether through ignorance or by design) denied the existence of such fundamental cultural differences in formulating, conducting and interpreting their "cross-racial" studies. Most of the measures used in this literature have been developed in terms of the conceptual framework of the European worldview. As was noted earlier, in the tradition of Western social science with its emphases on individualism, materialism, determinism, dualism, reductionism and mechanical explanations, these measures have been designed to assess black people's self-orientation or self-concept as it is defined (misperceived or distorted) by the European cosmology. That is, the racial preference and supporting studies have used measures designed specifically for European-American cultural reality to assess African American's self-conception, which limits our ability to truly understand this phenomenon. The one-dimensional race/color (materialistic-racist) emphasis of these measures, as well as the individualism emphasis, the underlying assumption of a compartmentalized human phenomenology and its linear related components (among other Eurocentric value referents implicit in these measures) all converge to blatantly distort and misrepresent the true nature of the African American self-orientation.

While it is rather obvious that much of the earlier research on black self-hatred was clearly steeped in the Eurocentric conceptual framework which undergirds Western psychology and social science (Akbar, 1984, 1985; Baldwin, 1979; Carruthers, 1972; Nobles, 1976a), it is most interesting to note that much of the contemporary research that has arisen to refute, and apparently redefine these earlier notions are also guided by this same Eurocentric paradigm, albeit more subtle in occurrence in some instances (see Banks, 1984; McAdoo & McAdoo, 1985; Parham & Helms, 1985; Semaj, 1980; Spencer, 1982a, 1982b, 1984). These more recent approaches designed to counter the earlier notions have seemingly attempted to eliminate or minimize many of the methodological flaws plaguing the earlier literature.

Notwithstanding the fact that much of this contemporary research makes a valiant effort to rebut some of the pejorative conclusions found in the earlier literature, it cannot be overlooked that serious theoretical and methodological questions remain. For example, Semaj (1980) (study described earlier) postulates that race consciousness is predicated upon the linear stage development of race constancy. That is, the older the child becomes the more likely he/she will have mastered the concrete operational stage of cognitive development and consequently will have mastered the understanding that race is a permanent characteristic in the person. According to Semaj, it is this ability of racial constancy that enables the child to be racially aware. His data, however, argue for a curvilinear relationship since only the children between ages 6-9 years show a strong black preference, while the youngest group (4-5 years) evidenced no preference and the oldest group (10-11 years) tended toward a white preference. Semaj suggested that only a longitudinal analysis can extricate substantive meaning from these trends. By his own admission, his findings could have been an artifact of the methodological limitations of the types of materials employed in the study, as well as the inability to control for the variety of perceptions such materials could have spawned in the children. To his credit, Semaj acknowledges the fact that a trend toward a so-called "bicultural" orientation among older black children would be desirable only among those advocating the assimilationist-integrationist ideology resulting from Eurocentric cultural oppression. This phenomenon, however, would represent a cause for concern among the more psychologically liberated, culturally-orientated African American social scientists.

Unfortunately, the same cannot be said of the work of Spencer (1984) and others (Banks, 1984; H. McAdoo, 1985). Spencer argued, based on her findings, that for some African American children to simultaneously maintain positive self-concepts and pro-white cultural values is evidence of the ability of black children to effectively compartmentalize personal identity (i.e., self-concept) from racial attitudes or racial preferences. Thus, Spencer (1982a, 1984) as well as other contemporary authors have begun to advocate this conceptualization of the African American's self-concept as essentially a personal-individualized identity independent of the collective (racial group) identity. This approach directly contradicts the Africentric or African worldview perspective in which the self is inextricably tied to the collective (racial group), because the self derives its significance by virtue of one's immersion into the collective or group reality.

It is entirely plausible that this compartmentalization thesis may in actuality be no more than a response to the unhealthy oppressive influence of the sometimes not so subtle and consistent messages of white supremacy that are presented to black children by all of the basic institutions of American society. Rather than labeling these black children as exemplary of healthy psychological functioning, these findings (to whatever extent they hold validity) should, more importantly, sound the alarm among black social scientists to begin to address the implications of this psychological inconsistency between personal identity and racial group orientation among victimized black youngsters. Instead, what we find is that the black social scientist once again cannot free him/herself from the oppressive shackles of Eurocentric conceptual incarceration and psychological misorientation, both of which implicitly embrace and project the European worldview (Baldwin, 1984, 1985; Nobles, 1976a).

Thus, a basic problem with these more contemporary studies by black social scientists is that they continue to accept uncritically the basic Eurocentric cultural assumptions undergirding this overall literature. That is, they continue to operate under the assumption that the various Eurocentric constructs, measures, instruments, etc., represent the appropriate framework for conceptualizing, measuring and explaining the black self-concept (e.g., personal versus reference group orientation, cognitive and affective self-concepts, "racial" objects and stimuli, etc.). Virtually all of these approaches, both the earlier and recent ones, implicitly accept the value of individualism as the paradigm appropriate to conceptualizing and assessing African (African American) people. Hence, the contemporary black researchers in this area have persisted in making some of the most fundamental and dangerous errors that social scientists can make (particularly black social scientists) in conducting research with black populations. They have used European cultural definitions and Eurocentric measures of self-conception in an effort to refute the conclusions which these definitions and measures have been designed to confirm (Akbar, 1985; Baldwin, 1976, 1979, 1985; Carruthers, 1972; Nobles, 1973, 1976a).

It is therefore clear that those theories and research findings claiming support for the existence of a condition of self-hatred (either personal or extended) in black people do not have any meaningful empirical basis upon which to stand especially from a true cultural relativistic perspective. Where the black self-concept in general is concerned, progressive African American theorists have convincingly argued that the black self-concept is a far more global and complex phenomenon than is indicated by the concerted focus on the single dimension of race-color as the presumably salient and generalizable factor involved (Baldwin, 1979). Thus, the basic issue of the black self-concept itself is seriously obscured by the various simplistic conceptions implicit in this literature. Given that virtually all of the black self-hatred literature clearly assumes Eurocentric cultural monisms, and therefore the existence of cultural homogeneity between black and white people in this country, it must be concluded that this literature is totally irrelevant to a valid inquiry into the nature of black self-concept, black personality and black experience in general. Thus, this literature makes little or no contribution to our understanding of African American behavior because it obscures and misrepresents, as well as outrightly denies, the existence of fundamental differences in cultural realities between black and white people. Regarding the issue of the black self-concept specifically, this literature erroneously assumes that African Americans should necessarily view themselves as European-Americans are presumed to view themselves, and interprets all deviations from the Eurocentric behavioral norm as potentially pathological. Let us now turn our attention to what we have argued in this paper is the valid and appropriate paradigm for conceptualizing and conducting research on the African American self-concept.

The Africentric Paradigm and the Concept of Self

From the Africentric perspective, the concept of "self" is defined within the context of the African ethos or the set of guiding principles which constitute the traditional African cosmology. The genesis of this ethos lies in the African conception of the universe as a totality composed of interdependent elements. This ontological conception of the universe as an interdependent totality has been variously regarded as a sense of "Oneness" or "Harmony with Nature" or the Universe, or a "Oneness of being" (Akbar, 1975; Erny, 1973; Mbiti, 1970; Nobles, 1972). The sense of oneness of being is reflected in the traditional African belief that man is inextricably tied to his surroundings as a part of the harmonious rhythm of nature. This belief contributes to another basic principle in the African ethos—"Survival of the group." Not only is the human being an integral part of his/her ecological setting, but he/she is also harmoniously bound to his/her bio-social community or group. These guiding principles of the African cosmology influence all aspects of African life. The African ethos endorses the value for unity, cooperative effort, collective responsibility and concern for the community among black people.

Nobles (1976a) and others (Akbar, 1979; Baldwin, 1981; Williams, 1981) have convincingly argued that this Africentric orientation or sense of Africanity, which highlights collectivity, interdependence and shared responsibility, is the most appropriate paradigm for understanding the nature of the concept of self among people of African descent.

According to Nobles (1976a), "when we examine the African philo-sophical tradition, particularly the ethosic orders of *survival of the people* and *one with nature*, we logically recognize that from this philosophical position an *extended* definition of self evolved." Mbiti (1970) further notes that the traditional African conception of the self is best ex-pressed in the belief that "I am because We are, and because We are therefore I am." From the Africentric view, then, the emphasis on the collective identity transcends individual identity, and the individual's conception of self extends to include one's self and kind. Nobles (1976a) argues that "This transcendent relationship (that between self and kind) is the 'extended-self.'"

Based on this analysis, it becomes clear that the African concep-tion of the self reflects several discernible and noteworthy qualities. First, the African self is not treated as separate from the group. This means that there exists an interdependence between the self and the group (others) in which the self derives is significance from its group affiliation. This also connotes an appositional rather than oppositional relationship between the self-concept and the group concept. In this sense, for the African the exercise of personal identity is tempered by an overriding concern for how the individual contributes to, and anchors him/herself in the survival of the collective.

Finally, this Africentric conception of self is based on internal metaphysical or spiritual imperatives (Akbar, 1979; Baldwin, 1981; Mbiti, 1970). The essence of the African self derives from its intercon-necting ontological orientation to the universe manifested in a spiritu-alistic commitment to the collective. The philosophical imperative that the self has meaning only to the extent that it is reflected of the collec-tive will of the group is the embodiment of this spiritual (intercon-nected) self definition. Hence, the interconnecting principle of a communal phenomenology among African people represents the spiri-tual core of the African self. The Africentric approach to the African American self-conception has been described as a "self-extension orien-tation" in which the black person consciously and unconsciously an-chors him/herself in a group or corporate definition, i.e., a communal phenomenology (Akbar, 1976; Baldwin, 1976, 1981, 1984; Nobles, 1976a, 1980). According to Baldwin (1981), this "African self-extension orientation" represents the unconscious and conscious operation of the spiritual core of the African American self-concept. This tendency to consciously and unconsciously extend one's self by defining self in group/corporate terms is evidenced in a variety of ways in the African American community. For example, the notion of the extended African family, (as opposed to the nuclear European family) is based on the principle that both immediate and distant relatives can be legitimately considered a part of the immediate family household. That is, the family household may not only consist of parents and siblings, but also of aunts, uncles, cousins, nieces, nephews and grandparents (Billingsley, 1968; Nobles, 1974; White, 1984). This self-extension orientation can be seen in the fact that both consanguineal and non-consanguineal persons are considered "family" in the African American community. The custom of incorporating a "play brother" or "play sister" into one's concept of family is exemplary of the African American's self-extension tendency (Nobles, 1974).

Another manifestation of the African self-extension orientation, or the collective sense of self which typifies the African American cultural reality is the "call-and-response" behavioral pattern found in most, if not all black churches (White, 1984). A rhythm is established between minister and congregation in which the congregation responds collectively to the query and interrogatories of the minister as if they were of one mind. This shared participation phenomenon characterizes most speaker/actor-audience interactions (sacred and secular) in the African American community (Akbar, 1975; Baldwin, 1976; White, 1984). Some other manifestations of the African self-extension orientation among African Americans have been noted in the following observations: (a) the strong social-affiliating tendency whereby African Americans seek out social or group situations as opposed to isolation and individualized experiences; (b) the strong shared feelings of victory and/or defeat among African Americans when one or more black persons engage in public-sanctioned competition against whites (e.g., in athletics-entertainment, academics, politics, etc.); (c) the intense practice of religion among African Americans which emphasizes the interconnectedness between humanity and God, including all of nature; (d) the long standing practice of informal adoptions among African Americans; (e) the reverence for the elderly and the norm of their continued involvement in the African American community; etc. (see Akbar, 1979; Baldwin, 1976, 1981; Dixon, 1976; Jones, 1972, 1980; Khatib et al., 1979; Nobles, 1978, 1980; Williams, 1981).

An Africentric analysis thus identifies and emphasizes these African cultural parameters which define the black self-conception as a self-extension orientation deriving from and reflective of the spiritualistic core of the African cultural reality. Baldwin (1981, 1984) and others (Azibo, 1983a, 1983b; Baldwin & Bell, 1985) have translated this African self-extension orientation core of the black self-concept into anther heuristic construct called African self-consciousness. African self-consciousness is therefore an extended self-consciousness; a communal phenomenology which manifests itself in a wide variety of self affirming, positive (pro-black) beliefs, attitudes and behaviors among African Americans. Given this overall analysis, two (Africentric) avenues for future research in this area of black psychology would appear to be necessary, if we are to change the current consequences of Eurocentric cultural oppression on the psyche of the African American community, and liberate its full Africentric potential. One line of Africentric research in this area must address the effects of the process of Eurocentric cultural oppression and racism on the Africentric or pro-black referent that naturally develops in black children in black families. Research in this area should be concerned with whether and under what conditions black children can be resocialized to adopt an anti-self (Eurocentric-type) orientation. The question of what factors are operating at the societal, community, and family and personal levels that are responsible for such a cultural aberration must be addressed by future research in this area.

The other line of Africentric research in this area, and in our view the most important research thrust, must be focused on uncovering the nature and character of the African referent in African American self-concept formation. What social environments, socialization processes, institutional and developmental social systems are most conducive to the formation of this kind of self-referent are critical research issues that must be addressed.

Naturally, Africentric research requires the development and construction of Africentric instruments, assessment techniques and research strategies or methodologies. Recent work by Baldwin and his Associates (Baldwin & Bell, 1985; Baldwin, Duncan & Bell, N.D.), and a small number of other researchers (Azibo, 1983a, 1983b; Nobles, 1978; Williams, 1981) have begun to address these kinds of Africentric research thrusts in this important area of concern. These Africentric research efforts are focused on such issues as: the nature and development of the Africentric self-orientation among African Americans; the various manifestations of this phenomenon in the everyday life activities of African Americans; and the manner in which the Africentric self-orientation influences other important (adaptive-survival oriented) functioning and behaviors among African Americans. This kind of analysis (Africentric analysis), then, represents the only valid and reliable approach to our understanding and explaining the so-called black self-concept. As we have tried to show, the theorists and researchers in this area must liberate themselves from their Eurocentric cultural incarceration in order to engage in authentic study of the African American self-concept from the perspective of its own "legitimate" cultural reality.

Conclusion

In concluding, this analysis has tried to show that when theory and research are focused on black people without giving systematic consideration to the existence of basic cultural differences between the European-American and African American communities, such studies contrasting (directly or indirectly) black-white attitudes, behaviors, etc., cannot make valid and definitive claims about basic aspects of the black personality based on their findings. The culturally relative meanings of the concepts, stimuli, resulting responses and the overall situations involved are never even seriously considered, if understood at all. Hence, we have attempted to demonstrate in this analysis the limiting potential of applying the Eurocentric paradigm to conceptualize and explain African psychological phenomena. The net effect of this paradigmatic misapplication has allowed for the construction of what has come to be known as the racially dissonant reaction called "black self-hatred." This analysis has also tried to demonstrate the Eurocentric conceptual incarceration of contemporary black thought in this (in our view) largely bankrupt and obsolete area of Eurocentric mythology. In this regard, we showed how contemporary black researchers have introduced the equally racially dissonant construct of a "bi-cultural" orientation among African Americans as an alternative to the notorious black self-hatred phenomenon. Certainly most black social scientists recognize the great danger in labeling psychologically aberrant behavior as normative, healthy and desirable. This is the dangerous consequence, as we have shown, of black social scientists operating from a perspective other than the Africentric cultural framework (i.e., from the Eurocentric cultural framework).

The implications of this analysis, of course, go well beyond the limited area of the self-concept literature. It recommends that *black social scientists must reject the Eurocentric paradigm as a strategy for theory and research concerning the psychological functioning and behavior of black people. We believe very strongly, and hope that we have demonstrated convincingly, that Africentric analysis must be brought to bear on this literature in order to clarify its severe limitations and dangerous social and psychological implications for the survival and liberation of the African American community. We have tried to accomplish this in our examination of the black self-hatred literature from a genuine cultural relativistic perspective.*

References

African Psychology Institute, (1982). *The African Psychology Institute Training Module Handbook.* Atlanta: The African Psychology Institute.

Akbar, N., (1985). Our destiny: Authors of a scientific revolution. In H. P. McAdoo & J. L. McAdoo (Eds.), *Black children: Social, educational and parental environments.* Beverly Hills: Sage.

Akbar, N., (1984). Africentric social sciences for human liberation. *Journal of Black Studies, 14* (4), 395-414.

Akbar, N., (1981). Mental disorders among African-Americans. *Black Books Bulletin, 7* (2), 18-25.

Akbar, N., (1979). African roots of black personality. In W. D. Smith et al. (Eds.), *Reflections on black psychology.* Washington, D. C.: Univ. Press of America.

Akbar, N., (1976). Rhythmic patterns in African personality. In L. M. King et al. (Eds.), *African philosophy: Assumptions and paradigms for research on black persons.* Los Angeles: Fanon, R & D Center.

Akbar, N., (1975). The rhythm of black personality. *Southern Exposure, 3* (1), 14-19. (AKA L. X Weems)

Azibo, D., (1983a). Some psychological concomitants and consequences of the black personality: Mental health implications. *Journal of Non-White Concerns,* 59-66.

Azibo, D., (1983b). Perceived attractiveness and the black personality. *The Western Journal of Black Studies, 7* (4), 229-238.

Baldwin, J. A., (1986). African (black) Psychology: Issues and synthesis. *Journal of Black Studies, 16* (3), 235-249.

Baldwin, J. A., (1985). Psychological aspects of European cosmology in American society. *The Western Journal of Black Studies, 9* (4), 216-223.

Baldwin, J. A., (1984). African self-consciousness and the mental health of African-Americans. *Journal of Black Studies, 15* (2), 177-194.

Baldwin, J. A., (1981). Notes on an Africentric theory of black personality. *The Western Journal of Black Studies, 5* (3), 172-179.

Baldwin, J. A., (1980). The psychology of oppression. In M. K. Asante & A. Vandi (Eds.), *Contemporary Black thought.* Beverly Hills: Sage.

Baldwin, J. A., (1979). Theory and research concerning the notion of black self-hatred: A review and reinterpretation. *Journal of Black Psychology, 5* (2), 51-77.

Baldwin, J. A., (1976). Black Psychology and black personality: Some issues for consideration. *Black Books Bulletin, 4* (3), 6-11, 65.

Baldwin, J. A. & Bell, Y. R., (1985). The African self-consciousness scale: An Africentric personality questionnaire. *The Western Journal of Black Studies, 9* (2), 61-68.

Baldwin, J.A., Duncan, J.A. and Bell, Y.R.(N.D.) Assessment of African self consciousness among black students, from two college environments. Talahassee, FL: Department of Psychology, Florida A&M University.

Banks, J. A., (1984). Black youths in predominantly white suburbs: An exploratory study of their attitudes and self-concepts. *Journal of Negro Education, 53*(1), 3-17.

Barnes, M. E. & Farrier, S. C., (1985). A longitudinal study of the self-concept of low income youth. *Adolescence, 20* (77), 199-205.

Bevis, W. M., (1921). Psychological traits of the southern Negro. *American Journal of Psychiatry, 78,* 69-78.

Billingsley, A., (1968). *Black families in white America.* Englewood Cliffs, N. J.: Prentice-Hall.

Carruthers, J. H., (1972). *Science and oppression.* Chicago: Center for Inner City Studies.

Clark, M. L., (1982). Racial group concept and self-esteem in black children. *Journal of Black Psychology, 8* (2), 75-88.

Clark, K. B. & Clark, M. P., (1950). Emotional factors in racial identification and preference in Negro children. *Journal of Negro Education, 19,* 341-350.

Clark, K. B. & Clark, M. P., (1939). The development of consciousness of self and the emergence of racial identification in Negro school children. *Journal of Social Psychology, 10,* 591-599.

Cooley, C. H., (1902). *Human nature and social order.* New York: Scribner.

Davis, A. & Dollard, J., (1940). *Children of bondage.* New York: Harper & Row.

Delaney, M., (1856, 1968). *The condition, elevation, immigration and destiny of the colored people of the United States.* New York: Arno Press.

Dixon, V. J., (1976). World views and research methodology. In L. M. King et al. (Eds.), African philosophy: Assumptions and paradigms for research on black persons. Los Angeles: Fanon R & D Center.

Dollard, J., (1937). *Caste and class in a southern town.* Garden City, New York: Anchor.

DuBois, W. E. B., (1946). *The world and Africa.* New York: International.

DuBois, W. E. B., (1902, 1961). *The souls of black folk.* New York: Fawcett.

Erny, P., (1973). *Childhood and cosmos: The social psychology of the black-African child.* New York: New Perspectives.

Farrell, W. C., Jr. & Olson, J. L., (1983). Kenneth and Mamie Clark revisited: Racial identification and racial preference in dark-skinned and light-skinned black children. *Urban Education, 18* (3), 284-297.

Grier, W. & Cobbs, P., (1971). *Jesus bag.* New York: McGraw-Hill.

Grier, W. & Cobbs, P., (1968). *Black rage.* New York: Basic.

Guthrie, R. V., (1976). *Even the rat was white: A historical view of psychology.* New York: Harper & Row.

Jones, R. L. (Ed.), (1972, 1980). *Black Psychology.* New York: Harper & Row.

Jordan, T. J., (1981). Self-concept, motivation and academic achievement of black adolescents. *Journal of Educational Psychology, 73* (4), 509-517.

Karenga, M., (1982). *Introduction to black studies.* Inglewood, Ca.: Kawaida.

Khatib, S., McGee, D. P., Nobles, W. W., & Akbar, N., (1979). Voodoo or I.Q. : An introduction to African Psychology. In W. D. Smith et al. (Ed.), *Reflections on black Psychology.* Washington, D. C.: University Press of America.

King, L. M., Dixon, V. J., & Nobles, W. W., (1976). *African philosophy: Assumptions and paradigms for research on black persons.* Los Angeles: Fanon R & D Center.

Mbiti, J. S., (1970). *African religions and philosophy.* New York: Anchor.

McAdoo, H. P., (1985). The development of self-concept and race attitudes of young black children over time. In H. P. McAdoo & J. L. McAdoo (Eds.), *Black children: Social, educational and parental environments.* Beverly Hills: Sage.

McAdoo, H. P. & McAdoo, J. L. (Eds.), (1985). *Black children: Social, educational and parental environments.* Beverly Hills: Sage.

McAdoo, J. L., (1985). Racial attitudes of Black pre-school children: Approaches to modification. In H. P. McAdoo & J. L. McAdoo (Eds.), *Black children: Social, educational and parental environments.* Beverly Hills: Sage.

Mead, G. H., (1934). *Mind, self and society.* Chicago: University of Chicago Press.

Nobles, W. W., (1972, 1980). African philosophy: Foundations for black psychology. In R.L. Jones (Ed.), *Black Psychology.* New York: Harper & Row.

Nobles, W. W., (1978). Toward an empirical and theoretical framework for defining black families. *Journal of Marriage and Family, 40,* 679-687.

Nobles, W. W., (1976a). Extended self: Rethinking the so-called Negro self-concept. *Journal of Black Psychology, 2* (2), 15-24.

Nobles, W. W., (1976b). African science: The consciousness of self. In L. M. King et al (Ed.), *African philosophy: Assumptions and paradigms for research on black persons.* Los Angeles: Fanon R & D Center.

Nobles, W. W., (1976c). Black people in white insanity: An issue for black community mental health. *Journal of Afro-American Issues, 4,* 21-27.

Nobles, W. W., (1974). African root and American fruit: The black family. *Journal of Social and Behavioral Sciences, 20,* 66-77.

Nobles, W. W., (1973). Psychological research and the black self-concept: A critical review. *Journal of Social Issues, 29,* 11-31.

Nobles, W. W. (Forthcoming). African consciousness and liberation struggles: Implications for the development and construction of scientific paradigms. In N. Akbar & J. Baldwin (Eds.) *Back to the source: Introduction to African psychology.* Los Angeles: University of Sankore Press.

Ogletree, K., (1976). Internal-external control in black and white. *Black Books Bulletin, 4* (3), 26-31.

Parham, T. A & Helms, J. E., (1985). Attitudes of racial identity and self-esteem of black students: An exploratory investigation. *Journal of College Student Personnel,* 143-147.

Porter, J. R. & Washington, R. E., (1979). Black identity and self-esteem: A review of studies of black self-concept, 1968-1978. *Annual Reviews of Sociology, 5,* 53-74.

Sattler, J. M., (1973). Racial experimenter effects. In K. S. Miller & R. M. Dreger (Eds.), *Comparative studies of blacks and whites in the United States.* New York: Seminar.

Semaj, L., (1980). The development of racial evaluation and preference: A cognitive approach. *Journal of Black Psychology, 6* (2), 59-79.

Smith, W. D., (1980). The Black self-concept: Some historical and theoretical reflections. *Journal of Black Studies, 10* (3), 355-366.

Spencer, M. B., (1984). Black children's race awareness, racial attitudes and self-concept: A reinterpretation. *Journal of Child Psychology and Psychiatry, 25* (3), 433-441.

Spencer, M. B., (1982a). Personal and group identity of black children: An alternative synthesis. *Genetic Psychology Monograph, 106,* 59-84.

Spencer, M. B., (1982b). Preschool children's social cognition and cultural cognition: A developmental interpretation of race dissonance findings. *Journal of Psychology, 112,* 275-286.

Welsing, F., (1981). The concept and the color of God and black mental health. *Black Books Bulletin, 7* (1), 27-29, 35.

White, J. L., (1984). *The psychology of blacks.* Englewood Cliffs, N. J.: Prentice-Hall.

Wilkinson, D., (1980). Play objects as tools of propaganda: Characterizations of the African-American male. *Journal of Black Psychology, 7* (1), 1-16.

Wilkinson, D., (1974). Racial socialization through children's toys: A socio-historical examination. *Journal of Black Studies, 5,* 96-109.

Williams, C., (1976). *The destruction of black civilization.* Revised edition. Chicago: Third World Press.

Williams, R. L., (1981). *The collective black mind: An Afrocentric theory of black personality.* St. Louis: Williams & Associates.

Delayed Gratification in Blacks

Wanda E. Ward, W. Curtis Banks and Sheri Wilson

Introduction

In the study of self-regulation, considerable attention has been paid to psychological constructs such as delay of gratification. Mischel (1974) proposed a two-staged process in the delay of gratification. The first stage focuses on the determinants (e.g., expectancies) of one's choice to delay and the second stage focuses on factors that facilitate delay behavior (e.g., desired rewards are not visibly present; cognitive representations and ideational activity which distract a subject from the consummatory qualities of the reward he/she is awaiting). While much of the recent research has focused on the second stage of the process (see Mischel, 1986), it is additionally useful to continue to examine research done on the choice to delay and the type of delay chosen. For example, early research in this area studied racial and class differences in delay behavior. As we will demonstrate below, it is important to examine carefully such reports in terms of their accuracy in characterizing black populations.

In addition to the theoretical and empirical issues that warrant further investigation in the study of delay of gratification among blacks, certain broader socio-political issues that potentially impact the experimental investigation of this topic warrant consideration. For example, throughout the long and arduous struggle for freedom and equal opportunity, blacks in this country and abroad have demonstrated persuasively and in very real-life and practical ways their ability to forego immediate gains of lesser value in favor of more highly prized, but distant goals (e.g., in the form of boycotts). The intriguing research issue this raises is the need to investigate the choice by massive numbers of *individuals* to delay gratification for the sake of greater but more temporally remote gains to the benefit of not only the individual, but one's ethnic/racial *group* as a whole. One might construct a taxonomy of delay behavior on the basis of personal and ideological aspects of the choice to delay (e.g., similar to the distinction made by Gurin, Gurin, Lao, and Beattie, 1969, in their work on locus of control). An important prelude to such investigations, however, is an assessment of the status of the evidence on delay of gratification among blacks. Therefore, in this paper we describe the basic construct and paradigm, and provide an updated review of the research on this topic.

Delay of Gratification: Construct and Methodology

The Construct   Banks, McQuater, Ross, and Ward (1983) stated that delay of gratification has been conceptualized to be the ability to forego immediate opportunities to satisfy impulses in favor of alternative opportunities that usually are both of greater value, but more temporally remote. The ability to delay is thought to distinguish two groups of individuals: those who succeed and prosper by hard work, thrift, and self-control (i.e., delayers) versus those who yield to the enticement of short-term gains and impulsivity.

A number of analyses of this construct have been performed, including those of: a) class differences in sociopsychological functioning (Davis & Dollard, 1940; Drake & Cayton, 1945; Schneider & Lysgaard, 1953); b) cultural differences that distinguish national groups (Mischel, 1961b); and c) race differences in personality characteristics (Lessing, 1969; Mischel, 1958; Price-Williams & Ramirez, 1974; Strickland, 1972). More recent studies have been conducted to validate the earlier, more impressionistic views about the inability to delay gratification among blacks. Toward that end, experimental research has been directed at establishing the relationship of immediate gratification preferences to academic success (Lessing, 1969), achievement motivation (Mischel, 1961a), social responsibility (Mischel, 1961a, 1961c), and psychopathology (Unikel & Blanchard, 1973) among blacks. Furthermore, some theorists (e.g., Rainwater, 1970) have even surmised that an "orientation toward immediate gratification (p. 230) is a result of a sense of impotence, unstable interpersonal relationships, and a disinclination to think about the future" (see also Pettigrew, 1964). Much of this line of reasoning is related directly to the empirical literature concerning father-absence (Mischel, 1958; 1961b), trust (Price-Williams & Ramirez, 1974; Seagull, 1966; Strickland, 1972), locus of control (Strickland, 1972; Zytkoskee, Strickland, & Watson, 1971), and conceptions of time (Mischel, 1961c).

Typical Methodology   The standard paradigm employed in the study of delay of gratification was devised by Mischel (1958) as a means of investigating the phenomenon experimentally. Mischel's research began with the study of black populations in the Caribbean, research which suggested to him the existence of a distinct tendency in Trinidadian blacks toward immediate gratification (see Mischel, 1971) in contrast to the postponed gratification and self-deprivation characteristics of the East Indian population. The basic paradigm consists of presenting subjects with the choice between two alternative rewards for their participation in an experiment. Typically, subjects choose between a small reward to be presented immediately by the experimenter or a larger, more valued reward to be presented at a later point in time by the experimenter. For example, Mischel (1958) offered the alternative of a one-cent candy immediately or a ten-cent candy after one week. Most investigations in this area employ the actual reward choice and/or hypothetical inquiries.

Review of the Body of Evidence on Delay of Gratification in Blacks

It is noteworthy that past reviews have devoted little critical attention to the evidence on delay of gratification reported on black populations (see Mischel, 1966; Renner, 1964). Banks et al. demonstrated the marked contrast between the actual data and the inferences drawn by theorists from past research, as well as their conjectures about "a preference for smaller, immediate rewards" among blacks (Mischel, 1966, p. 125). In fact, the accumulated evidence largely refutes rather than supports the construct validity of immediate gratification preference among blacks and, with minor exceptions, the evidence fails to even substantiate that such a preference characterizes the behavior of that population.

Specifically, we have found that: 1) five investigations reviewed showed black samples as either entirely or primarily nonpreferential toward the delay of gratification, and four studies contained subsamples responding in the same manner; 2) six studies revealed either entire samples or subsamples reflecting a pattern of preference for delayed gratification among American, Trinidadian, and Grenadian blacks; and 3) only four investigations within the experimental research literature supported the notion that primarily relatively limited subsamples of blacks exhibit immediate reward preferences.

Nonpreferential Delay of Gratification

In his initial examination of delay behavior, Mischel (1958) presented 35 black male and female 7-to-9 year-olds and a comparative sample of 18 East Indian children the choice between a one-cent candy immediately and a ten-cent candy after one week. The results were as follows: 37% of the black sample chose the larger, delayed reward alternative, while 63% chose the smaller, immediate one. In contrast, 67% of the East Indian children selected the larger, delayed reward, while 33% chose the smaller, immediate one. In an absolute sense, neither of these choice patterns could be characterized as preferential. That is, by statistical (z) test, blacks would have had to choose the smaller, immediate reward at a rate of a least 66% to reject the null hypothesis of chance (p = .05) selection of that reward. Similarly, the sample of 18 East Indian subjects would have had to choose the larger, delayed reward at a rate exceeding 70% that alternative.

In a subsequent study of a sample of black Trinidadians (Mischel, 1961a), based on their responses subjects were assigned to one of three groups: (1) consistent delay [three delay responses], (2) inconsistent delay [one or two delay responses], or (3) consistent immediate [zero delay responses]. Combining those who made two or three delay responses, 49% of the subjects can be described to have made delay responses. Using those who made either one or no delay responses, such combined immediate groups totaled 51% of the overall sample. Even if one considered the consistent delay (n = 37) and the consistent immediate (n = 30) groups only, the dichotomy of choice would be 55% and 45%, respectively, rates which again fail to deviate significantly from chance, although they are in the direction of preference for the larger, delayed alternative. The rates do not deviate significantly from chance.

Our analysis also revealed nonpreferential response patterns in studies of black fourth graders in a midwestern city (Herzberger & Dweck, 1978), black delinquents classified as psychopathic versus those classified as nonpsychopathic (Unikel & Blanchard, 1973), black Trinidadian children (in a study of Trinidadian and Grenadian children) (Mischel, 1961b), Trinidadian delinquents (Mischel, 1961c), black third graders in the Northeastern United States (Seagull, 1966), and lower and middle class boys and girls ages 7-11 (Freire, Gorman, & Wessman, 1980).

Preference for Delayed Gratification

In the earlier cited Mischel (1961b) study of Trinidadian and Grenadian children, although the Trinidadian black sample conformed to chance, the Grenadian black sample displayed delay behavior: 24% chose the smaller immediate reward while 76% preferred the larger, delayed reward, a statistically significant difference.

Also, in the earlier cited Mischel (1961c) study of the relationship between immediate preference and delinquency, within the overall sample of 206 Trinidadian black children, 68% selected the twenty-five-cent candy to be received in a week rather than the immediately available five-cent candy (32%). (This pattern of preference for the larger delayed reward was statistically significant at the .05 level). A similar significant preference for the delayed reward was found for the nondelinquent subsample.

Preference for delayed gratification was found in studies by Lessing (1969) (who devised seven hypothetical items that pertained to choice situations [e.g., "If wearing ugly braces would make my teeth look prettier later on, I would put up with looking awful for a year or two"]), Seagull (1966), and Price-Williams and Ramirez (1974).

Pattern of Preference for Immediate Gratification

We have presented evidence revealing nonpreferential as well as delayed gratification patterns. Mischel (1958) found that his entire, although small, subsample of Trinidadian black children who reported their fathers as not living at home chose the immediate reward alternative. Also, he reported in a later study (1961b) that a subsample of "father-absent" Trinidadian blacks preferred the smaller, immediate reward at a rate (74%) which exceeded chance. The interpretation offered by Mischel in both of these instances was that of trust. He asserted that father-absence may have undermined these children's confidence in any promises made by authority figures. Continuing in this line of reasoning, Strickland (1972) investigated the effects of the promise-maker's race and found that black children in her sample preferred the immediate reward (67%) in a white experimenter condition.

Based on Mischel's (1974) earlier mentioned two-staged model of an individual's tendency to delay gratification, Greenberg and Holmes (1978) studied the effects of the experimenter's race and sex and the visual presence or absence of rewards on black children's preference for larger, delayed versus smaller, immediate rewards. Greenberg and Holmes hypothesized that children would view the actions of a reward agent who was racially dissimilar from themselves with less confidence and would experience different ideational activity concerning the rewards than they would with a racially similar reward agent. Specifically, they proposed that a delay period may be highly frustrating for black children who are tested by a racially dissimilar reward agent because of the perceived uncertainty of receiving the reward, and that the already frustrating situation may be exacerbated further by the absence of rewards. On the other hand, they proposed, when the reward agent is racially similar to the child, the presence of the reward ought to heighten the frustration of the delay period and thus inhibit delay behavior, a result consistent with that of Mischel and Ebbesen (1970).

Greenberg and Holmes found that black males in their study

showed: 1) significantly greater delay preference with a black versus white experimenter, 2) significantly greater delay preference with a male versus a female experimenter, and 3) contrary to the repeated finding of Mischel and colleagues, greater delay with rewards present rather than absent. Greenberg and Holmes pointed out, however, through further examination of some of the findings, that when the experimenter was white and female, the absence of rewards inhibited rather than facilitated the preference for delayed rewards. They suggested that when the reward agent is racially and sexually dissimilar to the individual, the presence of rewards may actually reassure the subject that the rewards will be delivered rather than increase the frustration of the delay period. Finally, they suggested that an important contribution of such research is the demonstration of the specificity or discriminativeness of the preference for delayed rewards.

Looking at the broader picture of delay of gratification among blacks, it is clear that most of the evidence, contrary to prior conjectures, demonstrates a pattern of nonpreference for either smaller, immediate or larger delayed rewards. Nonetheless, more of the available evidence reviewed indicates preference for delayed gratification than does that which demonstrates immediate gratification preference. We have considered that one possible interpretation of the overall results is that, in fact, some blacks may prefer immediate rewards some of the time, and that the aggregate trend of chance- like responding veils a truly consistent response pattern in two distinct preference groups. Although the bulk of the evidence indicating immediate preference in blacks pertains to the father-absence (or trust) construct, other research efforts also address this general line of reasoning. Some of that evidence is reviewed in the following sections.

Trust and father-absence   In one of the earliest experimental studies, Mahrer (1956) examined the hypothesis that acquired expectancies determine an individual's willingness to forego immediate rewards in favor of postponed alternatives. Accordingly, Mahrer presented lower socioeconomic children with experimentally manipulated experiences of fulfilled and unfulfilled promises of delayed reinforcements. In subsequent trials, those children subjected to expectancy disconfirmations chose the delayed rewards less often than children who had experienced confirmation of expected rewards. Moreover, the effect of experimentally controlled trust was highly specific to the identity of the agent of past experience. That is, acquired expectancies were specific to the agent from whom they were learned; disconfirmed expectancies in the context of one agent did not affect later delayed reward choices in the context of a new agent.

Precisely what identifying characteristics of agents serve to establish the specificity or generality of acquired expectancies is not clear. Studies by Mischel (1958, 1961b), Mahrer (1956), Strickland (1972), Price-Williams and Ramirez (1974), and Seagull (1966) have explored this matter in detail.

A reasonable conclusion from a diverse literature is that, although specific experiences may have significant potential for shaping expectancies and resultant behaviors, blacks may show a certain resilience which defies the generalization of effects. For example, Seagull (1966) reported that an experimental manipulation of trust, similar to that of Mahrer's (1956), significantly affected preferences for immediate and delayed rewards among black third-graders. However, he also observed a recurring pattern of delaying behavior in "lower working class . . . Negro children who are overly trusting even in the face of repeated disconfirmation" (p. 350), prompting him to conclude that "delay choice was a situationally determined variable," often defying "consistently broken promises" (p. 351) in that population.

Social responsibility Early experimental research also sought to establish the inability to delay gratification as a factor in social deviance. Mischel (1961c) compared juvenile delinquents with controls from a population of Trinidadian blacks. He reported that a significantly larger proportion of delinquents than of controls selected a five-cent candy to be received immediately. However, the proportion of juvenile delinquents choosing the smaller, immediate reward was actually smaller than the proportion choosing the larger, delayed alternative, although both proportions conformed to chance for that group. Furthermore, juvenile delinquents who chose the immediate reward were undifferentiated on Harris' (1957) measure of social responsibility from juvenile delinquents who chose the delayed reward. Finally, when reward choices were combined with verbal responses to two hypothetical queries, the resultant pattern of "delay" responses permitted the classification of "consistent delayers" and "consistent nondelayers." Only these extreme subgroups of the juvenile delinquent sample were different on the Harris measure.

In a similar investigation of lower and lower-middle class black Trinidadian children (Mischel, 1961a), those children who gave 2 or 3 delay responses had higher social responsibility scores than those who gave 0 to 1 delay responses.

As mentioned earlier, however, Unikel and Blanchard (1973) failed to find any significant differences in delayed reward choice between black delinquents classified as psychopathic and those classified as nonpsychopathic. This finding is in direct contrast with the hypothesis that social responsibility among blacks is related to delay behavior.

Achievement   Early theorists argued that the ability to delay gratification is a critical factor in distinguishing those who persevere in hard work toward valuable long-range goals. Mischel (1961a) hypothesized that achievement motivation, as measured by fantasy expressions (McClelland, Atkinson, Clark, & Lowell, 1953) is a central aspect of the personality of socioeconomically and academically successful persons, and that the construct validity of delayed reward choices should be reflected in a positive association between that behavior and *n* Achievement. He predicted that individuals who are high in delayed reward preference would be those who "have learned to like work" (p. 544), and, in turn, are those who are high in *n* Achievement. He found a moderate correlation (.27) between the number of delayed choices and *n* achievement scores in a sample of black Trinidadian 11- to 14-year-olds.Whether such an association establishes the validity of delayed-reward choices as a construct implicated in actual academic and economic success is quite another matter, one which is empirically testable. Considerable argument has been advanced against the ability of the *n* Achievement measurement itself to predict achievement outcomes for blacks or distinguish them from other customarily successful populations in American society (e.g. Katz, 1967).

Locus of control and acquiescence   Another way research has attempted to establish the validity of immediate gratification preference in blacks is through its association with the locus of control and acquiescence constructs. Mischel (1961a) hypothesized that preference for immediate reward would be positively related to acquiescence in blacks. Lessing (1969), Strickland (1972), and Zytokoskee, Strickland, and Watson (1971) hypothesized that such preferences would be positively related to an external locus of control, or a sense of powerlessness in blacks.

Mischel asked his sample of black Trinidadian youngsters to imagine that he (Mischel) was thinking of something with which they might agree or disagree. Without their actually knowing exactly what he was thinking, subjects were asked to indicate whether they believed they would agree (by indicating yes) or disagree (indicating no). Those children who were high in delayed-reward choices more often indicated disagreement than children who were high in immediate reward choices. The validity of this measure of acquiescence, however, was unsubstantiated.

In a series of studies that employed a more generally validated measure, Strickland and her associates have found no association in blacks between external locus of control and preference for immediate rewards. The locus of control scores in the Nowicki-Strickland 40-item instrument were virtually identical for black 11- to 13-year-olds choosing immediate or choosing delayed rewards (Strickland and Mowicki, 1971). Similarly, Zytkoskee, Strickland, and Watson (1971) found no significant correlation between the Bialer Locus of Control Scale (Bialer, 1961) and their five-item measure of immediate- versus delayed-reward preference in a sample of black ninth-graders. Furthermore, Lessing (1969) found that blacks were significantly differentiated by a measure of locus of control, but they were not differentiated by a measure of delayed gratification preference.

Despite the characterization offered of blacks in much of the published literature (Mischel, 1971; Pettigrew, 1964; Rainwater, 1970), experimental data largely represent blacks either as preferring delayed gratification or as indifferent toward immediate versus delayed rewards. The meaning of such a characterization is not immediately apparent. The overall picture of the correspondent evidence also indicates the equivocal status of research on delayed gratification in blacks. Preference for immediate rewards has occasionally distinguished black children of father-absent homes from those of father- present homes (Mischel, 1958). More often it has not (Mischel, 1961b). This failure of father-absence to consistently distinguish delayed gratification preferences might rest largely with its rough approximation to the more specific variable of trust. Yet theorists have seldom been clear about precisely what cues evoke trust in blacks (cf. Price-Williams & Ramirez, 1974; Strickland, 1972; Greenberg & Holmes, 1978), or whether such sentiments, when aroused, play a significant role in the behavior of blacks in the real world (Seagull 1966). Mischel's findings suggested that the sex of a rewarding agent is sufficient to cue learned distrust; Strickland argued later that the agent's race was the critical feature; Price-Williams and Ramirez's results suggest that neither is necessary nor sufficient; and Greenberg and Holmes argued that sex, race and the presence or absence of rewards influence black children's tendency to delay gratification. Seagull strongly argued that for those most likely to feel distrust, it might not matter anyway.

Although blacks who prefer immediate rewards may be more acquiescent than others (Mischel, 1961a), they do not perceive themselves as less capable of controlling their reinforcement outcomes (Strickland, 1972; Zytkoskee, Strickland, & Watson, 1971). Indeed, some have found no relationship between locus of control and delay of gratification (Kinard, 1979). Blacks may display less achievement in their fantasy expressions (Mischel, 1961a), but it is not clear whether such expressions distinguish them from high achievers (Katz, 1967) or whether such gratification preferences influence their actual success (see, for example, Lessing, 1969; Tracey & Sedlacek, 1984, 1985). With respect to social responsibility, it is paradoxical that the same characteristic that distinguishes between normal and juvenile delinquent youngsters (Mischel, 1961c) fails to distinguish individual differences in either measured social responsibility attitudes (Mischel, 1961c) or psychopathology (Unikel & Blanchard, 1973) within delinquent populations.

Conclusion

Further comments are in order concerning the delay of gratification construct, not only as it pertains to blacks, but the nature of the construct as a whole. It is clear that inherent in early theorizing about this phenomenon was the belief that the ability to forego immediate, smaller gratification for larger, delayed gratification reflected healthy, adaptive psychological functioning and that such ability distinguished the successful members of society (e.g., through fortitude, etc.) from the more unsuccessful ones who succumbed to impulsivity and more immediate gains. These early trait approaches received less attention as state approaches gained more momentum in the field. Throughout the discussion of delay of gratification in this paper, mention has been made of the importance of considering situational as well as personal influences (e.g., Greenberg and Holmes, 1978; see also Herzberger and Dweck, 1978).

This latter approach reflects the influence of Bem and Allen's (1974) argument that personal and situational effects are weighted differentially depending upon the given individual studied, and that therefore on any given dimension some individuals will be more cross-situationally consistent than others. Such a perspective suggests then that a needed direction of research in this area is the systematic identification and separation of consistent and inconsistent delayers and nondelayers of gratification (see Herzberger & Dweck, 1978; Mischel, 1974, 1986), so that researchers can gain a more comprehensive understanding of how this phenomenon operates.

Another issue that warrants fuller examination is the assumed functionality of delay behavior in general. The value of the ability to delay gratification under some circumstances is indisputable. However, the value of the indiscriminate disposition to do so raises some concern. Such a tendency can, in fact, be maladaptive to the circumstances at hand (e.g. see Mischel, 1974). It is interesting that there exist reports of shifts in behavior that reflect a relative lack of delayed gratification preferences in the real world. For example, in educational and business circles, some have noted an increase in the tendency of some of today's youth to forego a college experience as a means of achieving gainful employment for a more immediate, short-term gain through direct work experience. Such a tendency might reflect the belief that delayed behavior might not yield its assumed benefits after all. The point to be considered is that delay of gratification for the sake of delay may actually be dysfunctional, and researchers might explore avenues of investigation that help individuals distinguish when such behavior is functional and when it is not. As Mischel (1986) has pointed out, the issue is not delay of gratification per se, but the appropriateness of the delay behavior, i.e., when, how, and for what one ought to delay.

Final comments concern the paradigm used to study delay behavior. In addition to reviewing early theoretical discussions of delay of gratification and demonstrating the equivocal status of published evidence of this phenomenon in blacks, Banks et al. (1983) raised a fundamentally important issue concerning the basic paradigm typically employed to investigate this construct. Specifically, we pointed out that the paradigm in which a sensitivity to reward latency was to be inferred from choices between two available alternatives consisted of a confounding between reward latency and reward quantity. We noted then that the standard paradigm makes it impossible to distinguish preference for immediate alternatives from preference for small ones, or preference for delayed rewards from preference for large ones and, further, that a complete factorial design would have eliminated the problem. Moreover, individuals might feel indifference toward the available alternatives if the net values of small, immediate rewards and delayed, large rewards are conjectured to be equal. Recent research bears out this line of thinking (McQuater, 1980; Ward, 1976; Banks, McQuater, Pryor & Salter, 1976) as well as its implications for choice behavior across the full range of delay and quantity permutations.

Closely akin to this perspective of indifference toward available alternatives is recent research conducted by Thomas and Ward (in press; 1979). Exploring the relationship between temporal perspective and time-related behaviors, we have conceptualized temporal preference in some ways similar to the standard delay of gratification paradigm. That is, both approaches involve the choice between an immediately available smaller reward or a larger reward at a later time (despite legitimate concerns about a paradigm which confounds reward latency with reward quantity, such a paradigm reflects the realistic conflict that individuals face in many everyday situations). The uniqueness (both conceptually and methodologically) of Thomas and Ward's approach as compared to the standard approach, however, is that we assume that for most individuals there exists a point at which the individual is equally likely to choose either of the options.

In that work, we defined time orientation measures (i.e., focus and preoccupation), time preference measures (i.e., discount rate and inflation rate), and summaries of spending behavior (e.g., immediate value of commodities and impatience for the unavailability of a commodity). We applied two mathematical models to questionnaire data and found that persons with an orientation towards the near future had higher discount rates and higher immediate values than persons with a more distant future orientation. We argued that both discount rate and immediate value are inverse measures of a person's tendency to delay gratification. With this assumption, our results appeared consistent with earlier theorizing that a preference to delay is associated with a temporal focus on the distant future and a preoccupation with the future. (See Thomas & Ward, in press, for a full discussion of this work).

One strength of this approach is that it enhances our understanding of basic processes that influence time-related behaviors such as delay of gratification. Further investigation of this approach is needed, however. For example, in that initial study, we did not target blacks as subjects. Therefore further delineation is needed of how time preference operates within and between different racial groups. It is of interest, for example, to see if different ethnic or racial groups differ in important ways in their temporal preferences.

Author Note

Some of the preparation of this article was supported by a Summer Research Fellowship to the first author by the Office for Research Administration, University of Oklahoma.

References

Banks, W.C., McQuater, G.V., Pryor, J., & Salter, B. (1976). *The effect of reward amount, delay interval, and work on incentive value.* Unpublished manuscript.

Banks, W.C., McQuater, G.V., Ross, J.A., & Ward, W.E. (1983). Delayed gratification in blacks: A critical review. *Journal of Black Psychology, 9,* 43-56.

Bem, D.J., & Allen, A. (1974). On predicting some of the people some of the time: The search for cross-situational consistencies in behavior. *Psychological Review, 81,* 506-520.

Bialer, I. (1961). Conceptualization of success and failure in mentally retarded and normal children. *Journal of Personality, 29,* 303-320.

Davis, A., & Dollard, J. (1940). *Children of bondage.* Washington, DC: American Council on Education.

Drake, S., & Cayton, H.R. (1945). *Black metropolis.* New York: Harcourt Brace.

Freire, E., Gorman, B., & Wessman, A. (1980). Temporal span, delay of gratification, and children's socioeconomic status. *Journal of Genetic Psychology, 137,* 247-255.

Greenberg, M.S., & Holmes, R. (1978). Effect of experimenter's race, sex, and presence of rewards on delay preference of black males. *Social Behavior and Personality, 6,* 155-162.

Gurin, P., Gurin, G., Lao, R.C., & Beattie, M. (1969). Internal-external control in the motivational dynamics of Negro youth. *Journal of Social Issues, 25,* 29-53.

Harris, D.B. (1957). A scale for measuring attitudes of social responsibility in children. *Journal of Abnormal and Social Psychology, 55,* 322-326.

Herzberger, S.D., & Dweck, C.S. (1978). Attraction and delay of gratification. *Journal of Personality, 46,* 215-227.

Katz, I. (1967). The socialization of academic motivation in minority group children. In D. Levine (Ed.), *Nebraska symposium on motivation.* University of Nebraska Press, *15,* 133-191.

Kinard, J.A. (1979). Effect of race of experimenter, perceived outcome and locus of control on gratification preference of black grade-school children. *Dissertation Abstracts International, 37,* (9-B), 4618-B.

Lessing, E. (1969). Racial differences in indices of ego functioning relevant to academic achievement. *The Journal of Genetic Psychology, 115,* 153.

Mahrer, A. (1956). The role of expectancy in delayed reinforcement. *Journal of Experimental Psychology, 52,* 101-105.

McClelland, D.C., Atkinson, J.W., Clark, R.A., & Lowell, E.L. (1953). *The achievement motive.* New York: Appleton-Century-Crofts.

McQuater, G.V. (1980). Delay of gratification: A theoretical and methodological address. Doctoral dissertation. Princeton University. *Dissertation Abstracts International.* Sept.-Oct., *42-03,* 1162B. (University Microfilms No. 80-1866-4).

Mischel, W. (1958). Preference for delayed reinforcement: An experimental study of a cultural observation. *Journal of Abnormal Social Psychology, 56,* 57-61.

Mischel, W. (1961a). Delay of gratification, need for achievement, and acquiescence in another culture. *Journal of Abnormal and Social Psychology, 63*(3), 543-552.

Mischel, W. (1961b). Father-absence and delay of gratification: Cultural comparisons. *Journal of Abnormal and Social Psychology, 63*(1), 116-124.

Mischel, W. (1961c). Preference for delayed reinforcement and social responsibility. *Journal of Abnormal and Social Psychology, 62,* 1-7.

Mischel, W. (1966). Theory and research on the antecedents of self-imposed delay of reward. In B.A. Maher (Ed.), *Progress in Experimental Personality Research, 3.* New York: Academic Press.

Mischel, W. (1971). *Introduction to personality.* New York: Holt, Rinehart & Winston.

Mischel, W. (1974). Processes in delay of gratification. In L. Berkowitz (Ed.), *Advances in experimental social psychology* Vol. 7. New York: Academic Press.

Mischel, W. (1986). *Introduction to personality: A new look.* New York: Holt, Rinehart & Winston.

Mischel, W. & Ebbesen, E.B. (1970). Attention in delay of gratification. *Journal of Personality and Social Psychology, 16,* 329-337.

Pettigrew, T.F. (1964). *A profile of the Negro American.* New York: Van Nostrand.

Price-Williams, D.R., & Ramirez, M. (1974). Ethnic differences in delay of gratification. *Journal of Social Psychology, 93,* 23-30.

Rainwater, L. (1970). *Behind ghetto walls: Black family life in a federal slum.* Chicago: Aldine Publishing Company.

Renner, K.E. (1964). Delay of reinforcement: A historical review. *Psychological Bulletin, 61,* 341-361.

Seagull, A.A. (1966). Subpatterns of gratification choice within samples of Negro and white children. *Papers of the Michigan Academy of Science, Arts, and Letters, 51*(2), 345-351.

Schneider, L., & Lysgaard, S. (1953). The deferred gratification pattern: A preliminary study. *American Sociological Review, 18,* 142-149.

Strickland, B.R. (1972). Delay of gratification as a function of race of the experimenter. *Journal of Personality and Social Psychology, 22*(1), 108-112.

Strickland, B.R., & Nowicki, S. (1971, September). *Behavior correlates of the Nowicki-Strickland locus of control for children.* Paper presented at the Annual Convention of the American Psychological Association, Washington, DC.

Thomas, E.A.C., Ward, W.E. (In press). Temporal preferences: Future directions for study of time related behaviors. In R.L. Jones (Ed.). *Advances in Black Psychology,* Berkeley, CA: Cobb & Henry.

Tracey, T.J., & Sedlacek, W.E. (1984). Noncognitive variables in predicting academic success by race. *Measurement and Evaluation in Guidance, 16,* 171-178.

Tracey, T.J., & Sedlacek, W.E. (1985). The relationship of noncognitive variables to academic success: A longitudinal comparison by race. *Journal of College Student Personnel, 26,* 405-410.

Unikel, I.P., & Blanchard, E.B. (1973). Psychopathy, race, and delay of gratification by adolescent delinquents. *Journal of Nervous and Mental Disease, 156*(1), 57-60.

Ward, W.E. (1976). *The use of internal-external locus of control and delay of gratification constructs in explaining black behavior.* Unpublished senior thesis, Princeton University.

Ward, W.E., & Thomas, E.A.C. (1979, April). *Time orientation, optimism and quasi-economic behavior.* Paper presented at the Western Psychological Association Conference, San Diego.

Zytkoskee, A., Strickland, B.R., & Watson, J. (1971). Delay of gratification and internal versus external control among adolescents of low socio-economic status. *Developmental Psychology, 4*(1, Pt. 1), 93-98.

Are Blacks External: On the Status of Locus of Control in Black Populations

W. Curtis Banks, Wanda E. Ward, Gregory V. McQuater, and Ann Marie DeBritto

In their report on educational opportunity in the United States, Coleman and his associates (1966) identified the black child's sense of powerlessness as the construct most significantly related to academic failure. With the simultaneous emergence of the construct of locus of control, and its extension beyond white standardization samples into the domain of black and other minority populations, externality and sense of powerlessness have become synonymous as a relatively stable feature of personality (Gore & Rotter, 1963) which characterize many of the unsuccessful and disadvantaged in our society (Lefcourt, 1972).

While still other concepts have come to be part of the scientific lexicon which relates this characteristic to blacks, and while a proliferation of instruments directed at its reliable measurement have swelled the literature, the fundamental meaning of the construct has remained surprisingly explicit and univocal. Certain individuals are characterized by a belief or expectancy that significant reinforcements in their experiences are determined by factors which lie outside their own behavior or their capacity for control (external locus of control). Patterson (1973) has argued that this deterministic orientation in blacks underlies a moral inferiority which impedes their success, enhances a sense of low self-concept, discourages hard work, and fosters political apathy. Moreover, a considerable body of research has subjected these and related hypotheses to systematic empirical examination, with results that have been admittedly inconclusive (see, e.g., Lefcourt, 1972).

Like some other prominent psychological constructs and paradigms, the constructs of externality and sense-of-powerlessness have failed to predict consistently, concur with, and discriminate, logically related aspects of personality and social behavior in blacks. This failure has consequently led to a preoccupation with problems of the validity of such traits. These considerations seem premature in light of a more fundamental recognition that there is no solid evidence that blacks possess the traits.

A detailed inspection of most measures of the locus of control construct strengthen our challenge of the entire approach. Most measures of the construct consist of some variation of a forced-choice verbal response instrument. Subjects are presented with statements in written or oral form which express an assessment of some familiar situation as indicative of causal influences which are under the willful control of the actor or outside the actor's sphere of influence (the larger social system, powerful others, or fate/chance). In response to each pair of statements, individuals select one with which they agree more. When all such forced choices made in the criterion (external or internal) direction are summed, the score yielded represents a point somewhere on the range of possible response preferences.

The character of the construct of locus of control and the measures by which it is assessed yield three possible categories into which the status of any individual or group may fit. First, the pattern of response may be characterized as internal, or the predominant belief in the capacity of individuals to influence their own reinforcement experiences. Scoring in this category is characterized by a significant deviation from the midpoint of the possible total range, in the internal direction of the measure. Second, the pattern of response may be external, or the predominant belief that causal factors outside the control of the individuals are determinants of their reinforcement experiences. Likewise, external scoring is characterized by significant departure from the midpoint of the possible total distribution of scores, in the external direction of the measure. Third is the pattern of responses which defies characterization as either predominantly internal or predominantly external, since the scores lie close to the midpoint of the measure.

Initial validation research indicated that whites are characterized by internality, since their response tendencies significantly departed from chance, in the direction of belief in internal control. On the other hand, the literature for blacks has suggested quite a different pattern. But a systematic review of the data from that literature yields results which stand in marked contrast to the conventional assumption of external locus of control in blacks.

The most striking aspect of the accumulated evidence is its categorical failure to establish external locus of control as characteristic of blacks. Of the 39 investigations reviewed which report scores for blacks, only 1 was found in which the overall mean of the scores differed from the midpoint of the scales in the external direction. Moreover, there were only a very few studies in which the several separate means reported differed from the midpoint in the external direction.

Internality in Blacks

The majority of the empirical evidence establishes internal responding as predominantly characteristic of the locus of control orientation of blacks. Twenty-two investigations were found to have reported patterns of response clearly within the internal range of various measures of locus of control, 17 with sufficient data to establish that trend as statistically reliable.

Coleman and his associates (1966), in their classic study of educational opportunity, reported the responses of black school children to three locus of control items: "Every time I try to get ahead something or somebody stops me"; "People like me don't have much of a chance to be successful in life"; "Good luck is more important than hard work for success." Subjects from three nonmetropolitan and five metropolitan regions were asked to indicate their agreement, disagreement, or uncertainty in response to each of the above. Results were reported as the percent of subjects responding in each category.

In the case of each query, what Coleman et al. referred to as a "high" rate of "low control" (i.e., external) responses among blacks represented less than 25% of the responding black subjects. Twenty-two percent overall reported agreement with the statement that something or someone impedes their progress. Fully 33% indicated either uncertainty or no response to the statement. The largest single proportion of subjects responded with disagreement (45%).

Moreover, in response to the statement that "People like me don't . . . (succeed)," blacks disagreed 58% of the time. They agreed with that statement only 12% of the time. In fact, the rate of disagreement was significantly greater than would be expected by chance. Similarly, blacks overwhelmingly disagreed with the statement that luck is more important than hard work (63%); while 12% agreed with that statement, 25% either expressed uncertainty or no response.

Clearly, then, there was no instance in which the rate of agreement even approached a substantial minority of respondents, while in all instances it fell below that of "neutral" responding. The clear majority of responses was, in fact, in the internal, or "high" control direction.

Our analysis of data from numerous other studies support a black internal locus of control orientation include Gore and Rotter, 1963 (black undergraduate students, in a southern black university); Battle and Rotter, 1963 (black middle school children in the midwest); Epstein and Komorita, 1971 (black males ages 10-13; Garrahan, 1974 (black undergraduate students in a compensatory education program in an eastern university).

Our examination of additional investigations which used a variety of locus of control measures have typically yielded similar results.

Internality in black studies examined include Buck and Austrin, 1971 (black children ages 14-16 in a midwestern city); Strickland, 1965 (politically active and politically non- active black students); Garcia and Levenson, 1975 (black college students); Rabinowitz, 1978 (sixth grade black children); Brown, Fulkerson, Furr, Ware & Voight, 1984 (third to sixth grade black and white boys and girls; also see, Ward 1986 for a detailed review of this work); and Riordan, 1981 (black, colored, and white South African boys and girls). Internal responding by blacks was also found in Berzins and Ross, 1973; Cross and Tracy, 1971; Garrett and Willoughby, 1972; Gruen, Korte and Baum, 1974; Gutkin, 1978; Lessing, 1969; Stephan and Kennedy, 1975; Valecha and Ostrom, 1974; Will and Verdin, 1978; Williams and Stack, 1972.

Neutral Responding

Three investigations do establish that externality may occur in some blacks, at least some of the time. For example, Orpen (1971) translated Rotter's 23-item locus of control scale for a sample of African adults in the Republic of South Africa. The black subjects were clerks and manual workers, classified racially as "Colored." Of the total sample, the mean for the 51 subjects who worked as clerks is significantly different from the midpoint, in the external direction. However, the 62 subjects in the manual workers' group showed a mean score which is not different from the neutral midpoint. In fact, taken together, the combined sample means would not allow a rejection of the null hypothesis of neutral responding to the Rotter scale for this African population.

Harris and Phelan (1973) studied black teenagers (16-18 years old) in the Los Angeles, California area schools. Their sample consisted of 28 students attending schools in which the population was 75% white (integrated) and 27 students attending schools in which the population was less than 1% white (segregated). Integrated children had a mean score significantly above the midpoint, in the external direction. However, the segregated black children were internal, with a mean score which is significantly below the midpoint.

This inconsistency across subgroups of subjects dissuades any uniform characterization of blacks as a population, but it seems unsurprising for a trait characteristic which is expected to discriminate among individual differences. A trait theoretical analysis, however, would not predict differences within black individuals to be demonstrated across time. Yet, Leon (1974), in a sample of 87 (mostly black) minority college students, found significantly different scores for the Rotter scale when administered in separate Fall and Spring semesters. Subjects in the Fall were found to be significantly external while the same subjects were found to be internal in the Spring.

In this light, it is not surprising that the net pattern of responding in so many investigations seems largely neutral in character. The total sample of scores in Leon's study and in Harris and Phelan's investigation each conforms to the midpoint of Rotter's measure of locus of control, in much the same way as does the overall Orpen sample. Indeed, a number of the studies reviewed yield evidence of this status, including Naditch, 1974 (black adults); Segal and DuCette, 1973 (black high school-aged females); Scott and Phelan, 1969 (black adults); Pedhazur and Wheeler, 1971 ("minority" sixth graders); Furnham and Henry, 1980 (African, Indian and South African nurses); and Maqsud, 1980 (Nigerian secondary school students); DuCette and Volk, 1972; Felton and Biggs, 1972; and Levenson, 1974.

In a progressive line of research examining the multidimensionality of locus of control, Gurin and colleagues (Gurin, Gurin, Lao, & Beattie, 1969; Gurin, Gurin, & Morrison, 1978) have stressed the importance of distinguishing between personal control and control ideology. In a sample of 1297 subjects, 53 of whom were black males and 84 of whom were black females, Gurin et al. (1978) reported that personal control only was related to higher socioeconomic status and to efficacious efforts in areas of personal life where individual effort can have some impact. Regarding political behavior among groups that challenge the status quo, the researchers reported that personal control was unrelated to political behavior, whereas external control ideology was related to greater political participation.

However, among political conservatives, Rotter's unidimensional conception was borne out in that internality on both personal control and control ideology was related to greater political participation. Gurin et al. (1978) confirmed their hypotheses that race and sex differences would obtain on the personal control dimension, but not on the control ideology dimension; namely, they found that white men expressed a greater degree of personal control than any other group studied, presumably because they have faced relatively fewer external obstacles to controlling their own lives. Examination of blacks' absolute I-E scores reveal, however, that they fell in the neutral or internal region of the scale.

Externality in Blacks

One study reviewed did indicate an overall external pattern of responding. In an investigation of the relationship of locus of control, self-concept, and masculinity-femininity to fear of success in black freshmen and senior college women, Savage, Stearns, and Friedman (1979) administered the Gurin Multidimensional Internal-External Locus of Control Scale (Gurin, Gurin, Lao, & Beattie, 1969) to 50 black female undergraduates (24 seniors and 26 freshmen). The mean locus of control score for this sample differed significantly from the scale's midpoint, in the direction of externality.

Conclusion

With respect to the status of black populations, there are three possible fundamental patterns of the evidence on locus of control. Blacks may be largely internal, largely external, or largely neither. These categories are not exclusive, and neither are they as discrete as an idealized typological system. However, the evidence is clear, especially in one respect: blacks have not been shown to be external. In fact, more than half of the explicit evidence reported for black samples indicates a clear internal pattern of responding. Roughly 45% of the published data fail to establish blacks as either internal or external.

On the face of it, these findings are not surprising. However, these findings stand in sharp contrast to conventional conceptions. At least one reason for this is readily apparent: the reports of the findings within the published literature are inconsistent with the findings themselves. Forty-seven percent of the investigations reviewed here refer narratively to blacks either as external or as more external than whites and others (e.g., Coleman et al., 1966; Epstein & Komorita, 1971; Lefcourt & Ladwig, 1965; Jacobson, 1972). Although nearly 60% of the studies reveal clearly internal data for blacks, only 20% refer to blacks as either internal or as simply less internal than whites and others. In one sense, it seems an almost trivial semantic question whether blacks are described as more external or less internal than whites within the largely comparative research paradigms employed in this area. But such a trivial decision would not be expected so often to be made in one direction. In 14 cases where the option clearly existed, 12 resulted in a "more external" characterization, only two resulted in the "less internal" alternative. What makes this choice of words the more curious is that comparatively whites are virtually never external. So how may blacks be more so?

Coleman and his associates, for example, reported that black children in their national sample made low control responses in some cases at twice or even three times the rate as did white children. They then referred to the rates of such responses for other minority children as "similarly higher" (p. 289) as those of blacks. Yet these "high" rates never exceeded 23% of the black sample; on 2 of the 3 items, the rates of such responses were less than 12%. At the same time, the relatively high rate among blacks of explicit nonendorsement of the Coleman et al. low control items went unmentioned, despite the fact that they exceeded the overall endorsement rate of low control responses by threefold in that sample, or the rate expected by chance alone.

Previous reviews of the literature have extended this misunderstanding. Joe (1971) reported that ". . . Almost all the previous studies indicate that Negroes . . . have higher external scores . . . ." Lefcourt (1972) went further, arguing that the accumulated research on blacks has supported the position that external control expectations develop among the disadvantaged. Of course, neither these nor earlier reviews were concerned primarily with the absolute status of the evidence for blacks per se. Most research has focused on the relative status of group and individuals with respect to this trait, and the correlation of that trait status with other trait characteristics. Accordingly, reviews have tended to focus upon the resultant evidence of the validity of externality in blacks, rather than upon the existence of that trait characteristic.

However, the accumulated evidence suggests that the construct has validity properties for blacks which are different from (or even opposite) those that derive from the theory on which the construct is based. Even revisions of the construct aimed at its refinement (see Gurin, Gurin, Lao, & Beattie, 1969) have not led to consistent findings (Guttentag & Klein, 1976) for black populations. Several examples may be cited.

Valecha's (1972) findings that the Rotter locus of control measure failed to differentiate work-related experiences for internal and external blacks led him to conclude that the ". . . construct . . . appears to have a much better construct validity for whites than for (b)lacks" (p. 456). Thurber, Heacock and Brown (1973) found that while degree of externality predicted scoring and number of assists for black basketball players, degree of internality predicted scoring and assists for whites. In an attempt to establish the relationship between locus of control orientations and political activism in blacks, Gurin and her associates (1969) revealed that a system-blame subcomponent of externality in blacks was associated with political participation. But Guttentag and Klein (1976) reported that no such differentiation within externality emerged for their sample of black fifth to eighth-graders. Strickland (1965) found that among her black college student sample, internality was related to activism. But civil rights activism was unrelated to either internality or externality in Evans and Alexander's (1970) black college sample. In sum, then, considerable speculation surrounds the question of whether locus of control is always measuring the same thing (see Stephens,

1972), or even whether, for blacks, it can be said to measure anything at all. Moreover, the validity of externality in blacks seems at least as questionable as its existence (See Note 1).

Ironically, the heuristic success of the locus of control construct in the domain of black populations has led far less to establishing the existence of an external belief system within the black community than to establishing a relatively stable belief system within the research community in externality for blacks. Few investigators have taken pains carefully to report the status of the evidence for blacks per se. Even when they have (see Strickland, 1965, p. 35), reviewers often distort the initial characterization (see Lefcourt, 1972, p. 16). This is, of course, the kind of looseness of language and communication of which most misunderstandings are borne. At the same time, an aggregate of conceptual misunderstandings is likely to have given this issue an initial momentum. Since validation research with white samples seemed to establish a relationship between externality and low achievement (Crandall, Katkovsky, & Preston, 1965; Coleman et al., 1966; McGhee & Crandall, 1968; Nowicki & Roundtree, 1971), low self-concept (see Fitch, 1970) and immediate gratification preferences (Bialer, 1961; Zytkoskee, Strickland, & Watson, 1971), it seemed inevitable that external locus of control should obtain in blacks. But recent reviews of the empirical literature deny a characterization of blacks as low in self-concept (Banks, 1976; Baldwin, 1979), in achievement motivation (Banks, McQuater, & Hubbard, 1978), or as preferring immediate gratification (Banks, McQuater, Ross, & Ward, 1983). Therefore, while on the face of it, the evidence of nonexternality in blacks may not be so obvious, neither should it any longer be surprising.

Notes

Some of this work was prepared while the second author was visiting the Center for the Study of Reading, University of Illinois at Urbana-Champaign.

We gratefully acknowledge A. Babatunde and Philip G. Zimbardo for comments on a draft of this article.

1. In fact, reviews on locus of control for other racial groups have also been done, where similar issues were raised. For example, Trimble and Richardson (1983) question the legitimacy of generalizing externality to American Indians because of the

failure to find large or consistent differences, the lack of socioeconomic controls, and the failure to consider the dimensionality of the locus of control construct.

References

Baldwin, J.A. (1979). Theory and research concerning the notion of black self-hatred: A review and reinterpretation. *Journal of Black Psychology, 5*(2), 51-77.

Banks, W.C. (1976). White preference in blacks: A paradigm in search of a phenomenon. *Psychological Bulletin, 83*(6), 1179-1186.

Banks, W.C., McQuater, G.V., & Hubbard, J.L. (1978). Toward a reconceptualization of the social-cognitive bases of achievement orientations in blacks. *Review of Educational Research, 48*(3), 381-397.

Banks, W.C., McQuater, G.V., Ross, J., & Ward, W.E. (1983). Delay of gratification in blacks: A critical review. *Journal of Black Psychology, 9*(2), 43-56.

Battle, E., & Rotter, J.B. (1963). Children's feelings of personal control as related to social class and ethnic groups. *Journal of Personality, 31*, 482-490.

Berzins, J.I., & Ross, W.F. (1973). Locus of control among opiate addicts. *Journal of Consulting and Clinical Psychology, 40*(1), 84-91.

Bialer, I. (1961). Conceptualization of success and failure in mentally retarded and normal children. *Journal of Personality, 29*, 303-320.

Brown, D., Fulkerson, K.F., Furr, S., Ware, W.B., & Voight, N.L. (1984). Locus of control, sex role orientation, and self-concept in black and white third- and sixth-grade male and female leaders in a rural community. *Developmental Psychology, 20*(4), 717-721.

Buck, M.R., & Austin, H.R. (1971). Factors related to school achievement in an economically disadvantaged group. *Child Development, 42*(6), 1813-1826.

Coleman, J.S., Campbell, E.Q., Hobson, C.J., McPartland, J., Mood, A.M., Weinfeld, F.D., & York, R.L. (1966). *Equality of educational opportunity.* Washington, D.C.: United States Government Printing Office.

Crandall, V.J., Katkovsky, W., & Preston, A. (1965). Motivational and ability determinants of young children's intellectual achievement behaviors. *Child Development, 33*(3), 643-661.

Cross, H.J., & Tracy, J.J. (1971). Personality factors in delinquent boys: Differences between blacks and whites. *Journal of Research in Crime and Delinquency, 8*(1), 10-22.

DuCette, J., & Volk, S. (1972). Locus of control and levels of aspiration in black and white children. *Review of Educational Research, 42*(4), 493-504.

Epstein, R., & Komorita, S.S. (1971). Self-esteem, success-failure, and locus of control in Negro children. *Developmental Psychology, 4*(1), 2-8.

Evans, D.A., & Alexander, S. (1970). Some psychological correlates of civil rights activity. *Psychological Reports, 26*, 899-906.

Felton, G.S., & Biggs, B.E. (1973). Psychotherapy and responsibility: Teaching internalization behavior to black low achievers through group therapy. *Small Group Behavior, 4*(2), 147-155.

Fitch, G. (1970). Effects of self-esteem, perceived performance, and choice on causal attributions. *Journal of Personality and Social Psychology, 16*(2), 311-315.

Furnham, A., & Henry, J. (1980). Cross-cultural locus of control studies: Experiment and critique. *Psychological Reports, 47*(1), 23-29.

Garcia, C., & Levenson, H. (1975). Differences between blacks' and whites' expectations of control by chance and powerful others. *Psychological Reports, 37*(2), 563-566.

Garrahan, D.P. (1974). The relationship between social activism and feelings of powerlessness among low socioeconomic college students. *Journal of College Student Personnel, 15*(2), 120-124.

Garrett, A.M., & Willoughby, R.H. (1972). Personal orientation and reactions to success and failure in urban black children. *Developmental Psychology, 7*(1), 92.

Gore, P.M., & Rotter, J.B. (1963). A personality correlate of social action. *Journal of Personality, 31*(1), 58-64.

Gruen, G.E., Korte, J.R., & Baum, J.F. (1974). Group measure of locus of control. *Developmental Psychology, 10*(5), 683-686.

Gurin, P., Gurin, G., & Morrison, B.M. (1978). Personal and ideological aspects of internal and external control. *Social Psychology Quarterly, 41*(4), 275-296.

Gurin, P., Gurin, G., Lao, R.C., & Beattie, M. (1969). Internal- external control in the motivational dynamics of Negro youth. *Journal of Social Issues, 25*(3), 29-53.

Gutkin, T.B. (1978). Modification of elementary students' locus of control: An operant approach. *Journal of Psychology, 100*(1), 107-115.

Guttentag, M., & Klein, I. (1976). The relationship between inner versus outer locus of control and achievement in black middle school children. *Educational and Psychological Measurement, 36*, 1101-1109.

Harris, H.F., & Phelan, J.G. (1973). Beliefs in internal-external control of reinforcement among blacks in integrated and segregated high schools. *Psychological Reports, 32*, 40-42.

Jacobson, C.K. (1972). The effects of black power and the locus of control variable on performance and self-depreciation of junior high school students in biracial pairs. *Dissertation Abstracts, 32*, 7109-7110.

Joe, V.C. (1971). A review of the internal-external control construct as a personality variable. *Psychological Reports, 28*, 619-640.

Lefcourt, H.M. (1972). Recent developments in the study of locus of control. In B.A. Maher (Ed.), *Progress in experimental personality research* Vol. 6 (pp. 1-39). New York: Academic Press.

Lefcourt, H.M., & Ladwig, G.W. (1965). The American Negro: A problem in expectancies. *Journal of Personality and Social Psychology, 1*, 377-380.

Leon, G.R. (1974). Personality change in the specially admitted disadvantaged student after one year in college. *Journal of Clinical Psychology, 30*, 522-528.

Lessing, E. (1969). Racial differences in indices of ego functioning relevant to academic achievement. *Journal of Genetic Psychology, 115*(2), 153-167.

Levenson, H. (1974). Activism and powerful others: Distinctions within the concept of internal-external control. *Journal of Personality Assessment, 38,* 377-383.

Maqsud, M. (1980). Locus of control and stages of moral reasoning. *Psychological Reports, 46*(3), 1243-1248.

McGhee, P.E., & Crandall, V.C. (1968). Beliefs in internal-external control of reinforcement and academic performance. *Child Development, 39,* 91-102.

Naditch, M.P. (1974). Locus of control, relative discontent and hypertension. *Social Psychiatry, 9,* 111-117.

Nowicki, S., & Roundtree, J. (1971). *Correlates of locus of control in secondary school age students.* Unpublished manuscript, Emory University.

Orpen, C. (1971). Internal-external control and perceived discrimination in a South African minority group. *Social and Personality Research, 46,* 44-48.

Patterson, O. (1973). The moral crisis of the black American. *The Public Interest, 32,* 43-69.

Pedhazur, L., & Wheeler, L. (1971). Locus of perceived control and need achievement. *Perceptual and Motor Skills, 33*(3), 1281-1282.

Rabinowitz, R.G. (1978). Internal-external control expectancies in black children of differing socioeconomic status. *Psychological Reports, 42*(3), 1339-1345.

Riordan, Z.B. (1981). Locus of control in South Africa. *Journal of Social Psychology, 115*(2), 159-168.

Savage, J.E., Jr., Stearns, A.D., & Friedman, P. (1979). Relationship of internal-external locus of control, self-concept, and masculinity-femininity to fear of success in black freshmen and senior college women. *Sex Roles, 5*(3), 373-383.

Scott, J.D., & Phelan, J.G. (1969). Expectancies of unemployable males regarding source of control of reinforcement. *Psychological Reports, 25,* 911-913.

Segal, S.M., & DuCette, J. (1973). Locus of control and premarital high school pregnancy. *Psychological Reports, 33,* 887-890.

Stephan, W.G., & Kennedy, J.C. (1975). An experimental study of interethnic competition in segregated schools. *Journal of School Psychology, 13*(3), 234-247.

Stephens, M.W. (1972). Dimensions of locus of control: Impact of early educational experiences. *Proceedings of the Annual Convention of the American Psychological Association, 7,* 137-138.

Strickland, B.R. (1965). The prediction of social action from a dimension of internal-external control. *Journal of Social Psychology, 66,* 353-358.

Thurber, S., Heacock, D., & Brown, B. (1973). The control orientation of black athletes in relation to unobtrusive tasks of skill. *Journal of Psychology, 85,* 43-44.

Trimble, J.E., & Richardson, S.S. (1983). Perceived personal and societal forms of locus of control measures among American Indians. *White Cloud Journal, 3*(1), 3-14.

Valecha, G.K. (1972). Construct validation of internal-external locus of reinforcement related to work-related variables. *Proceedings of the Annual Convention of the American Psychological Association, 7,* 455-456.

Valecha, G.K., & Ostrom, T.M. (1974). An abbreviated measure of internal-external locus of control. *Journal of Personality Assessment, 38*(4), 369-376.

Ward, W.E. (1986). Comment on Brown et al.'s "Locus of control, sex role orientation, and self-concept in black and white third- and sixth-grade male and female leaders in a rural community." *Developmental Psychology.*

Will, E.E., & Verdin, J.A. (1978). Social desirability response bias in children's locus of control reports. *Psychological Reports, 43*(3), 924-926.

Williams, J.G., & Stack, J.J. (1972). Internal-external control as a situational variable in determining information seeking by Negro students. *Journal of Consulting and Clinical Psychology, 39*(2), 187-193.

Zytkoskee, A., Strickland, B.R., & Watson, J. (1971). Delay of gratification and internal versus external control among adolescents of low socioeconomic status. *Developmental Psychology, 4*, 93-98.

The Testing Game

Robert L. Williams and Horace Mitchell

By the time the fool has learned the rules of the game, the players have dispersed.

An Ashanti Proverb

Educational testing is not only big business in this country, it is also a big game. The "testing game," as we prefer to call it, is an ongoing series of transactions with ulterior motives which progress to well-defined, predictable outcomes.

Since most of us play this game or have played it, it is only fair that we all understand its framework. The game is played by individuals at four levels: (1) *game producers* (test publishers) who construct the game and make the rules, (2) *game advocates* (schools, colleges, universities and employers) who support the game through acceptance and reliance on its rules and outcomes; (3) *game dealers* (counselors, psychologists, teachers, etc.), the users who run the game although they may or may not always know or understand the rules; and (4) *game pawns* (students, employees) who play the game but don't know the rules. The motivation for playing the testing game is found in the payoff which involves profit, winners and losers.

The Game Producers

The game producers are the originators of the transactions in the testing game. Usually they devise not one but a recurring set of transactions or a series of moves variously called "validity," "reliability," "norming," "tryouts," etc. It is within these moves that the game producers can be honest or dishonest. The truth is that they have been basically dishonest in their moves by developing culturally biased tests.

The most common game played by test producers is "Tell me what you've learned about my culture." This game suggests that while individuals may understand various concepts and know particular information, they must be able to articulate this understanding in majority culture terms in order to be "given credit" for this knowledge. While test publishers talk glibly about the "objective" nature of standardized tests, we realize that the whole game is quite subjective. This subjectivity is usually not recognized since it occurs in test development. This first subjectivity occurs in the definition of constructs (i.e., intelligence, aptitude, achievement). Theoretical statements and test manuals contain dozens of definitions of "intelligence." There are also numerous definitions of "aptitude." Which of them is the "objective" definition? There is none. Therefore, each test developer makes a subjective decision about what "intelligence" will mean for his test.

Therefore, the construct validity of a test depends on how you (subjectively) define the construct. While some testing advocates would attempt to attribute to tests the accuracy of science, the testing enterprise fails to be scientific because it lacks a commonly agreed upon set of well-defined constructs. In sum, the whole enterprise is a subjective one which is made to appear objective.

The primary problem with intelligence and aptitude tests is that they are highly inferential and based on unsupportable assumptions. If we define intelligence broadly as the individual's ability to profit from his experiences, then we must know what his/her experiences were, rather than to assume that he/she has had the same experiences as the standardization group. In fact, one of the cardinal principles in research is that one cannot generalize one's research results to populations which were not represented (or underrepresented) in the sample. If we were to accept the proposition that experiences are individual and are determined to some degree by choice, we are still required to assume (for our instrument to be valid) that each individual had an equal opportunity to make the choice as to what his experiences would be. Again, we realize that for many people, particularly minorities and the poor, no such choice is available.

There are no "aptitudes" which can be shown to exist in the absence of some prior exposure to the "aptitude" being measured or to some component parts of the aptitude which are used to infer the presence of the aptitude. The person who is likely to do best on a "Test of Bricklaying Aptitude" is a person who has had some exposure to bricklaying. Even scores on performance items of tests (e.g. puzzles, picture arrangement, block design, etc.) are likely to be largely dependent on whether or not the person has had some exposure to these things as part of his experience.

In sum then, the minority individual is being judged by a test which is based on an experience which he has not been allowed to have and which gives no credibility to his actual experiences. Test scores are a result of subjective cultural references where some individuals have been excluded by segregation (school and housing) from participating in the culture on which the test is based. In most standardized tests, subtests are heavily loaded with content from the white middle-class culture. Therefore, it should not be surprising that individuals from that group do better on such tests than individuals from minority groups.

For minority groups, therefore, these tests measure only their familiarity with white culture which is operationally defined as "intelligence." Since these tests are based on a white frame of reference, the mind-set of some black children causes them to be penalized. For example, one item on the WAIS asks, "When is Washington's birthday?" If the black child answered by giving the birthday of Booker T. Washington, this would be marked wrong. The item takes for granted that the examinee knows that the question refers to George Washington. Secondly, is it more indicative of "intelligence" for a black child to know "who wrote Faust" than to know "who wrote the Black National Anthem?"

When a test is based on a minority group's perspective and experiences, that group will do better on the test than the majority group. Experience with the Black Intelligence Test of Cultural Homogeneity, a black, culture-specific test, shows that blacks score consistently higher than whites on this test, which is based on black culture (Williams, N.D.). The means of white samples on the BITCH-100 tend to be around 51 (out of a possible 100), while the black means tend to be around 87. Blacks show up consistently superior to whites on this test which has more content validity for blacks than for whites. This illustrates that if a test is made specifically for a particular group (as most standardized tests are made for the white middle class) one would expect members of that group to score higher on the test than members from out-groups.

To be fully honest about what their instruments are able to do, test publishers should first delete the words "intelligence" and "aptitude" from all test titles. At best they can substitute the word "achievement." They should also have the following statement in a visible place on all tests and in all test instructions and manuals: "Research studies have demonstrated that this instrument may be biased against certain minority groups. Therefore, a score on this test may or may not represent what the examinee knows about this subject, posed in this manner, under these circumstances and at this point in time."

The Game Advocates

The game advocates have acquiesced to the game producers in their decision-making processes about students and employees. These schools, colleges, universities and employers are in a good position to force the producers to improve the game since they are the conduits through which the tests must pass (test adoption) before they get to the test dealers. They could demand a better and non-biased product. But rather than approaching test publishers, stating what their needs are, and requiring the development of tests to meet those needs, most institutions and employers have been passive, underinformed, multi-million dollar *purchasers* of almost any test *sold* by major testing *corporations*. To accept a simple test score is easier than systematically analyzing the strengths and weaknesses of applicants in terms of valid, criterion-related, variables. Therefore, the game advocates give in to expediency with no concern for fairness because the game works for their overall purpose—sorting applicants.

Institutions and employers are in the best position to make test publishers accountable, but since this would also require more work on their part, they support the game through acceptance of and reliance on its rules and outcomes.

Game Dealers

The game dealers are the counselors, teachers, psychologists and others who actually run the game. They have the responsibility of carrying out the game for the advocates and are singled out by the producers as being the most appropriate target for testing critics. The typical game is "blaming the dealer."

The dealers are usually unskilled in principles of test development, underskilled in test interpretation and perform the mechanical role of giving the tests and reporting the results with little, if any, meaningful enlightened professional perspective. They often perceive their role as that of carrying out policy, rather than influencing policymaking. Their feedback to advocates tends to reinforce test use rather than to call test use and abuse into question. Many game dealers who are aware of the dangers of the testing game rationalize that "If I don't give the tests, they'll hire someone else who will, and where will I be?" Thus the dealers are the hired guns who wittingly or unwittingly play out the script as prepared by the producers and as encouraged by the advocates. Again, no one wants to be accountable for the consequences of testing.

While the game dealers must bear significant responsibility for giving tests and writing interpretations which have adverse effects on the game pawns, the dealers are not alone in their culpability. They have justifiably come under severe attack, but the attack must also extend to the publishers who are responsible for the development of biased instruments and to institutions and employers who provide for their dissemination and extensive use.

Game Pawns

Game pawns are the students and employees who don't understand the rules of the game and whose future moves are heavily determined by the outcomes of the game. Pawns can be divided into two subgroups: (1) those who "luck out" (usually majority group persons) because the game is based on their perspective and gives validity to their experiences; and (2) those who "lose out" (usually minority group persons) because the game is not based on their perspective and gives no validity to their experiences. The winners are not adversely affected by the testing game. In fact, because they "lucked out" they sometimes become supporters of the game and look questioningly at the losers who bitterly charge that the game is unfair.

It is the losers who are victimized by the testing game. The testing of minority students and job applicants has tended to serve only a sorting function, a basis for deciding which of these persons should be excluded from educational and economic opportunities. The testing game starts in elementary school when it is used as a basis for deciding which students should be removed from the educational mainstream and placed into second or third rate programs which tend to restrict severely, if not end, their equal educational opportunity. In virtually every school system having large enrollments of minority students, these students are assigned (on the basis of test scores) to "terminal education," "slow learner," "EMR" and other such pejorative classifications in numbers which are overrepresentative of their percentage of the school population. All students labeled by such classifications usually experience lowered self-esteem and fall victim to that self-fulfilling prophecy which starts with the statement, "They can't learn," continues when the teacher decides not to teach them anything and ends with "I told you so" when the minority child shows no improvement after further "instruction." We must put an end to this scenario which has resulted in the educational stagnation and psychological abuse of so many minority children.

The economic implications of such classifications are clear. The completion of only a second-rate or third-rate educational program places such individuals at distinct disadvantages for college admission and in the job market. Consequently, they must generally accept low-paying, unskilled jobs which are most frequently unrewarding and which often result in the individuals' being unable to provide the resources necessary for their children to break out of the poor education-poor opportunity-poor education cycle.

Despite the staggering odds against them, some potential "losers" are able to escape the consequences of the testing game. Two brief case histories follow:

Not many folks have heard of Earl "Duke" Harvey, a black student who was in the lowest percentage of his graduating class from Central High School in St. Louis. Earl scored only 74 on the IQ test. He has a severe speech impediment. He was advised not to go to college because his SAT scores were too low.

Yet, Earl Harvey—through determination, perseverance and stamina, refused to let a speech impediment, ridicule from his peers and the worst kind of degradation a youth can face—rejection—stop him in his drive for success.

Earl "Duke" Harvey went on to attend Tennessee Agricultural and Industrial University in Nashville where he made the Dean's List and graduated with a 3.5 grade point average (4.0 scale). In addition, against all odds, Earl Harvey received his doctorate in Secondary Education from Michigan State University on June 12, 1976. On September 3, 1976 Earl Harvey received a Testimonial Resolution from the Detroit City Council stating that:

> Dr. Harvey has set an example for youth everywhere who may be touched by adverse conditions that success is possible if self value is maintained. Now therefore, Be it Resolved that the Detroit City Council commends Dr. Earl Harvey for his personal achievements . . .

Another example is Ronnie L. Collins, a black student who attended Pocomoke Maryland High School. Before he graduated in 1970, Ronnie was advised by a white counselor that he should forget about college and that, if he insisted on further schooling, he should go into vocational training because of his low test scores.

Collins ignored the advice, however, and enrolled in Bowie State College. In June 1974, he graduated with honors in the top ten percent of his class. He was president of his senior class and consistently made the Dean's List. He won both a Fulbright-Hayes Scholarship and a Danforth Fellowship. The prestigious Fulbright-Hayes Scholarship enabled Collins to attend the University of Scotland at Edinburgh where he studied Comparative Linguistics. Collins will receive full tuition and living expenses for four years to pursue his Ph.D. in preparation for a career for college teaching. It would be a gross understatement to say that Harvey and Collins were misjudged. In fact, such an assessment would be completely false. The point is that untold thousands of black students, Puerto Rican, Chicano, Asian and other minority students are being denied access to institutions of higher education today because of what game producers call "error variance," but what we prefer to call "intentional variance" or the zero-sum game. It is no accident that Harvey and Collins were advised not to go to college; the educational system in this country is structured so that similar tragedies befall many other similar students.

This explanation of the testing game should make all players—producers, advocates, dealers and pawns—very aware of the rules of the game, the parts which they play in the script, the payoff for producers, advocates, and dealers and the consequences for pawns.

Despite widespread calls for testing moratoria, the development of valid tests and better training of all involved in the game, the game continues to run "as usual."

The Rise of College Testing Games

One of the primary arenas in which the testing game is played is higher education and the "game kits" have such names as SAT, ACT, GRE, MAT, LSAT, MCAT, etc.

The College Entrance Examination Board, a major game producer consisting of a membership of more than 2,000 colleges and secondary institutions, was founded in 1900. The CEEB established the Educational Testing Service (ETS) to administer its testing games.

ETS began its game operations in 1948 by administering the CEEB's SAT to 76,000 pawns. Since 1948, ETS's gross annual payoff has doubled in amount every five years.

Briefly put, in the SAT game scores are reported in numbers ranging from 200 to 800; about two-thirds of the pawns who take the SAT score between 400 and 600. On a standard scale of 0 to 100, a score of 200 is equal to zero and 800 is equal to 100. Therefore, on the SAT, a pawn cannot receive a score below 200 or one above 800. An average SAT score on either the verbal or numerical portions is 500. In 1962-63 the mean SAT verbal and math scores were 475 and 502, respectively. Ten years later, in 1972-73, the mean scores declined to 445 and 481, respectively. One conclusion reached was that college pawns were getting dumber. The other conclusion reached was that the scores of minority pawns had been bringing down the means. As Chuck Stone (1974), of the Philadelphia Daily News says:

> The American educational system is not prepared to admit that its students are actually getting dumb, but the drop in the SAT average score, whatever it is supposed to mean, is interpreted to be an indication the black students' scores are bringing down the average.

College admission testing games are based on a normative assumption—an upper half and lower half. The tests yield a distribution in which 50% of the pawns score above the mean and 50% of the pawns score below the mean. In other words, the sum of the scores above the mean and the scores below the mean is zero. Thus, the present system requires that someone fall off at the bottom half. There will be winners and there will be losers. Earl Harvey, Ronnie Collins and other black pawns were designated to be the losers.

Robert Green presents the most comprehensive review of the issues relating to the admission of black students to colleges and universities in terms of modifying existing criteria. Green (1972) suggests taking into account motivational and attitudinal characteristics as well as the intellectual factors. Green points out further, "Educators should realize that tests are tools which can be used wisely or harmfully, to help or to hinder the educational growth of children." We add, however, that if the tool doesn't fit, put it back in the toolbox where it belongs.

The question under consideration here, then, is whether the SAT or similar tests are biased against black students. An article by Davis and Temp, both employees (or former employees) of the Educational Testing Service, answers this concern ambiguously and inconclusively. In their study Davis and Temp conclude that the validity of the SAT in predicting grades of black and white pawns is the same in some institutions while in others it differs. The authors concluded that there is no evidence of bias against blacks in spite of the fact that they find differences in the relationship between the SAT scores of black pawns and their ultimate college grades. Of the 19 institutions studied, the SAT scores *did not* accurately predict grades for blacks in 37% of the institutions studied. In the same study, the SAT scores *did* accurately predict college grades for white pawns in 18 of the 19 institutions or in 95% of the cases.

It is a well-known fact that blacks make lower scores on the SAT than whites. Whereas 50% of the white pawns score above 500 on the SAT, S.A. Kendrick, Executive Director of Research and Development of the College Board, estimated that "not more than 15% and perhaps as few as 10% of Negro high school seniors would score 400 or more on the verbal section of the SAT. Only one or two percent would be likely to score 500 or more." In other words, 85-90% of black pawns score below 500! If this is true, increasingly fewer numbers of blacks will be entering college over the next two or three decades, especially if a mean within the 400-500 range is to be used as a cut-off point. Since 200 is the lowest score than can be attained, then the range for selection for black pawns cannot be very broad.

A major fallacy exists here. It has been assumed that the SAT is used to predict success in college. This is not true; the SAT is used primarily as a predictor of first and second semester grades, not college success. The criterion for a predictive test should not be just the first year in college but the entire four-year period, or for college success in general. The first year of college tends to be the most difficult year. In the

Davis and Temp study (1971), a correlation was made between the SAT (verbal and mathematical) and only freshman grades in 19 institutions. It would be instructive to determine what that prediction would be for the overall success in college. As Davis and Temp (1971) point out in their study:

> ... the SAT is a product developed from the majority or elite culture ... the curriculum and instructional strategy in colleges and universities are also products of the majority culture and the SAT has been developed faithfully, even tediously to reflect the traditional systems of instructions. (In this and other cases, there may be bias against blacks in grading procedures.)

In fact, most if not all of the research that has been done on the predictive validity of SAT and ACT scores relates to predicting freshman grades for blacks. Using the SAT or the ACT predictions of first year or first semester grades for black pawns as a basis for predicting total college success is similar to attempting to predict the winner of a football or basketball game based on first quarter scores. A student's performance in the first year is not necessarily predictive of what he will do in subsequent semesters, but if he is not admitted, the answer to the problem will never be known. The SAT has been used mainly, then, to predict only part of the criterion measure, and not total success in college. Lanier and Lightsey (1972) argue that SAT scores should be used for general predictions and not for specific letter grades. They stated that the majority of research indicates that high school rank was the best single predictor of success in college. Another study was conducted to examine the relationship between high school rank and the ACT scores and first semester grade point average. The study included a sample of 981 students at Texas A & M University. The study concluded that high school rankings were better indicators of potential college achievement than the ACT. Male students tended to score higher than female students on the ACT, but they also earned a lower grade point average. Cherdack (1971) studied minority students enrolled in the Educational Opportunity Program at UCLA. Black, Mexican-American and Caucasian students were all included in this sample. His purpose was to determine the degree to which the SAT scores and high school grades are effective in predicting the freshman grades of "disadvantaged" minority pawns. The result of the study once again demonstrated that the high school average was the best predictor of college grades for all pawns. On the whole SAT scores were lower for minority students.

Clark and Plotkin (1964) found also that the SAT is not a valid predictor of academic success in integrated colleges. They found that attained success for black pawns was far beyond the level predicted by the SAT. We contend that the SAT and other college admission games produce numerous "false negatives." There are many who are refused

admission through the usual selection processes, but who might succeed in college if greater weight were given to motivation and nonacademic indications of ability. Earl Harvey and Ronnie Collins are
excellent examples of false negatives. Dr. Harvey still has an IQ of 74; he
still has the speech problem; but he also now holds a doctorate and is
making significant contributions to his people. What would have happened to him if he had listened to the game dealers?

According to Hernstein (1974) " . . . there is a powerful trend toward meritocracy, the advancement of people on the basis of ability,
either potential or fulfilled, measured objectively." At the end of the
paper Hernstein concludes:

> When people can freely take their natural level in society, the
> upper classes will, virtually by definition, have greater capacity
> than the lower. The measurement of intelligence is one of the
> yardsticks by which we may assess the growing meritocracy . . .

It is clear that ability tests and scholastic aptitude tests such as the
SAT, are inherently connected with the so-called meritocracy game.
Equality of opportunity means more than an opportunity to take a test.
It means equality in acquiring the skills necessary to pass the test; it
means real diversity of educational opportunity. The question remains,
however, is the meritocracy game a fair one? We must answer in the
negative, especially where blacks and other oppressed people remain
the pawns and the losers.

The Need for Game Referees

Game producers continue to take no responsibility for their central role in the testing game, preferring instead to point an accusing
finger at the game dealers. They assert that the tests are valid, but are
sometimes misused, and that this misuse is not their responsibility.
Game advocates have decisions to make and they want the easy way out
(playing the testing game) even though it leads to many poor decisions.
By asking rhetorically, "What else can we do?" they take no responsibility. Game dealers insist that they are caught in the middle and that the
actual culprits are the institutions and employers (advocates) who require that they run the game. No one wants to be accountable for the
consequences that fall on many game pawns.

Since the testing game is produced, advocated and run by people
who have vested interests, the deck is usually stacked against minority
pawns. Therefore, there is a need for an outside referee to assure that the

rights of the pawns are protected when they are subjected to the testing game.

Blacks and other minorities have, historically, relied heavily on the courts to assure them "equal protection of the laws" whenever they have been dealt with unfairly in many of this society's games (e.g. the housing game, the employment game, the education game, the health care game, etc.). Within the last ten years the courts have served as referees in the testing game. But the current trends do not appear very bright. The decisions of the present Supreme Court are so unfavorable to minority pawns that the future strategy may not be how to forge new changes through litigation, but how to prevent the chipping away of legal supports already obtained. The gains of the fifties and sixties are being neutralized or cancelled out by the losses of the seventies. We may have moved from a period of "benign neglect" to one of "litigation retreat" in every area, including the testing game. This is particularly true in the case of *Defunis* vs. *Odegaard*—a case of so-called reverse discrimination.

In 1971, Marco Defunis, a Jewish student from southern California, applied to the University of Washington Law School. He was rejected in spite of the fact that 36 "minority applicants" who were admitted had scored lower than he did on a scale (composed of LSAT and undergraduate grades) the school used to evaluate applicants. The reason was that the law school at the University of Washington gave preference to certain ethnic groups that are underrepresented in the legal profession.

The Supreme Court decided 5-4 not to rule on Defunis' challenge to the constitutionality of this policy because Defunis was about to graduate from the school (Washington Post, 1974). Justice Douglas vehemently dissented by arguing that the Court should order another lower court test of the Defunis case. In his discussion he attacked the inadequacy of standard aptitude tests as university admission criteria. He equated the inadequacy of the aptitude tests with unconstitutionality. Douglas is saying that when college aptitude tests are involved, cultural differences result in discrimination. And he insists that abolition of the LSAT "would be a first step toward eliminating racism in college admissions."

On February 21, 1977 the same Burger Court agreed to rule on a crucial testing case of whether university quotas favoring blacks and other minorities violate the constitutional rights of whites. The widely publicized case involves a prospective medical student at the University of California Medical School at Davis: Alan Bakke (Arkansas Gazette, 1977). He sued after failing twice to be admitted and blamed his rejection on the University's special admission policies favoring disadvantaged applicants of racial or ethnic minority group status. The

University of California program was designed to compensate for past discrimination against minorities, and to eliminate traditional barriers to medical careers.

The California Supreme Court ruled Alan Bakke had been denied his rights under the equal protection clause of the Fourteenth Amendment because 16 places in the University of California Medical School were reserved for minorities. Bakke argued that he would have been admitted without the special admission policies because his grades and test scores were superior to those of the minority applicants.

The Bakke case has provoked considerable controversy and has called into question similar admission programs favoring minorities at most colleges and universities. If the Court orders Bakke admitted to medical school, the game producers and game dealers will have won again. (N.B. Bakke won.) Much of the court activity around testing has centered on laws which are fairly general in nature (e.g. the Fourteenth Amendment) or on "guidelines" that have been established by various federal agencies. Since these have been ineffectual in guaranteeing fairness in the testing game, a stronger tact is needed. Since the huge testing industry is accountable to no one, we urge the following steps:

1. A congressional investigation, initiated by the Black Caucus, into the testing game.
2. A surge of class-action lawsuits against the game producers, game advocates and game dealers.

It is about time that we put an end to this evil testing game. *Resispa loquitur* (The situation speaks for itself).

References

Arkansas Gazette, February 23, 1977. p. 5A.

Cherdack, A. N. (1971). The predictive validity of the SAT for disadvantaged college students enrolled in a special education program. Dissertation Abstracts, April, vol. 31, (10-A).

Clark, K. B. & Plotkin, I. (1964). *The Negro student at integrated colleges*. New York: National Scholarship Service for Negro Students.

Davis, J. A. & Temp, G. (1971) Is the SAT biased against black students? *College Board Review*, no. 81, Fall, 4-9.

Green, R. L. (1972). The black quest for higher education: An admissions dilemma. In R.L. Jones (Ed.), *Black psychology* New York: Harper & Row, pp. 95-103.

Green R. L. (1974) The awesome danger of "Intelligence" tests. *Ebony*, vol. 29, no. 10, pp. 68-72.

Herrnstein, R. (1974). I.Q. *The Atlantic Monthly*, no. 228, September, pp. 43-64.

Washington Post, June 10, 1974.

Kendrick, S. A. (1967-68). The coming segregation of our selective colleges. *College Board Review*, 66, Winter pp. 6-13.

Lanier, D. & Lightsey, R. (1972). Verbal SAT scores and high school averages as predictors. *Intellect*, November.

Stone, C. (1974). Colonialism in college admissions. Second Annual Conference in Counseling Minorities, Michigan State University.

Williams, R.L. (N.D.). The BITCH-100: A Cultural Specific Test. Williams & Associates, Inc., 6374 Delmar Blvd., St. Louis, MO 63130.

Black Social Scientists and the Mental Testing Movement, 1920-1940

V. P. Franklin

In the last few years, several works have appeared which documented many of the racist premises which underlie the field of psychology in the United States. Robert V. Guthrie, for example, pointed out that "the profession of psychology had maintained an unhealthy alliance with several racist themes." Guthrie, however, was much too generous in his description of mainstream American psychology and psychologists in the twentieth century. Psychological research was often used to support overtly racist ideas and practices in American society. The theories, methodologies, findings, and conclusions generated by many American psychologists have been used to try and demonstrate that blacks and other racial minorities are mentally inferior to whites. The conclusions of such leading American psychologists as Lewis Terman, Edward Thorndike, Carl Brighman, Henry E. Garrett, and many others, as to innate mental inferiority of blacks, were considered respectable and generally accepted in the social scientific community and American society at large (See Note 1).

From the earliest years in the twentieth century, however, black social scientist challenged many of the findings and conclusions of the "mental testers." In the process of attacking the validity of certain findings, black social scientists made important contributions to the field of psychological testing. These black researchers between 1920 and 1940 not only pointed out the flaws in the methodologies, test procedures, sampling, and other aspects of mental testing, but also contributed to our general knowledge of what the so-called "intelligence tests" were actually measuring. In this essay, I will examine some of the research and statements of black social scientists which challenged the belief that the intelligence tests demonstrated the innate mental inferiority of blacks to whites, and discuss the overall significance of these activities to our understanding of the black intellectual tradition in the United States.

Race Differences and Mental Abilities

Records exist from very ancient times which suggest that men have long been aware of racial (physical) and cultural differences among the various peoples of the world. Ancient philosophers and historians recounted the various explanations and myths which attempted to explain these differences among men. The Greek historian, Herodotus, for example, recorded the myth of Phaeton, who rode the chariot of the sun god too close to the Earth and burned the faces of the people in the area we now know as "Africa." Throughout the medieval and early modern eras men recorded and preserved their observations of exotic peoples in distant lands. The travels of Marco Polo, Prester John, and innumerable adventuresome sea captains fed the imaginations and the desires for wealth and fame of many fifteenth and sixteenth century western Europeans. During the Age of European Enlightenment, however, several researchers began to apply the new "scientific method" to their observations and classifications of mankind. In the early eighteenth century, Linnaeus and Johann Friedreich Blumenback divided mankind into first four, then five varieties or races: Ethiopian, American, Mongolian, Malay, and Caucasian. Then in 1853 the Count Joseph de Gobineau began publishing his multivolume *Essay on the Inequality of the Human Races*, in which he concluded that the white race was innately superior to the darker ones, and that the so-called "Aryans" should be considered the "summit of civilization."

The classic early American statement on the innate inferiority of blacks and Native Americans in both "mind and body" to whites was made by Thomas Jefferson in his *Notes on Virginia* (1781). Jefferson entertained few doubts about the innate mental inferiority of blacks:

> Comparing them by their faculties of memory, reason, and imagination it appears to me, that in memory they are equal to whites, in reason much inferior; as I think one could scarcely be found capable of tracing and comprehending the investigations of Euclid; and that in imagination they are dull, tasteless, and anomalous.

He did venture one qualification, however, which has become one of the major "indoor sports" of American psychologists:

> The opinion, "that they are inferior in the faculties of reason and imagination," wrote Jefferson, "must be hazarded with great diffidence. To justify a general conclusion, requires many observations, even more where the subject may be submitted to the Anatomical knife, to Optical glasses, to analysis by fire, or by solvents.

Opposition to this viewpoint has been recorded from the early nineteenth century. Early antislavery spokespersons and leaders supported the position that the reason for the apparent lack of mental acuity of the Negro was his "depraved and degraded condition" in American society. Rev. Samuel Stanhope Smith, a leading abolitionist, in 1801 wrote that:

> the abject servitude of the Negro in America, condemned to the drudgery of perpetual labor, cut off from every means of improvement, conscious of his degraded state in the midst of freedmen who regard him with contempt, and in every word and look make him feel his inferiority; and hopeless of ever enjoying any great amelioration of his condition, must condemn him, while these circumstances remain, to perpetual sterility of genius.

The environmentalist position on black intellectual ability was later upheld by many of the more "radical abolitionists' of the 1830s, 1840s, and 1850s. Theodore Tilton summarized the environmental argument in an article which appeared in 1862. "We put a stigma upon the black man's color, and then plead that prejudice against the commonest fair dealing; we shut him out of schools, and then bitterly inveigh against the ignorance of his kind." Tilton continued:

> We shut up all the learned professions from his reach, and withhold the motives for ordinary enterprise, and then declare that he is an inferior being, fitted only for the menial services.

The antislavery vanguard gave voice to few doubts about the "childlike and dependent nature" of the Negro, but this was considered to be part of the legacy of the "peculiar institution." As Theodore Tilton put it in 1863, "Two centuries of slavery must needs have molded the character of the slave . . . . The faults of the slave . . . come from training, rather than of natural endowment."

It should be pointed out, however, that the radical abolitionist did not usually express the idea that blacks and whites were equal; most believed that the races were just "very different." Whereas it was fairly clear that blacks were intellectually inferior to whites, blacks did have their strong points. Rev. James F. Clarke, another antislavery advocate, in a sermon published in 1843 made clear many of the differences.

> The colored man has not so much invention as the white, but more imitation. He has not so much of the reflective, but more of the perceptive powers. The black child will learn to read and write as fast or faster than the white child, having equal advantages. The blacks have not the indomitable perseverance and will, which make the Caucasian, at least the Saxon portion of it, masters wherever they go—but they have a native courtesy, a civility . . . and a capacity for the highest refinement of character. More than all, they have almost universally, a strong

religious tendency, and that strength of attachment, which is capable of any kind of self-denial, and self-sacrifice. Is this an inferior race—so inferior as to be fit only for chains?

In the last quarter of the nineteenth century and first quarter of the twentieth, few white researchers even gave blacks credit for these dubious virtues. In 1859 Charles Darwin's *Origins of Species* was published in which the existence of evolutionary change in nature was posited. Darwin's ideas about the struggle for survival in nature was almost immediately applied to man's social environment. The "social Darwinist" came to believe there that were some races and societies (white Anglo-Saxon Protestants, for example) that were winning in the struggle for survival, while other groups were obviously doomed to extinction. Social Darwinian notions also supported the white supremacy movement and imperialistic adventures of the United States and Western Europe in the late nineteenth century. Although blacks may have been considered "gentle" and "humble," the social Darwinists came to believe that unless American blacks could take on a few of the "finer characteristics" of the white race, they would soon die out.

One of the main reasons for these pessimistic opinions about blacks was the general belief that they were particularly deficient in "gray matter." Throughout the nineteenth century many researchers tried to demonstrate the mental inferiority of blacks and other darker peoples through measurement of "cranial capacity" (size of the brain cavities). But the results of these investigations were inconclusive. With the development of the Binet-Simon Intelligence Test in 1905, however, many white Americans finally had an instrument which they believed would "accurately" measure their mental superiority.

In 1905 the first "intelligence test" was produced by Alfred Binet and Theophile Simon in France in order to detect mentally deficient children in the French public schools. This test was revised and published in 1908. Henry H. Goddard translated and published Binet's "Measuring Scale for Intelligence" in the United States in January 1909. After testing four hundred feeble-minded and two thousand "normal" white children, Goddard concluded, "first, that the Binet Scale was wonderfully accurate; and second, that a child cannot learn the things that are beyond his grade of intelligence. He may be drilled upon them but can only give rote work and will fall down upon them if carefully questioned." Thus after only two administrations, Goddard suggested that the Binet-Simon Test measured how much a child was capable of learning at a given chronological age.

During the same school year that Goddard was testing the two thousand normal white children in Vineland, New Jersey (1910-1911), Howard Odum was using the new intelligence test on black children in the Philadelphia public schools. Odum had been commissioned by the

Board of Public Education to undertake an investigation of the increasing number of black pupils in the schools, and decided to administer the new Binet Test to the children and compare the results with those of Goddard in New Jersey. This was probably the first attempt to use the new mental tests to compare the intellectual and scholastic abilities of blacks and whites in the United States.

The use of the Binet-Simon test to measure the "mental abilities" of various groups spread rapidly throughout the country. As early as 1912 Henry Goddard was asked by the U.S. Public Health Service to apply the new mental tests to newly arriving immigrants on Ellis Island. As a result, according to Goddard, the number of "feebleminded" aliens entering the country was greatly reduced. The first major revision and standardization of the Binet-Simon test was carried out at Stanford University by Lewis Terman in 1916. In his book, *The Measurement of Intelligence*, published that year, Terman discussed the poor showing of black, Indian, and Mexican children on the tests.

> Their dullness seems to be racial, or at least inherent in the family stocks from which they come. The fact that one meets this type with such extraordinary frequency among Indians, Mexicans, and Negroes suggests quite forcibly that the whole question of racial differences in mental traits will have to be taken up anew . . . there will be discovered enormously significant racial differences . . . which cannot be wiped out by any scheme of mental culture.

During World War I the first mass testing program was developed and administered in the United States. American soldiers were given either the Alpha (for literates) or Beta (for illiterates) tests in order to determine what positions and ranks they should hold in the United States Army. And during the 1920s numerous articles, monographs, and books appeared which attempted to interpret the results of these tests. Several black social scientists openly challenged many of the interpretations which appeared during that decade, and launched the ongoing black critique of the mental testing movement in the United States.

The Black Critique

Black scholars began to systematically critique the findings and conclusions of white social scientists about black life during the last decade of the nineteenth century. In 1897 the American Negro Academy published Kelly Miller's review of a study of the black population in the United States by Frederick Hoffman in which he concluded that American Negroes were "doomed to extinction" within the next few centuries. Miller pointed out that Mr. Hoffman's evidence was inadequate for such a conclusion, and that many of the more unfortunate "race traits" exhibited by American Negroes were actually due to the social and economic conditions under which blacks were forced to live in this country.

The Atlanta University Studies of Negro Life (1897-1914) also contained more important information which tended to refute the conjectures of many "white experts" on the Negro. W.E.B. DuBois, who was the editor of most of the reports, often publicized the research of white researchers who did *not* enter into discussions of black life in the United States with a number of preconceptions about the "Negro Problem." In the 1906 report on *The Health and Physique of the Negro American*, DuBois reprinted an article by Dr. Herbert A. Miller on "some Psychological Considerations on the Race Problem." Dr. Miller had developed a series of tests of memory, perception, and logical relationships, and found that "so far as the original endowment of the Negro is concerned, I would conclude that there is nothing to differentiate him particularly as a different psychic being from the Caucasian."

The Crisis magazine, published by the National Association for the Advancement of Colored People and edited by DuBois between 1910 and 1934, almost monthly reported and criticized the various reports of mental testing of black children and adults throughout the United States. Moreover, between 1920 and 1940 there were basically four areas where black social scientists openly challenged the findings of the mental testers. First, they attacked the generally accepted beliefs about what the "intelligence tests" were measuring. Second, they conducted research which undercut the so-called "mulatto hypothesis." Third, they attacked the attempts to use mental tests results to justify the further segregation of black children in American public schools. And finally black researchers exposed the general misuse of mental tests and test results with respect to blacks throughout the United States.

In the early 1920s several statements and discussions appeared in psychological journals and books evaluating the new intelligence tests. In 1921 psychologist Robert Yerkes published the results of the Army testing program and pointed out that blacks and immigrants scored lower on both the Alpha and Beta tests. Also in 1921 the *Journal of Educational Psychology* published a symposium on "Intelligence and its Measurement" in which seventeen leading American educators and psychologists were asked to define "general intelligence," and to describe how it can best be measured. Although there were some minor differences, most of the respondents agreed that general intelligence was the ability to learn and adjust to the conditions of life. Thus, an individual was "intelligent" to the extent that he was able to adjust to his environment. And the intelligence test score was important, according to Edward L. Thorndike, because of "its value in prophesying how well a person will do in other intellectual tasks."

The National Society for the Study of Education in its 1922 yearbook examined *Intelligence Tests and Their Use.* "General Intelligence" was again defined as the capacity to learn and the contributors to the yearbook recognized several types of intelligence, such a motor, verbal, and social intelligence, which could be measured by the various intelligence tests. Stephen Colwin of Brown University, however, cautioned that "little or no value can be attached to the results of tests in which individuals tested vary in any marked degree as to their opportunity and desire to become familiar with the materials of the test employed." This important caveat, published in 1922, was generally ignored by most mental testers in the 1920s and 1930s.

In 1923 Carl Brigham published the first major reanalysis of the Army Test data. He concluded that the Alpha and Beta tests measured the "native or inborn intelligence" of the soldiers. Also in 1923 there appeared the first major examination of the studies which compared the results of the intelligence testing of blacks and whites in the United States. Joseph Peterson, a noted psychologist who helped develop the Army tests, published a monograph on *The Comparative Abilities of White and Negro Children*, in which he discussed how blacks and whites compared on numerous tests of "rational learning," "sensory responses," "ability to learn," and other behaviors. Peterson examined the literature on "the effect on the [mental test] score of different degrees of white blood in the negroes." Opinions, observations, and experiments on the topic were discussed in detail, and the results of his own research were reported. In the conclusion Peterson summarized his findings:

> Our results with young subjects, in agreement with those of investigators studying older subjects, both Negro and American Indian, indicate an increase of ability to achieve success in simple abstract learning with an increase in the degree of white blood. That is to say, were the factor arising from hybridization eliminated from our Negro group, the differences between the two races would be greater than those revealed by this investigation.

With regard to the overall issue of the mental differences between the races, Peterson was very explicit:

> We believe that the intelligence of the Negro race as represented in America is about that which will give him an I.Q. of approximately 0.75 to 0.80 when compared with the whites of his own section of the country or with fair samples of American white people generally. The disadvantages of the Negro's inferior school and home environment and of his general social status, as these factors will affect the test scores, will be at least

partly balanced by the fact that these are results on the colored subjects as found in America with a large percent of individuals containing white blood in varying degrees. Intelligence test results, as far as they go, indicate that the mulatto, or the mixed blood Negro in America generally, is a little more efficient than the pure Negro. This statement, however, does not contradict the fact that there are to be found a small percent of pure Negroes that rank with the best whites.

Then Professor Peterson launched into a "cultural deficit" explanation of the mental differences:

There can be little question that in most tests the Negro suffers considerably in comparison with the white man in the lack of social inheritance from cultured ancestors. What he has that serves him well in America is obtained from former slave-owning whites and from his contemporary white neighbors and employers who as a rule have every advantage over him.

Peterson pessimistically concluded that "the outlook for the bright and capable Negro is dark at the best. He can find little encouraging appreciation in the members of his own race and his recognition by the whites, beyond certain rather narrow limits, is impossible." Thus by the early 1920s, most of the mental testers were telling other psychologists, educators, and laymen that the new intelligence tests measured innate mental abilities, and that these tests had demonstrated the inherent mental inferiority of blacks to whites.

In March 1923, in an article entitled, "Race and Mental Tests," Howard Hale Long, a professor at Paine College in Georgia, called into question several of Lewis Terman's statements and conclusions about the Army test results. Terman believed that the "Army mental tests have shown that not more that 15 percent of American Negroes equal or exceed in intelligence the average of our white population, and that the intelligence of the average Negro is vastly inferior to that of the average white man." Long, however, pointed out that with respect to these Army test scores, "greater differences were found between Southern whites and a selected group of whites, than between Southern whites and Northern blacks . . . In other words, the situation in the field of mental testing agrees with the general findings in anthropology that variation of individuals and groups within races is greater than the variation between the races of major groups." Long went on to discuss the findings of psychologists who had found that "environment" was a much greater influence on "intelligence" than was "heredity."

In June 1924, Horace Mann Bond, who was then Director of the School of Education at Langston University, reviewed the book by Carl Brigham, *A Study of American Intelligence*, in an essay entitled, "Intelligence Tests and Propaganda" which appeared in *The Crisis*. Among other things, Brigham believed that the Army test results had demonstrated that "Negroes, of all racial groups, possess the least intelligence," and that "Negroes from Northern states possess larger increments of intelligence than Negroes from Southern states." But Bond asked, Why should this be the case?

> Mr. Brigham says that this is because the more intelligent have immigrated northward; a very pretty explanation, but not one which can be taken to justify the fact[s]. There is only one obvious explanation; the Negro from the North, because of infinitely superior home, civil and above all school conditions, has been favored by environment in just as great a degree as his Southern brother has been deprived of the same.

In another essay on "What the Army Intelligence' Tests Really Measured," Bond showed that the blacks who migrated to the North must have also left their "duller and less accomplished *white* fellows in the South" as well, since the average scores of blacks from several northern states were higher than those for whites in many southern states. Bond went on to emphasize that the Army test scores reflected the social and educational environment of the individuals who took the tests, rather than any innate or native "intellectual" abilities.

By the late 1920s several mental testers recognized the need to try and demonstrate experimentally that "heredity" was a much more important determinant of "intelligence" than was "environment." The 1928 yearbook of the National Society for the Study of Education, edited by Lewis Terman, dealt with *Nature and Nurture: Their Influence upon Intelligence, and Their Influence upon Achievement.* It contained a number of studies of the intellectual levels within families, among siblings, and between twins; and reached the general conclusion that "heredity" was by far a greater influence upon intelligence than was environment." This conclusion, however, was not accepted by many black and white social scientists, and from the early 1930s onward, numerous experiments were undertaken which demonstrated the overwhelming effects of environmental conditions upon the performance of blacks and whites on mental tests.

Black social scientists during the 1920s and 1930s were also active in research which tended to undercut the belief that any "intelligence" exhibited by an individual black was probably due to white ancestry. Originally, the so-called "mulatto hypothesis" stated that the offspring of interracial unions were inferior in physical and mental ability to either parent. But when it became clear that many Negro leaders and professionals were mulattos (or at least, fair-skinned), the hypothesis was changed to state that the children of a black-white union were usually mentally superior to the pure Negroes, but inferior to whites. Thus, if one found a group of blacks who scored high on the intelligence tests, it was probably due to the large number of mulattos in that group. Many early mental testers got around this problem by reporting intelligence test results for "full-blooded," "three-quarters," "mulatto," and "quadroon" Negroes; or for "blacks, browns, and yellows."

In 1927, Horace Mann Bond published an article on "Some Exceptional Negro Children," and reported the results of his testing of thirty black youngsters in Chicago with the original Stanford-Binet Intelligence test. Bond was very careful in his administration of the tests, and tried to establish and maintain a positive "rapport" with the children. He reported that 63 percent of the children made I.Q. scored above 106, whereas Terman had stated that only 33 percent of white children score in this range. Forty-two percent of these black children scored above 125, and 26 percent above 130. With regard to the "mulatto hypothesis," Bond, with a bit of sarcasm, indicated that "the most fortunate part of the whole study is that these children have not yet achieved prominence and accordingly, have not yet been classified as mulattoes. One little girl made a score of 142. Neither the child nor her parentage evidences any admixture of white blood. Of the five children with the highest scores, not one was any lighter in complexion than the brown races of Africa." Bond knew that some would argue that these children "come from homes on the whole superior to the 'typical' Negro home," but he reiterated the fact that this very small group, tested under more positive conditions, contained a large number of exceptional black children.

Other black educators and psychologists administered the "intelligence tests" to black children and reported similar results. In 1930 Howard H. Long and Martin D. Jenkins began a series of investigations which produced mental test scores for blacks that were much higher than those reported during the 1920s, and which tended to refute the claims of the "Mulatto hypothesis." Long, who became Associate Superintendent for Research in the District of Columbia Public Schools, administered a battery of mental tests to black and white children in the schools in 1929 and 1930. He found that the average I.Q. for the black children in the public schools, and born in the district, as 95.25; while for comparable white children it was 100. This score for the black children was much higher than the scores reported for other groups of blacks before this time.

Long believed that one of the reasons why blacks in Washington scored higher on the intelligence tests was because the expenditures for black education in that city were much higher than in other places. He noted that children who recently migrated to Washington from other parts of the South usually scored lower on the mental tests than children born in the District. But, at the same time, Long reported that the average scores for black children in the upper grades was much lower than the averages in the lower grades. He suggested that this occurred because black children in the upper grades were not being taught the subject matter on the advanced mental tests.

Martin D. Jenkins while a graduate student at Northwestern University in the 1930s carried on a number of investigations of exceptional black children in the Chicago public schools. He identified and studied the background of over 120 black children with (Stanford-Binet) I.Q. scores over 120. With respect to the incidence of Negro children of superior intelligence within the black school population, he reported that "superior Negro children are spread rather evenly throughout the various age and grade levels, no age or grade having a preponderance of subjects." The overall socioeconomic status of these superior black students was high, and "in home background, in developmental history, in physical development, in school progress, in educational achievement, in interests, in activities, and in social and personal characteristics; Negro children of superior intelligence resemble other American children of superior intelligence."

In this research Jenkins directly addressed several aspects of the mulatto hypothesis:

> That Negro ancestry is not a limiting factor in intelligence test performance is suggested further by the racial composition of our subjects. In racial composition an American "Negro" may range from practically pure white to "pure" Negro. Now, if whites are superior to Negroes in intelligence-test performance *because of a racial factor*, a group of Negro children of superior intelligence should be composed predominantly, if not exclusively, of children with large amounts of white ancestry. This group of Negro children of superior intelligence, however, constitutes a typical cross-section in racial composition, of the American Negro population. The findings of this study suggest that the differences in the test performance of white and Negro children found by so many investigators are *not* due to inherent racial factor.

In his investigations of gifted black children Jenkins reported identifying a black girl, age 9, in the Chicago public schools with an I.Q. of 200. Her mother was a teacher and her father was an electrical engineer. With regard to her "racial composition," Jenkins stated that "the mother reports 'B' to be of pure Negro stock. There is no record of any white ancestors on either the maternal or paternal side."

Many black educators and psychologists made it clear they believed that the administration of intelligence tests to black children and comparing the results with those of whites was unfair under most circumstances because of the great disparity in the social and educational opportunities between blacks and whites in this country. During the period 1920 to 1940, most blacks lived in the South and the segregated public school systems to which they were subjected were grossly inadequate by any standards. Even in the North, predominantly black schools were known to be inadequately maintained, overcrowded, and lacking in many of the basic materials for instruction. Thus it was to be expected that blacks would not do as well as whites of the same age and grade levels on these intelligence and achievement tests. However, the poor performance of blacks on these tests led some white researchers to suggest that given the "mental inferiority" of Negroes, they should not be taught in the same classes as whites since they would probably retard the educational progress of the white children. From as early as 1913, the mental testers were stating that the inferior mental abilities of the Negro required that he be educated in "separate schools" with a "special (industrial) curriculum."

Joseph St. Clair Price of West Virginia State College examined in 1929 the numerous studies of the intellectual and physical development of blacks and whites and pointed out that most of the investigations concluded that black children developed physically more rapidly than did whites. With regard to intelligence, however, most of the social science research maintained that blacks were inferior. Price concluded that the reason for the poor performance on the mental tests was most likely the result of the inferior education which blacks received in the segregated schools of the South.

Doxey Wilkerson in an article entitled, "Racial Differences in Scholastic Achievement," published in the *Journal of Negro Education* in 1934, reviewed the studies of black and white performance and achievement tests and found that "the disparity between the scores of Negro and white children on standard achievement tests is in general greater than on standard tests of intelligence." This finding, however, had no "logical implications for education," according to Wilkerson, because "individual members of both races are to be found on the highest and lowest levels of scholastic achievement." After a lengthy analysis of many of the reports on the scholastic achievement of blacks and whites in segregated schools, Wilkerson concluded that "Negro school children in general, particularly in the segregated school systems, achieve on a lower level than white children in the same school systems." As was the case with "intellectual abilities," he found that "racial differences in home and school environment are probably the major causes of racial differences in scholastic achievement." Though many other researchers, both black and white, were to conclude that the poor performance of many blacks on intelligence and achievement tests was very likely due to lack of educational opportunities for black children in this country, the results of these mental tests were continually dragged out in order to demonstrate why segregated schooling was best for blacks as well as whites.

Some white researchers went so far as to try and demonstrate that blacks performed better in segregated schools. In 1929 L.A. Pechstein published a report in which he concluded that "segregation of Negro and white children in separate schools accomplished far more for the black race than can be gained in mixed classes." His evidence for this conclusion was the fact that the separate black high schools produced more black graduates than did mixed high schools; the results of a study of 100 Negroes of eminence which showed that 83 percent attended separate elementary schools; and a study of 3000 Negro pupils which showed "much mental deficiency and retardation." W.E.B. DuBois responded to this report in *The Crisis* in September 1929 in his famous editorial, "Pechstein and Pecksniff." DuBois blasted Pechstein for being "narrow in reasoning and ignorant of all the facts." He also informed Pechstein and any others who were interested that "most Negroes had to be educated in separate schools or not be educated at all since for a hundred years more than 9/10 of them were offered 'Jim Crow' schools or nothing."

> It is obvious that the well-known and magnificent Negro high schools of Baltimore and Washington send out a much larger proportion of well trained Negro graduates than the Negro-baiting mixed high schools of a hundred different Northern cities. But Merciful God! is this an argument *for* segregation, or *against* discrimination, cruelty, cheating and hate on the part of white pupils, teachers, and officials? . . . The success of some separate Negro schools is a crushing indictment of hatred and prejudice and not a demand for further segregation. If Negroes have done well in certain separate Negro schools, two speculations arise: how much more might Negroes have done if all their separate schools had been adequately equipped and taught; and further what might not the Negro pupil have done if without hurt of hindrance the whole educational opportunity of America had been open to him without discrimination.

DuBois in *The Crisis* and Charles Johnson in *Opportunity* magazine provided a running commentary on the activities of the mental testers during the 1920s. With the advent of the *Journal of Negro Education* in 1932, edited by Charles Thompson, black social scientists had an important organ for criticizing and disseminating their own research findings on the intellectual and scholastic abilities of black Americans. In the July 1934 yearbook issue of the *Journal*, which was devoted to an examination of the research on "the Physical and Mental Abilities of the American Negro," Joseph St. Clair Price reviewed the various studies of "Negro-White Differences in General Intelligence" and concluded that "there has been no adequate comprehensive measurement of Negro intelligence." Price was able to support this contention by demonstrating that:

> "on the one hand, the tests used have been standardized upon Northern whites, largely, whose schooling has been different in amount and kind from the great bulk of Negroes who, of course, are in the South. And, on the other hand, the sampling has neither been random nor representative, for the groups compared have either (or both) been too small and/or they have been unlike in socio-economic status, school training and cultural background."

Price reiterated the findings of many previous researchers that the differences between blacks and whites on the various mental tests were attributable, either in whole or in part, to environmental factors. In 1939 Martin Jenkins came to the same conclusions after a thorough review of the major studies of black-white mental differences, and concluded that "any program looking toward the development of the American Negro must be based on the assumption that the race is fully capable, from the standpoint of mental ability, of assuming a position of equality in the social order."

There is evidence that by 1940 the general social science community began to take seriously the objections of these black social scientists to the studies of the comparative mental abilities of blacks and whites. The 1940 yearbook of the National Society for the Study of Education was devoted to a "Comparative and Critical Exposition" of *Intelligence: Its Nature and Nurture.* In contrast to the Society's "Terman Yearbook" of 1928, this later assessment contained studies which attempted to demonstrate the significance of environmental conditions upon mental test performance as well as investigations which tried to substantiate the belief that heredity was the major determinant of "intellectual abilities."

The 1940 yearbook also contained a section on "Intelligence as Related to Race." Leta S. Hollingsworth, Professor of Education at Teachers College, Columbia University, discussed the "Problem of Comparing Races." She began by quoting the unanimous resolution of the American Anthropological Association, passed 1938, which stated that "race involves the inheritance of similar physical variations by large groups of mankind, but its psychological and cultural connotations, if any exist, have not been ascertained by science . . . Anthropology provides no scientific basis for discrimination against any people on the ground of racial inferiority, religious affiliation, or linguistic heritage." She also pointed out that psychologists "have not yet ascertained whether differences in mental ability, or mental pattern exist among the races of men. More specifically, the position would be that it is at present wholly

unknown whether there are differences in intelligence as related to ethnic species."

In his discussion of the "Research Upon the American Negro," Paul
Witty of Northwestern University reviewed the research findings of
Martin Jenkins and others, and concluded that "results from extensive
and thorough research have demonstrated, of course, that there are
differences between the races, and in subgroups within each race-*not*
that there are true racial differences in innate or inherited intelligence."
Thus one of the major American research societies, which from 1922
had been active in gathering and publishing the major research findings
on "intelligence testing," reported in 1940 that to that date the much-
discussed innate mental inferiority of blacks to whites had not been
demonstrated. And in drawing this conclusion, the commentators cited
the work of one of the leading black psychologists in the area.

The emphasis in this essay has been placed upon the research and
other activities of black social scientists in bringing about the shift in the
beliefs of some members of the social scientific community about differences in the mental abilities of blacks and whites. However, several
white researchers were also active in this area. Melville Herskovits carried out a great deal of research which demonstrated the inadequacies
of the so-called "mulatto hypothesis." Otto Klineberg's famous study of
Negro Intelligence and Selective Migration demonstrated that with respect
to mental test results, "the superiority of the Northern over the Southern Negroes, and the tendency of Northern Negroes to approximate the
scores of whites, are due to factors in the environment, and not to the
selective migration" of the more intelligent Negroes from the South.
And the seminal work of anthropologist Franz Boas on the mental abilities of so-called "primitive" peoples paved the way for much of the
research of later social scientists on the mental abilities of black and
white Americans.

In focusing on the activities of black educators and psychologists
in mental testing between 1920 and 1940, however, we are able to gain
several important insights into the role of the black scholar and intellectual in the advancement of blacks in this country. The findings and
conclusions of the mental testers became one of the major components
of "Jim Crow's Defense" in the twentieth century. Black social scientists
directly challenged the conclusions of the mental testers, and indirectly
assisted in loosening the grip of racial discrimination and segregation
on American society.

In reviewing the historical and sociological literature on black
Americans, one gets the impression that blacks had no intellectual heritage. Some works point out that there were blacks who "thought," but
few would acknowledge the existence of a scholarly or intellectual tradition in black America. However, the activities of black social scientists

with regard to the mental tests serves as one important example of how black intellectuals functioned historically in the United States. These black researchers were aware of the research in the field of mental testing, received the necessary training and carried out their own experiments and investigations, disseminated their findings and conclusions in the leading educational, psychological, and popular journals of the period; and eventually had their conclusions accepted generally in some sectors of the social scientific community. Hopefully, other historians and sociologists will begin to systematically document and interpret the role of the black scholar and intellectual and other teachers, and the average American citizen will become aware of the significance of the black intellectual tradition in this county.

Note

1 I would like to acknowledge the financial assistance of a Summer Faculty Fellowship from the National Academy of Education in the completion of this article.

References

Boas, F. (1911). *The mind of primitive man*. New York: The Macmillan Co.
Boas, F. (1910). The real race problem. *The Crisis, 1*, 22-25.
Bond, H.M. (1924). Intelligence tests and propaganda, *The Crisis, 28*, 63.
Bond, H.M. (1927, October). Some exceptional Negro children. *The Crisis 34*, 257-259.
Bond, H.M. (1966). *The education of the Negro in the American social order*. Reprinted New York: Octagon Books.
Bond, H.M., & Johnson, C. (1934, July). The investigation of racial differences prior to 1910. *The Journal of Negro Education, 3*, 328-339.
Brigham, C. (1923). *A study of American intelligence*. Princeton, NJ: Princeton University Press.
Canady, H. (1936). The effect of rapport on the I.Q.: A new approach to the problem of racial psychology. *Journal of Negro Education, 5*, 209-219.
Colwin, S. (1922). Principles underlying the construction and use of intelligence tests. In The Twenty-First Yearbook of the National Society for the Study of Education (NSSE), *Intelligence tests and their use*, p. 43. Bloomington, IL: Public School Publishing Company.

DuBois, W.E.B. (1929). Pechstein and Pecksniff. *The Crisis, 36*, 336-350.

Fredrickson, G. (1971). *The black image in the white mind: The debate on Afro-American character and destiny, 1817-1914* (pp. 97-129). New York: Harper & Row.

Goddard, H.H. (1910). Four hundred feeble-minded children classified by the Binet method. *Pedagogical Seminary, 17*, 390-398.

Goddard, H.H. (1911). Two thousand normal children measured by the Binet measuring scale of intelligence, *Pedagogical Seminary, 18*, 233.

Gossett, T.F. (1963). *Race: The history of an idea in America*, Dallas, TX: Southern Methodist University Press, pp. 5-9, 9-29.

Guthrie R.V. (1976). *Even the rat was white: A historical view of psychology*. New York: Harper & Row.

Herskovits, M. (1934). A critical discussion of the 'Mulatto Hypothesis'. *Journal of Negro Education*, 389-402.

Hollingsworth, L.S., (1940). The problem of comparing races. In *The Thirty-Ninth Yearbook of the NSSE*, p. 257-258.

Jenkins, M.D., & Witty, P. (1934). The educational achievement of a group of gifted Negro children, *Journal of Educational Psychology, 25*, 585-597.

Jenkins, M.D., & Witty, P. (1935). The case of 'B' —A gifted Negro girl. *Journal of Social Psychology, 6*, 119.

Jenkins, M.D. (1936). A socio-psychological study of Negro children of superior intelligence. *Journal of Negro Education, 4*, 190.

Jensen, A. (1975). Can Negroes learn the way whites do? In C. Karier, *Shaping the American Educational State*, pp. 342-348.

Johnson, C. (1923). Mental measurement of Negro groups. *Opportunity, 1*, 21-28.

Jordan, W.D. (1969). *White over black: American attitudes toward the Negro 1550-1812. Baltimore, MD: Penguin Books.*

Kamin, L. (1974). *The science and politics of IQ*, Potomac, MD: L. Earlbaum Associates.

Karier, C.J. (1973). Testing for order and control in the corporate liberal state. In *Roots of crisis: American education in the twentieth century* (pp. 108-137). Chicago, IL: Rand McNally.

Kamin, L. (1975). Heredity, intelligence, politics, and psychology. In *Shaping the American educational state, 1900 to the present*. New York: Free Press.

Karier, C.J. (1975). *Shaping the American educational state, 1900 to the present*, New York: Free Press.

Klineberg, O. (1935). *Negro intelligence and selective migration*, (pp. 1-62). New York: Columbia University Press.

Loehlin, J.C. (1975). *Race differences in intelligence*, San Francisco, CA: W.H. Freeman.

Long, H.H. (1923, March). Race and mental tests, *Opportunity, 1*, 22-25.

Long, H.H. (1925). On mental tests and racial psychology: A critique. *Opportunity, 3*, 134-138.

Long, H.H. (1934). The intelligence of colored elementary pupils in Washington, D.C. *Journal of Negro Education, 4*, 205-222.

Long, H.H. (1935). Test results of third grade Negro children selected on the basis of socio-economic status. *Journal of Negro Education, 4*, 192-212, 523-552.

Lyons, C. (1975). *To wash an aethipe white: British ideas about black African educability, 1530-1960*, (pp. 52-85). New York: Teachers College Press.

MacPherson, J. (1964). *The struggle for equality: Abolitionists and the Negro in the civil war and reconstruction*, (pp. 144, 149-150). Princeton, NJ: Princeton University Press.

Meier, A. (1963). *Negro thought in America: racial ideologies in the age of Booker T. Washington*. Ann Arbor, MI: University of Michigan Press.

Meier, A. (1969). *Black protest thought in the twentieth century*. Indianapolis, IN: Bobbs-Merrill.

Miller, K. (1897). *A review of Hoffman's race traits and tendencies of the American Negro*. Washington, DC.

Miller, H.A. (1906). Some psychological considerations on the race problem. In W.E.B. DuBois, (Ed.), *The health and physique of the Negro American*. Atlanta, GA: Atlanta University Press.

Newby, I.A. (1965). *Jim Crow's defense: Anti Negro thought in America, 1900-1930*. Baton Rouge, LA: Louisiana State University Press.

Odum, H. (1913). Negro children in the public schools of Philadelphia. *The Annals of the American Academy of Political and Social Science, 49*, 186-208.

Price, J. St. C. (1929). Negro-white differences in intelligence. *Opportunity, 7*, 341-343.

Price, J. St. C. (1934). Negro-white differences in general intelligence. *Journal of Negro Education, 3*, 424-452.

Peterson, J. (1923). *The comparative abilities of white and Negro children*. Baltimore, MD: The Williams and Wilkins Company.

Reuter, E. (1928). The American mulatto. *The Annals of the American Academy of Political and Social Science, 140, 36-43.*

Terman, L. (1922, October). Were we born that way? *World's Work, 44*, 660.

Thorndike, E.L. (1921). Intelligence. *Journal of Educational Psychology, 12*, 123-147.

Twenty-Seventh Yearbook of the National Society for the Study of Education, (1928), *Nature and Nurture: Their influence upon achievement*. Bloomington, IL: Public School Publishing Company.

Thirty-Ninth Yearbook of the National Society for the Study of Education, (1940). *Intelligence: Its nature and nuture, comparative and critical exposition*. Bloomington, IL: Public School Publishing Company.

Viteles, M. (1928). The mental status of the Negro. In *The Annals of the American Academy of Political and Social Science, 140*, 166-177.

Wilkerson, D. (1934). Racial differences in scholastic achievement. *Journal of Negro Education, 3*, 477.

Witty, P. (1940). Research upon the American Negro. In *The Thirty-Ninth Yearbook of the National Society for the Study of Education*, p. 262.

Yerkes, Robert, (1921). *Memoirs*. Washington, DC: National Academy of Sciences.

Reconstruction

IV. Reconstruction

The papers in this section have been written to provide, on the basis of present knowledge and conceptualizations by African American scholars, a psychological portrait of African Americans. The work presented projects African Americans in a positive light, and without defensiveness. Some of the analyses and conclusions are based on black-white comparisons, but much written here represents new conceptualizations and interpretations or reinterpretations of the literature—with African Americans as the frame of reference and the point of departure. The intention is to be relatively wide-ranging in the topics covered. Thus, literature on cognitive as well as non-cognitive attributes is covered, including personality, cognitive style, non-verbal behavior, language, and psychological health and disorder.

How do African Americans come to know the world? Answers to this question are basic to our understanding of many aspects of the psychological functioning of African Americans. Shade ("African American Patterns of Cognition"), working under the assumption that "Americans of African descent have developed a unique culture as a result of coping with and adapting to a color conscious society and a part of that culture includes specific and unique cognitive strategies," examines patterns of knowing that have been developed and transmitted within the African American community. In addressing the question posed above, Shade reviews a sizeable body of literature in such areas as modality preference, cue selection, and information analysis and organization. Her analyses provide strong support for the existence of distinctive African American cognitive styles.

We have come to realize that the behavior of African Americans is more than the sum of self-conception, motivation and identity, but there are unique patterns of verbal and nonverbal behavior as well. Work on these topics is covered in papers by, respectively, Smitherman, and Majors. Smitherman ("Talkin' and Testifyin': Black English and the Black Experience") focuses on Black English. After introducing the landmark Martin Luther King Junior Elementary School v. Ann Arbor School District Board case, that ". . . reaffirmed the legitimacy of Black English and the existence of its African substratum," Smitherman goes on to describe the nature of Black English, its history, and its present-day status and future, and presents what she believes should be the elements of a language policy for the African American community.

In the most comprehensive paper on the subject to date, Majors ("Nonverbal Behaviors and Communication Styles Among African

Americans") describes and evaluates a vast literature on African American nonverbal behavior and communication styles, including research and writing on such topics as African American kinesics (including walking, stances, handshakes, facial expressions, eye and visual behavior, etc.), proxemics, hairstyles, dance, clothes, automobiles, and sports. As do several authors in the present volume, Majors discusses areas needing additional research and study.

Investigation of black self concept has been an area of considerable study. An underlying assumption is that exposure to racism and oppression has damaged the African American's psychological makeup. The papers by Nobles ("Extended Self: Rethinking the So-Called Negro Self-Concept") and James Jones ("The Politics of Personality: Being Black in America") reject such a notion but do, nevertheless, hold different points of view concerning the origins of African American personality. Nobles' view might be considered Afrocentric, while Jones' orientation embraces a more multidimensional explanation. As was seen in earlier papers (Baldwin and Akbar, for example) some tension exists among scholars concerning the framework that most appropriately accounts for the psychological dimensions of African American life, including personality generally and self-concept specifically. Nobles asks basic questions about the philosophical and referential bases of conceptualization and study. He indicates, for example, that the conceptions and research on black self-concept have been controlled by others, with the consequence that the kinds of questions asked have already predetermined the realm in which the answers will fall. Nobles argues for a conception of self rooted in the African world view and philosophical tradition. Jones, does not deny that the African legacy is one element in the development of black personality. Rather, he argues for a theory of black personality organized around racism and black responses to it.

Several propositions and theories about black identity development and transformation were introduced in the early 1970s. The most developed of the formulations, that by Cross and his associates, was introduced in the first edition of *Black Psychology*. The paper made extensive reference to the work of the late Charles Thomas, who, during the same period, was formulating somewhat similar notions about the nature and development of black identity. These early writings introduced provocative and fundamental hypotheses about identity development and transformation and sought to explain the changes in self-conception that seemed to be occurring. With repeated exposure to black power and black is beautiful slogans, and in the face of riots, bombings, and burnings, it was difficult to deny that changes in black behavior, and undoubtedly in black identity and self-conception, were taking place. It remained for Cross and Thomas, however, to advance explanations which illuminated the processes underlying these hypothesized changes.

The paper by Cross, Parham and Helms ("The Stages of Black Identity Development: Nigresence Models") summarizes the early work and thinking on the topic and introduces recent theoretical advances and empirical studies, the most significant of which are an extension of the Nigresence model from late adolescence to late adulthood, and consideration of the identity stages as world views.

While much has been written about African American psychopathology, as Akbar ("Mental Disorder Among African Americans") reminds us in a provocative paper, we need to develop our own classification system because "the ability to decide who in your community is sane or insane is one of the ultimate measures of power and community integrity." Akbar goes on to suggest that rather than "preoccupation with disorders which threaten the life of the predators" we should direct our focus "toward those ideas and behaviors which threaten the life of the victims". Akbar classifies and describes mental disorders of African Americans from an Afrocentric perspective.

Very little has been written about African American psychological health, strength, and resilience. These topics are the subject of papers by Ramseur ("Psychologically Healthy Black Adults") and Hayles ("African American Strengths: A Survey of Empirical Findings"). Ramseur discusses the social/cultural situation of African Americans, essential elements of an ideal model of adult psychological health, and models of African American personality and identity that have psychological health implications. And in one of the first and by far the most systematic coverage of the subject to date, Hayles summarizes a sizeable literature on African Americans psychological strengths, superiority, and distinctive competencies and covers such topics as cognitive performance, interpersonal perception, field independence-dependence, psychomotor functioning, sensorimotor development, coping with confinement, role taking and role taking skills, family functioning, and functioning in organizations.

African American Patterns of Cognition

Barbara J. Shade

Cognition, in its broadest definition, represents the act of knowing. Within the act are the processes of perception, memory, mental elaboration and reasoning. Although, as Cole and Scribner (1974) point out, the processes are basically the same for all individuals, differences are noted in the way the processes are used. The basis of these variations is found in the demands of a specific ecocultural environment (Thompson, 1969; Berry, 1976). The purpose of this paper is to examine the patterns of knowing which have been developed and transmitted within the Afro-American community. Such a search is built on the premise that Americans of African descent have developed a unique culture as the result of coping with and adapting to a color-conscious society and a part of that culture includes specific and unique cognitive strategies.

Identifying African American differences is a perilous task in that the identified variations are generally interpreted as deficient and in negative terms. In spite of this difficulty, differences in the use of cognitive processes will be explored with the hope that these will be viewed as preferences or stylistic dimensions rather than badges of inferiority.

In this exploratory effort, questions undoubtedly will be raised about the wisdom of depicting African Americans as a monolithic group. This occurs for several reasons. First, there is the recognition that "color" affects the environmental responses of all African Americans, regardless of social class. In addition, at this point in history, there still remains a viable social-cultural system which transmits both the African American world view and cognitive-behavioral patterns to all levels of the community (Blackwell, 1975).

The third reason for the assumption of homogeneity stems from the study by Stodolsky and Lesser (1967). They found that, although class differences were present in levels of performance, an ethnic group's overall pattern was essentially the same.

There are, of course, reasons to believe that there may be developmental and gender differences within the African American community as there are in other groups. Unfortunately, the current studies of African American cognition have neglected these variables, thus, individual differences are difficult to ascertain. Within the studies reviewed here, neither social class nor gender differences were identifiable.

The studies chosen for this review will deal with children and youth, aged 3-21, who are native-born African Americans. Studies using international samples of individuals with African heritage were not selected as it was felt that the ecological demands are not equivalent in both societies; therefore, cognitive patterns might not be similar. Also, the patterns to which we allude are not seen as innate characteristics, but socialized environmental behavior. To use Africans or African Americans from another culture and environment seems to suggest that genetic factors are involved rather than ecocultural dimensions.

A second, and equally important, characteristic of the subjects in the studies chosen for review is that they represent a "normal" population. As Bruner (1968) points out, "Our insights into mental functioning are too often shaped by the observations of the sick and the handicapped. It is difficult to catch . . . man's mind . . . at its best." (p. 15) It was this reviewer's wish to understand African American cognition at its best, not after it had succumbed to the pressures of the environment.

With these general guidelines in mind, let us return to the examination of the important question: Do African Americans have a unique pattern of cognitive strategies or a cognitive style? To determine the answer, it is necessary to use the information processing paradigm and examine the way in which African Americans perceive, encode, represent and analyze information.

African American Information Processing

The information processing model which has emerged in the last decade assumes that man's internal structures perform certain behavioral processes (Strom & Bernard, 1982). More important, the paradigm assumes an interaction between the environment and the organism rather than a reaction.

Numerous models have emerged to depict the process (Gagne, 1977; Das, Jarmon, & Kirby, 1975; Anderson, 1980). In general, the models suggest that:

1. The information is registered through the preferred sensory modality or modalities and preferred cues are selected for attention.
2. The information is then placed in short-term memory for recognition and labeling.

3. The information is sorted, classified, and organized.
4. Following organization, the information is analyzed and incorporated; then, performance requirements specified.
5. The individual decides to act or respond on the basis of the analysis of the information.

The major variation in this processing of information which seems to be uniquely African American occurs in the preprocessing and central processing stages, e.g., in patterns of perception.

African American Patterns of Perception

Perception is the basic process of cognition as it is the process through which the living organism maintains contact with the environment (Travers, 1982). Research in the area stipulates that perception is heavily influenced by one's socialization and past experiences. As J.J. Gibson (1950) points out, individuals are taught to "see the world." This process of "seeing" involves not only the sensation or reception of the sensory stimuli, but also involves an analytical process. There is reason to believe that the perceptual process of African Americans differs in style from other groups.

The question of a unique perceptual style within the African American community has been around for some time. It was first raised by Tyler in 1956 and again by Mandler and Stein in 1977. Mandler and Stein point out in their examination of this issue that the question has been reinterpreted as a truism without any substantial empirical documentation. Although it is an issue which has not been confronted directly, it is one which seems to manifest itself continually as we look for a pattern which represents how African American culture trains its children to learn.

Sensory Modality Preference

One of the first variations noted in African American perceptual style is in the preference of modalities for receiving information. Information present in the environment is registered in all six sensory channels. However, there appears to be a hierarchy of development which leads to the efficient and preferential use of the channels. According to Barsch (1971), the younger child makes the most efficient use of the gustatory, olfactory, and tactile senses. However, as learning occurs and cognitive effectiveness increases, the kinesthetic, auditory, and visual modes become the ones most heavily relied upon. As we examine the mode most emphasized in mainstream American culture, we note that emphasis is placed on perceiving via the visual channel.

The majority of information in our society is transmitted through visually oriented material. Vision is seen as the "queen" of the sensory registration modes and is the medium through which we attempt to assess learning ability and other aspects of cognition. If one examines the instruments on which many judgments about individuals are made such as the Raven's Progressive Matrices, the Bender-Gestalt Test, the Thematic Apperception Test, the Group Embedded Figures Test, and the performance tasks of the intelligence tests, one notes that these are predominantly, and almost exclusively, visual information processing tasks.

It is, however, an error to assume that all individuals have the same modality preference or the same efficiency in use. Barbe and Swassing (1979) found that individuals have a modality through which they prefer to receive information and that the preferred modality may not be vision. Wober (1966) agrees and further suggests that the demands of the environment develop this preference.

To support his point, Wober worked with the Embedded Figures Test, the Rod-and-Frame Test, the Kohs Block Design and the Raven's Progressive Matrices. In addition to the visually oriented versions, the tests were converted into tactile and proprioceptive versions as well. The results demonstrated that the style of processing information in one modality does not correlate highly with the ability to process information in another modality. Individuals who had performed at the lower end of the continuum on the visually oriented tasks did better on the kinesthetic/tactile versions of the instruments. Wober concluded that there are different *sensotypes*. By sensotypes, Wober means the modality pattern preferred by the child for perceiving the world and upon which the child develops his or her abilities. This concept is much the same as Barsch's (1971) processing mode hierarchy which is said to represent the rank order of the sensory modes in which individuals prefer to receive information.

The idea of an individual preference in modality dominance is another resurrected idea. Fernald presented the same hypothesis in 1912 and later conducted a study to identify visual learners, auditory learners, and kinesthetic learners (Fernald, 1943). Like Barsch and Barbe, Fernald promotes the belief that, while all modalities are active, individuals find some modalities more effective and efficient than others. This premise leads to the question: Is there a more effective modality for learning than vision for African Americans?

Charles Keil (1966) noted in his book, *Urban Blues*, that there are certain modes of perception more characteristic of the black community than the white community. In his explication of the various cultural components of the community, Keil writes:

> . . . its modes of perception and expression, its channels of communication are predominantly auditory and tactile rather than visual and literate . . . the prominence of the aural perception, oral expression and kinesic codes . . . sharply demarcate the culture from the white world. (p. 16-17).

Other indications that African Americans may have a different modality preference come from the ethnographic study done by Pavenstedt and her associates of thirteen low income children from problem families. In the report (Pavenstedt et al, 1967), the observers commented that the children were rather advanced in their motor development and seemed to use visual perception differently than usually observed. Malone (1967) noted in his part of the study that the children used vision as ways of protecting and orienting themselves in the environment rather than for gathering information.

Although the aural mode is undoubtedly a very important channel in African American culture, it seems very probable that the kinesthetic mode is the primary mode of information induction for the majority of the members of the community. This supposition is based upon the literature in the field of motor learning. The evidence has been around for some time that African Americans have a high motoric capability due to their apparent sensorimotor precocity (Morgan, 1981). They also appear to use kinesics more than most groups. Guttentag (1972) for example, studied the difference in the number and variety of movements of African American and Euro-American four year olds. She found that African American children emitted significantly greater movement responses and a greater variety. Van Alstyne and Osbourne (1937) examined the rhythmic responses of black and white children between the ages of two and six. African American children were found to be 50% better than Euro-American children in following rhythms. In a similar study, Stigler (1940) compared the capacity of the two groups to perceive minute body movements by attaching a kinesimeter to study peripheral acuity. African Americans were superior in their ability to perceive the slightest body movements. One might conclude from these studies that African Americans are adept at gathering, using and analyzing kinesthetic information.

In his book, *The Mind's Eye*, Sommers (1978) details the characteristics of individuals who are high in kinesthetic imagery. These individuals can take in and elaborate in great detail spontaneous motoric responses. The description presented by Sommers closely parallels the descriptions often noted by sociologists and anthropologists of African American rhythm, spontaneity and movement as exhibited in walks, stance, dance, and athletic encounters (Pasteur & Toldson, 1982; Kochman, 1972). Apparently, imagery is one of the best ways to study modal preferences. For example, Colvin and Meyer (cited in Barsch, 1971) read a story comprised of visual, auditory, and motor words to a group of children. The children were then asked to write the story the following day. The number of words recalled in each modality was judged to indicate the primary modal preference. Perhaps the closest use of this approach to study African American modalities is the work done by Kochman in black idiom. In his study of the communication pattern to which most African Americans revert when interacting with one another, Kochman found that there was a preponderance of words which possess the quality of rapid and unrestricted movement or have the potential for such movement. Conversely, words which suggest static or impeded movement have unfavorable connotations. Kochman (1972) goes on to suggest that patterns such as the identified kinetic quality of the language have a significant influence on the minds and habits of the speakers. We assume that this pattern of kinetic preference is also operating within the African American perceptual process.

Cue Selection

In addition to a difference in sensory modality preference, there appears to be a variation in African American cue selection.

The number and types of information to which an individual is exposed are massive; therefore, choices must be made about the cues or information an individual can address. Thompson (1969), Gibson (1969) and others suggest that a culture trains its children to tune in on certain types of information and filter out others. Young (1974) in her examination of the socialization process, suggests that African Americans are trained to concentrate on people rather than non-people types of information. This is essentially a dichotomy of looking at people and events as opposed to ideas and objects.

Evidence of cue preference is found in several studies. Damico (1983) examined the person-vs-object hypothesis by permitting black and white sixth grade children the opportunity to photograph school as they perceived it. Although the findings were apparently an artifact or secondary finding of a larger study, the significant difference in the types of photographs taken to depict the meaning of school seemed to support the hypothesis. African American children chose to include people such as teachers or classmates in their pictures while the Euro-American children depicted objects or physical settings. Damico concluded that African American children were significantly more people than object oriented.

In another study, Eato and Lerner (1981) asked 183 African American sixth graders to indicate their perceptions of their physical school environment and their social environment in the school. The researchers were attempting to determine which of the factors seemed to influence the children's adaptive behavior. The major factor which seemed to be most important to all children was the people in the environment, particularly the teachers. The physical environment seemed important only to the males and at a fairly minimal level.

Other indications that African Americans seem to have a preference for social and human cues is found in the literature on recognition of faces and emotions. It has been found that not only are African Americans better able to recognize faces and emotions than groups with which they are compared (Galper, 1973; Chance, Goldstein, & McBride, 1975; Luce, 1974; Gitter, Black, & Mostosoky, 1972) but they also are extremely sensitive to social situational nuances (Hill & Fox, 1973; Witmer & Ferinden, 1970). This attention to social nuances may have led to the results which Sherif (1973) observed about the differences in categorization of situations. In his study, African American and Euro-American students were asked to analyze and sort out situations which were acceptable for participation in terms of interracial interactions and those which were unacceptable. African American students were found to make their decisions based upon the interpersonal demands and the possible social effects on the person while Euro-American students categorized situations based upon the formal demands of the setting. Again, for African Americans, people took precedence over rules and context.

Other indications that the interpersonal domain has a primary spot in African American attention is found in the research on learning styles. African Americans seem to prefer affective materials to facilitate their learning (Rychlak, 1975), warm and supportive teachers (St. John, 1971), and a socially interactive environment (Slavin, 1983; Cureton, 1978). As Morgan (1981) points out in his examination of the learning style of African American children, "It appears as though the social interaction model provides an atmosphere in which black children can do well."

This information preference pattern probably is best represented in the behavioral dimension as *extroversion*. Although there are many interpretations of the extroversion-introversion dimension, the one which seems to fit the information processing paradigm best is the conceptualization by Carl Jung. According to Jung (1923), extroversion represents a preference for and attention to the external world rather than the internal world of ideas, concepts or insights (introversion). The choice manifests itself in the preference for action, for involvement and for being a part of the human scene (Myers, 1980). The Myers-Briggs Type Indicator measures extroversion based upon Jung's interpretation.

Using a group of 758 undergraduates at Howard University, Levy, Murphy, and Carlson (1972) administered the Myers-Briggs Type Indicator at two different times in order to establish the test's reliability for their population. A comparison of the 146 males of the sample with a Euro-American sample from Amherst revealed that a larger percentage of the African American population fell in the extroversion category than in the introverted categories that occurred with Euro-American males. A similar finding emerged in a recent study of ninth grade students done by this author (Shade, 1983). When viewed *in toto*, both the African American and Euro-American groups were extroverted. However, when divided by achievement level, the African American high achievers and the Euro-American low achievers were extroverted while the Euro-American high achievers and the African American low achievers preferred their internal world.

When Morris (1979) reviewed the literature on extroversion-introversion, he noted that in general most children are externally oriented until around ages 12 and 13, and up to that point extroversion is highly correlated with school achievement. After that age, students who do well become more introverted and introversion becomes more highly correlated with achievement. For African Americans, it is interesting to note that the developmental change occurs only for the high-risk students who are not finding much success in school while African American students who manage to succeed maintain their orientation toward social interaction and involvement.

Farley (1974), in his studies of cue preference and motivation, has proposed that extroverts are individuals seeking stimulation from their outside world and in their search, they look for a variety of stimuli, complexity, novelty, and activity. Although he uses a different terminology, it appears that this is the same description Boykin (1979) gives of African American children in his discussion of psychological and behavioral verve. According to Boykin, African American children seem to prefer and need a variety of information at a constantly changing pace and seem to have little tolerance for monotonous or low-level activity. Euro-American children, on the other hand, seem to be able to tolerate a more low-keyed and less varied type of activity.

An interesting by-product of this orientation, according to Farley (1981), is that this preference for high stimulation or extroversion is believed to be predictive of creative performance and a highly creative personality. Perhaps it is. In a study of the performance of 70 African American eighth grade students in northeast Georgia on various creative and cognitive measures, Richmond (1971) found that African Americans were superior to Euro-Americans on the test of figural elaboration. This task is seen as a test of ability to elaborate, embellish, and develop ideas, and a demonstration of high sensitivity in observation.

It is one of Torrance's tests of creativity. While the evidence that this group of students was extroverted comes from the author's own observation of their intensity and personal involvement in the testing situation and their friendliness toward the examiners, the finding does raise the question of the possibility of a relationship between African American cue preference and creativity as suggested by Farley.

Information Analysis and Organization

In addition to the differences in modality preference and cue selection, variations are also noted in the second component of perception —analysis and organization.

To handle the many types of information with which individuals are bombarded, it is necessary to learn to discriminate and group the various bits of data into broad and generalizable categories. This segmentation and division of the world is quite arbitrary and many theories suggest that the categorization of information is rooted in the cultural dimension of the individual (Rosch, 1974).

The evidence about African American encoding patterns is rather limited with the majority of the evidence found in the studies of conceptual differentiation. Of the studies available, it appears that African Americans group information about objects, as well as people and events, differently than other groups. Sigel, Anderson, and Shapiro (1966), for example, found that African Americans tended to categorize objects based upon pictorial representations of those objects in a more relational or holistic manner rather than an analytical or detail-oriented manner. Orasanu, Lee and Scribner (1979) found that African Americans tended to sort word lists on the basis of their functional use while Euro-Americans used a more taxonomic, descriptive approach. As previously mentioned, Sherif (1973) found that African Americans categorized situations differently than Euro-Americans.

The difference manifested in the sorting behavior of African Americans may be a difference in cognitive strategies with African Americans apparently proceeding with a top-down processing approach rather than the bottom-up approach most often used in teaching (Anderson, 1980). On the other hand, this variation noted in perceptual analysis and organization may be based upon "what" is being discriminated. This is to say that the types of tasks used to assess categorization behavior may not be registering a difference in processing but rather in what is being perceived (Cole, Gay, Glick, & Sharp, 1972). Sigel, Anderson, and Shapiro (1966) noted, for example, that while class and IQ did not seem to make a difference in the sorting behavior manifested, the method of presentation did have an effect. Some children within their sample did not respond to pictorial representations of the objects at all, but did very well in response to the objects themselves. In research by this author, only a slight difference was noted between African American and Euro-American students on the Clayton-Jackson Object Sorting task which is a written list of objects to be categorized. A highly significant difference was noted, however, in a pictorial task in which the students were asked to discern similar characteristics of objects and select another which was comparable (Shade, 1983).

There is a general assumption that any mode of presentation will elicit the same type of categorizing behavior (Sigel, Anderson, Shapiro, 1966). This may not be the case. Mangan (1978), Kennedy (1974), and Hagan and Jones (1978) point out that interpretations of visual images are learned within the cultural milieu of the individual. Images which may have cultural interpretations include photographs, images representing spatial information, geometric forms, and line drawings. Teaching the decoding of these representations is analogous to teaching children to read the written word (Mangan, 1978). Thus, a pictorial image should not be expected to convey the same information to all individuals or groups. If we assume, then, that the pictorial representations as found in the Matching Familiar Figures Test, the Raven's Progressive Matrices, the Bender-Gestalt Test and other such instruments are *not* the nonsymbolic representations of the world they are purported to be, we can also assume that African American children may be seeing and registering different information from these tasks than expected.

The possibility that variation in performance on pictorial psychometric tasks is due to processing differences rather than ability differences was the basis for the study conducted by Blaha, Fawaz, and Wallbrown (1979). These researchers administered the Bender-Gestalt, the Goodenough Draw-A-Person Test, and the Matching Familiar Figures Test to 74 middle class African American students in the first grade. The tasks were then correlated on the basis of the subprocess involved in the information processing paradigm and IQ. The results demonstrated that 9% of the variance in performance was accounted for by intelligence, 6% of the variance by visual-motor integration and coordination, 3% by the response time, and the remaining variance, 16%, was accounted for by the perceptual process in the information processing model.

Using the supposition that there may be a difference in what is being perceived when the information appears in pictorial form, previous studies of African American cognitive patterns were reexamined by identifying the task requirements of the tasks African American students were asked to complete.

In the study of various ethnic groups, Stodolsky and Lesser (1967) used four tasks: a verbal ability task which required memorization of verbal labels; a reasoning task which required the formation of concepts; a number facility task in which students used various arithmetic processes; and a space conceptualization task which required students to interpret pictures by visualizing movement, spatial relationships, or size. Results indicated that African Americans did best on the verbal, then the reasoning and number tasks, and ended up as the lowest of the four ethnic groups on the space conceptualization task. This pattern was found for both the middle and lower class sample as well as in the sample from another city.

Rohwer (1971) also examined the cognitive patterns of African and Euro-American children who were five to eight years of age. Large differences were found between the groups on the pictorial vocabulary task (the Peabody Picture Vocabulary Test) and the Raven's Progressive Matrices, a test which requires the completion of a pictorial pattern series. Little, if any, difference was found on the learning proficiency task which required the learning and transformation of verbal pairs. This same type of disparity is found throughout the literature with African Americans doing as well, if not better, than their age group on tasks using aural perception, but poorly on tasks requiring visual picture perception (Hall & Kaye, 1977; Guinaugh, 1971).

Backman (1972), in her study of patterns of cognitive abilities of talented youngsters from four racial groups in the ninth through the twelfth grades, compared the groups using several achievement tests, a visual reasoning task, and a task measuring perceptual-motor coordination and memory. The results reported indicated that African Americans, regardless of socioeconomic status, had high scores on the perceptual speed and accuracy task but ended up as the lowest of all the ethnic groups on the visual reasoning task.

In their review of the perceptual difference manifested by people of African American heritage, Mandler and Stein (1977) point out that this same pattern between verbal and pictorial representations appears in the literature on intelligence test performance. When the verbal and performance IQ scores are compared, little, if any, difference is noted on the verbal subtests, but consistently lower scores are found on the visual-spatial performance tasks, i.e., the Block Design Test, the Object Assembly, and the Picture Completion tasks (Young & Bright, 1954; Davidson, 1950; and Teahan & Drews, 1962). A similar pattern emerged in a study done by Vance, Hankins, and McGee (1979) using the WISC-R. Farnham-Diggory (1970) reported similar findings in her examination of information processing by young children. She found that

African American children did well in the processing and synthesizing of verbal material, but poorly on visual material which required analysis and organization.

A similar pattern of verbal and pictorial processing differences was found in the study by A.R. Jensen (1973). Children in the fourth, fifth, and sixth grades, representing three ethnic groups, were given a rather extensive battery of standardized tests. Rather than identify differences on each measure, basic underlying processes were factored out and three factors emerged. Factor one was found to load heavily on all of the verbal-type tests in the battery; factor two was represented in the pictorial type tasks; and factor three included those tests requiring memorization. Although Jensen labeled each factor as a type of intelligence, each could just as easily have been labeled types of information to be processed.

In addition to the intelligence measures and such tests as the Raven's Progressive Matrices, attention must also be paid to tests such as the Bender-Gestalt, the Thematic Apperception Test, and the Rorschach. In studies using each of these measures which require pictorial/visual information processing, African Americans end up with lower or different than expected performances (Henderson, Butler, & Goffeney, 1969; Albott & Gunn, 1971; Marmorale & Brown, 1977). It is also interesting to note that the Alpha and Beta tests used by the Army as the first classification test and which set the stage for the consistent labeling of African Americans as inferior also contained a substantial number of subtests which required visual information processing (Jenkins & Paterson, 1961).

Finally, attention must also be given to the test most often used to study cognitive style, i.e., the Embedded Figures Test, another visual processing task. As with the instruments, African Americans end up with lower scores suggesting that they are more likely to be field-dependent (Perney, 1976; Ritzinger, 1971; Schratz, 1976; Gamble, 1971; Shade, 1984).

For each of these instruments, a less than expected performance by African Americans has been interpreted as a deficit. Mandler and Stein (1977) suggest that a deficit approach is inappropriate. A more plausible explanation may be that African Americans have merely been taught to perceive, that is, to visually transform, the world differently.

Conclusion

How do African Americans come to know the world? From all indications, their knowledge is gained most effectively through kinetic and tactile senses, through the keen observation of the human scene, and through verbal descriptions. This difference in perception manifests itself, not only in world view, but also in modality preference, cue selection, and pictorial perception. Although our examinations of the effect of melanin may lead to an additional factorial contribution to the difference in the perceptual process (Pasteur & Toldson, 1982; Stewart, 1981), at this point in time, culture appears to be the major "progenitor" of this variation.

The evidence that these patterns exist, while sufficient to produce a strong intuitive argument, is really insufficient to produce the types of changes necessary in the teaching-learning process and in the assessment of skills. There is an overwhelming need for a cadre of scholars to examine these issues in the laboratories and in the field in an effort to support these propositions. With substantiation, it would then be possible to encourage a more concentrated and positive look at modality-based instruction, a less value oriented approach to the differences in cognitive style, and perhaps a process, rather than ability, orientation to the concept of intelligence.

The type of learner described by these patterns who can tolerate and live with diversity and variety, who can conceptualize the world as a whole rather than just in its parts, who is personable and an exceptional observer and interactor with society is exactly the type of person Toffler suggests will do well in "The Third Wave" civilization. If this is the case, these traits not only epitomize African Americans, but will be the type of cognitive patterns promoted for society in general. Understanding these dimensions, then, becomes not only a defense against past judgments, but also and more importantly, the basis for the development of the capacity to adapt to our future existence.

References

Albott, W.L., & Gunn, H.E. (1971). Bender-Gestalt Performance by culturally disadvantaged first graders. *Perceptual and Motor Skills, 33,* 247-250.

Anderson, J.R. (1980). *Cognitive psychology and its implications.* San Francisco: W.H. Freeman.

Backman, M.E. (1972). Patterns of mental abilities: Ethnic, socioeconomic status, and sex differences. *American Educational Research Journal, 9,* 1-12.

Barbe, W.B., & Swassing, R.H. (1979). *Teaching through modality strengths: Concepts and practices.* Columbus, OH: Zaner-Bloser.

Barsch, R.H. (1971). The processing mode hierarchy as a potential deterrent to cognitive efficiency. In J. Hellmuth (Ed.), *Cognitive studies: 2: Deficits in cognition*. New York: Brunner/Mazel.

Berry, J.W. (1976). Human ecology and cognitive style: *Comparative studies in cultural and psychological adaptation*. New York: John Wiley & Sons.

Blackwell, J.E. (1975). *The black community: Diversity and unity*. New York: Dodd, Mead.

Blaha, J., Fawaz, N., & Wallbrown, F. (1979). Information processing components of Koppitz errors on the Bender-Gestalt. *Journal of Clinical Psychology, 35*, 784-790.

Boykin, A.W. (1979). Psychological/behavioral verve: Some theoretical explorations and empirical manifestations. In A.W. Boykin, A.J. Franklin, & J.F. Yates (Eds.), *Research directions of black psychologists* (pp. 351-367). New York: Russell Sage Foundation.

Bruner, J.S. (1968). *On knowing: Essays for the left hand*. New York: Atheneum.

Chance, J., Goldstein, A., & McBride, L. (1975). Differential experience and recognition memory for faces. *Journal of Social Psychology, 97*, 243-253.

Cole, M., Gay, J., Glick, J., & Sharp, D.W. (1971). *The cultural context of learning and thinking*. New York: Basic Books.

Cole, M., & Scribner, S. (1974). *Culture and thought: A psychological introduction*. New York: John Wiley & Sons.

Cureton, G.O. (1978). Using a black learning style. *The Reading Teacher, 1*, 751-756.

Damico, S.B. (1983). *The two worlds of school: Differences in the photographs of black and white adolescents*. Paper presented at the annual meeting of the American Educational Research Association, Montreal.

Das, J.P., Kirby, J., & Jarmon, R.F. (1975). Simultaneous and successive syntheses: An alternative model for cognitive ability. *Psychological Bulletin, 82*, 87-103.

Davidson, K.S. (1950). A preliminary study of Negro and white differences on Form I of the Wechsler-Bellevue scale. *Journal of Consulting Psychology, 6*, 489-492.

Eato, L.E., & Lerner, R.M. (1981). Relations of physical and social environment perceptions to adolescent self esteem. *Journal of Genetic Psychology, 139*, 143-150.

Farley, F.H. (1974). *A Theoretical-predictive model of creativity*. Paper presented at the annual meeting of the American Psychological Association, New Orleans.

Farley, F.H. (1981). Basic process individual differences: A biologically based theory of individualization for cognitive, affective and creative outcomes. In F.H. Farley, & N.J. Gordon (Eds.), *Psychology and education: The state of the union*. Berkeley, CA: McCutchan.

Farnham-Diggory, S. (1970). Cognitive synthesis in Negro-white children. *Monograph of the Society for Research in Child Development, 35* #4.

Fernald, G.M. (1912). Diagnosis of mental imagery. *Psychological Review*, Monograph Supplement, #58.

Fernald, G.M. (1943). *Remedial techniques in basic school subjects*. New York: McGraw-Hill.

Gagne, R.M. (1977). *The conditions of learning* (3rd ed.). New York: Holt, Rinehart & Winston.

Galper, R. (1973). Functional race membership and recognition of faces. *Perceptual and Motor Skills, 37,* 455-462.

Gamble, J.F. (1971). *Cognitive and linguistic style differences among educationally advantaged and disadvantaged eighth-grade boys.* Doctoral dissertation, University of Tennessee.

Gibson, E.J. (1950). *The perception of the visual world.* Boston: Houghton Mifflin.

Gibson, E.J. (1969). *Principles of perceptual learning and development.* New York: Appleton-Century-Crofts.

Gitter, A.G., Black, H., & Mostofsky, D. (1972). Race and sex in the perception of emotion. *Journal of Social Issues, 28,* 63-78.

Guinagh, B.J. (1971). An experimental study of basic learning ability and intelligence in low socioeconomic status children. *Child Development, 42,* 27-36.

Guttentag, M. (1972). Negro-white differences in children's movement. *Perceptual and Motor Skills, 35,* 435-436.

Hagan, M.A., & Jones, R.K. (1978). Cultural effects on pictorial perception: How many words is one picture really worth? In R.D. Walk, & H.L. Pick, Jr. (Eds.), *Perception and experience.* New York: Plenum.

Hall, V.C., & Kaye, D.B. (1977). Patterns of early cognitive development among boys in four subcultural groups. *Journal of Educational Psychology, 69,* 66-87.

Henderson, N.B., Butler, B.W., & Goffeney, B. (1969). Effectiveness of the WISC and Bender-Gestalt test in predicting arithmetic and reading achievement for white and non-white children. *Journal of Clinical Psychology, 25,* 268-271.

Hill, W.H., & Fox, W.M. (1973). Black and white marine squad leaders' perception of racially mixed squads. *Academy of Management Journal, 16,* 680-686.

Hirschberg, N., Jones, L., & Haggerty, E. (1978). What's in a face: Individual difference in face perception. *Journal of Research in Personality, 12,* 488-499.

Jenkins, J.J., & Patterson, D.G. (1961). *Studies in individual differences: The search for intelligence.* New York: Appleton-Century-Crofts.

Jensen, A.R. (1973). Level I and Level II abilities in three ethnic groups. *American Educational Research Journal, 10,* 263-276.

Jung, C. (1923). *Psychological types.* London: Routledge & Kegan Paul. (Translated in 1949 by H. Goodwin Baynes.)

Keil, C. (1966). *Urban blues.* Chicago: University of Chicago.

Kennedy, J.M. (1974). *A psychology of picture perception.* San Francisco: Jossey-Bass.

Kochman, T. (1972). The kinetic element in black idiom. In T. Kochman (Ed.), *Rappin' and stylin' out: Communication in urban black America.* Urbana: University of Illinois.

Levy, N., Murphy, C., & Carlson, R. (1972). Personality types among Negro college students. *Educational and Psychological Measurement, 32,* 641-653.

Luce, T.S. (1974). The role of experience in interracial recognition. *Personality and Social Psychology, 1,* 39-41.

Malone, C.A. (1967). Developmental deviations considered in the light of environmental forces. In E. Pavenstedt (Ed.), *The drifters: Children of disorganized lower-class families.* Boston: Little, Brown.

Mandler, J.M., & Stein, N.L. (1977). The myth of perceptual defect: Sources and evidence. *Psychological Bulletin, 84*, 173-194.

Mangan, J. (1978). Cultural conventions of pictorial representation: Iconic literacy and education. *Educational Communication and Technology Journal, 26*, 245-267.

Marmorale, A., & Brown, F. (1977). Bender-Gestalt performance of Puerto-Rican, white and Negro children. *Journal of Clinical Psychology, 33*, 224-228.

Morgan, H. (1981). Factors concerning cognitive development and learning differentiation among black children. In A.E. Harrison (Ed.), *Conference on empirical research in black psychology, 6*, 14-22.

Morris, L.W. (1979). *Extroversion and introversion: An interactional approach.* Washington: Hemisphere.

Myers, I.B. (1980). *Gifts differing.* Palo Alto: Consulting Psychological Press.

Orasanu, J., Lee, C., & Scribner, S. (1979). Free recall: Ethnic and economic group comparisons. *Child Development, 50*, 1100-1109.

Pasteur, A.B., & Toldson, I.L. (1982). *Roots of soul: The psychology of black expressiveness.* Garden City, NY: Anchor Press/Doubleday.

Pavenstedt, E. (Ed.) (1967). *The drifters: Children of disorganized lower-class families.* Boston: Little, Brown.

Perney, V.H. (1976). Effects of race and sex on field dependence-independence of children. *Perceptual and Motor Skills, 42*, 975-980.

Richmond, B.O. (1971). Creative and cognitive abilities of white and Negro children. *Journal of Negro Education, 40*, 111-116.

Ritzinger, F.C. (1971). *Psychological and physiological differentiation in children six to eleven years of age.* Doctoral dissertation, Washington University, St. Louis, MO.

Rohwer, W.D. (1971). Learning, race, and school success. *Review of Educational Research, 41*, 191-211.

Rosch, E. (1975). Universals and cultural specifics in human categorization. In R.W. Brislin, S. Bochner, & W.J. Lonner (Eds.), *Cross cultural perspectives on learning.* Palo Alto: Sage Publications.

Rychlak, J.F. (1975). Affective assessment, intelligence, social class, and racial learning style. *Journal of Personality and Social Psychology, 32*, 989-995.

St. John, N. (1971). Thirty-six teachers: Their characteristics and outcomes for black and white pupils. *American Educational Research Journal, 8*, 635-648.

Schratz, M. (1976). *A developmental investigation of sex differences in perceptual differentiation and mathematics reasoning in two ethnic groups.* Doctoral dissertation, Fordham University.

Shade, B.J. (1983). *Afro-American patterns of cognition.* Unpublished manuscript. Madison, WI: Wisconsin Center for Educational Research.

Shade, B.J. (1984). *Is there an Afro-American cognitive style?.* Unpublished manuscript.

Sherif, C.W. (1973). Social distance as categorization of intergroup interaction. *Journal of Personality and Social Psychology, 25*, 327-334.

Sigel, I.E., Anderson, L.M., & Shapiro, H. (1966). Categorization of behavior of lower and middle-class Negro preschool children. *Journal of Negro Education, 35*, 218-229.

Slavin, R.E. (1983). *Cooperative learning.* New York/London: Longman.

Sommers, R. (1978). *The mind's eye: Imagery in everyday life.* New York: Delacore.

Stewart, M.D. (1981). *Sensori-motor abilities of the African-American infants: Implications for developmental screening.* Doctoral dissertation, George Peabody College for Teachers of Vanderbilt.

Stigler, R. (1940). Comparison of the capacity to perceive minute movements in the visual periphery in whites and Negroes. *Biological Review, 30,* 114-126.

Stodolsky, S., & Lesser, G. (1967). Learning patterns in the disadvantaged. *Harvard Educational Review, 37,* 546-593.

Strom, R.D., & Bernard, H.W. (1982). *Educational psychology.* Monterey, CA: Brooks/Cole.

Teahan, J.E., & Drews, E.M. (1962). A comparison of northern and southern Negro children on the WISC. *Journal of Consulting Psychology, 26,* 292.

Thompson, L. (1969). *Secrets of culture: Nine community studies.* New York: Random House.

Toffler, A. (1980). *The third wave.* New York: William Morrow.

Travers, R.M.W. (1982). *Essentials of learning* (5th ed.). New York: Macmillan.

Tyler, L.E. (1956). *The psychology of human differences* (2nd ed.). New York: Appleton-Century-Crofts.

Van Alstyne, D., & Osbourne, E. (1937). Rhythmic responses of Negro and white children two to six. *Monographs of the Society for Research in Child Development, 2,* #4.

Vance, H., Hankins, N., & McGee, H. (1979). A preliminary study of black/white differences on the revised Wechsler Intelligence Scale for Children. *Journal of Clinical Psychology, 35,* 815-819.

Witmer, J., & Ferinden, F. (1970). Perception of school climate: Comparison of black and white teachers within the same schools. *Journal of the Student Personnel Association for Teacher Education, 9,* 1-7.

Wober, M. (1966). Sensotypes. *Journal of Social Psychology, 70,* 181-189.

Young, M.F., & Bright, H.A. (1954). Results of testing 81 Negro rural juveniles with the WISC. *Journal of Social Psychology, 39,* 219-226.

Young, V.H. (1974). A black American socialization pattern. *American Ethnologist, 1,* 405-413.

Talkin and Testifyin: Black English and the Black Experience

Geneva Smitherman

In the Beginning

As with other aspects of African American life, the question of Black English (See Note 1) continues to be governed by shifting paradigms of intellectual thought and consciousness and by changing social, political and economic currents. The motive forces of history in America and throughout the world fundamentally altered black-white relations in the U.S. and concomitantly affected research and study on black speech. For example, we must credit the Black Liberation Struggle of the 1960's for the fact that 80% of all black Ph.D.'s in our entire history in America were produced since 1960. Among these intellectuals was the first group of African American linguists. Lorenzo Dow Turner (1949), the lone African American linguist in our past, had left a rich legacy for black linguist-activists, but it lay buried until the 1960's.

There is an old proverbial tale about a son who asked his father why it was that in all the stories he read about lions and men fighting in the jungle, the lion always loses. The father replied, "Son, it will always be that way until the lion learns how to write." This account of Black English will be told from the perspective of the lions who, in the liberation movements of the past generation, have learned how to write.

King v. Ann Arbor: Language, Policy and the National Black Community

During the late spring and early summer of 1979, a rather obscure Federal court case, begun on behalf of fifteen African American children attending the Martin Luther King Elementary school, gained international attention and prominence as the "Black English Case." While African Americans have been in the courts countless times fighting U.S.

oppression, this was the first time we went to court on the issue of our language. And we won. The decision reaffirmed the legitimacy of Black English and the existence of its African sub-stratum, and it laid the basis for this language to become a part of the educational process which has generally denigrated and excluded black speech.

Though it has been suggested by African American linguist Wayne Williams (1982) that the "Black English Case" was "premature," nonetheless, it marked the beginning of national dialogue among both professionals and lay people about language policy in the African American community. Further, the recent formation of movements against linguistic minorities (Note 2) and the possibility of a counter formation in the form of a "rainbow coalition" on language issues remind us that the motion of history does not wait for political maturity.

Briefly, the background facts of the "Black English Case" (which should be referred to by its more appropriate designation, *King*) are as follows. On July 28, 1978, attorneys Gabe Kaimowitz and Kenneth Lewis of Michigan Legal Services filed suit in the U.S. Eastern District Court, located in Detroit, Michigan, on behalf of fifteen African American underclass children residing in a low-income housing project in Ann Arbor, Michigan. Shortly thereafter, I was asked to join the case as chief expert witness for the children in a capacity in which I worked for the next two years. The case of *Martin Luther King Junior Elementary School Children v. Ann Arbor School District Board* (1977-79) became the first to be tried under the language barrier provision of the 1974 Equal Educational Opportunity Act (EEOA). Provision 1703(f) of that Act reads in part:

> No state shall deny equal educational opportunity to an individual
> on account of his or her race, color, sex, or national origin, by . . . the
> failure to overcome language barriers that impede equal participa-
> tion by its students in its instructional programs.

On July 12, 1979, using the "existing knowledge" garnered in years of research on Black English and the courtroom testimony of a team of national researchers organized by myself, a white judge, Charles C. Joiner, himself a resident of Ann Arbor, issued a ruling in our favor. That ruling legitimated Black English within a legal framework; it mandated that the Ann Arbor School District "take into account" Black English in the educational process, and it reaffirmed the obligation of educational institutions to teach black children "to read in the standard English of the school, the commercial world, the arts, science, and professions" (Joiner, 1979).

The School District was given thirty days to present a plan to Judge Joiner to remedy the situation. The chief component of that remedy was special training and orientation for the School District's teachers in Black English and in its educational implications. It was a historic moment in the lives of a people struggling for literacy and freedom for the present generation and those yet to be born in this post-industrial, technological center of the crisis-ridden capitalist world.

It has been suggested that *King* may be viewed in a narrow sense as simply a case about teaching little African American children to read (Bailey, 1981). Yet the case generated a voluminous amount of written material and public outcry. Not only were there numerous academic articles, there were over three hundred newspaper and magazine articles, some of them in the foreign press. There were dozens of local and national radio and television programs about the case. In community forums, churches, school meetings, and other gatherings, there were intense and heated local and national debates as well as occasional outbursts of hysteria about *King*. The British Broadcasting Corporation journeyed to Detroit to produce a film about the case. The magnitude of this public arousal and attention clearly demonstrates the broad significance and socio-political ramifications of the "Black English Case."

The critical issues raised by *King* have been integral to the struggles of African Americans throughout our history. The essence of these issues can be captured in terms of the following questions: What is the nature of Black English, its linguistic character and origin? How are the socio-historical and politico-economic experiences of African Americans reflected in the development, history, and future of Black English? How does the question of Black English relate to literacy and freedom for the African American population?

Nature of Black English

When the EEOA became Federal law in 1974, legislation governing bilingual approaches in education had already been in existence for some years. Thus the inclusion of provision 1703(f) raises the question of whom this obscure language provision was designed to protect. The Ann Arbor School District took the position that it applied only to those with foreign language backgrounds. We argued, citing former Health, Education and Welfare Secretary Elliott Richardson, that the statute protected the "legal right of any child with a language handicap" (1972). Judge Joiner agreed and denied Ann Arbor's motion for dismissal on these grounds, asserting that:

> ... The statutory language places no limitations on the character or source of the language barrier except that it must be serious enough to impede equal participation by ... students in ... instructional programs ... 1703(f) applies to language barriers of appropriate

severity encountered by students who speak 'Black English' as well as to language barriers encountered by students who speak German (1978). The "barrier," or "handicap," of course, as the judge was later to rule, was not Black English, in and of itself, but institutional attitudes toward it in the Nation's schools, which reflected the larger society.

Yet the question of the nature of Black English—what is it, where did it come from, who speaks it—was an issue which never left the case. Linguists define Black English as a hybrid language. It contains elements of Euro-American English (today's so-called "standard" English, that is, White English), elements of West African languages (surviving Africanisms from Yoruba, Ibo, Ewe, etc.), and elements manifesting the uniqueness of the African American experience in this country (servitude, institutionalized racism, rural and urban modal existences). Some of the illustrative features of Black English are given below:

1. *Indicating habitual action through verb structure, notably using the form "be" as a verb.* For example, from the children in *King*: "He *be* hollering at us and stuff"; He *be* going to summer school"; "They *be* hitting on peoples"; "I like the way he *be* psyching people out." This use of *be* derives from an aspectual verb system that is also found in many African languages, in Creole language forms of the Caribbean, in West African Pidgin English, and in the Gullah Creole spoken by blacks living in the Sea Islands along the Southeastern seaboard of the U.S. Its use conveys the speaker's meaning with reference to the qualitative character and distribution of an action over time. In White English, there is no uniform way of conveying this same meaning although the simple present tense tends to be used for this purpose. Thus, the White English equivalent for the first example above would be something like: *He is always (or, constantly) hollering at us; He frequently (or, often) hollers at us; He sometimes (or, occasionally) hollers at us;* or simply, He *hollers*.
2. *Indicating remote past through verb structure, notably using "been" with stress.* For example, "We had *been* (pronounced with stress) finished our schoolwork"; "She *been* gone"; "I *been* doing that." The only way of conveying this meaning in White English would be with some kind of adverbial construction, such as "a long time ago," or "for a long time." Thus the White English equivalent for the first example might be: "We had finished our schoolwork a long time ago."
3. *Predication with optional copula.* The sense of complete predication can be conveyed in Black English by a noun followed by an adjective, adverb, verb, noun, or prepositional phrase. White English, however, requires a form of the verb "to

be" for completion. Examples: "He real little"; "She six"; "My momma name Annie"; "She my teacher"; "They in the house"; "Them boys always fighting"; "He not here." This feature of Black English is common in many West African languages, e.g., in Kimbundu, *Ene macamba*, literally "They friends."

4. *Semantic inversion, turning a word into its opposite.* For example, from Mandingo, *a ka nyi ko-jugu*, literally, "It is good badly," meaning "it is very good," or it is so good that it's bad." Semantic inversion is the process that produces much of what is imprecisely labelled "Black slang." For instance, the often-used Black English adjective "bad" refers to the highest good, most omnipotent, most powerful, etc.

A classical example here is that of Muhammad Ali who nearly caused an international diplomatic disaster in referring to the superpower heads of state when he said, "There are two bad white men in the world, the Russian white man and the American white man. They are the two baddest men in the history of the world." Though castigated for using a term interpreted among White English speakers as evil, wicked, or negative, Muhammad Ali was simply using the semantic inversion of his African ancestors, clearly referring, in this context, to the omnipotence and toughness of the Russian and American leaders, with their capacity to destroy the world through their power.

5. *Appropriating and secularizing church terms.* Many other terms in the semantics of Black English come out of the Traditional Black Church, where the worship patterns infuse African form with Judaeo-Christian content. Both in the Traditional African World and in Black America, there is no sharp division between the sacred and the secular; all of life is deemed holy. One or two examples will have to suffice.

On T. "On time," from the Traditional Black Church saying and Gospel song, "He may not come when you want Him, but He's right on time." This a way of distinguishing physical time from spiritual or psychic time, as when basketball player Magic Johnson suddenly whips a lightning-fast pass to Kareem Abdul-Jabbar, having anticipated—read Kareem's mind—where on the basketball court Kareen would position himself after the fast break. The pass is said to be "on T."

Testify. Giving verbal recognition to the power of an experience (in the Traditional Black Church, the experience of being "saved"). Thus one finds in the black blues song, the recurring line: "I just want to testify what your love done did for me."

6. *Pronominal apposition, that is, repeating the subject for emphasis.*

Examples: "*Her brother, he* got sent up"; "*The men, they* was fooling around too much"; "*All the preachers, they* start talking about what could they do." This is another feature of Black English that is common in several West African languages, e.g., from Yoruba, *Eya me, ot cu*, literally, "My mother, she has died."

7. *Widespread use of speech acts, that are either not in White English at all, not used as frequently by White English speakers, or not used according to the same set of social rules of speaking.* Space will allow for only two illustrations.

   Consider the verbal art of *signifyin'*. This is the verbal tradition in Black English of using language to admonish, to teach a lesson, to disparage, or sometimes just for verbal fun and play. It demands verbal wit, clever repartee and powerful speaking ability. Reverend Jesse Jackson, in a call for black unity across class lines, uses this bit of signifyin': "Pimp, punk, prostitute, Ph.D.—all the P's, you still in slavery!" (Jackson, 1970).

   Consider the use of *proverbs*. In the Black English-speaking tradition, there is a much more extensive use of this speech act than is the case among White English speakers. Thus blacks use proverbs as rhetorical strategy, as corrective guidance in the socialization of black children, in Traditional Black Church sermons, in black popular hit songs, and in general conversation. Moreover, there are certain distinctive proverbs used almost exclusively by blacks, such as "What go round come round"; "A hard head make a soft behind." The proverb tradition is found throughout African communities, as writers like Achebe (1959) tell us, not only in conversational speech but even in the courtroom and in legal proceedings.

8. *Signalling of possession by context and/or juxtaposition.* To convey this meaning in White English requires the inflectional *-z* (written as *-s* preceded or followed by an apostrophe). Black English has no such obligatory rule. Examples: "She took him to his *grandmother house*"; "*Popeye girlfriend* saw him"; "My *daddy name* John."

The foregoing examples of black language are obviously not meant to be exhaustive. The subject has been the concern of several full-length works. For those interested in a more thorough inventory and description of Black English, consult Smitherman (1969, 1977); Major (1970); Labov (1972); Dillard (1972); Rickford (1975, 1979); Kochman (1972, 1981); Baugh (1979, 1983); and Spears (1982, 1984). Judge Joiner's earlier ruling in *King* dismissed the problem of our having to demonstrate, during the trial itself, that Black English is a language. But the issue of whether Black English is a language or a dialect continues to be raised on several grounds. It if is a language, then African

Americans do indeed constitute a nation within a nation since language is taken to be one of the defining characteristics of a nation. If it is merely a dialect, then African Americans are simply a sub-group of white America just as dialects are simply sub-languages of any given national language.

From the vantage point of linguistics, the Black English language-dialect issue reflects a fundamental contradiction within linguistics itself as to how language is to be defined, conceptualized and studied (Smitherman, 1983a). I refer to the classic dichotomy between *langue* and *parole* and to the current split between the Cartesian (e.g., Chomsky, 1966, 1972) and the socially constituted, ethnographic (e.g., Hymes, 1974) schools of linguistics. While Cartesian linguists focus on language structure and syntax, ethnolinguists focus on the use and users of language; their history, culture, values, world views and social structure are considered fundamental to understanding and analyzing linguistic data. Cartesian language models are viewed as falsely separating language from speech and abstracting communication from social reality. Further, the social unit is the *speech* community, not the *language* community because linguistic intelligibility depends not only on shared rules of grammar and structure but also on shared social norms about when, where and how to use the grammar and structure. Put simply, you can have two speakers ostensibly speaking the same language, but if they do not share what I have termed the sociolinguistic construction of reality (Smitherman, 1976, 1983a), they literally cannot understand one another. (The Muhammad Ali example mentioned earlier is illustrative.)

The Black English language dialect issue is compounded by the dilemma in linguistics regarding the classification of pidgins, Creoles and interlanguages. That is, where you have speech phenomena comprised of features from two or more source languages widely used in a speech community, how much or how many differences are required to constitute a "foreign language?" For instance, the co-occurrence of Black English features within a single statement creates intelligibility problems between black and non-Black English speakers. Consider the statement: "She the bad girl momma." Does this mean that the person being referred to is the mother of the girl in question; or that the person is a very young girl who happens to be a mother; or that the person is simply a girl being pointed out to the speaker's mother? And is the girl being referred to as "bad-*good*" girl or a "bad-*bad*" girl? Such examples—and they are much more numerous than space will permit me to deal with here—strengthen the case for viewing black speech as a separate language.

Finally, there is the dimension of social perception. That is, do the speakers perceive themselves as speaking a different language? If so, then for all practical purposes, the language mixture is a "language," not a "dialect."

Linguistics, as a science, cannot and does not offer the definitive word on language-dialect differentiation in general, nor in the case of Black English in particular. The point is that differences between Black and White English create barriers and points of unintelligibility and have significant impact on African Americans in the American political economy. Further, because of U.S. society's treatment of these differences, as we demonstrated in *King*, they become barriers to literacy, perpetrate educational underachievement and contribute to the growing formation of an African American underclass in the U.S.

Is Black English a language or a dialect, then? Ultimately, it comes down to who has the power to define. As the linguist Max Weinreich once put it, the difference between a language and a dialect is who's got the army.

Black English and the Black Experience

The history, present-day status and future of Black English can be best understood against the backdrop of the long-standing controversy about the existence and role of Africanisms in the black experience. Two schools of thought have emerged: The Anglian-based tradition; and 2) the African-based tradition.

The Anglian tradition of scholars (e.g., Krapp, 1924, 1925; Kurath, 1949) asserts that what is called "*Black*" English is really "*White*" English, traceable to British dialects of Old and Middle English which slaves picked up from white immigrants of British East Anglia (large numbers of whom settled in the South during the Colonial era in U.S. history). So black speech is simply outdated or archaic white speech, sustained in the black community by forces of social and hence, linguistic isolation. Actually, this line of thinking simply replaced Nineteenth Century theories of biological determinism which explained African American speech and other cultural differences on the basis of physiognomy and genetics (e.g., Harrison, 1884). In either case, the African American still has not quite caught up with the white in the scheme of human evolution, and you have simply moved from biology to socio-biology (Wilson, 1975; Olson, 1977; Farrell, 1983.)

The Anglian origins theory of Black English is the linguistic version of the socio-historical school of thought that argues that everything African was eradicated from African American communities during the hardship of the Middle Passage (Note 3) and the aftermath of slavery creating a cultural *tabula rasa* filled with European American

(white) culture (e.g., Park, 1950; Stampp, 1956). Even one of our notable, highly respected African American scholars (Frazier, 1939) attributed the cultural differences to the degradation of poverty and hard
times, rather than to residual Africanisms.

The African-based tradition asserts that Black English is really
Africanized English, traceable to the formation of English pidgins and
Creoles during the slave trade and the reign of the slavocracy. (A *pidgin*
is a mixture of two languages, with a simplified structure, to facilitate
communication. A *pidgin* becomes a *Creole* when it is in widespread
use and is the first and only language of a speech community.) What
happened, then, in the African-European language contact situation,
in the slave trade and in slave communities in the "New World," was
the formation of a language mixture, a combination of a given European language vocabulary—English, Dutch, Portuguese, French, etc.—
with West African grammatical and phonological patterns. While
much of the lexicon was derived from the European language, the way
the Africans used the lexicon was African. The result produced various
African-European pidgins and Creoles—e.g., Dutch Pidgin, French Creole, etc. Thus, in the U.S., despite the variety of West African language
groups (deliberately mixed on American slave plantations so as to foil
communication and rebellion), a common linguistic system evolved
because the African slaves shared two linguistic denominators: the
English vocabulary they picked up from whites and the African meaning systems.

The African origins school is the linguistic version of the DuBois
(1903), Herskovits (1949) socio-historical school which asserts that New
World black cultural distinctiveness results from retentions and adaptations of African cultural consciousness. Such scholars disavow the cultural *tabula rasa* theory as a logical impossibility for human societies,
even under enslavement and poverty. Moreover, these scholars point
out that the segregation and racism which created separate black and
white institutions and living conditions effectively ensured the retention of Africanisms.

As Labov (1982) noted, by the time of *King*, there had emerged a
consensus among linguists about the Africanized, Creole formation of
Black English. While not everything can be accounted for in terms of
African linguistic antecedents, much of Black English is similar to the
Creole of speech communities throughout the African Diaspora. That
is, the linguistic adaptations to the material circumstances of enslavement and colonization are all highly similar among groups of African
descendants who have never had any contact with one another.

Because U.S. blacks, except for the Gullahs (Note 4), were and are,
in the minority (in contrast to the situation of blacks elsewhere in the
Diaspora and in Africa, where blacks are clearly the dominant group, at

least numerically), there has been greater pressure on black Americans to assimilate, linguistically and culturally. Thus slavery and post-slavery blacks (as psychiatrist Frantz Fanon tells us colonized people are prone to do) began to opt for the language and "ways of white folk" (Hughes, 1934). The linguistic manifestation of this assimilationist effort is *decreolization*, the gradual levelling out of the African component of Black English in the direction of White English. The Black English of North America represents a more highly *de-creolized* (i.e., *de-Africanized*) variety of the African-European language mix.

Because of the incomplete assimilation of African Americans into American social, political and most importantly, economic life, *decreolization* remains incomplete, particularly among those African Americans whose contact with whites and education has been minimal, that is, the African American underclass. In times past, when residential and geographical isolation of all African Americans—regardless of class—existed, Black English was retained by the middle class, educated and professional blacks for community solidarity. These same blacks, though, while "talkin dat talk" developed code-switching facility (i.e., from Black to White English) as a survival mechanism in American educational and socio-economic life. However, no such switching facility exists among the African American underclass. Thus, it was that in *King*, the black children experiencing educational underachievement were those from the low-income Green Road housing project area. The other black children at the school, middle class and thus possessing code-switching ability, were not confronted by language barriers. This contradiction between race and class required some creative legal maneuvering on our part because American law opposes discrimination based on race, national origin, or ethnicity, but not on class. There is no U.S. law which prohibits discrimination against the poor, be they black or white.

While *King* had to be won on the basis of race, the question of Black English clearly reflects the interaction of *race and class*. Thus, it was that in the Black Liberation Movement of the 1960's, there was a move to *re-creolize* Black English, to make the medium fit the message of liberation (e.g., Henderson, 1973; Smitherman, 1973). Among many African American intellectuals, artists and activists—particularly those of middle class origins—*re-creolization* became the linguistic symbol of class suicide. (The brilliant writer-activist Amiri Baraka is an outstanding example of this.)

Language and Liberation

The schematic in Table 1 traces the development of Black English over time and plots its interaction with the material conditions and modal experiences of African Americans. Throughout it all, the quest has been for freedom and literacy. Freedom: historically defined as freedom from enslavement, contemporaneously meaning political and economic liberation. Literacy: historically defined as the ability to read and write, now and for the future survival of African Americans, meaning the ability to read not only the word but the world.

Just as the status of African Americans themselves has been ambiguous in white America, there has existed a DuBoisian "double consciousness" (1903) about black language. This linguistic push-pull (Smitherman, 1981) evidences itself, on the one hand, in the use of Black English for selling and advertising in America's capitalist marketplace and in the adoption of black lingo by those whites seeking hipness, such as star athletes, musicians, entertainers, up and coming swinging singles, etc. Because Black English springs from soul and style, it is the language of a group viewed as in touch with the nitty-gritty realities and pleasures of life, and is *real*, it is appropriated by whites and sustained by blacks. Beyond all this, for African Americans, it represents group solidarity. We may deem this the *push* toward linguistic Africanization.

On the other hand, Black English had its formation in the slave era, it is a language of rebellion and protest from an outsider, downgraded nation within the American nation, and it has been kept alive in the segregated and now urban, underclass communities. Whites reject this deep structure dimension of Black English, and, when convenient, use the language as a tool of racist oppression to justify black exclusion from the social, political and economic rewards of American life. African Americans, particularly those of the middle class, thus become negative about Black English and may reject it, as well as its speakers. We may deem this the *pull* away from linguistic Africanization.

The race-class contradiction, and its corollary, linguistic push-pull, is unfolding in developing class tensions in America, both in the black and white communities. The cities of the U.S. are increasingly home only for the African American underclass, as both white and black "flight" out of America's urban areas continues. Recent research by Labov (1985) and associates in Philadelphia shows that Black English is diverging greatly from White English, contrary to the predictions of two decades ago, at which time it was believed that the era of black pride and black liberation would usher in greater literacy and greater economic development for the African American community. Had this happened, so this line of reasoning goes, Black English would

Table 1
Black English and the Black Experience

1619	1700	1808	1863
20 African slaves/indentured servants arrived at Jamestown on Dutch ship	Slave codes circumscribing activities and life of slaves	Outlawing of Slave Trade; rise of Aniti-Slavery Movement	Emancipation

PIDGIN	CREOLE	DECREOLIZATION	
No direct evidence of slave speech during this period but note Barbardian slave Tituba's "He tell me he God," recorded by Justice Hathorne at Salem Witch Trial in 1692.		This period, as well as earlier, characterized by: 1) West African language use; 2) Black English; 3) Standard ("White") English	
Modal existence was rural, agrarian, slave; quest was for freedom		Modal existence rural, sharecropping; quest for literacy	

A pidgin is a mixture of two languages, with a simplified structure, to facilitate communication. As a result of the slave trade, various African-European pidgins evolved—Dutch Pidgin, Portuguese Pidgin, English Pidgin, etc. A pidgin becomes a Creole when it is in widespread use and is the first and only language of a speech community, as was the case of the plantation English Creole used in slave communities in America. (Some linguists maintain that a Creole represents a more fully developed and sophisticated stage of the language mixture.)

Excerpted from *Language, Politics, and Ideology* by Geneva Smitherman, work in progress.

Table 1 (continued)

1877	1914-1945	1966	1980's
Reconstruction; institutionalization of "separate but equal"	World Wars I & II; vast urban migration of Blacks out of South	Black Power Movement; push for integration comes to halt	Capitalist, post industrial crisis creating severe survival problems for Blacks
		RECREOLIZATION	
De-creolized forms solidify, especially among underclass	De-creolization continues	De-creolization halted; conscious attempt to recapture earlier Black English forms (in interature, speeches, etc.)	Emergence of strong bilingual/ bidialectal consciousness
Modal existence urban, industrial; quest for literacy and freedom (i.e., political & economic liberation)		Modal existence in transition, to post-industrial, technological; continued quest for literacy and freedom	

De-Creolization refers to the linguistic de-Africanization of Black speech varieties, a force that can be accounted for by political, economic and educational pressures from the dominant language community—e.g., during the slave period in America, speaking "good English" was often a mark of free Blacks who did not reside in the slave community, and after emancipation, speaking standard "White English" was a way of demonstrating that "I too sing America."

by now look much more like White English (i.e., *de-creolization* would be virtually complete.) Yet, the Black Liberation Struggle was aborted when it came too close to confronting the capitalism beneath the racism, and the rewards of President Johnson's Great Society became co-optive forces for the African American middle class, passing over the masses of African American people in the process. Thus, the "two separate societies" which the Kerner Commission on Civil Disturbances (1968) warned the Nation about has continued to flourish with the additional complication that black society is itself subdividing into a small group of "have's," and a very large and troubled group of "have not's." Linguistically, the black speech community is increasingly becoming one where the Black English of the African American underclass is not only diverging from White English but from the English of the African American middle class as well.

The children of the black underclass are rejecting the bourgeois sociolinguistic character of the schools and dropping out or being forced out of school at a rate of 50-75% in some cities. The goal of literacy, reading the word and the world, which leads to liberation, is becoming far removed from this group, and economic forces threaten to cast them upon the ash heap of society. At the same time, the African American middle class is being jolted out of its complacency by the reemergence of racism and other reactionary forces (e.g., blind patriotism) being re-legitimated by the current national administration and ideology.

The unity of "all of the P's" (as Reverend Jesse Jackson would say) is the salvation of the black community. This salvation depends on the development of common terms of communication and understanding. In the post-industrial, technological era, African Americans have become surplus labor and the "white man's burden" as social and economic deterioration wreak havoc in urban communities. The clarion call from African American linguists is for a language policy for the African American community to lay the foundation for our coming together once again before time runs out. It is possible here only to sketch the broad outlines of this policy.

First, a language policy for the African American community must stress the legitimacy of Black English, and call for its use as a co-equal language of instruction, particularly in African American underclass schools. Over fifty years ago, two of the most important black scholar-activists in our history, although they were not linguists, advocated the use and study of our speech. DuBois urged educators to use "that variety of the English idiom which Negroes understand" (1933), and Woodson contended that we should "study the background of the Negro dialect as a broken-down African tongue" (1933). In recent years, African linguists have argued for mother tongue instruction as a "passport to literacy," both for Africans (e.g., Bamgbose, 1976) and African Americans (e.g., Bokamba, 1981). And finally, it was our position in *King*, which was reaffirmed in Judge Joiner's *Opinion*, that Black English be "taken into account" in the teaching of standard English.

Secondly, the language policy must reinforce the need for standard English, presently either rejected out of hand by the black underclass and its children, or accepted only half-heartedly and self-consciously. This is because the schools do not use the native tongue as an instructional bridge, and social attitudes allow only lip service acceptance of the language of the black speech community. The black underclass rejects the ambivalence of the black middle class and the white mainstream about Black English. Simultaneously they reject the standard (White) English which is the language of literacy in the U.S. Yet when there is security about the legitimacy of one's native language, including Black English, as Williams (1982) shows in his research among African Americans in Seattle, Washington, there is a greater willingness to learn a second language, and even a third language.

Thirdly, our language policy must promote one or more Third World languages so African Americans can carry on independent dialogue with other persons of color—the majority population in today's world (Smitherman, 1984). Possibly Spanish would be one of the Third World languages because of its large numbers of speakers both in the U.S. and in the Western Hemisphere.

It is not only that we need such a policy to "protect the interests of the black community" (Williams, 1982). Over and beyond that, a language policy for the national black community can be the basis for preparation in world leadership by African Americans. The lions have learned to write. Our time has come.

Notes

1. The terms Black English, Black Speech, Ebonics, Black Language will be used interchangeably throughout.
2. I refer, for example, to attempts in the State of California to overturn the tradition of printing election ballots in languages other than English. This, of course, would effectively disenfranchise large numbers of Spanish-speaking voters who are on the verge of becoming a dominant population in that State. Further, not only has the Reagan administration proposed

severe cuts in the Federal budget that assists bilingual education in the States, there is now a proposal to amend the U.S. Constitution to make English the official language of the U.S. A national, well financed organization, "U.S. English," under the leadership of Senator Hayakawa—ironically, a semanticist Japanese-American himself, who merely labels the U.S. incarceration of Japanese-Americans during World War II as "unfortunate"—has been established in Washington, D.C. "U.S. English" distributes a newsletter-journal, called *Update*. (See *New York Times*, 1984; *Update*, 1984; *Washington Times*, 1984; *Florida Legionnaire*, 1985.)

3. This refers to the voyage by slave ships from the West Coast of Africa to the Americas. In this "veritable nightmare," slaves were packed like cattle, chained, with no standing, lying or sitting room. Smallpox, disease, filth and stench were rampant and it is estimated that no more than half of all slaves shipped from Africa ever became "effective workers in the New World" (Franklin, 1947).

4. Gullahs, also known as "Geechee's," are rural and urban blacks living in the coastal regions of the States of South Carolina and Georgia. They have remained fairly isolated from contact with the U.S. mainland and were rather late arrivals to America, e.g., as late as 1858, just three years before the U.S. Civil War—in which slavery was a dominant issue—and long after the 1808 Slave Trade Act outlawed the importation of slaves, over 400 slaves were bootlegged directly from African to Georgia (Bancroft, 1931).

References

Achebe, C. (1959). *Things fall apart.* New York: Fawcett.

Bailey, R. (1981). Education and the law: The King case in Ann Arbor. In G. Smitherman (Ed.), *Black English and the education of black children and youth*, pp. 94-129. Detroit: Wayne State University, Center for Black Studies.

Bamgbose, A. (1976). Introduction: The changing role of the mother tongue in education. In A. Bamgbose (Ed.), *Mother tongue education: The West African experience*, pp. 9-26. Paris: Unesco Press.

Bancroft, F. (1931). *Slave-trading in the Old South.* Baltimore.

Baugh, J. (1979). *Linguistic style shifting in Black English.* Ph.D. Dissertation, University of Pennsylvania.

Baugh, J. (1983). *Black street speech: Its history, struture, and survival.* Austin: University of Texas Press.

Bokamba, E. (1981). Language and national development: Black English in America. In G. Smitherman (Ed.), *Black English and the education of black children and youth*, pp. 278-88. Detroit: Wayne State University Center for Black Studies Press.

Chomsky, N. (1966). *Cartesian linguistics: A chapter in the history of rationalist thought*. New York: Harper & Row.

Chomsky, N. (1972). *Language and mind*. (enlarged edition). New York: Harcourt Brace Jovanovich.

Dillard, J.L. (1972). *Black English*. New York: Random House.

DuBois, W.E.B. (1969). *Souls of black folk*. New York: New American Library. (Originally published in 1903).

DuBois, W.E.B. (1973). Field and function of the Negro college. In H. Aptheker (Ed.), *The education of black people*, pp. 83-102. Amherst: University of Massachusetts Press. (Originally published in 1933).

Farrell, T.J. (1983). IQ and standard English. *College Composition and Communication, 34*, 470-484.

Florida Legionnaire (1985). *Se habla Espanol: U.S. English fighting back*. Author, 30, No. 7.

Franklin, J.H. (1969). *From slavery to freedom* (3rd ed.). New York: Vintage Books. (Originally published in 1947).

Frazier, E.F. (1966). *The Negro family in the United States*. Chicago: University of Chicago Press. (Originally published in 1939).

Harrison, J. (1884). Negro English. *Anglia, VII*, 232-279.

Henderson, S. (1973). *Understanding the new black poetry: Black speech and black music as poetic reference*. New York: Morrow.

Herskovits, M. (1941). *Myth of the Negro past*. Boston: Beacon Press.

Hughes, L. (1934). *The ways of white folk*. New York: A.A. Knopf.

Hymes, D. (1974). *Foundations in sociolinguistics*. Philadelphia: University of Pennsylvania.

Jackson, J. (1970). *I am somebody*. Volume I. Memphis, TN: Respect Record Album (Division of Stax Records).

Joiner, C.C. (1978). *Opinion*. 451 F. Supp.,(E.D. Mich.)

Joiner, C.C. (1979). *Memorandum and opinion*. 473 F. Supp. 1371 (E.D. Mich.)

Kerner Commission on Civil Disturbances (1968). *U.S. National Advisory Commission on Civil Disorders Report*. Washington, D.C.: U.S. Government, Print Office.

Kochman, T. (Ed.), (1972). *Rappin and stylin out: Communication in urban Black America*. Chicago: University of Illinois Press.

Kochman, T. (1981). *Black and white styles in conflict*. Chicago: University of Chicago Press.

Krapp, G. (1924, May-August). The English of the Negro. *The American Mercury, II*, pp. 190-195.

Krapp, G. (1925). *The English language in America*. New York: Modern Language Association.

Kurath, H. (1949). *A word geography of the Eastern United States*. Ann Arbor: University of Michigan.

Labov, W. (1972). *Language in the inner city*. Philadelphia: University of Pennsylvania Press.

Labov, W. (1982, August). Objectivity and commitment in linguistic science: The case of the Black English trial in Ann Arbor. *Language in Society*.

Labov, W. (1985). *The increasing divergence of black and white vernaculars.* March, 1985. Four Research Reports on National Science Foundation Project, "The Influence of Urban Minorities on Linguistic Change," 1981-84. Available from William Labov, Director, Linguistics Laboratory, University of Pennsylvania, Philadelphia, Pennsylvania, U.S.A.

Major, C. (1970). *Dictionary of Afro American slang.* New York: International Publishers.

Martin Luther King Junior Elementary School Children v. Ann Arbor School District Board. (1979) Civil Action No. 7-71861 (E.D. Mich).

New York Times. (1984). *The mother tongue has a movement.* June 3.

Olson, D.R. (1977, August). From utterance to tests: The bias of language in speech and writing. *Harvard Educational Review, 47,* 257-281.

Park, R. (1950). *Race and culture.* Glencoe, Ill.: Free Press.

Richardson, E. (1972). 118 U.S. Congressional Record 8929.

Rickford, J.R. (1975). Carrying the new wave into syntax. In R. Fasold, & R. Shuy (Eds.), *Analyzing variation in language.* Washington, D.C.: Georgetown University Press.

Rickford, J.R. (1979). *Variation in a creole continuum: Quantitative & implicational approaches.* Ph.D. Dissertation, University of Pennsylvania.

Smitherman, G. (1969). *A comparison of the oral and written styles of a group of inner-city black students.* Ph.D. Dissertation, University of Michigan.

Smitherman, G. (1973, October). The power of the rap: Black idiom and the new black poetry. *Twentieth Century Literature,* pp. 259-74.

Smitherman, G. (1976). *Language of black workers.* Unpublished manuscript.

Smitherman,G. (1977). *Talkin and testifyin: The language of Black America.* Boston: Houghton Mifflin.

Smitherman, G. (1981). *Black English and the education of black children and youth: Proceedings of the National invitational symposium on the King decision.* Detroit: Wayne State Univeristy, Center for Black Studies Press.

Smitherman, G. (1983, April). *Language, consciousness and auto workers: Who are the nigguhs?.* Paper presented at Marxist Scholars Conference.

Smitherman, G. (1983, Winter). Language and liberation. *Journal of Negro Education, 52*(1), pp. 15-23.

Smitherman, G. (1984, February). *If you got good religion, show some sign: Toward a language policy for the black community.* Keynote presentation at Howard University Black Communications Conference.

Smitherman, G. (work in progress). *Language, politics and ideology.*

Spears, A.K. (1982). The Black English semi-auxiliary *Come. Language, 58,* 850-72.

Spears, A.K. (1984). Towards a new view of Black English. *The Journal, 1,* 94-103.

Stampp, K.M. (1956). *The peculiar institution: Slavery in the ante-bellum South.* New York: Knopf.

Turner, L.D. (1949). *Africanisms in the Gullah dialect.* Chicago: University of Chicago Press.

Update. (1984, September-October). Volume II, No. 4.

Washington Times (1984, May 31). *Hayakawa sees big trouble from bilingual movement push.*

Williams, W. (1982, March). *Language consciousness and cultural liberation in Black America*. Paper delivered at the Sixth Annual Conference of the National Council for Black Studies, Chicago.

Wilson, E.O. (1975). *Sociobiology: The new synthesis*. Cambridge: Harvard University Press.

Woodson, C. (1933). *Miseducation of the Negro*. Washington, D.C.: Associated Publishers.

Nonverbal Behaviors and Communication Styles Among African Americans

Richard Majors

Nonverbal Behaviors in African American Culture: Overview

Since Darwin's publication of *The Expression of the Emotions in Man and Animals* in 1872, interest and research on nonverbal behavior and communication has grown steadily. Research on nonverbal behavior and communication in African American culture, however, has been limited (cf. to Cook, 1980; Johnson, 1971). Therefore, the purpose of this chapter is to discuss and describe the significance, importance and current status of nonverbal behaviors and communication among African Americans.

Definition and Categorization

There is no consensual definition of nonverbal communication. Definitions range from very broad to very narrow. Knapp (1972), a respected scholar in the field of nonverbal behavior wrote: ". . . most researchers have assumed that if words are not spoken or written, the behavior involved is nonverbal in nature" (p.4). Knapp suggests that "nonverbal communication should not be studied as an isolated unit, but as an inseparable part of the total communication process" (1978, p. 5).

Most scholars in the field of nonverbal communication categorize nonverbal communication into the following areas: *kinesics or body motion* (i.e., gestures, movements of the body, e.g., hands, limbs, head, feet and legs); *facial expressions* (e.g., smiles); *eye behavior* (e.g., blinking, direction and length of gaze, and pupil dilation); *posture, touching behavior* (e.g., stroking, hitting, holding); *paralanguage* (i.e., vocal qualities, e.g., pitch, tempo, etc. and nonlanguage sounds, e.g., moans, yells, etc.);

I am indebted to Carol Brooks, Blaine Peder, Michael Nakkula and Esther Gross for their editoral assistance on an earlier draft of this paper.

physical characteristics (physique, body shape, general attractiveness, body or breath odors, hair, weight, height, and skin color); *proxemics* (people's use and perception of personal and social space); *artifacts* (e.g., perfume, clothes, lipstick, eye glasses, false eyelashes, wigs, etc.); and *environmental factors* (e.g., architecture, furniture, lighting, crowding, music and noise, geography, smells, weather, or related factors that could affect the communication process).

Expressive and Performance-Oriented Behaviors

To cope with the "invisibility" and frustration resulting from racism and discrimination, many African American people have channeled their creative talents and energies into the construction and use of particular expressive and conspicuous styles of nonverbal behaviors (e.g., in their demeanor, gestures, clothing, hairstyles, walk, stances, and handshakes, among other areas). For many African American people these unique, expressive, colorful, stylish and performance-oriented behaviors are ways to act "cool," to be visible and show pride. Elsewhere these behaviors have been referred to as "Coolpose" (Collias, 1988, Doyle, 1989; Majors, 1983, 1986a, 1987, 1989b; Majors, in press; McLeod, 1986; Messner 1987, 1989; Page, 1986; Peterman, 1988; Sariola & Naukkarinen, 1989). African Americans use such nonverbal behaviors to accentuate the self, appear urbane, suave and charming, and to show adherence to cultural norms. These behaviors are also used to keep whites off guard about one's intentions, to exercise power and control, express pride, dignity and respect for themselves and their race; to release pent-up aggression and obtain entertainment, gratification and stimulation.

Kochman (1981) (*Black and White Styles in Conflict*) discussed the significance of expressive, stylish and performance-oriented behaviors in African American culture (see Majors, 1986, 1987; Majors, 1990; Pasteur & Toddson, 1982). He described expressive and performance-oriented behaviors among African Americans as spontaneous, intuitive, improvisational, emotional, rhythmic, assertive, confrontive, direct, and animated. On the other hand, he described white culture as a low-stimulus culture: dispassionate, nonchallenging and impersonal. African Americans, Kochman stated, tend to be emotionally expressive and less able (or willing) to control impulses, while whites value and have a more emotionally self-restrained style and often attempt to understate, avoid, ignore, or diffuse intense or unpleasant situations.

Dramaturgy

Dramaturgy is a framework that is concerned with analyzing and understanding expressive, performance-oriented behaviors, impression management, communication techniques, roles, and symbolic behaviors among individuals (Brissett & Edgley, 1975; Combs & Mansfield, 1976; Haas & Shaffir, 1982; Zurcher, 1982). Dramaturgy is potentially an important concept in helping us to understand nonverbal behaviors and communication styles (in clothing, grooming, mannerisms, gestures, stances, handshakes, walk, dance, etc.) among African Americans.

Erving Goffman popularized the concept of dramaturgy, but the intellectual roots of dramaturgical social psychology are found in the work of Kenneth Burke (Peribanayagam, 1982). In an attempt to describe dramaturgy, Zurcher (1982) writes: "Dramaturgy . . . is helpful for revealing how emotional expression is socially influenced within the immediate situation of groups of people who have assembled in accordance with institutional patterns" (p. 3) . . . .Dramaturgically [then] . . . emotions, or more accurately the performance of emotions, is enacted by the individual in terms of his or her understanding of appropriate emotional behaviors in particular situations" (p. 2). Messinger, Sampson and Towne (1962) add: "The outcome of interest to the [individual] is the 'effective' creation of a 'character' which by 'taking in' the audience, or failing to do so, will permit the individual to continue a rewarding line of activity or to avoid an unrewarding one, which will result in his being 'discredited'" (pp. 77-78).

The above descriptions of dramaturgy have particular importance for African Americans. A long history of socio-economic oppression, discrimination, and racism has taught African Americans to distrust whites. This distrust prompted African Americans to use dramaturgical roles for the purposes of scrutinizing, calculating and managing behavior (i.e., what they say, what they do, how they act) for their survival, and as a way to satisfy mainstream norms and expectations. Dramaturgical roles then are not used by African Americans as much out of dishonesty, cunning or manipulative purposes as they are necessary for survival. Thus, role-playing, role-taking, and anticipatory and performance-oriented behaviors have become functional survival mechanisms in the African American life-style.

Messinger, Sampson and Towne (1962) use the late Sammy Davis, Jr. to illustrate how some African American people have learned to develop and make use of different roles because of distrust of whites and in an attempt to survive. Specifically, the authors describe Sammy Davis, Jr., as an individual who learned how to perform and "to be on" at the right time. Davis is quoted as saying "As soon as I go out the front door of my house in the morning, I'm on, daddy, I'm on . . . but when

I'm with the group, I can relax. We trust each other" (p. 74). Messinger, et al. also say that by "Drawing on his experience in the theater, Davis seems to be saying that there are times when, although 'off stage,' he feels 'on-stage' (p. 74). The authors conclude with a statement from Bernard Wolfe:

> "seldom out of sight of a white audience, Negroes in our culture spend most of their lives 'on' . . . Every Negro is to some extent a performer. At other times, 'relaxing among themselves, Negroes will 'mock' the type of personalities they are obliged to assume when they are 'on' . . . We may expect, perhaps, that members of any oppressed group will have similar experiences" (Messinger, Sampson & Towne, p. 74).

From this perspective, African Americans regard presentations of self-to-others and impression management as the key to control and survival. Dramaturgy then is not only useful for analyzing how African Americans react to and express distrust towards whites, it is also a useful framework for understanding and analyzing nonverbal behaviors and communication styles among African Americans.

Although dramaturgy is applicable and relevant for the study of nonverbal behaviors in African American culture, its use has been limited, by and large, to white middle-class groups. That is to say, scholars have not used dramaturgy to study gender, race and socioeconomic status. Yet, dramaturgy can be a helpful framework in which to advance our understanding of nonverbal behaviors and communication styles among African Americans.

Culture and Nonverbal Behavior

There is a lack of agreement among scholars as to whether nonverbal behaviors are universal or cultural (Eibl-Eibesfeldt, 1972; Ramsey, 1979; Obudho, 1979; Rich, 1974). In "The Expression of Emotion in Man and Animal", Darwin proposed that human movements were universal (innate) rather than culturally learned. Recently, however, LeBarre, concluded that expressions of emotion in one culture could be open to serious misinterpretation in another (cited in Rich, 1974). Birdwhistell takes a similar view by noting, for example, that a smile is a universal expression, but its meaning must be studied within the framework of a specific culture (Rich, 1974).

Nonverbal Behavior and Communication Styles in African American Culture

What is the origin of nonverbal behavior and communication styles in African American culture? Some scholars view the origins of these nonverbal behaviors as beginning in Africa (Johnson, 1971), whereas other scholars view nonverbal behaviors in African American as being a product of both the African American community and white European cultures. Still others reason that nonverbal behaviors in African Americans are a product of African American intergroup dynamics, independent of African or European culture. That is to say, the isolation of African Americans from African culture since the days of the slave trade, and the isolation of African Americans from whites at different times in history may have influenced the development of unique and original nonverbal behaviors among African Americans in this country. Whatever the case, it appears that particular nonverbal behaviors in African Americans have taken on distinctive qualities as a consequence of the "history of conflict" with whites in this country (slavery, servitude, racism, discrimination). Because of this history, I believe that survival, pride, solidarity, camaraderie, entertainment, and bitterness have become the impetus for and raíson d'etre of many culture-specific nonverbal behaviors in present-day African American culture.

Two of the most widely cited articles on nonverbal behaviors and communication in African American culture are "Black Kinesics: Some Nonverbal Communication Patterns in Black Culture" (Johnson, 1971) and "Nonverbal Communication Among Afro-Americans: An Initial Classification" (Cooke, 1980, originally published in 1972). Johnson and Cooke's articles were written during the ascendancy of the Black power movement. The Black power movement, during the late 1960s and early 1970s reflected "a period of symbolism," i.e., a period when African Americans more often than not used nonverbal behaviors and communication styles in clothes, (e.g., dashikis), handshakes, hairstyles, stance, walking styles, etc., to symbolize power, struggle, anger, strength, protest, defiance, unity, pride, independence, and solidarity. However, for many African Americans, nonverbal behaviors of the past go against the ideology, needs and etiquette of today. Thus, many nonverbal behaviors in African American culture have changed to reflect today's needs, taken on new forms, or have disappeared altogether; African American culture is a dynamic, rather than a static culture. Therefore, the development and use of nonverbal behaviors among African Americans can be considered an "art form," because new nonverbal behaviors evolve regularly.

African American Kinesics

Efron's (1941) classic book *Gesture and Environment* introduced innovative ways of studying body language by emphasizing the importance of culture. Like Efron, other scholars have concluded that kinesic behaviors are cultural-specific and therefore must be studied within a cultural framework (Dodd, 1977; Knapp, 1980).

Birdwhistell (1970), who popularized and legitimatized the study of kinesics, used the term kineme to categorize and describe various body movements. Kinemes are the smallest set of body movements that have structural meaning. Kinemorphs are the next unit of categorization, which consist of a combination of kinemes (Harper, Wien & Matarazzo, 1978).

Birdwhistell hypothesized the existence of some 50 or 60 kinemes. The significance of these numbers can be appreciated by the following statement: "Physiologists have estimated that the facial musculature is such that over twenty thousand different facial expressions are somatically possible. At present we have been able to isolate thirty-two kinemes in the face and head area (in Harper, Wien & Matarazzo, 1978, p. 123).

New forms and manifestations of kinesics and other nonverbal behaviors and communication styles currently being used by African Americans are described in the following sections. The reader should be aware that not all behaviors described are exhibited by all African Americans; some behaviors or patterns may be modified by region, class, age, or gender.

Walking: Males

Because many African American men in this country have been viewed as "invisible," the conspicuous and expressive nature of the African American male's walk has become a way in which to gain visibility, to accentuate the self, gain the attention of females, and proclaim, "see me, I'm alive, I breathe, I am." Hence, the African American walk provides African American males with a strong sense of self-esteem, masculinity, power, and pride in self and race. Those who cannot walk black, or prefer not to walk black in the African American community, may be seen as "corny" or uncool and thus are often candidates for ridicule, abuse, or harm.

Even though there appears to be a basic African American male walking style (with some regional differences) there are a variety of different styles. The mainstay of the African American walk is its rhythm and style (as opposed to the white male's walk that has been referred to as "robot-like" and mechanical). For example, Johnson (1971) described the African American walk as being a somewhat slower walk—almost like a stroll. The head is slightly elevated and tipped to one's side. One arm will swing at the side while the hand is slightly cupped. At the same time, the other arm hangs to the side or is put in the pocket. "The gait is slow, casual, and rhythmic. The gait is almost like a walking dance, with all parts of the body moving in rhythmic harmony" (p. 185).

Hannah (1984) reported that "macho" sixth grade boys often used the African American walk. She writes, "along with a swagger, the head tips to one side, one arm swings at the side; the other is tucked in a pocket . . . . The polyrhythmic walk included dynamism as parts of the torso moved counter to each other; hips shifted or rotated sideways as the upper torso was held relatively upright. Boys often walked with a springiness, the heel only momentarily placed on the ground. Some children trembled their shoulders and rippled their spines" (p. 381). (Also, see Rich, 1974, for discussion of the African American male walk). Hence, rhythm and style permeate the African American walk.

Walking: Females

There is less research on the walk of African American females than on African American males. One reason may be that the African American female's walk is not as conspicuous, dramatic, expressive, or as creative as the African American male's walk. Hence, because African American males have had a greater history of *direct* oppression as victims of police abuse, murders, lynchings, capital punishment, imprisonment, unemployment, etc., it is likely that this history has influenced African American males use of walking as a means of "symbolic empowerment." Because African American females have not experienced oppression in the same direct way as African American males, they may not have had the same need to use or develop walking as a means of symbolic empowerment and pride.

Nevertheless, African American females use walking for some of the same reasons as males—e.g., as a way to attract the attention of the opposite sex. For example, Cooke (1980) refers to the black female walk as "shaking it up." He describes the female African American walk as "a forward-and-backward motion of the shoulders which creates movement in the breast area. This kind of walk ". . . involves movement of many parts of the body (hips, shoulders, breasts) . . ." (p. 155).

Cooke (1980) described the female shaking it up walk on the basis of data collected in the 1960's (I am not certain this walk is used today; rather, there are probably a number of variations). Because of individual differences, females, like males, also improvise, create, and use a variety of various walks. Therefore, the African American female walk has the potential to be as varied as the African American male walk.

Stances: Males

Stances are among the most recognized and discussed nonverbal behaviors in African American culture because they are used, in part, like African American walking styles, to impress and gain the attention of females.

Even though Cook's (1980) article on nonverbal behavior in African American culture contributed to the literature on stance behaviors among African Americans, some of his findings are questionable. Specifically, I question Cooke's tendency of suggesting more names for African American male stances than there were actual stances (player stance, pimp stance, rapping stance, cat stance) at the time. Nevertheless, I think Cooke's "lowered shoulder kineme" stance (Cooke, 1980) can be viewed as the basic African American male stance, and the source of any number of variations.

In the lower shoulder kineme stance, one shoulder is tilted higher (in almost a "crunched" position) than the other. The head usually leans toward (chin often protrudes) the tilted shoulder. Many black males "sport" the lower shoulder kineme with one or both hands in their pockets, by tucking their hand under their belt, or by cupping their hands over their genitals (Cooke, 1980).

African American males also use the "stationary pimp strut" stance (Johnson, 1971). Males using this stance will often put their hands in their pockets and "move in a rhythmic fluid dance-type way (without actually walking) to accentuate this behavior. The free arm will swing, point, turn, and gesture, as conversation proceeds. It is as if they are walking in place" (p. 186).

Other contemporary stances include the "forward-lower-shoulder kineme" and "peeping" (Cooke, 1980). The forward lower shoulder kineme is much like the lower shoulder kineme, but the shoulders are tilted forward—as opposed to the side.On the other hand, in "peeping" males will lift their shoulders upward, in a raised and crunched-like position, while slightly tilting one shoulder higher in the air than the other. At the same time, the head tilts and is slanted in the opposite direction of the body. One of the more noticeable characteristics of peeping include staring, gazing, and fixed eyes. The same variations of hand placement used with lowered shoulder kineme (or forward- lower-shoulder-kineme) may be used and applied to peeping.

The lower shoulder kineme, forward-lower-shoulder kineme, and peeping are all used in courtship (e.g., as a prelude to "rapping" with a female, catching the eye of or observing and watching females, etc.). During courtship the goal of such stances is to accentuate and advertise the self.

Many stances described above are largely used by lower socioeconomic status African American males who live in urban metropolitan areas, but variations of these stances are also used in other regions of the country, and by other socioeconomic groups. Research is needed to substantiate who uses what kind of stances, when, where, and in what situations.

Stances: Females

Cooke (1980) in his description of the "shaking it up walk" discussed and described the dominant stance females used:

"Her walk is sufficient to draw attention. [But] there are various stances she may employ to further indicate her mood. Standing with her hands resting . . . her derriere thrust outward . . . , she bends one leg forward, somewhat in front of the other leg, which is held straight in back . . . a variation of this stance is achieved . . . by resting one arm on the bar, pushing out the hip and placing the other hand on the hip. Again, one leg may be bent in order to accentuate the touching of the hip" (p. 157). Similarly, Johnson (1971) describes the African American females' stance (especially when interested in a member of the opposite sex) as a fixed stance usually with one hip extended, the body weight is placed on the back foot, buttocks protruding and one or both hands are often placed on or near the hip area.

Because research on African American females and nonverbal behaviors is either outdated or limited, contemporary descriptions of female stances (and other areas of female nonverbal behaviors) are needed.

Handshakes

During the late 1960s and early 1970s, few nonverbal behaviors symbolized the consciousness of African American people and the black power movement in the way that black handshakes and hand gestures did (e.g., see Rich, 1974 discussion of black Olympic medal winners, Tommie Smith and John Carlos, who both raised black gloved fists toward the flag as an act of defiance). There were so many different handshakes and hand gestures during this time that the creation of new handshakes and hand gestures were only limited by one's imagination.

Cooke (1980) referred to handshakes and hand gestures as "giving skin" and "getting skin." Some of the names and ways in which a person in the 1960s and 1970s "gave skin," or "got skin," were as follows: "palm-to-palm," "agreement skin," "complimentary skin," "greeting skin," "emphatic skin," "superlative skin," "parting skin," "five on the sly skin," and "regular skin." Other handshakes and hand gestures used during this time included the black thumb grasp" (i.e., mutual encircling of the thumb, while grasping each other's hands with bended fingers), placing hands on shoulders, raising of the arms, flexing the biceps, and making a fist (Cooke, 1980) among others.

In the 1960s and 1970s many of these handshakes and hand gestures were used to make symbolic statements of agreement, approval, compliment, introduction, greetings, farewell, intimacy, support, solidarity, power, pride, and identity (Cooke, 1980; Shiffrin, 1974; Labarre, 1974). There are a variety of meanings associated with "handwork," however, the only real way to interpret handwork is to analyze the entire communication act (how the body moves, how you feel, etc.) (Schiffrin, 1974).

There is no doubt that many of the above handshakes and hand gestures were in use in some form during the 1960s and 1970s. However, as with stances, Cooke (1980) overstated the uses of handshakes and hand gestures by suggesting more names (as opposed to variations) than actual handshakes and hand gestures. Although some of these handshakes and hand gestures are in use today in some form (and some handshakes and hand gestures are more popular in certain regions than others), I view the "African American thumb grasp," which involves the mutual encircling of thumbs while hands are grasped together, as the dominant hand gesture in use in African American culture today. Another contemporary handshake and hand gesture, among others, is the "high five" which involves the mutual raising of the arms, high in the air, with open palms while individuals grasp or touch each other's palms. The high five appears to be used most often in sporting events. In fact, some African American athletes, and their white team mates on the Oakland A's baseball team, have begun to use a new variation of the high five referred to as the "elbow-bash" high five. This high five is used to show recognition, approval and is a way to act cool.

On the other hand, the "low five" involves the mutual downward extension of the arms with open palms, while individuals mutually grasp or touch each other's palms. For example, in some college basketball events, during pre-game introductions, starting basketball players, with hands extended downward and palms out, bend down and run one by one through a line of non-starting players (in similar bent positions) and cheerleaders giving each other low fives.

African American fraternities, gangs and other formal and informal organizations have their own "secret" handshakes and hand gestures. For example, certain black fraternities use a "hand-body shake" which involves any number of hand grasps used concomitantly with some kind of body embracing between persons. Others have referred to the hand-body shake as the "frat shake" (Greg Foster, personal communication, June 23, 1988). However, one fraternity member prefers to call the frat shake "givin up the da-dap" (John Barnes, personal communication, April 14, 1988; for discussion of a black military shake—"clap hand-to-hand greeting" see Hannah, 1984). The above descriptions do not comprise a comprehensive list of handshakes and hand gestures in use today. Because of the innovative and creative nature of African American culture, new handshakes and hand gestures are constantly evolving.

Facial Expressions

Ekman's (1972) research on facial expressions are valuable for understanding facial expression in various cultural groups, including African Americans. Ekman and Friesen (1967) developed the "neurocultural theory of facial expressions of emotion" (in Harper, Wien and Matarazzo, 1978). The theory describes how cultural display rules modify elicitors from the environment to produce behavior. In this theory, Ekman and Friesen believe facial behaviors are both universal and cultural-specific. As Ekman writes: "What is universal in facial expression of emotions is the particular set of facial muscular movements triggered when a given emotion is elicited" (in Harper, Wien and Matarazzo, 1978, p. 100). Hence, Ekman and Friesen (1967) believe some elicitors of facial expressions are unlearned even though most facial expressions are learned—for example, a look of disgust on a person's face in response to a bad taste or smell.

However, Ekman and Friesen argue that because of cultural norms, individual expectations, socio-histories, etc., eliciting events for the same emotions can vary from person to person. That is to say, after an eliciting event occurs, more often than not there is some kind of cognitive processing by the person just prior to activation of facial affect. For example, if a basketball player makes a winning basket with two seconds remaining on the clock, he must first find and identify his teammates before he can react with happiness.

Ekman and Friesen also argue that facial expression can be modified by voluntary muscular control, by unconscious behavior or by automatic habit—which Ekman refers to as "display rules." Depending on the circumstance, then display rules modify or alter facial behavior (i.e., exaggerate emotions, understate emotions, neutralize or, mask emotions, e.g., laughing and smiling to cover up anger, sorrow or disgust) (Harper, Wiens & Matarazzo, 1978).

Ekman (1972) uses the term "blends" or multiple emotions (Ekman posited seven primary emotions: happiness, anger, surprise, fear, disgust, sadness, and interest) to describe how display rules and culture effect facial expressions. Blends may occur when a stimulus event elicits more than one emotion, as when winning a lottery may produce both surprise and happiness. Gender and facial expression research has shown that females exhibit more facial displays of emotions than males (LaFrance, 1981; Eakins & Eakins, 1978) and that females generally smile more than males (Frances, 1979). Smith (1983) extended findings on smiling behaviors to African Americans and gender. She found no significant differences in smiling behavior between African American males and African American females. However, she concluded that females may smile more at opposite sex partners, but not when interacting with the same sex.

Eye and visual behavior Visual behavior (eye contact, gaze, staring, "rolling of the eyes," "cutting of the eyes," etc.) plays a major role in African American nonverbal behavior (see Watson, 1970 for extensive review of cultural gaze). In particular, eye and visual behavior play an important role in interpersonal communication, interpersonal attraction and arousal (Cooke, 1980 refers to eye usage among African American males-females as the "silent rap").

Lafrance and Mayo's (1976) research indicates that African Americans tend to have lower eye contact and gaze than whites. For this reason, these researchers believe white authority figures (e.g., administrators, teachers, educators, etc.) often misread African American eye behavior (e.g., African Americans are uninterested, less honest, withhold information and have poor concentration). Thus, Lafrance and Mayo conclude that a cultural framework should always be used in interpreting eye contact and gaze. Hanna's (1984) research on cultural eye behaviors indicate that whites associate eye contact and eye gaze with affiliation, positive attitudes between communicators, trustworthiness, forthrightness, and sincerity. On the other hand, African Americans may associate eye contact and gaze with negative overtones and a lack of respect. Hanna's data also showed some African Americans were reluctant to look directly in the eye of persons who occupied an authority position.

The eye and visual literature shows that overall, females use eye contact more frequently than males (Smith, 1983; Exline, Gray & Schuette, 1965; Eakins & Eakins, 1978). It is generally believed that females establish greater eye contact than males because of the propensity toward social and interpersonal dynamics. As such, females may establish more eye contact when compared to males, as a way to show sensitivity and emotional expression (Eakins & Eakins, 1978; Exline, 1963). These sex differences also seem to be generally consistent across age. For example, Kagan and Lewis (1965) found that female infants attend to human faces more at 6 months than male infants do at the same age, suggesting that looking may be an innate sex-related characteristic.

Research on eye contact across race generally shows that African Americans look at others while listening, with less frequency than whites (Smith, 1983; Harper, Wiens & Matarazzo, 1978; Lafrance & Mayo, 1976; Hanna, 1984; LaFrance, 1974; Hall, 1974; Shuter, 1979). Typically, whites look at others more when listening than speaking, whereas blacks do the opposite (LaFrance & Mayo, 1976; Hanna, 1984). Overall, LaFrance and Mayo (1976) found that looking while listening occurred less for black males and most for white females.

On cultural eye contact behaviors, Smith's (1983) findings indicate that: (1) African American females showed significantly less gazing behavior than white females; (2) African American females showed more gazing while listening versus other groups; (3) African American females versus African American mixed sex pairs revealed no significant differences, while African American male pairs showed significantly less gaze behavior than African American mixed sex pairs; and (4) white females showed significantly more gaze behavior than white mixed sex pairs. However, on same and cross-sex pairing, Harper, Wiens and Matarazzo (1978) found that male-female African American pairs did not gaze significantly less than white male and white female pairs but African American female pairs gazed less than white male pairs or white male and female pairs. LaFrance and Mayo (1976) and Smith (1983) caution that such variables as the history of the relationship, intimacy, setting, etc. should be taken into consideration when analyzing and interpreting data on cultural eye contact and gaze behavior.

As mentioned above "staring, "rolling of the eyes," and "cutting of the eyes" are eye behaviors African Americans often use. Scholars have well documented the effects of staring on humans and animals (Eibl-Elbesfeldt, 1972; Eakins and Eakins, 1978; Ellsworth, Carlsmith and Henson, 1972). Ellsworth, Carlsmith & Henson (1972) and Eakins and Eakins (1978) suggested that staring acts as a threat display that evokes tension and arouses hostility. Ellsworth, Carlsmith & Henson (1972) studied the effects of staring in humans in a variety of different situations. In one study, researchers either stood at the street corner or were sitting on motorcycles staring at people as they crossed the street. Time spent crossing the street was found to be significantly affected by staring: people who were stared at crossed the street much faster. Interestingly, "subjects who were stared at for less than 5 seconds drove off just as fast as those who were stared at for 10 seconds or more" (cited in Harper, Wien & Matarazzo, p. 205). Do these findings have any implications for understanding staring behaviors among African Americans?

In this country, African Americans staring at whites often has been associated with tension bitterness, distrust and hostility between African Americans and whites (Majors, 1987; Rich, 1974). One example of African Americans' use of staring at whites as a demonstration of anger, frustration, distrust, etc. was noted in an interview study of African American male coolness (Majors, 1987). One informant discussed the importance of staring at whites as a form of coolness:

> ... "You're going to find that when you start getting out there dealin [with whites], that you're going to have to use a type of cool somewhere. Watch him, and look him in the eyes. He can't stand that! Look at him dead in his eyes and talk to him and don't take your eyes off him. You might burn your eyes, but ... you've psyched him out ... that's another cool system" (p. 77).

"Rolling the eyes" is yet another eye behavior often associated with African Americans (Cooke, 1980; Johnson, 1971; Hanna, 1984; Pennington, 1979; Blubaugh & Pennington, 1976; Ramsey, 1989; Rickford & Rickford, 1976). "Rolling the eyes" is a nonverbal eye behavior that often communicates general disapproval, anger, and dislike of others. "Rolling the eyes" is described as an initial glare, but not actually a stare. Following the initial glare, the eyes move from one side of the socket to the other in an upward arc, with lowered eye lids.

On the other hand, "cutting of the eyes" is eye behavior that is directed toward a person rather than directed away from someone as in the case of "rolling the eyes" (Pennington, 1979; Johnson, 1971). After the eyes are fixed on the person (i.e., after the "cutting") the eyes often remain in a temporary focused state (Johnson, 1971).

Touching Research on touching clearly shows race and gender differences (Smith, 1983). Some scholars suggest that as a result of socialization females use touching more for intimacy, friendship, and warmth, while males use touching more for status and power (Eakins & Eakins, 1978; Smith, 1983). Such scholars believe that females are conditioned by society to show feelings and emotions whereas males are conditioned not to show feelings and emotions. Also, most research seems to indicate that females are touched more by others than males are touched by others. Eakins & Eakins (1978) suggest this may be age-related because mothers touch their female children more often than their male offspring, from the age of six months on. Their data clearly showed a higher being-touched mean score for females than males.

Hence, gender-related differences in touching may have been established early as a result of socialization.

Although female touching behaviors may be a product of socialization and intimacy, males on the other hand, often use touching to express status and power. Therefore, when males touch females they may be symbolizing chauvinistic attitudes. That is to say, touching for males may connote dominance, possession, etc. towards others. As Henley and Thorne wrote: ". . . the wholesale touching of women carries the message that women are community property" (Eakins and Eakins, 1978, p. 394).

Race research on touching behavior has shown that African Americans, as contrasted with whites, touch others in a wider variety of different situations. For example, Smith, et al. (1980) found a higher rate of touching among African Americans than whites in expression of congratulations on a bowling team. Heinig (1975) reported that African American students touched teachers more than their white counterparts. Willis, Reeves, and Buchman (1976) showed that touching behavior among African Americans was much greater than the touching behavior among white children (Hanna, 1984). Willis and Hoffman (1975) observed touching behaviors among African Americans and white female pairs while waiting in elementary school cafeteria lines during their lunch. These authors concluded there was "more frequent touching in same sex and same race dyads than in dyads of other race/sex combinations (Smith, 1983, p. 58). In a similar study with junior high students, Willis and Reeves (1976) discovered that touching was more likely to occur in black-black dyads with females touching more frequently than any other group. The authors concluded that black females use touching behaviors as a way to communicate intimacy. Taylor and his colleagues (1974) in yet another study, found racial differences in touching in the military: African Americans were "turned off" when whites touched their hair, buttocks, or shoulders.

There are also class differences in touching. For example, Henley (1977) found that people in higher income brackets touched less whereas those in lower income brackets touched more. Similarly, Hall (1974) noted that when comparing working class African Americans to Northern European middle-class whites and working class Hispanics, working class blacks, as contrasted with other groups, showed a greater tendency toward bodily contact in interpersonal interactions.

Proxemics The term personal space was first coined by Katz (1937). However, Hall (1955, 1966) was the first researcher to study personal space, systematically referring to the study of spatial usage as proxemic. Proxemics is a term that describes the study of the individual's use and perception of social and personal space. The study of proxemics includes fixed features of space (i.e., buildings), semi-fixed features (i.e., seating and furniture arrangements) and personal space (Dodd, 1977; Knapp, 1978). Personal space orientation is sometimes referred to as territoriality. That is to say, the term territoriality often is used in the study of proxemics to describe what seems to be a tendency for humans to "stake out" personal territory—much in the same way that animals do (Knapp, 1978).

In regards to gender, it is often said that the male's need and desire for control of greater territory and space (LaFrance, 1981) is a sublimal expression of dominance and status. Hence, it is not unusual for males to believe they are entitled to more personal space. For example, Eakins and Eakins (1978) noted that males compared to females, usually have larger houses, land-holdings, automobiles, offices, and desks. Additionally, Eakins and Eakins reported that males also used more personal space in their body spread. It is not surprising, therefore, that women's territory is perceived as smaller by both females and males. In other words, women seem to have become accustomed to, and tolerant of, invasions of their personal space.

Hall (1955, 1966), who studied cultural differences and personal space, discovered that Germans used greater areas of personal space and were less flexible with their personal space than Americans. On the other hand, Arabs, French, and Latin Americans were more tolerant of sharing space and allowed much more flexibility than Americans. On sex differences, Hall found that American males preferred to stand 18-20 inches from other males during face-to-face interactions. However, females under these same circumstances preferred 22-24 inches (Obudo, 1979). McCroskey (1975) found that males tended to establish greater interpersonal distances from other males, but were more flexible with females. McCroskey also found that females establish less interpersonal distance with males and other females. Overall, women were shown to interact at closer interpersonal distances than males. Some scholars suggest that womens' feelings often may be inferred from how close they sit or stand to someone (Smith, 1983; Heshka & Nelson, 1972).

In a study of middle-class populations, Willis (1966) reported that African Americans greeted other African Americans at greater distance than whites greeted other whites. Moreover, whites greeted African Americans at further distances than they greeted other whites. Baxter (1970), in a study of personal space usage of three subcultural groups, reported that African Americans stood furthest apart, followed by whites, Mexican Americans were the closest. Baxter also found that whites interacted at "comparable distances" irrespective of being indoors or outdoors, while African Americans gathered closer when indoors. Knapp (1978) found that black-white pairs maintained greater interpersonal distances than white versus white or African Americans versus African American dyads. Similarly, Hanna, (1984) reported that African Americans preferred greater interpersonal distance from whites. Also, Smith (1983) found that African American females leaned synchronously more than white females or African American male dyads. Smith suggested that African American women use leaning as a way to convey intimacy and rapport.

In regards to race differences and personal space usage Scherer found that middle-class children maintained greater conversational distance than lower-class children. However, he found no differences in personal space usage between middle-class blacks and whites nor lower-class blacks and whites (cited in Knapp, 1978). Nevertheless, Harper, Wiens and Matarazzo, (1978) cautioned that to ensure accuracy all findings should be controlled for individual differences in age, personality, psychiatric disorders, acquaintance, interpersonal similarity, intimacy, etc.

Hairstyles In the 1950s and 60s, many African Americans, especially males, wore their hair straight, or "processed." Also, during the 1950s and 1960s black Americans wore their hair cropped short, (often wavy) with the front, temples, sides and back "edged up" by clippers or a razor. However, by late 1960 until about the mid-1970s, the predominant hairstyle worn by African Americans was the "Afro" or "natural."

During the Black Power movement, (of the late 1960s and 1970s) the Afro or natural reflected the "spirit" of the movement by symbolizing solidarity, identity, and pride (of self and race). Thus, by the late 1960s, straightening the hair and "processes" were considered demeaning by African Americans because such hairstyles were associated with "wanting to look white" and lacking self-esteem and/or pride. However, since the mid 1970s, the Afro, or natural hairstyle, has not been in vogue with African Americans. Hence, since the mid 1970s, African Americans have worn a variety of new and different hairstyles. Many of these hairstyles are fashionable and in use today. Because African American culture is not static but is creative, expressive, and action-oriented, new forms of hairstyles are constantly evolving. As such, any discussion of "fashionable" and vogue hairstyles is always subject to change.

Some of the more popular contemporary hairstyles are "the shag" (shorter on the top, while longer in the back) the "sculpture-block" look, "the flat top" (hair that is cut flat on the top, and usually cropped short on the sides, or shaved off on the sides). Other popular contemporary hairstyles are: the "Boxcut," "hightop fad," the "Gumby" (André Brown, personal communication, March 15, 1990), and dreadlocks. While these hairstyles are often worn in any number of combinations and forms, an individual may "sport" a "tail" (a piece of hair in the back of the neck that is permitted to grow at length, then is braided), or shave multiple "parts" on the side (usually no more than 2-4 "parts" are cut in to the side of the head) of the head. "The fade" (hair can be a number of lengths on top, while the sides are decreasingly shorter and may even be shaved off around the temple and ears) is yet another contemporary African American hairstyle. The Punk-rock movement has also influenced African American hairstyles. In fact, it is vogue for some blacks to wear "buzzcuts," or "mohawk cuts," (occasionally with dyed hair).

Among contemporary African American women, cornrows and braids remain in vogue. Braids are often worn by themselves or with beads. Recently, however, some white employers have opposed African Americans wearing braids in the workplace (see Shipp, 1988 for an excellent discussion of this issue). Popular chemically treated hairstyles African Americans wear today include, but are not limited to, "Jeri curls," and "perms" (both tight curls and loose curls, or "relaxed") (see Fornay, 1984, for discussion of chemically-treated hairstyles among African Americans).

Finally, many contemporary African American males wear the "wavy-look" hairstyle. In this hairstyle the hair is cut close to the scalp, pomade is put on the hair usually at night before bed, and stocking cap is then placed over the hair, to promote waves.

Dance Dancing is a nonverbal behavior that African Americans use primarily as a means of entertainment. Dancing expresses creativity (e.g., spontaneity, improvisation) and the "rhythmic style" in African American culture (Lomax, 1982) (see Hanna, 1984, for discussion of how African American children spontaneously create different dances inside and outside of the classroom).

In the 1950s and 1960s, such dances as the "Cool jerk" and the "twist" were popular in African American culture. However, today such dances as the "pop," the "humpty-hump," the "cabbage patch," the "snake," the "moonwalk," the "electric boogie" and the "butt," among others, are popular. But no recent new dance form in African American culture in the 1980s gathered as much attention from adolescents, choreographers, movie producers, advertisers, and even gymnastic officials and gymnasts (Towson, 1986) as breakdancing has (Rosenwald, 1984; Cox, 1984; Grubb, 1984). The term breakdancing or 'breaking' "has come to be used generically to describe all modern street dancing, but the individual forms, although having some similarities, are myriad. Breakdancing is based on centripetal force (movement directed toward center) and spinning on an axis, with all the low-level movement done on or close to the floor" (Rosenwald, 1984). Breakdancing is often done on flattened cardboard boxes spread out on the sidewalk, or concrete. Rosenwald (1984) reports that breakdancing probably emerged from the ghetto neighborhoods of the South Bronx as a macho street-dance for the purpose of entertainment.

There are a number of various styles and forms of breakdancing: "Egyptian," "popping," "floating," "slam-dancing," among others (see Rosenwald, 1984 for an excellent discussion and overview of break-dancing. This article also includes a glossary of terms "breakers" use). Breakdancing is thought to help prevent violence, bloodshed, and fighting among adolescents in our large cities. Some writers suggest that adolescents and gang members often use breakdancing rather than street fighting as a form of "positive" competition, self-expression, brotherhood, and "macho" entertainment (Cox, 1984; Rosenwald, 1984).

Clothes During the black power movement, African Americans wore African-style clothing (dashikis) and jewelry to express and symbolize pride and identity. However, present day African Americans use clothes more for fashion, and as status symbols. Nevertheless, Knapp (1978) suggested that clothes help individuals to communicate attitudes, interests and values. In addition, individuals use clothes to attract attention and, as ways to enhance self-esteem (for additional discussion of how African Americans use clothes for purpose of styling, attention, respect, etc., see Folb, 1980; Majors, 1987).

Today, clothes among adolescents have been associated with violence, fighting, and even death. For example, some gangs use certain clothing, (e.g. baseball caps) and "colors" as a way to show affiliation, and gang membership. As such, some gangs have killed individuals in certain areas of the city for wearing the wrong "colors" or clothes. Gangs and adolescents have also fought, and sometimes killed, over certain brand-name clothes (e.g., Georgio, Gucci, etc.,), basketball sneakers, or items like gold chains. However, some organizations, such as black fraternities, use and wear clothing without incident and show others the same respect (i.e., wearing what they want without fear of abuse).

Automobiles African Americans often make nonverbal statements about themselves by the kinds of cars they drive. Also, the nonverbal behaviors and body gestures one uses while driving or sitting in a car also say something about the person. In other words, cars for African Americans (and no doubt other groups), are not only a status symbol, but much like clothes, are a kind of symbol that allows "one to be seen."

One of the best ways to be noticed or receive attention while driving or sitting in a car is "leaning" or "low-riding" (Folb, 1980; Majors, 1987). Leaning and low-riding are stylized types of physical posturing that African American males often use while driving or sitting in cars to "show off"; gain the attention of females, or for the purpose of just being cool. On leaning and low-riding, Folb (1980) writes: "This particular posture, assumed by the driver (and sometimes by passengers), is where a person sits as low in one's seat as possible, so all that is visible is the top of the person's head and eyes peering over the steering wheel. Like leaning, low-riding is a strategy designed to call attention to driver and car" (p. 115).

Sports African Americans, especially black males, use sports to communicate nonverbally. In many ways, the channels or avenue for sports has always been much more accessible than such areas as the classroom or employment. Because of this, black males have come to use sports as a way to express masculinity (Majors, 1990), accentuate or display themselves, obtain gratification, release pent-up aggression, gain prestige and recognition, exercise power and control, and show pride for self and race. Moreover, African American males use sports as a means of creativity and self-expression (e.g., "to style," play it cool, perform, etc.).

Some of the ways in which African American males demonstrate expressive behaviors nonverbally in sports are: fancy dances in the end-zone, "spiking" the football, fancy moves (e.g., "Dr. J" was known for his very creative, graceful and athletic abilities on the basketball court: agility, flexibility, and "air-hang" time), "dunking" (e.g., basketball's Michael Jordan's "Air-Jordan" dunk, Darryl Dawkins' "gorilla dunk"), the wearing of towels that hang from pants and multiple wristbands, "low and high fives" and other hand gestures. Athletes who are known for their exhibited expressive behaviors in sports include Muhammad Ali (boxing) (i.e., fast hands, foot speed, e.g., "Ali Shuffle," displays of tassels on shoes, ritualistic hair-combing in mirror after bouts, etc.), Reggie Jackson (standing at the plate and watching his home run balls leave the park) Connie Hawkins (Fancy moves), Thomas "Hollywood" Henderson (football) (bragging behavior, colorful personality), and more recently, Jeff Leonard (known for his "one flapdown homerun trot") and Magic Johnson's (basketball) "no look" passes.

Future Work

The literature on language and especially sociolinguistics has made a major contribution to the understanding of African American culture. On the other hand, literature that addresses nonverbal behaviors and African American culture is limited at best. If we are to appreciate and understand African American culture, much more research on nonverbal behavior is needed. It is especially important to study non-verbal behavior of African Americans concomitantly with race, class and socioeconomic status. Such efforts collectively can advance our knowledge of African Americans.

References

Abrahams, R. (1976). *Talking black*. Rawley, MA: Newbury House.

Birdshistell, R.L. (1970). *Kinesics and context: Essays on body motion communication*. Philadelphia: University of Pennsylvania Press.

Baxter, J.C. (1970). Interpersonal spacing in natural settings. *Sociometry, 33*, 444-456.

Blubaugh, J.A., & Pennington, D.L. (1976). *Crossing difference: Interracial communication*. Columbus, Ohio: Merrill.

Boykin, W. (1983). The academic performance of Afro-American children. In J. Spence (Ed.), *Achievement and achievement motives*. San Francisco, CA: W.H. Freeman.

Brissett, D., & Edgley, C. (Eds.) (1975). *Life as theater: A dramaturgical sourcebook*. Chicago: Aldine.

Burke, K. (1945). *Grammar of motive*. New York: Prentice-Hall.

Chance, M.R., & Russell, W.M. (1959). *Protean displays: A form of allaesthetic behavior*. Proceedings Zoological Society London, 132, 65-70.

Collias, E. (1988). *The "mask" in black poetry*. Unpublished manuscript. De Kalb, Illinois: Northern Illinois University.

Combs, J.E. & Mansfield, M.W. (Eds.) (1976). *Drama in life: The uses of communication in society*. New York: Hasting House.

Cooke, B. (1980). Nonverbal communication among Afro-Americans: An initial classification. In R.L. Jones (Ed.), *Black psychology* (2nd ed.) New York: Harper & Row.

Cox, D. (1984). Brooklyn's furious rockers. *Dance Magazine*.

Cully, J.F,. & Legon, J.D., (1976). Comparative mobbing behavior of Scrib and Mexican Jays. *Auk, 93*, 116-125.

Darwin, C. (1872). *The expression of the emotions in man and the animals*. London: J. Murray.

Dodd (1977). *Perspectives on cross-cultural communication*. Dubuque, IA: Kedall/Hunt.

Eakins, B., & Eakins, G. (1978). *Sex differences in human communication*. Boston: Houghton-Mifflin.

Edmund, M. (1975). *Defense in animals*. New York: King's Crown Press.

Efron, D. (1941). *Gesture and environment*. New York: King's Crown Press.

Ekman, P. (1972). Universal and cultural differences in facial expression of emotion. In J.K. Cole (Ed.), *Nebraska symposium on motivation*. Lincoln: University of Nebraska Press.

Ekman, P., & Friesen, W.V. (1967). Origin, usage, and coding: The basis for five categories of nonverbal behavior. Paper presented at the Symposium on Communication Theory and Linguistic Models, Buenos Aires.

Eisenberg, J.F. & Lockhart, M. (1972). An ecological reconnaissance of Wilpattu National Park, Ceylon. *Smithsonian Contributions of Zoology, 101*, 1-118.

Eible-Elbesfeldt, I. (1972). Similarities and differences between cultures in expressive movements. In R.A. Hinde (Ed.), *Nonverbal communication*. London: Cambridge University Press.

Eible-Elbesfeldt, I. (1975). *Ethology: The biology of behavior*. New York: Holt, Rinehart & Winston, Inc.

Ellsworth, P.C., Carlsmith, J.M., & Henson, A. (1972). The state as a stimulus to flight in human subjects: A series of field experiments. *Journal of Personality and Social Psychology, 21*, 302-311.

Exline, R.V. (1963). Explorations in the process of person perception: Visual interaction in relation to competition, sex, and need for affiliation. *Journal of Personality, 31*, 1-20.

Exline, R.V., Gray, D., & Schuette, D. (1965). Visual behavior in a dyad as affected by interview content and sex of respondent. *Journal of Personality and Social Psychology, 1*, 201-209.

Fagen, R. (1981). *Animal play behavior*. New York: Oxford University Press.

Farris, H.E., & Otis, R. (1980). Sexual behavior: Courtship and mating. In R. Denny (Ed.), *Comparative psychology*. New York: Wiley & Sons.

Folb, E. (1980). *Runnin' down some lines: The language and culture of black teenagers*. Cambridge, MA: Harvard University Press.

Frances, S.J. (1979). Sex differences in nonverbal behavior. *Sex Roles, 5*, 519-535.

Goffman, E. (1959). *The presentation of self in everyday life*. Garden City, N.Y.: Doubleday.

Grubb, K. (1984). Hip-hippin' in the South Bronx: Lester Wilson's beat street. *Dance Magazine, 58*, 76-78.

Haas, J., & Shaffir, W. (1982). Taking on the role of doctor: A dramaturgical analysis of professionalization. *Symbolic Interaction, , 2*, 187-203.

Hall, E.T. (1955). The anthropology of manners. *Scientific American, 192*, 85-89.

Hall, E.T. (1964). Adumbration as a feature of intercultural communication. *American Anthropologist, 66*, 154-163. Hall, E.T. (1974). *Handbook for proxemic research*. Washington, D.C.: Society for the Anthropology of Visual Communication.

Halonen, J., & Denny, R. (1980). Defense against predation. In R. Denny (Ed.), *Comparative psychology*. New York: Wiley & Son.

Hammond, E. (1965). *The contest system: A survival technique*. Unpublished manuscript. St. Louis, MO: Washington University.

Hanna, J.L. (1984). Black/white nonverbal differences, dance and dissonance: Implications for desegregation. In A. Wolfgang (Ed.), *Nonverbal behavior: Perspectives, applications, intercultural insights*. Lewiston, N.Y.: C.J. Hogrefe, Inc.

Harper, R.G., Wiens, A.N., & Matarazzo, J.D. (1978). *Nonverbal communication*. New York: Wiley & Son.

Harre, E., & Secord, P.F. (1972). *The explanation of social behavior*. Great Britain: Basil Blackwell.

Harrison-Ross, P., & Wyden, B. (1973). *The black child*. Berkeley: Medallion.

Heinig, R.M. (1975). *A descriptive study of teacher-pupil tactile communication in grades four through six*. Doctoral dissertation. Pittsburgh, PA: University of Pittsburgh.

Henley, N.M. (1977). *Body politics: Power, sex, and nonverbal communication*. Englewood Cliffs, N.J.: Prentice-Hall.

Heskha, S., & Nelson, Y. (1972). Interpersonal speaking distance as a function of age, sex, and relationship. *Sociometry, 35*, 491-498.

Hinde, R.A. (1972) (Ed.). *Nonverbal communication*. New York: Cambridge University Press.

Hudson, J. (1972). The hustling ethic. In T. Kochman (Ed.), *Rappin' and Stylin' out*. Urbana: University of Illinois Press.

Huxley, J. (1914). The courtship habits of the great crested grebe (pidiceps cristatus): With an addition to the theory of sexual selection. *Proceedings Zoological Society London, 35*.

Johnson, K.R. (1971). Black kinesics: Some nonverbal communication patterns in black culture. *Florida Foreign Language Reporter, 9*. 17-20.

Kagan, J., & Lewis, M. (1965). Studies of attention in the human infant. *Merrill-Palmer Quarterly, 2*, 95-122.

Katz, N. (1937). *Animals and men*. New York: Longman, Green.

Kochman, T. (Ed.) (1972). *Rappin' and stylin' out*. Urbana: University of Illinois Press.

Kochman, T. (1981). *Black and white styles in conflict*. Chicago: University of Chicago Press.

Knapp, M.L. (1972). The field of nonverbal communication: An overview. In C.J. Stewart, & B. Kendall (Eds.), *On speech communication: An anthology of contemporary writings and messages*. New York: Holt, Rinehart & Winston.

Knapp, M.L. (1978). *Nonverbal communication in human interaction*. New York: Holt, Rinehart & Winston.

Knapp, M.L. (1980). *Essentials of nonverbal communication*. New York: Holt, Rinehart, & Winston.

Korshgen, C.E., & Fredrickson, L.H. (1976). Comparative displays of yearling and adult male wood ducks. *Auk, 93*, 783-807.

Kortlandt, A. (1967). Experimentation with champanzees in the wild. In R. Schneider, & H.J. Kuhn (Eds.), *Neue ergbrisseder primatology: Process in primatology*. Struttgart: Gustav Fischer Verlag.

Kortlandt, A. (1972). *New perspectives on ape and human evolution*. Amsterdam: Stichting voor Psychobiologie.

Kruuk, H. (1975). *Hyaena*, London Oxford University Press.

LaBarre, W. (1947). The cultural basis of emotions and gestures. *Journal of Personality, 16*, 49-68.

LaFrance, M. (1974). Nonverbal cues to conversational turn taking between black speakers. Paper presented at the meeting of the American Psychological Association, New Orleans.

LaFrance, M., & Mayo, C. (1976). Racial differences in gaze behavior during conversations: Two systematic observational studies. *Journal of Personality and Social Psychology, 33*, 547-552.

LaFrance, M., & Mayo, C. (1978). *Moving bodies: Nonverbal communication in social relationships.* Monterey: Brooks/Cole.

LaFrance, M. (1981). Gender gestures: Sex, sex-role, and nonverbal communication. In C. Mayo, & N.M. Henley (Eds.), *Gender and nonverbal behavior.* New York: Springer-Verlag.

Loizos, C. (1966). Play in mammals. *Symposium of the Zoological Society of London, 18,* 1-10.

Loizos, C. (1967). Play behavior in higher primates: A review. In D. Morris (Ed.), *Primate ethology.* London: Weidenfeld and Nicolson.

Lomax, A. (1982). The cross-cultural variation of rhythmic style. In M. Davis (Ed.), *Interaction rhythms.* New York: Human Science Press.

Majors, R. (1983). *Coolpose: A new hypothesis in understanding antisocial behavior in lower socioeconomic status males.* Unpublished manuscript, University of Illinois, Urbana-Champaign.

Majors, R. (1986a). Coolpose: The proud signature of black survival. *Changing men: Issues in gender, sex, and politics, 17,* 5-6.

Majors, R. (1987). *Coolpose: A new approach toward a systematic understanding and studying of black male behavior.* Unpublished doctoral dissertation, University of Illinois, Urbana IL.

Majors, R. (1989). Coolpose: The proud signature of black survival. In M. Messner, & M. Kimmel (Eds.), *Men's lives: Readings in the sociology of men and masculinity,* (pp. 83-87). New York: Macmillan.

Majors, R. (1990). Coolpose: Black masculinity in sport. In M. Messner, & D. Sabo (Eds.), *Sports, men and the gender order: Critical feminist perspectives.* Champaign, IL: Human Kinestics.

McLeod, M. (1986). Psychologist examines black males' "Cool Mystique". *The Orlando Sentinel.*

Messner, M. (1987). Masculinity, ethnicity, and the athletic career: A comparative analysis of the motivation and experiences of white men and men of color. Paper presented at the meeting of the American Sociological Association.

Messner, M. (1989). Masculinities and athletic careers. *Gender and Society, 3,* 71-88.

Obudhe, L.E. (1979). *Human nonverbal behavior: An annotated bibliography.* Westport, CT: Greenwood Press.

Overington, M.A., & Mangham, I.L. (1982). The theatrical perspective in organizational analysis. *Symbolic Interaction, 5, 2,* 173-185.

Page, C. (1986). Here's some hot dope on being cool. *Chicago Tribune.* November 30.

Pasteur, A.B., & Toldson, I.L. (1982). *Roots of soul: The psychology of black expressiveness.* Garden City, NY: Anchor Press.

Pennington (1979). Black-white communication: An assessment of research. In M.K. Asante, E. Newmark, & C.A. Blake (Eds.), *Handbook of intercultural communication.* Beverly Hills, CA: Sage.

Perinbanayagam, R.S. (1982). Drama, metaphors, and structures. Symbolic Interaction, 5, 2, 259-276.

Peterman, P. (1988). The cool look. *St. Petersburg Times,* p. 1-D. January 4.

Pool, T.B. (1966). Aggressive play in polecats. *Z. Tierpsychology, 24,* 35-369.

Portmann, A. (1961). *Animals as social beings.* New York: Viking Press.

Prestrude, A.M. (1977). Some phylogenetic comparisons to TI with special reference to habituation and fear. *Psychological Record, 1*, 21-40.

Prosser, M.H. (1978). *The cultural dialogue: Introduction to intercultural communication.* Boston: Houghton Mifflin Co.

Rainwater, L. (1966). The crucible of identity: The lower-class Negro family. *Daedalus, 95*, 172-1216.

Ramsey, S. (1979). Nonverbal behavior: An intercultural perspective. In M. Asante, E. Newmark, & C. Blake (Eds.), *Handbook of intercultural communication.* Beverly Hills, CA: Sage.

Rather, S.C. (1977). Immobility of invertebrates: What can we learn? *Psychological Record, 1*, 1-14.

Rickford, J.F., & Rickford, A.E. (1976). Cut-eye and suck-teeth: African words and gestures in New World guise. *Journal of American Folklore, 89*, 294-309.

Rich, A.L. (1974). *Interracial communication.* New York: Harper and Row.

Rosenwald, P. (1984). Breaking away 80's style. *Dance Magazine.*

Rutledge, A. & Gass, G. (Eds.) (1967). *Nineteen Negro men.* San Francisco: Jossey-Bass.

Sariola, S., & Naukkarinen, P. (1989). Coolpose-Rokote Alkoholismia Vastaan? *Tiimi-A-Klin Ikkassaatio.* (Finland), 22-23.

Schiffrin, D. (1974). Handwork as ceremony: The case of the handshake. *Seriotica, 12*, 189-202.

Shipp, E.R. (1988). Are cornrows right for work? *Essence, 18*, 109-111.

Shuter, R. (1979). The day in the military: Hand-to-hand communication. *Journal of Communication.* 136-142.

Shuter, R. (1979). Gaze behavior in interracial and intra-racial interaction. In N.C. Jain (Ed.), *Intercultural communication annual, 5.* Falls Church, VA: Speech Communication Association.

Sike, S.K. (1971). *The natural history of the African elephant.* New York: Elsevier.

Simpson, M.J. (1973). The social grooming of male chimpanzees. In J. Crook & R. Michael (Eds.), *The comparative ecology and behavior of primates.* London: Academic Press.

Slater, P.B. (1985). *An introduction to ethology.* Cambridge: Cambridge University Press.

Smith, A. (1983). Nonverbal communication among black female dyads: An assessment of intimacy, gender and race. *Journal of Social Issues, 39*, 55-67.

Smith, D.E., Willis, F.N., & Gier, J.A. (1980). Success and interpersonal touch in a competitive setting. *Journal of Nonverbal Behavior, 5*, 26-34.

Stanback, M., & Pearce, B.E. Man (19). Some communication strategies used by members of subordinate social groups. *The Quarterly Journal of Speech, 67*, 21-30.

Taylor, O.I., Min, L., Spears, A., & Stoller, P.A. (1974). *Problems in crosscultural communications: A study of blacks and whites in the U.S. Army.* Washington, D.C.: Center for Applied Linguistics.

Tinbergen, N. (1952). Derived activities: The causation, biological significance, origin, and emancipation during evolution. *Quarterly Review of Biology, 27*, 1-32.

Watson, O.M. (1970). *Proxemic behavior: A cross-cultural study.* The Hague: Mouton.

Willis, F.N. (1966). Initial speaking distance as a function of the speaker's relationship. *Psychonomic Science, 5,* 221-222.

Willis, F.N., & Hoffman, G.E. (1975). Development of tactile patterns in relationship to age, sex and race. *Developmental Psychology, 11,* 866.

Willis, F.N., Reeves, D.L., & Buchman, D.R. (1976). Interpersonal touch in high school relative to sex and race. *Perceptual and Motor Skills, 43,* 843-847.

Willis, F.N., & Reeves, D.L., (1976). Touch interactions in junior high school students in relation to sex and race. *Developmental Psychology, 12,* 91-92.

Wittenberger, J.F. (1981). *Animal social behavior.* Boston: Duxbury Press.

Wolfgang, A. (Ed.), (1984). *Nonverbal behavior: Perspectives, application, and intercultural insights.* Toronto: C.J. Hogrefe, Inc.

Zurcher, L.A. (1982). The staging of emotion: A dramaturgical analysis. *Symbolic Interaction, 5,* 1-22.

Extended Self: Rethinking the So-Called Negro Self-Concept

Wade W. Nobles

> "For the oppressed to be really free, he must go beyond revolt, by another path he must begin other ways, conceive of himself and reconstruct himself independently of the master." Memmi, 1969.

It is indeed no accident that in this society the subjects of social and psychological studies are in some capacity the powerless. It is, in fact, the powerful who study the powerless. Social scientist of all disciplines have traditionally occupied positions of economic, political, and psychological superiority over the people they select to study. In a very real sense, the position of the social scientist is similar to that of the colonial master and his subject people. In this regard, Lewis (1973) has noted the relationship between colonialism and anthropology; and like Galtuny (1967) she has recognized the parallels between the exploitation by social scientist (in terms of data and the creation of information) and the political and economic exploitation by colonists (in terms of natural resources and wealth). Both Galtuny and Lewis note that to exploit data from a country or community to one's own country or community for processing into manufactured goods such as books and articles, is no different than exporting raw materials and wealth from a colony for the purpose of "processing" into manufactured goods. Galtuny argues that in the academic arena this process is no less "scientific colonialism," whereby the "center of gravity for the acquisition of knowledge about a nation is located outside the nation itself." We note, in this analogy, that just as the colonial power felt it had the right to claim and use for its benefit any product of commercial value in the colonies, so too the major aspect of scientific colonialism is the "idea" of unlimited *right of access* to data and the creation of information (See Table 1).

Nowhere has social science been more guilty of scientific colonialism than in the disciplines of psychology and anthropology. Psychology especially has contributed more clearly to the domination and continued oppression of people of color. It, in fact, has become the single most powerful tool of oppression and its single most effective technique has been to place itself, its conceptions, and formulations as the standard by which all peoples of the world are to be understood.

Table 1. Comparative Colonialisms

Colonialism Manifested by:	Political Colonialism	Scientific Colonialism
1) Removal of wealth:	Exportation of raw materials and wealth from colonies for the purpose of "processing" it into manufactured wealth and/or goods.	Exporting raw data from a community for the purpose of "processing" it into manufactured goods (i.e., books, articles, wealth, etc.).
2) Right of Access and claim:	Colonial Power believes it has the right of access and uses for its own benefit anything belonging to the colonized people.	Scientist believes he has unlimited right of access to any data source and any information belonging to the subject population.
3) External Power Base:	The center of power and control over the colonized is located outside of colony itself.	The center of knowledge and information about a people or community is located outside of the community or people themselves.

Following the "scientific colonialism" model further, one can see where psychologists and social scientists in general, like other colonialists, have historically reaped huge economic and political benefits in the form of better jobs, ease of publication, and recognition and fame, and like many anthropologists who returned from the "bush," the psychologists who returned from our communities to create information on the lives and people of the ghetto, most often found a "prestigious" institution of learning as a consequence of their trek into the "unknown." Western psychology as a tool of oppression and domination is probably best seen in this country in the scientific investigation of "Negro" intelligence and self-conception. The remainder of this paper will, however, address itself to only the scientific investigation of the so-called "Negro" self-concept.

Clearly, the assessment of the "Negro" self-concept literature and its creators, in terms of (1) data being exported from the community to foreign shores (i.e., the university) for processing into manufactured goods (i.e., books and articles), (2) the center of gravity for the acquisition of knowledge about "Negro" self-concept being located outside of so-called "Negroes" themselves, (3) the unlimited *right of access* to data and the creation of information, and (4) the profitable enterprise of studying and creating information about the lives and "people of the ghetto," qualifies this literature as a prime example, almost by defini-tion, of "scientific colonialism."

However, of the aspects which define this literature as scientific colonialism, the understanding of how raw material (data) was *processed* is far more critical than the actual technique of raiding black communi-ties to capture the raw material. The process is critical solely because it is here that the scientist's own assumptions, guiding principles, ways of thinking and perceiving the world, are "forged" with the raw material to produce the created information.

In terms of the so-called "Negro" self-concept, the process by which information was created naturally reflected the thinking, percep-tions, assumptions, and guiding principles of the investigators who con-ducted the studies. The "process" is most clearly seen in the major philosophical and theoretical approaches of the study of "Negro" self-concept.

We contend that the "process" factor (i.e., philosophical/theoreti-cal assumptions, etc.) is directly related to the nature of the findings, (i.e., finished product) characteristic of the literature. The way in which information concerning self-conception, particularly the so-called "Negro" self-concept, was "processed" is indeed revealing given the above-mentioned relationship. The "process" factor for the study of "Negro" self-conception like the self-concept literature in general, is characterized by four major philosophically-based approaches (see No-bles, 1973).

It is this relationship, (i.e., the relationship between philosophy and scientific evidence or results) of which black psychologists particu-larly must be aware. More directly, we need to recognize in what manner the literature created by non-African investigators represents a valid picture of black reality. The key to this understanding is, of course, in the fact that the kinds of questions asked pre-determine the type of answers possible (Clark, 1972). It is, however, the scientist's philosophy which determines the kinds of questions he will, in fact, ask. There is not only a clear and particular relationship between the kinds of ques-tions you ask and the kinds of answers you will get, but there is also an even stronger relationship between one's guiding beliefs or philosophy and the kinds of questions one will ask. Thus, one can see that once you accept the *a priori* assumptions and subsequent questions (i.e., philo-sophical orientation) concerning a particular issue, one has at the same time pre-determined the realm in which your answers may fall.

Answers are consistent with the questions asked. It is consistent, therefore, that if one asks a question (for instance, why are so-called

"Negroes" inferior to whites?) that the question itself will predetermine the realm of the answer. That is, the answer can only relate to the already accepted assumption (philosophy or guided belief of), in this example, the inferiority of black people.

We contend, however, that the above-mentioned characteristics of the so-called Negro self-concept literature, combined with the philosophy-questions-answers relationship, require one to conclude that if you believe the Euro-American *a priori* assumptions and ask questions consistent with it, then one must, in turn also accept the answers (results) characteristic of the research. That is, having accepted Euro-American assumptions about black (African) reality, one's questions and answers about black (African) people will be—in a pre-determined manner—in response to the Euro-American reality.

The "philosophical and theoretical assumptions" affecting the "findings" relationship is particularly critical for understanding Western scholarship as it relates to African peoples. We contend that through the recognition of this relational aspect one can best illustrate (1) the fundamental relationship between the scientist's guiding principles (philosophy) and his scientific investigations (results), and (2) the point at which the scientist's guiding principles invalidate his analysis of a particular area or subject.

We note that the general characteristics of Euro-American philosophy or guiding principles are different from those of African philosophy and consequently, when African "data" are processed by the guiding principles of Euro-Americans, the finished product (results) distorts the integrity of the original nature of the data. For instance, the European world view is tempered with the general guiding principle of (1) "survival of the fittest" and (2) "control over nature." These, in turn, naturally affect the nature of European values and customs. The emphasis on "competition," "individual rights," and the position of "independence" and "separateness" are clearly linked to the above-mentioned guiding principles. Likewise, the overemphasis on "individuality," "uniqueness," and "difference" in European-based psycho-behavioral modalities is traceable to the values and customs characteristic of that community and the guiding principles reflected in it.

On the other hand, if one examines the African world-view and compares it with the European, one can readily note the differences and their implications for understanding black self-conception. Rather than survival of the fittest and control over nature, the African world-view is tempered with the general guiding principle of (1) survival of the tribe and (2) one with nature. In contrast with the European world view, the values and customs consistent with the African world view are characteristically reflective of the sense of "cooperation," "interdependence," and "collective responsibility." Similarly, the emphasis in African psycho-behavioral modalities is not on individuality and difference. The modalities consistent with the African world-view, we note, emphasize "commonality," "groupness," and "similarity (See Figure 1 below)."

The effects of these two different world views on the understanding of black self-concept is critical. The nature of the "processing" of data regarding black people and our self-conceptions was, in fact, filtered through the European world view and to the extend that black people are an African people, the "process" has significantly distorted the validity of black self-conception.

We have contended that African psychology is rooted in the nature of black culture which is based on particular forms of African philosophical principles (Nobles, 1972). Consequently, the understanding of the psychology of black people (more appropriately classified as Americanized Africans) must be African-based. Similarly, if we are to rid the literature of its scientific, colonialistic tone, the proper understanding of black self-concept must be based on African assumptions and must incorporate African-based analyses and conceptualizations. In this regard, we can clearly see the importance of understanding the African self-concept and its psychological basis for black self-concept.

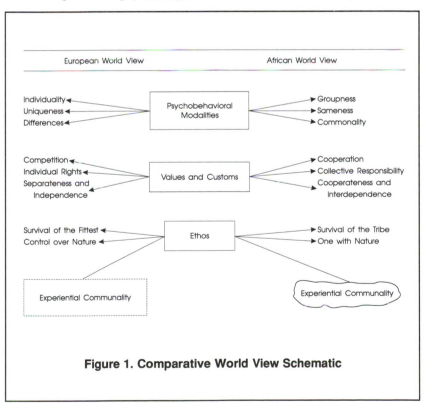

Figure 1. Comparative World View Schematic

African Self-Concept: The Extended Self

When we examine the African philosophical tradition, particularly the ethosic orders of *survival of the people* and *one with nature*, we logically recognize that from this philosophical position an *extended* definition of self evolved. That it to say, the African self-concept was (is) by philosophical definition the *WE* instead of the *I*. Hence, in terms of self-conception, the African philosophical tradition, unlike Western philosophical systems, does not place heavy emphasis on the "individual" or "individuality." It recognizes, rather, that only in terms of one's people does the "individual" become conscious of one's own being (cf: Mbiti, 1970). It is, in fact, only through others that one learns his duties and responsibilities toward himself and the collective self (tribe or people).

In terms of the African *ethos*, then the first order or guiding belief (one with nature) suggests that African peoples believe themselves to be part of the natural rhythm of nature. The second order or guiding principle (survival of the tribe) suggests that African peoples believe in the cosmological and ontological importance of life, which in turn suggests that life never ends (cf: Mbiti, 1970). Hence, the life of one's people is "paramount" and "permanent." In accordance with the notions of *one with nature* and *survival of the tribe*, the Africans consequently think of experience as an intense complementary rhythmic connection or synthesis between the person and reality.

The cardinal point, therefore, in understanding the traditional African conception of self, is the belief that *I am because We are, and because We are, therefore I am* (cf: Mbiti, 1970). Descriptively, we have defined this relationship (the interdependence of African peoples) as the "extended-self" (cf: Nobles, 1972).

In recognizing that in terms of self-conception, the relationship of interdependence (and oneness of being) translates to an "extended" definition, we note again that the African feels himself as part of all other African peoples or his tribe. One's self-definition is dependent upon the corporate definition of one's people. In effect, the people definition *TRANSCENDS* the individual definition of self, and the individual conception of self *EXTENDS* to include one's self and kind. This transcendent relationship (that between self and kind) is the "*extended-self.*"

The notion of the "we" instead of the "I" may become clearer through the following ontological analysis of the "self." It is generally safe to say that the establishment of self is accomplished by (1)*recognizing* qualities or characteristics similar to one's own and/or (2)*denying* qualities or characteristics similar to one's own and/or other people. The self, therefore, can be considered the consequences of either of two processes—opposition and/or apposition. The way, however, in which African peoples are extended into themselves is not clear in this kind of simplistic distinction. What one must distinguish between is the levels and relativity of "reality."

The meaning that one has for being one *within* himself and his universe (The Oneness of Being) or what is felt as an inner feeling of oneness with oneself is the result of an interpretive process which evolved over the course of hundreds of millions of years. This inner "something" which is called the self, is, in fact, the result of an evolutionary production which in the end left man believing in the consistency of his own internalized organized system. The evolution and consistency of the internalized systems of varying groups of people is not, however, always the same.

The philosophical notion of the Oneness of Being, for instance, is predicated on Man being an integrated and indispensable part of the universe. For the African, the Oneness of Being suggests that Man participates in social space and elastic time as determined by the character of the universe. Hence, it is true, that *to be* is to be what *you are* because of your historical past as well as what you anticipate to be your historical future. In an existential manner, therefore, having recognized the historical grounding of one's being, one also accepts the collective and social history of one's people. African people, in turn, realize that one's self is not contained only in one's physical being and finite time. The notion of *interdependence* and *Oneness of Being* allows for a conception of self which transcends, through the historical consciousness of one's people, the finiteness of both the physical body, finite space, and absolute time.

Self-awareness or self-conception is not, therefore, limited (as in the Euro-American tradition) to just the cognitive awareness of one's uniqueness, individuality and historical finiteness. It is, in the African tradition, awareness of self as the awareness of one's historical consciousness (collective spirituality) and the subsequent sense of "we" or being One.

It is in this sense that the self is portrayed as a TRANSCENDENCE INTO EXTENDATION. That is, the conception of self transcends and extends into the collective consciousness of one's people.

Black Self-Concept

At this point in history, one cannot, however, talk about the African self-concept without talking about the effect of African peoples being dominated, oppressed, and subjugated by European peoples. In noting that the juxtapositioning of Africans and Europeans affected the traditions of both the Europeans and the Africans, we do not believe that the negative contact with Europeans resulted in the total destruction of things African. We do believe, however, that each system was different and that even now, after a relatively long period of contact, the systems of consciousness (i.e., self knowledge) are still different.

For example, the European philosophical tradition bases the notion of self on the concept of independence (Brown, 1972). Consequently, the Euro-Americans' self is believed to develop through the process of establishing one's "uniqueness" and "separateness" (i.e., "I am (my)self by virtue of setting (my)self off and away from others, by opposing (my)self to others—Jasper, 1959). To "discover" oneself, therefore, in this tradition is to establish one's "individuality."

In accordance with the African philosophical tradition, the analysis is different. Here, we find, as alluded to earlier, very little importance or significance given to "individuality." When one takes into account the notion of *interdependence* and the *Oneness of Being*, then one can rightfully see that a single person's conception of self and/or his self-identity is rooted in being whatever his people's definition is or was. Tribal or people membership, the "we," in accordance with the extended definition of self, becomes the most fundamental and critical identity. One's conception of self is thus rooted in being an Ashanti, or Ibo, or Black, or African.

Clearly, the physical situation in which Africans— particularly in the Americas—find themselves involves the domination and imposition of a fundamentally European system of "reality" on a non-European people. This situation naturally has caused psychological confusion, because by the nature of European "reality" it denied the most compelling property (cosmological grounding of self in the collective, social and spiritual sense of history) of the African conception on self.

Parenthetically, it is suggested that this situation produces the pseudo-entity referred to as the "Negro." The concept "Negro" refers to the African person who attempts to deny or is forced to (or convinced to) deny the philosophical basis of his Africanity, even though he cannot negate the recognizable properties (psychological facts) of his Africanity (cf: Brown, 1972). This denial, it is believed, is due to the person being caught in the contradiction between the two philosophical systems, i.e., the African (black) and the Euro-American (white). To be a "Negro," therefore, is to be in a natural state of philosophical confusion (cf: Muhammed, 1965).

The infliction of the Euro-American philosophical tradition, as it relates to self-conception (i.e., individuality, separateness, etc.) for African peoples causes many of us to falsely believe that our natural temperamental tendencies and characteristic spirit were and are "wrong" and/or "uncivilized." This confusion is fundamentally based on the fact that the Euro-American tradition denies the African his historical roots or the grounding of self into the collective and social definition of one's peoples, and that the so-called "Negro" is taught (tricked) that the Euro-American culture is (1) the "right" (only civilized) culture and (2) that he will or can be (under prescribed conditions) assimilated into it. Hence, the black self-concept is reflective of a situation *Dubois (1903) described well over seventy years ago. It is, in fact, "two warring idols in one dark body, one Negro and one American." It is clearly the African in us that has never been acknowledged and until this aspect is shared, the self-concept of the black man will never be fully and accurately understood.*

References

Brown, B. (1967). The assessment of self-concpet among four-year old Negro and white children: A comparative study using the Brown-IDS self-concept referents test. New York: Institute for Developmental Studies. (Mimeo).

Brown, S.K. (1972). Empathic process as a dimension of African reality. Unpublished Doctoral Dissertation, Stanford University.

Clark, C. (1972). Black studies or the study of black people. In R.L. Jones (Ed.) *Black psychology*, New York: Harper and Row.

Clark, K.B., Clark, M.P. (1947). Racial identification and preference in Negro children. In T.M. Newcomb and B.L. Hartley (Eds.) *Readings in social psychology*, New York: Holt, Rinehart and Winston.

Cooley, C.H. (1972). *Human nature and social order*. New York: Scribners.

Deutsch, M. (1960). Minority group and class status as related to social and personality factors in scholastic achievement. Monograph No. 2, Society of Applied Anthropology.

Dubois, W.E.B. (1903). *The souls of black folks: Essays and sketches*. Chicago: Chicago Press.

Galtuny, J. (1967). After Camelot. In Irving Hurowitz (Ed.), *The rise and fall of project camelot*. Cambridge: MIT Press.

Lewis, D. (1973). Anthropology and colonialism. *Current Anthropology*, Vol. 14.

Mbiti, J.S. (1970). *African religions and philosophy*. New York: Anchor.

Memmi, A. (1967). *The colonizer and the colonized*. Boston: Beacon Press.

Muhammed, E. (1965). *Message to the black man*. Chicago: Muhammed's Mosque of Islam No. 2.

Nobles, W.W. (1972). African philosophy: Foundations for black psychology. In R.L. Jones (Ed.), *Black psychology*. New York: Harper and Row.

Nobles, W.W. (1973). Psychological research and the black self- concept: A critical review. *Journal of Social Issues, 29 (1)*.

Pettigrew, T.F. (1944). *A profile of the Negro American*. Princeton, N.J.: Van Nostrand.

Tiryakan, E.A. (1968). Existential self and the person. In C. Gordon and K. Gergen (Eds.), *The self and social interaction*, Vol. 1. New York: Wiley.

The Politics of Personality: Being Black in America

James M. Jones

Introduction

Black personality is in part an adaptation to the political contours of racism. The conflict between the freedoms and rights of United States citizens is juxtaposed to the denial of freedom and rights that is the history of the African American presence in this country. If we view personality as the resultant of coping patterns and socialization directives, then black personality is, in part, the cumulative representation of the effects of racism over four centuries. It reflects over time, the effects of the form and structure racism takes, and comes to signal the nature of race relations at any point in time.

However, the only systematic statements of black personality present it as a debilitating self-defeating reaction to at best difficult circumstances. While this may to some degree apply, it in no way can account for the resilience and resourcefulness of black personality—the continuing growth and accomplishment of African Americans against perpetually disadvantageous odds. In this paper I will discuss ways we may move beyond this conception towards a view that offers a perspective that fits the reality.

I will not deal with the content of personality, as a fundamental aspect of my view is that personality is a consequence of adaptation. In the absence of thorough finegrained analyses of the environmental exigencies to which black personality adapts, it would be premature to focus on that content. Such as we have in psychology focused on the content of black personality, it has been from a single-minded perspective that assumes (1) the only impact of racism is debilitating and negative; and (2) the modal content of personality is that which sustains an individualistic, materialistic, quantitative, and future-oriented behavioral style. A thorough response to the ideas contained in this paper will hopefully help chart a theoretical and empirical course that will illuminate such issues with greater clarity and relevance to the real experiences and capabilities of African Americans.

The presence in the United States of persons of African descent has been a constant source of conflict from the time the first African set foot in Virginia. This conflict has produced behaviors at various times violent, heroic, inspired, pathetic and disgraceful. While the racial conflicts have continued in various forms for nearly four centuries, the problematic has been more frequently cast in simple political terms. The Constitution that governs this Republic set forth the definition that these Africans were to be counted as three-fifths the man for purposes of determining taxable wealth, while at the same time, the Declaration of Independence declared the inalienable rights of men. The political practice and philosophy that governed this Nation then, and governs it now, is confused, ambiguous and, we might say, schizophrenic when it comes to understanding the American of African descent.

The Eminent Swedish Sociologist, Gunnar Myrdal understood this fundamental problem as *An American Dilemma* (1944). He described the manifestation of that problem as the Negro problem, in these terms:

> There is a Negro problem in the United States . . . The very presence of the Negro in America; his fate in this country through slavery, Civil War and Reconstruction; his recent career and his present status; his accommodation; his protest and his aspiration; in fact his entire biological, historical and social existence as a participant American represent . . . an anomaly in the structure of American society." (p. lxix.)

While this reflection of America's ambivalence and ambiguity on African Americans has laid heavy on the Nation for four centuries, the *EXPERIENCE* of this ambivalence by persons of African descent has not always been properly understood. The expression of that experience is given as long ago as 1903 in clear, compelling and commanding terms by W.E.B. DuBois in his *Souls of Black Folks*, when he states:

> After the Egyptian and Indian, the Greek and Roman, the Teuton and Mongolian, the Negro is a sort of seventh son, born with a veil, and gifted with second-sight in this American world,—a world which yields him no true self-consciousness, but only lets him see himself through the revelation of the other world. It is a peculiar sensation, this double-consciousness, this sense of always looking at one's self through the eyes of others, of measuring one's soul by the tape of a world that looks on in amused contempt and pity. One ever feels his two-ness,—an American, a Negro; two warring ideals in one dark body, whose dogged strength alone keeps it from being torn asunder.
>
> The history of the American Negro is the history of this strife,— this longing to attain self-conscious manhood, to merge his double self into a better and truer self. In this merging, he wishes neither of the older selves to be lost. He would not Africanize America, for America has too much to teach the

world and Africa. He would not bleach his Negro souls in a flood of white Americanism, for he knows that Negro blood has a message for the world. He simply wishes to make it possible for a man to be both a Negro and an American, without being cursed and spit upon by his fellows, without having the doors of opportunity closed roughly in his face." (p. 214-215).

The political struggle, then, is double-edged. While the Nation struggles with its dilemma, embracing the concept of equality while practicing racism, African Americans struggle with their duality, an African heritage which bestows degradation and insult, and an American heritage which seems to offer promise and opportunity.

As a result, being black in America often leads to a bifurcation of self. As DuBois noted, there is a twoness which itself, as with the Nation in which it lives, creates political turmoil, conflict and compromise. "Are you a black man or an American?" Marvin Kalb queried Jesse Jackson on Meet the Press during his presidential campaign in 1984. Kalb demanded the two were mutually exclusive states of being, Jackson rejected the premise in defense of his person. The interchange went like this.

Kalb: The question . . . [is] . . . are you a black man who happens to be an American running for the presidency, or are you an American who happens to be a black man running for the presidency?

Jackson: Well, I'm both an American and a black at one and the same time. I'm both of these . . .

After a lengthy reply from Jackson detailing the issues he has addressed in his candidacy and asserting that they are fundamentally national issues that should be of concern to any American citizen, Kalb is still searching for an answer to the question that perplexes *him*.

Kalb: What I'm trying to get at is something that addresses a question no-one seems able to grasp and that is, are your priorities deep inside yourself, to the degree that anyone can look inside himself, those of a black man who happens to be an American, or the reverse?

Jackson: Well I was born black in America, I was not born American in black! You're asking a funny kind of Catch-22 question. *My* interests are *national* interests. (excerpted from *Meet The Press*, February 13, 1984)

To understand being black in America is in part to understand this Catch-22 political reality. In 1965, claiming to be black was a political decision with personal consequences. The bifurcation of self was portrayed graphically, if cynically, by the Oreo Cookie metaphor—black on the outside-white on the inside! The problem was made even more acute by Eldridge Cleaver's (1968) dictum, "You're either part of the problem *or* part of the solution! The politics of society are internalized as the politics of self. Growing up black in America is a political process which necessarily informs the psychological parameters of self-consciousness.

Politics as Conflict and Compromise

The political dimensions of patterns of inequality in a country whose basic Creed demands it has been the focus on several inquiries. Myrdal's (1944) analysis of the American Dilemma illustrates the problem with respect to African Americans. Roger Daniels' *Politics of Prejudice* (1968) documents a similar pattern regarding Japanese in California. Kate Millett's *Sexual Politics* (1970) catalogues the political dimensions of power and domination that characterize this patriarchal society. R.D. Laing's *Politics of Experience* (1969) shows that when one is alienated from his or her own experience, it often facilitates performance in this materialistic society and hence is encouraged, taught and viewed as normal. However, according to Laing, behavior is a function of experience, so this destruction of experience makes destructive behavior much easier to perform.

Personal politics might be broadly viewed as the art of obtaining desirable outcomes against competing alternatives and self-interests. The presence of black people in America is itself a political reality that has been a constant source of conflict for this nation as Myrdal suggested. That presence is clearly tracked by the United States Constitution, Presidential Executive Orders, Supreme Court Decisions, and Congressional legislation where specific actions, laws and directives can be shown to be responsive to black and other political agitation. What is important for us to recognize is that the political conflict that plays out on a public, organizational/structural level, has personal psychological parameters that, in my mind, *ought* to be a major concern of psychologists interested in understanding human psychological functioning. This continued political role of African Americans in this society has psychological ramifications for black life. These ramifications each imply psychological conflict. The following are some examples.

1. The force of racialism and racism makes the black presence one of political moment. The political conflict is defined in terms of the contradictions inherent in manifest inequality juxtaposed with a creed of freedom and natural rights.

2. Given the facts of the ambiguity and ambivalence suggested by racialism, the art of political behavior requires blacks and whites alike to adopt strategies for achieving the outcomes considered to be in their best interest. Defining black self-interest in a way that encompasses national self-interest seems to be a necessary political strategy for blacks, but one which, as Marvin Kalb illustrates, is not easy to accomplish.

3. The personal strategies for survival often create a conflict between that behavior regarded as appropriate in Mainstream America, and that behavior judged to be an expression of self and circumstance. Must one choose, as Kalb apparently wants, between being an American and being black? Is it true that there is no black culture beyond the parameters of lower income, rural or ghetto dwelling poverty? Once a black person becomes educated and middle-class, is blackness no longer relevant?

The questions raised above are not simply rhetorical but frame a crucial dimension of black experience. For van den Berghe (1967), race refers to a group that is socially defined on the basis of physical criteria (e.g., skin color). Ethnicity, on the other hand, refers to a group that is socially defined on the basis of cultural criteria (values, history, symbols and so on). African Americans are by these criteria, both a race and an ethnic group. To the extent that the political problem is seem as simple disaffection for skin color, then achieving a "color blind society" as the administration argues, will not solve the problem. However, if we view blacks as an ethnic group, then understanding the correlates and expressions of black culture is critical.

Now let me say what all this means to me. Being black in America means to be identified with a peculiar history that attaches itself to conflict, denial and negativity. When I ventured forth into the world, it was not a neutral place in which those with the most advantage and those with less stayed behind. Rather, it was very clear very early that power and control rested in white hands. Socialization was learning how, when and where to exercise talent, opinions, desires and beliefs. Being aggressive in certain contexts was a political decision. Socialization demanded that one know when and where it was appropriate, if at all. The consequences of the same behavior are not always the same for blacks and whites. For example, Henderson (1975) showed that while scores on the Edwards Personality Preference Schedule did not vary between black and white policeman in a large northern city, scores for aggression, assertiveness and heterosexuality were negatively correlated with *performance* evaluations for black policemen, but uncorrelated with evaluations for white policemen. Thus behaving in ways that might be seen as efficacious and normal, may have negative consequences for African American men. If one surmises this to be true, what does he do? Whatever decision is made, the situation calls for political compromise. Learning the consequences of behavior is often an act of political socialization for African American children.

Let's turn our attention now to black personality.

Black Personality

As a frame of reference for what I mean by personality, I adopt Gordon Allport's 1937 working definition

> PERSONALITY IS THE DYNAMIC ORGANIZATION WITHIN THE INDIVIDUAL OF THOSE PSYCHOPHYSICAL SYSTEMS THAT DETERMINE HIS (SIC) UNIQUE ADJUSTMENTS TO HIS (SIC) ENVIRONMENT (p. 48).

Put another way, personality is that creative adjustment to environmental circumstances and as such is a mode of survival. It is quite clear that the predominant and recurring environmental reality for African Americans is racialism, oppression, racism and discrimination. Black personality, then, is inevitably, but not exclusively, that composite individual adaptation to racism. DuBois acknowledged this fact in 1903 with his idea of double-consciousness. Social scientists have addressed this issue of black personality over the years, always from this adaptation-to-racism perspective. However, what has dominated the thinking and reasoning of social scientists has been the belief that the personality that adjusts to racism is *necessarily* a neurotically driven defensive reaction to racism. This view has spawned the self-hate theories of black personality, and failed to understand the complexity of personality that adjustment to racist circumstances requires. This view is at best incomplete for several reasons.

The first reason is that personality reactions to extreme hostile and difficult circumstances are not always negation, defeat and doubt. Gail Sheehy (1986) has elaborated the idea of the "triumphant personality" in her recent book. She documents those personal triumphs over adversity and specifies several features that characterize such victorious persons. As it applies to the black personality, racism presents not only a problem but an opportunity to develop resilience, creative problem solving, discipline and resolve.

The second reason is that because of segregation, cultural differences and racism itself, black people spend a vast majority of their time in contact with other black people. Thus, systems that confer self-esteem and accomplishment and love and respect can do so to a large degree independent of whites and the specific problem of discrimination.

A third reason, is that many black people *prefer* to be with people who share their values, preferences and behavioral styles. Thus, whether racial integration happens and to what degree is not going to materially affect the kind of life led by a large number of black people.

It might be useful to briefly touch upon the most thoroughly elaborated self-hate theory of black personality to learn of its presumptions and concepts. Abram Kardiner and Lionel Ovesey published *The Mark of Oppression* in 1951. They conducted psychoanalytic interviews with 25 black urban men and women of varying ages and socioeconomic circumstances. They summarized their analysis of these case studies in the following terms:

> The Negro, in contrast to the white, is a more unhappy person; he has a harder environment to live in, and the internal stress is greater. By "unhappy" we mean he enjoys less, he suffers more. There is not one personality trait of the Negro the source of which cannot be traced to his difficult living conditions. *There are no exceptions to this rule.* The final result is wretched internal life. (p. 81).

For Kardiner and Ovesey, the mark of oppression is low self-esteem tantamount to self-contempt which leads to idealization of whites, frantic attempts to be white, which because it is unattainable, leads to self-hatred, hostility toward whites, introjection of white ideals and a resultant projection of hatred to other blacks. This is a rather grim psychological scenario. This unrelenting psychological suffering, according to Kardiner and Ovesey, is due simply to the recurring and continuing problem of racism.

A somewhat more versatile view was offered by Pettigrew (1964) when he acknowledged that at least three different kinds of responses to racial oppression could occur. One could move *toward* the oppressor seeking acceptance for his humanity and determined to be treated equally. One could move *against* the oppressor as the so-called militancy of the Civil Rights movement was perceived as doing; or one could move *away from* the oppressor, establishing independence and autonomy of values, custom and culture. Which of these modes of response occur and in what combination might be viewed as a pattern of personal adaptation to a racialist world. Perhaps one of the most clear expressions of the politics of black personality is shown by the social science statement on race which informed the Supreme Court in its 1954 desegregation ruling. This statement was based in part on research by Kenneth and Mamie Clark (1947) which showed that African American children rejected their black or Negro identity as demonstrated by their selection of a white doll in response to instructions to select the doll that looks like you; is a nice doll; that you like to play with. This finding dovetailed with the mark of oppression idea to leave one with the view that the inevitable and inexorable effect of racism on black personality was negative and debilitating. The history of the survival of black Americans could hardly be as it is if this were the whole story.

Black psychologists have recently mounted a systematic effort to alter this view of black personality. In general, this approach emphasizes the African cultural contribution to the style and content of black adaptation to racism (i.e., black personality). This view takes an Afrocentric approach and holds as essential, the understanding of the political dimensions of black adaptation.

Charles Thomas (1969) coined the term Negromachy to describe the negative mental health state associated with self-hate and internalized white standards proposed by Kardiner and Ovesey. William Cross (1975) extended Thomas' notion in a stage-model of the Negro-to-black conversion experience. Cross' model followed the development of black personality from the negative aspects of Negromachy, to a positive immersion in blackness that resulted in a new self-definition based on positive, effective and desirable identification with a black collective.

Semaj (1979) presented a three-phase model of extended identity anchored at the low end by what he calls "Alien" personality. This personality finds blackness alien, internalizes European standards, is individualistic in orientation and rejects or denigrates his African origins. In a middle phase, the person is "Diffused" as he tries to balance a positive view of blackness with a recognition that power resides in the majority white culture. The third phase is the "Collective" in which commitment to the well-being of blacks as a group is of paramount concern.

In general, black personality theories of black psychologists share three main features:

1. Each sees the negative consequences of reactions to racism in the form of internalized white standards and rejection of black self-images.
2. Each view projects a dynamic by which this negativity is transformed into a positive growth that involves rejection of the internalized white ideal, and the development of an active engagement with the collective black group identity.
3. Each position posits an acceptance of the existence and value of African cultural origins.

In comparing the self-hate portrayals of Kardiner and Ovesey with the stage-developmental models of black psychologists, we find that both identify the pivotal role of racial discrimination and oppression in the unfolding of black personality. Both perspectives view these influences as restrictive, negative and undesirable. However, black psychologists see a positive identity evolving from a political perspective in which one's personal role in the politics of group racial conflict offers the opportunity of growing self-expression. The strong black personality is the one rooted in an affinity for the African legacy and a commitment to positive collective black outcomes.

There is merit to both views. However, both fall short of providing a comprehensive account of the variable contexts of black personality. The old view sees self-hate as the *only* response to racism. This may have been more *apropos* in its time, but it greatly overstated the case then, and is of relatively little use to us now. The new view gives a better account of positive developments in black personality, but seems to limit it to group identity. While this might be politically desirable, it is not required in a healthy personality, and tends to ignore or reject those black persons whose lives are not intimately tied to visible black group identity. Neither position seems to specify the potential positive consequences of coping with a hostile and subtle resistant environment for the emergence of positive personality structures. In my mind, this is where the most fruitful work lies.

Not only do the major theoretical positions on black personality fall short, but the empirical literature is paltry indeed. A search of the computerized PASAR data-base of published articles and dissertations for the twenty year period from 1966-1985 retrieved 176 entries to the index terms, black and personality. While there may well have been other studies relevant to black personality that focused on specific attributes such as locus of control, achievement and so on, it is significant that we do not have more empirical interest in the question of black personality.

Of those entries retrieved, over half (N = 91) were dissertations, and over 70% (N = 125) were published during the first half of the time period, prior to 1976. In addition, these published articles by and large are not found in APA sponsored journals. The leading journal for black personality articles is *Psychological Reports* (n = 10) followed by the *Journal of Negro Education* (n = 9). APA journals produced nine articles or 10.6% of the total. The absence of published research on black personality in primary, refereed journals, combined with a preponderance of studies done as dissertations, suggests that the subject does not enjoy major standing in the research enterprise of psychology, but does seem to be a subject of concern to young investigators beginning their research careers.

I'd like to turn now to a presentation of what this state of affairs suggests about understanding black personality.

Towards an Understanding of Black Personality

Division 8 of the American Psychological Association gives the H.A. Murray award each year for excellence in research that deals with "the thematic unity of individual lives in the midst of phenotypic diversity." I am here arguing that the meaning of black personality derives from the thematic unity of black consciousness in a racist society.

While there is phenotypic diversity in the lives of African Americans, the goal of a theory of black personality is to understand how racism provides a thematic unity that brings black Americans into a common orbit. However, the unity of reactions to racism is not equivalent to sameness. Thus, I am arguing that reactions to racism form a common bond or unity among black Americans, *but* the behavioral and even psychological manifestations of those reactions will vary from person to person.

Shweder and Bourne (1984) have shown that members of individualistic societies prefer trait labels, whereas members of sociocentric societies prefer context-qualified descriptions. Black personality emerges as a context-qualified expression of modes of adjustment to a complex circumstance.

Boykin (1985) captures this complexity in his notion of the Triple Quandary. In his model, black Americans live as Americans and pursue mainstream goals and participate in mainstream life. They also are associated with minority status and thus join other groups who face political, social and economic disadvantage. Finally, they live out a black cultural legacy that includes an African ethos as well as a peculiar history of slavery, and oppression and centuries of coping with them. Martin Kalb tried to pin Jessee Jackson to the mutual exclusivity of black and mainstream American life. Jackson rejected this dichotomy, and further, seized the middle ground in establishing his Rainbow Coalition, a common minority fate.

There are a number of questions and perspectives one can bring to understanding the dynamic of black psychological life in the United States. Following are some ways we could view the intersection of racism and black personality.

1. The thematic unity of black personality exists both in the cumulative reactions to racism and in the ways in which an African cultural legacy influences the unfolding of black culture.
2. If black personality reflects cumulative adaptation to racial discrimination, then changes in black personality should reflect changes in society. We often talk about Neo-Racism, Symbolic Racism, Aversive Racism and other new forms of systematic and subtle discrimination. What new coping strategies do they

require, what changes in black personality must transpire to meet this challenge?

3. It is often argued that adapting to negative environments lead to the establishment of disadvantageous personality traits, those viewed as undesirable in mainstream America. This Catch-22 situation sees society creating ghetto conditions leading to adaptations which are then judged to reflect personal and collective deficiencies because they do not conform to mainstream expectations. In these instances, there is a tendency to attribute inferior psychological functioning to persons who have low social standing. It is not necessarily the case that the two are correlated, and failure to recognize that fact often means that evidence of psychological strength will go unnoticed.

4. Any theory of black personality must account for

a) the diversity of adaptations to the fundamental realities of racialism in this society;

b) the fact that coping with the subtle and sometimes blatant forms that racism takes will often lead to strength of character and creativity in its expression.

5. Because the unity of being black and American has been politically disconnected, black personality is often expressed as a bifurcation of self. This bifurcation may present psychic conflict when it produces approach-avoidance tensions at a single instant, or it may be a source of adaptation when one selectively calls upon the self that is most suited to handle a given situation. When we take a nomothetic approach, as personality theorists have so long favored, the psychic tension is the preferred account of this bifurcation and the result is a mark of oppression analysis. If, however, we take an idiographic view, one based on the variance of expression across situations, then the bifurcation works as expanded possibilities for coping. This conflict is most crucially revealed when behaviors that are expressive-of-self are often detached from behaviors that are instrumental-for-self. The decision processes that guide acts of expression and instrumentality are among the most politically crucial to black psychological functioning.

Now what has been lacking in conceptions of black personality is a consideration of the dynamic organization, motivation and self-regulating features of that personality. That is, what are the determinants of how black personality is organized and expressed? The Kardiner and Ovesey view simply states that without exception, racism leads to a low self-esteem which is manifested in self-hate, internalization of white values, and ultimately apathy, hedonism, criminality. Black theorists see the emergence of three basic personality structures, one that is neg-atively conditioned as suggested by Kardiner and Ovesey; one that is marginally in two worlds as implied by DuBois and given popularity by E. Franklin Frazier; or one that is emersed in a black group context. Each of these views, to my mind, presents a linear possibility that fails to account for the multidimensional complexities of black life in America.

For the sake of discussion, and in keeping with the politics meta-phor, let's consider the dynamic forces in black personality as political platforms that give meaning to the psychic structures. I envision four such platforms within which, variations will determine the personality structure and its behavioral manifestation.

1. *Individual versus group identity.* In essence, one can escape the limitations of a negative group identification by espousing individuality. Both the mark of oppression and black liberation models assume the pre-eminence of group identification, the former as negative and the latter as positive. However, I simply assert that black people vary in the degree to which and the circumstances under which group identity is espoused. The argument on behalf of a 'colorblind' society is an argument for individual identification. To understand one of the fundamental dynamics of black personality is to understand how a given person handles the individual versus group identity decision.

2. *Trust versus mistrust.* Following the Eriksonian (1965) emphasis on trust as the cornerstone of personality development, it is clearly a crucial aspect of black personality. Given a hostile environment in which majority culture has systematically earned mistrust, one must nevertheless develop strategies to work with the system. The behavioral style and psychic motivation for that interaction will certainly be different if it follows from a basic trust in the system (or at least a belief in its *potential* for fairness), or mistrust.

3. *Personal accountability versus contextual blame.* This platform is a variant of the locus of control concept. However, unlike the locus idea which seeks to locate causal effects on personal outcomes, accountability refers to the acceptance of responsibility for personal outcomes *regardless of the locus of causation.* By choosing to be accountable, one is acknowledging the determinacy of intention. Clearly we see this distinction when for example, an account of a black teenage mother shows her overcoming the difficulty of teenage poverty and motherhood to complete high school, care for her child, and build a career for herself. She accepted personal accountability, even though it might have been easy to blame her context for her misfortune.

4. *Minority versus majority*. This final platform is a matter of perspective. William McGuire (1982) and his colleagues have shown that one's spontaneous self-concept includes gender and ethnicity to the degree that one is in the minority in a family or peer situation. According to this view then, the person who is in a racially mixed environment is more likely to find his or her racial characteristics more salient. This may well account for some of the negative findings of the effects of bussing. Bussing makes race more salient while at the same time, continues the domination of white cultural standards.

These four dynamics of personality organization impart structure and guide behavior among African Americans. Because of the bifurcation of self, it is possible to move across the spectrum of these platforms mixing and combining perspectives, preferences and styles as the situation demands. Indeed, this is one of the major strengths of the reactions to racism—multi-dimensionality and biculturality. By considering this dynamic, one may now find a way to include the wide diversity of black experiences of racism, and the variation in black responses to it, within a comprehensive theory of personality.

The research agenda must direct itself at how these dynamics are socialized, chosen, experienced and expressed. As we saw, the empirical work in black personality has not been vital. To tackle the implications of the above formulation would make a vital research endeavor. To understand how African Americans have survived the hostilities of racism and discrimination with psychic strength is an important goal of psychology. In the process of understanding this profound dynamic of African Americans, we may well hold up a mirror to the soul of this society.

References

Allport, G.W. (1937). *Personality: A psychological interpretation*. New York: Henry Holt & Company.

Boykin, A.W. (1986). The triple quandry and the schooling of Afro-American children. In U. Neisser (Ed.), *The school achievement of minority children: New perspectives*. Hillsdale, NJ: Lawrence Erlbaum.

Clark, K.B., & Clark, M.P. (1947). Racial identification and preference in Negro children. In T.M. Newcomb, & E.L. Hartley (Eds.), *Reading in social psychology*, (1st Ed.). New York: Holt.

Cleaver, E. (1968). *Soul on ice*. New York: McGraw-Hill.

Cross, W.E. (1979). The Negro-to-black conversion experience: An empirical analysis. In A.W. Boykin, A.J. Franklin, J.F. Yates (Eds.), *Research directions of black psychologists*, pp. 107-130. New York: Russell Sage Foundation.

Daniels, R. (1968). *Politics of prejudice: The anti-Japanese movement in California and the struggle for Japanese exclusion*. Berkeley, University of California Press.

DuBois, W.E.B. (1903). *Souls of black folks*. Chicago: A.C. McClurg and Company.

Erikson, E.H. (1968). *Identity: Youth and crisis*. New York: W.W. Norton.

Henderson, N.D. (1979). Criterion-related validity of personality and aptitude scales: A comparison of validation results under voluntary and actual test conditions. In C. Spielberger (Ed.) *Police selection and evaluation*. pp. 179-196. Washington, D.C.: Hemisphere Publications.

Jones, J.M. (1972). *Prejudice and racism*. Reading, MA: Addison Wesley Publishing.

Jones, J.M. (1986). Racism: A cultural analysis of the problem. In J.F. Dovidio, & S.L. Gaertner (Eds.), *Prejudice, discrimination and racism*, pp. 279-314. Orlando, FL: Academic Press.

Jones, J.M. (1988). Racism in black and white. In P.A. Katz, & D.A. Taylor (Eds.), *Towards the elimination of racism: Profiles in controversy*, pp. 117-136. New York: Plenum.

Kardiner, A., & Ovesey, L. (1951). *The mark of oppression*. New York: W.W. Norton.

Laing, R.D. (1969). *The politics of experience*. New York: Pantheon Books.

McGuire, W. (1983). The phenomenal self: Beyond self-esteem and the reactive self. In R.A. Zucker, J. Arnoff, & A.I. Rabin (Eds.), *Personality and the prediction of behavior*. New York: Acadmic Press.

Millet, K. (1970). *Sexual politics*. New York: Avon.

Myrdal, G. (1944). *An American dilemma*. New York, London: Harper & Brothers.

Pettigrew, T.F. (1964). *A profile of the Negro American*. Princeton, N.J.: D. Van Nostrand Company.

Semaj, L. (1981). The black self, identity, and models for a psychology of black liberation. *The Western Journal of Black Studies, 6*, 116-122.

Sheehy, G. (1986). *Spirit of survival*. N.Y.: Morrow.

Shweden, R.A., & Bourne, L. (1984). Cross-cultural variation in the concept of the person. In R.A. Shweden, & R.A. Levine (Eds.), *Culture theory: Essays on mind, self and emotions*. New York: Cambridge University Press.

Thomas, C. (1969). *Boys no more*. Beverly Hills, CA: Glencoe Press.

van den Berghe, P. (1967). *Race and racism: A comparative perspective*. New York: Wiley.

The Stages of Black Identity Development: Nigrescence Models

William E. Cross, Jr., Thomas A. Parham, and Janet E. Helms

". . . And on the 12th of May, 1828, I heard a loud noise in the heavens, and the Spirit instantly appeared to me and said the Serpent was loosened, and Christ had laid down the yoke he had borne for the sins of men, and that I should take it on and fight against the Serpent, for the time was fast approaching when the first should be last and the last should be first."

Confession of Nat Turner, 1831

"It is a peculiar sensation, this double-consciousness . . . , one ever feels his twoness-An American, a Negro; two souls, two thoughts, two unreconciled strivings, two warring ideals in one dark body, whose dogged strength alone keeps it from being torn asunder."

Souls of Black Folks, by W.E.B. DuBois, 1903

"In the last decade something beyond the watch and guard of statistics has happened in the life of the American Negro and the three norms who have traditionally presided over the Negro problem have a changeling in their laps. The Sociologist, the Philanthropist, the Race-leader are not unaware of the New Negro, but they are at a loss to account for him. He simply cannot be swathed in their formulae. For the younger generation is vibrant with a new psychology; the new spirit is awake in the masses, and under the very eyes of the professional observers is transforming what has been a perennial problem into the progressive phases of contemporary Negro life."

The New Negro, by Alain Locke, 1925

"I still marvel at how swiftly my previous life's thinking pattern slid away from me, like snow off a roof. It is as though someone else I knew of had lived by hustling and crime. I would be startled to catch myself thinking in a remote way of my earlier self as another person."

The Autobiography of Malcolm X, 1964

"Black as a physical fact has little significance. Color, as a cultural, social, and political fact, is the most significant fact of our era. Black is important because it gives us ground from which to fight—a way to feel and think about ourselves and our own reality—a way to define."

Black Arts Notebook, by John O'Neal, 1971

Introduction

Psychologically speaking, the social history of African Americans has been dominated by two competing processes: deracination or the attempt to erase black consciousness, and nigrescence or the development of an African American identity. Up until the mid-1960s, the exploitation of black labor was an important dimension of American commerce, and in anticipation that African Americans would attempt to counter the forces of oppression through various collective enterprises, racist whites sought to control the political and cultural socialization of blacks in order to (a) increase the probability of deracination and false consciousness, which in turn would (b) decrease the probability of the development of individuals and, more importantly, collective awareness around issues of culture and class. Thus, whether it be the "breaking in process" during slavery, or the miseducation of blacks in the 20th century, adult African Americans have repeatedly commented that to varying degrees their experiences as children and youth in formal educational institutions seemed deliberately designed to promote confusion and a self-blame perspective, regarding the problems black people confront, and a diminished appreciation, if not outright ignorance, about the evolution and existence of African American culture.

Given the ubiquity of the white emphasis on deracination, it comes as no surprise that within African American history are accounts of blacks who, having first been successfully deculturalized, experienced revitalization through the process of nigrescence. Nigrescence is derived from French and means "to become black," and as the five quotes in the epigraph attest, black figures out of the distant past through the present have traversed a Negro-to-Black identity conversion. Sometimes it was recorded in history as a singular metamorphosis in isolation from the community, as was the transformation of Nat Turner in 1831, other times as the parallel experience of hundreds of cohorts involved in various black social movements, such as the Garvey Movement and Harlem Renaissance of the twenties, or in the case of the more recent epochal period of nigrescence, the contemporary Black Consciousness Movement of the 1960s and 1970s.

Evolution of Nigrescence Models

While the search for an authentic (cultural) self-image is an omnipresent theme in black social history, the appearance of nigrescence models for application in the analysis of the psychology of black identity change is a fairly recent phenomenon, dating back no further than 1968 or 1969. Recall that the contemporary African-American social movement, which lasted from about 1954 to 1975, had two phases: A civil rights phase (1954-1967) and a black power or black consciousness period (1968-1975). While today the concept of black identity is generally taken for granted and is sometimes associated with the Movement as a whole, in point of fact notions of blackness, black identity and nigrescence stem from the dynamics and ideological emphasis of the second and not the first phase.

The earliest attempts to analyze the blackness phenomena led many researchers to construct psychological profiles which differentiated "black militants" from "traditional" Negroes (Cross, in press; Caplan, 1970; McCord, et al., 1969), but this approach more often than not led to a pejorative and stereotypical vision of black identity, a perspective which, amazingly enough, still finds favor in some circles, as evidenced by the pathetic and pseudo-scientific diatribe against any and all forms of black identity recently offered by Wortham (1981). Almost from the onset, the profile approach came under considerable criticism. For example, in 1971 Cedrick Clark commented that . . . "the language of contemporary psychology, particularly dealing with black Americans, is basically monodic: phenomena are described in terms of entities and characteristics which a person possesses instead of the processes in which he/she is engaged (Clark, 1971; p. 33)."

Comments like Clark's calling for a developmental perspective struck a strong cord amongst black psychologists trained in the more process oriented fields of psychology (developmental, personality, psychotherapy, sensitivity training, etc.), and in the aftermath of the assassination of Martin L. King, Jr., the literature exploded with nigrescence models as evidenced by the works of Gerlach and Hine (1971); Crawford and Naditch (1970), Downton (1973); Sherif and Sherif (1970); Napper (1973); Pinderhughes (1968); Kelman (1970); Toldson and Pasteur (1975); Milliones (1973); Jackson (1976a); Thomas (1971); and Cross (1971).

Summary of Stages

In this current review, we will not attempt a microscopic analysis of the eleven or so process models. However, a summary of the stages common to most nigrescence models will be presented, with highlights drawn from the works of Thomas (1971), Cross (1971) and Jackson (1976a).

Nigrescence models tend to have four or five stages (we will stress four stage summary) and the common point of departure is not the change process per se but an analysis of the identity to be changed. The person is first described as functioning in an ongoing steady-state (Stage 1) with a deracinated or "Negro identity"; following this, some event or series of events compel the person to seek and be a part of change (Stage 2); this is followed by psychological metamorphosis (Stage 3) and finally the person is described as having internalized the new black identity and enters another steady-state (Stage 4). The period of metamorphosis or transition is depicted as an intense struggle between the "old" and emerging "new" self; consequently, *the process writers saw the change process as being informed by rather than divorced from the character of the identity to be transformed.*

Stage 1: Setting the Conditions for Change

This stage describes the nature of the old identity or frame of reference to be changed. The process writers seem to understand that the Negro community reflects a great deal of psychological diversity in that Negroes differ in their personalities, lifestyles and behavior. Nevertheless, they have attempted to isolate a modal pattern Negroes employ when dealing with the issue of race. Thus, Stage 1 focuses on the central ideas, basic attitudes, value systems, frames of reference and world views linked to Negroism:

> "It (Negroism) is an American concept not based on economic deprivation or lack of education or cultural sterility, but on white America's idea of the African type of (black person) and that person's place in American society. It is an American concept that is socially derived, politically sanctioned, and economically abused" (Onwauchi, 1967).

At the core of the Stage 1 description is an aggressive assimilation-integration agenda, an agenda linked not only to the search for a secure place in the socio-economic mainstream, but motivated as well by a desperate attempt to escape from the implications of being a "Negro." In this light, the Stage 1 Negro is depicted as a *deracinated* person who views being black as an obstacle, problem or *stigma* and seldom a symbol of culture, tradition or struggle. The Negro is thus preoccupied with thoughts of how to overcome his stigma, or how he can assist whites in discovering that he is "just another human being" who wants to assimilate.

The process writers depict the Negro as someone who has nothing to offer whites in exchange for social acceptance. Since whites might question Negro humanity based on their (white) interpretation of slavery, African and contemporary Negro life, a perspective no doubt shared by the Negro, the Stage 1 person is said to be *very* defensive about race issues and burdened with a sense of shame about his/her African roots, slave heritage, and the lowly condition of rural and urban Negro communities. *In a sense, the Negro is depicted as one who views herself or himself and her or his group from the perspective of whites, and will do almost anything to overcome the stigma of race in order to obtain white approval.*

More often than not, the Stage 1 person rejects the notion that he or she is personally inferior and sees the problem as the stigma attached to his/her *group identity*. Consequently, since identifying with the group might well impinge upon his/her search for *personal approval*, the Stage 1 person is often described as an uncompromising *individualist* who marks progress by how far he/she, or other individuals progress in a system rather than how the system treats the group.

In his model, Cross stressed that the Negro identity is in evidence across social class but that its manner of expression varies by class. For instance, middle class and lower class Stage 1 Negroes share a common distaste for the quality of their hair texture. Lower class blacks might "straighten" their "bad" hair to make it "better" whereas middle class blacks might prefer a "very short" style in which the "bad" hair is cut away. Either class-based style is traceable to the same theme: discontent with one's body features.

The extent to which the Stage 1 identity is also linked to behavioral problems differs from writer to writer. Thomas associates conformity, compliance, subservience, repressed rage and unproductive lifestyles to the Stage 1 identity, while in their respective models, Jackson and Cross spend more time describing the peculiar features of the Negro value system and world view than on the possible correlation of this world view with general personality variables. In any case, implicit in all of the models is the notion that the Stage 1 identity reflects some level of impaired mental health. What seems necessary for this review, however, is the recognition that a deracinated personality influences cognitions, affect, *and* behaviors, all of which are interrelated. That each model may have a different focus (i.e., behaviors versus values or world view) is less important than highlighting the degree of thematic congruence each seems to share.

Stage 2: "Pulling the Rug from Under One's Feet"

The Stage 2 identity is the product of traditional macro-temporal developmental experiences and as is the case for any steady-state identity, it performs its functions in a habitual and unconscious manner, a point stressed in the Jackson model. Furthermore, while people may gradually change modest dimensions of their identity, they tend to resist wholesale identity change. In fact, the *stability* and *predictability* functions of identity converge to form a barrier against major change. Such a notion is analogous to the development of psychological defense mechanisms which help to fortify one's ego against any threat of anxiety.

The second stage focuses on an event or series of events that manage to work around this resistance or even *shatter* the person's current feeling about herself/himself and his or her interpretation of the condition of blacks in America. In brief, the Stage 2 "encounter" has the effect of "pulling the rug" from under the feet of the person operating with the Negro identity. The change event or encounter involves two steps: first, experiencing and personalizing the event and, secondly, beginning to reinterpret the world as a consequence of the encounter. The second part is depicted by Cross as a testing phase during which the individual cautiously tries to validate his/her new perceptions. When the person absorbs enough information and receives enough social support to conclude that (a) the old identity seems inappropriate and (b) the proposed new identity is highly attractive, the person throws caution to the wind and begins a frantic, determined, obsessive and extremely motivated search for black identity. At the end of the second stage the person is not depicted as having obtained the new identity, *but as having made the decision to start the journey toward the new identity.* The person feels less internally secure and seeks authentication through external validation.

Stage 3: The Agony, Comedy, Tragedy and Romance of Metamorphosis

This stage encompasses the most sensational aspects of black identity development, as it is the vortex of psychological metamorphosis. The nigrescence writers see this as the period of transition in which the struggle to destroy all vestiges of the "old" perspective occurs simultaneously with an equally intense concern to clarify the personal implications of the "new" frame of reference.

There is nothing subtle about this stage, and for good reason. Although the new recruit has just affirmed a desire for change, in point of fact he or she is more familiar with the identity to be destroyed than the one to be embraced. Having lost patience with the past, the boundaries and essence of the old self are truncated, collapsed and codified in "very" pejorative terms, images and emotions. On the other hand, he/she is "unfamiliar" with the new self, for that is exactly what he/she hopes to *become*; thus, the person is forced to erect simplistic, glorified, highly romantic and speculative images of what he or she assumes the new self will be like. Under the spell of this dynamic, the person can be vicious in attacks on aspects of the old self that appear in others or her/himself, and he or she may even appear bizarre in his or her affirmation of the new self. It is one of the ironies of social change that the most demonstrative displays of a new (black) identity are generally performed by people who are the least at ease with the new identity.

The potential personal chaos of this stage is generally tempered by the social support a person gains through group activities. The groups joined during this period are "counterculture institutions" (i.e., counter to the "Negro" culture) which have rituals, obligations and reward systems that nurture and reward the developing identity, while inhibiting the efficacy of the decaying "old identity". In fact, in the midst of rebellion against the larger society, the Stage 3 person is described as being quite *conforming* within black consciousness groups. Since the new black identity is something yet to be achieved, the Stage 3 person is generally anxious about how to demonstrate to others that he/she is becoming the right kind of black person. Demonstrating and "proving" one's level of blackness, of course, requires an audience before which to perform, and a set of group standards toward which to conform. A great deal of comedy and tragedy related to the late 1960s can be traced to those acts and activities of commitment and conformity designed to "prove one's blackness" (this remains true of any conversion).

Although the initial part of Stage 3 involves total immersion and personal withdrawal into blackness, the latter segment of this stage represents emergence from the reactionary, "either-or" and racist aspects of the immersion experience. The nigrescence writers claim that the person's emotions begin to level off, and psychological defensiveness is replaced by affective and cognitive openness. This allows the person to begin to be more critical in his or her analysis of what it means to be black. The strengths, weaknesses and oversimplifications of blackness can now be sorted out as the person's degree of ego-involvement diminishes, and her or his sense of "perspective" expands. The person begins to feel in greater control of himself/herself and the most difficult period of nigrescence comes to an end.

Stage 4: Internalizing the New Identity

Following the depiction of the transition period, all nigrescence models present a fourth or fifth stage describing the habituation and internalization of the new identity. The fourth stage signals the resolution of conflicts between the "old" and "new" world view, thus tension, emotionality and defensiveness are replaced by a calm, secure demeanor. Ideological flexibility, psychological openness, and self-confidence about one's blackness are evident in interpersonal transactions. Anti-white feelings decline to the point that friendships with white associates can be renegotiated. While still using blacks as a primary reference group, the person moves toward a pluralistic and nonracist perspective, although relationships are negotiated from a position of strength rather than weakness.

In the Thomas model, persons who have incorporated the new sense of self are said to have a clearer understanding of where they want to go in life on the basis of resources that are actually available; evidence an increased capacity to respond and act effectively across a variety of situations, and are capable of more extensive self-criticism and self-evaluation. Thomas argues, however, that blackness involves more than a positive feeling of self, it also includes "assertive behavior" within a social context. Upon gaining a stable sense of self, the (new) African American assaults oppressive institutions that brought about the necessity for a search for black identity in the first place, with an eye on affecting change for the benefit of one's people rather than just oneself. Certainly, Thomas' position reflects a more collective view of self which is philosophically consistent with an African American frame of reference.

For Baily Jackson, the nigrescence process at first involved the isolation and the reformulation of a single dimension of a person's self-concept, followed by the reconstitution of the total self-system through the syntheses of the new black self component during Stage 4:

> "For the person who sees him/herself as a black only or to view his/her blackness completely separate from the other aspects of the person is seen as a dysfunctional fragmentation of self. While recognizing the necessity for the separation of the person's blackness from other parts of him/herself in earlier stages as a strategy for making sense of that aspect of self, the person now needs to complete the developmental process by internalizing and synthesizing this new sense of blackness" (Jackson, 1976a, p. 42). Being black is placed into perspective and balanced with the other demands of one's personhood (gender identity, spiritual identity, various role identities, etc.) of which some are quite race neutral.

Stage 4 is also a point at which the person re-examines the bi-cultural nature of black existence, a factor which requires explication. The nigrescence writers note that in a generic sense, any identity reflects and is a product of the physical and metaphysical realities that frame the childhood and adolescent socialization process. Then as the person develops and becomes more and more an actor in his/her own right, one's identity enables the person, given adequate ego structures and interpersonal skills, to exploit and conduct social and material exchanges with one's reality. Blacks tend to live in *two* material and cultural realities, realities which at times are quite distinctive and at other moments are so interwoven as to give the appearance of a common fabric. From this perspective, Cross and Jackson stress that all blacks, to one degree or another, have a *bi-cultural identity structure*. It is this notion of a bi-cultural identity structure that helps to connect the struggles of the contemporary black American with the legacy of Negro America captured in the writings of W.E.B. DuBois (1903). As Americans, blacks have as part of their overall identity, components of self *commonplace to the identity of most Americans*, and as blacks, there is a sphere of self which is ethnically and psychologically unique. Part of the work of Stage 4 is coming to accept the enigmatic, conflictual as well as advantageous and supportive aspects of being an "American," but most of all, Stage 4 is coming to grips with the incontestability of one's Americanness. This fact, along with being black, is the ubiquitous "twoness" found in all black psyches. During the earlier transition stage, blackness was romanticized and played off against the "evils" of whiteness. Not only did the new convert denigrate all that was white, he or she frequently proclaimed that in becoming black, one ceased to be an American, and at best, the convert saw no value in such a predicament (i.e., being American). Just as Stage 4 saw movement away from a "blind faith" analysis of blackness, likewise this period of resolution and internalization leads to a rapprochement with one's Americanness. To paraphrase Bailey Jackson, in Stage 4, the bi-cultural basis of black existence ceases to be disarming, psychologically speaking, and instead comes to be viewed as a multifaceted reality which, depending on one's circumstances, can be personally advantageous, supportive, as well as at times perturbing and problematic. In a more recent publication he elaborates in the following way:

> The individual (in Stage 4) also has a new sense of the American culture. The person is able to identity and own those aspects of the American culture that are acceptable (e.g., materials possessions, financial security, independence, etc.) and stand against those aspects which are toxic (racism, sexism, war, imperialism, and other forms of oppression). The ownership of the accept-

able aspects of the American culture does not preclude or override the ownership of black culture" (Jackson, 1976b, p. 62).

This notion of the factual acceptance and selective ownership of one's Americanness is not to be confused with assimilation, for we are speaking here more of an anthropologically derived concept of acceptance. Perhaps the following hypothetical situation will help clarify the point. Two people of African descent meet at a conference, one from Brazil, the other from the United States. Both agree that historically and metaphysically speaking, each is an African person, but neither wastes time trying to deny the non-African elements of their respective world views and cultural frames of reference. Thus, they compare notes not only on their shared Africanity, but on the manner in which that Africanity has been reformulated through either the North American or South American experience. *It is from this same type of vantage point that the Stage 4 person has learned to accept the reality that she or he is neither solely black nor American, he or she is very much an African-American.*

It has already been noted that one's identity is a cognitive map which functions to guide intercourse with society and the physical environment. As a way of bringing to a close our brief summary of the nigrescence paradigm, let us focus on the functions of black identity as revealed in the discussion of internalization by Jackson, Thomas and Cross. For the person who has reached Stage 4 and beyond, the internalized black identity tends to perform three dynamic functions: (1) to defend and protect a person from psychological insults, and, where possible, to warn of impending psychological attacks that stem from having to live in a racist society; (2) to provide social anchorage and meaning to one's existence by establishing black people as a primary reference group; (3) to serve as a conduit or point of departure for gaining awareness about, and completing transactions with, the broader world of which blackness is but a part.

1. Defensive Mode An easily perceived but nonetheless essential function of the stabilized black identity which the nigrescence writers address is the protection of the individual from psychological harm that may result from daily existence in a racist society. A person with a well developed defensive modality is aware that racism exists, anticipates encounters with racism, has developed reactive strategies for use in racist situations, and has a keen sense of personal efficacy. Black identity helps the person to be aware that oppressive and racist factors are realities in everyday life in America and that personal encounters with racism should come as no surprise. This sense of awareness combined with the "anticipatory set" function to buffer or blunt the impact of racist encounters. Through experience and maturity the person develops and learns to apply strategies of withdrawal, avoidance and assertiveness when confronted by racist circumstances. In the past, withdrawal, avoidance and passive-aggression were the hallmark of black survival, but the new black identity stresses effective counterattacks and personal aggressiveness. Finally, one of the primary consequences of racism is that many blacks are forced to live in poverty and degradation, and some blacks may blame such circumstances on themselves. However, in a properly functioning defensive mode, self-blame, depression and despair are less likely because the person combines a high level of personal efficacy with a system blame orientation. The lowly state of one's material conditions are linked to oppression and racism rather than being viewed as an extension of one's self-concept.

The nigrescence writers point out that there are two extremes to this modality: in one, the person may deny the significance of racism in which case the defensive function will be inadequately developed and the person's self-protection abilities will be nil. In the other, the person may be overly-sensitive or even paranoid, "seeing" racism where it does not exist.

2. Reference Group Functions   It is generally the case that each black person has a number of options from which to satisfy one's group affiliation needs. However, in the case of an individual with a black identity, social anchorage and a sense of being, existence or purpose of life derives from making black people a primary, although not necessarily the only, reference group. While religion, occupational status, political affiliation, gender, etc. will all constitute some component of the self, having a black identity means that one's personal interpretation of the meaning of blackness will frame one's value system, aesthetics, personal social network, daily interactions, and personal conduct. In one of two ways, and perhaps a mixture of both, "race" becomes highly salient to the person. When viewed as a socio-historical variable, "race" refers to an *experientially derived perspective* or world view; from the vantage point of a reactionary ideology, one's perspective flows "naturally" from one's racial or biogenetic characteristics. At its best, the reference group functions of black identity lead to the celebration of blackness, the press to solve black problems and a desire to promulgate black culture and history. At its worst, it provides the basis for inhibiting, if not destructive social conformity, ethnic chauvinism, reactionary cultural ideologies (biogenetically based ideologies) and a tendency to view as less than human, to one degree or another, those who are "not black" (such negative and positive potential goes along with any and all forms of nationalism, ethnicity or group affiliation and is thus not unique to the black experience; one can embrace a cultural perspective without being reactionary, but all biogenetically defined notions of culture are inherently reactionary).

3. Proactive and Transcendental Functions   When Malcolm X returned from Mecca, he was no less committed to black people; however, his "tunnel" vision had been expanded, enabling him to see blackness and black people as but *one* cultural and historical expression of the human condition. His new vision did not question the basic integrity of the black experience, rather it made blackness his point of departure for discovering the universe of ideas, cultures, and experiences beyond blackness in place of mistaking blackness as the universe itself. It is often assumed that ethnicity acts as a barrier to humanism, but in its highest expression black identity functions as a window on the world. The humanism, ever present in the life of Martin Luther King and increasingly apparent in the final period of Malcolm X's life, did not represent a contradiction to their blackness; on the contrary, it was a product of blackness. In coming to know black people, both Malcolm and King had to explain black diversity. In tracing this diversity to the various cultural, economic, linguistic, social and political *systems* under which blacks lived throughout the diaspora, it was only natural that each should eventually try to make sense of the behavior of non-black people and nations through a similar analysis. Thus, the more deeply blacks explore themselves and the lives of those around them, the more likely they are to understand people as reflections of systems and personal experiences, and less so as clusters of ever distinct "racial groups".

The development of the capacity to proactively perceive and transcend one's blackness is the primary function of the third and final functional mode of the Stage 4 black identity. The nigrescence theorists see it as a mediating or *bridging mode* which links the person to other spheres such as the world of work, politics, gender, social class, international affairs and religion. Some critics have suggested that in the transcendence of Stage 4, the nigrescence writers are depicting a person who ceases to be anchored in a black world, but this is a gross distortion of their use of the term. Transcendence depicts a person who *is black oriented* but has the capacity to interact with and comprehend non-black social systems, cultures and individuals, which in effect is all of the world beyond blackness. It is through mediation, proactivity and transcendence that the stage is set for future identity growth. Finally, this last mode helps people to feel reasonably comfortable with unanswered questions, life's contradictions, and the rapid change in American society. In today's ever-changing world, learning to live with ambiguity in juxtaposition with a firm sense of self (blackness) are at the vortex of modern mental health for black people, as it is for most Americans.

As in the case of the other two functional modes, there are extremes to which the third mode can descend: (a) For some, having the "correct" ideology and a rigid sense of self precludes "learning to live the questions" and facing ambiguity; consequently, transcendence is seldom experienced; (b) either because they are overwhelmed by the need to compromise or are tempted by opportunism, another group makes so many compromises that eventually having a sense of blackness ceases to have meaning; (c) finally, others become enveloped in the world of Eurocentric or pseudo-humanism and forsake any commitment to blackness, seeing blackness as a contradiction to humanism rather than its expression within a particular social-historical context.

Recent Theoretical Advances

Parham's Lifespan Nigrescence Model and the Concept of Recycling

In the opinion of the two senior authors of this review, perhaps the most important theoretical advance in the field of nigrescence is Parham's application of a lifespan perspective to the study of nigrescence. In an article titled "Cycles of Psychological Nigrescence," Parham presents a life cycle nigrescence model based on a modification of the Cross Model:

> "... within the context of normal development, racial identity is a phenomenon which is subject to continuous change during the life cycle. While the psychological nigrescence research certainly documents how a person's racial identity can change from one stage to another (i.e., Pre-encounter to Encounter to Immersion-Emersion to Internalization), previous research has failed to detail how the various stages of racial identity will be accentuated at different phases of life. My model seeks to describe how the stages of racial identity are manifested at three phases of life, (late adolescence/early adulthood, midlife, and late adulthood) and how each phase of life is characterized by a central underlying theme" (Parham, in press).

The first object of Parham's concern is pinpointing the earliest phase of the life cycle at which one is capable of experiencing nigrescence. He presupposes that the manifestation of identity during childhood are "more the reflection of parental attitudes or societal stereotypes which a youngster has incorporated", than the integrated, cognitively complex, identity structures found in adults. Consequently, Parham hypothesizes it is during adolescence and early adulthood that one might first experience nigrescence, and thereafter the potential is

present for the remainder of one's life. Parham then notes there is probably a qualitative difference between the nigrescence experience at adolescence or early adulthood, than say nigrescence at middle or late
adulthood, because a black person's concept of blackness will be influenced by the distinctive developmental tasks associated with each
phase of the adult life span. A major portion of the remainder of his
article is then devoted to walking the reader through nigrescence, first
as might be experienced by an adolescent or young adult, then by a
middle aged adult and finally by an elderly black person.

Perhaps the most profound issue Parham raises is not so much
that aspects of the *initial* nigrescence episode varies with age, but having completed nigrescence, he sees the demand characteristics of each
phase of adult development making more likely a person's recycling
through the stages:

> "*Recycling* is defined as the reinitiation into the racial identity
> struggle and resolution process after having gone through the
> identity process at an earlier stage in one's life. In essence, a
> person could theoretically achieve identity resolution by com-
> pleting one cycle through the nigrescence process (internaliza-
> tion), and as a result of identity confusion, recycle through the
> stages again" (Parham, in press).

Parham's use of the term, "identity confusion" is misleading, for
recycling may have less to do with confusion, disintegration or regression, and more to do with a mid-life challenge for which one's initial
nigrescence cycle, experienced during an earlier period of development,
provides few answers. For example, having experienced nigrescence as a
single person, marriage and/or the challenge of raising one's progeny,
especially during *their* adolescence, is enough to drive any otherwise
normal person to "rethink" attitudes about blackness. From Parham's
perspective, recycling does not mean the person reverts back to the old
(Pre-encounter) identity and then traverses all the stages. Rather he is
inclined to believe that the challenge or trauma acts as a new *Encounter
episode* which exposes small or giant gaps in the person's thinking
about blackness, and the person recycles in order to fill such gaps. Thus
depending upon the nature of the challenge or new encounter, recycling may mean anything from a mild "refocusing experience" to one
involving full fledge Immersion-Emersion and Internalization episodes.

Another important advancement in Parham's model is his recognition that a person's initial identity state is not restricted to Pre-encounter attitudes. This assertion represents a significant departure from
the traditional nigrescence models (i.e., Cross, Jackson, Thomas), which
implicitly and explicitly suggest that one's racial identity development
begins with a pro-white/anti-black frame of reference or world view.
Parham speculates, for example, that if a young adolescent is exposed

to and indoctrinated with parental and social messages which are very pro-black in orientation, the reference group orientation initially developed by that youngster might be pro-black as well.

A third point of interest in Parham's model is his articulation that identity resolution can occur in at least three ways: stagnation (failure to move beyond one's initial identity state), stage-wise linear progression (movement from one identity state to another in a sequential, linear fashion), and recycling. The Cross (1971), B. Jackson (1976a), and Thomas (1971) models imply that nigrescence occurs in a linear fashion, with no other alternatives being proposed.

Helm's Concept of World View

Recall that the origin of the field of nigrescence was in part a reaction against the tendency to apply typological profiles to people who, because they were in the midst of identity change, were likely to have a *continuously changing profile*. The typology or non-process approach was said to obscure process.

> "... the non-process studies relied on a "single snap-shot" of the (new) black person, generally at the height of militancy. The process writers ... noted that militancy was less an identity and more a trait of identity during metamorphosis. In place of a single snapshot, they would require a series of pictures, if not a motion picture. We should note however, that the process writers were not rejecting the non-process research strategies. They generally understood that once large numbers of black people had internalized the new black identity, a non-process or steady state profile of the new identity would be extremely important. They did object to the application of research techniques which assumed steady state conditions when all the evidence seemed to point to a condition of identity in transition" (Cross, in press).

History has now made clear, however, that a process orientation is subject to the reverse error, in that the attributes associated with anything other than the Internalization stage are treated as diaphanous and evanescent, and thus the identity implication of each earlier stage is underestimated, if not overlooked all together. Recent research, which we will review shortly, has led to the perception that in steady-state or non-change conditions (periods in history in which there are no ongoing large scale social movements which induce nigrescence), the stage related profiles constitute identities in their own right, and not necessarily transition points toward nigrescence. Perhaps the only stage for which there is an inherent change component is the Encounter Stage which describes the event or events that cause a person to be conscious of the need to change. Otherwise, each stage related profile may reflect a complete identity.

Helms (1986a; 1986b), in synthesizing the work of Cross (1971) and Sue (1978), has taken this a step further and asked that we consider each stage profile as a distinctive *world view*.

> "In explicating his model of racial identity development, Cross . . . used the concept of 'stages of identity' to describe the different ways in which black people may resolve the identity issues caused by their need to function in a racist society. If one reads Cross's descriptions of the stages carefully, one comes to realize that in each of the stages, he is describing a complex interaction between feelings, cognitions, attitudes, and behaviors. In my opinion, Cross uses stages as a synonym for what Sue . . . called 'world views,' . . ." (Helms, 1986a; p. 62).

Quoting Sue, Helms (1986a) defines world view as "the way in which people perceive their relationship to nature, institutions, other people, and things. World view constitutes our psychological orientation in life and can determine how we think, behave, make decisions, and define events" (Sue, 1978, p. 458). The racial identity stages refer to that portion of the person's world view that is designed to organize and interpret one's personal (internal) and society's (external) definition of the worth and salience of the group to which one is ascribed. Thus, Helms attempts to provide a broader cognitive definition of the stages and to suggest the ways in which identity might function even in the absence of an ongoing large scale social movement.

In recent discussions between the first author and Bailey Jackson of the University of Massachusetts, one of the most active of the nigrescence theorists, Jackson stated that the Pre-encounter, Immersion-Emersion and (new) black identities are *not* period specific in the sense that each can only be found in the dynamics of contemporary black life. Instead, Jackson sees the three identities as ever present throughout the social history of black America. At any particular historical period, one identity may be normative for reasons unique to that period, while the other identity profiles, though in evidence, may take on less significance. As time progresses, the ancillary identity may become normative, and the previously normative identity, less popular. Together, Helms' notions of world view and Jackson's historical perspective bring the field of nigrescence ever closer to the capacity to articulate a comprehensive psychohistory of black America. While such a venture is beyond the purview of the current effort, an outline of the psychohistory will likely be based on the following four points:

> 1. Slavery in the Americas Begins: Africans are introduced to the Americas as slaves, and various deracination schemes are de-

vised to mute and disable their Afrocentric perspective. Also, in the course of simply learning to adopt to their new circumstances, a degree of acculturation occurs and Africans, at least over several generations of slavery, become African-Americans.

2. Effects of the Institutionalization of Slavery: In an anthropological sense, slavery fails to dehumanize blacks, and it fails in its attempt to destroy all vestiges of Africanity, although deracination and acculturation result in blacks themselves no longer being able to *consciously* identify the Africanity in their daily life. It is in the realm of identity and world view that slavery is *most* successful in a destructive sense, for early on, the historical record shows many black slaves with a Pre-encounter oriented world view, as the dialectics of oppression (deracination) and liberation (nigrescence) are etched in stone. In the aftermath of slavery's destruction of a conscious African world view, slaves forge new ways of codifying their vision of themselves and the world around them. Some like Phyllis Wheatley, Benjamin North, Booker T. Washington, and the African-Americans who "colonize" Liberia, exhibit a Pre-encounter perspective, unique not so much by themes of self-hatred (the notion of self-hatred has been exaggerated in depictions of Pre-encounter), but in the tendency to view the world from a Euro-American perspective. Others, from a very early age, are socialized into pro-black orientations, and their identity never seems to necessitate conversion. In fact, Sojourner Truth and Frederick Douglas even exhibit the qualities of transcendence. But Douglas and Truth seem more the exception than the rule, and the successes of deracination makes slavery the initial theater for nigrescence, with the life of Nat Turner being one of its most demonstrative performances.

3. The Post-Slavery Experience, 1865-1975: After slavery, the three world views are easily spotted in autobiographies written by blacks between 1870 and 1900, but in the formation of black urban America at the turn of the century a new phenomena is revealed in the black response to oppression. In place of singular conversions experienced in isolation from the community, the dynamics of black social movements show thousands of blacks moving through the stages of nigrescence together. This first epoch of collective nigrescence is the Garvey Movement and the Harlem Renaissance. However, the forces of deracination, in conjunction with the effects of the Depression, dilute the gains made toward nigrescence in the 1920s and 30s. Furthermore, the McCarthy era destroys the lives of many blacks who might otherwise act to bridge the generations of the sixties with the earlier nigrescence period. In their place, the McCarthy debacle helps evolve a moderate (mainstream) black leadership that is assimilationist to the extreme. As the limitations

of the deracinated assimilationists unfold, the stage is set for the most recent epoch of nigrescence, the black Consciousness Movement of the sixties.

4. Nigrescence in the Present and Future: although the actual date can be debated, the Movement of the sixties and seventies seems to lose its mass movement dynamics by the mid-nineteen-seventies. In accordance with anyone's standards, the Movement is only partially successful in creating sustained and meaningful opportunities for *some* blacks. On the other hand the accumulated victories of historical racism give birth to the black underclass. Ironically, the *success* of the Movement has meant a socialization period (1975-1985) in which for some blacks, race has taken on less significance, and merit more importance. Thus, while yesterday's Pre-encounter Negro displayed a strategy of *seeking* approval and acceptance, today's Pre-encounter Negro is more the product of perceptions that she/he has *gained* acceptance and approval. The new Negro, in effect, rejects blackness from both a cultural and class position. In any case, it takes no magician to predict that the forces are building toward another period of nigrescence, one in which social class issues may be as dominant as cultural factors. Should it come soon enough, the black Community will likely be prepared, for the personalities and organizations which might bridge such a movement with the events of the sixties continue to have status in the black community.

In explicating our psychohistorical scenario of nigrescence, we have not done justice to another important factor, that being Parham's notion of recycling. This would become evident were we to examine in comprehensive detail the individual lives of blacks for any of the periods (slavery, 1865-1900, 1900-1920, etc.) to which we made reference. It probably has not escaped the attention of some readers, however, that perhaps recycling can also be applied to the black community as a whole, in that periodically our communities, and not simply individuals, seem in need of recycling.

This descriptive summary of the models is only half the story, for as of 1988, well over 75 empirical studies that focus on the nigrescence phenomena have been conducted. For an examination of the empirical literature, see the recent review article by Cross, Thomas & Helms (in press). [In point of fact, the above summary of the models has been taken from the first part of the review article by Cross, Thomas & Helms (in press), *Advances in Black Psychology*, Reginald Jones (Ed.).]

References

Caplan, N. (1970). The new ghetto man: A review of recent empirical studies. *Journal of Social Issues, 26,* 57-73.

Clark, C. C. (1971). General systems theory and black studies: Some points of convergence. In C. W. Thomas (ed.), *Boys No More,* 28-47. Beverly Hills: Glencoe Press.

Crawford, T. J., & Naditch, M. (1970). Relative deprivation, powerlessness and militancy. *Journal of Psychiatry, 33(2),* 208-223.

Cross, W. E., Jr. (1978). The Thomas and Cross models of psychological nigrescence: A review. *Journal of Black Psychology, 5(1),* 13-31.

Cross, W. E., Jr. (July, 1971). The Negro-to-Black conversion experience. *Black World,* 13-27.

Cross, W. E., Jr. (In press). *Black identity: Theory and research.*

Downton, J. V. (1973). *Rebel leadership: Commitment and charisma in the revolutionary process.* New York: The Free Press.

Gerlach, L. P., & Hine, V. H. (1970). People power and change: Movements of social transformation. New York: Bobbs-Merrill.

Helms, J. E. (1986a). Expanding racial identity theory to cover counseling process. *Journal of Counseling Psychology, 33(1),* 62-64.

Helms, J. E. (1986b). Black psychology: Stages of nigrescence. Paper presented at the University of Pennsylvania Conference on Leadership, Afro-American Studies Department. Philadelphia, PA., November 19, 1986.

Jackson, B. W. (1976a). The functions of black identity development theory in achieving relevance in education. Unpublished doctoral dissertation, University of Massachusetts.

Jackson, B. W. (1976b). Black identity development. In L. Golubschick and B. Persky (Eds.), *Urban Social and Educational Issues,* 158-164. Dubuque: Kendall-Hall.

Kelman, H. C. (1970). A socio-psychological model of political legitimacy and its relevance to black and white student protest movements. *Psychiatry, 33(2),* 224-246.

McCord, W., Howard, J., Friedberg, B., & Harwood, E. (1969). *Life styles in the black ghetto.* New York: W. W. Norton.

Milliones, J. (1973). Construction of the developmental inventory of black consciousness. Unpublished doctoral dissertation, University of Pittsburgh.

Napper, G. (1973). *Blacker than thou.* Michigan: W. B. Eerdmans.

Onwuachi, P. C. (March, 1967). Identity and black power: An African viewpoint. *Negro Digest,* 31-37.

Parham, T. A. (In press). The psychodynamics of dissent. In J. H. Masserman, (Ed.), *The dynamics of dissent,* 56-79. New York: Grune and Stratton.

Sherif, M., & Sherif, C. (1970). Black unrest as a social movement toward an emerging self-identity. *Journal of Social and Behavioral Science, 15(3),* 41-52.

Sue, D. W. (1978). World views and counseling. *Personnel and Guidance Journal, 56,* 458-462.

Thomas, C. W. (1971). *Boys no more.* Beverly Hills: Glencoe Press.

Toldson, I., & Pasteur, A. (1975). Developmental stages of black self-discovery: Implications for using black art forms in group interaction. *Journal of Negro Education, 44*, 130-138.

Wortham, A. (1981). The other side of racism: A philosophical study of black race consciousness. Ohio: Ohio State University Press.

Mental Disorder Among African Americans

Na'im Akbar

The African American has been the victim of oppression both on the physical and the mental planes. He has endured the atrocities of physical abuse and then his mental efforts to cope have been subjected to intellectual oppression. Intellectual oppression involves the abusive use of ideas, labels and concepts geared toward the mental degradation of a people (or person). There is no area in which mental or intellectual oppression is more clearly illustrated than in the area of mental health judgments.

Traditional definitions of mental health in the Western world have been normative definitions. In the context of considerable uncertainty as to what constituted a normal human being, a kind of "democratic sanity" has been established. This "democratic sanity" essentially applies the socio-political definition of majority rule to the definition of adequate human functioning. As a result, the mental health practitioner determines insane behavior on the basis of the degree to which it deviated from the majority's behavior in a given context. The typical textbook in abnormal psychology such as Coleman (1972) states forthrightly: "On a psychological level, we have no 'ideal model' or even 'normal' model of man as a base of comparison." ". . . the concepts of 'normal' and 'abnormal' are meaningful only with reference to a given culture: normal behavior conforms to social expectations, whereas abnormal behavior does not." The consequence of such "democratic sanity" is that entire communities of people with seriously inhuman behaviors can be adjudged sane and competent, even exemplary human specimens, because the majority of people in that particular context either participated in the questionable behavior or refused to question the strange behavior.

As a consequence of "democratic sanity" no one has raised a question about the mental competence of a people who enslaved as cattle, thousands of non-hostile human beings. The question of the possible mental incompetence of a people who terrorized and murdered thousands of non-hostile inhabitants in the name of exploration and geographical expansion has never been raised. The persistent oppression and support of oppression of non-hostile human being simply on the basis of a shared hallucination of color differential has not received consideration by the world's scientists and philosophers who have studied human mental functioning.

Recently, some African American scientists such as Wright (1975), Welsing (1972) and Clark et al., (1976) have suggested the possible pathological origin of such humanly questionable behavior. More commonly, the tendency has been to justify and explain the behavior of the victims of such insanity on the basis of the assumed sanity of the victimizers and the context of the victimization. Such efforts have proven circular in their logic, at best, and have served as the basis for continued intellectual oppression, at worst. The question of emotional disturbance among African Americans has been one of the most frequently addressed issues among many Jewish American and African American social scientists, primarily Clark (1965), Figelman (1968), Grier and Cobb (1968), Kardiner and Ovesey (1962), Karon (1958), and many others. This preoccupation with the lack of mental health among African Americans has not only presented a distorted image of the American of African descent, but has failed to address the real problems of this substantial constituent of the American community.

The classic work from the early 1960's which tackled the issue of mental health for the African American from a scientific basis was *The Mark of Oppression* (1962) by two Jewish psychoanalysts, Abram Kardiner and Lionel Ovesey. This was the first literature of any great significance which even warrants serious consideration. Previously, the mental health scientists involved themselves in documentation of such dubious notions as "freed slaves showed a much greater proneness to mental disorder because by nature the negro required a master" (quoted by Thomas and Sillen, 1972). The conclusion reached by Doctors Kardiner and Ovesey based on their analysis of a select number of "emotionally disturbed" African Americans was that all or most of the personality characteristics of both sane and insane African Americans could be accounted for on the basis of the experience of oppression. There is much to be said for their hypothesis because as we shall discuss below, oppression is an inhuman condition which stimulates unnatural human behavior. It is ultimately to a source of inhuman conditions that we can trace the roots of mental disorder. At a time when social scientists were acquiring great scholarly renown for documenting the human deficits of African Americans, these observers did attempt to provide a comprehensive psychohistorical analysis of the condition of the "Negro," using slavery as their historical vantage point. The over-riding problem with this book and the subsequent numerous related ones was the perspective of pathology accepted by these writers. All of the case histories presented in the Kardiner and Ovesey (1962) document suffer from some type of sexual and/or aggressive malady, not unlike any human being subjected to the Freudian microscope. The analysis of incompetent mental functioning is concluded based on the norm and the context of the"sanity democracy" standards set by the middle class European American.

An indication of the severity of intellectual oppression is reflected in the fact that African American scholars have characteristically followed the lead of European American scholars in both conceptualizing and analyzing their problems. (The reader is referred to Baldwin, 1981; Hare, 1969; and Mahdubuti, 1976, for extensive descriptions of this phenomenon). Grier and Cobbs (1968) are probably the supreme example. Their promising document of 1968 offered the opportunity for an alternative perspective to be offered by African American mental health scientists about African American mental health conditions. Instead, these accomplished psychiatrists presented a European American social worker's handbook and guide to the neurotic "Negro," on how to understand the justifiable hatred of the "blacks." The most frequently made criticism of the book *Black Rage* is its tendency to overgeneralize. This objection is not nearly so disturbing as is the persistence of these scholars to redefine within the traditional context of Western psychology—with its emphasis on pathology—the cause and character of the "limited" mental health and "pervasive" mental disorder facing African American communities. The assumption underlying this study by Grier and Cobbs and related ones (such as *Dark Ghetto* by Kenneth Clark) is that to be psychologically healthy is to conduct oneself as much as possible like a middle class European American. They also assume that the behavior that produces problems for European Americans is the same behavior that produces problems for African Americans. It is further assumed that the standards set by "sanity democracy" are in fact reflective of human standards documented by thousands of years of human history.

These writers fail to address the importance of two essential variables in determining the adequacy of human behavior: (1) the historical antecedents or determinants of that behavior and (2) the effects of a functionally inhuman environment and conditions of the human being. As a result of the failure to take account of these variables, there has been a concerted effort to rehabilitate, correct, modify or resocialize many of the behaviors which have been and still are critical to the survival of the African American. There has been a systematic disregard for those qualities of humanity which have persisted despite oppression, while they have disappeared among the historical oppressors. There has also been a failure to address those issues of intellectual oppression which persist even when the more obvious conditions of physical oppression have been reduced.

The classification and description of African American mental health has failed to utilize one of the few "universals" associated with a meaningful definition of mental health. This definition of mental health has its origin in the unalterable laws of physical life, which when transposed to mental life maintains its essential identity. Physical health means that the naturally disposed tendency to maintain life and perpetuate itself is functional. Physical illness is concluded when forces or processes within the physical body begin to threaten the natural disposition to live. The transposition of this concept would suggest that mental health is reflected in those behaviors which foster mental growth and awareness (i.e., mental life). Mental illness would then be the presence of ideas or forces within the mind that threaten awareness and mental growth. From an ontogenetic or extended concept of self or mind (Nobles, 1972) we could conclude that mental illness is seen in any behavior or ideas which threaten the survival of the collective self (or tribe). With such a definition, we could understand the classification of an entire society as mentally ill if that society were entrenched in a set of ideas geared toward the self-destruction of the people within that society. On the other hand, we could understand the apparently contradictory behavior of a people who have formulated their survival on the domination of others. Domination, though insane from the perspective of survival of the victim, is the very essence of sanity for the dominant who requires a victim in order to survive. When two life processes or entities are opposed in such a relationship then one is obligated to assess "health" or "sanity" from the perspective of the life process which you are seeking to understand and/or preserve. Then both processes must be subjected to the universal standard of natural law to determine which is correct in its oppositional force: is it the unprovoked attacker or is it the innocent victim of attack who must seek to define and assure its own survival in defense from such an attack?

The effort of this discussion is to classify the mental disorders of African Americans from the perspective of universal mental health—that which fosters and cultivates survival of itself. This model equips the African American community with a vehicle by which it recognizes "anti-life" forces (Moody, 1971) within itself and threatening from without. Rather than the more typical preoccupation with disorders which threaten the life of the predators, the focus is directed toward those ideas and behaviors which threaten the life of the victims.

The four classifications of disorders from this perspective include (1) the alien-self disorder; (2) the anti-self disorder; (3) the self-destructive disorder; and (4) the organic disorder. We accept the basic argument of Thomas Szasz and others that mental "illness" is actually a myth. There is no particular behavior that is sick in and of itself. Therefore, one cannot assume a disease entity being present for the production of certain specific behaviors. We can accept the allegorical relationship between disorders in the body and disorders in the mind since they both signal danger to the life of their separate planes of being. We do submit, however, that there are socially, mentally and spiritually destructive patterns of behavior which we will describe here as disorders in contrast to the self-surviving and perpetuating forces which operate in an ordered mind. "Disorder" is used in this discussion in preference to "mental illness" because we stand opposed to the position of the Western psychologists who assume that man has no natural order. We claim in accord with the African scholars and scientists from the eastern part of the world that there is a "natural order" for man (Akbar, 1977).

The Alien Self Disorder

The alien-self disorder represents that group of individuals who behave contrary to their nature and their survival. They are a group whose most prevalent activities represent a rejection of their natural dispositions. They have learned to act in contradiction to their own well-being and as a consequence they are alien from themselves. These are the growing number of African Americans in recent years who have been socialized in families with primarily materialistic goals. They see themselves as material and evaluate their worth by the prevalence of material accouterments which they possess (Braithwaite, et al., 1977). These families are usually preoccupied with materialistic values, social affluence and rational priorities (to the exclusion of moral imperatives). The socialization of these alien-self persons has been geared toward a denial of social realities particularly as they relate to issues of race and oppression. They are encouraged to ignore the blatant inequities of racism and to view their lives as if slavery, racism and oppression never existed. They are asked to pretend that there are not forces of injustice threatening their collective survival. They are encouraged to always adopt the perspective of the dominant culture even if it means a condemnation of self.

The outcome for the alien-self disorder is a symptom picture not dissimilar to the rather traditional neurotic in Caucasian society. He is a person who condemns his natural dispositions and tries, ineffectively, to live in a dream world. Such persons are usually wrought with anxiety, tension and existential stress. They remain in conflict as to their true identity and go from one social charade to another. A typical example is the sorority socialite who becomes the miserable suburbanite playing at happiness in a glass palace. They are burdened with sexual problems and perversions because the natural sexual disposition has either been disproportionately eliminated or accentuated for the developing person.

The African American homosexual is another example of the alien-self disorders. The severity of his confusion about his identity (ethnic and interpersonal) has penetrated to his confusion about his sexual identity. He has usually been raised to deny his own masculine disposition because the assertiveness which characterizes boyish emergence was viewed as potentially threatening by the dominant culture and by his confused family circle. The similar feminine pride is associated with Caucasian images of beauty which frustrate the girl's search for identity. They are both encouraged to restrain their natural dispositions which merely generalizes to their sexuality resulting in a disorder which perpetuates a pattern disruptive to natural family functioning. The female homosexual has often simply retreated from the field of femininity because the standards of Caucasian "acceptability" were recognizably unattainable for a woman of African descent. Another variation on this theme is the boy who becomes delinquent because of his refusal to accept such restraint and rather than relinquish his masculine identity as does the homosexual he defines his masculinity by aggressive rebellion, excessive and precocious sexual activity, criminality, etc. Such a revolt is also found in the female who becomes a teenage mother, young prostitute, or female criminal who rebels by her indulging those feminine drives which she is not "supposed to have" as a young black woman.

This alien-self disorder is occurring with alarming frequency in middle class and professional African American communities. The particular manifestation of this disorder in alien sexual behavior is increasingly evident in all segments of African American society. The tremendous need to assimilate into the dominant society and to deny those factors which have affected us historically and continue to shape us in the contemporary society has succeeded in alienating increasing numbers of African Americans from themselves. Such persons bring the unique contribution of their heritage to these disorders, but the essential problem is that they have assimilated into a life style which is alien to themselves. They, therefore, are substantially similar to that dominant society which fosters material acquisition rather than natural human cultivation.

Affectation best describes the person with an alien-self disorder. They speak, walk, dress, act, even laugh as they visualize the dominant group. At great pains they live in neighborhoods predominantly or exclusively populated by other ethnic groups; their children attend the same exclusive schools; they attend exclusive churches and aspire to join exclusive clubs. The outcome is that they belong to neither group: African American nor certainly the European American group. The consequence is loneliness and confusion. They often end up living in a no-man's land unwilling to seek the acceptance of others like themselves, and unable to be accepted by those whose acceptance they passionately desire.

The Anti-Self Disorder

The anti-self disorder adds to the alien-self disorder overt and covert hostility towards the group of ones origin and by implications towards oneself. The anti-self disorder not only identifies with the dominant group but essentially identifies with the projected hostility and negativism towards his group of origin. In the terms of Frantz Fanon (1968), they represent the true "colonized mentality." They have so thoroughly identified with the colonizer or slave-master that they desire to replicate the structure which existed prior to their physical liberation.

The dangerous aspect of this group is that unlike the alien-self disorder, they feel quite comfortable with their alien identification. Most often, they exemplify the very epitome of mental health according to the standards of the "democratic sanity." They are usually the very model of stability in the context of the dominant group. The danger from this group with the anti-self disorder is that they are unlikely to seek help as is the case with the previous group. Neither are they likely to be coerced into treatment by the legitimized authorities since they are the model of legitimate behavior, from the perspective of the outer group.

These are the politicians who will join any faction in order to further their careers. They are elected leaders who are more committed to the "system" than to their constituency; the policemen who beat black heads with a vengeance. These are the African American scholars who are more concerned about scientific credibility than about community facility. These are the businessmen who are more concerned about their own economic solvency than they are about the communities from which they came. These are the educators and administrators who ask first if they have the approval of the dominant group and secondarily (if at all) if they have provided a service of enlightenment to their group. Included in this group are the African Americans who reach the apex of their self-rejection by choosing a marriage partner from the alien group. To the extent that a mate represents the extension of oneself, their statement of who they are is reflected in the identity of that mate. The fact that such blatant betrayal of oneself is done without remorse and with excessive justification reflects the intensity of self-rejection in the anti-self disorder. There is nothing implicitly self-destructive in choosing an outer group marriage partner. However, when such partners have historically demonstrated themselves to be in opposition to your group's survival then such choices are clearly self-destructive and are symptomatic of an anti-self disorder. This is especially true in instances where the person actively rejects potential partners within his own group in order to select a member of the outer group.

The anti-self disorder is more out of contact with reality than the alien-self disorder. Therefore, in terms of severity, he is more disturbed than the alien-self group. When he has fleeting glimpses of his isolation, he merely intensifies his efforts to acceptability by the dominant group and becomes even more aggressive towards the group of his origin.

This personal rejection of self for the purpose of becoming like the aggressor results in a form of psychological perversion which is at best only damaging to the African American community and at worst could be the instrument of destruction of our communities. Victims of this disorder are most vulnerable to the manipulation of unscrupulous persons who play upon their need for outer group approval and flattery as a means of utilizing them to control the self-affirmative progress of African American communities.

The Self Destructive Disorders

Inhuman conditions bring about insanity. Oppression in its varied and sundried forms constitutes one of the most inhuman conditions. The unnatural pressures exerted on human life by the human abuse of oppression drives beings away from reality. A system of oppression erects several critical blockages to human growth which stimulate a retreat from reality: (1) The destruction of human dignity and self-respect is a component of oppressive systems. In order to operate effectively in the world of reality, human beings must see themselves as worthy and effective. (2) The systematic blockages to human development such as masculine responsibility, feminine receptivity, self-determination and social productivity thwarts necessary human expansion. (3) Systematic injustice destroys trust and predictability of the social environment facilitating retreat from the world of reality.

Victims of the self-destructive disorders are the most direct victims of oppression. These disorders represent the self-defeating attempts to survive in a society which systematically frustrates normal efforts for natural human growth. This group is typified by the pimps, pushers, prostitutes, addicts, alcoholics and psychotics and an entire array of conditions which are personally destructive to the individual and equally detrimental to the African American community. These are the individuals who have usually found the doors to legitimate survival blocked and out of the urgency for survival have chosen personally and socially destructive means to alleviate immediate wants such as pimping, pushing drugs, or prostituting. Black-on-black homicide and crime is an acting-out of the self-destructive disorder. The addicts, alcoholics and psychotics in varying degrees of intensity have retreated from reality into their respective worlds of dreams. The addict and alcoholic find greater solace in the chemically induced world of fantasy. The psychotic, who for various direct and indirect reasons of oppression never developed sufficient involvement in reality, persists in his world of fantasy which despite all of its torment often offers greater order than the world of oppression.

These victims have refused to accept (or have not had the opportunity to develop) the alien self-identity. Often as a consequence of great struggle they have acquired an African American identity which is inconsistent with Caucasian American achievement. The pimp has succeeded in maintaining an African disposition of male dominance and flamboyance. In order to do so he had to become a sadistic brute and exploiter in order to actualize these traits in a society which had defined the concept of masculinity as inconsistent with being African American and masculine self-confidence as "nigger arrogance." The junkie, often painfully sensitive to the realities of his environment retreats from those realities which have defined him as zero even before he picked up a needle.

It takes the most devastating of environments to reverse the most natural trend of life which is SURVIVAL. The conditions experienced by these self-destructive disorders have made them enemy forces to their immediate selves and to their extended selves in the African American community.

The deadlines of human degradation in the American system of human oppression is reflected in the kind of self-destructive minds which are produced. The fact that such self-destructive disorders do not only occur in oppressed communities is indicative of the shared dehumanization which occurs to the oppressor who seeks to dehumanize. We shall discuss elsewhere the nature of disorder in the Western world which makes it the exclusive producer of mass murderers, child molesters and other perverted minds which are occurring with increased frequency within this society. Suffice it to say that there is a universal backlash which brings the human suffering meted out back to the door of the oppressor.

The psychotic is much more complicated than might be suggested by the conciseness of these concepts. For the purpose of my argument which views sane behavior as self-preservative and insane behavior as counter self in some form, then the psychotic clearly falls into the category of the self-destructive. Mental life is nourished by awareness of reality. Withdrawal from that reality constitutes the same kind of mental self-destructiveness that exists in physical suicide or drug abuse. Despite the rather dramatic form of many psychotic behaviors we wish to suggest that the psychotic is using mechanisms at his disposal in order to self-destruct reality just as is the alcoholic and the pimp. The alcoholic accomplishes chemically what the pimp accomplishes socially and what the psychotic accomplishes psychologically.

Organic Disorders

This group represents those conditions which, insofar as present information suggests, are the result of physiological, neurological or biochemical malfunction. The group includes the severely mentally defective, organic brain disorders and most of the commonly recognized forms of schizophrenia. We are unwilling to accept that all such "organic" disorders are the result of physical defects alone and therefore do not raise questions about the social environment. For one thing, we do not operate under the mistaken Western assumption of dualism whereby physical causation occurs in isolation from social and mental influences. Despite the unquestioned predominance of symptoms which suggest physical defect, we are concerned about the potentially correctable contribution made by the social, mental or physical spheres.

There is growing evidence that "freaks of nature" may be freaks of society. Each year scientists are increasingly able to isolate the effects of tobacco, commonly dispensed drugs, alcohol and diet on the unborn offspring. The responsibility for life seems to extend far beyond individual survival but for generations ahead. A recent discovery that birth control pills affect the growth of tumors in second generation female children demonstrates the long range influence of the folly of meddling with nature's order. The point is that the organic disorder may be the outcome of a disordered society as is the case with the three groups discussed above.

Intellectual defectives seem to be products of poor nutrition, unspecified chemical conditions such as controllable toxic intake and defective environments. Those defective environments seem to result from an increasing neglect and outright abuse of the young. In other words, the self-destructive disorders discussed above are likely to manifest their self-destructive state of mind by abusing their own flesh, in the form of their offspring which gives rise to the organic defectives of this group. Genuine poverty conditions are as much the direct cause of both poor diet and poor environment as is the physical abuse. In such instances the oppressive system remains the essential cause of mental disorder within the African American community.

Another condition which is often classified in this group of organic disorders is senility. This incapacitating disorder of the elderly is on the increase in African American communities as we increasingly adopt the alien life style of the European American. This life style requires the premature burial of our aged in homes which feed mental deterioration. The urgency of the upwardly mobile family to be freed from the inconvenience of elderly parents requires the disposal of this burden to a sanitary field of inactivity—a kind of living death. So an entire population of formerly active, productive and exceedingly valuable members of the community are converted as specimens for organic deterioration.

There is an increasing emphasis on the organic basis for all forms of mental disorders. It is unfortunately an effort to deny the contribution of the society in the shaping of firm mental life or disordered mental life. It is also an effort to disavow the subtle interaction between social, psychological and physical phenomenon. The African American practitioner must maintain an awareness of the unity of these influences as he attempts to address the cause of conditions affecting all human beings.

Summary

What's the point of another classification system for mental disorders? Why another rehearsal of the disastrous consequences of oppression? Mental disorder is a social, political, economic, philosophical, even spiritual phenomenon. Both the occurrence, its cause and its management is deeply tied into the historical, social and political status of its victims. We do ourselves a disservice to let the psychiatrists, psychologists and other so-called specialists from other cultural persuasions define the mentally disordered. Paradoxical as it may sound, the ability to decide who in your community is sane or insane is one of the ultimate measures of power and community integrity. As long as this definition comes from outside of the community, one's community is controlled by outside influences.

Any type of classification should be not only descriptive and orderly but functional. In the case of identifying pathology, the classification system should be able to isolate the dangerous conditions, it should suggest the origins of that condition and it should contain implications for correcting that condition. We have attempted in this discussion to classify mental disorders, not as the European American classifies it for his convenience and protection, but as African Americans should begin to see it for the preservation of our communities. The classical "bad nigger" is classified as an assaultive paranoid by the European American psychiatrist because he actively combats oppression. The exasperated welfare mother is called psychotically depressed because the case workers can more conveniently transfer her to the psychiatric social workers.

Each of the four classifications discussed here represents separate types of danger to African American communities. Each group of disorders emanate as radials from a common axis, i.e., a psychopathic society typified by oppression and racism (See Figure 1). These disorders usually do not endanger the broader European American society. In fact, the alien self disorder and the anti-self disorder are usually the primary agents for intransigence in the African American community.

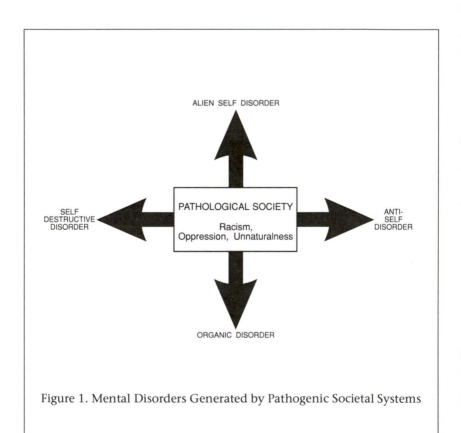

Figure 1. Mental Disorders Generated by Pathogenic Societal Systems

Until African Americans are able to effectively define what is normal for our communities, we remain as subjects to an alien authority. Until we recognize the forces which operate to alienate us from ourselves, we will continue to lose our mental power and commitment to anti-community forces. The definition of normality and abnormality is one of the most powerful indications of community power. So long as these definitions come from outside of the community, the community has no ability to grow nor can human beings within those communities realize the full power of their human potential.

References

Akbar, N. (1974) Awareness: The key to black mental health. *Journal of Black Psychology, 1(1)*.

Akbar, N. (1977). *Natural psychology and human transformation.* Chicago: World Community of Islam.

Braithwaite, H., Taylor, K., & Black H. (1977). *Materialistic depression.* Unpublished manuscript.

Clark, C. (1972). Black studies or the study of black people. In R. Jones (Ed.), *Black psychology.* New York: Harper & Row.

(Clark) X, C. (1975). Voodoo or IQ: An introduction to African psychology. *Journal of Black Psychology, 1*(2), 9-29.

Coleman, J. (1972). *Abnormal psychology and modern life* (4th ed.). Glenview, Ill.: Scott & Foresman.

Fanon, F. (1968). *The wretched of the earth.* New York: Grove Press.

Figelman, M. (1968). A comparison of affective and paranoid disorders in Negroes and Jews. *International Journal of Social Psychiatry, 14*.

Grier, W., & Cobbs, P. (1968). *Black rage.* New York: Basic Books.

Hare, N. (1969). A challenge to the black scholar. *Black Scholar*, 2-7.

Kardiner, A., & Ovesey, L. (1962). *The mark of oppression.* Cleveland, OH: World Publishing Company.

Karon, B. (1958). *Negro personality: A rigorous investigation of the effects of culture.* New York: Springer.

Lee, D. (aka Mahdubuti, H.) (1976). *From plan to planet.* Chicago: Third World Press.

Moody, L. (1977). *The white man as anti-life force.* Unpublished manuscript. Norfolk State University.

Nobles, W. (1972). African philosophy: Foundations for black psychology. In R. Jones (Ed.), *Black psychology.* New York: Harper & Row.

Szasz, T. (1960). Myth of mental illness, *American Psychologist, 15*, 113-118.

Thomas, A., & Sillen, S. (1972). *Racism and psychiatry.* New York: Bruner/Mazel Publishers.

Welsing, F.C. (1970). *The cress theory of color confrontation*. Washington, D.C.: C-R Publishers.
Wright, B. (1975). *The psychopathic racial personality*. Chicago: Third World Press.

Psychologically Healthy Black Adults

Howard P. Ramseur

> ... the Negro has no possible basis for a healthy self-esteem and every incentive for self-hatred. A. Kardiner and L. Ovesey, *The Mark of Oppression* (1951, p. 297)

> ... the experience of being black in a society dominated by whites does *not*, as is sometimes incorrectly assumed, lead to deep and corrosive personal demoralization. Blacks live with greater stress, but they have the personal and social resources to maintain a perspective which keeps the stress external, does not permit it to become internalized or to disrupt personal integration (J. Veroff, E. Douvan, and R. A. Kulka, *The Inner American* 1981, p. 437).

Overview

What are the psychological and social characteristics of psychologically healthy black American adults? How do these characteristics develop and change over the life cycle? Until now these significant questions have not been comprehensively addressed. They have not been addressed partly because of the lack of consensus and conceptual clarity in the literature about what represents "psychological health" or "healthy development" for adults, black or white. In addition, the idea that black American adults could be psychologically healthy, however defined, is one that mainstream social scientists and much of the lay public would find unacceptable. The vast literature on blacks in psychology, sociology, social work, and psychiatry converges on the assumptions embodied in the quote from Kardiner and Ovesey (1951) above. That is, given the social and cultural conditions under which black Americans live, psychological health is an impossibility.

The 1960s and 1970s saw theoretical and empirical challenges to mainstream social science theories, particularly to their predictions that black adults were self-hating or had self-esteem lower than white Americans. Recently, some social scientists have moved beyond the mainstream view, or simply challenging it, have begun to focus on specific aspects of psychological functioning or development they have defined as healthy; e.g., high self-esteem, positive racial identity, or adaptive coping styles. While a number of interesting empirical findings have emerged, little general theorizing about black adult psychological health over the life cycle, or about the implications of these findings for psychological treatment, has occurred.

This chapter will review theory and research on psychological health among black American adults by discussing the social/cultural situation of black Americans, "universal" models of psychological health, and theories of black personality and identity that have psychological health implications. The chapter will then turn to empirical research and associated theorizing in three areas that have been linked to black psychological health: self-conception (self-esteem and racial identity), the "competent" personality, and black coping resources and styles. Finally, the chapter will examine the implications of recent theory and empirical research for creating models of black adult psychological health and future research.

Models of Psychological Health

How should "psychological health" be defined? How does it change over the adult life cycle? No theory or model of adult psychological health has achieved a consensus or accumulated a convincing body of empirical evidence to address these questions. In addition, while existing models of psychological health claim to be "universal," that is applicable and explanatory for all persons, in fact, they usually have little or nothing to say about the unique social/cultural circumstances of black Americans and the impact of such circumstances on black adult psychological health. Existing theories of black adult psychological health will be reviewed by focusing on the unique social/cultural situation of blacks and the issues that it raises, and by examining the two existing bodies of theory: "universal" models of psychological health and models of black personality and identity.

The Social/Cultural Context of African Americans

Black adults must live and adapt to a unique social and cultural environment as well as history in the United States. That environment and the necessity that they adapt to it has implications for any model that claims to define and understand psychological health for black American adults. Certain issues seem important in characterizing the aspects of that environment that are relevant to psychological health:

white racism, the need to adapt to white institutions and culture, adapting to the black community—family, institutions, and culture, and coping with poverty and political powerlessness (See Jones, 1972; Pierce, 1974; Barbarin, 1983; Cross, 1984, for extended discussions).

Pierce (1974) argues that the overriding psychiatric (psychological) problem for blacks is the "withering effect of racism" (p. 512). Jones (1972) and Pierce (1974) have extensive discussions of racism and its impacts on blacks and the black community. While Pierce defines white racism as behavior that results from the attitude that white skin (and whites) are always superior to black skin (and blacks), Jones has a more detailed discussion of the different levels of racism: individual, institutional and cultural. For Jones, individual racism refers to individual acts of discrimination or violence and attitudes of prejudice and paternalism that grow out of a belief in the genetic inferiority of blacks to whites. Institutional racism refers to institutional patterns—of resource allocation, entry, expectation, or outcome—that consistently lead to different and more negative status for blacks than for whites. Cultural racism refers to the ideologies and values that undergird the other forms of racism; racist values that are perpetuated by the mass media, schools, and churches. While Jones (1972) and other writers emphasize different themes, three key racist cultural themes emerge from a survey of the literature: 1) blacks as unattractive and not socially valuable; 2) blacks as unable to be effective in the world: unable to achieve, to effectively manage people or events, unable to compete with whites; and 3) what Pettigrew (1964) calls Id-oriented stereotypes—blacks as sexually and aggressively impulsive and uncontrolled. These, then, may be key cultural themes of racism to which the black individual (and community) are forced to adapt.

Most black Americans must adapt to both the black community and its culture as well as white American culture and institutions. While most blacks live, have families, social friends and churches within the black community, they still must adapt to white-run schools, workplaces, military settings, and media, an adaptation that often requires them to juggle different values, behavioral styles and aspirations. This situation has led some social scientists to postulate that many blacks become bicultural; i.e., able to function in both cultures.

There is another aspect of social reality that blacks must adapt to as well. Cross (1984) exhaustively documents a family poverty rate and an adult unemployment rate for black Americans that are double those for whites. He notes the family income and wealth gap and lower access to quality medical and other social services that blacks suffer from as well. Cross also demonstrates the continuing relative political and economic powerlessness of blacks and the black community. He links these social conditions to the historic and current discrimination and institutional racism that he sees as continuing constraints and frustrations for blacks. Barbarin (1983) points out that these social conditions mean more stressors for blacks and fewer resources than whites have to cope with them.

In summary, black adults must adapt to racism in its different variants, black and white cultures, poverty, and political powerlessness. They often have the support of black families and friends, the black community and its institutions, and black culture in their attempts to successfully adapt. Which issues and conflicts are the central ones they must adapt to, given the social/cultural context, and which psychosocial characteristics are "adaptive" or "healthy" for black adults are questions any adequate model of black adult psychological health must address.

"Universal" Models of Psychological Health

What do existing "universal" models of psychological health contribute to an understanding of black adult psychological health? This review of existing models will utilize the work of George and Brooker (1984), who analyzed conceptions of psychological health and came up with four categories that grouped them. Modifying their format by drawing on the work of Lazarus (1975) yields six categories that will organize a brief discussion of existing "universal" models of psychological health. The categories are: 1) freedom from illness; 2) being average; 3) an ideal personality type; 4) using multiple criteria to determine psychological health; 5) a developmental/life-span perspective; 6) a stress/adaptation approach.

Freedom from symptoms or illness is the most medical model of psychological health. Health is the absence of illness, and implicitly the ability to function adequately. Psychological health defined as being essentially like the average or "modal" member of society, or being "adjusted" to one's social/cultural surroundings were once common models in the literature. However, both concepts are rarely used now. "Adjustment" seems to evoke conformity and blandness for many theorists, and a culture-bound notion that they want to transcend. Health as the absence of illness has also been criticized by theorists (see Maslow, 1968) who stress the importance of "positive" characteristics like creativity, "growth," and self-actualization in psychological functioning. The "ideal personality" approach has a number of exponents: S. Freud and his concept of the "genital character" and A. Maslow's model of the "self-actualizer" are the most widely known. Freud is reputed to have said that the healthy person should be able to "love and to work," that is, to make a balanced commitment to a heterosexual love "object" and productive work. The abilities to have unconflicted sexual and emotional expression and to work productively are expressions of the full maturity of the "genital character." The final stage of psychosexual development, the genital stage, is reached by those whose sexual, emotional, and interpersonal development was not damaged and fixated at an earlier psychosexual stage. The genital character is an ideal of balanced psychological forces, functioning, and rationality that is never actually attained by any individual.

A. Maslow (1968), writing from a humanistic perspective, described a healthy person as a "self-actualizer," someone who is moving towards fulfilling (or has fulfilled) their unique human potential. We all have an inherent motivation towards growth or self-actualization, Maslow felt, that would flower if society allowed more primitive needs to be satisfied (e.g., hunger, safety). Maslow investigated the personality characteristics of self-actualizers by reviewing biographies of prominent figures and his friends and drawing up a list of common traits. He arrived at fifteen, ranging from accurate perception of reality, the ability to be intimate with others, and the capacity to have mystical experiences, to creativity. Self-actualizers are rare, and probably should be seen as the Olympic athletes of mental health—if, as many wonder, they exist.

Marie Jahoda's (1958) classic discussion of the six themes of "positive mental health" perhaps best represents the "multiple criteria" approach to psychological health. "Positive mental health" refers to the stance that psychological or mental health is more than the absence of symptoms of mental disorder, it involves the presence of "positive," "healthy" characteristics. Based on the social science literature and discussions with colleagues, she came up with six aspects of the healthy person: 1) positive and realistic attitudes towards the self; 2) growth and self-actualization,; 3) integration or a balance of psychological forces and consequently stress resistance; 4) autonomy; 5) accurate perception of reality; and 6) environmental mastery—the ability to love, work, and play, efficiency in problem solving, etc. Jahoda did not specify how, or if, the six criteria are interrelated.

Erik Erikson's (1968) elaboration and extension of Freud's model is probably the most sophisticated example of the developmental/life-span approach to psychological health. Erikson analyzed the human life cycle in terms of eight different stages of ego development. Each stage is a crisis or turning point that involves a basic psychological issue that can have a healthy or pathological outcome that has implications for the next stage of life. Erikson emphasized the role of social and cultural factors on development, as well as sexual and unconscious ones, and analyzed their impact on personality development over the whole life cycle. He postulated that four stages (of eight) are adulthood:

V) Ego identity vs. role confusion—where the healthy outcome is identity and role confusion the pathological outcome; VI) Intimacy vs. Isolation; VII) Generativity vs. Stagnation; and VIII) Ego Integrity vs. Despair. Erikson states that the outcome of each of these stages is a dynamic balance; with health representing a favorable ratio, not perfection. His work is the basis for much of the recent life-span developmental research focusing on mid-life.

A sizeable amount of literature has developed in recent decades that examines the stress/adaptation model and the links between stress, coping mechanisms, and the level of subjective well-being or distress experienced by an individual or group. Stress has been defined in many ways; but all definitions involve an environmental demand to which the person must react, one that is perceived of as at least potentially exceeding the person's ability or resources to meet it. Coping refers to efforts to master environmental demands when a previous response is unavailable or ineffective. The stressor and the coping response(s) are linked by the cognitive appraisal of the stressor and the internal/external resources of the individual. Cognitive appraisal refers to the significance and meaning attached to the stressor. Internal resources are individual factors; i.e., personality traits, racial identification, social class, and cultural beliefs. External resources refer to family or social ties, work relationships, church affiliation, etc. Outcome refers to either short or long-term psychological distress and symptoms or adaptive behavior and subjective health. The model then is: stressor(s), an appraisal of the stressor(s) and the person's internal/external resources which in turn produces a coping response that leads to an adaptive or distressful outcome. There is also feedback between elements of the model; i.e., the outcome can modify the coping response and/or appraisal of the stressor (see Barbarin, 1983; and Cervantes and Castro, 1985 for extended discussions).

While all existing models of psychological health fail to meet the criteria for an ideal model of black adult psychological health, each has its areas of strength and weakness. "Freedom from symptoms" and being average" or "adjusted" have the virtues of being straightforward and potentially measurable. However, their atheoretical nature, and for "adjustment," culture-bound stance, limit their usefulness. The "ideal personality" model, especially Freud's "genital character," has the asset of being tied to personality theory and more general psychological theories. It also presents a unified, detailed picture of the psychologically healthy adult, and in Freud's case a picture of development and pathology. However, the lack of a social/cultural framework for understanding adult psychological health and the neglect of development(s) during the adult years are real weaknesses. The difficulty in empirically defining and investigating the model as well as the implicit assumption that either no actual adult or very few are psychologically healthy limits its usefulness.

The multiple criteria, developmental, and stress models all seem to be more useful in understanding psychological health among blacks. The multiple criterion approach specifies that psychological health has a number of definable dimensions that may be related, but may also be independent of one another. Implicit in the approach is the idea that the dimensions are measurable and can be empirically investigated. However, variants of this model are often not tied to theory, don't have a developmental or social/cultural perspective, and don't consider gender differences. Because Erikson discusses the whole life cycle, points to the importance of society and culture, and forges clear links to theory, his developmental approach has a number of strengths. He also points out that psychological health is a matter of a "dynamic balance" or a favorable ratio of positive to negative psychological aspects—not perfection—a useful corrective. Unfortunately, relatively little empirical investigation of his work has occurred. The stress/adaptation model has a number of strengths too: it inherently takes the social/cultural environment of the person into account, can look at different points in the life cycle, is open to empirical measurement and investigation, and is linked to social/psychological theory. However, generally work based on this model has been focused at the group level of analysis, rather than the individual, so that applying findings to assess or describe a psychologically healthy individual is often difficult.

R. Lazarus (1975), in a comprehensive review of existing models and research on psychological health, makes two observations that are important for a discussion of "universal" models. First, Lazarus points out a central issue: the role of values. The question of why "autonomy might be considered an essential characteristic of health and "creativity" not, confronts the role that the values of the theorist, investigator, or community play in defining psychological health. Lazarus argues that it is impossible to objectively define "optimal," "effective," or "healthy" functioning because at least implicit in the discussion is a conception of what is a good or desirable behavior, emotion, or way of life. Lazarus argues that theorists and investigators need to explicitly state their position in this inevitable aspect of describing or defining psychological health and attempt to empirically investigate the consequences of favoring one value over another (e.g., autonomy over creativity). Implicit in his discussion is the question of whose values, or which community's perspective, will determine what are "healthy" or "positive" characteristics or functioning.

Second, Lazarus addresses the issue of the central characteristics of the psychologically healthy person. He does so by surveying the major theorists and attempting to identify areas of consensus on central characteristics. He identifies five: 1) Acceptance of self; 2) The ability to be intimate with others; 3) Competence (Freud's work?); 4) Accurate perception of reality; 5) Autonomy and independence (Lazarus, 1975, pp. 16-18). Relating the social/cultural realities facing the black individual and the central characteristics of the healthy person listed by Lazarus, it seems clear that the social/cultural context facing the black individual compromises or renders more difficult attainment of a positive status on Lazarus' characteristics. For example, Lazarus lists acceptance of self and a sense of competence as key aspects of the healthy person. Certainly for blacks, given their unique social/cultural circumstance and its demands, attaining both is a more complex and problematic enterprise than it is for their white American peers. Unfortunately, existing "universal" models of psychological health give little guidance in understanding that complex process.

Traditional Theories of Black Personality and Identity

While little direct theorizing or research on the topic of psychological health among black adults occurred in mainstream social science literature, a substantial literature on black personality and identity was produced. Given the prevailing assumptions and findings about black personality or black identity, little needed to be said about psychological health; rather, the focus was on emotional disorder and social pathology among blacks. A brief review of mainstream work about black personality will point out the assumed barriers to black psychological health more clearly and put recent work in context. The mainstream view of black personality and identity has a number of variants; but the basic model is that living in a racist white society, where blacks are viewed and treated as inferior, and where they are in poverty in a powerless community, leads blacks early in life to internalize negative beliefs and negative feelings about themselves and other blacks. Explanations of exactly how the internalization occurs and its precise impacts vary with the theoretical orientation of the writer (see Kardiner and Ovesey, 1951; Karon, 1958; Pettigrew, 1964; Thomas and Sillen, 1972). The most influential example of the psychological approach has been Kardiner and Ovesey's *Mark of Oppression* (1951). Kardiner and Ovesey were Freudian psychiatrists whose central idea was that a group of people who live under the same institutional and environmental conditions will have similar mental and emotional processes, or a "basic personality" in common. Since American blacks live under similar caste and social class barriers they should possess a basic personality that differs from that of American whites. To understand "black personality," they studied 25 black New York City residents. Their subjects were psychoanalytically interviewed for from 20 to 100 sessions and administered the Rorschach and T.A.T. tests. Male and female as well as lower and middle class blacks were studied; 12 were patients in psychotherapy, 11 were paid subjects, and two volunteered.

Kardiner and Ovesey concluded that blacks did have a "basic personality" that was different and more damaged than that of white Americans. Black personality was centrally organized around adapting to social discrimination (racism) they argued. Racist behavior by whites reveals an unpleasant image of the self to the black individual who internalizes it and feels worthless, unlovable, and unsuccessful. In essence, he or she feels low self-esteem that eventually is elaborated into self-hatred and idealization of whites. In addition, the frustrations of racist behavior arouse aggression, which cannot be expressed because of the caste situation, so it must be controlled and contained. Kardiner and Ovesey argued that this repressed aggression usually led to low self-esteem, depression and passivity.

Grier and Cobbs (1969) used a number of elements of this approach in their discussion of black psychology in the book *Black Rage*. They seem to differentiate between a male and female basic personality. Black male personality revolves around the control of aggression through repression, passivity, or explosion. The family, particularly mothers, socializes males against the direct expression of aggressiveness in childhood and their social roles in adult life reinforce the lesson. Black women have their feminine narcissism (self-love) wounded because they cannot be the white ideal of femininity; their central concern, therefore, becomes maintaining self-esteem. Grier and Cobbs saw turning away from heterosexual life towards maternal functions or becoming depressed as typical ways black women cope with this dilemma.

Grier and Cobbs (1969) also developed a model of black psychological health that they called the *Black Norm*. The *Black Norm* is a body of personality traits that all American blacks share. "It also encompasses adaptive devices developed in response to a peculiar environment," which are seen as "normal devices for making it in America" for blacks (p. 178). The black norm consists of cultural paranoia, cultural depression and masochism, and cultural anti-socialism. While providing little detail for their formulations, Grier and Cobbs seem to say that American blacks share a mistrust of whites as individuals, distrust white society's laws, and have each developed a sadness and an "intimacy with misery" in reaction to racism. Grier and Cobbs say little about variation by age, class, gender, or region in these characteristics, nor do they provide any non-clinical empirical evidence for them.

While the "Mark of Oppression" model and traditional social science approaches have substantial theoretical and empirical support (see

McCarthy and Yancey, 1971; Taylor, 1976 for reviews), challenges to them have recently developed. Social scientists have questioned the model's assumptions, noting that given the social and cultural diversity of the black community, postulating one reaction pattern to racism or one set of personality traits seems unreasonable. Some observers have also noted that the black family, institutions, and community can serve as mediators of the negative messages from white society (see Barnes, 1980) and as sources for alternative frames of reference and significant others for black children and adults (see Taylor, 1976). In addition, black identity need not be negative or only have an insignificant effect on the psychological functioning or behavior of the black individual (see Cross, 1980).

The most striking challenge to this tradition has been the findings of recent studies that run counter to the predicted personality characteristics of blacks. In fact, black children and adults have been shown to have equivalent levels of self-esteem when compared with whites (see McCarthy and Yancey, 1971; Taylor, 1976 for reviews; Heiss and Owens, 1972; Edwards, 1974; Veroff, Douvan, Kulka, 1981; Jensen, White, and Galliher, 1982), and to show no more symptoms, diagnoses of psychopathology, or reported psychological distress than whites (Yancey, Rigsby, and McCarthy, 1972; Veroff, Douvan, & Kulka, 1981; see Neighbors, 1984 for review). In addition, the prediction of more repressed aggression or more aggression directed against other blacks rather than whites receives only mixed support in a brief review of studies by Guterman (1972, 231-233).

To summarize, how successful are existing theories in explaining and describing black adult psychological health over the adult life cycle? Clearly no existing theory meets the criteria for an "ideal" model of black adult psychological health. A number of the "universal" theories have positive points and ideas; e.g., Erikson's life-cycle perspective, and his idea that health is a dynamic balance, not perfection. However, all of them leave large areas unexplored, often the social/cultural factors that have an impact on health—a crucial lack for a model of black American adult psychological health. While theories addressing black personality and identity do discuss social and cultural factors, their focus on the "inevitable" pathological outcome and impact for the black adult, and their assumption of little diversity in reactions to social factors and in the black community limit their explanatory usefulness as well.

While no existing theory will serve as a satisfactory explanatory or descriptive model of black adult psychological health, it is possible to synthesize aspects of existing theory, the discussion of the social/cultural situation of American blacks, and Lazarus' "consensus" characteristics to point to central issues an adequate theory would address. Based on the work cited earlier, several psychological issues can be hypothesized as important for the black individual throughout the adult life cycle: 1) maintaining an overall positive conception of the self; 2) maintaining a positive conception of blacks as a group and a positive sense of connection and involvement with the black community and its culture; 3) maintaining an accurate perception of the social environment (including its racism); 4) adapting to both black and white community/cultures and using effective, non-destructive ways to cope with both; 5) developing and maintaining emotional intimacy with others; 6) maintaining a sense of competence and the ability to work productively. How successfully an individual confronts these issues and the balance between successful and dysfunctional adaptation may be the measure of psychological health for a black adult. Certainly, an adequate theory of black adult psychological health would have to describe and explain how the black person developed and maintained a positive status on these issues.

Recent Empirical Research

The findings of recent empirical studies of self-esteem and psychological distress cited above stand in stark contrast to the conclusion that no black American adults are able to successfully adapt to the key psychological tasks that face them. Investigations of blacks in several other areas also challenge the mainstream view and address issues central to black psychological health as well—specifically studies in the areas of racial identity, the competent personality, and coping with stress. Unfortunately, no general model and little theorizing has emerged from this work. In addition, only scattered work has emerged in other areas related to psychological health, like intimacy and interpersonal relations or involvement in group or individual action to combat racism—an important lack. Existing research will be reviewed in the areas of self-conception—self-esteem and racial identity, competent personality, and coping with stress in order to assess current findings and draw theoretical implications where appropriate. This review will cite studies that are central to the area discussed or ones that illustrate important trends in the literature. Comments in each area will be based on cited studies as well as a wider reading of the literature.

Self-conception

Self-conception, variously defined and conceptualized, has been at the heart of much of the research and theorizing done about African

Americans. Low self-esteem, self-hatred, and a negative racial identity have been the characteristics traditionally attributed to black children and adults. Recent research on self-esteem and racial identity challenges these traditional findings and offers new evidence about how some blacks positively adapt to one of the central psychological tasks facing them: establishing and maintaining a positive sense of self— both individually and as a member of a group.

Self-esteem Self-esteem is usually defined as the evaluative dimension of the self-concept. The person is thought to have global, i.e., overall, self-esteem that can range from very positive to very negative. Global self-esteem is often thought to be the summing up of the person's self-esteem in a number of specific areas, ranging from physical self to academic self. Adult self-esteem is typically measured using paper and pencil personality or self-esteem inventories or projective tests or, more rarely, interviews.

A number of comprehensive reviews and excellent studies of black self-esteem have been published in the last 15 years. Perhaps the most comprehensive was done by Cross (1985), who reviewed 161 studies of black self-concept done between 1939 and 1977, studies conducted using child and adult subjects. Some 101 of these studies involved self-esteem; of those, 71% showed black self-esteem to be equal to or to exceed that for whites, 16% found whites with higher levels of self-esteem, and 13% had mixed results. Taylor (1976) in a comprehensive review of theory and studies of child and adult self-esteem, reached similar conclusions. Large sample studies of black and white adult self-esteem by Yancey, Rigsby, and McCarthy (1972) and by Heiss and Owens (1972) found that the two groups had essentially equal overall self-esteem. Veroff, Douvan, and Kulka (1981), using national survey data, found blacks and white American adults to have equivalent overall self-esteem and equivalent self-esteem in a number of areas. Unfortunately, little information about black self-esteem at different points in the adult life cycle exists.

What are the sources of positive black self-esteem? Discussing children and youth, Taylor (1976) and Gibbs (1985) found that the key factor for the level of a black child's self-esteem is the general attitude of significant others towards the child. Parents, peers, and teachers are significant others for black children. For the vast majority of black children, and by extension black adults, these significant others are black. Therefore, a black social context is their primary source of social comparisons and self-evaluation—evaluations that are often positive. Barnes (1980) also argues that, under certain conditions, the black family and community can act as mediators or filters of negative, racist images and messages for the black child or youth (and adults). McCarthy and Yancey (1971) argue that black adults use other blacks as significant others, that they use criteria of worth relevant to the black community to evaluate themselves, and that a "system-blame" explanation of failure is available to cushion blows to self-esteem. Heiss and Owens (1972) empirically investigated these ideas with a large-sample study of black and white adults. They looked at global self-esteem and how these adults evaluated different aspects of the self (e.g., self as parent, intelligent, athlete). While they found rough equality overall between groups, there was variation between each race on different traits (and by the four race-sex groups as well). They argued that their results indicated that variation occurred because of the variations in the type of significant others used by blacks, likelihood of blacks using dominant society standards of evaluation (vs. black community ones), and differences in the availability of a system-blame explanation for each aspect of self-esteem.

In summary, recent research points out that: 1) blacks and whites have equivalent global self-esteem; 2) blacks often use other blacks, not whites, as their significant others; 3) other mechanisms may be available to insulate black self-esteem, e.g., a "system blame" explanation of negative events, or the use of black cultural (vs. white) standards of evaluation; and 4) blacks and whites may not have equivalent evaluations of different aspects of the self.

Racial Identity

Racial identity has been discussed extensively in the social science literature using various terms and measures. Black identity, group identity, group self-concept, "sense of peoplehood," "sense of blackness" are all terms used and measured by workers in the field. No consensus on concept definition, measurement technique, or links to personality theory has emerged, however. Much of the work in the field seems to assume that black identity is strongly linked to personal self-esteem, but usually makes that link a theoretical postulate rather than empirically demonstrating it.

Cross (1985), in a comprehensive review of 22 studies of "reference group orientation" (group identity, race awareness) done from 1968 to 1977 found that in 68% (15 studies) black subjects (children and adults), showed positive black identities, in 27% (6) negative ones, and in 5% (1) a mixed pattern. Surveying studies back to 1939 and one longitudinal study, he argues that "black parents present both the black and white worlds to their children . . . black children, and perhaps black people in general, have a dual [black and white] reference group orientation" (Cross, 1985, p. 169). Cross sees this dual reference group orientation as adaptive and healthy for black Americans.

Although few studies have investigated the racial identities of black adults a number have looked at the racial identities of black adolescents. Gurin and Epps(1975) investigated black identity and self-hatred by interviewing 600 southern black college students in 1965 as part of a larger study. They found what they saw as a typical pattern of black identity: a predominantly positive black identity for most black students and a small subgroup of students who had a predominantly negative identity. Ramseur (1975) looked longitudinally at the racial identities of black freshmen and cross-sectionally at a sample of black upperclassmen at Harvard College. He found two independent dimensions: "Salience of racial issues" and "Acceptance of black ideology" (separatism, community control). Both dimensions were significantly linked to race-related social/extracurricular activities at college, but not to academic achievement. Gibbs (1974) interviewed 41 black college student clients at Stanford's Counseling Center and categorized them based on their orientation towards the dominant white culture at the university. Her categories were affirmation, assimilation, separation, and withdrawal. Affirmation was the most adaptive mode, involving "movement with the dominant culture". It was a mode marked by "self-acceptance, positive[black] identity . . . high achievement motivation, and autonomous self-actualizing behavior" (Gibbs, 1974, p. 736). Perhaps the best known and most widely researched model of black identity and identity development is Cross's (1980) model of the conversion from "Negro" to "black." He has sometimes referred to his (and Charles Thomas') perspective as that of "psychological nigrescence," the process of becoming "black." He describes five stages: 1) Pre-encounter—the person is a "Negro" and accepts a "white" view of self, other blacks, and the world. 2) Encounter—some shocking personal or social event makes the person receptive to new views of being black and the world. This encounter precipitates an intense search for black identity. 3) Immersion—an emotional period ensues where the person glorifies anything black and attempts to purge him or herself of their former world-view and old behavior. 4) Internalization—the person makes his/her new values their own and blacks their primary reference groups. This stage and the next, 5) Internalization-Commitment, are characterized by positive self-esteem, ideological flexibility and openness about one's blackness. In the fifth stage the person finds activities and commitments to express his or her new identity.

Cross clearly sees the person in stage Five-Internalization-Commitment as the "ideal," that is, psychologically healthy black person. They have made their new pro-black identity and values their own. They have a "calm, secure demeanor" characterized by "ideological flexibility, psychological openness and self-confidence about one's blackness" (Cross, 1980, p. 86). Blacks are a primary reference group, but the person has lost his prejudices about race, sex, age and social class. He or she also struggles to translate their values into behavior that will benefit the black community. Cross seems to see the "Negro to black" conversion process as an African American model of self-actualization under oppressive social conditions. Blacks in Stage Five would then be black self-actualizers. Cross has yet to follow up this idea, and says elsewhere that basic personality structure remains the same after the process. It seems that key aspects of racial identity change, however.

Cross (1980) points to a number of studies that seem to validate his stage model and to say that his stages exist independently and occur in the sequence he describes. However, the family and social conditions that lead all blacks to the "Pre-encounter" stage or that support the Stage 5—Internalization/Commitment phase are unspecified. In addition, class, gender, and regional differences in the prevalence of people at different stages and theorizing about those differences are largely missing from his work as well (For a comprehensive review of research in this area see Cross, Parham, & Helms, in press).

In summary, 1) many blacks have a predominantly positive racial identity, with perhaps a minority having a negative identity; 2) black identity has links to behavior; and 3) black identity can have links to other attitudes and personality characteristics. However, the issue of whether an individual's type (positive, negative) of black identity is linked to their level of personal self-esteem seems unresolved. While Cross (1985), Clark (1982), and Houston (1984) find no evidence for such a link, Gibbs (1974), Parham and Helms (1985a, 1985b), and Wright (1985) do find empirical evidence for it.

Competent Personality

M. B. Smith (1968) describes competence as an important aspect of personality functioning. He bases his discussion on the theoretical work of Robert White (1960) and his empirical study of "competent" Peace Corps volunteers. Smith sees the competent person as having views of the self, the world and behaviors that fit together, and are trans-cultural (and trans-racial). The person has positive self-esteem, but more importantly a sense of potency and efficacy in the world—a sense he or she can cause desirable things to happen. The person also has "hope" about the world—an attitude that effort can achieve results in the real world. Smith also describes a behavioral component to competence, since he expects the competent person to set "realistic," moderately challenging goals for himself. Tyler (1978), with a conception of competence similar to Smith's, explored the idea that competence is a configuration of personality traits, attitudes toward the world, and behaviors. Focusing on Rotter's Internal-External control dimension, level of trust (rather than Smith's hope) and an "active coping orientation" that has behavioral attributes like realistic goal setting, he surveyed three samples of college students. He found that the configuration held across the three samples and was independent of social desirability and aptitude.

Unfortunately, studies focusing on "competent" adult blacks are sparse. Ramseur (1982), in a study of stress and coping mechanisms among "successful" (competent) black administrators at white universities, surveyed the literature and interviewed six "successful" male and female black administrators. The interviewed administrators were found to have high self-esteem and realism about the self and their work environment. They were also planful and had set career strategies for themselves in ways that pointed to a high sense of internal control. These administrators also seemed to positively identify with being black and took a pragmatic view of race-related issues and problems they confronted.

A number of studies have had adolescents as their focus. Looney and Lewis (1983) examined 11 "competent" working-class black adolescents and 11 upper-middle class white ones. The black (and white) youngsters were strikingly secure and open, were described as "doers"—active and self-assertive, as generally good students, and as having wide networks of friends. The authors described their "competent" families, all of whom were two-parent ones, as having open communication, openness with affection, a focus on efficiently solving problems, as encouraging the development of autonomy, and as showing high emotional support of members. Lee (1984,1985) studied competent black adolescents in a rural county in the deep South. In his 1984 study of these academically and socially "successful" students, Lee found them to have "positive, but realistic" views of the self, an internal locus of control, high achievement motivation, and strong social networks outside the family. Students described their families as having a high degree of open communication, and their parents as "strict," or close to it, in terms of rules and discipline. Lee rated most of them as having low to moderate levels of "black consciousness". Griffin and Korchin (1980) initially interviewed 6 junior college faculty members for their descriptions of the "ideal" competent personality for an adolescent black male. These faculty members then nominated "competent" black male students (13) who were studied along with "average" peers (10) who volunteered for the study. Faculty members, both black and white, saw competent male black adolescents similarly: as able to adapt to many different settings—academic and social; as goal oriented, with realistic, flexible goals; and as able to be disciplined and self-confident in the face of difficult conditions. Both competent and average students scored as "well-adjusted," on Offer's self-image questionnaire and in general seemed to be functioning effectively. Competent males, however, were more inner-directed, more ambitious, goal-striving more vigorously, and less concerned with their acceptability to others than were their "average" peers.

The ability to draw conclusions from the studies in this area is limited by a number of methodological problems. The differing definitions of "competence" used in the studies, small sample sizes, the usual lack of a control group, the focus on adolescents as subjects (see also Edwards, 1976), and the lack of discussion of gender differences combine to limit the force of conclusions that can be drawn. However, trends do emerge: 1) Positive self-esteem, a high sense of efficacy, active coping strategies ("a doer"), being achievement oriented, and having good social relations, are characteristics that seem to regularly occur together; 2) At least a mildly positive identification with blacks and a pragmatic view of race relations were also regularly present; and 3) Certain family backgrounds seem most common for competent black individuals: high family stability, both marital and residential, high emotional support generally, and encouragement of academic achievement. Clear rules and regulations at home ("strictness") was another common finding, along with "competents" being first-borns.

Stress/Adaptation

In recent years, a number of studies have looked at links between aspects of stress, (appraisal, coping resources, coping styles) and the level of psychological well-being or distress of black adults. This section will briefly review work on the appraisal of stress, external and internal coping resources, and the coping styles of black adults.

Appraisal   Do blacks and whites differ in their appraisal of the severity or meaning of different stressors? Little systematic information exists on these questions, but there are some suggestive studies. Komaroff, Masuda, and Holmes (1968) compared whites, blacks, and Mexican-Americans on their assessment of the amount of adaptation required by certain life-change events (e.g., marriage, moving). The three groups of low income subjects rank-ordered the items in similar fashion, with blacks and Mexican-Americans in closest agreement.

Barbarin (1983) in a review of stress and appraisal among black families, pointed to three factors that might be important in blacks' appraisal of stress: religious orientation, causal attributions of undesirable events to racial discrimination, and "paradoxical" control beliefs. He argued that personal religiosity and involvement in organized religion can enhance coping by providing a basis for optimism and a cognitive framework for understanding stressful episodes. He also found in an empirical study (Barbarin et al., 1981) that blacks more frequently interpret negative life outcomes in terms of individual and institutional discrimination than do whites. In addition, based on that 1981 study, he argued that blacks often have "paradoxical" control attributions. This means they have a sense of personal efficacy but at the same time the sense that blacks as a group have little control over their destiny. Overall, then, his work suggests a type or style of appraisal for African Americans that differs from that of white Americans.

External coping resources A number of researchers have examined the topic of external resources that blacks use to cope with stress. A quote cited by George and McNamara (1984) summarizes many of the findings well:

> We know black people have a history of being religious and oriented towards their kinship and friendship networks for buffering the stresses of life, but we were surprised by the extent to which the data [from American blacks] reveal family and church to be essential elements in the lives of our respondents (*ISR Newsletter*, 1983: 7).

Neff (1985), in a brief review, points out that adjusting for age and social class, blacks show higher levels than whites for church attendance, interaction with friends, enjoyment of clubs, and help from both friends and relatives. Blacks also more often had a family member nearby, had contact with relatives living close by, and were somewhat more likely than whites to perceive relatives as available sources of help.

Blacks have also been found to rely more than whites on informal social networks (family, friends) than formal ones to cope with stress (Gibson, 1982; Barbarin, 1983). Neighbors, Jackson, et al. (1983) found that for *all* socio-demographic groups of black adults in a national survey sample, informal social networks were used first and more substantially than formal sources of help. Gibson (1982), in a reanalysis of national survey data from 1957 and 1976, looked at middle-aged and elderly black adults' resources and coping styles. She found that blacks in middle and late life were more likely to seek help from friends (1957) and from a combination of family members (1976) than were whites. That is, whites were more likely to only turn to a spouse or one family member with their worries than were blacks. This difference held even when all social variables were held constant. Gibson also found that blacks shifted from talking with friends in middle years to multiple family members in later years.

In addition, other studies point to the importance of supportive social and kin networks. For example, Holahan, et al. (1983) studying working-class black and white women found that black women with high social network scores (friends, neighborhood contacts, job) showed mental health levels similar to white women. Those black women low in social integration showed mental health scores in the pathological range. All measures of social integration showed a much greater relation to mental health scores for black women than white. Dressler (1985) studied the ability of the extended black family to buffer stress. He linked recent stressful events, chronic stress, kin and non-kin support, and depression for black subjects. Those black adults who perceived their kin to be supportive reported fewer symptoms of depression. The number of kin and non-kin support sources were not related to depression. However, there was no buffering effect for chronic stressors, like economic problems. Dressler defined support as money, information, and help with tasks for both sexes.

Internal coping resources   Religion has historically played a powerful role in the life of the black community and for black individuals. It apparently continues to do so given recent research findings. George and McNamara (1984) note that studies have found blacks to be more frequent church attenders than whites. Their re-analysis of 1972-1982 national survey data which looked at religion, subjective life satisfaction, and health produced several striking findings: 1) For blacks, far more than for whites, a sense of well-being seems markedly enhanced by religious attendance and by stated strength of religious affiliation, at *all* levels of age, education and income. Black women seem to derive most life satisfaction from church attendance and black men from stated strength of religious affiliation ("religiosity"). For both sexes, their respective measures of religious involvement are highly predictive of global happiness, subjective health, and satisfaction with family life.

Bowman (1985) used a national survey sample of black husband/fathers to examine the links between stress (employment difficulties and consequent difficulties fulfilling the provider role in the family), coping resources, and psychological well-being (here, "subjective life happiness"). Bowman examined five coping resources—multiple economic providers, family closeness, non-kin friendship, racial ideology (system-blame), and religious orientation. He found that religious orientation had a much stronger positive effect on the level of life happiness among black fathers than did family cohesion or any other informal coping resource investigated.

Harrison, Bowman, and Beale (1985) used a national sample of black working mothers to investigate the links between stress (role strains from being a worker and a mother), coping resources, and psychological well-being. They examined five coping resources—religious orientation, family closeness, best friend, child care availability, and child care advice. They found that religious orientation was the most important coping resource followed by family closeness. They also found that the five coping resources together significantly offset the stress from role strain these black mothers experienced and therefore positively affected their psychological well-being.

Coping styles   Neighbors, Jackson et al. (1983), Barbarin (1983), and Gibson (1982) found prayer to be the most common coping response to worries or stressful episodes for blacks. Moreover, prayer was used substantially more by black adults at all age ranges than by whites. Neighbors found that the coping response ranked "most helpful" by blacks after prayer was an instrumental one: "Facing the problem squarely and doing something about it." Neighbors found that among subjects with economic difficulties lower income people were more likely to use prayer as a coping strategy; and that overall a majority of blacks using prayer found that it made economic troubles "easier to bear" (Neighbors & Jackson et al., 1983). Perhaps there is a fusion of external resource (church association) with internal resource (religiosity), and coping style (use of prayer) for many black adults.

Lykes (1983) studied how 52 "successful" black women coped with incidents of racial and sexual discrimination over their life histories. The women were 70 or older at the time of the study and Lykes worked from transcripts of their oral histories. The study and findings were complex; but, in part, she found that these black women were discriminating and adaptive in their use of coping responses in response to situational demands and constraints. She also found that directness (confrontation vs. indirect) and flexibility (use of several strategies) of coping were independent dimensions of coping style for these women.

Several findings emerge from these studies of stress and coping: while black adults may not differ from others in their appraisal of the stressfulness of particular events, they may have a cognitive framework for appraising stress that is significantly different from that of white Americans. In addition, blacks seem to rely on informal social networks (kin, friends) to buffer stress to a significantly greater degree than white adults. Religious involvement—church attendance, "religiosity"—is also an important factor in buffering stress for many black adults. There are some suggestive findings that point to typical patterns of coping with stress by black adults, that is, use of resources and coping styles, that may differ significantly from those of their white peers.

Conclusion

What are the social and psychological characteristics of psychologically healthy black adults and how do they change over the life
cycle? No existing theory or model satisfactorily addresses these questions. While "universal" models of psychological health offer some positive perspectives and ideas, they generally have little to say about the
unique social-cultural context of African Americans. Other models that
focus on black personality and identity have generally assumed pathological reactions and a lack of diversity of reaction to the social/cultural
context by blacks. While neither body of theory provides an adequate
model, taken together, along with work on the social and cultural situation of American blacks, they do provide a basis for hypothesizing
about the central psychological issues for black adult psychological
health. Those issues are: 1) maintaining globally positive self-conception; 2) maintaining a positive group (black)identity and community
connection; 3) maintaining an accurate perception of the social environment—including its racism; 4) effectively adapting to the social environment confronting a black individual—coping with its stressors
and adapting to both black and white cultures; 5) developing and maintaining emotional intimacy with others; 6) maintaining a sense of competence and the ability to work productively.

What are the major findings of recent empirical research in areas
important for black adult psychological health? In the area of self-conception recent research has pointed out that many black adults have
positive self-esteem, that they use blacks as significant others, and that
they use a black social context for their social comparisons and self-
evaluations. In addition, black adults may use "system-blame" explanations of failure to protect their self-esteem. Other studies point out that
many blacks have positive or largely positive racial identities and that
racial identity has links to behavior and other personality characteristics. Black adults may also have a cognitive framework for appraising
stress that is significantly different from their white peers. They also
appear to use different internal and external resources to buffer stress:
relying on informal social networks and religious involvement to a
greater degree than do whites. These different types of appraisal and
resource use may be tied to unique black coping styles. Other research
on competence indicates that positive self-esteem, a sense of personal
efficacy, active coping strategies, achievement orientation, good social
relations, and a positive racial identity may regularly occur together to
form what might be called a "black competent personality". Certain
family backgrounds and childrearing practices also seem associated
with these characteristics.

What are the implications of these theories and recent research?

Several central ones stand out: 1) Some black American adults possess "positive" or "healthy" psychological characteristics and functioning. Theories or models that postulate universal pathology or pathological outcomes are clearly unhelpful and do not fit current findings; 2) Particularly in the area of self-esteem, some of the sources and mechanisms that maintain these "healthy" characteristics are being identified, theorized about, and empirically investigated; 3) Developing new models and expanding current theory is a vital task at this point, particularly outside of the area of self-esteem. For example, a rigorous definition of the dimensions of black identity and its links to other aspects of self-conception, personality, and behavior would be extremely useful. A clear definition and conceptualization of the black "competent personality" would also be helpful. Examining emotional intimacy and interpersonal relations among blacks would be a valuable addition. Forging theoretical links with other traditions and newer theories in psychology and sociology are other necessities. Rutter's (1979) discussion of "protective factors" and more recent discussions of the "invulnerability" of some children in the face of stress have obvious relevance; 4) Empirical research using adult subjects, with large samples, sophisticated designs and statistical rigor, is sorely needed. New research needs to be guided by theory and to be sensitive to gender differences and the diversity by class, region, and home country within the American black community. For example, research that investigated the actual degree of association of the characteristics said to comprise the "black competent personality" and that looked at gender, class, and regional differences would be extremely valuable. 5) Perhaps the model of the "competent personality" has the ability to unite and make sense of recent research findings on self-concept, personality characteristics, and coping styles. It also offers a link to a theoretical/research tradition in psychology that has been fruitful. Finally, recent theorizing and empirical findings and the increasing research interest in areas this chapter identified as central to understanding black adult psychological health mark this as an important and productive period for the field.

References

Abatso, Y. (1985). The coping personality: A study of black college students. In M. Spencer, G. Brookings, & W. Allen (Eds.), *Beginnings: The social and affective development of black children* (131-144). Hillsdale, NJ: Lawrence Erlbaum.

Barbarin, O. (1983). Coping with ecological transitions by black families: A psychosocial model. *Journal of Community Psychology, 11*, 308-322.

Barbarin, O., Maish, K., & Shorter, S. (1981). Mental health among blacks. In O. Barbarin, P. Good, O. Pharr, & J. Siskind (Eds.), *Institutional racism and community competence.* Rockville, MD: U.S. Department of Health and Human Services (DHHS Publication #ADM81-907).

Barnes, E. J. (1980). The black community as a source of positive self-concept for black children: A theoretical perspective. In R. Jones (Ed.), *Black psychology*, 106-138. New York: Harper & Row.

Bowman, P. (1985). Black fathers and the provider role: Role strain, informal coping resource, and life happiness. In W. Boykin (Ed.), *Proceedings.* Seventh Conference on Empirical Research in Black Psychology, 9-21. Rockville, MD: N.I.M.H.

Cervantes, R. C., & Castro, F. G. (1985). Stress, coping, and Mexican American mental health: A systemic review. *Hispanic Journal of Behavioral Sciences, 7(1)*, 1-73.

Clark, M. L. (1982). Racial group concept and self-esteem in black children. *Journal of Black Psychology, 8(2)*, 75-89.

Cross, T. (1984). *The black power imperative: Racial inequality and the politics of non-violence.* New York: Faulkner Books.

Cross, W. E. (1980). Models of psychological nigrescence: A literature review. In R. Jones (Ed.), *Black psychology.* New York: Harper & Row.

Cross, W. E. (1985). Black identity: Rediscovering the distinction between personal identity and reference group orientation. In M. Spencer, G. Brookings, & W. Allen (Eds.), *Beginnings: The social and affective development of black children*, 155-173. Hillsdale, NJ: Lawrence Erlbaum Associates.

Cross, W. E., Parham, T., & Helms, J. (In press). Nigresence revisited: Theory and research. In R. L. Jones (Ed.), *Advances in black psychology.*

Dressler, W. W. (1985). Extended family relationships, social support, and mental health in a southern black community. *Journal of Health and Social Behavior, 26*, 39-48.

Edwards, D. W. (1974). Blacks versus whites: When is race a relevant variable? *Journal of Personality and Social Psychology, 29(1)*, 39-49.

Edwards, O. L. (1976). Components of academic success: A profile of achieving black adolescents. *Journal of Negro Education, 45*, 408-422.

Erickson, E. (1968). *Identity, youth, and crisis.* New York: Norton.

Gary, L. E. (Ed.) (1978). *Mental health: A challenge to the black community.* Philadelphia: Dorrance & Co.

George, A., & McNamara, P. (1984). Religion, race and psychological well-being. *Journal for the Scientific Study of Religion, 23(4)*, 351-363.

George, J. C., & Brooker, A. E. (1984). Conceptualization of mental health. *Psychological Reports, 55*, 329-330.

Gibbs, J. T. (1985). City girls: Psychosocial adjustment of urban black adolescent females. *Sage, 2(2)*, 28-36.

Gibbs, J. (1974). Patterns of adaptation among black students at a predominantly white university: Selected case studies. *American Journal of Ortho-Psychiatry, 44*, 728-740.

Gibson, R. (1982). Blacks at middle and late life: Resources and coping. *Annals of the American Academy of Political and Social Science, 464*, 79-90.

Grier, W., & Cobbs, P. (1969). *Black rage*. New York: Basic Books.

Griffin, Q. D., & Korchin, S. J. (1980). Personality competence in black male adolescents. *Journal of Youth and Adolescence, 9(3)*, 211-227.

Gurin, P., & Epps, E. (1975). *Black consciousness, identity, and achievement: A study of students in historically black colleges*. New York: John Wiley & Sons, Inc.

Guterman, S. (1972). *Black psyche: The modal personality patterns of black Americans*. Berkeley, CA: Glendessary Press.

Harrison, A. O., Bowman, P., & Berale, R. (1985). Role strain, coping resources, and psychological well-being among black working mothers. In W. Boykin (Ed.), *Proceedings*. Seventh Conference on Empirical Research in black Psychology, 21-29. Rockville, MD: N.I.M.H.

Heiss, J., & Owens, S. (1972). Self-evaluations of blacks and whites. *American Journal of Sociology, 78*, 360-370.

Holahan, C. J., Betak, J. F., Spearly, J. L., & Chance, B. J. (1983). Social integration and mental health in a biracial community. *American Journal of Community Psychology, 11(3)*, 301-311.

Houston, L. (1984). Black consciousness and self-esteem. *Journal of Black Psychology, 11(1)*, 1-7.

Institute for Social Research (1983). Black Americans surveyed. *I.S.R. Newsletter*, 5-6. Ann Arbor: Institute for Social Research.

Jahoda, M. (1958). *Current concepts of positive mental health*. New York: Basic Books.

Jensen, G. F., White, C. S., & Galliher, J. M. (1982). Ethnic status and adolescent self-evaluations: An extension of research on minority self-esteem. *Social Problems, 30(2)*, 226-239.

Jones, E. E., & Korchin, S. J. (1982). *Minority mental health*. New York: Praeger.

Jones, J. M. (1972). *Prejudice and racism*. Reading, MA: Addison-Wesley Publishers.

Kardiner, A., & Ovesey, L. (1951). *The Mark of Oppression: Explorations in the personality of the American Negro*. New York: World Books.

Karon, B. P. (1958). *The Negro personality: A rigorous investigation of the effects of culture*. New York: Springer.

Komaroff, A. C., Masuda, M., & Holmes, T. H. (1968). The social readjustment rating scale: A comparative study of Negro, Mexican, and white Americans. *Journal of Psychosomatic Research 12(2)*, 121-128.

Lazarus, R. (1975). The healthy personality—A review of conceptualizations and research. In L. Levi (Ed.), *Society, stress and disease* (Vol. 2). *Childhood and adolescence*, 6-35. New York: Oxford U. Press.

Lee, C. C. (1984). An investigation of psychosocial variables related to academic success for rural black adolescents. *Journal of Negro Education, 53(4)*, 424-434.

Lee, C. C. (1985). Successful rural black adolescents: A psychosocial profile. *Adolescence, 20(77)*, 129-142.

Looney, J. G., & Lewis, J. M. (1983). Competent adolescents from different socioeconomic and ethnic contexts. *Adolescent Psychiatry, 2*, 64-74.

Lykes, M. B. (1983). Discrimination and coping in the lives of black women: Analyses of oral history data. *Journal of Social Issues, 39(3)*, 79-100.

Maslow, A. (1968). *Towards a psychology of being.* (2nd ed.) Princeton, NJ: Van Nostrand.

McCarthy, J., & Yancey, W. (1971). Uncle Tom and Mr. Charlie: Metaphysical pathos in the study of racism and personal disorganization. *American Journal of Sociology, 76*, 648-672.

Neff, J. (1985). Race and vulnerability to stress: An examination of differential vulnerability. *Journal of Personality and Social Psychology, 49(2)*, 481-491.

Neighbors, H. W. (1984). The distribution of psychiatric morbidity in black Americans: A review and suggestions for research. *Community Mental Health Journal, 20(3)*, 169-181.

Neighbors, H., Jackson, J., Bowman, P., & Gurin, G. (1983). Stress, coping, and black mental health: Preliminary findings from a national study. *Prevention in Human Services, 2*, 1-25.

Parham, T., & Helms, J. (1985a). Relations of racial identity attitudes to self-actualization and affective states of black students. *Journal of Counseling Psychology*, Vol. 32 *(3),*, 431-440.

Parham, T., & Helms, J. (1985b). Attitudes of racial identity and self-esteem of black students: An exploratory investigation. *Journal of College Student Personnel*, Vol. 26, 143-147.

Pettigrew, T. W. (1964). *A profile of the Negro American.* Princeton, NJ: Van Nostrand.

Pierce, C. (1974). Psychiatric problems of the black minority. In A. Arieti (Ed.), *American Handbook of Psychiatry*, (2nd ed.), *2*, 524-534.

Porter, J., & Washington, R. (1979). Black identity and self-esteem: A review of studies of black self concept 1968-1978. *Annual Review of Sociology, 5*, 53-74.

Ramseur, H. (1975). *Continuity and change in black identity: black students at an interracial college.* Cambridge, Mass: Unpublished Ph.D. dissertation, Harvard University.

Ramseur, H. (1982). Major sources of stress and coping strategies of black administrators at white universities. *Proceedings.* First National Conference on Black Administrators at White Universities. Cambridge, MA: Massachusetts Institute of Technology Black Administrators Association.

Rutter, M. (1979). Protective factors in children's responses to stress and disadvantage. In M. Kent, & J. Rold (Eds.), *Primary Prevention of Psychopathology, 3*, 49-79. Hanover, NH: University Press of New England.

Smith, M. B. (1961). "Mental health" reconsidered: A special case of the problem of values in psychology. *American Psychologist, 16*, 299-306.

Smith, M. B. (1968). Competence and socialization. In J. Clausen (Ed.), *Socialization and society*, 270-320. Boston: Little, Brown and Co.

Smith, W. D., Burlew, A. K., & Mosley, M. H. (1978). *Minority issues in mental health.* Reading, Mass.: Addison-Wesley.

Spurlock, J. (1986). Development of self-conception in Afro-American children. *Hospital and Community Psychiatry, 37(1)* January, 66-70.

Stock, W. A., Okun, M. A., Haring, M. J., & Witter, R. A. (1985). Race and subjective well-being in adulthood: A black-white research synthesis. *Human Development, 28,* 192-197.

Taylor, R. L. (1976). Psychosocial development among black children and youth: A reexamination. *American Journal of Orthopsychiatry, 46(2),* 4-19.

Thomas, A., & Sillen, S. (1972). *Racism and psychiatry.* Secaucus, N.J.: Citadel Press.

Thomas, C. S., & Comer, J. (1973). Racism and mental health services. In C. Willie, B. Kramer, & B. Brown (Eds.), *Racism and Mental Health.* Pittsburgh: University of Pittsburgh Press.

Tyler, F. (1978). Individual psychosocial competence: A personality configuration. *Educational and Psychological Measurement, 38,* 309-323.

Veroff, J., Douvan, E., & Kulka, R. A. (1981). *The inner American: A self-portrait from 1957 to 1976.* New York: Basic Books.

White, R. (1960). Competence and the psychosexual stages of development. In M. Jones (Ed.), *Nebraska symposium on motivation 1960,* 97-141. Lincoln: University of Nebraska Press.

Wilcox, C. (1973). Positive mental health for blacks. In C. Willie, B. Kramer, & B. Brown (Eds.), *Racism and Mental Health.* Pittsburgh: University of Pittsburgh Press.

Wright, B. (1985). Effects of racial self-esteem on personal self-esteem of black youth. *International Journal of Intercultural Relations, 9(1),* 19-30.

Yancey, W. L., Rigsby, L., & McCarthy, J. D. (1972). Social position and self-evaluation: The relative importance of race. *American Journal of Sociology, 78,* 338-359.

African American Strengths: A Survey of Empirical Findings

V. Robert Hayles, Jr.

Introduction

The purpose of this paper is to summarize research on African American strengths and distinctive black competencies. My objectives are to: (a) stimulate non-comparative research on African American people; (b) encourage research in which positive and negative outcomes are possible but not distorted by inappropriate paradigms, unsuitable methods, or transubstantiative errors, and (c) provoke discussion of and stimulate research on distinctive black competencies. The chapter is neither anti-white, nor ethnocentrically pro-black. While some comparative data are reported, group comparisons are not the chapter's main focus.

Historical Viewpoint

The author accepts the following facts:

1. The earliest human was found on the continent known today as Africa, and this human was dark skinned (McGee, 1976).
2. Early (pre-B.C.) Africans possessed a sophisticated long term education system (Hilliard, 1978). Many scholars and historians (especially Europeans and Greeks) state they were educated in Africa and that their teachers were dark skinned with woolly hair (James, 1954).
3. Early (pre-B.C.) African civilization was characterized by such scientifically documented achievements as design and construction of earthquake-proof structures (Hilliard, 1978), therapeutic use of the *modern* antibiotic called tetracycline

The author acknowledges and extends sincere appreciation to Bill and Gladys Commons for critical and supportive comments on earlier drafts of this chapter, and to Deborah Francois and Beverly Harris for their assistance in typing the manuscript.

(Bassett, et al., 1980), the formulation and use of spermicides and other sophisticated pharmacological agents (Hilliard, 1978; and National Geographic, July 1974), and religious doctrine which formed the basis of later Protestant, Catholic, and other religions (Mbiti, 1970; Ben-Jochanan, 1970).

4. In general, African civilization, as the parent civilization, spread itself world-wide and is reflected even today in the religion, politics, economics, and creativities of many of the world's peoples including, especially, Europeans (Hilliard, 1978).

5. Early African civilization was systematically destroyed by foreign invaders (Williams, 1974). Because of that destruction and the later developed viewpoint that there was nothing of value in Africa, many 19th and 20th century technological, cultural and other achievements are reinventions.

Bringing this historical viewpoint up to the 1990's, the world is repeating the history it ignored. Specifically, we are destroying rather than fully utilizing the expertise and skills possessed by African American people. These skills could make significant contributions to the solutions of major problems like war, pollution, resource shortages, substance abuse and health. Furthermore, drugs, incarceration, miseducation, racism and poverty continue to destroy present and future generations.

Discussion of and research on distinctive black strengths and competencies are presented in the sections following.

Individual/Group Performance

Cognitive Tests

A brief and insightful discussion of IQ testing can be found in the APA Monitor (January 1986). More detailed discussions are available in a report by the NAACP (1976), a special issue of the Negro Educational Review (1977), and a volume by Kamin (1974). Kamin (1974) documents the outright falsification of data used to 'prove' black inferiority. The above and other sources cite the inappropriate uses of tests, psychometric and substantive inadequacies of many standardized tests, and noteworthy achievements by African Americans with low scores on IQ tests.

Many African Americans have excelled far beyond what would have been predicted based on ability and aptitude tests. Hilliard (1977) lists several holders of doctoral degrees from top ranked predominantly white colleges and universities with IQ test scores below 90. Some of these achievers were labelled *mentally retarded* while in school. Hilliard also presents data showing that one-fifth of a sample of 123 African American doctoral degree holders had below average General Classification Test scores (exam used by the military to screen personnel). Nine of these Ph.D. holders were classified as *retarded*. Such findings reinforce the fact that existing tests are inadequate for predicting the accomplishments of African American people.

While African American children tend to score lower (one-half to one standard deviation lower) than white children on most IQ tests, there are exceptions. For example, Williams (1972) showed consistently superior black performance on the BITCH (a culturally oriented test of vocabulary and concepts unique to the African American community). Franklin and Fulani (1973) demonstrated that African American youths perform much better than white youths on a free word recall task when half of the categories and their corresponding words are pertinent to the experiences of African American youth. For example, words like ribs and greens were added to the food category. The remaining words were common in the American workplace (e.g., hat, shoes, shirt).

On measures of divergent thinking ability (creativity) African American and other minority group children typically do as well and frequently better than majority group children. For example, Mexican and African American males scored significantly higher than Anglo males on fluency and flexibility as measured by the Unusual Uses Test (Price-Williams & Ramirez, 1977). Moreover, African American females produced the highest flexibility/fluency ratio (an efficiency index) of all groups. Torrance (1967 and 1971) administered his Tests of Creative Thinking to African American and white children. In his study, African American children scored significantly higher than white children on measures of figural fluency, flexibility and originality.

Academic and Job Performance

There has been much research and debate on the differential predictive validity of achievement and aptitude tests. Noteworthy in this research is the consistency in the direction of findings. For aptitude and ability tests, performance of black students scoring in the lower two or sometimes lower three quartiles is consistently underpredicted (Byham & Spitzer, 1971; Farr, et al., 1971; Mattison & Northrup, 1975; and Hayles, 1974). Why do ability and aptitude tests often underpredict African American performance? The more heuristic question is *what causes many African Americans to perform above predicted levels?* In addition to the predictive deficiencies of existing tests, factors not measured by tests also determine performance. These unaccounted for factors may be different and/or more powerful for blacks. The empirical research on this issue consistently points to African American strengths like:

1. An achievement and future oriented personality (Booth & Berry, 1978; Goodstein & Heilbrun, 1962; Hakel, 1966; Lunneborg & Lunneborg, 1967; and Epps, 1969a and 1969b).
2. Achievement motivation nurtured by family and friends (Epps, 1969a, 1969b; Grande & Simons, 1967; Rowland & Del Campo, 1968; Guthrie, 1977; and Curtis, 1978).
3. A cluster of traits like strong ethnic identity, value for independence for all black people, self-determination, and value for equality (Ross & Glaser, 1973; and Hayles, 1974).

In summary, a good case can be made for asserting that many African Americans possess attributes that enable performance above *measured* ability and aptitude levels.

Face Recognition

Face recognition has been the subject of substantial research (Lavrakas, Buri & Mayzner, 1976; Goldstein, Stephenson & Chance, 1977; Feinman & Entwisle, 1976; and Barkowitz & Brigham, 1982). Poor face recognition has been described as a correlate of the tendency to stereotype; good face recognizers stereotype less than poor face recognizers (Garfield, 1979) and tend to have good pattern recognition and memory functions, particularly those occurring in the right hemisphere of the brain (Levin, Hamsher & Benton, 1975; Moscovitch, Scullion & Cristie, 1976). Good recognizers are field independent (Hoffman & Kagan, 1977) or able to function well in the field independent mode (implied by Ramirez, 1983). Field independence is characterized by the ability to view objects without perception being distorted by the field in which the object appears. It is associated with being task oriented, formal and having a tendency to focus on details.

Barkowitz and Brigham (1982), in a review of the literature on face recognition, concluded that the research unambiguously supports the position that African American children are significantly better than white children at face recognition. More specifically, African American children are significantly better at recognizing both white faces and African American faces, and consequently, tend to engage in less stereotyping behavior. This is an obvious benefit in their interactions with persons from different ethnic groups, since they are more likely to see the unique qualities and characteristics in each individual.

Bicognitive Ability

Face recognition findings also indicate that more accurate recognizers have superior pattern recognition and memory, at least for certain types of information. Moreover, research by Thompson (described by Gloye, 1980) reported that the right hemispheres of most persons are specialized in processing visual images and spatial information—non-verbal data. On two tests requiring superior right hemisphere processing for superior performance, the Mooney Closure Test and the Benton-Van Allen Test of Facial Recognition, African Americans (in particular, African American subjects from economically poor communities) outperformed Anglo Americans by a significant margin. The Mooney Closure Test required subjects to identify objects in incomplete pictures. The Benton-Van Allen Test of Facial Recognition involved recognizing pictures of human faces from different angles. Thompson's findings support the view that African Americans as a group may excel in certain types of information processing tasks. In the case of face recognition, African American children appear less fettered by negative attitudinal inputs (stereotypic thoughts) and/or have exceptional cognitive ability for such tasks.

A related issue is cognitive performance in the field independent mode. Hoffman & Kagan (1977) state that field independent persons are better at face recognition than field dependent persons. Field dependent or field sensitive (a less perjorative term) persons are affected by backgrounds and have difficulty separating objects from their contexts. They tend to have a social orientation and focus on global aspects. While African American children have been shown to be better at face recognition, researchers have also argued that they tend to be field sensitive (Ramirez & Castaneda, 1974; and Ramirez, 1983). How is this contradiction reconciled? First, the key terms must be defined. Ramirez (1983) defines field independent, field sensitive (dependent) and bicognitive as follows:

> Field independent. Individuals who are predominately field independent are characterized by task orientation in interpersonal relationships, a tendency to use an impersonal, formal style in communicating with others, a preference for nonsocial rewards, and a tendency to focus on details of ideas, problems, and documents.
>
> Field sensitive. Predominately field sensitive individuals are characterized by a strong social orientation in interpersonal

relationships with a tendency to personalize communications, a preference for social rewards, and a tendency to focus on the global aspects of ideas, problems, and documents.

Bicognitive. Bicognitive individuals are characterized by the ability to use the field independent and field sensitive cognitive styles interchangeably, and by a tendency to combine elements of these two styles to arrive at new approaches to coping with life's problems and to problem solving. (Although most adults are bicognitive to some degree, they often exhibit a preference for either field sensitivity or for field independence). (p. 155)

The contradiction is easily resolved by acknowledging the existence of bicognitive individuals. Price-Williams and Ramirez (1977) document the existence of bicognitive African Americans and Valentine (1971) has described biculturality in the African American population. Smith (1977) argues in support of biculturalism and bilingualism among African Americans. Although the data for this argument are limited to a few studies, they are unambiguous. Bilingual/cultural/cognitive talent is very special and provides the potential for such individuals to bridge gaps between very diverse groups and among heterogeneous individuals. Bicultural youngsters are better adjusted than monoculturals (Szapocznik, Kurtines & Fernandez, 1980). Bilingual students show higher self-esteem than monolinguals, especially in terms of self-confidence and social ease (Pesner & Auld, 1980). Underutilization of this African American and Latino talent clearly suboptimizes contemporary efforts to achieve peace at individual, group, national and global levels. Especially encouraging is the conclusion by Ramirez (1983) that bicognitive skills can be developed through the use of appropriately designed educational programs.

Psychomotor Functioning

No sophisticated analyses are needed to confirm African American dominance in many sports. The number of African Americans who achieve the highest levels of psychomotor proficiency is several times the number predicted by assuming parity with respect to the percentage of African Americans in the general population. Even adjusting the calculations to take into account the younger average age of the African American population fails to eliminate disproportionate dominance. Edwards (1982) provides data on the African American presence in certain professional sports. He notes, for example, that in 1955 black players comprised over 55% of the National Football League. In 1981, 74% of the National Basketball Association's roster was black. About 20% of America's major baseball league players in 1981 were black. Even larger figures are found upon examination of black participation among starting lineups, Heisman Trophy winners (all Black from 1974 to 1981), leading football running backs (36 out of the top 40 in 1986 were black), etc. On the other hand, black participation as quarterbacks in football, pitchers and catchers in baseball, in certain sports such as golf, tennis and hockey, and as coaches and general managers, is as dismal as participation in certain other positions and sports is overwhelming.

The Alley-oop Play

An excellent description of black intellectual and physical prowess was written by Fairchild (1983). He described a mentally and physically demanding play in basketball involving a high pass over the rim followed by slamming the ball into the basket. Fairchild provides analytical details that portray the complex perceptual, sensory and decision-making processes involved in this lob-pass play:

> The play begins with a rebound. A player's rebounding ability is no doubt conditioned by experience, so that even as the ball is approaching the basket, the experienced rebounder begins to *position* for the rebound. As a result, good rebounders are constantly making subtle position adjustments during the flight of the ball to the basket. During this time the player must also confront attempts by the opposing team to thwart his/her efforts at getting the rebound. As the ball hits the rim and bounds up, the defensive player sneaks around the opposition, and leaps for the ball. Jumping for the ball is no small feat. The *timing* of the jump is what makes the difference between a great rebounder and an average one. While height is certainly an important asset in basketball, the greatest rebounders in the game are not necessarily the tallest players. Thus, certain players get more than their fair share of rebounds. This is because of their ability to quickly judge the flight and trajectory of the errant shot, and make the decision to leap at precisely the right instant to complete the rebound. Rebounding, then, is fundamentally a question of perception, encoding, processing or decision making, and acting. After getting the rebound, the player, still aware of the presence and location of opposing players, spins and pushes the ball up the floor.
>
> Dribbling also requires considerable cognitive and physical ability. The bounce of the ball is a quick event, and on closer analysis may be seen to involve the real-world use of applied geometry, trigonometry, and even physics. Certainly the laws of motion are involved during dribbling, and the player is constantly pushing the ball *ahead* while running down the floor, thus necessitating extrapolations into the future. The ball then carves a sine-like wave as it moves down the floor, and the

player must coordinate the movement of the ball, body speed and hand motion to simply keep the dribble going.

While the player is dribbling the ball down the court, he/she looks left and notices an opponent's speed and direction in relation to his/her own, and concludes help is needed from a teammate. Past experience (i.e., long-term memory) indicates that a teammate is probably following the flow of the play on either the left or right wing. The player looks right and sees a teammate streaking down the right sideline. Close behind may be an opponent desperately trying to catch up. In successful executions of this play, the dribbler must accurately *read* the court and anticipate future court positions. A fix on range and position of the basket is obtained.

The player looks to a teammate on the right wing, and when eye contact is established, lofts the pass high on the right side of the rim. This pass represents yet another complex information processing task. Using past experience as a guide, the distance to the basket is estimated, the speed and motion of the teammate is examined, and an extrapolation into the future occurs. Most importantly, all of these considerations must be followed by a complex behavioral response: Passing the ball at the right time, with the right trajectory, and with an appropriate amount of force. Kinesthetic feedback, between musculature and the central nervous system, regulates this complex response.

On seeing the pass leave the passer's hands, the receiving player must quickly adjust speed and direction so as to leap at the appropriate instant. The jump is not directed at the ball, but at the space where the ball *is going to be*. Such a feat requires precise calculations of speed, trajectory, and timing. Grabbing the ball above the rim is perhaps the easiest part, and a quick look to the rim assures the two points as the player slams it home. The play is over when the scorer lands from the ten foot altitude and, frequently, shares *high-fives* with teammates.

The alley-oop, then, is a complex series of events that requires an assessment of the situation (perception), an internal imagery of that external situation (sensation), an interpretation of that imagery (based on short-term and long-term memory), calculations of future images, the making of decisions, and appropriate behavioral responding—all at a high rate of speed.

Sensorimotor Development

Werner (1979) conducted an international cross-cultural study on sensorimotor development and reached these conclusions:

Of all ethnic groups studied, Negroid samples showed the greatest early acceleration of psychomotor development, the Caucasian samples the least, and the Central American Indian and Asian samples occupied an intermediary position—even if they lived in the same ecological setting (p. 164).

To explain differential performance some authors describe ethnic differences in proportions of body fat, differential neural system reactivity, variation in the lenghts of muscle fibers, variation in unsolicited early psychomotor activity, and so on. Generally the within group variation on most such variables makes it difficult to draw simple and unambiguous conclusions.

Tyndall (1986) describes research on the pineal gland, which is the only gland known to be wired into the brain with nerve-like connections. While its function in humans is not fully understood, it has been shown, in animal studies, to function as a light receptor with an endocrine function of stimulating production of the hormone melatonin; it acts as an interpreter, translating signals from the environment to the brain. Other animal research shows the pineal gland to be part of a neural circuitry that has a timing clock that can operate independently of the circuit and send out signals that cause the gland to release a chemical substance sending impulses across the tiny gaps between nerves. The nerve endings, receptors, respond and produce melatonin. Melatonin acts on the hypothalamus in ways we do not yet fully understand. The hypothalamus controls body temperature, thirst, hunger, and sexual function. It is also associated with mood and sleep patterns.

McGee (1976) believes that the pineal gland, melatonin, melanin and the hypothalamus are related in ways that help explain the exceptional mental and physical performance (e.g., long-term survival under hostile/difficult conditions) of African American people. Melanin comes from the Greek word 'melanos' meaning 'black' and is produced and dispersed by cells called melanocytes. Melanin production is the result of a series of enzymatic biochemical reactions. When the essential enzymes are present, sufficient melanin is produced to provide dark skin, hair and eyes. Nearly all humans produce some melanin. It is the genetic inability to produce melanin which results in only one tenth of the world's population being classified as non-colored or white. A low level of melanin is significantly correlated with a higher incidence of such diseases as Parkinson's, PKU and skin cancer. These diseases are rarely found among people of color, especially blacks. McGee also argues that melanin plays a key role in the development of the neural matter responsible for impulses which facilitate muscle contraction. In other words, melanin may be relevant to the explosive grace demonstrated by even average black athletes.

Noncognitive Attributes and Abilities

Coping with Confinement and Crowding

Black people are disproportionately represented in prisons. Figures range from a low of less than ten percent black inmates in Navy prisons (Hayles & Perry, 1981) to 42% in local jails (U.S. Bureau of the Census, 1974) to 49% on death row (Jones, 1978). The range in State prisons is 12 to 77% with an overimprisonment rate of 20% (computed using Blumstein's formula to correct for arrest rates and population demographics (Hawkins, 1986). How have blacks coped?

Carroll (1976) conducted a participant observation study of inmates in a California jail. Her sample was small/limited and included 21 white and 5 African American women. Among her observations were the following:

> African Americans tended to be stoical about their deprivations. Whites demonstrated a far weaker coping attitude, with much *bitching, whining, cursing, pouting, railing and ranting.*

> Four out of five African American girls in the dormitory attended the jail school morning and night. Of the 21 white women, *one attended occasionally, to be joined later by a second.*

> Unlike many white inmates, African Americans *were not only concerned with their own individual physical welfare but with one another's as well.*

> Depression was the normative white tone. *Set alongside the liveliness and sparkle of the African Americans, whites looked drab, remote, and sad.* (p. 5)

McCain, Cox and Paulus (1979) examined the effect of prison crowding on inmate behavior in the entire Oklahoma prison system. They studied general relationships between such variables as institution size, change in size, violent death rates, nonviolent death rates, etc. Their results showed that institutions with larger populations had disproportionately more negative outcomes (deaths, psychiatric commitments, illness complaint rates, self-mutilations, and attempted suicides). In general, individuals who perceived themselves as being more crowded tended to respond more negatively (e.g., more illness complaints) than those who saw themselves as being less crowded. Within this larger scale study, a comparative analysis of African American, Hispanic and Anglo American inmates reinforced Carroll's small scale study (1976) findings: African American and Mexican-American prisoners had the least negative responses, fewer negative mood states and more feelings of choice and control.

In summary, African Americans are among the most effective groups in dealing with a crowded and unpleasant environment like jail. Moreover, it has also been shown that strong ethnic identity enhances survival in situations like jail and concentration camps (Sarason, 1979). While this may be so, we must realize that jails are extremely punitive and that effective coping should be viewed as adjustment to a punitive environment.

Expressiveness

Expressiveness is a well documented African American attribute. Staples (1974) traces expressiveness in sexual and religious matters to experiences in slavery. Taylor (1969), Abrahams (1963) and Kochman (1972) document the expressiveness used in the language spoken by many African Americans. Garner (1985) describes how African American children learn rhetorical competency and also points out the centrality and high importance given to oral communication effectiveness within black communities. Baumrind (1976) described African American people in the following ways: *have style; improvisational flare in conversation, personal presentation, and clothing, and soul, the capacity for human compassion and empathy achieved through suffering and aptly expressed in the blues; an awareness of the value and integrity of the human personality is an intrinsic part of the black experience; expressive skills in language, movement and music*; and more (pp. 21-22). The above attributes, and others are discussed extensively by Majors (present volume).

Role-Taking and Role-Playing Skills

Turner (1956) defines role-taking as the ability to orient one's self in social interaction through the creation, modification and coordination of conceptions of the self and others. Role playing is the ability to understand enough about the perspective of another person or role to behave as if one is that other person or in that other role. These skills are most evident in actors, empathic therapists, scam artists, effective law enforcement personnel, and so on. It seems likely that part of the foundation for the development of role-playing and role-taking skills among African American children is their strong attentiveness to affective cues (discussed by Boykin, 1977a). Thomas, Franks and Calonico (1970) concluded that the lack of social power among African Americans is associated with (i.e., facilitates, encourages, stimulates skill building, etc.) the development of greater role-taking competence. Role-playing skills are essential to the survival of oppressed people. Role-taking and role-playing skills are necessary to cipher the informal implicit rules of the dominant society. Baumrind (1976) cites several empirical studies documenting exceptional role playing and taking skills among African Americans. Newmeyer (1970) reported that young African Americans were consistently better at enacting emotions in ways that maximized correct perceptions on the part of observers. Newmeyer's African American subjects were also significantly better at interpreting the emotions of other actors. Gitter, et al. (1972) studied African American and white American college students and found that African American subjects made correct judgments about emotions displayed in photographs of professional actors significantly more often. Since these skills are enhanced through heterogeneous social contact, Baumrind (1976) suggests that integration may be of greatest value to white Americans.

Equity and Fairness

In thinking about how African American people have been treated, many believe that an exceptional internalized sense of justice is developed. This sense has been documented in at least one empirical investigation. Ruhe and Allen (1977) studied military leaders and found that African American officers were consistently rated by African American and white raters as superior in handling issues of fairness and equity.

The Costs to Excel

While such qualities as physical fitness, resiliency, and ability to role play seem highly positive, the abilities to endure and repress anger have severe negative consequences. Major results of continued repression are the buildup of rage and associated inevitable adverse impacts on mental and physical health (Grier & Cobbs, 1968; and Braxton, 1983). Paranoid-like behaviors, black-on-black crimes, stress-related disorders (e.g., high blood pressure, diabetes, high blood sugar, gastrointestinal malfunctions), and other psychosomatic problems result from the sustained repression of anger.

In thinking about black strengths and competencies, we must be mindful of the benefits as well as the potentially adverse effects of their development and maintenance.

Effective Family Functioning

Although the literature on effectively coping African American families is limited, it is well documented due to the efforts of African American scholars like Harriette McAdoo, Wade Nobles, Robert Staples, Robert Hill, Janice Hale, Albert McQueen, Joyce Ladner, and others.

Some scholars (Bronfenbrenner, 1977 and Etzioni, 1977) expressed the view that the family as we know it is rapidly changing and becoming extinct. Others believe the family is still strong and resilient (Libman & Lawson, 1976; Daedalus Spring 1977 issue; and Bane, 1978). Hayles (1978) argued that in spite of a long history of racial atrocities, black and ethnic minority families have continued to survive and grow. Hayles and Nobles (1978) concluded that black families were more marriage and family oriented than the majority society. Excellent reviews of the history of black family research can be found in Billingsley (1968) and Nobles (1976).

There has been a small thread of positively (strength) oriented research including studies by Frazier (1932 and 1939), Willie and Weinandy (1963), Billinglsey (1968), Grier and Cobbs (1968), Joint Commission on Mental Health of Children (1969), Scanzoni (1971), Hill (1972), Staples (1974), Nobles (1976), Guthrie (1977), McQueen (1977), Hayles and Nobles (1978), Martin and Martin (1980), Werner and Smith (1982), McAdoo and McAdoo (1985), and Lewis and Looney (1986).

Drawing heavily from the above sources, the empirically documented strengths of African American families are:

1. Kinship networks and extended family systems;
2. Value systems that emphasize such things as harmony, cooperation, interdependence, acceptance of difference/ diversity, internal development, strong work and achievement orientation, and traditionalism;
3. Strong male/female bonds;
4. Role adaptability and flexibility;
5. Roots, emotional support and buffers or consolations against racism;
6. Respect, appreciation, and full utilization of the skills and wisdom of senior family members; and
7. Child centeredness.

Hayles (1978) describes how the above strengths were developed and are maintained. It must be noted that special attention is still desperately needed to address the debilitating conditions (e.g., poverty, racism, crowding) imposed on African American families.

Black Participation in Organizations

Most of the world's largest corporations are either multinational or becoming multinational. This movement comes during an era when at least minimal efforts are being made to insure the participation of previously underrepresented groups such as women and members of many ethnic minority (numerical) groups. Historically, equal opportunity and affirmative action efforts tend to be applied at the lowest levels. As pressure builds for these participants to be promoted, the issue of costs and benefits becomes increasingly important. The major costs of this increase in diversity are added recruitment expenses, training for new and existing staff (job and human relations), more social stress, attributional conflict, accommodation to cultural differences (holidays, food, dress, etc.), and more time and energy needed for effective communications (Hayles, (1982).

The benefits far outweigh the costs. The performance of diverse (in terms of personality, sex, and racial/ethnic composition) problem-solving groups on many tasks is superior to that of homogeneous groups (Ziller, 1972). Triandis, et al., (1963) indicated increased productivity when diverse groups received training to facilitate mutual understanding of each others' points of view. When combined with the results of other research, the Triandis study suggests superior performance for heterogeneous groups when creativity is the criterion. Ziller (1972), who reviewed heterogeneous versus homogenous group performance, found superior performance on the part of heterogeneous groups on complex problems when quality was the criterion. The differences brought into play by creating cultural diversity include thinking styles (field sensitive and field independent, analytical, intuitive, etc.), decision making approaches (top-down, consensus, etc.), information sources, communication networks, linguistic resources, and more. Increased black participation along with that of women and other ethnic groups will bring the strengths created through diversity to bear on corporate functioning.

Tucker (1980) discusses the unique capabilities of blacks as well as differences between African black people and those with European white origins. He argues that a combination of the strengths of both perspectives could result in a *balanced white-African American dialectic that can yield the negotiated perception of truth that is needed to improve the social contract between black and white people within organizations and within this country.* A similar point is made by Kanter (1983) whose research provides data that allowed her to conclude that *The companies with reputations for progressive human-resource practices were significantly higher in long term profitability and financial growth than their counterparts* (p. 19). Since her study was a post-hoc analysis and not an experiment, cause and effect could not be confirmed. However, the statistical relationships she reported were very strong. Since strong affirmative action programs were a major element of *progressive human-resource practices*, her conclusion reinforces the argument that African American participation is good for business.

Values

Significant changes must occur if the world is to survive for longer than a few more decades. Central to the requisite changes are the values held and espoused by the world's inhabitants. Values *denote an evaluative representation of a person's or group's perception of his/her or their relationship to the social/physical environments* (O'Driscoll, 1976, p. 8). Borsodi (1965) believes that values are important because *every human action is the reflection of an individual value, and every human institution is the outgrowth of a social value* (p. 433). Sperry (1974) has gone so far as to advocate that *among the vast complex of forces that influence and control the brain and behavior of man, human values stand out as a universal determinant of all human decisions and actions* (p. 9). Sperry further asserts that:

> the future will be unique only if we acquire the power and values to shape it in our own image, to reclaim and reconstruct our lives in more human terms. It will not be unique because there are more machines, but because the masses have struggled and succeeded in bringing into being a new society and world, a new woman, man and child, people with new values and vision, living and enjoying a free, fuller and higher level of human life (p. 38).

Authors from a wide variety of disciplines have examined this issue and delineated the changes, circumstances and values necessary for individual, group, and global survival. Stern (1978) noted that people often fail to act in the long range best interest of humanity in spite of claiming to be interested in the future. Prime examples of such behavior are evident among many inhabitants of developed nations who fail to conserve obviously scarce resources and continue to pollute the air, land and water. Of special significance is Stern's point that Western development, formal traditional higher education, and the like do not seem to lead to future-oriented behavior. There are, on the other hand, numerous examples of *developing* nations whose people created social systems that successfully preserve their ecosystems and resources over many generations. In fact the oldest societies in the world exist in the least *developed* areas (Africa, South Pacific, Australia, South America, etc.).

The values essential for global survival seem more prevalent among people of color, and the ones most detrimental to survival seem more prevalent among the rest of the population.

While many authors (viz., Wilson, 1975; Bennis, 1970; Toffler, 1970; and Lynn & Oldenquist, 1986) describe the changes in values that are needed, few if any, cite any of the voluminous literature by black authors.

Black Values

Values evident among or espoused for African people throughout the diaspora have been discussed by a number of scholars. Both Karenga (1967) and Baraka (1969) delineate/advocate Seven Principles for the growth and survival of black people.

Umoja (unity)—to strive for and maintain unity in the family, community, nation and race.

Kujichagulia (self-determination)—to define ourselves, name ourselves, and speak for ourselves, instead of being defined and spoken for by others.

Ujima (Collective work and responsibility)—to build and maintain our community together and to make our Brothers' and Sisters' problems our problems and to solve them together.

Ujamaa (cooperative economics)—to build and maintain our own stores, shops and other business and to profit from them together.

Nia (purpose)—to make our collective vocation the building and developing of our community in order to restore our people to their traditional greatness.

Kuumba (creativity)—to do always as much as we can, in the way we can in order to leave our community more beautiful and beneficial than when we inherited it.

Imani (faith)—to believe with all our hearts in our parents, our teachers, our leaders, our people and the righteousness and victory of our struggle.

Nobles (1967a), having studied the scholars mentioned earlier in this chapter along with others such as Memmi (1967), summarized the African world view as follows: Psycho-behavioral modalities—Groupness, Sameness and Commonality; Values and Customs—Cooperation, Collective Responsibility, Cooperateness and Interdependence; and Ethos—Survival of the Tribe, and One with nature.

Summary of African and Anglo Value Systems

Drawing from material cited in this section and previous ones, African American value systems can be summarized by pointing to their emphasis on harmony and rhythm; soul and internal development or consciousness (Cook and Kono, 1977); and one's tribe or nation. Anglo systems can be summarized by indicating their emphasis on the individual (rugged individualism) and competitiveness. Global survival requires more of the world's population to shift toward values prevalent among black people. Baumrind (1976) and Kanter (1983) have observed and noted that many of the values and behaviors found among predominantly black people and ethnic minority groups are essential for global survival. They also suggest that the adoption of such behaviors and values will lead to superior individual, organizational and societal functioning.

In general, black people throughout the diaspora need to enhance and maintain such values. Essential to that enhancement and maintenance is the avoidance of total assimilation.

References

Abrahams, R.D. (1963). *Deep down in the jungle*. Chicago: Aldine Publishing Company

Bane, M.J. (1978). *Here to stay*. New York: Basic Books

Baraka, I.A. (1969). A black value system. *The Black Scholar, 1 (1)*, 54-60.

Barkowitz, P. & Brigham, J.C. (1982). Recognition of faces: Own-race, incentive, and time delay. *Journal of Applied Social Psychology, 12* (4), 225-268.

Bassett, E.J., Keith, M.S., Armelagos, G.J., Martin, D.L., & Villanueva, A.R. (1980). Tetracycline-labeled bone from ancient Sudanese Nubia (A.D. 350). *Science, 209*, 1532-1534.

Baumrind, D. (1976). Subcultural variations in values defining social competence: An outsider's perspective. Paper presented at the Society for Research in Child Development, Western Regional Conference.

Ben-Jochanan, Y. (1970). *African origin of the major 'Western Religions'*. New York: Alkebu-Lan Books.

Bennis, W.G. (1970). A funny thing happened on the way to the future. *American Psychologist, 25 (7)*, 595-608.

Billingsley, A. (1968). *Black families in white America*. New Jersey: Prentice-Hall, Inc. Englewood Cliffs.

Booth, R.F. & Berry, N.H. (1978). Minority group differences in the background, personality, and performance of Navy paramedical personnel. *Journal of Community Psychology, 6*, 60-68.

Borsodi, R. (1965). The neglected science of values: Eight propositions about values. *Journal of Human Relations, 13*, 433-445.

Boykin, A.W. (1977a). Experimental psychology from a Black perspective: Issues and examples. *The Journal of Black Psychology, 3 (2)*, 29-49.

Braxton, E.T. (1983). Psycho-spiritual and energetic approaches to the management of rage and pain in black client populations. Presentation at the 16th Annual Convention of the Association of Black Psychologists, Washington, D.C.

Bronfenbrenner, U. (1977), Nobody home: The erosion of the American family. *Psychology Today, 10 (12)*, 41-47.

Byham W. & Spitzen, M. (1972). *The law and personnel testing.* New York: American Management Association.

Carroll, S.J. (1976). The topsy-turvy world of a Califorina prison. *Behavior Today*, 12-6, 4-6.

Cook, N.D. & Kono, S. (1977). Black Psychology: The third great tradition. *The Journal of Black Psychology, 3, (2)*, 18-28.

Curtis, W.M.J. (1978). The black adolescent's self-concept and academic performance. *Western Journal of Black Studies, 2 (2)*, 125-131.

Daedalus (1977), The family. 2, 106. Author.

Edwards, H. (1982). On the issue of race in contemporary American sports. *The Western Journal of Black Studies, 6 (3)*, 138-144.

Epps, E.G. (1969a). Negro academic motivation and performance: An overview. *Journal of Social Issues, 25 (3)* 5-11.

Epps, E.G. (1969a). Correlates of academic achievement among Northern and Southern urban Negro students. *Journal of Social Issues, 25 (3)*, 55-70.

Etzioni, A. (1977). Science and the future of the family. *Science, 196*, 4289, Editorial.

Fairchild, H.H. (1983). A micro-analysis of the Alley-Oop with notes on the race and IQ controversy. Paper presented at the 16th Annual Convention of the Association of Black Psychologists, Washington, D.C.

Farr, J.L., O'Leary, B.S., Pfeiffer, C.M., Goldstein, I.L., & Bartlett, C.J. (1971). Ethnic group membership as a moderator in the prediction of job performance, Technical Report No. 2, American Institutes for Research, Silver Spring, MD.

Feinman, S. & Entwisle, D.R. (1976). Children's ability to recognize other children's faces. *Child Development, 47*, 506-510.

Franklin, A.J. & Fulani, L. (1974). Cultural content of materials and ethnic group performance in categorized recall. Paper presented at the Empirical Research Conference of Black Psychologists, Ann Arbor, Michigan.

Frazier, E.F. (1932). *The Negro family in Chicago.* Chicago, IL.: University of Chicago Press.

Frazier, E.F. (1939). *The Negro family in the United States.* Chicago, IL.: University of Chicago Press.

Garner, T. (1985). Developing rhetorical competency in oral culture. *Western Journal of Black Studies, 9*, 17-22.

Gitter, A.G., Black, H. & Mostofsky, D.I. (1972). Race and sex in perception of emotion. *Journal of Social Issues, 28*, 63-78.

Gloye, E. (1980). Culture and right brain processing. Behavioral and Social Sciences Report, Pasadena, California: Office of Naval Research, 20, May-June 1980.

Goodstein, L.D., & Heilbrum, A.B., Jr. (1962).Prediction of college achievement from the Edwards Personal Preference Schedule at three levels of intellectual ability. *Journal of Applied Psychology, 46*, 317-320.

Grande, P.P. & Simons, J.B. (1967). Personal values and academic performance among engineering students. *Personnel and Guidance Journal, 45 (6),* 585-588.

Grier, W.H. & Cobbs, P.M. (1968). *Black rage.* New York: Bantam Books.

Guthrie, R.V. (1977). *Even the rat was white.* New York: Harper and Row.

Hakel, M.D. (1966). Prediction of college achievement from the Edwards Personal Preference Schedule using intellectual ability as a moderator. *Journal of Applied Psychology, 50 (4),* 336-340.

Hayles, R. (1974). The role of values in the achievement of black freshmen at the University of Colorado. Unpublished doctoral dissertation. University of Colorado in Boulder.

Hayles, R. (1978). Psychological health among culturally different families. Paper presented at the 4th International Association of Cross Cultural Psychology Congress, Munich, Germany.

Hayles, R. & Nobles, W.W. (1978) (Eds.) The effectively coping black family. In E.J. Hunter and D.S. Nice (Eds). *Military families: Adaptation to change.* New York: Praeger.

Hayles, R. & Perry, R.W. (1981). Racial equality in the American naval justice system: An analysis of incarceration differentials. *Ethnic and Racial Studies, 4 (1),* January, 44-45.

Hayles, R. (1982). Costs and benefits of integrating persons from diverse cultures into organizations. Twentieth International Congress of Applied Psychology, Edinburgh, Scotland.

Hill, R. (1972). *The strengths of black families.* New York: Emerson Hall.

Hilliard, A.G. (1977). The predictive validity of norm-referenced standardized tests: Piaget or Binet? *The Negro Educational Review, 28 (3-4),* 189-201.

Hilliard, A.G. (1978). Free your mind, return to the source. The African origin of civilization and European scientific colonialism. Notes and outline for presentation.

Hoffman, C. & Kahan, S. (1977). Field dependence and facial recognition. *Perception Motor Skills, 44,* 119-124.

James. G.G.M. (1954). *Stolen legacy.* New York: Philosophical Library.

Joint Commission on Mental Health of Children. (1969) Digest of crisis in child mental health: Challenge for the 1970's. New York: Harper and Row Publishers.

Jones, T. (1978). The court system and black America: A critical analysis. *The Western Journal of Black Studies, 2 (4),* 259-267.

Kanter, R.M. (1983). *The change masters: Innovation and entrepreneurship in the American corporation.* New York: Simon and Schuster, Inc.

Kamin, L. (1974). *The science and politics of IQ.* Potomac, MD: Lawrence Erlbaum.

Karenga, R. (1967). *The quotable Karenga.* Los Angeles, CA: U.S. Organization.

Kochman, T. (1972). Toward an ethnography of black American speech behavior. In A. L. Smith (Ed.) *Language, communication and rhetoric in black America.* New York: Harper & Row, 1972.

Lavrakas, P.J., Buri, J.R. & Mayzner, M.S. (1976). A perspective on the recognition of other-race faces. *Perception, Psycho-physics and Physiology, 20,* 475-481.

Levin, H.S., Hamsher, K. & Benton, A.L. (1975). A short form of the test of facial recognition for clinical use. *Journal of Psychology, 91,* 223-228.

Lewis, J.M. & Looney, J. G. (1986). *The long struggle: Well-functioning working-class black families.* New York: Brunner/Mazel.

Libman, J. & Lawson, H. (1976). The future revised: The family, troubled by changing morals, still likely to thrive, *The Wall Street Journal, 94 (54).*

Lunneborg, C.E. & Lunneborg, P.W. (1967). EPPS patterns in the prediction of academic achievement. *Journal of Counseling Psychology, 14 (4),* 389-390.

Lynn, M. & Oldenquist, A. (1986). Egoistic and nonegoistic motives in social dilemmas. *American Psychologist, 41 (5),* 529-534.

Martin, E.P. & Martin, J.M. (1980). *The black extended family.* Chicago: University of Chicago Press.

Mattison, E.G. & Northrup, J.R. (1975). *Minority upgrading and mobility in the Navy and Marine Corps.* Industrial Research Unit Report No. 20. Philadelphia: The Wharton School, University of Pennsylvania.

Mbiti, J.S. (1970). *African religions and philosophies.* New York: Anchor Books, Doubleday.

McAdoo, J. & McAdoo, H. (1985). *Black children: social, educational and parental.* Beverly Hills: Sage.

McCain, G., Cox, V.C. & Paulus, P.B. (1980). The effects of prison crowding on inmate behavior, Final Report, LEAA Grant, 78-NI-HX-0019, University of Texas, at Arlington.

McGee, D.P. (1976). An introduction to African psychology: Melanin, the psysiological basis for psychological oneness. In King, Lewis M., Dixon, Nervon J., & Nobles, Wade W. (Eds.). African philosophy: *Assumptions & paradigms for research on black persons.* Fanon Research & Development Center, Charles R. Drew Postgraduate Medical School, Los Angeles, California.

McQueen, A. J. (1977). The adaptations of urban black families: Trends, problems, and issues. Conference on families in contemporary America: Varieties of form, function and experience. Sponsored by the Department of Psychiatry and Behavioral Sciences, George Washington University, School of Medicine and the Center for Continuing Education in Mental Health, Psychiatric Institute Foundation, Washington, D.C.

Memmi, A. (1965). *The colonizer and the colonized.* New York: The Orion Press, Inc.

Monitor, (1968, January). American Psychological Association, pp. 7-9.

Moscovitch, M., Scullion, D., & Cristie, D. (1976). Early versus late stages of processing and their relation to functional hermispheric asymmetries in face recognition. *Journal of Experimental Psychology and Human Perceptual Performance, 2,* 401-416.

National Association for the Advancement of Colored People, (1976). *NAACP report on minority testing.* New York: NAACP Special Contribution Fund.

National Geographic, (1974). Ancient pharmacy. Washington, D.C., July issue.

Negro Education Review, (1977). Issue on testing black students, *28* 3, 4.

Newmeyer, J.A. (1970). Creativity and nonverbal communication in pre-adolescent white and black children. Unpublished doctoral dissertation, Harvard University.

Nobles, W.W. (1976a). Extended-self: Rethinking the so-called Negro self-concept. *The Journal of Black Psychology, 2 (20),* 15-24.

Nobles, W.W. (1976). A formulative and empirical study of black families. A Final Report submitted to the Office of Child Development under contract number 90-C-255.

O'Driscoll, M.P. (1976). Values and culture contact: Some perspectives and problems. In Brislin, Richard W. (Ed.) Topics in Culture Learning, Honolulu: East-West Center, 4, 8-9.

Pesner, J. W., & Auld, F. (1980). The relationship between bilingual proficiency and self-esteem. International Journal of Intercultural Relations, 4, 339-351.

Price-Williams, D. R. & Ramirez, M. (1977). Divergent thinking, cultural deficiencies and civilizations. The Journal of Social Psychology, 103, 3-11.

Ramirez, M.T. (1983). Psychology of the Americas: Mestizo perspectives on personality and mental health. New York: Pergamon Press.

Ramirez, M., & Castaneda, A. (1974). Cultural democracy, bicognitive development and education. New York: Academic Press.

Ross, H.L. & Glaser, E.M. (1973). Making it out of the ghetto. Professional Psychology, 347-356.

Rowland, M.K. & Del Campo, P. (1968). The values of the educationally disadvantaged. How different are they? Journal of Negro Education, 37, 86-89.

Sarason, I.G., (1979). Life stress, self-preoccupation, and social supports. Technical Report. Seattle: University of Washington.

Scanzoni, J.H. (1971). The black family in modern society. Boston: Allyn and Bacon, Inc., 1971.

Smith, E. A. (1977). A case for bilingual and bicultural education for United States slave descendants of African origin. Department of Linguistics, Seminar Paper Series, Paper No. 39, California State University, Fullerton, 1977.

Sperry, R.W. (1974). Science and the problem of values. Zygon, 9, 7-21.

Staples, R. (1974). The black family in evolutionary perspective, The Black Scholar, 5 (9), 2-9.

Stern, P.C. (1978). When do people act to maintain common resources? A reformulated psychological question for our times, International Journal of Psychology, 13 (2), 149-158.

Szapocznik, J., Kurtines, W.M., & Fernandez, T. (1980). Bicultural involvement and adjustment in Hispanic-American youths, International Journal of Intercultural Relations, 4, 353-356.

Taylor, O. (1969). Historical development of black English and implications for American education. Center for Applied Linguistics, Howard University, Washington, D.C.

Thomas, D.L., Franks, D.D., & Calonico, J. (1970). Role-taking and power in social psychology. American Sociological Review, 37, 605-614.

Toffler, A. (1980). The third wave. New York: Bantam Books.

Torrance, E.P. (1967). Understanding the fourth grade slump in creative thinking. Final report on Cooperative Research Project No. 944, Office of Education. Athens, Georgia: Georgia Studies of Creative Behavior, University of Georgia.

Torrance, E.P. (1971). Are the Torrance Tests of Creative Thinking biased against or in favor of the "disadvantaged" groups?, Gifted Child Quarterly, Summer, 75-80.

Triandis, H.C., Bass, A.R., Ewen, R.B., & Mikesell, E.H. (1963). Team creativity as a function of the creativity of the members. *Journal of Applied Psychology, 47 (2)*, 104-110.

Tucker, R.C. (1980). Towards a philosophy of science for black-white studies. Paper presented at the 13th annual convention of the Association of Black Psychologists, Cherry Hill, New Jersey.

Turner, R.H. Role-taking: Process versus conformity. (1956). In A.M. Rose (Ed.), *Human behavior and social process: An interactionist approach.* Boston: Houghton-Mifflin, Co.

Tyndall, K. (1986). Interpreter gland, *Insight*, March 3, p. 64.

U.S. Bureau of the Census (1974). Current Population Reports, Special Studies, P-23 No. 54. The social and economic status of the Black population in the United States. Washington, D.C.

Valentine, C. (1971). Deficit, difference and bi-cultural models of Afro-American behavior. *Harvard Educational Review, 41*, 137-157.

Wells, L. (1985). Misunderstandings of and among cultures: The effects of transubstantiative error. *Sunrise Seminars, 2*, 51-57.

Werner, E.E. (1979). Cross-cultural studies of sensorimotor development in infants. In E.E. Werner, *Cross-cultural child development.* Monterey, CA: Brooks Cole.

Werner, E.E. & Smith, R.S. (1982). *Vulnerable but invincible: A longitudinal study of resilient children and youth.* New York: McGraw Hill.

Williams, C. (1974). *The destruction of black civilization: Great issues of a race from 4500 B.C. to 2000 A.D.* Chicago: Third World Press.

Williams, R.L. (1972) *The black intelligence test for cultural homogeneity manual.* St. Louis: Williams & Associates, 1972.

Willie, C.V. & Weinandy, J. (1963). The structure and composition of "problem" and "stable" families in a low-income population. *Marriage and Family Living, 25*, 439-446.

Wilson, I.H. (1975). Business and the future: Social challenge, corporate response. In A.A. Spekke (Ed.), *The next 25 years: Crisis and opportunity.* Washington, D.C.: World Future Society.

Ziller, R.C. (1972). Homogeneity and heterogeneity of group membership. In C.G. McClintock, *Experimental social psychology.* New York: Holt, Rinehart and Winston.

Applications of
Black Perspectives

V. Applications of Black Perspectives

In a 1980 paper, White, Parham, and Parham introduced the notion of Black psychology as a unifying force in psychology. Their view emphasized that Black psychology was not an isolated body of ideas with relevance only to African Americans, but that the views, constructs, and perspectives of black psychologists have the potential for informing much wider arenas of psychological concern. Papers in the present section show how black perspectives can inform and direct research in the more traditional areas of psychology and are written to whet the reader's appetite and hopefully encourage wide applications of black perspectives to more conventional psychological subject matter, especially as the subject matter relates to African Americans.

Fields of Psychology

The papers in this section show how black scholars have looked at several subdisciplines in psychology—educational, social, developmental, physiological, experimental, and organizational. The papers included here are not conventional critiques from African American perspectives of the full range of subject-matter of the subdisciplines represented. Such a task would be formidable, and far beyond the scope of the present volume. It is possible, nevertheless, to give the reader a flavor of the kinds of concerns, issues, and approaches that black psychologists have used in their disciplinary-based research and writing. White and Johnson ("Awareness, Pride and Identity: A Positive Educational Strategy for Black Youth") are engaged in model building. Strongly rejecting the practice of determining the educational needs of culturally different youth on the basis of white middle class norms and standards (acculturistic models), they present a model of education based upon the unique characteristics and learning styles of low-income urban black children and youth. White and Johnson then go on to examine educational programs of acculturation with attention to the deficiencies of these approaches, and folklore about how black children and youth learn. An important section of White and Johnson's paper is their attention to building theories which incorporate the world view of black children and youth. They conclude with a set of recommendations for fostering the optimal development of black youth in educational settings.

It is incumbent upon black scholars to review and critically evaluate the psychological literature on black people and to note trends, to identify shortcomings and to point to areas needing further study and attention. Content analysis is one method that can be used to systematically evaluate a large body of literature. In the present section, the approach has been used to look at certain topics in developmental and social psychology. In the first paper, McLoyd ("What Is the Study of African American Children the Study of?") uses content analysis and her own analytical skills to review the ways in which African American children have been studied and described in the psychological literature, to examine the extent to which comparative methodology has been used in the studies, to investigate differences between research on the black child reported in major developmental and other journals, and to look at the extent to which the study of African American children has changed over time. McLoyd relates her findings to social and political changes in American Society.

In the next paper, James Jones ("The Concept of Race in Social Psychology") reviews the treatment of race in social psychology journals and textbooks and uses the results of content analysis to propose reasons for the patterns revealed. Jones concludes by suggesting how social psychology might be enriched by a consideration of cultural differences and by the inclusion of culture-relevant concepts and variables.

Boykin ("Black Psychology and Experimental Psychology A Functional Confluence") provides an enlightening critique of the strengths and limitations of experimental psychology and draws on his own ingeneous studies and those of his colleagues and others to convincingly demonstrate how true experiments that protect and incorporate the integrity of the black experience can be conducted.

In an area that has received very little attention from black psychologists, Harrell, Clark, and Allen ("That Ounce of Value: Visualizing The Application of Psychophysiological Methods in Black Psychology") discuss the research of three black psychopsychologists and show how laboratory-based psychophysiological studies can be used to address issues of interest to black psychologists.

In a review that includes an impressive body of literature, including his own work, Bowman ("Organizational Psychology: African American Perspectives") discusses "critical issues that must be addressed to better understand the experience of African Americans in organizational settings." Bowman's adoption of Boykin's triple quandry paradigm is a particularly powerful framework for conceptualizing the unique problems of African Americans in organizations.

Counseling and Psychotherapy

Research and writing on the counseling of blacks continues to increase and develop. Papers in the first edition were devoted to establishing the views that counseling strategies and techniques ought to take account of the unique history, culture, and experiences of African Americans, and that the conceptual framework from which most counselors worked was dysfunctional for African American—views that did not enjoy widespread currency in the late 1960s and early 1970s.

Within recent years there has been much activity in addressing concerns highlighted in the previous editions. Just how much progress has been made and the forces leading to the changes is subject of papers by Jackson ("The African Genesis of the Black Perspective in Helping") and Lee ("Counseling African Americans: From Theory to Practice"). Jackson contrasts the European perspective in helping with that of the African perspective and draws specific implications from the African perspective for the treatment of African American clients.

Lee gives a brief overview of the black perspective in counseling, admonishes to us to avoid considering all black people as alike, advises counselors to take a proactive approach to their work with African American clients, and provides us with directions for promoting career and personal-social development and fostering African American psychological health—all of which should inform counselor training and research.

We are beginning to apply the new concepts and ideas of black psychologists to actual clinical intervention with African American clients. One approach is by Arthur Jones ("Psychological Functining in African Americans: A Conceptual Guide for Use in Psychotherapy") who develops a model that accounts for individual differences among African Americans. Jones' model includes four classes of variables: 1) reaction to racial oppression; 2) influences of the majority culture; 3) influence of traditional African American culture; and 4) individual and family experiences and endowments. Drawing upon his own clinical experiences, Jones illustrates how each of the variables can be used as a basis for conceptualizing therapeutic approaches with African American clients.

Psychologists and Psychology in the Community

An early and continuing concern of black psychologists has been the application of psychological concepts and interventions in the African American community. Up to and including the 1960s, the stance of black psychologists was largely reactive. That is, the vast majority of black psychologists devoted their energies to the perceived misapplication of psychology in African American communities. The situation is much different in the early 1990s. The stance of black psychologists is now proactive: their energies are being turned to what must be done to make psychology more useful in the community. Examples of this activity are reflected in papers in the present section which address such issues and questions as: What are the dilemmas faced by black psychologists in their work in the community and how can they be resolved? How can the black community facilitate positive self-identity in the black child? What do black psychologists have to contribute to understanding and dealing with the criminal justice system as it relates to African American people?

Jones ("The Black Psychologist As Consultant and Therapist") deals with issues of the individual black professional in the delivery of consultation services. Jones identifies inner problems faced by the black psychologist who is forced to face the fact that even his Ph.D. degree indicates a certain establishment orientation. But he, no less than the client, is struggling with his blackness. We must understand, Jones notes, that the society in which his personal and professional success was achieved exists simultaneously in a personally destructive context. Through many examples from clinical practice, Jones highlights issues and dilemmas faced by the black psychological consultant working in the African American community.

What mechanisms lead to the development of healthy self-image and high personal regard? In the next paper ("The Black Community As the Source of Positive Self-Concept for Black Children: A Theoretical Perspective"), Barnes reviews data from social and psychological sources on the development of the black child's self-concept and questions many of the hypotheses and findings in this area. Barnes warns against using research based on low-income blacks as a basis for generalizing about all African Americans, and against assuming that the generalized other to which the black child responds is synonymous with white society. Barnes also highlights conditions and characteristics of the African American community that facilitate development of a positive self-identity in the black child.

In the final paper of the section, Thomas Hilliard ("Application of Psychology and the Criminal Justice System: A Black Perspective"), presents substantive analyses of jury selection, criminal responsibility, and penal reform, with particular attention to how racism may affect African Americans in relationship to the above areas. In addition to his astute analyses, Hilliard emphasizes psychological literature, action models, and techniques that may help address problems faced by African Americans who are involved with the criminal justice system.

Racism

As the authors of a number of papers in this volume indicate, psychology and other social sciences have embraced a number of racist themes in describing, explaining, and attempting to modify the behavior of African Americans. These themes can be seen in every section of this volume—in conceptions of black people's abilities and personality, in suggestions for the education of blacks, and in suggestions for work with African Americans in counseling and psychotherapy, to name a few. Refuting these notions, while simultaneoulsy presenting a black perspective, is a central concern of contributors to the present volume. This refutational work by African American scholars is valuable and must be continued, but we also need to turn our attention to the concept of racism itself. The purpose of this section, therefore, is to present research and writing on racism by African American scholars.

In the first paper ("White Racism: Its Root, Form, and Functions"), Comer traces the development of white racism in the United States. He outlines the function it has served and suggests how it is transmitted from one generation to the next. Given the great racial awareness and pride characterizing contemporary African Americans, Comer concludes that without a significant reduction in white racism now, African American reactions can only be intensified and form the basis for a "more widespread and malignant form of black racism."

The late Lloyd Delany's "The Other Bodies in the River" views white racism as classic pathology. Using examples from the past and contemporary history, Delany examined the acting out, denial of reality, projection, transference of blame, disassociation, and justification components of white racism.

James Jones ("Racism: A Cultural Analysis of The Problem") reminds us of the continuing presence of racism in this country and the need to sensitize those in power to the potential of non-whites as a source of strength in this society. Jones gives us definitions of key terms and the rememdies associated with each of these terms. His focus, however, is upon contrasting models on the sources of racial disparities: 1) system blame and 2) individual blame, and upon suggestions as to how problems associated with these models can be overcome. A key element of his approach is TRIOS, which is an acronym for Time, Rhythm, Improvisation, Oral Expression, and Spirituality.

While African American social scientists have written about racism from social, psychological, educational, sociological, and political contexts, especially to clarify its nature and to document its impact on African Americans, they have conducted little research on the topic. The work by Taylor ("Dimensionalization of Racialism") is an exception. Emphasizing that *racialism* (a term Taylor uses to refer to prejudice developed along racial lines, "a term which distinguished it from other forms of social prejudice") is a complexly organized process, Taylor offers a conceptual taxonomy that generates a number of types of racialism. When all combinations of content, incident, and sociogenic variables are considered, 144 varieties of racialism are identified. Taylor suggests that specific typing promises "important information regarding differential vulnerability to change, direction and expected extent of change, and strategy for change." A variety of empirical studies supporting Taylor's conceptualization are reported—with the promise of more to come.

Research

The three papers in this section deal with research on African Americans, including a discussion of Eurocentric and Afrocentric paradigms of research, specific issues in mental health research, and ethical issues.

Observing that "traditional scientific paradigms have served the function of perpetuating oppression and erroneously depicting the reality of the victims of oppression," Akbar ("Paradigms of African American Research") takes a critical look at traditional paradigms for investigations of the black community, which he finds to be "counteractive to the needs of African Americans." Akbar then suggests an alternative paradigm and models, methods and modalities he believes are "consistent with the survival, growth and perpetuation of African American communities".

Next, Gary ("Mental Health of Black Americans: Research Trends and Directions") takes a critical look at the research industry and black participation in it and reviews relatively recent research on African American mental health, with special attention to major theoretical and methodological problems in the research. Gary also addresses the rather infrequently discussed topic of intragroup comparisons of African American mental health and includes as a part of this discussion a number of studies he and his colleagues conducted at the Institute for Urban Affairs and Research at Howard University. Finally, Gary offers directions for future research.

Bowman, in the final paper, ("Race, Class and Ethics in Research: Belmont Principles to Functional Relevance") takes a critical look at ethical issues in research and draws upon the Tuskegee Syphlis Experiment and the National Surveys of African Americans to illuminate crucial ethical issues, principles and guidelines that have relevance for the conduct of research on African Americans and other vulnerable race and class groups.

Awareness, Pride and Identity: A Positive Educational Strategy for Black Youth

Joseph L. White and James A. Johnson, Jr.

> The systematic application of ethnic awareness, identity, and pride can substantially contribute to the understanding and solution of a variety of individual, group and institutional problems. Each time black is used it must express thoughts, attitudes, and feelings that are embodied in the black experience. It must also provide the strategies and goals for correcting defective self-concepts . . . (Thomas, 1974, pp. 68-69).

Traditionally, educational needs have been determined by comparing student behavior with existing institutional norms. The use of such a model is appropriate for children and youth who have learned a culture or lifestyle that overlaps the cultural lifestyle that is valued by the school. However, the use of the same model for students who come from lifestyles or cultures that significantly differ from the school-valued culture results in the labeling of those students as deficient. Such a model is acculturistic. For those of us who value cultural pluralism, especially in education, acculturistic models are unacceptable. The purpose of this paper is not to criticize the acculturistic model, but rather, to present the reader with an alternative model which is pluralist in nature. Pluralist models are designed to help educators meet the needs of children from specific ethnic classes. At issue here is the low-income, urban black ethnic class (black children and youth).

> . . . low-income, urban black children and their families constitute a fairly significant proportion of the ethnic and social minority population in this country, and compared with other ethnic classes, are among those suffering most from existing societal conditions (Johnson, 1973, p. 130).

The making of decisions with respect to the educational needs of black children and youth is of extreme importance. Jacobs, for example, concluded from his interviews with black citizens after the Watts Rebellion that four primary agents of oppression were salient. Those four primary agents of oppression are the police, welfare personnel, merchants, and agents of the school. Schooling agents view their primary purpose as that of actualizing and enabling children and youth. However, these data suggest that they are oppressing and disabling black children and youth. This conflict of perceptions indicates that something in the way of dramatic change must take place before educators will be able to play useful and productive roles in the growth and development of black children and youth. Dramatic change cannot, in our judgement, be achieved by utilizing acculturistic models. Such models are not perceived as legitimate by a sizable number of visible and powerful black opinion-makers. Furthermore, there is irrefutable evidence that these models do not work.

One example of an acculturistic model that, by all evidence, has failed to work is Compensatory Education. Beginning in the 1960s and continuing into this decade, the blame for the failure of American Public Schools to effectively educate black children and youth was and is, by this model, placed squarely on the shoulders of black children and youth and their families. The cultural deprivation model, from which Compensatory Education stems, states, in essence, that black children come from homes which are incapable of simulating Euro-American and middle class intellectual, cognitive and social development. Put another way, cultural deprivation is predicated upon the tenuous proposition that a nurturing environment in which Euro-American and middle class actors (or actors who aspire to Euro-Americaness and middle classness) are dominant is critical to healthy child growth and development. A related proposition is that if a child is not nurtured in such an environment, and the effects of the "inadequate nurturing environment" are not compensated for, then the child's performance will be inconsistent with institutional expectations.

Compensatory Educational Programs can be trichotomized into programs that purport to treat superficial, deep, and profound "deficiencies." Programs purporting to treat "superficial deficiencies" are characterized by an "enrichment ethic." The initial Head Start programs, designed to undo "superficial deficiencies," that were imputed to black children and youth are examples of the operationalization of an "enrichment ethic." "Deep deficiency" programs are characterized by the "total immersion ethic." Typically, these programs treat children for periods of time as long as three and one half years prior to kindergarten or first grade. Treatment is directed toward supplanting the child's language, culturally determined preferences with respect to music, dance, food, pre-interaction, and expectations as to how child behavior will be managed by adults. Examples of "deep deficiency" programs or programs which operationalize a "total immersion ethic" are longitudinal Head Start programs, Parent Child Centers, and other "home grown" programs such as Get Ready and Get Set. It should be noted that programs that would treat "superficial" and "deep deficiencies" are a function of time. They provide treatment in an institution separate and apart from the home and focus on modifying the behavior of the child.

"Profound deficiency" programs focus on the child's home and can be characterized by a "causal analysis ethic." The child in these programs is perceived as a manipulative non-cause and the child's mother is perceived as a manipulative cause. Therefore, efforts are made to render the mother's behavior more consistent with behavior imputed to Euro-American and middle class mothers. It is argued that if the mother can be induced to behave in the preferred manner, then it is likely her child will be socialized to the preferred norms.

After more than a decade it is clear that, on purely pragmatic grounds, Compensatory Education has not worked. The drop/push-out rate among black children and youth remains high. Black children and youth in elementary schools throughout the Nation continue to fail to be presented with appropriate opportunities to master basic skills in reading and mathematics. Assertions that the behavior of black children and youth and their mothers have changed in the "preferred direction" as a result of their being manipulated by Compensatory Education strategies are not supported by empirical evidence. Additionally, our experience is that black children and youth and their mothers, not withstanding the imposition of these "treatments," continue to eat grits, greens, and maws; "boog-a-loo," "bump and grind," manifest "soul and style"; speak both "radio-announcer English" and Ebonics, and in general, behave independent of the acculturative objective and mission of the educational technocracy.

In addition to problem areas associated with acculturation and cultural deprivation there exists a third problem area, that of folklore about how black children and youth learn. Here we have limited ourselves to four salient elements of this folklore: (1) relationships between research methodology and outcomes of schooling, (2) relationships between teacher expectations and outcomes of schooling, (3) relationships between learning and achievement motivation, and (4) relationships between language and learning. Sectors of the educational technocracy babble the findings of Moynihan, Coleman, and Jencks as though those findings were consistent with truth. Yet, little or no emphasis has been placed on the reality that: (1) the input-output model utilized by these social scientists is fraught with deficiencies and untenable assumptions, (2) because researchers cannot find statistically significant differences among phenomena does not mean that differences do not exist, (3) that data utilized by these researchers were secondary and tertiary and subject to the possibility of error at their source, and (4) that many significant events occur in processes that are ignored by researchers who use this model. In short, while the technocrats would lead us to believe that the truth with respect to the educational and social outcomes of schooling for black children and youth is known, it is our position that their reported findings are suspect. Educational and social outcomes of schooling for black children and youth need to be looked at from other perspectives using alternative research models.

A second element of this folklore derives from the findings reported by Rosenthal and Jacobson in their book, *Pygmalion in the Classroom*. The controversial proposition tested by Rosenthal and Jacobson, that learning is a function of teacher expectations, is difficult for us to assess because the literature is contradictory and confusing. While our objective here is not to list all possible substantive and procedural problems with the study, we will point out two problems with that study which support our position. First, the authors of the study failed to define the term "expectation." It is impossible to determine from the text whether the authors are referring to teacher *anticipation* of specific student behavior independent of institutional norms, or teacher *anticipation* of student behavior in relation to institutional norms. Second, we are not sure of the source of the expectations imputed to the teachers by the authors of the study. Was prior teacher knowledge of the child, siblings, or peers seminal to the expectations, or were status variables such as the child's home, address, sex, or appearance associated with the expectation? For these reasons, among others, we argue that relationships that are believed to exist between teacher expectations for and outcomes of schooling of black children and youth are, at best, speculation.

A third dimension of technocratic folklore with which we find problems is associated with the interaction of learning and achievement motivation. Professors Atkinson and McCelland of Harvard University define achievement motivation as competition with a standard of excellence. The argument states that since black children and youth do not achieve effectually in school (or are not schooled effectively) black children and youth have low achievement motivation. Note two things: first, the assumption is made that a standard of excellence is embedded in urban schools and that black children and youth are not motivated to compete with these standards. Second, the problem is defined in terms of child-failure while little or no attention is given to the fact that agents of urban schools fail to recognize the nature and meet the needs of black children and youth. Were the latter position given serious attention, we would be forced to approach questions associated with the technocracy's motivation, ability, proclivity, or disposition to motivate black children and youth to compete with standards of excellence.

A fourth element of the folklore fabric is language. Technologists argue that education involves communication between teachers and students and the language by which education is accomplished is "radio-announcer" English. The argument goes on to state that since black children and youth do not typically speak "radio-announcer" English, it can be predicted that those children will have difficulty communicating with their teachers and, by extension, learning. This argument assumes that teachers speak "radio-announcer" English. The argument also makes the ethnocentric assumption that "radio-announcer" or "standard" English is preferable to Ebonics. The argument further denies the fact that persons with extreme hearing loss and mute persons learn not withstanding the fact that they do not speak or understand "radio-announcer" English. We do not deny the importance of teacher-pupil communication to learning. What we do take issue with is the position that communication must take place in a language which is often foreign to black children and youth in order for learning to occur.

The juxtaposition of these three problem areas yields a triangle. Leg one may be labeled "acculturation," leg two, "deficiency," and leg three, "folklore." The interaction of legs one and two ("acculturation" and "deficiency") has been discussed above under Compensatory Education, which, in effect, denies the black experience and self-actualization in black children and youth. The interaction of legs one and three explicates the futile and illogical nature of the "acculturation ethic." First, acculturation is a term that is easily expressed. However, the application of resources to understanding and solving individual, ethnic class and institutional problems associated with acculturation has not been forthcoming. Second, it is difficult, and less than reasonable, to believe that black children and youth will become white and middle class because their teachers want, anticipate, or expect these metamorphoses to take place. Third, there is no reason to believe that white and middle classness and standards of excellence are coterminous. And fourth, we are less than fully convinced that if all black children and youth were competent utilizers and generators of "radio-announcer" English, other "defects" would not be identified and targeted.

The interaction of legs one and three yields several rhetorical questions: 1. To what extent are perceived "deficiencies" imputed to black children and youth as a function of folklore? 2. To what extent are these perceived "deficiencies" a function of the fact that these children have been socialized to different norms? 3. To what extent are the academic and social outcomes of schooling for black children and youth a function of barriers imposed by societal institutions which inhibit access to the "good life"? 4. To what extent have agents of schools been socialized to believe that black children and youth are not educable? 5. To what extent are standards of excellence embedded in urban schools? 6. To what extent is learning dependent upon language? 7. To what extent is the nation serious about solving problems associated with the schooling of black children and youth?

We contend that realistic answers to these questions would yield the following picture: 1. The schooling of black children and youth takes place in a society that is ethnocentric—as Stokely says, " . . . from top to bottom, left to right" (Carmichael, 1971). 2. Early in the growth and development of white and middle class children and youth society strikes a bargain. By age five or six those youngsters are on a conveyor belt labeled "school," and whenever those youngsters leave the conveyor belt (whether it be high school, college, or the university) they inherit a range of choices that have been reinforced from day one of that youngster's life. That is, with slight exception, the butcher, the milkman, the principal of the school, the mayor, and the president are Euro-Americans. 3. Black children and youth are encouraged to stay on the same conveyor belt notwithstanding the fact that they do not inherit the same range of choices. 4. When a youngster knows that he is not going to inherit an equal range of choices with respect to admission to union programs, private business, politics, and other offices, statuses and positions, it is difficult to hold the value that that youngster should conform to what is expected by agents of the educational technocracy. 5. The black child's experience is constantly negated by schooling agents. This negation results in the questioning by the child of his own self-worth and the creation of retroactive inhibition and interference modification which black children and youth are left to their own devices to manage. 6. Black children and youth should enter the adult world with enabling managerial strategies and skills. These skills should facilitate the commanding of a wide-range of economic, occupational and psychosocial options. This condition has not been achieved for black children and youth in this complex, oppressive society.

Such a picture causes us to raise the question, "What are the kinds of experiences necessary for the development of enabling managerial strategies and skills in black children and youth?" Prior to addressing such a question, the following observations about human interactions are in order. This is necessary due to the critical nature of the interaction of black children and youth and schooling agents. We have observed that it is difficult for human beings to interact if they do not consent. We have further observed that the consent to interact is best obtained when, at the least, the rules which govern the interaction are agreed upon and, at best, the participants engaged in the interaction contribute to the definition of those rules. Those rules typically govern: (1) the conditions under which any interaction may be said to have commenced, (2) the behavior of each of the participants, and (3) the conditions under which the value of the interaction is assessed to determine the worth or value of the interaction for each participant. These observations can be summarized as follows: 1. All interactions are rule-governed. 2. All interactions are commenced (or have an opening move). 3. All interactions include intermediate behavior or moves. 4. All interactions are terminated (by a terminal move). 5. The value or worth of all interactions is subject to assessment.

Given this background, let's now return to the question which was raised above vis-a-vis the kinds of developmental experiences necessary for the creation of strategies in black children and youth as they move toward becoming adults. Gerald West, a psychologist at San Francisco State College elicited from black children and youth responses to the question, "What kinds of experiences will enable you to effectually handle the world around you?" West's work is instructive because it represents an attempt to build a theory which incorporates the views and experiences of the children and youth at issue. This is a welcome departure from the typical practice of social scientists and educators who build theories about black persons without incorporating the points of view and perceptions of their experience. West asked black children and youth to relate to one primary thematic question: "Given the world we live in, what do you have going for you in order to get yourself together?" Subsequently, Joseph White and West have sequentially ordered the primary themes that were reported by the youngsters into the conceptual language of psychology.

Initially, the youngsters seemingly agreed that one had to have what they referred to as a "stick" or something one could use as an "opener" (an opening move) in combating the world. A "stick" or "opener" was defined to include mastery in such areas as verbal skills (a "bad rap"), an engaging personality, mechanical skills, mathematical ability, and musical talent. In a sense, a "stick" is an area of perceived mastery which generates self-confidence. Among child development technocrats it is generally agreed that self-confidence and mastery are highly intertwined. Avoiding the "chicken and egg" problem, it seems sound to reason that perceived mastery builds the kind of self-confidence that is necessary to reaching out and exploring new areas of mastery. Conversely, children without perceived areas of mastery and self-confidence tend to be reluctant to reach out for new areas of mastery believing that by doing so they expose themselves to the risk of failure.

Next, the youngsters placed great emphasis on the necessity of having "partners or dudes and chicks to hang out with." While they were obviously talking about what many of us label as "peer group relationships," the vital psychological input from one's partner seems to be positive recognition of, and reinforcement for, perceived areas of mastery. Furthermore, in the black community, the peer group, as a part of the "extended family," helps the black child fulfill the need for belongingness—the apparent psychological opposite of real and perceived alienation. To the extent that a black child possess self-confidence, which is reinforced by reality-bound perceived areas of mastery, the child has a framework for the development of a positive self-image and a sound notion of their own identity. We take this to mean that the black child or youth who has multiple areas of perceived mastery, that are recognized as such by significant others, is in the position to make strong and bold opening moves with authority and competence.

As the analysis of the data continued, a third area emerged which had to do with making decisions about alternatives (or intermediate vs. terminal moves). In the words of the respondents, "You have to lay back and check it out." In brief, one has to learn to sequentially analyze situations in such a way that one can accurately and comprehensively list alternative moves, and having the alternatives before oneself, select the alternative move which is in one's best interests. Hard drugs represent an excellent illustration of the process of sequential analysis. A youngster with a reasonable degree of reality-based predictive skills knows that "tasting" is an intermediate move and that "being strung out" is a terminal move. However, to the extent that black children and youth are lacking in self-confidence, mastery, recognition, and belongingness they may be vulnerable to choosing the ultimate terrors that heroin will finally bring down on them. That is, they may lack the ability to distinguish between intermediate and terminal moves.

Adult managerial strategies and sequential analysis, or the ability to "read" the social-cultural context competently, has, historically, been where black folks are concerned. This was due to the fact, that the ability to evoke and use these skills directly affected their total range of perceived options. One of the primary effects of oppression is the limiting of the range of choices; economically, occupationally, and psychologically. Thus, in order for black persons to approach a range of choices which is equivalent to that enjoyed by middle class and Euro-American persons, we must have, or be caused to have, a psychological style which enables us to create new alternatives, choices, and options which are based upon sound, sequential analysis of situations which face black persons as an ethnic class or as individuals.

To make some opening and intermediate moves toward such a condition, we present the following set of recommendations: 1. We must take a closer look at the interaction between black children and youth and schooling agents from a bicultural frame of reference. In doing so, it is incumbent upon us to examine the concepts which educational technocrats utilize in exploring why some children are able to learn and others are not and how the operationalization of these concepts negatively affects the self-image of black children and youth. 2. We must bring more black role models into the educational arena as practitioners and managers. It is our contention that when black children and youth can concretely see, through the presence of role models, that they can approach a range of choices that is equivalent to that range of choices available to Euro-American and middle class income children and youth, they will then have reality-based rationales for aspiring to roles to which they have not typically aspired. 3. We must further provide these technocrats with the capability to create and utilize data which are consistent with the experiential frames of reference and life experiences of black children and youth. 4. We must begin to help educational technocrats see the value of and utilize the experience bases which black children and youth bring to schooling. 5. We must reorganize delivery systems in such a way that black children and youth develop areas of mastery, self-confidence, self-recognition, and belongingness. We view such outcomes of schooling as these to be requisite to the development of the kind of successful managerial strategies that will enable black children and youth to become adults who can make decisions that are in their best interest. This paper began with a quote from Charles Thomas, but the quote was not finished. We would like to finish that quotation here. Thomas went on to say:

> . . . as well as the defective social system. Through such means we mount the challenge of those social forces whose function it is to perpetrate deficient-deficit sanctions in people of color (Thomas, 1974, pp. 68-69).

Here we have made, what is in our judgment, a viable opening move toward furthering the agenda of which Thomas speaks. We trust that this challenge is of vital concern to all of us who are concerned with the delivery of educational services to black children and youth. Accordingly, we invite you, in the words of the youngsters to "lay back and check it out."

References

Atkinson, J. W. (1966). *A Theory of achievement motivation*. New York: Wiley.

Carmichael, S. (1971). *Stokely speaks*. New York: Vintage.

Coleman,J., Campbell, E. K., Hobson, C. J., McPartland, J., Mood, A. M. Veinfeif, F. D., and York, R. L. (1966). *Equality of educational opportunity*. Washington, D. C.: U.S. Government Printing Office.

Jacobs, P. (1967). *Prelude to riot*. New York: Random House.

Jencks, C., et al. (1972). *Inequality: A reassessment of the effect of family and schooling in America*. New York: Basic Books.

Johnson, J., Jr. (Ed.) (1973). *On the interface between low-income, urban, black children and their teachers during the early school years*. San Francisco: Far West Laboratory for educational research and development.

Moynihan, P. (1967). *The Negro family, The case for national action.* In Lee Rainwater and William Yancy (Eds.) *The Moynihan report and the politics of controversy.* Cambridge, Ma.: M.I.T. Press.

Rosenthal, R. (1968). *Pygmalion in the classroom.* New York: Holt, Rinehart and Winston.

Thomas, C. W. (January, 1974). The significance of the E (throcentrism) factor in mental health. *Journal of Non-White Concerns in Personnel and Guidance, 22.*

What is the Study of African American Children the Study of?

The Conduct, Publication, and Changing Nature of Research on African American Children

Vonnie C. McLoyd

Almost since its inception, the psychology study of African American children has spawned heated debate. At issue most often have been the appropriateness of inferring competence on the basis of performance in environments deemed to be contrived, foreign, and suboptimal, comparing the behavior of African American children to that of European American children, interpreting differences between these two groups as evidence of deficits in American children, and using tests normed on European American children to assess the development of African American children (Howard & Scott, 1981; Labov, 1970; McLoyd, 1990; Myers, Rana & Harris, 1979). At the root of this controversy is a troika of circumstances whose impact on the lives of African American children is both certain and incalculable, namely, economic deprivation, minority status, and stigmatization growing out of the unique history of oppression and racism experienced by African Americans in the United States. These circumstances have shaped the criticisms of both early (Guthrie, 1976) and contemporary scholars about prevailing methods used to study African American children and the alternative research strategies and interpretations of data they have proposed. In this chapter I review these critiques and proposals and summarize the contributions my collaborators and I have made to this discourse (McLoyd & Randolph, 1984; McLoyd & Randolph, 1986; Washington & McLoyd, 1982).

A Tradition of Dissent

In 1916, an anonymous author expressed doubt that the Binet test of intelligence was appropriate for African American children. In addition, the author underscored the effects of rapport on performance and made clear that performance under certain circumstances may lead to underestimation of competence. It was the author's contention that in view of the tendency of African American children "not to let a white person know anything about him . . . it is not too much to say that the mere presence in the room of a member of the dominant race creates an atmosphere in which it is impossible to get a normal response" (Some Suggestions . . . , 1916, p. 202). These claims prompted an empirical investigation in 1928 by Herman Canady (cited in Guthrie, 1976), a prolific African American research psychologist, of the effects of the race of the experimenter on IQ test performance of African American and European American children. Canady (1936) found that both African American and European American children showed depressed performance when tested by a different race experimenter. His work was followed by a spate of research studies by a small contingent of African American psychologists that documented the effects of rapport and environmental conditions on IQ test performance and counteracted the popular belief that African Americans were intellectually inferior (Guthrie, 1976).

Instigating much of the early debate about the study of African American children was Horace Mann Bond (1924), the first African American president of Lincoln University in Pennsylvania. In his view, the comparison of lower-versus middle-class children was both invidious and spurious. He argued that intelligence tests were useful in monitoring the differential progress of children exposed to the same curricular and pedagogical conditions but decried their use to compare the abilities of children from unequal socioeconomic backgrounds. As he put it, "To compare the crowded millions of New York's East Side with the children of some professorial family on Morningside Heights indeed involves a great contradiction; and to claim that the results of the tests given to such diverse groups, drawn from such varying strata of the social complex, are in any wise accurate, is to expose a fatuous sense of unfairness and lack of appreciation of the great environmental factors of modern urban life" (Bond, 1924, p. 64).

Echoes of these early dissident voices that challenged the ecological and interpretative validity of research on African American children, running the gamut in focus from language to patterns of mother-child interaction, reached a crescendo during the early to mid-1970's (e.g., Bay Area Association of Black Psychologists, 1972; Clark, 1972; Cole & Bruner, 1971; Hall, 1974; Labov, 1970; Tulkin, 1972; Weems, 1974; Williams, 1972). This development coincided with an increase in both the study of African American children and the number of African Americans awarded Ph.D.'s in psychology and allied disciplines (Bayton, 1975; Guthrie, 1976). Perhaps most eminent and influential of the critiques were those of Cole and Bruner (1971) and Labov (1970). Labov challenged the validity of controlled experiments that purported to demonstrate that African American children are impoverished in their means of verbal expression. Like the early anonymous author (Some Suggestions . . . , 1916) cited above, he was sensitive to the inhibitory effect racial barriers might have on the behavior of African American children in the presence of European American examiners. Labov found that lower-income African American children who showed defensive monosyllabic behavior when tested by a white interviewer in an academic setting exhibited much improved performance when tested by a "regular" African American interviewed in a nonacademic setting designed to be minimally threatening. He concluded (1970, p. 171):

> Controlled experiments that have been offered in evidence [of verbal deprivation in Afro-American children] are misleading. The only thing that is controlled is the superficial form of the stimulus. All children are asked, "What do you think of capital punishment?" But the speaker's interpretation of these requests, and the action he believes is appropriate in response is completely uncontrolled. One can view these test stimuli as requests for information, commands for action, or meaningless sequences of words . . . With human subjects it is absurd to believe that identical stimuli are obtained by asking everyone the same question. Since the crucial intervening variables of interpretation and motivation are uncontrolled, most of the literature on verbal deprivation tells us nothing of the capacities of children.

Cole and Bruner (1971) applied Labov's arguments more broadly to the concept of competence, resurrecting and popularizing the competence versus performance distinction in their classic article "Cultural Differences and Inferences About Psychological Processes." They argued forcefully that groups typically diagnosed as culturally deprived have the same underlying competence as those in the mainstream of the dominant culture, that differences in performance derive from the situations and contexts in which competence is expressed, and that a simple equivalence-to-test-procedure is not sufficient to make inferences about the relative competence of different groups of children.

Comparative Study: A Question of Goals

Of the many characteristics of the study of African American children, perhaps none is more conspicuous and venerable than the tendency to compare African American children with European American children. McLoyd and Randolph (1984) found that African American children were compared to European American children (race-comparative studies) in 69% of studies published between 1973 and 1975 whose abstract in *Child Development Abstracts and Bibliography* indicated that African American children comprised at least 10% of the total study. In another study, McLoyd and Randolph (1986) found that African American children were compared to European American children in 47% of all studies of African American children published in *Child Development* between 1936 and 1980, while the remaining studies were equally divided between those in which African American children (comprising at least 10% of total sample) were grouped with, but not compared to, racially-or-ethnically-different children (race-heterogeneous studies) and those in which the research sample was comprised exclusively of African American children (race-homogeneous studies).

There is also evidence that the race-comparative paradigm even exerts influence on the conduct of race-homogeneous studies. Myers et al. (1979) compiled an annotated bibliography of the literature published on African American children in major social science journals between 1927 and 1977. They found that in a substantial portion of studies whose samples were comprised exclusively of African American children, standardized tests normed on European American children were administered to African American children to measure the variables of interest. The rationale often given for this practice was that it facilitated comparability of findings from studies based on European American children.

The tendency to study African Americans in terms of how they differ from European Americans is a salient one not only in developmental psychology, but in the discipline of psychology in general. Evidence of this trend comes from Caplan and Nelson's (1973) examination of abstracts reported in *Psychological Abstracts* that either mentioned African Americans specifically or were included under the index heading "Negro." These researchers found that 48% of the studies compared African Americans with European Americans.

The popularity of race-comparative studies stems, in part, from the nature of the basic model of behavior in the field of psychology. This model is a normativistic one that sets up criteria of behavior against which individuals and groups are measured (Hall, 1974). Riegel (1972) argued persuasively that the current normativistic model was nurtured by the political and economic ideologies within which developmental psychology developed in England and the United States during the second half of the 19th century and the early 20th century. According to Riegel (1972, p. 130), Darwin's view of human development as a "process of continuous competition and selection whose direction and goals are represented by the 'successful' survivors here and now" gained widespread acceptance in 19th century England, in part, because it was in keeping with the political-economic ideals of a free market competitive trade system. Because of the fit between his activities and societal demands, the "white, middle-class adult most likely engaged in manufacturing or business enterprises" was thought, at that time, to be the successful survivor and thus the standard or ideal (Riegel, 1972, p. 130). One result of the strong emphasis on competition was that the young, the old, the deviant and, generally, the different were placed into inferior positions and evaluated negatively. This "capitalistic" orientation found its way into the emerging discipline of child psychology in the United States. A legion of early descriptive studies of child development contributed to establishing trends and standards with which the performance of "differents" could be compared and found wanting in comparison with the standard-ideal, i.e., white, middle-class adults.

In contrast to the "capitalistic" orientation of England, the "mercantilistic-socialistic" orientation of continental Europe, according to Riegel (1972), fostered a relative disregard for competition between classes and groups. This was due, in part, to the fact that the development of manufacturing was largely initiated and supervised by the state rather than by individuals. These factors made possible the emergence of an ethos appreciative of multicultural and multigenerational differences. It was in this milieu that Rousseau outlined an educational philosophy that affirmed the equality of people and set children apart from the adult world to be educated and evaluated according to the standards of their peer group alone. This tradition, according to Riegel (1972), is reflected in developmental psychology, to varying degrees, in the work of Piaget and Vygotsky. Interest in links such as those proposed by Riegel between the institutions and values of society and the practice, canons, and knowledge base of psychology has increased dramatically in the past two decades and has led to efforts to formalize a new subdiscipline of psychology termed the sociology of psychological knowledge (Buss, 1975).

It is the hegemony of the comparative paradigm that occasioned Myers et al.'s (1979) pessimism about the capacity of future research to deepen and expand significantly our understanding of development in African American children. In the introduction to their selective annotated bibliography of research on African American children, these researchers concluded (Myers et al., 1979, p. xiv):

> The research on black child development with its consistent practice of defining black behavior exclusively in terms of white normative behavior perpetuates the mystification and idealization of the white norm. In so doing, very little can be said about variation among black children within the phenomenal black reality. What, for example, is normative black development? What factors seem to account for deviations from this norm, both positive and negative, among black children? . . . Questions such as these are not currently being asked by researchers, nor are they likely to be explored as long as a black-

white comparison model of inquiry is used exclusively (p. xiv). The theoretical and practical importance of studying intragroup variation in minority groups is illustrated convincingly by evidence that differences within certain minority groups in, for example, achievement, are best accounted for by variables that are different from those that explain between-group differences (Gallimore, Boggs & Jordan, 1974; Howard & Scott, 1981).

That many students of African American behavior eschew the race-comparative paradigm is surprising at first glance. After all, how can one measure the effects on African Americans of poverty and racism, demonstrate the need for remedies, or document the unique qualities of African American culture and behavior except through comparative studies? This paradigm has been criticized not so much because of its focus on contrast per se but because of the restricted nature of the information it yields, the intellectual foreclosure it encourages (e.g., documenting race differences as an end in itself and devoting little effort to identifying and understanding the proximal causes of these differences), and the characteristic interpretation of comparative data.

Specifically, critics argue that comparative studies (a) point to the ways in which African American children do not behave rather than how they do behave, yielding data that are limited in their informative value, virtually useless in generating theory and ultimately, capable of supporting only superficial analyses of individual differences and their determinants among African Americans (Howard & Scott, 1981; Myers et al., 1979), (b) foster indirectly the views that African American children are abnormal, incompetent, and changeworthy since differences between African American and European American children are typically interpreted, if not by the author, by a significant portion of the readers, as deficiencies or pathologies in the former rather than in cultural relativistic or systemic terms (Hall, 1974; Myers et al., 1979; Washington & McLoyd, 1982), and (c) promote person-blame interpretations of social problems rather than thoughtful treatments of the roles of situational and systemic factors, since they emphasize the race of the subjects or personal characteristics associated with race (Caplan & Nelson, 1973). These putative characteristics are not inherent to race-comparative studies themselves but appear to derive from the stigmatized and marginal existence of African Americans in American society.

Criticisms leveled against the comparative paradigm might lead one to conclude that race-comparative research is qualitatively different from research in which the sample is comprised exclusively of African American children. We conducted a content analysis of selected research to determine if indeed systematic differences exist between these two types of studies (McLoyd & Randolph, 1984). Our purpose was not to review the results of these studies but, rather, to assess their theoretical framework and methodology. We predicted, first, that race-comparative studies would be more likely than race-homogeneous studies to be based on the premise that African American children are deficient because they either exhibit or fail to exhibit certain behavior and, second, that race-comparative studies would be less likely than race-homogeneous studies to focus on the situational determinants of behavior.

To identify a pool of relevant studies, we reviewed volumes 47 (1973) through 51 (1977) of *Child Development Abstracts and Bibliography* (CDAB) to locate journal articles published between 1973 and 1975. It was necessary to search volumes of CDAB that were published after 1975, the last target year, because of the lag between publication of a journal article and publication of an abstract of that article in CDAB. We selected any study whose abstract in CDAB indicated that African American children comprised at least 10% of the total study sample (roughly equivalent to the proportion of African Americans in the total United States population according to the 1970 census). If the abstract did not explicitly state that the research sample included or was comprised entirely of African American, black, or Negro children, labels such as race, ethnicity, ethnic group, disadvantaged, and deprived served as cues that African American children may have comprised some portion of the sample. Because we were concerned with the study of the normal population of African American children, we excluded, first, any study whose research sample was comprised solely of adults (i.e., persons over 18 years of age) or children of African descent who lived outside the United States and, second, any study in which the sample of children was labeled retarded, institutionalized, or delinquent. Finally, we excluded books, case studies, and review articles that were not data based.

Subsequent to the selection process, we verified that the study summarized in each abstract selected from CDAB was appropriate for inclusion in the study. Each article was located in its respective journal and reviewed briefly. If the study reported therein met the criteria outlined above, the article was included in the study. In those cases in which two or more studies were reported in one article, we randomly chose one study for review so that some articles did not contribute more than others to the overall findings of the present study. These procedures yielded the data base of our study, namely, 117 studies, each of which was coded for a series of variables. The reliability of the selection and coding of articles was very high (see McLoyd and Randolph, 1984, for details on the reliability procedures).

The Nature of Research on African American Children: Research Findings

Of a total of 117 studies, 35 were published in 1973, 37 in 1974, and 45 in 1975. African American children were the sole research subjects in 30 studies (race-homogeneous studies) (26%), while in four studies, African American children were grouped with, but not compared to, racially or ethnically different children (race-heterogeneous studies)(3%). In keeping with the impressions and allegations of many scholars, the overwhelming majority of studies (83 studies, 71%) compared African American children to racially or ethnically different children. Specifically, African American children were compared solely to European American children in 64 studies (55%), solely to Hispanic children in three studies (2%), and to both European American children and ethnic minority children, typically Hispanic, in 16 studies (14%). Within each type of study and for each category of each variable, a proportion was computed by dividing the number of studies in the category by the total number of studies.

Several characteristics of the corpus of 113 studies (the four race-heterogeneous studies were excluded in all analyses) bear mention. We found strong support for the claim of some critics that research on African American children is essentially an atheoretical undertaking in which raw empiricism typically triumphs over thoughtful conceptually grounded inquiry. First, only 25% of the 113 studies were designed explicitly to test components of a theory or theoretically derived formulations. Second, despite the marked tendency to compare the behavior and responses of African American children to those of ethnically-different children (typically European American), researchers generated hypotheses or predictions about racial or ethnic differences in only 26 (31%) of the 83 race-comparative studies. Because race differences so often are explored in the absence of a theoretical framework that provides the raison d'etre for comparison and guides interpretation of differences that are found, it is hard not to suspect that many of the race differences reported are banal, insular, and void of real significance. We were surprised that so few authors explicitly acknowledged deficiency (16%) or person-blame (8%) as heuristic concepts.

Several forces conspire with the historical ones suggested by Riegel (1972) to impel researchers to compare African American children with ethnically different children in the absence of compelling theoretical rationales for the comparison. First is the difficulty of convincing the gatekeepers of knowledge (i.e., reviewers) of the merit and interpretability of data about African American children in the absence of comparable data on the standard-bearer (i.e., European American children). Often, their skepticism is almost palpable. After reading a manuscript that I submitted for publication that reported the findings of an experimental study of intrinsic motivation in African American children, an editorial reviewer concluded:

> The primary problem [with this study] is the use of only black children as subjects. While race as a summary variable for socialization experiences is indeed of interest for developmental investigations, the fact that it may contribute to the observed findings raises the possibility that the present results are not truly generalizable or interpretable as they reflect upon findings from prior research. In order to achieve its primary goal, the present study should have had two samples of children, one white and one black, in which case the author(s) would have been able to satisfy any personal intrinsic interest in the black population, tell other investigators something about the effects of those variables assumed to index intrinsic interest and could have spoken to the prior literature to boot. In the present case, this cannot be done and with the possible differences in subjects between this study and prior ones it is essentially impossible to evaluate it on the dimension providing foundation for its self-justification: the previous literature on intrinsic interest . . . If the present study were expanded to include a white population, then, I think the author(s) should be encouraged to resubmit it for further consideration.

The professional risks of studying African American children without a comparison group of European American children are not lost on the neophyte researcher, especially if she or he has a plain-spoken mentor and has experienced rejection of a manuscript or grant proposal partially because no race comparison was done or planned. One effect of this infatuation with and press for race-comparison, then, is that comparisons are often undertaken for pragmatic, rather than substantive theoretical reasons.

Second is the press for integrated samples by those who control access to children, a common result of which is the introduction of race as a variable. Research review committees and other entities of school systems charged with the responsibility of deciding whether to permit the conduct of a study under their auspices are often disquieted by requests to recruit only African American children and, indeed, often make their approval contingent on inclusion of European American children. Their reasons may range from fear of the ire of parents who regard participation of solely African American children in research studies as evidence of unequal treatment of the races, to concern about the psychological effects on African American children of being singularized (e.g., if child is in an integrated classroom), to a genuine desire to know whether race influences the relationships the researcher proposes to test. Often left with few alternatives and facing a time schedule, the researcher may capitulate and retain the original research design but double the size of the sample so that variance due to race can be estimated, or retain the original sample size, jettison some other independent or predictor variable and replace it with race. Again, pragmatics, rather than theory, provokes the researcher to take up the question of how the behavior or African American children differs from that of racially different children.

In our investigation, the majority of studies focused on cognitive development (53%) and were conducted with lower-class African American children (60%). In most studies (63%), children's social class was determined on the basis of inference (e.g., locale of school attended by child, attendance at a Head Start center) rather than direct assessment (e.g., Hollingshead, knowledge of the income, occupation, and/or educational status of individual parents). Samples typically were selected on the basis of some special person characteristic (e.g., underachiever) other than age, sex, or social class; rarely was a random sample drawn (15%). The major dependent variable typically was assessed via a test, interview, or self-report (80%); in most cases the race of the experimenter or examiner was unspecified (59%). A substantial proportion of the research reports concluded with caveats about possible threats to the internal validity of the study (47%), though very few cautioned readers against overgeneralizing the findings (14%).

Differences Between Race-Comparative and Race-Homogeneous Studies

Statistical analysis (chi square) was used to determine if race-comparative studies and race-homogeneous studies were significantly different from each other with respect to the relative frequency with which cases fell in the categories for each variable. Note that race-heterogeneous studies were again excluded. Contrary to our predictions, type of study was unrelated to espousal of the deficit model or focus on situational determinants of behavior. The lack of support for our predictions may suggest the need for finer distinctions among studies. As we noted earlier, Myers et al. (1979) found that research in which only African American children are studied is often guided implicitly by the race-comparative paradigm, suggesting the need for further differentiation of race-homogeneous studies.

However, a number of statistically significant differences were found between race-comparative and race-homogeneous studies. A summary of the most notable ones follows: (a) Reports of race comparative studies were more likely to omit information about the social class backgrounds of the research subjects, an omission that probably signals that race and class were confounded. Lower-class children were more likely to be the exclusive subjects of interest in race-homogeneous studies, while race-comparative studies were more likely to focus on both lower and middle-class African American children (a statistically significant difference). Indeed, social class was an independent or predictor variable more frequently in race-comparative studies than in race-homogeneous studies (16 vs. 3%, respectively). (b) The samples in race-comparative studies were more likely to be random or representative, while in race-homogeneous studies, the subjects were more likely to be chosen because they embodied some special person characteristic, without regard to randomness (a statistically significant difference). This finding suggests that the findings of race-comparative studies may have more generalizability than those of race-homogeneous studies. On the other hand, it will be recalled that a substantial proportion of the race-comparative studies, compared to the race-homogeneous studies, failed to provide information about the social class background of the African American children studied, information essential to determining the appropriate generalization of findings. As others have indicated, even if random sampling is conducted as a basis for external validity, the appropriate generalization of findings is dependent on adequate definition and description of the sample and the target and accessible population (Kerlinger, 1973; Shaver & Norton, 1980). Thus, on the basis of the variables examined in our study, we regard as problematic the external validity (generalizability) of a substantial proportion of both race-homogeneous studies and race-comparative studies, in the first case, largely because samples were not drawn randomly, and in the second case primarily because descriptions of the samples are inadequate. (c) Researchers who conducted race-comparative studies were less prone to draw attention to the limitations and deficiencies of their research. Specifically, they were less likely than researchers who conducted race-homogeneous studies to caution readers in the discussion section about potential threats to the internal validity of the study. One effect of this omission may be that readers accord greater credibility to the findings of race-comparative studies. (d) Race-comparative studies were less likely than race-homogeneous studies to focus primarily on cognitive development as a dependent variable (correlational studies were excluded from this analysis) and were (e) less likely to be conducted for the explicit purpose of unraveling variables confounded in previous research.

Differences Between Major Developmental Journals and Other Journals

In this study, we also sought to determine in what ways studies of African American children varied as a function of the journal in which they are published. There exists among researchers an informal lore about the differences among journals in terms of variable preferences, methodological orientation, and relative emphasis on empirical research versus theory. Kail and Herman (1977) used quantitative procedures to assess differences in the qualitative nature of six journals devoted primarily to research in developmental psychology. They concluded on the basis of citations that appeared in these journals during the selected years that *Child Development, Developmental Psychology*, and the *Journal of Experimental Child Psychology* are the data producers, providing the primary data base of developmental psychology, while *Human Development, Merrill-Palmer Quarterly*, and the *Journal of Genetic Psychology* are generally data consumers, publishing manuscripts that seek to advance theories of development or explore topics of interest to small groups of developmental psychologists and other scholars.

In our study, journals were distinguished on the basis of their visibility as outlets for empirical and theoretical articles on human development (McLoyd & Randolph, 1984). Peery and Adams (1981) conducted a survey in which randomly selected members of the Society for Research in Child Development (SRCD) were asked to list and rank order the ten journals in which the best developmental articles are published. *Child Development, Developmental Psychology, Merrill-Palmer Quarterly, Human Development, Monographs of SRCD*, and the *Journal of Genetic Psychology* emerged as the most visible and credible journals that concentrate on human development but do not limit their foci, as do some journals, in terms of research methodology or variables of interest. We distinguished these journals from other journals that publish research on African American children in an attempt to determine if the major developmental journals differ from less visible journals in the nature of research reported therein about African American children. Evidence of differences between journals would suggest that certain theoretical and methodological perspectives themselves enjoy varying degrees of visibility and prestige among scholars seeking information about African American children. We predicted that major developmental journals would publish proportionately more race-comparative studies than other journals on the grounds that highly visible and prestigious journals are more likely to support a traditional approach and discourage less venerable approaches to the study of African American children.

The two journals that published the most research articles about

African American children were *Developmental Psychology* (23) and the *Journal of Educational Psychology*. (23). Contrary to our prediction, major developmental journals i.e., *Developmental Psychology, Child Development, Monographs of SRCD, Human Development*, and *Journal of Genetic Psychology* (no relevant studies were found in *Merrill-Palmer Quarterly*) published relatively fewer race-comparative studies and more race-homogeneous studies than other journals (statistically significant difference). One possible explanation for this finding is that specification of the theoretical framework that guides and undergirds research and makes plain its significance to the area of inquiry is applied more rigorously as criteria for publication in more prestigious journals. If the presentation of theoretical rationales, or lack thereof, for comparing African American children with racially or ethnically different children can be used as a crude estimate of the overall theoretical strength of race-comparative research, one might argue that race-comparative studies tend to be theoretically anemic and, thus, are less likely to be published in more prestigious journals. Recall that hypotheses or predictions about racial or ethnic differences (which generally necessitate clarification of the theoretical justification for comparison) were made in only 31% of the race-comparative studies. Studies published in major developmental journals were more likely to be guided explicitly by a competence model of behavior in African American children, and to be interpreted in relation to the child's family or cultural milieu (statistically significant differences).

The findings of this study verify the contention of many scholars that the study of African American children, in the main, is the study of how African American children differ from European American children. It should be clear that race-comparative studies *can* provide important information about the adverse effects of racism and economic oppression and the unique qualities of African American culture and behavior. This potential notwithstanding, it no doubt is the case that the dominance of the race-comparative framework has resulted in an impoverished body of knowledge about African American children and stymied the advancement of theory about development in these children. Sorely needed as a counterweight to the study of race and ethnic differences is study of African American children qua African American children. Ogbu (1981) argues convincingly that a requisite to understanding the origins and development of human competence is insight into the nature of culturally defined adult tasks, particularly subsistence tasks. Because certain competencies meet the needs of the society, adults adapt their childrearing techniques to ensure that children acquire them. Researchers need to launch systematic efforts to understand the processes of transmission and acquisition of required competencies in the context of the cultural and survival tasks presented by the immediate environments of African American children. The prospects of significant progress toward this goal, argues Ogbu, are infinitely better when we study African American children qua African American children since they (especially those from lower-class backgrounds) are confronted with cultural and survival tasks that are different, in important ways, from those faced by European American children. Such study would significantly enrich our knowledge and understanding of development in African American children.

Secular Trends in the Study of African American Children

How has the study of African American children changed over time? This question was the focus of a second study. In particular, we examined secular trends in studies of African American children published in *Child Development* between 1936 and 1980. We focused on *Child Development*, only one of several outlets for research findings in the field of child development, because of its prestige, interdisciplinary focus, longevity as a serial publication, and wide dissemination among professionals in several disciplines (Peery & Adams, 1981; Super, 1982). Though publication of this journal began in 1930, we chose 1936 as the point of departure because it was in this year that *Child Development* became an official publication of the Society for Research in Child Development (SRCD), the major professional organization of research-oriented developmentalists.

Of particular interest were shifts in research procedures that have engendered considerable debate, such as comparing African American children with European American children (Washington & McLoyd, 1982), confounding race and social class (Myers et al., 1979), and using non-African Americans as experimenters and observers of African American children (Oyemade & Rosser, 1980). We also examined secular trends in less controversial aspects of research, such as the major dependent or criterion variable of interest, ages of the children studied, and size of the research sample. Underlying this study was the assumption that published research defines a scientific field (Kail & Herman, 1977) and represents an archive of the paradigms of research in that field (Super, 1982).

The method section of each article published in *Child Development* between 1936 and 1980 was examined to identify those studies in which African American children constituted at least 10% of the research sample. Excluded from our study were (a) literature reviews or articles of a primarily theoretical nature that were not data based,

(b) studies in which the subjects were mentally retarded and/or institutionalized (e.g., juvenile delinquents), and (c) studies in which the research findings related only to adults. In all but a few cases, only one study was reported in each article. In cases of multiple-study articles, one study was randomly selected for coding. Using these criteria, a total of 215 articles/studies were identified. Articles were coded for type of study (i.e., race-comparative, race-homogeneous, race-heterogeneous) and additional variables related to the characteristics of the research sample, research topics and methods, and the nature of the discussion of the research. Details of the procedures used to establish reliability, which was quite high for both selection and coding of articles are presented elsewhere (McLoyd & Randolph, 1986).

Data analyses consisted of calculating for each variable the percentage of articles/studies falling into each category of each variable. Because the articles included in this study represent virtually the entire population of data-based articles published about normal African American children in *Child Development* between 1936 and 1980, these percentages are regarded as descriptive parameters that obviate the use of inferential statistics (Games, 1967).

Major Findings

The total number of studies per year was extremely low prior to mid-1960, necessitating the pooling of articles across several of the early years. The articles were grouped into four periods of publication: (a) 1936-1965 (33 articles), (b) 1966-1970 (39 articles), (c) 1971-1975 (91 articles), and (d) 1976-1980 (52 articles). The first publication period, then, covers a span of 30 years, while the second, third, and fourth publication periods each cover a total of 5 years. The frequency of all three types of studies peaked during the third publication period, a trend largely due to the number of articles published in 1971 (8 of the 24 race-homogeneous studies, 16 of the 39 race-comparative studies, and 10 of the 28 studies of the third publication period were published in 1971).

Within each publication period, the proportion of race-comparative studies was almost twice that of race-homogeneous studies. In 85 of the 102 race-comparative studies, African American children were compared solely to European American children, while in the remaining 17, they were compared to both European American children and ethnic minority children (typically Puerto Rican or Mexican-American). Thus, a question posed by all race-comparative studies was how African American children differed from European American children.

In order to assess secular changes in the characteristics of studies, a proportion was computed for each category of each variable of interest within each publication period by dividing the number of studies in the category by the total number of studies published within the respective publication period (the proportions are converted to percentages in the tables). In these analyses, we combined race-homogeneous and race-comparative studies (N = 157). Race-heterogeneous studies were excluded because, compared to race-homogeneous and race-comparative studies, they provide information that is less particularistic, at least with regard to race and ethnicity. They neither describe normative behavior in African American children per se nor, by definition, demonstrate how the behavior of African American children compares to that of children from other racial or ethnic backgrounds. A second rationale for our exclusion of these studies was our belief that scholars are unlikely to look to or draw from them in their search for knowledge about African American children.

Our findings indicate that the most notable changes in the study of African American children occurred during the third publication period, that is, between 1971 and 1975. Of the four publication periods, the relative frequency with which the following occurred was highest in the third period: (a) study of preschoolers, (b) study of children from urban environments, (c) study of the effects of environmental factors on behavior, (d) control of social class in race-comparative studies, (e) use of an African American as experimenter/observer, (f) identification and discussion of factors that threatened the internal validity of the reported findings, (g) discussion of the external validity of the findings, and (h) discussion of the educational and social policy implications of the research.

In addition, of the four publication periods, the relative frequency with which the following occurred was lowest in the third period: (a) failure to specify the race of the experimenter/observer and (b) failure to specify the socioeconomic status of the African American children studied.

Two findings that depart from this patterns of marked change during the third publication period are noteworthy. First, specification in the abstract of the article that race or ethnicity was a variable of interest or that some or all of the research subjects were African American declined consistently over the four publication periods (83%, 72%, 56%, and 46%). There were no articles in which race and ethnicity-related information was specified in the title but not in the abstract. Excluded from analyses of abstracts were studies published during or prior to 1963 (N = 15), as the publication format of *Child Development* did not include abstracts until 1964. Second, the relative frequency with which studies were supported by research grants from various sources (e.g., federal agency, private foundation, and university) increased substantially from the first to the second publication period, held steady in the third period, but dropped precipitously in the fourth (48%, 81%, 81%, and 69%).

The Role of Social and Political Change in Scholarship about Development in African American Children

Several of the secular trends found in this study no doubt reflect real changes in research practices and values within the discipline of psychology, whereas others may be epiphenomena caused by changes in the editorial policies (and values) of *Child Development*. In either case, it is our belief that the positive changes that marked the period between 1971 and 1975 are related to several social and political changes in American society (extrascientific forces) and to forces within the discipline of psychology itself (intrascientific forces).

The most obvious of these influences is the Head Start Program, established in 1965 as part of President Johnson's War on Poverty. Head Start had as one of its goals the "inoculation" of poor children against the adverse effects of poverty and racial discrimination on social and intellectual development by insuring that they had mastered the educational prerequisites necessary to take advantage of formal, traditional schooling. Environmentalism was a cornerstone of Head Start and, indeed, had become the "zeitgeist" during the 1960s according to Zigler and Anderson (1970). These researchers contended that "the public hailed the construction of a solid foundation for learning in preschool children as the solution to poverty and ignorance . . . . Great expectations and promises were based on the view that the young child was a plastic material to be molded quickly and permanently by the proper school environment . . . For policymakers, legislators, and the public the theory had a common-sense appeal (Zigler & Anderson, 1979, pp. 7-9).

Two scholars played a key role in the 1960s in increasing awareness of the role of the child's environment on intellectual growth and affirming the social policy initiatives that resulted in Head Start (Steiner, 1976; Zigler & Anderson, 1979). Bloom (1964) made the argument in *Stability and Change in Human Characteristics* that intellectual growth occurs most rapidly during the first 4 or 5 years of life. Thus the critical time to enrich the child's environment should be during the preschool years. Hunt (1961), in his book *Intelligence and Experience*, challenged the beliefs in fixed intelligence and predetermined development and emphasized the ways in which the child's environment influences intellectual growth.

With the establishment of Head Start and other antipoverty

programs came vast sums of money from federal agencies and private foundations for the conduct of scholarly research consistent with the philosophy undergirding these initiatives. These developments, we believe, resulted in the increase between 1971 and 1975, first, in the number of studies that focused on African American children, and second, in the proportion of studies that focused on preschoolers and children from urban environments and sought to demonstrate the effects of environmental factors on behavior. Because of the lag between the spawning of research studies and the publication of these studies it is understandable that the new research on African American children did not appear in the pages of *Child Development* until the third publication period (1971-1975).

The decline between 1971 and 1980 in the explicit espousal by *Child Development* authors of a deficit model of development in African American children and the increased attention given to validity issues between 1971 and 1975 may be linked to two developments, namely, the publication of two iconoclastic papers that rendered decisive criticism of prevailing research on African American children and set new research priorities (Cole & Bruner, 1971; Labov, 1970) and the rise of Black Nationalism between 1965 and 1970. As noted earlier, the compelling calls by Labov and by Cole and Bruner for the conduct of research in environments conducive to the display of intellectual and social skills by African American and other minority children preceded a barrage of similar criticisms (e.g., Clark, 1972; Hall, 1974; Tulkin, 1972; Williams, 1972).

Around 1965, following the successful desegregation of places of public accommodation and the enfranchisement of millions of African Americans in the South, the appeal of the nonviolent, integrationist ideology of the civil rights movement began to wane and give way to Black Nationalism (Brisbane, 1974). Various groups called for black separation and emigration to Africa, affirmed their African heritage (e.g., dress, customs, and names), and proclaimed the legitimacy and richness of African American culture (Brisbane, 1974; Lester, 1971). The reverberations of this movement were to be felt in the halls of academe, where there emerged a demand for inclusion in the curricula of predominantly white colleges and universities courses in African American history, culture, and behavior. By 1970 Black studies programs had been established at Yale, Harvard, Cornell, Columbia, and the University of Michigan, and by 1972 more than 600 colleges and universities were offering black studies courses (Brisbane, 1974). The veneration of African American culture during this period may have served as an antidote to the cultural imperialism and calm ethnocentrism that hitherto appeared to inform so much of the research on African Americans conducted by European Americans.

It is interesting that the lessening of expressed concern about validity and methodological issues from the third (1971-1975) to the fourth period (1976-1980) coincided with a decline in social and political activism among African Americans. We saw other unpropitious changes during the fourth period, including a decline in the number of studies of African American children, an increase in the proportion of studies that did not specify the race of the experimenter/observer, an increase in the proportion of race-comparative studies that did not specify the social class of one or both of the groups compared, and an increase in the relative frequency with which race and social class were confounded.

Two of our findings collectively may signal a waning of prestige or interest in race-comparative study, at least among contributors and editors of *Child Development*. First, while interest in how African American children differed from European American children remained conspicuously high in each publication period, the proportion of race-comparative studies declined significantly after the second publication period. Second, we found a steady decline in the tendency to report in the abstract that the subjects included African American children or that race or ethnicity was a variable of interest. While race-related information was provided in the abstracts of almost all relevant articles published between 1964 and 1970, it was provided in less than half the articles published between 1976 and 1980. The practical significance of this shift is increased difficulty in accessing information published about African American children in *Child Development*. Scholars who rely on the abstracts of *Child Development* articles to locate recent research on African American children may commit significant errors of omission because many abstracts of relevant articles do not report that race was a variable of interest or that the subjects included were exclusively African American children. Even more articles may be missed by scholars who rely on *Child Development Abstracts and Bibliography*, as the abstracts in this publication are often abridged versions of the authors' abstracts that appeared in *Child Development*.

The "research-on-research" approach (Jones, 1973) used in this study has been applied to literature on African American families (Johnson, 1981; Peters, 1981) and to articles published in the *Joural of Black Psychology* (Steele & Davis, 1983). Collectively, this work confirms that the social scientific study of African Americans is constantly undergoing change and is not impervious to nonscientific social and political transformations within larger society. Further attention should be given to the sociology of psychological knowledge about African Americans. Issues of particular interest include the publication and review process of professional journals, the demographic characteristics of the editorial boards of professional journals, changes in editorial policies of these journals, and the role of graduate training programs. It is my hope that increasing numbers of scholars will provide analyses and comment on the study of African Americans with a view toward charting new directions for research and theory, revealing the links between social science, social structure, and the values of society, and nurturing a self-consciousness among scholars about their unique role in creating and perpetuating positive and negative images of cultural groups and society.

References

Bay Area Association of Black Psychologists. Position statement on use of IQ and ability tests. (1972). In R. L. Jones (Ed.), *Black Psychology*. New York; Harper & Row.

Bayton, J. A. (1975). Francis Sumner, Max Meenes, and the training of black psychologists. *American Psychologist, 30*, 185-186.

Bloom, B. S. (1964). *Stability and change in human characteristics*. New York: Wiley.

Bond, H. M. (1924) Intelligence tests and propaganda. *Crisis, 28*, 61-64.

Brisbane, R. H. (1974). *Black activism: racial revolution in the United States*. Valley Forge, PA: Judson.

Buss, A. R. (1975). The emerging field of the sociology of psychological knowledge. *American Psychologist, 30*, 988-1002.

Caplan, N., & Nelson, S. D. (1973). On being useful: The nature and consequences of psychological research on social problems. *American Psychologist, 28*, 199-211.

Canady, H. G. (1936). The effect of "rapport" on the IQ: A new approach to the problem of racial psychology. *Journal of Negro Education, 5*, 209-219.

Clark, C. (1972). Black studies or the study of black people? In R. L. Jones (Ed.), *Black Psychology*. New York: Harper & Row.

Cole, M., & Bruner, J. (1971). Cultural differences and inferences about psychological processes. *American Psychologist, 26*, 867-876.

Gallimore, R., Boggs, J., & Jordan, C. (1974). *Culture, behavior and education: A study of Hawaiian-Americans*. Beverly Hills: Sage.

Games, P. A. (1967). *Elementary statistics*. New York: McGraw-Hill.

Guthrie, R. V. (1976). *Even the rat was white: A historical view of psychology*. New York: Harper & Row.

Hall, W. S. (1974). Research in the black community: Child development. In J. Chunn (Ed.), *The survival of black children and youth*. Washington, D.C.: Nuclassics & Science Publishing.

Howard, A., & Scott, R. A. (1981). The study of minority groups in complex societies. In R. H. Munroe, R. L. Monroe, & B. Whiting (Eds.), *Handbook of cross-cultural human development*. New York: Garland.

Hunt, J.M. (1961). *Intelligence and experience.* New York: Ronald Press.

Johnson, L. B. (1981). Perspectives on black family empirical research: 1965-1978. In H. P. McAdoo (Ed.), *Black Families.* Beverly Hills: Sage.

Jones, R. (1973). Proving blacks inferior: The sociology of knowledge. In J. A. Ladner (Ed.), *The Death of White Sociology.* New York: Random House.

Kail, R. V., & Herman, J. F. (1977). Structure in developmental psychology: An analysis of journal citations. *Human Development, 20,* 309-316.

Kerlinger, F. N. (1973). *Foundations of behavioral research.* New York: Holt, Rinehart & Winston.

Labov, W. (1970). The logic of non-standard English. In F. Williams (Ed.), *Language and poverty.* Chicago: Markham.

Lester, J. (1971). The angry children of Malcolm X. In A. Meier, E. Rudwick, & F. L. Broderick (Eds.), *Black protest thought in the twentieth century.* Indianapolis: Bobbs-Merrill.

McLoyd, V.C. (1990). Minority children: Introduction to the Special Issue. *Child Development, 61,* 263-266.

McLoyd, V. C., & Randolph, S. M. (1984). The conduct and publication of research on Afro-American children: A content analysis. *Human Development, 27,* 65-75.

McLoyd, V. C., & Randolph, S. M. (1986). Secular trends in the study of Afro-American children: A review of *Child Development* 1936-1980. *Monographs of the Society for Research in Child Development, 50* (4-5 Serial No. 211), 78-92.

Myers, H. F., Rana, P. G., & Harris, M. (1979). *Black child development in America, 1927-1977.* Westport, CT: Greenwood Press.

Ogbu, J. U. (1981). Origins of human competence. A cultural-ecological perspective. *Child Development, 52,* 413-429.

Oyemade, U. J., & Rosser, P. J. (1980). Development in black children. In B. Camp (Ed.), *Advances in behavioral pediatrics* (Vol. 1). Greenwich, CT: JAI.

Peery, J. C., & Adams, G. R. (1981). Qualitative ratings of human development journals. *Human Development, 24,* 312-319.

Peters, M. F. (1981). Parenting in black families with young children. In H. P. McAdoo (Ed.), *Black Families.* Beverly Hills: Sage.

Riegel, K. F. (1972) Influence of economic and political ideologies on the development of developmental psychology. *Psychological Bulletin, 78,* 129-141.

Shaver, J. P., & Norton, R. S. (1980) Randomness and replication in ten years of the *American Educational Research Journal. Educational Researcher, 9,* 9-15.

Some suggestions relative to the study of the mental attitude of the Negro. (1916). *Pedagogical Seminary, 23,* 199-203.

Steele, R. E., & Davis, S. E. (1983). An empirical and theoretical review of articles in the *Journal of Black* Psychology: 1974-1980. *Journal of Black Psychology, 10,* 29-42.

Steiner, G. Y. (1976). *The children's cause.* Washington, D.C.: Brookings Institution.

Super, C. M. (1982, Spring). Secular trends in child development and the institutionalization of professional disciplines. *Newsletter of the Society for Research in Child Development,* 10-11.

Tulkin, S. R. (1972). An analysis of the concept of cultural deprivation. *Developmental Psychology, 6,* 326-339.

Washington, E. D., & McLoyd, V. C. (1982). The external validity of research involving American minorities. *Human Development, 25,* 324-339.

Weems, L. (1974). Black community research needs: Methods, models and modalities. In L. Gary (Ed.), *Social research and the black community: Selected issues and priorities.* Washington, D.C.: Institute for Urban Affairs and Research, Howard University.

Williams, R. (1972). Abuses and misuses in testing black children. In R. L. Jones (Ed.), Black Psychology. New York: Harper & Row.

Zigler, E., & Anderson, K. (1979). An idea whose time had come: The intellectual and political climate. In E. Zigler & J. Valentine (Eds.), *Project Head Start: A Legacy of the War on Poverty.* New York: Free Press.

The Concept of Race in Social Psychology: From Color to Culture

James M. Jones

In *Prejudice and Racism* (Jones, 1972), I began to consider the ways in which social psychology has dealt with racism. The title originally proposed for the book—a volume in the *Topics in Social Psychology* series (Kiesler, 1969)—was simply *Prejudice*. As I worked on the book it became obvious that the concept of racism should be more central and in fact deserved to be included in the title. I found that social psychology had extensively addressed the concept of prejudice, but in order to analyze racism I had to look elsewhere: to anthropology, sociology, political science, and the law. Social psychologists had focused on prejudice partly because of their field's preoccupation with *attitude*, which is primarily an intrapsychic construct. Racism, in contrast, concerns real-life behavior: competition, power, and discrimination.

My purpose became not only to review what social psychology had said about racism—or, in its own terms, about prejudice—but also to examine factors that affect the dynamics of interracial relations as they unfold over time in a particular sociocultural context. Thus, while the analysis necessarily began with prejudice, it pointed to the need to advance beyond an individualistic attitudinal orientation. The problems of racism are woven into the fabric of the American society; to analyze them thoroughly one must use a multifaceted, multileveled approach.

I therefore sought to account for racism at the multiple levels at which people (primarily blacks, in this country) suffer its consequences, namely at the individual, institutional, and cultural levels. Racism at the individual level, in my scheme, was simply a segue, a bridge from the familiar concept of prejudice to the more appropriate concept of racism. "Institutional racism" was a new concept at the time, used or implied by the Kerner Commission (U.S. Commission on Civil Disorders, 1967) and Carmichael and Hamilton (1967), and was formalized by Knowles and Pruitt (1969). According to this notion, the charge of racism does not require proof of intent or evilmindedness; it requires only the assessment of patterns of outcomes by race. For many this was a breakthrough: it implied a remedy—affirmative action—for the problems of institutional racism. However, I went a step further to what, for me, is the most consequential of causes, *cultural racism*.

Individuals are socialized in and by institutions, which in turn are influenced by a set of philosophies, a cultural worldview. The set of values and assumptions underlying this worldview are not adequately implicated by the concept of institutional racism. Nor does the proposed remedy, affirmative action, directly address the problem of cultural values. And until we do, I submit, we will be dancing around the core of the issue.

Both the traditional analysis of prejudice and the analyses of individual and institutional racism ignore the fact that this society's cultural prescriptions are Anglo-European in origin and therefore predicated on a set of values and a sense of history that place other groups (e.g., black people) at a fundamental disadvantage. Because the fact of cultural difference is not addressed, while individual and institutional biases are, we tend to invent head-counting *numerical* concepts—affirmative action, minority groups—and continue to overlook culture. As I hope to show in the present analysis, social psychology, despite its presumed logical affinity for cultural concepts, has followed the larger society in ignoring cultural aspects of race in its theoretical and empirical inquiries.

In the following pages I will argue that social psychology has evolved a conception of race and its role in social life that is unfocused, underdeveloped, simpleminded, atheoretical, and consequently of little value in understanding contemporary trends in the world arena. "Cultural diversity" is not just a term in the liberal lexicon; it is an accurate description of the way the world really is: occupied by a diverse array of human cultures. Of course, the world was this way too during the years of social psychology's emergence as a respectable intellectual discipline, but certain features of the field's development caused it to neglect culture and focus instead on individual's thoughts, attitudes, and actions without attending to the fact that these are organized by culture. The result is a deficient, indeed largely myopic and sterile, view of both American culture and world-historical social trends.

I intend to examine the ways in which social psychology has dealt with racial issues and with the concept of race, and to suggest how we might approach them more productively. I want to argue, moreover, for the inclusion of persons of color and of diverse cultural backgrounds in the field of social psychology. They can play significant roles in the development of our important ideas, not just those specifically concerning race-relevant phenomena (prejudice, discrimination, and the like), but also those having to do with general human capacities and tendencies that are significantly influenced by culture. The cliche about fish being unaware of the existence of water applies to much of social psychology; its practitioners live and breathe Anglo-European culture without realizing the extent to which it influences their work. Just as a science of fish must eventually say something about water, social psychology remains woefully deficient as long as it neglects culture and cultural racism.

Race in Social Psychology: A Brief Historical Overview

In his classic analysis of the origin and development of social psychology, Allport (1968) defined the field as a forum on the ways in which the thoughts, feelings, and behavior of individuals are influenced by other people. The importance of cultural/normative pressures was acknowledged in concepts such as "group mind," "national character," and "*Volkgeist.*" Race was one such cultural and group concept, and it played a prominent, if not very pleasing, role in the early history of social psychological inquiry. As Samelson (1978) has noted, the Psychological Index revised its classification scheme in 1912 to give greater emphasis to "race." In addition to the old "Race Pathology" subsections entitled "(a) Criminology" and "(b) Degeneration and Sex Pathology," a new major heading was added, "Individual, Racial, and Social Phenomena," which included a new subsection: "Race Psychology and Anthropology."

Samelson's (1978) brief but provocative review outlines the major aspects of race psychology, which was aimed primarily at proving the basic inferiority of black and other Third World peoples, and documents the major shift away from it and toward the study of racial prejudice. Samelson attributes the shift to three events: (1) the Immigration Registration Law of 1924, which dramatically reduced the influx of immigrants, thereby making it less necessary to disparage immigrant races; (2) the rise in prominence of psychologists with other than Anglo-Saxon background, including Jews and eastern and southern Europeans who had an interest in prejudice directed against their own ethnic groups; and (3) the onset of the great Depression, which according to Samelson pushed many social psychologists to the left on the political spectrum and moved social issues in general—and race relations in particular—to the top of the research and theoretical agenda. This trend can be contrasted with the earlier worries of the well-known social psychologist William McDougall. In his book, *Is America Safe for Democracy?* (1921), McDougall concerned himself with what he considered to be the adverse effects of mixing people of different races under the aegis of American democracy. He feared that the factors that had made the United States a strong nation would be eroded if too much social equality were permitted. He pointed to the work of "mental anthropology" as supporting the intellectual inferiority of blacks and other groups, and compared various racial groups to demonstrate the superiority of certain Anglo-Saxon character traits such as will, curiosity, providence (the ability to delay gratification), individualism (as opposed to sociability), and reflectivity (as opposed to impulsiveness). McDougall argued that these important positive traits could be preserved and fostered if society would take a more active social-engineering approach based on "social and behavioral science."

Another trend in the treatment of race by social psychologists is revealed by changes in the *Handbook of Social Psychology*. The first edition, edited by Carl Murchison (1935), included an entire section of 210 pages devoted to four chapters addressing the sociocultural histories of the black, red, yellow, and white citizens of the United States. These chapters stressed the cultural diversity of the four groups and documented their unique histories and their special statuses within a heterogeneous American society. Herskovits (1935), for example, identified at least nine African cultural groups that were funneled into three major black groups in the New World: Spanish (Brazil, Cuba), French (West Indies, Louisiana), and British (West Indies, Eastern United States). His analysis made it reasonable to expect cultural differences between black and white Americans.

The 1954 edition of the *Handbook*, edited by Gardner Lindzey, dropped these chapters and added a major new section on research methodology. In addition to chapters on experimental methods, quantitative techniques, attitude and sociometric measures, observation and interview methods, and content analysis, there was a chapter on cross-cultural research methods (Whiting, 1954). According to this chapter, the focus of cross-cultural research was changing from an attempt to describe the cultural evolution of various institutions within different societies (institutions such as marriage, lineage, and religion) to the test of cross-culturally universal theories:

> In the last fifteen years, the cross-cultural method has not only become more popular but has changed in its theoretical orientation. *It has drawn upon the theory of general behavioral science rather than that of cultural evolution* [p. 523; emphasis added].

Thus, rather than attempting to understand the origin and perhaps unique functions of family organization within a given culture, an effort was made to test "general" hypotheses about family organization in cultures other than the investigator's own. It is very likely, of course, that the theories being tested in this way (e.g., the psychoanalytic theory of oedipal conflicts) were rooted in the investigator's own culture. Although this new hypothesis-testing approach, coupled with the elimination of the substantive sociohistorical analysis of cultures, may have increased the precision of investigations of certain race-related variables, it seems to have done so at the expense of a meaningful understanding of many other race-related phenomena.

Another change in the 1954 edition of the *Handbook* was the addition of a section on applied social psychology, which contained chapters on voting, industry, mass media, and, most important for present purposes, prejudice and ethnic relations (Harding, Kutner, Proshansky, & Chein, 1954). Harding and associates defined ethnic groups as consisting of people who perceive themselves, or are perceived by others, as similar on the basis of (1) religion, (2) racial origin [physically determined], (3) national origin, and (4) language and cultural traditions. They defined prejudice simply as a negative ethnic attitude and, in developing their analysis of the social problem of prejudice in the United States, referred to two distinct research traditions. These were (1) the group focus associated with Park (1913, 1950), Thomas and Znaniecki (1918), and Myrdal (1944), which emphasized historical development, cultural traditions, migration, and changing political and economic fortunes; and (2) the individual focus, associated with Bogardus (1925) and Adorno, Frenkel-Brunswik, Levinson, and Sanford (1950), which emphasized social attitudes. Harding and associates mention that the latter approach best represented the field's emphasis during the previous fifteen years.

To summarize social psychology's first half century, then, the field began with a major interest in race, albeit a concept of race rooted in racism and biological determinism. For a while the differences between racial and ethnic groups were examined in terms of cultural evolution and cultural diversity. Before this approach had a chance to become firmly established as a part of social psychology, however, it was overshadowed by new emphases on the testing of hypotheses derived from general psychological theories and an approach to prejudice that centered on individuals' attitudes. The cultural bases of these attitudes received progressively less attention.

The rising emphasis on methodology inadvertently discouraged a sophisticated analysis of race-related issues. The experimental method, combined with enthusiasm for quantification and causal hypotheses, made it desirable to assign subjects randomly to experimental treatment and control groups. Since it is impossible to assign subjects randomly to races, race was forced to join other culture—and social system—related variables on social psychology's back burner. Moreover, the mass movement into university social psychology laboratories encouraged an emphasis on *molecular* levels of analysis. Modern equivalents of concepts such as group mind and *Volkgeist* rarely appeared in accounts of social behavior once the experiment took center stage. Instead, analogies between the individual mind and computers dominated the field. (This trend continues, as evidenced by the recent creation of the journal *Social Cognition*.)

It is in this context that the quantitative and cultureless concepts of "minority" and "affirmative action" should be examined. Whereas race was once an anthropologically rich concept, and race ranked as a social problem because of its association with cultural conflict and cultural influence, it has now been diluted into an issue of bureaucratic counting, as if cultural differences would dissolve once a certain institutional *number* was reached.

This summary of trends in the use of race as a social psychological concept suggests some hypotheses: (1) Research on race declined as social psychology became more "rigorous" (i.e., more experimental). (2) Cultural interpretations of race differences are considered less significant now than they were decades ago. (3) The ethnicity/race of writers and researchers will have an important effect on the questions they ask and the variables they study.

In the following sections I would like to explore some implications of these hypotheses by (1) examining the number and nature of published articles in major social psychology journals and the amount of attention given in certain social psychology textbooks to race and race-related subjects; (2) proposing reasons for the patterns revealed by these analyses; (3) considering ways in which the theories and methodological practices of social psychology might be revised to offer a more cogent and useful treatment of race; and (4) reviewing selected works of black psychologists to see how social psychology might be enriched by cultural differences and the inclusion of culture-relevant concepts and variables.

Race: Its Use in Social Psychology Journals and Textbooks

It would be a massive task to review all of the empirical work published over the past 60 years in a search for race-related studies and findings. It is possible, however, to examine the bulk of work done since the implementation of the automated retrieval system associated with *Psychological Abstracts*. In the first part of this section, I will report the preliminary results of such a search. Because the retrieval system contains only articles published since 1968, it will be necessary to look elsewhere for information on the use of the concept of race before that time. In the second part of this section I will report findings from a survey of social psychology textbooks, including several published in the decades before 1968. Both of these surveys will be rather global because of time constraints: I will summarize the race-relevant literature in social psychology in terms of themes and gross topographical features, such as obvious changes in emphasis over time, journal-related topical foci, and implicit choices revealed by dominant methodological orientations. Desirable but not attempted here would be micro-analysis of the empirical findings, a review of the methodological-conceptual critiques, and an attempt to formulate a useful conceptual integration of race-related theory and data. I hope that each of these important tasks will be made easier by the efforts described here.

A Survey of Race-Related Articles in Social Psychology Journals, 1968-1980

A search was conducted through the Psych-Info data base developed and maintained by the American Psychological Association. This data base contains over 350,000 documents abstracted from more than 950 journals that publish psychological work. The search procedure is known as PASAR (Psych-Info Assisted Search and Retrieval). The article titles and the text of their abstracts are scanned for key index terms selected by the investigator. Index terms for the present study included all of those associated with race, in alphabetical order: Afro-American, African American, American Indian, Asian American, Blacks, Chicanos, Chinese, Cubans, Culture, Ethnic, Eskimo, Gypsies, Hispanic, Japanese, Mexican, Minority, Negroes, Pacific Islander, Puerto Rican, Race, Spanish American, and Tribes.

Seven journals were selected as representative of mainstream work in social psychology. Other possible journals were not selected because, although they often included social psychological work, they were either too pointedly concerned with race/ethnicity to be reflective of the mainstream (*Journal of Black Psychology, Hispanic Journal of Behavioral Science, Journal of Cross-Cultural Psychology*), redundant with journals already selected (e.g., *American Journal of Social Psychology*), or based on an atypically broad conception of social psychology (e.g., *British Journal of Clinical and Social Psychology*). The following journals were selected:

Journal of Personality and Social Psychology (JPSP)
Journal of Social Issues (JSI)
Personality and Social Psychology Bulletin (PSPB)
Journal of Social Psychology (JSP)
Journal of Applied Social Psychology (JASP)
Journal of Experimental Social Psychology (JESP)
Social Psychology Quarterly (SPQ)

Using the 22 index terms, all articles in the seven journals were searched for the period 1968-1980. The search produced a complete citation and abstract for each relevant article, 751 in all. Each citation-plus-abstract was pasted on a 4" x 6" file card, and analyses were performed by sorting the cards.

Results

The breakdown of articles by journal and year reveals that JSP yielded the most articles, followed, in order, by JPSP, JSI, PSPB, JASP, SPQ and JESP. The enormous number of JSP articles is primarily due to this journal's strong commitment to cross-cultural research. Nearly 60% of the JSP articles uncovered by the search were cross-cultural in focus.

While the number of race-related articles published in each journal is approximately what one would expect, the temporal patterns are perhaps less predictable. There is a clear increase from 1968 to 1973, after which the curve drops off sharply. The increase is understandable; the volatile 1960s made race a salient issue and won for it the designation of an important social problem. More surprising is the dropoff after 1973. Anyone who is familiar with American society knows that the problem is still far from solved.

Experimental Rigor and Race-Relevance

I hypothesized earlier that increasing scientific rigor, defined mainly in terms of the use of laboratory experiments, discouraged research based on a molar, cultural view of race. One way to test this hypothesis is to see whether the journals judged to be more rigorous are also less likely to publish race-relevant research. To explore this possibility I had a panel of five expert judges, all senior researchers in social psychology, rank the seven journals according to "the degree of rigor and/or sophistication of research exemplified by the articles published in them."

The rank order of each of the journals with regard to methodological rigor was JESP, JPSP, SPQ, PSBP, JASP, JSP and JSI. Analysis was also undertaken of the relative concern for race-relevant issues, expressed in terms of the relative proportion of race-relevant articles appearing in each journal. This analysis revealed 35% of the 6684 articles published in the seven target journals between 1968 and 1980 were contributed by JPSP, while JSP contributed only 19.4%. Comparing these figures with the percentages of race-relevant articles contributed by the same journals, we find that JPSP contributed only 19.4% of them, 15.6% less than their contribution to the total. JSP, in contrast, contributed 47.2% of the race-relevant articles, which is 19.1% more than their contribution to the total of all articles. It is clear that as one looks from less to more rigorous journals, the relative contribution of race-relevant articles declines correspondingly. While this obviously does not prove that an increased emphasis on experimental rigor is responsible for the recent decline in race-relevant studies, the results are compatible with that interpretation, and it is certain that the two do not enjoy a positive relationship. Evidently, race and rigor are perceived as somehow incompatible.

Categorization by Race of Subjects

We can ask another kind of question about the data: What are all of these studies actually about? What do they tell us about race? What conclusions can be drawn from them? Unfortunately, the answers are not very satisfying to the psychologist with a serious interest in race.

I first sorted the 751 articles into two categories, empirical versus nonempirical. (The latter typically do not include subjects.) Only 55 articles fell into the nonempirical category (reviews, essays, and so on), and of these fully 31 appeared in JSI. In further subdividing the empirical articles, I employed three categories suggested by Pepitone (1975) in his brief for a normative approach to social psychology:

- *Intra-Subcultural*: Studies of subjects who belong to a single subcultural group in the United States (including whites). (Recall, all of the articles had something to do with race or culture, though not necessarily the race of the subjects involved.)
- *Cross-Subcultural*: Studies involving comparisons between one or more racial/ethnic groups. Subcategories include black-white, white-other, and multiple (e.g., black-white-Chicano).
- *Cross-Cultural*: Studies in which at least one of the subject populations is not from the United States. Subcategories include U.S.—other culture, two other cultures compared, and an examination of one non-U.S. culture.

The majority of studies fell into the cross-cultural category (37.4%). Of these, a whopping 93% were published in JSP. The next largest category was cross-subcultural (213 or 28.3%). Of these, 133 (62%) compared blacks and whites. The remaining category, intrasubcultural studies, concerns studies that tell us something about a particular race or ethnic group. Of the 202 articles in this category, 116 (57.4%) concern whites, 51 (25.2%) concern blacks, and the remainder (17.4%) are divided among studies of Chicanos, Puerto Ricans, Asian Americans, Hawaiians, and Eskimos.

These results deserve comment. Remember, my search of the data base resulted in 751 articles that had something to do with race or culture. That left 5933 articles from the seven journals that did not have anything special to say about these topics. It can be assumed, I believe, that the vast majority of empirical articles in this category were based on white subjects or involved random assignment of white and nonwhite subjects to conditions, thus burying any cultural differences in the analysis. Until normative influences associated with race/ethnicity are shown to be trivial, I assume that they operate in most social psychology experiments. Therefore, the overwhelming bulk of social psychological studies in recent years have been intrasubcultural and have been based on an inadvertent exploration of the dominant white subculture. While it may seem extreme to view nearly all such studies as inherently cultural or normative rather than universal in application, the thrust of this view is not inconsistent with arguments made recently by others (e.g., Boykin, 1983; McGuire, 1974; Pepitone, 1975).

A few speculations may be useful to future investigators of these matters. First, when blacks and whites are compared in a single study (as happened 133 times in the articles retrieved), it is reasonable to guess that the hypotheses were derived from knowledge of the white subculture, even though researchers do not typically mention this. Second, as I explained earlier, there has been a move away from thinking of race in normative terms and toward an emphasis on prejudice. Almost always the focus is on prejudice of the majority (whites) against the minority (blacks, in most of the studies sampled). This makes it seem acceptable or even appropriate to devote exclusive attention to members of the white subculture.

Combining these ideas with the notion that experimental rigor tends to militate against intrasubcultural study of the black subculture from a normative perspective, one can predict, even when considering only race-relevant studies, that the more rigorous journals will tend to include a disproportionate number of studies involving white subjects. This hypothesis was supported.

Before proceeding to the next section, it may be helpful to summarize the main points of the analyses conducted so far:

(1) From 1969 to 1980, only 11.2% of all articles published in seven major social psychology journals concerned race, ethnicity, or culture.

(2) During the same period, the number of race-relevant articles

evidenced a dramatic curvilinear trend, increasing from 1968 to 1973 and then declining rapidly to pre-1968 levels.

(3) The experimental rigor of a journal seems to be negatively related to the journal's likelihood of published race-relevant articles.

(4) Published empirical studies can be distinguished in terms of the race-ethnicity of the subjects used and also in terms of the intergroup comparisons made, if any. The data indicate that when the more rigorous journals do publish race-relevant studies the subjects are likely to be whites (examined for prejudice) or white and African Americans who are being compared (most likely on measures and in terms of theories derived from the white subculture). Journals judged less rigorous are more likely to include intrasubcultural studies of nonwhites and cross-cultural comparisons.

These findings are generally in line with the argument I developed earlier. To the extent that race has been viewed as a mainstream issue by social psychologists, it has entered their analysis mainly in terms of the prejudicial attitudes held by members of the white subculture. As a result, social psychology has contributed relatively little in recent years to cultural (normative) analyses of nonwhite subcultures in the United States or to theories concerning intercultural relations.

A Survey of Race-Related Terms in Social Psychology Textbooks 1908-1981

For present purposes, a social psychology textbook will be defined as any book located in the HM251 section of the Dewey Decimal System that has the phrase "social psychology" in its title. All books at that location are highly relevant to social psychology, although not all important social psychology books are located there. I scanned these books with an eye for five major race-related concepts: (1) race/ethnic/ethnicity, (2) culture/cross-cultural, (3) racism, (4) black/Negro, and (5) prejudice/discrimination. For sake of simplicity, other relevant terms such as stereotype and national character and other ethnic groups (e.g., Japanese, Chinese, and Spanish Americans) were ignored. Anti-Semitism, which has been a major concern of social psychologists, was often retrievable under the heading "prejudice/discrimination."

Three measures of conceptual representation can be determined while skimming a textbook: (1) appearance of a term in a chapter title, (2) appearance of a term in a subheading, and (3) number of pages allocated to a subject. Since reading all of the relevant books was out of the question, page allocation was determined from each book's subject index.

The 653 psychology textbooks contained 25,408 pages. Of these, 3,128 (12.3%) contained discussions of race-related terms. (This is a somewhat inflated figure because the same pages were sometimes referred to under more than one heading, and I did not attempt to correct for this.) There were 77 relevant chapter titles and subheadings. The more interesting results concern trends over time in the treatment of race-related issues. To look for such trends, the texts were divided into those with pre-1960 and those with post-1960 publication dates. This particular dividing line was chosen because 1960 was the beginning of the decade in which social psychology witnessed a proliferation of experimental methodology. There proved to be only a very slight trend toward greater representation of race-related terms in the older texts (13.4% versus 11.3%). Of considerable interest, however, is the heavy representation of "culture" in the pre-1960 texts (43% of chapter headings and 44% of all pages), and the corresponding emphasis on "prejudice and discrimination" after 1960 (37% of chapter heading and 34% of pages). These results are consistent with the arguments and results presented earlier.

Reflections on Changes in the Use of Race as a Social Psychological Concept

It is illuminating to read textbooks and journal articles that appeared fifty or sixty years ago in comparison with those that flood the market today. The surveys I have presented thus far really cannot do justice to the overwhelming change in the feel and tone of these writings. Collective histories and experiences were extremely prominent in early attempts to account for the social behavior of individuals and groups. McDougall (1921), for example, even tried to explain the differential success of British and French colonialism in terms of different national characters (a cultural notion with racial undertones). He divided the cultures of Europe into three categories, labeled "races": Nordic, Alpine, and Mediterranean. Social psychological analyses in those days were aimed at social processes of global interest, nation states were asserting themselves all over the world, emigration to the United States was high, and racial/cultural mixing was occurring at a rapid rate.

Contrast these grand ideas and feelings, whatever their scientific merit, with the contemporary scene. Affirmative action has rendered numbers the major factor in race and ethnicity. Our research, perhaps picking up this cue or being influenced by common forces, emphasizes perceptual and cognitive processes associated with numbers: illusory correlation (Hamilton & Gifford, 1976), solo behavior in groups (Taylor, et al., 1977), and minority influence (Latane & Wolfe, 1981). Racial and ethnic variables have more meaning as stimuli for white subjects' judgments than as vital aspects of collectivities of people whose experiences have a long socio-cultural-historical continuity. What has brought us to this point?

Race is a second-class variable. Important social-scientific investigations are, according to mainstream beliefs, those with universal applicability and those involving experimental methods. Race loses out on both counts. Each racial-ethnic group is unique in certain important respects and so calls as much for ethnography as for experimental manipulation. As mentioned earlier, subjects cannot be randomly assigned to races (except in a special sense to be discussed in a subsequent section). Of course, to someone like me who believes that many social psychological processes are likely to be affected by race/ethnicity, it is an illusion to view studies of white American college students as generating universal principles or conclusions. Nevertheless, a study based only on white students is thought not to need a racial-ethnic comparison group (even though most editors would probably be uncomfortable with a study that claimed to generate universal principles using only a small sample of black subjects).

Race is perceived to be less of a social problem these days. Because today there are few race riots, noisy demands for black studies programs, affirmative action demands for blacks, and the like, it is easy to believe that race is less of an issue than it was 10 or 15 years ago. Nevertheless, surveys show that Los Angeles Mayor Bradley, a black man, probably lost his 1982 bid for the governorship of California because of over 200,000 people who explicitly voted against him on racial grounds. Several years ago, thousands of lifelong Democrats in Chicago chose to vote Republican because a white Republican is running against a black Democrat, Harold Washington. This is hardly what an African American would call the absence of a social problem. Still, a national survey by Kluegel and Smith (1982) revealed that 73% of white adults believe that the chances for blacks and other minority groups to get ahead are equal to or greater than the chances for whites. Thus, presto, the race problem is declared no longer problematic.

There is a second sense in which race might be perceived to be less of a social problem than it once was. A host of issues now compete for social problem status, as can be seen by examining recent issues of JSI. Whereas in the late 1960s and early 1970s several issues dealt with black-white social relations, one now reads about sex-role changes, drugs, violence, rape, jury decision-making, abortion, and so on. Race, if it is perceived to be a social problem at all, is now just one among many.

Race is confounded with ethnicity, culture, and social class. Race is intertwined with several other important concepts and in fact has little clear social meaning without them. The nature of the relationships can be clarified with the help of some standard definitions.

> RACE (in its basic biological sense): a major segment of a species originally occupying since the first dispersal of mankind a large geographically unified and distinct region touching on the territory of other races only by relatively narrow corridors. Within such a region, each race acquired its distinctive genetic attributes with its visible appearance and its invisible biological properties, through the selective forces and all aspects of environment including culture [Bloom, 1966].

This definition emphasizes genetic distinctiveness but implies a relationship between this and both environment and culture. Van den Berghe (1977) draws an additional distinction, between race and ethnicity:

> RACE: The human group that defines itself, and/or is defined by other groups as different by virtue of innate of immutable characteristics. These physical characteristics are in turn assumed to be intrinsically related to moral, intellectual and other non-physical attributes or abilities. A race, therefore, is a group that is *socially defined on the basis of physical criteria.*

> ETHNICITY: [refers to] a group that is *socially defined on the basis of cultural criteria.*

To the extent that the massive racial segregation documented by Taeuber and Taeuber (1965) continues (88.6% of African Americans would have to move to create racial integration) and combines with substantial genetic inbreeding, one might wish to think of race in biological terms. Or, one could accept the view of Van den Berghe, noting that whites experience blacks as a racial group (that is, blacks are socially defined as a race based on skin color and other physical attributes but are also seen as having distinctive values and behavior patterns). However, black people define themselves primarily in cultural terms, hence for them ethnicity rather than biological race is the more appropriate characterization. Kroeber and Kluckhohn (1954) define culture as:

> Transmitted by symbols, constituting the distinctive achievement of human groups including their embodiment of artifacts, essential beliefs consisting of traditional (i.e., historically derived) and selected ideas, especially their past values. Culture systems may, on the one hand, be considered as products of

action, on the other hand, as conditioning elements of future action [p. 18].

Thus, culture is a historically derived pattern of beliefs, values, symbols, behaviors, and so on that serves as a meaningful structure and guide for future behavior. Too often social scientists have considered black culture to be merely a reaction to suppression by whites; but black psychologists and other black social scientists, while certainly not denying the effects of slavery, discrimination, and so on, seek to focus attention as well on the positive components of black culture, a culture that evolved in Africa long before suppression by whites occurred.

Finally, race is sometimes used almost synonymously with social class (e.g., Lewis, 1961). The so-called "culture of poverty" argument acknowledges the intertwining of culture and race but attributes the character of black culture almost entirely to poverty. Once again, therefore, the positive traditional aspects of black culture are ignored. (In a later section I will outline ways in which black psychologists are attempting to construct a more balanced picture of black culture.)

Shifts from group to individual focus. In recent years, not only have social psychologists largely abandoned the study of culture and institutions, they have devoted more and more attention to individuals and less and less to groups and intergroup relations. In my earlier treatment of racism (Jones, 1972), I emphasized the independent-variable status of culture; culture influences the establishment and functioning of institutions whose consequences are not neutral for certain racial/ethnic groups. Social psychology's emphasis on experimental studies of supposedly universal processes in social cognition leave little place for racial variables. Their only natural place is on the stimulus side of the equation, hence the everpresent tendency to use photographs of minority faces, essays supposedly written by minority authors and so on—in conjunction with white subjects whose reactions form the dependent variables of interest. The investigator with a cultural/normative perspective on racial issues is locked into a Catch 22 bind: one can either study race using correlational and ethnographic techniques and suffer consignment to second-class nonexperimental journals or use experimental methods and abandon some of the most intellectually and practically important research problems. This places minority psychologists in a difficult position.

Reorganizing Social Psychology's Approach to Race

In this section I would like to offer some concrete suggestions for improvement in the way race is conceptualized and studied by social psychologists.

Definition. As I have shown, race can refer to biological/physical features of a person (e.g., skin color) or to a person's cultural background, in which case the more appropriate term is "ethnicity." If we use, say, stimulus pictures of black people in an experiment on white subjects' attitudes, the biological concept of race may or may not be sufficient, depending on what inferences the subjects draw concerning the pictured people's motives, characteristic social behaviors, and the like. Certainly though, if we are trying to understand the thoughts, feelings, and behaviors of a particular racial group, we cannot do justice to the topic without a careful consideration of culture (ethnicity). This requires a knowledge of sociohistorical context that is very rare among contemporary social psychologists.

Two Research Examples

In a recent study by Sagar and Schofield (1980), junior high school boys were given descriptions of ambiguously aggressive actions committed by black or white boys (manipulated by drawings of the perpetrators). In the context of the experiment, the only relevant variables were race of the actor, race of the target (also established by drawings), and race of the subjects (a biological and cultural reality). When asked to describe how mean and threatening the actor was, both black and white subjects saw the black actor as more extreme on these dimensions.

Schofield wrote: "The lack of any statistical interaction between race of subject and race permutations . . . suggests . . . that the ratings reflect a general bias among this male population, rather than a uniquely white response" (p. 594). However, if we include the notion of cultural differences in our interpretation, the meaning of the actions might well vary with race of the subject. If one assumes, for example, that the baseline level of aggression represented by the ambiguous actions is best represented by the within-racial judgments (white ratings of white actors, black ratings of black actors), then the effect of race should be assessed in terms of deviations, if any, from this within-racial/cultural baseline. My portrayal of the possibility revealed that the absolute level of aggressiveness perceived by black and white subjects was about the same when they judge actors of their own race. However, whites judge black actors to be far more aggressive than white actors, and blacks judge whites to be far *less* aggressive than blacks.

My interpretation fits with facts supplied by the authors: The school where the study was conducted had been recently desegregated by bringing middle class whites (about a third of the school population) into an environment of black children with lower achievement and SES levels. Although overt racial conflict was reportedly minimal, "This generally positive picture was balanced by interview data in which both black and white students reported that white students were more likely to be intimidated by their black peers than vice versa" (p. 593). Given this cultural context of interracial interaction, what seems significant to me is that black subjects do not perceive black actors to be any more aggressive than white subjects perceive white actors. My reanalysis considers it be part of a cultural complex.

Word, Zanna, and Cooper (1974) conducted a pair of studies that also break new ground in the study of race-related processes. In the first study, white male undergraduates interviewed black and white high school students for a final spot on a competitive team. The interviewees had been trained by the experimenters to behave in comparable ways. The results indicated that interviewers reacted differently depending on the interviewee's race. Black interviewees were treated in a more negative nonverbal manner (greater interpersonal distance, more speech errors indicative of anxiety, quicker termination of interviews). The second study involved white subjects being interviewed for a job by a white interviewer who was a confederate of the experimenters. In each experimental condition, the interviewer acted in one of the two ways revealed in the first study, in a way characteristic of a white interviewing a black or of a white interviewing a white. An independent panel of judges then rated the performance of these white subjects, who were functioning (without knowing it) as blacks or whites. The functional black subjects were judged to be less competent, less confident, and overall less desirable as job candidates. The beauty of this study is that by experimentally reproducing an aspect of the usual treatment received by black interviewees, the researchers were able to understand a black behavior pattern while detaching it from physically black subjects.

The study suggests that some cultural aspects of interracial interactions can be studied experimentally, but only if we are able to identify and isolate particular culture-based processes and then bring them under experimental control. It is likely that members of the racial-ethnic groups in question can be very helpful in specifying these processes and so should be actively involved in social psychology. That Word, first author of the article from which I have taken this example, is black supports my point.

Sampling

Does a sample of white sophomores from a midwestern university represent the white race. Does it represent the white ethnic groups of America? As I mentioned earlier, if all of the subjects in a social psychology experiment are white, researchers and readers of their articles seem not to perceive the study as involving race or ethnicity. Add an additional group of black students from the same university, however, and suddenly white subjects become representative of their racial/ethnic group (as the black students do of theirs). I submit that with no better definition of group membership than skin color it is gratuitous to consider such research an adequate contribution to the study of race or racial differences. This may be one reason for the inconsistency of previous race-related findings. It is not uncommon in such studies to use whites from one economic level (upper middle) and blacks from another (always lower). Usually the different selection histories of members of the two groups are ignored.

Several years ago, Worthy and Markle (1970) argued that whites are better baseball pitchers than blacks, citing as evidence the fact that major league pitchers were overwhelmingly white. In looking more carefully at available statistics, I found (Jones & Hochner, 1973) that black pitchers actually had better performance records than white pitchers on virtually every measurable dimension. Does this mean that blacks were actually better pitchers than whites? Not at all. There were only 12 black major league pitchers at the time, compared with 144 whites. The black pitchers undoubtedly had to be exceptionally good to make it into a major league pitching position; the selection criteria were, in effect, more stringent for them than for their white counterparts. The general point is that experimental and psychometric rigor mean relatively little if the groups compared in a particular study are different in a host of ways that aren't taken into account. It is rather amazing that so much effort has been devoted to laboratory technology and so little to sampling problems.

Theory

To put it bluntly, there is almost no sound social psychological theorizing about race or ethnicity. There are many studies of prejudice, and these are certainly of value, but I hope I have shown that these do not substitute for an understanding of any particular racial/ethnic group's value orientation or behavior. There are also some promising studies of "subjective culture" (Triandis, 1972), but these have not yet had a large impact on the field. (They have been used primarily to teach people about other cultures.) Black psychology, Chicano psychology, and the works of other psychologists of color attempt to clarify and specify the parameters of membership in particular racial/ethnic groups. Theoretical ideas about biculturalism are emerging from this work which may have an important organizing influence on race-relevant research in social psychology. (I will consider black psychology in more detail in the next section of this chapter.)

Another important emerging idea is that culture can be viewed as both a dependent and an independent variable. American social scientists have tended to view African American culture as a reaction to devastation by the white majority, beginning with slavery and continuing down to the economic and political discrimination of today. While there is certainly one useful perspective, when taken alone it tends to rob minority ethnic groups of the opportunity to consider positive aspects of their own lives and to American society's cultural diversity. The dependent-variable view of culture adopted by social scientists is based on the implicit assumption that there is, on the one hand, a dominant culture (with its positive personality characteristics, historical accomplishments, and so on) and, on the other, a handful of minority groups that have yet to adapt themselves fully to this culture. Actually, of course, each of America's minority groups already had a highly developed culture of their own. This culture influences their choices, feelings, and behaviors—that is, it acts as a constellation of independent variables in determining their actions, and so should not be ignored by social scientists.

Perspectives from Black Psychology

Over the past few decades, psychological analysis of race has identified an unending stream of dysfunctions, maladaptations, deficient social organization, poor intellectual performances, inadequate motivation, restricted ego domains, doubts, stresses, and fears. One wonders, on the basis of this extensive literature, how African Americans have managed to survive. The genetic versions of these negativistic analyses are based on the assumption that deficient genes explain the poor adaptation to American society; the environmental versions instead point the finger at poverty and racist oppression. While the environmentalists often accuse the geneticists of racism, black psychologists cannot help noticing that neither position recognizes a single attribute, capacity, or contribution of black people that could be considered positive, desirable, or worth preserving. An essential goal of black psychology, then, is to go beyond the reactive conception of African Americans' history to develop a cultural-evolutionary perspective that recognizes African origins, and more recent developments in the United States (and other countries), and the effects of prolonged oppression. This new perspective should include what is distinctively good and useful in the African American experiences.

Nobles (1980), for example, argues that the unique state of black psychology "is derived not from the negative aspects of being black in white America, but rather from the positive features of (Black) African philosophy which dictate the values, customs, attitudes, and behavior of Africans in Africa and in the New World" (p. 23). This philosophy emphasizes the inclusion of human beings in nature (rather than the technological subjugation of nature) and the fundamental identity of self and other ("I am because we are, and because we are therefore I am"—which might be contrasted with Descartes' "I think, therefore I am"). Nobles also talks about the fundamental differences between African and Anglo-American conceptions of the relations between opposites; between mind and body; and between past, present, and future.

Dixon (1976) discusses the different philosophies inherent in different world views. He argues that research methods are influenced by philosophical differences in axiology, epistemology, and logic—the study of values, methods or ways of knowing, and the criteria for the validation of knowledge, respectively. According to Dixon, there are striking differences between what he calls the Euro-American and African orientations (see Table 1). This depiction of the differences clearly implies that black (African) heritage is highly social rather than individualistic, and highly affective-symbolic, present-oriented, and nonlinear. The implications of these differences for life in American society need to be explored.

Table 1
Dixon's Comparison of Euro-American and African Philosophical Orientation

Orientation	Euro-American	African
Axiologies		
Human/Nature	Human-to-object	Human-to-person
Relations	(I/It)	(I/Thou)
	Mastery over Nature	Harmony with Nature
	Individualism	Communalism
Time	Future, Divisible	Past-present,
	Linear clock	Continuous Felt
Activity	Doing	Being
Epistomology	Object-measure	Affect-Symbolic
	Cognition	Imagery
Logic	Either-Or	Diunital

Source: Dixon (1976). Reprinted with permission of the Famon Center.

Cole (1970) identified three principal components of black culture that derive from black people's participation in American society: an "American mainstream" component (including aspects of material culture, mainstream values, mainstream behavior patterns, and so on); a "minority sense" component (which involves continual monitoring of the dominant society's hostility and continual acts of self-protection); and a "blackness" component (including the African and African American cultural heritage with its many positive elements). The first and second components are common to many other disadvantaged groups: racial/ethnic groups, women, the elderly, gays, and the like. The third is unique to the black experience and has evolved into what Cole calls "soul" (a product primarily of sociality combined with hardship) and "style" (characteristic ways of walking, talking, dressing, and thinking). At the very least, in order to understand much of an African American person's feelings and behavior one would need to know something about his or her standing in terms of these three components of black culture. So far, social psychology has not moved very far in that direction.

Boykin (1983) has provided an extensive and thoughtful review of the issue of culture as it affects the academic performance of black children. He considers the traditional "victim-blame deficit model" and finds it severely lacking. He also considers the social-structural view and the cultural difference view, finding that both have problems. The first is unnecessarily pessimistic about the possibility of improving black performance, the latter too simplistic in ignoring the societal context in which performance must take place. Like other black psychological theorists, Boykin outlines some realms or dimensions of black culture which are of relevance to psychological research:

- Spirituality—recognition of the power of immaterial forces in everyday life
- Harmony—interconnectedness of self with surroundings
- Movement—personal conduct organized through movement
- Verve—propensity for energetic, intense, and stimulating experience
- Affect—integration of feelings with thoughts and actions
- Communalism—social interdependence
- Expressive individualism—distinctive personality expressed with style
- Orality—knowledge gained and transmitted orally and aurally
- Social time perspective—marking of time is based on socially meaningful events

The complexity of the black experience is indicated by what Boykin calls the "triple quandary." African Americans must participate in mainstream American society, cope with unfairness of past and present treatment, and decide what to do about their unique cultural orientations (this is an elaboration of Cole's analysis).

Finally, I also have attempted to delineate some of the basic facets of human experience that may be useful in thinking about minority cultures. These categories, summarized in the acronym TRIOS (time, rhythm, improvisation, oral expression, and spirituality; see my chapter in the present volume, Racism: A Cultural Analysis of the Problem for elaboration), are based on several sources, including cross-cultural studies of humor (Jones, 1976), evaluation of individual athletic styles (Jones, & Hochner, 1973), and various culturally based forms of expression (Jones, 1974). I have been interested in exploring the TRIOS categories because they represent some of the main areas in which the dominant culture may conflict with minority cultures. Insisting on a narrow range of acceptable values and behavioral styles, and basing equity (reward and resource allocation) decisions on them, is one of the most conspicuous and damaging ways in which cultural bias operates. The TRIOS categories might encourage social psychologists to consider a broader range of human capacities and contributions and to view differences as positive outcomes of cultural diversity and cultural evolution. Determining what these various contributions are is one important goal of black psychology and other ethnic psychological analyses.

Concluding Comments

I began by showing that race, once an important concept in social psychology, has been redefined and conceptually demoted to such an extent that it now occupies a second-class position in the field's prestige hierarchy. When race does appear in contemporary experimental studies, it is usually operationalized in a physical way (e.g., by a picture of a black person's face) and serves to manipulate an independent variable. If black or other minority subjects are included in the study—and usually they are not—they are randomly assigned to conditions so that cultural differences between them and white subjects get lost in the analysis. To the extent that experimental procedures dominate the field and other social problems compete with race for research attention, very little is learned about race except what is written by minority psychologists for each others' consumption. Not only will this state of affairs delay our understanding of minority-group and intergroup behavior, it contributes to social psychology's general retreat from cultural concepts—a retreat that is, in my opinion, intellectually disastrous. Human behavior is, to a large extent, a cultural creation; to ignore this fact cannot be healthy for a major subdivision of American social science.

I view race-related research as a potentially central and vital component of mainstream social psychology, not just as a sub-sub-specialty of interest only to minority academics. I cannot help thinking that the impact of minorities on majorities discussed by Latané and Wolfe (1981) in their article on group process applies as well to the impact that properly conceived and carefully executed research into race/ethnicity/culture could have on our field:

> In the face of changing times and conditions, majorities continue to convince each other of the truths of the past, whereas minority positions may be fresher, more elegant or realistic than those of the outmoded majority. The insistent behavior of the minority thus forces the majority to attend to the discrepancy between its position and the current state of the world, creating the conditions for a profound and often rapid change in the status quo. Thus the minority may serve mainly as a trigger to create an explosive release from the powerful conformity pressures exerted by the majority. [pp. 451-452].

In order for race/ethnicity research to have this liberating effect on social psychology, we need to improve our conceptualization of race-related variables, broaden the kinds of studies we design, and consider alternative interpretations of studies that have been done in the past. We also need to pay more attention to the theoretical and empirical work of ethnic minority psychologists and consider the different perspectives that minority students and colleagues could add to our interpretations of social events. Finally, we need to take culture seriously, perhaps by returning to some of the fundamental ideas of earlier thinkers whose work has been squeezed out of recent accounts of the field. Social psychology has unnecessarily traded its substantive soul for a sparkling collection of powerful methods. It is time to apply these methods to the field's originally challenging problems. I will be pleased if the present paper stimulates further thinking along those lines.

Notes

1. Lest my negative comments be construed as opposition to affirmative action, let me say quite clearly that affirmative

action is necessary and must be continued for the foreseeable future. However, the notion of affirmative action neglects the possibility that different cultural groups have different strengths and may contribute to society in different but equally beneficial ways. Affirmative action by itself, concerned only with head counts, makes it seem that full absorption into the dominant culture is and should be everybody's goal. Also, thoughtless emphasis on head counts, makes it seem that a person's actual contribution to society is irrelevant. This leads to the belief that affirmative action is inequitable and brings charges of "reverse discrimination" or, in Glazer's (1975) paradoxical phrasing, *Affirmative Discrimination*.

2. I have focused in this paper on the difficulty of studying many race-related issues with laboratory-experimental methods. In recent years a host of new statistical methods have been proposed for the study of naturally-occurring, complex social processes. These new procedures—for instance, PLS, LISREL, path analysis, and various methods for analyzing longitudinal data—may well contribute substantially to the causal analysis of racial and cultural phenomena. To date they have not, however, so my analysis of racial and cultural research remains timely. It would be a pleasure to admit, sometime in the near future, that the bulk of the critique no longer applies.

3. I am extremely grateful for the help, constructive criticism, and insightful observations of several people: Wade Boykin and Harriet McAdoo provided the opportunity to clarify my ideas and offered cogent criticism of an early version of this manuscript at the Seventh Conference on Empirical Research in Black Psychology, Hampton University; Olive Jones helped me to get straight what I wanted to say and encouraged me to say it; Samuel Gaertner was continually available and nudged me toward greater clarification of several confusing points; and Brenda Rawls, who typed the manuscript skillfully and swiftly. Finally, I thank the editors of the volume in which this paper first appeared: Ladd Wheeler for his patience and belief that I could eventually say something useful, and Phillip Shaver for jumping in with undaunted optimism to create a finished manuscript that would do justice to my ideas and the purpose of the volume.

References

Adorno, T.W., Frenkel-Brunswik, E., Levinson, D.J., & Sanford, N. (1950). *The authoritarian personality*. New York: Harper.

Allport, T. (1924). *Social psychology*. Boston: Houghton Mifflin.

Allport, G.W. (1954). *The nature of prejudice*. Reading, MA: Addison-Wesley.

Allport, G.W. (1968). History of modern social psychology. In G. Lindzey, & E. Aronson (Eds.), *Handbook of social psychology*, (Vol. I). Reading, MA: Addison Wesley.

Bayton, J.A., McAlister, L.B., & Hamer, J.R. (1956). Race-class stereotypes. *Journal of Negro Education 41*, 75-78.

Banks, W.C. (1976). White preference in blacks: A paradigm in search of a phenomenon. *Psychological Bulletin, 83*, 1179-1186.

Bloom, L. (1971). *The social psychology of race relations*. Cambridge, MA: Schenkman Publishing.

Bogardus, E.S. (1925). Measuring social distance. *Journal of Applied Sociology, 9*, 299-308.

Boykin, A.W. (1983). The academic performance of Afro-American children. In J. Spence (Ed.), *Achievement and achievement motives*. San Francisco, CA: W.H. Freeman.

Campbell, D.T., & Stanley, J.C. (1966). *Experimental and quasi-experimental designs for research*. Chicago, IL: Rand McNally.

Carmichael, S., & Hamilton, C.V. (1967). *Black power: The politics of liberation in America*. New York: Vintage Books.

Clark, K.B., & Clark, M.P. (1950). Emotional factors in racial identification and preference of Negro children. *Journal of Negro Education, 19*, 341-350.

Cole, J. (1970). Negro, black and nigger. *Black Scholar, 1*, 40-44.

Deutsch, M., & Collins, M.E. (1951). *Interracial housing*. Minneapolis: University of Minnesota Press.

DeVos, G.A., & Hippler, A.E. (1968). Cultural psychology: Comparative studies of human behavior. In G. Linzey, & E. Aronson (Eds.), *Handbook of social psychology* (Vol. 4). Reading, MA: Addison-Wesley.

DuBois, W.E.B. (1903). *Souls of black folk*. Chicago: A.C. McClurg.

Gaetner, S., & Bickman, L. (1971). Effects of race on the elicitation of helping behavior: The wrong number technique. *Journal of Personality and Social Psychology, 20*, 218-222.

Glazer, N. (1975). *Affirmative discrimination: Ethnic inequality and public policy*. New York: Basic Books.

Hamilton, D.L. (1979). A cognitive-attributional analysis of stereotyping. In L. Berkowitz (Ed.), Advances in experimental social psychology (Vol. 12). New York: Academic Press.

Hamilton, D.L., & Gifford, R.K. (1976). Illusory correlation in interpersonal perception: A cognitive basis of stereotypic judgment. *Journal of Experimental Social Psychology, 12*, 392-407.

Harding, J., Kutner, B., Proshansky, H., & Chein, I. (1954). Prejudice and ethnic relations. In G. Lindzey (Ed.), *Handbook of social psychology* (Vol. 2). Reading, MA: Addison Wesley.

Harvey, E.D. (1935). Social history of the Yellow man. In C. Murchison (Ed.), *Handbook of social psychology*. Reading, MA: Addison-Wesley.

Herrnstein, R. (1971). I.Q. *Atlantic Monthly, 228(3)*, 43-64.

Herskovits, M. (1935). Social history of the Negro. In C. Murchison (Ed.), *Handbook of social psychology*. Reading, MA: Addison-Wesley.

Hraba, J., & Grant, G. (1970). Black is beautiful: A reexamination of racial identification and preference. *Journal of Personality and Social Psychology, 16,* 398-402.

Jones, J.M. (1972). *Prejudice and racism*. Reading, MA: Addison-Wesley.

Jones, J.M. (1974). The art of black psychology: Rejecting the null hype. *Proceedings of the Annual Convention of the Association of Black Psychologists*. Nashville, TN.

Jones, J.M. (1979). Conceptual and strategic issues in the relationship of black psychology to American social science. In A.W. Boykin, A.J. Franklin, & J.F. Yates (Eds.), *Research directions of black psychologists*. New York: Basic Books.

Jones, J.M. (1980). The concept of racism and its changing reality. In B. Bowser, & R. Hunt (Eds.), *Impacts of racism on white Americans*. Beverly Hills, CA: Sage.

Jones, J.M., & Hochner, A.R. (1973). Racial differences in sports activities: A look at the self-paced versus reactive hypothesis. *Journal of Personality and Social Psychology, 27* 85-95.

Jones, J.M., & Liverpool, H. (1976). Calypso humour in Trinidad. In A. Chapman, & H. Foot (Eds.), *Humour and laughter: Research and theory*. London: John Wiley.

Katz, D., & Braly, K.W. (1933). Racial stereotypes of 100 college students. *Journal of Abnormal and Social Psychology,* 280-290.

Kiesler, C.A. (1969). *Topics in social psychology*. Reading, MA: Addison-Wesley.

Kluegel, J.R., & Smith, E.R. (1982). Whites' beliefs about blacks' opportunity. *American Sociological Review, 47,* 518-532.

Lewis, O. (1961). *Children of Sanchez: Autobiography of a Mexican family*. New York: Random House.

Lindzey, G. (1954). *Handbook of social psychology*. Reading, MA: Addison-Wesley.

Lindzey, G., & Aronson, E. (Eds.) (1968). *Handbook of social psychology* (3rd ed.). Reading, MA: Addison-Wesley.

Linville, P., & Jones, E.E. (1980). Polarized appraisals of out-group members. *Journal of Personality and Social Psychology, 38,* 689-703.

McDougall, W. (1921). *Is America safe for democracy?* New York: Scribners.

McGuire, W.J. (1973). The yin and yang of progress in social psychology. *Journal of Personality and Social Psychology, 26,* 446-456.

Mischel, W. (1958). Preference for delayed reinforcement: An experimental study of a cultural observation. *Journal of Abnormal and Social Psychology, 56,* 57-61.

Mischel, W. (1961). Delay of gratification, need for achievement, and acquiescence in another culture. *Journal of Abnormal and Social Psychology, 62,* 543-552.

Moynihan, D.P., & Glazer, N. *Ethnicity*. New York: Free Press.

Murchison, C.W. (1935). *Handbook of social psychology* (1st ed.). Reading, MA: Addison-Wesley.

Myrdal, G. (1944). *An American dilemma: The Negro problem and modern democracy*. New York: Harper.

Nobles, W.W. (1980). African philosophy: Foundations for black psychology. In R.L. Jones (Ed.), *Black psychology* (2nd ed.) New York: Harper & Row.

Ornstein, R.E. (1969). *On the experience of time.* New York: Penguin Books.

Ornstein, R.E. (1977). *The psychology of consciousness* (2nd ed.). New York: Harcourt Brace Jovanovich.

Park, R.W. (1913). Racial assimilation in secondary groups with particular reference to the Negro. *Publication of the American Sociological Society, 8,* 66-83.

Park, R.W. (1950). *Race and culture.* New York: Free Press.

Pepitone, A. (1976). Toward a normative and comparative biocultural social psychology. *Journal of Personality and Social Psychology, 34,* 641-653.

Pettigrew, T.F. (1969). Racially separate or together? *Journal of Social Issues, 25,* 43-69.

Sagar, H.A., & Schofield, J.W. (1980). Racial and behavioral cues in black and white children's perceptions of ambiguously aggressive acts. *Journal of Personality and Social Psychology, 39,* 590-598.

Samelson, F. (1978). From "race psychology" to "studies in prejudice": Some observations on the thematic reversal in social psychology. *Journal of the History of the Behavioral Sciences, 14,* 265-278.

Taeuber, K.E., & Taeuber, A.F. (1965). *Negroes in cities.* Chicago: Aldine.

Taylor, S.E., Fiske, S.T., Close, M., Anderson, C., & Ruderman, A.J. (1977). *Solo status as a psychological variable: The power of being distinctive.* Unpublished manuscript, Harvard University.

Thomas, W.I., & Znaniecki, F. (1918). *The Polish peasant in Europe and America.* Boston: Richard Badger.

Triandis, H.C. (1972). *The analysis of subjective culture.* New York: Wiley-Interscience.

Triandis, H.C. (Ed.), (1976). *Variations in black and white: Perceptions of the social environment.* Urbana: University of Illinois Press.

United States Commission on Civil Disorders. (1968). *Report of the U.S. Commission on Civil Rights.* Washington, DC: Government Printing Office.

Van den Berghe, P. (1977). *Race and racism.* New York: John Wiley.

Wallis, W. (1935). Social history of the white man. In C. Murchison (Ed.), *Handbook of social psychology.* Reading, MA: Addison-Wesley.

Whiting, J. (1954). Cross-cultural methods. In G. Lindzey (Ed.), *Handbook of social psychology* (Vol. 1). Reading, MA: Addison-Wesley.

That Ounce of Value: Visualizing the Application of Psychophysiological Methods in Black Psychology

Jules P. Harrell, Vernessa R. Clark, and Brenda A. Allen

Twenty years ago, rather formal distinctions were made between two branches of biological psychology (Stern, 1964; Sternbach, 1966). One, designated physiological psychology, was seen as concerned primarily with behavioral output after the making of a surgical or pharmacological alteration in the nervous system of an animal. One thinks here of well known studies where brain structures in the limbic system were destroyed and the effects on eating, drinking, sexual or aggressive behavior were observed. The second branch, psychophysiology, traditionally manipulated the behavioral, affective or cognitive states of human beings and used a polygraph to measure the subsequent physiological effects of these manipulations. This approach is exemplified by those studies reported in the 1960's, where individuals were shown aversive films, performed reaction time tasks or were threatened with electric shocks while electrodermal or heart rate responses were recorded.

William Lawson (1976) argued that black behavioral scientists should attend assiduously to the activities in the area of biological psychology. In that paper, Lawson, a physiological psychologist and a psychiatrist, was concerned with behavioral genetics and findings emerging from traditional work in physiological psychology. Here it will be argued that the psychophysiological approach may be of significant use to black psychologists. The intent is to encourage students and those "retooling" for research careers to consider the kinds of contributions that can be made by those prepared to do work in this area.

The paper will describe the research programs of three black psychophysiologists. These programs are provided as sample applications of the paradigm, and as frameworks for providing some vision of the kinds of activities in which young black psychophysiologists might engage. Before these are presented, some general comments on the scope of the psychophysiological approach will be provided. The final section discusses some of the more practical considerations related to engaging in psychophysiological studies.

What is Psychophysiology?

The initial paragraphs of this paper are misleading. In fact, the term psychophysiology has no definition that is universally accepted. Since 1964 the Society for Psychophysiological Research has published the journal, *Psychophysiology*. Usually paradigms described in this bimonthly publication are consistent with the definition presented earlier. However, when Furedy (1983) proposed a similar definition of the field in the first issue of the *International Journal of Psychophysiology*, published by the International Organization of Psychophysiology, serious objections were raised. Mangina (1983) preferred a broader based definition designating psychophysiology as the study of the "physiology of psychic functions."

Even within the traditional psychophysiological paradigm significant modifications are found. For example, a recently reported line of research attempted to identify the neural pathways involved when psychological stressors influence the cardiovascular system (see Obrist, 1981). Earlier studies had demonstrated that impressive changes in blood pressure occur during reaction time tasks and mental arithmetic exercises. However, in order to specify the neural mechanisms causing these changes, a drug known to block the activity of a particular pathway within the autonomic nervous system was administered prior to the encounter with the stressful task. The contribution of a given neural system was inferred by the differences in reactivity in the heart when the neural system was blocked and when it was left intact.

Clearly, the inclusion of pharmacological agents in the psychophysiological paradigm represented a departure from the traditional approach. Still the research was psychophysiological in nature and much of it was published in *Psychophysiology*. It is pointless to quibble about definitions here. Most psychophysiologists are concerned with human cognitive and affective functioning. Most use electrophysiological measures and manipulate situational elements. If surgical or pharmacological elements are introduced, their purpose is to enhance our knowledge of the mechanisms involved in the functioning of whole organisms (Furedy, 1983).

One final comment on a troublesome issue is in order before specific applications of this paradigm are reviewed and other applications are projected. Plumpp (1972) phrased the matter in clear and stark terms. "The crisis a black man who studies psychology faces is whether he will create his own system for judging human behavior or whether he will try to squeeze out every ounce of value from the European model" (p. 84). Admittedly, this article takes the more conservative position. This article assumes black behavioral scientists can squeeze some drops of enlightening and healing information from the psychophysiological approach. But the approach should be viewed as a tool. Like all tools, its utility is determined by the facets and parameters of the task at hand. This article is written as a caution against a hasty dismissal of the paradigm. More unfortunate, perhaps, would be a deification of it.

Developmental Psychophysiology

Psychophysiological methods can be used to examine the status of the nervous systems of very young infants. The strategy is deceptively simple. Any number of physiological measures can be obtained while auditory, visual or tactile stimuli are presented. Simple responsivity in terms of orienting or defensive responses (Graham and Clifton, 1966; Graham, 1984), the habituation of physiological reactions or classically conditioned responses can be studied. Studies of the lateralization of electroencephalographic (EEG) activity (Fox and Davidson, 1984; Davidson and Fox, 1982) or of linkages between respiratory and heart rate activity (Porges, 1984; 1983) provide valuable insight into the status of the neonatal nervous system.

Emerging is a productive cadre of young black developmental psychologists. Their work often dominates the pages of collected volumes of empirical papers in black psychology (Boykin, 1985; Franklin, 1985). The work of Dr. David Crowell, director of the Newborn Research Laboratory at the University of Hawaii, may be of special interest to this new force of black professionals. Certainly Crowell, a leading international figure in the study of pathology in newborns, is the dean of black psychophysiologists. His work is marked by a creative handling of the quantification of the physiological dependent variable. Often responses are quantified in terms of amplitude or latency, that is, the size of the response or how long it took for the response to begin or return to baseline. Crowell has been concerned with the *periodicity* of responses. He examines the patterns of changes in physiological responses across time intervals. Hence, often his task is to determine the correlation between levels of physiological activity sampled at one interval and that sampled at later time intervals.

An example may be helpful. In one study (Crowell, Kapuniai and Jones, 1985) the sensitivity of the hearts of newborns (one to three days old) to tones of varying frequencies and amplitudes was demonstrated. Heart rate responses were averaged across many trials of tone presentations. An autoregressive technique was used to remove the time dependent relationship among the beat to beat heart rate changes. Subsequently, serial predictions of heart rate were made using heart rate levels at one instance to predict the next beat. T-tests were used to determine if actual heart rate levels differed from predicted values. The findings showed that in these very young babies, the heart is a sensitive index of the capacity to process auditory information.

Based on Dr. Crowell's past research strategy, one expects he will soon publish work related to the clinical utility of this "averaged heart rate response" to auditory stimuli. Several years ago his research group published reports of this kind where EEG measures were taken (see Crowell, Kapuniai and Jones, 1978; Crowell, Jones, Kapuniai and Leung, 1977). Again, using a time series analysis, EEG patterns of low birthweight and full-term neonates were classified. These classifications allowed for significant discriminations between the two populations of babies. What has been demonstrated here is a gauging of the maturation level of the brain through the quantification of EEG records.

The promise of this kind of research is impressive. Obviously, it will improve our technology for identifying pathological states within the nervous system immediately after birth. In addition, the capacities of young humans to process information from the environment are discernable with these methods. Those interested in charting norms of development for black children might find this approach useful. Who knows what light psychophysiological methods might shine on the functional capabilities of newborns.

Personality and Psychophysiology

The rudiments of an Afrocentric personality theory can be found in the writings of Diop (1974), Baldwin (1981), Akbar (1981) and Boykin (1983; 1986). Personality theories are comprised of core and peripheral components (Maddi, 1980). Core aspects refer to universal central structures and forces within the personality. Often these take the form of instincts, needs and drives. Peripheral characteristics differentiate people and include personality traits and types. Though one might conclude that psychophysiological techniques are best equipped to study the peripheral manifestations of personality (see Levenson, 1983), core aspects can be examined also.

Consider certain core features of personality advanced in the Afrocentric theory of Baldwin (1981). He maintained that rooted *biogenetically* in the core of the African personality are tendencies for "felt experiencing" and total involvement in experiencing (p. 174). Apparently, Baldwin is suggesting that nonverbal (felt) versus verbal modes of experiencing are dominant in the black personality. These modes of information processing should have correlates in EEG patterns. The obvious hypothesis is that a suppression of right hemispheric activation is not a common phenomenon in blacks. The technology and paradigms for testing this hypothesis are available. The imaginative researcher need only structure experiential stimulus chains of events theoretically linked to rather restricted verbal (left hemispheric) or to nonverbal or affective domains. Baldwin's theory would lead us to expect rather generalized cortical activation even when experiential events are theoretically linked to one cortical region. This facet of theory can be tested if psychophysiological methods are used in a creative fashion.

The studies of Thomas Robinson are excellent examples of the effective application of psychophysiological methods and findings to the study of human personality and personality theory (Robinson, 1981; Robinson and Zahn, 1979; 1985). Often construct validational studies reveal that personality tests are not measuring the dimensions they are purported to measure. Robinson's work suggests that one conventional personality scale, designed to measure psychoticism, may actually be measuring psychopathic tendencies (Robinson and Zahn, 1985). His own studies included an orienting task, a two-flash threshhold behavioral task as well as manipulations of arousal levels as the independent variables. Robinson, in conceptualizing his findings, adeptly integrated what is known about the psychophysiological reactivity of schizophrenics and psychopaths. The physiological reactivity and performance of those with elevated scores on the psychoticism scale under study, resembled that of psychopaths more so than schizophrenics. The line of research followed by Robinson shows that careful scrutiny of patterns of physiological reactions to psychological stimuli can provide important information about instruments used to measure personality traits and types.

It is anticipated that psychophysiological studies will be applied to the conceptual framework evolving in the studies of Boykin (1983; 1986). One facet of this framework is concerned with behavioral styles of Afro-American people. Afro-American culture is seen as encompassing three realms of experiencing, the mainstream, the minority and the black Cultural. Boykin (1983) holds that the black cultural realm is the most neglected and least understood of all the experiential realities. It is fundamentally the link between the contemporary Afro-American and the traditional West African worldview (Hale, 1982; Boykin, 1983). It is postulated that the black cultural realm manifests itself in cultural styles, and that these styles are linked to nine interrelated dimensions of the black cultural experience. These dimensions grew out of the traditional West African belief system. In fact, in some ways these dimensions resemble core aspects of personality.

Of the nine dimensions, *verve* has been subjected to the most intense empirical scrutiny (Boykin, 1982; Boykin, DeBritto and Davis, manuscript in review). Verve is defined as a special receptiveness to high levels of variability and intensity in stimulation. This receptiveness is proposed to be a function of continuous exposure to varied stimulation characteristic of the Afro-American home. To date, verve is measured through differential task performance under learning conditions defined as either high or low in stimulus variability. Also, inventories are available to assess individual preferences for stimulus variability when engaging in various activities. In addition, the verve concept lends itself to investigation through psychophysiological methods. For example, the receptiveness to stimulus variability can be studied through the habituation paradigm. Since verve is the result of constant exposure to variable stimulation, one would predict that individuals scoring in the higher ranges on measures of verve would require fewer presentations of interruptive stimulation before showing electrodermal or heart rate habituation. Hence in a relatively straight-forward paradigm, a facet of Boykin's interesting and rich framework can be examined.

Psychological Stress

In the instances discussed to this point, physiological measures were used as the basis for one of two kinds of inferences. The first is an inference about the clinical state of the nervous system of the organism. Here physiological measures are taken as sensitive indices of the integrity of biological structures. The second inference is to a facet of the psychological state of the organism. Again, the physiological measure is taken as a sensitive index. However, in this instance, the physiological measure is the basis for an inference related to the nature of the ongoing cognitive or affective commerce with the environment.

On the other hand, the physiological dependent variable may become of interest in and of itself in psychophysiologial studies. Often this is the case in research on the effects of psychological stress. For example, the effects of aversive or extremely challenging environments on secretions of stomach acids, blood pressure, respiration or muscle tension around the head and neck are often studied, and the physiological measure is of intrinsic interest.

We (Harrell, 1980) reviewed the literature on psychological variables and essential hypertension. Two conclusions drawn in that review set the direction for our psychophysiological investigations of stress and hypertension in black populations. The first conclusion was that, in many cases, early hypertension is a disorder of the heart. The peripheral vasculature and the kidneys become involved in high blood pressure at later junctures in the syndrome. In essence, in the initial phases, the amount of blood pumped (cardiac output) is in excess of what is needed to provide oxygen to the tissues of the body. A similar overperfusion of body tissues is known to occur when certain kinds of psychological stressors are encountered (see Turner and Carroll, 1985). The second conclusion was that extensive variability in cardiovascular reactions to psychological stressors persists across laboratories and types of stressors. Based on these conclusions, our studies involved a comprehensive monitoring of heart activity and an array of strategies for measuring individual differences in the person, variables that might affect physiological responding.

The first step was to obtain a fairly detailed picture of heart performance without causing our participants inordinate distress. We opted to use impedance cardiography (Miller and Horvath, 1978). An assessment of heart rate is easily obtained with this technology. It also provides, for each beat of the heart, an estimate of the amount of blood that was pumped and an index of the force with which the left ventricle contracted. We have examined how psychological events influence each of these parameters and how the parameters are interrelated in people without hypertension or heart disease. What became evident was a kind of wisdom in the cardiac system. When confronted with mild psychological challenges, heart rate increased considerably. However the force of the contraction of the heart muscles on each was reduced as was the amount of blood pumped on each beat. It was only when rather challenging tasks were imposed that we noted significant increases in the output of blood and the force of contraction (Harrell and Clark, 1985).

As expected, some individuals showed pronounced cardiac changes to very mild as well as to the more challenging psychological tasks. Others were impervious to changes of this type regardless of the nature of the task. The prediction of these differences in responsivity from traditional measures of personality dimensions are optimized when there is a link between situational elements and the dimension being measured. For example, we found that when individuals imagined a stressful event that was to try the patience of participants, the impatience dimension of the Jenkins Activity Scale (JAS) (a measure of the Type A coronary prone behavior pattern) predicted heart rate increases (Sutherland and Harrell, 1987). In like manner, in a recent dissertation study conducted by Vernessa Clark, when participants played a video game it was found that the tendency to experience anxiety in novel situations was a strong predictor of cardiac changes. The impatience subscale of the JAS was less effective as a predictor of physiological reactivity in this study.

However, the accounting for individual differences in physiological responsivity to psychological events is a difficult and frustrating task. The yield of the search for the source and correlates of hyperreactivity may be the early identification of those prone to hypertension and other stress related disorders. In effect, a set of "risk factors" for the development of disorders of these kinds in the black community may be identifiable. However, it will be necessary to cross-validate findings in several laboratories before risk factors can be established. A pooling project of this kind would be well suited for a group of energetic black psychophysiologists.

Some Cautionary Notes: A Preachment

People arrive at research in psychophysiology from disparate avenues. Medical doctors, physiologists and a full spectrum of behavioral scientists, including sociologists and psychologists of every kind, may become involved in psychophysiological research. The result is a rich research texture and a broad sampling of research questions. The focus can be quite applied, as is research on the physiological effects of relaxation training or lie detection research. On the other hand, topics can be of theoretical interest primarily. For example, much of the research on evoked potentials and memory and the studies of classical conditioning of electrodermal responses is best classified as basic science. Regardless of the kind of research one plans, there are certain basics that should be carried to this forum.

A knowledge of the general physiology of the response system that serves as the dependent variable is essential. The manner in which the levels of activity in this system are affected by circadian rhythms, posture, and the levels of activity in other systems should be known. This is an addition to an understanding of the neural and hormonal mediation of changes in the activity of the system. Certainly, one need not be a cardiologist to use heart rate as a dependent variable in a study of anxiety or a neurologist in order to study hemispheric assymetries in EEG activity. Still, a rule of thumb would be that the more known about the physiological influences on the system being measured, the safer the inferences about the significance of changes that occur after a psychological stimulus is encountered.

There is a body of knowledge in psychophysiology itself in which one should be girded. One should reflect on this information before conducting this kind of research. Here is a strategy for easing into this literature. There are three knotty problems that refuse to recede in psychophysiological research. One, the law of initial values insists that the prestimulus level of activity in a particular physiological system may affect the response to an imposed stimulus and therefore should temper our interpretations of responses to discrete stimuli. A second vexing phenomenon, known as situation stereotypy, is the finding that particular kinds of situations tend to elicit specific patterns of physiological activity. The third problem is a phenomenon known as individual response stereotypy. People tend to show characteristic patterns or configurations of physiological reactions to a range of environmental stimuli. Recently, two pioneering psychophysiologists, John and Beatrice Lacey, retired. On the occasion of their retirement, Coles, Jennings and Stern (1984) edited a collection of articles that discuss, in historical and current terms, these three problems as well as other concerns that are the daily lot of psychophysiologists. A good place to begin reflecting on the basics of the psychophysiological literature is with the articles by the Laceys and other psychophysiologists in the Coles et al. text.

Finally, something should be said of ethics. Black psychologists have been acutely aware of the ethical aspects involved in research with human populations. That concern should be heightened with the appliction of this paradigm. Two potential problems are apparent. The first is an unavoidable invasion of personal space that is inherent in psychophysiological measurement. The second is a kind of magic that may mistakenly be attached to the entire process of being involved in a psychophysiological experiment. The participants in our studies are shown pictures of electrode placements when they arrive at the laboratory. Then, all facets of the attachments and recording of signals are discussed. We still find the attachment of electrodes a psychologically delicate matter. It should be managed with the utmost of care and interpersonal skill.

It is essential to demystify the entire process of participating in studies of this kind. Some of this demystification takes place before volunteers participate in the studies. Certainly we strive to see that they leave the laboratory knowing that there is no magic involved in psychophysiological research. Physiological measurement is the amplifying of a bodily signal. The wonder and magic is in the bustling but ordered human system not in the activity of the psychophysiologists who briefly view only a small portion of this system.

The increased participation of black psychologists in psychophysiological research holds some potential for mitigating the effects of racism on both physical and mental health. It may also assist, in some small manner, as black psychologists develop more suitable theories and norms for conceptualizing black behavior. The psychophysiological paradigm might fit well into the armamentarium of black psychology.

References

Akbar, N. (1981). Mental disorders among African-Americans. *Black Books Bulletin, 7*, 18-25.

Baldwin, J.A. (1981). Notes on an Africentric theory of black personality. *The Western Journal of Black Studies, 5*, 172-179.

Boykin, A.W. (1986). The triple quandary and the schooling of Afro-American children. In V. Neisser (Ed.), *The school achievement of minority children*. Hillsdale, NJ: Erlbaum Associates.

Boykin, A.W. (1985). *The Seventh Conference on Empirical Research in Black Psychology*. Rockville, MD: NIMH.

Boykin, A.W. (1983). The academic performance of Afro-American children. In J. Spence (Ed.), *Achievement and achievement motives*. San Francisco: W. Freeman.

Boykin, A.W. (1982). Task variability and the performance of black and white school children: Vervistic explorations. *Journal of Black Studies, 12*, 469-485.

Boykin, A.W., DeBritto, A.M., & Davis, L.H. (under review). Social process factors, context variability and school children's task performance: Further exploration in verve.

Coles, M.G.H., Jennings, J.R., & Stern, J.A. (1984). *Psychophysiological perspectives*. New York: Van Nostrand Reinhold Co. Inc.

Crowell, D.H., Kapuniai, L.E., & Jones, R.H. (1985). Detection of averaged heart response to tones in human newborns. *Psychophysiology, 22*, 697-706.

Crowell, D.H., Kapuniai, L.E., & Jones, R.H. (1978). Autoregressive spectral estimates of newborn brain maturational level: Classification and validation. *Psychophysiology, 15*, 204-208.

Crowell, D.H., Jones, R.H., Kapuniai, L.E., & Leung, P. (1977). Autoregressive representation of infant EEG for the purpose of hypothesis testing and classification. *Electroencephalography & Clinical Neurophysiology, 43*, 317-324.

Davidson, R.J. & Fox, N.A. (1982). Asymmetrical brain activity discriminates between positive versus negative affective stimuli in human infants. *Science, 218*, 1235-1237.

Diop, A.C. (1974). *The African origin of civilization: Myth or reality*. Westport: Lawrence Hill & Co.

Fox, N.A., & Davidson, R.J. (1984). *The psychobiology of affective development*. Hillsdale, NJ: Erlbaum Associates.

Franklin, A.J. (1985). *The eighth conference on empirical research in black psychology*. Rockville, MD: NIMH.

Furedy, J.R. (1983). Operational, analogical and genuine definitions of psychophysiology. *International Journal of Psychophysiology, 1*, 13-20.

Graham, F.K. (1984). An affair of the heart. In M.G.H. Coles, J.R. Jennings, & J.A. Stern, *Psychophysiological perspectives*. New York: Van Nostrand Reinhold Co. Inc.

Graham, F.K., & Clifton, R.K. (1966). Heart rate change as a component of the orienting response. *Psychophysiology, 65*, 305-320.

Hale, J. (1982). *Black children: Their roots, culture and learning styles*. Provo, UT: Brigham Young Press.

Harrell, J.P. (1980). Psychological factors in hypertension: A status report. *Psychological Bulletin, 87*, 482-501.

Harrell, J.P., & Clark, V.R. (1985). Cardiac responses to psychological tasks: Impedance cardiographic studies. *Biological Psychological, 20*, 261-283.

Lawson, W.B. (1976). Psychobiology: Some consequences of the biological foundation of behavior. *Black Books Bulletin, 4*, 44-49.

Levenson, R.W. (1983). Personality research and psychophysiology: General considerations. *Journal of Research in Personality, 17*, 1-21.

Maddi, S. (1980). *Personality theories: A comparative analysis* (4th). Homewood, IL: Dorsey Press.

Mangina, C.A. (1983). Towards an international consensus in defining psychophysiology. *International Journal of Psychphysiology, 1*, 21-24.

Miller, J.C., & Horvath, S.M. (1978). Impedance cardiography. *Psychophysiology, 15*, 80-91.

Obrist, P.A. (1981). *Cardiovascular psychophysiology: A perspective.* New York: Plenum Press.

Plumpp, S. (1972). *Black rituals.* Chicago: Third World Press.

Porges, S.W. (1984). Heart rate oscillations: An index of neural mediation. In M.G.H. Coles, J.R. Jennings, & J.A. Stern (Eds.), *Psychophysiological perspectives.* New York: Van Nostrand Reinhold Co. Inc.

Porges, S.W. (1983). Heart rate patterns in neonates: A potential diagnostic window to the brain. In T. Field & A. Sostek (Eds.), *Infants born at risk.* New York: Grune and Stratton.

Robinson, T.N. Jr. (1981). Relationship of visual two-flash and absolute auditory perceptual sensitivity. *Perceptual and Motor Skills, 4*, 363-369.

Robinson, T.N. Jr., & Zahn, T.P. (1985). Psychoticism and arousal: Possible evidence for a linkage of P and psychopathy. *Personality and Individual Differences, 6*, 47-66.

Robinson, T.N. Jr., & Zahn, T.P. (1979). Covariation of two-flash threshold and autonomic arousal for high and low scorers on a measure of psychoticism. *British Journal of Social and Clinical Psychology, 18*, 431-441.

Stern, J.A. (1964). Towards a definition of psychophysiology. *Psychophysiology, 1*, 90-91.

Sternbach, R.A. (1966). *Principles of psychophysiology.* New York: Academic Press.

Sutherland, M.E., & Harrell, J.P. (1987). Individual differences in physiological responses to racially noxious and neutral imagery. *Imagination, Cognition and Personality, 6*, 133-150.

Turner, J.R., & Carroll, D. (1985). Heart rate and oxygen consumption during mental arithmetic, a video game and graded exercise: Further evidence of metabolically-exaggerated cardiac adjustments? *Psychophysiology, 22*, 261-267.

Black Psychology and Experimental Psychology: A Functional Confluence

A. Wade Boykin

The Liberalization of Experimental Psychology

Over the years, experimental psychology has been the bastion of orthodoxy for psychology and has greatly contributed to psychology's claim to scientific respectability (Altman, 1987). For most of this century, experimental psychology has been revered as the core that binds disparate arenas of psychology and has been seen as the pinnacle of what psychology ultimately represents (Boring, 1950; Hearst, 1979). Times have changed; experimental psychology has lost its luster, and perhaps for good reason. While the reverence is no longer there, at least not to the same degree as in the past, and while psychology as a discipline is no longer as coherent, the ideals, practices and focus identified with experimental psychology should be taken seriously—within certain boundary conditions—by those of us who wish to systematically pursue the psychological study of African Americans.

Recent arguments have been advanced that the core of experimental psychology is dissipating (Altman, 1987; Staats, 1983). We no longer have a monolithic entity that can be referred to as "experimental psychology." In its place, new disciplinary categories have emerged such as psychonomic science, neuroscience, cognitive science, and psychopharmacology. These new specialties cut across the traditional boundaries of psychology, and converge with fields such as neurology, pharmacology, cybernetics, and others. Indeed, the classic image of the experimental psychologist running laboratory animals through their experimental paces in order to examine "the" process of learning or motivation is steadily becoming outdated.

By convention, experimental psychology refers to both content and methodology. As a content domain, it has been classically referred to as the study of basic psychological processes. These processes have typically included learning, motivation, problem solving, thinking, language, perception, and attention (Woodworth and Schlosberg, 1954;

Stevens, 1951). Methodologically, experimental psychology connotes the utilization of "true" experimental procedures. As such, the method entails the employment of variables the experimenter directly manipulates and/or purposely holds constant in order to determine their effects on target responses or behaviors (*Snodgrass, Levy-Berg & Haydon, 1985*). Further, the method entails the random assignment of subjects to conditions. Under controlled conditions and randomization procedures, the experimenter is said to be able to ferret out cause and effect relationships (*Christensen, 1988*). That is, the manipulation makes the phenomenon occur. One is assured that differences in response or behavior are in fact *caused* by the experimenter's manipulation of the conditions to which the subjects have been assigned. Thus, in the purest and strictest sense, experimental psychology is the study of "basic psychological processes" through the utilization of the experimental manipulation of conditions and the random assignment of subjects to these conditions, with the expectation that causal inferences about the phenomenon under scrutiny can be drawn. Moreover, this constellation of practices is properly executed in controlled laboratory settings and unhinged from "real-life" behavioral demands to avoid explanatory tarnishment.

In recent years, processes like memory, thinking and motivation have been investigated through other than formal experimental paradigms (*Neisser, 1982; Weiner, 1986*). That is, traditional topics in experimental psychology have been investigated through the use of naturalistic observation, personal recollections, questionnaire surveys, and the like. Further, formal experimental methods have been applied to subject matter not classically identified with the content domain of experimental psychology. Indeed, such areas as experimental social psychology and experimental child psychology are viewed as subspecialties of their respective domains within psychology proper, and respected journals carry such phrases in their titles. Thus, while "pure" or classical experimental psychology does exist as an entity, legitimate hybrid forms have arisen; there now exists a more inclusive or liberal connotation for the domain of experimental psychology, and the field of psychology has been enriched by such developments (Hearst, 1979).

The hybrid forms have developed in part because some perceive experimental methods to be so scientifically credible that they can be extended to other content domains, while others believe that the classical content of experimental psychology is so fundamentally important that it can be used to obtain a more basic understanding of content issues in other arenas of psychology. But the liberalization also is due to disaffection with the straight-jacketing effect classical experimental psychology appears to have had on choice of problem or method of study. In no small measure, African American psychologists, many operating under the aegis of "black psychology," have been in the recent vanguard in calling into question the sacredness of classical experimental psychology (Clark, 1972; Gordon, 1973; Boykin, 1977; Jones, 1979; Akbar, 1985; Clark X., McGee, Nobles, & Akbar, 1976), but the advent of black psychology also represented collective responses to misgivings about much broader issues than those experimental psychology has embodied.

Limitations of Experimental Methods

Experimental methods are paradoxical: they remain revered in many circles and perhaps for good reasons. They have been scorned—also for good reasons—especially when deployed in a zealous and uncritical manner. Experimental methods, often mystified, are represented as the pinnacle of scientific methodology. Thus it is important, at the outset, to clearly depict assumptions, aspects and functions of the methods and to provide critical assessment of them. Through such exercises experimental methods can be placed in their proper perspective. With improved focus (and a healthy dose of humility now thrown in), the residual utility of experimental methods in the pursuit of understanding the African American psychological experience can be better appreciated. The presentation and critique which follow are principally aimed at experimental methods. Yet in some aspects the comments are applicable to the scientific method in general. In these cases, experimental methods are seen as exemplifying the scientific pursuit in psychology.

Objectivity

The scientific method is said to be the supreme form of knowledge acquisition. It is said to be superior to approaches such as revelation, authority and intuition because, principally, it possesses the characteristic of objectivity. Furthermore, pure experimental methods exemplify the objective quality of the scientific method above all other methods. As *Christensen, (1988)* has stated, "Because of its ability to identify causation, the experimental method has come to represent the prototype of the scientific method for solving problems . . ." (p.61). However, the impeccable objectivity of the scientific method has been called into question in recent years; its alleged objectivity does not exempt the methods from criticism. *Thomas (1970)* has persuasively claimed that you cannot separate the knower from the knowledge gained: the scholar cannot be separated from the scholarship. Indeed, before the very first shred of data is collected, prior decisions have been made by the investigator, even if tacit or implied ones. Decisions have already been made about the choice of problem to investigate, specification of the problem, the research questions deemed important to ask, the ways the experiences to be examined are categorized and understood, the type and scope of observations possible, and the meaning, significance and coding of behaviors of interest (*Boykin & Toms, 1985; Allen, 1978*).

Moreover, the constructs offered, the instruments employed for measurement and assessment, and the ways in which the independent and dependent variables are operationalized, are all based on prior assumptions, either those of the investigator or, by proxy, the originator of the instruments, constructs and variables to be operationalized. These prior decisions and assumptions have a fundamentally subjective cast, no matter what the pretensions. Indeed, the prior decisions and presuppositions inevitably flow from the philosophical persuasions, cultural orientation and personal biases and experiences of the investigator, or those of the originator of the constructs, variables and coding categories the investigator has incorporated (Sherwood & Nataupsky, 1968; Akbar, 1985; Clark, 1972; Scarr, 1985; Spence, 1985). In following this line of argument, the "objectivity" of scientific procedures largely results because a consensus is readily formed among the community of scholars and relevant consumers of research information. The consensus is readily formed because of converging or congruent cultural, philosophical and value assumptions of the pertinent producers and consumers of research information. The convergence and congruence allow for shared, often implicit understanding of what constitutes proper knowledge as well as the means by which to achieve it, giving rise to the aura of unimpeachable objectivity. Yet the accumulation of unambiguous facts which transcend subjective considerations through the employment of the "proper" scientific methods, whether experimental or otherwise is, at best, quite difficult to achieve.

"Objectively" observed behavior is open to multiple interpretations. Indeed, as *Gergen, (1978)* has argued, human actions are social actions, in the main, and as such are understood not because of universally obvious inherent properties but because of the existence of a consensus, that is, a shared agreement among the community of relevant "knowers" as to the "what" that is being observed. A given behavior thus can take on a range of meanings as a function of the subjective meaning bestowed on it within a subjectively defined social context; human action does not occur in a vacuum. Its very texture is derived from the context in which it is perceived to occur. Yet, the context which breathes significance into the behavior is itself open to multiple interpretations. Since no observation can be unambiguously linked to some absolute sense of knowing, and since behaviors, observations and "findings" are open to multiple interpretations, humility about the objectivity of the scientific method is absolutely essential. Again, pure experimental methods are surely no exception.

The entity called the "experiment" is not exempt from being viewed in relative terms. Indeed, the research experiment is a social institution (*Danzinger, 1985*). Role expectations for the various participants in the experimental setting abound. These expectations require coordination between the experimenter and the subjects in order to effectively play out the roles and rituals of this institution. The role expectations are often tacit. The rules of coordination, no matter how well choreographed, are open to differing interpretations by the various participants. No guarantees exist that experimenters and subjects are on the same expectational wavelength. Thus, the roles, rituals, expectations, interpretations of responsibilities or demands may not be the same for the experiment's participants. This account thus argues that true objectivity is compromised in that it may apply to inanimate subjects of experimentation, but surely not to humans who have the ability to interpret and give meaning to the experimental setting in which they find themselves. Further, subjects have the ability to interact with the experimenter directly and thus change the circumstances of experimentation in ways that can substantially deviate from the scripted objective setting as conceived by the investigator (Adair, 1973).

Quantification

Beyond the issue of objectivity, the scientific research method attaches considerable significance to quantification. This focus is most profoundly evident in experimental methods, because such methods are preoccupied with manipulation, control and prediction of relevant research variables. The prevailing wisdom is that if a phenomenon under scrutiny can be measured, if it can be conceived of in quantitative terms then: (1) it can be construed in a more rigorous and precise fashion, (2) its relevant parameters can be better manipulated and controlled and hence (3) it can be more properly, more fundamentally, more ultimately understood (Estes, 1979). Quantification is said to allow for more precise manipulation and control and ultimately greater predictive power for the research. Indeed, implied in experimental methods is that the knowing process proceeds from prediction . . . to controlling, manipulating and quantifying the input . . . to quantifying the output and thus . . . to precisely evaluating the prediction (Christensen, 1988). If we are successful in the manipulation, control and in turn were successful at confirming a quanitfied prediction then we have understood the phenomenon in its most fundamental form. It is well documented that this knowing sequence is fundamentally linked to the physical sciences and was conceived with the subject matter of the physical sciences in mind (Clark, 1972; Koch, 1985). It may work well for scrutinizing atomic particles, or for other inanimate objects that are essentially understood on a materialistic basis, but the fluidity and dynamic character of human action is not easily controllable, manipulable and in turn predictable. While the lack of controllability and predictability are treated as experimental or measurement error in scientific research, this "solution" in many ways is unsatisfactory, for the animate, dynamic nonmaterial fluid essence of human action itself may be the stuff to be studied. Such properties may be the things to be understood per se and not the part to be cast off as noise to be overlooked or minimized in the knowing/research process. Thus, excessive quantification and its corresponding trappings of prediction, manipulation and control may indeed be viewed as limiting our understanding of human psychology (Akbar, 1985).

On the other hand, quantification may be necessary to help capture a phenomenon efficiently and systematically. It can be a useful device for gaining a summary understanding or shorthand depiction of some psychological phenomenon. But this should not be confused with fundamental or ultimate knowing. Such efficiency and summarization may cloud a deeper, more profound understanding of the richer aspects of human action.

Causation

Psychology has inherited the notion of causation from the physical sciences. This is the notion that explanation per se should be understood in cause and effect terms. Indeed, cause-effect relationships are at the base of mechanical physics. Causation is a mechanistic orientation to explanation (Mischel, 1975). This machine-like mode of explanation was embraced wholesale by mainstream psychology upon its emergence as a "true" science. Indeed cause-effect was directly translated into stimulus-response by scientific psychology. The analogy to the action of billiard balls can be drawn. One billiard ball stays at rest until it is struck by a second billiard ball. The second billiard ball is seen as the causal agent in the first ball's activity (Hanson, 1958). The second ball is said to cause the first to respond the way it did. In a like manner, the search in scientific psychology especially through the experimental research process, has been to isolate the causes of behavioral effects. The approach has been to discern the cause of the effect—the effective stimulus for the response of interest. This mechanistic notion of causation which especially has been a methodological cornerstone of experimental psychology is quite discernible when the experimental research setting is examined. For the most basic case, let us call the experimental conditions treatment A, and also include a "control" or no treatment condition. Let us now suppose that subjects are randomly assigned to one or the other condition. Through this procedure it is argued we are "assured" that whatever differences we obtain between the typical response under treatment A and the no treatment condition is in fact caused by some quality of treatment A that is not conveyed in the control condition. If, for example, subjects who experienced treatment A had higher performance scores than those exposed to no treatment, it could be concluded that treatment A caused the increase in performance. This line of reasoning is not without merit. Clearly we have established directionality to the performance effects. That is, we know the higher performance did not precede treatment A. Further, we have isolated the locus of the effects. That is, we know that treatment A is somehow implicated in the obtained results.

Resorting to the notion of causation as the basis for explanation clearly implying that treatment A *causes* response X, may not only be an oversimplification of what actually did happen but may in fact distort the real processes at work (Hanson, 1958; Dewey, 1931). We don't know, for example, if the response increase is due to some process triggered by the introduction of treatment A and not by some quality of treatment A per se. We don't know if the presence of treatment A released some other process or operative factor from inhibition, thereby leading to enhanced performance. It may be that subjects perceive treatment A to be more compatible with their interests and thus exert more effort in this condition. The point here is that causation in its mechanistic sense easily may not do explanatory justice to the process at work in even this simple situation. The term causation, although conveying something quite scientifically definite may indeed serve to obscure the circumstantial complexity actually present here. Further, given the multiple interpretation and value assumption issues addressed earlier, we must also realize that the entities in the so-called causal chain are open to subjective delineation. As Hanson (1958) has stated, "What we refer to as 'causes' are theory-based from beginning to end. They are not simple tangible links in the chain of sense experience, but rather details in an intricate pattern of concepts" (p. 54).

Nomothetic Inferences

Another limitation concerns nomothetic inferences drawn from pure experimental research. The term nomothetic literally means "of general or universal laws." The nomothetic approach to knowledge acquisition is part of the Euro-American cultural tradition. It is characterized by what *Sampson, (1978)* has called the "democratization of equality." This is the notion that the same (universal) principles, the same explanations should be applied equally to all people. In this sense, equality is seen as synonymous with sameness. The kind of data typically sought through experimental methods is essentially nomothetic data (Hearst, 1979). That is, the goal is to provide a summary picture of the "typical" responses in the given setting to which the subject was randomly assigned. This summary depiction is represented in the form of a group score. It is construed to be a statement about how *people in general* respond to a given situation. As such we would get virtually no insight into how each individual subject responded except as represented by the relative general spread or closeness of the scores (limited exceptions include the single-subject designs executed by Skinnerian behaviorists). This relative spread is revealingly referred to, in statistical analysis, as "noise" or "error," so actually the uniqueness of individuals, the diversity in the ways people orient or respond to the conditions and stimuli and the demands they are placed under get minimized given the functional philosophy of "the" experimental situation. Furthermore, it is inconceivable, for example, to randomly assign people to cultural groups or races (*Jones, 1986*), so group diversity gets obscured in the orthodox use of the experimental process as well. A nomothetic orientation obscures the fact that different cultural groups might respond to the same situation, demands or stimuli in different ways, or that one group might respond in a particular way to one given context and other groups might respond in that same way to quite different contexts.

Nomothetic inferences may be good, broad brushstroke portrayals of the psychological landscape of interest, but they should not satisfy researchers who explore the psychological dynamics of African American life. Nomothetic statements often hide cultural or group experiential differences that may be at the heart of the researcher's interest. Researcher's must "go inside" the data to discern how factors of culture or ethnicity interact with the manipulated conditions. Indeed, ethnicity by treatment or cultural group by treatment interactions should be rigorously sought; they should form the backbone of the research questions. Of course research examining a single ethnic or cultural group per se should also be pursued. Indeed, such a methodological tactic has merit in its own right, especially for examining within group variation and the in-depth specification of attendant processes and characteristics (Banks, 1982; McLoyd & Randolph, 1984). The issue raised presently is that we should be extremely cautious about, if not outright avoid, within group research which attempts to draw nomothetic generalizations. All too often, universal claims have been made from data gathered solely with middle-class, "privileged" Euro-Americans. This is among the most widespread and egregious errors in all of scientific psychology. But curiously, it is almost never grounds for rejecting publication of an article in a so-called "mainstream" journal.

Laboratory Research

The appeal to universality and generality of explanation is linked to another limitation of empirical research, especially orthodox experimental methods. There is the persisting conviction that research is best conducted in a laboratory setting. There is an abiding belief that fundamental research is best conducted under "controlled, vacuum-like" conditions where a deliberate attempt is made to eliminate all extraneous influences. When research is conducted in this way, it is presumed that obtained motivational or learning effects, for example, would not be tarnished by artifacts of the setting in which they occur. Conversely, if the research had not been done in a laboratory setting, such artifacts or confounds could not be carefully held in check (Estes, 1979). In essence, traditionally laboratory research has striven to eliminate context from the obtained results. Also implied here is that laboratory-based effects and processes are universal in scope and general in their applicability.

This "laboratorization" of knowledge also is linked to scientific psychology's emulation of the "more established" sciences like physics. Laboratory research is thought to provide more fundamental, more precise, more unambiguous data. The knowledge gained and the responses obtained are seen as universal; they apply to all people and to the universe of possible settings. The purported generalizability to all settings implies the outcome(s) are acontextual as well. This position has been extensively challenged, especially in recent years (Bronfenbrenner, 1979). It is countered that the contrived and controlled laboratory setting produces contrived and controlled responses and in turn contrived, controlled explanations for the phenomena under scrutiny. Instead of producing information that transcends settings, laboratory research produces information that may be applicable to the particular laboratory setting in which it was generated and virtually nothing more (Spence, 1985). Such data may bear little resemblance to that generated in the "real world" or in distinctly different settings. Basic psychological processes must be understood in context. That is, their expression should be understood relative to the contexts in which they were generated.

It should be understood that even "sterile" experimental settings and manipulations convey more than connoted by the term "stimuli."

They are indeed contexts and should be understood as such. They are in fact contexts with qualitatively distinct characteristics; characteristics that should be understood on their own terms. These terms, this texture of the contexts, are often culturally informed. As such, they may afford salient, culturally distinct information or cues more consonant with cultural orientations of some groups and not others; or the contexts may be multidimensional to the point that different aspects will be differently responded to on the basis of cultural or individual predilections. Thus, the context of responding, even in spite of efforts to laboratize it, has implications for how to understand the responses expressed, what is expressed, how well it is expressed, and who expresses it. In sum, the understanding of the context for responding can very likely contribute to an understanding of individual and group diversity (Rogoff, 1982; Spence, 1985; Simmons, 1985).

Indeed, rather then attempting to isolate "the" effective stimulus which produces the response of interest, one could pursue the generation of effective contexts per se, especially if issues of culture or ethnicity are seen as crucial. Whenever feasible, this author advocates the employment of contextual variables rather than stimulus variables. Contextual variables connote a patterning of stimuli, a qualitative texture that is more "true to life" and more appropriate for exposing cultural or ethnic differences. Contexts indeed inform responses and psychological processes. We should also remain mindful that many of the most interesting psychological phenomena are contextually bound. Indeed, a more heuristic goal for empirical research would be not the pursuit of absolute, objective universal truth but the understanding of the range of contexts for which some particular psychological phenomenon holds (*McGuire, 1983*). This "contextualist" methodology thus argues that it is more important to generate the boundary conditions for obtained effects than to pursue the elusive "absolute truth"—to discern under what conditions targeted effects occur and do not occur. Such would not only be more realistic in a pragmatic sense, but more in touch with the real world by establishing realistic boundaries for what works, how, when, where, and for whom.

Experimental Psychology As Content

Much of our attention has been directed at experimental psychology considered as methodology. I argue that such methodology should be judiciously pursued. It is also crucial to pursue experimental psychology as subject matter. Such domains as motivation, problem solving, perception and memory are especially relevant not only to understand their extant manifestations in black people per se, but also because of their obvious implications for educational practice. Indeed, far too many black children are less than successful in formal schools (Neisser, 1986). If we do not do a better job of moving black students through the formal schooling process, then American society in general and black communities in particular will fail to develop fully an increasingly important pool of human talent and expertise. As we better understand the deployment, manifestation and promotion of motivational, perceptual and cognitive processes in black populations, we may also better understand ways and contexts that can serve to facilitate the academic performance of black students. Indeed, well-conceived and well-executed basic research on such basic psychological processes can be seen as exercises in "prescriptive pedagogy." That is, in the course of unveiling contexts which facilitate or more optimally elicit these basic psychological processes, we are simultaneously providing prototypes of academic contexts which may better facilitate academic performance.

In Defense of Experimental Methods

While this paper has discussed several limitations of empirical research in general and the experimental method in particular, the critical analyses are not grounds for abandoning experimental methods. Rather, they are reasons for appreciating why the methods should be used advisedly. Over the years, much of the work done under the guise of black psychology has sought to examine black people in their own proactive terms, derived from their own proactive experiences, with the aim of enhancing their life conditions (Boykin, Franklin & Yates, 1979). I believe this proactive use of psychological scholarship can be fostered by pulling from experimental psychology in its methodological sense and pulling from phenomena traditionally associated with the content domain of experimental psychology. And while certain cautions should be exercised, the judicious deployment of experimental psychology can be a useful and worthwhile endeavor.

If certain canons of scientific/experimental psychology are followed, benefits can accrue. Given the explicit rules of specification (embodied in the scientific method), replication of obtained effects at the aggregate level of analysis is possible; and consistency of observation across time and observers can be obtained. Moreover, especially through experimental procedures, such as random assignment to conditions, obtained effects can be directionalized and their boundaries localized; and certain competing explanations can be convincingly

eliminated. Thus, potentially reliable, systematic information and reasonably well-pinpointed explanatory insights can be gathered that do
not simply confirm the researcher's wishes about reality. Rather, the
gleaned findings can lead to the accumulation of "knowledge" that can
inform individuals providing services, implementing programs, and
building institutional structures that can be of benefit to African American people. All of this is possible if we eliminate the hypocrisy of the
detached, disinterested observer, but instead offer observational categories, presuppositions, research questions, and instruments that self-consciously convey the integrity, humanity and dignity of African
American people; and we accept that subjects can help to create the
situations in which they are placed. It is important to conduct scien-
tific/experimental research which is not quick to make mechanistic
causal claims; which is humble about the limitations on the level of
knowing that is available through quantification procedures; which acknowledges that different interpretations of the same phenomena are
possible as a function of cultural perspective or political/personal agendas; which accepts that psychological phenomena, however specified,
do have boundaries (that can be historical, phenomenological, thematic and/or cultural), and that specifying these boundary conditions
should be part of the investigative program.

New consensuses must be generated in which there is convergence on the need to understand the integrity and humanity of African
Americans on their own terms and from their own phenomenological
frame of reference; and in which behavioral research findings are connected to the complexity of real life, real world settings. With these
considerations in place it becomes quite possible to have persuasive,
useful information generated from scientific research which employs
experimental methods. These claims require further elaboration, con-
creteness, and the support of actual examples. I now turn to these ends.

Experimental Research From a Black Perspective

Experimental research conducted from a black perspective must
be mindful of the conceptual framework being served by the research in
question. Researchers who have not explicitly generated a conceptual
framework, should be very clear on what framework, even if un-
articulated, has fostered the research questions, the instruments, and
the observational categories. They should be mindful of the cultural
values and philosophical assumptions they are in fact subscribing to as
manifested in the research accouterments (i,e., instruments, coding
schemes, behavioral operationalizations and the like). They should be

mindful of whether their personal biases about the conditions and realities of black people are being served in the formulation of their research. If researchers are not sensitive to these considerations, other cultural, philosophical, political, conceptual and personal agendas will be served. Indeed, a considerable amount of intellectual work gets done before any data are collected. It is imperative that this work, if borrowed from others, does not contradict the African American researcher's intellectual agenda.

It also seems important that the researcher should accept that multiple interpretations of psychological phenomena are a fact of life, an occupational hazard as it were. Moreover, the researcher must accept that challenges and criticisms will occur in spite of the "rigor" of the experimental research methodology, especially as we pursue progressive, avant-garde conceptions that break with the traditions of mainstream psychology—conceptions which include the empowering interests of African Americans. Given this reality, the concerned researcher is likely to be disputed, undermined or criticized on alleged scientific grounds, when in truth the criticism is based on issues of power, ideology and politics. These challenges do not address the intellectual or scientific quality of the scholarship; they should be taken for what they are—ideological, cultural, and political differences. A useful check is to consult others who work inside the researcher's presuppositional boundaries. Indeed, criticism by kindred but judicious scholars should be welcomed. It is quite likely to be more valuable than that of "outsiders" who may be ideologically threatened by the frame of reference advocated.

The researcher must understand that subjects in experiments are not mechanical wind-up toys, so it is prudent to include the subjects' point of view as a part of the research procedures. Indeed, conventional wisdom has been that subjects are the worst source of information about the reasons for their responses. *Ericson and Simon (1980; 1984)* have helped put this notion to rest; they document the importance of seeking subjects' opinions as to the reasons for their responses. The subjects' points of view should be part of the database and will be useful in helping understand the functional connections between psychological events and outcomes.

Researchers should be encouraged to utilize quantification procedures in the collection of systematic empirical data. Such procedures can provide useful, efficient, rather crisp summaries and can inform decisions about the veracity or quality of ones' hunches. Yet the concerned researcher should also be mindful of the non-material, fluid dynamic character of human beings, which obviate precise prediction and control of human activity, even in the most contrived research setting. Indeed, the goal should be the pursuit of understanding. But understanding in this instance is not the same as prediction and control. Quantitative findings must be augmented by qualitative insights. Protocols of what individual subjects actually do can add important dimensions of understanding to the research endeavor. Yet, we must realize that richer, more profound knowing may elude us in the quantitative empirical pursuit of knowledge. We cannot, for example, use quantitative empirical research to understand fully the essence of spirituality per se or the core depths of the experience of being spiritual. The quantitative enterprise is simply ill equipped to handle this task. However, we can, for example, randomly assign individuals to "spiritual laden" and "non-spiritual laden" contexts and systematically examine the ensuing reactions. We can take people who score high vs. low on a spirituality scale and randomly assign equal numbers of them to a spiritual laden and a non-spiritual laden context and subsequently examine performance on dependent measures.

Indeed, random assignment to and deliberate experimenter manipulation of experimental conditions lie at the heart of the experimental method; and such procedures in and of themselves retain considerable merit despite the critical claims of this paper. For when subjects are randomly assigned to deliberately manipulated conditions, idiosyncratic characteristics of individual subjects are ruled out as a source of confound and explanation. Since these conditions, or contexts if you will, are deliberately shaped by the investigator, they are conceived to be essentially stripped of extraneous confounds and artifacts and thus differ only in terms of the dimensions of research interest. Conceivably then, there are reasonably localized explanations for the obtained results and there is less ambiguous insight into findings. In all, such procedures can yield a reasonably clearer, crisper and more incisive picture of what is going on in this research setting than would otherwise be the case.

Of course, if such procedures are to be effective, experimenters must include conditions (i.e., *contexts*) which, although harnessed for experimental purposes, still attempt to reflect the cultural and/or experiential realities of African Americans. The experimental contexts should afford cues and outlets for psychological/behavioral expression that are reminiscent of the ordinary, yet proactive life experiences of African American people.

In all, much is to be gained by using experimental methods to pursue an understanding of the African American psychological experience. But such pursuit does not require that we appeal to the physical sciences, that we appeal to mechanistic or machine-like metaphors, that we invest in rampant materialism or positivism or that we construe people as akin to billiard balls who can be ultimately controlled, manipulated and explained in knee-jerk terms. Nor does it mean we fail if the research does not produce universally applicable explanations.

Research Examples

The various admonitions, pitfalls and guidelines I have suggested may appear to be formidable, but they are not as prohibitive as they might seem. Indeed, there are many good examples in recent years that conform to the methodological and strategic guidelines provided here. I turn now to such examples.

In spite of the potential heuristic benefit of systematic, experimental research, those working from a black perspective have generally shied away from this research tactic. My survey of empirical articles appearing in the *Journal of Black Psychology* from its inception in 1974 through 1989, that only approximately 18% of articles published in the Journal had experimental manipulations, only 12% could be classified as containing experimental psychology subject matter, and only 7% contained both experimental methodology and content. Indeed, only one article appeared in this journal in the 1980s which contained both experimental psychology methodology and content. This dearth of experimental investigations must change; there is benefit to be accrued from such exercises, if the research tactics (and content) are put in their proper perspective and utilized to maximize their more positive attributes. Fortunately, examples of sound and heuristically appropriate experimental research consistent with a black perspective do exist. Investigations cited below show that such work can be done successfully; they exemplify the proactive attributes advocated in this paper and also help demystify experimental psychology by demonstrating that its deployment need not overwhelm us, even though we must attend to multiple considerations.

Smith and Lewis (1984) examined the phenomenon of "self-schemata" as it related to the recall of story information by African American children. Self-schemata were defined as cognitive structures which develop from attempts to account for ones own actions in some domain. As such they are seen as 'symbolic representations' of the self stored in memory. Smith and Lewis reasoned that black children should show more recall from stories containing black characters than from stories containing non-black characters because black characters would be more congruent with their existing racial self schemas. One hundred twenty, 6-7 year old low income African American children were randomly assigned to one of three experimental conditions. In one condition, each child was read a story that contained only African American people as characters. In a second condition, the story read only contained white characters. In the third condition, the story contained only animal characters. Two different stories were used under each condition, but each child only heard one of them. In each instance, the story depicted daily life experiences of the characters. In the stories containing human characters, the race of the characters could not be inferred from the story line. Every story was accompanied by picture panels illustrating the corresponding characters. Thus, the children could infer the race of the relevant characters from the pictures. After hearing their story, children answered a set of questions concerning what the story was about, what happened in the story, and how the story ended. Their answers were coded for amount of information recalled.

The results revealed that children who had heard a story with the African American characters recalled significantly more story information than those who heard a story with white characters. The recall from the animal character stories was essentially equivalent to that from the African American character stories.

The research design and results were actually more complicated than depicted here. But what has been presented illustrates several important points. The study represents an example of classic random assignment to conditions, and shows how such a procedure can be straightforwardly used to address an important question *within* a black population. It also quite directly tackles a topic classically identified with experimental psychology, namely recall—which combines elements of learning and memory processes. Moreover, the research question, centering on the notion of racial self-schemata, is clearly guided by presumed knowledge of the African American experience. Thus, such insights were used to construct the conditions to which subjects were randomly assigned. And by including the "control" condition with the "neutral" animal character stories, the investigators were in a position to gain insight into the nature of the effects. If recall under the white character and animal character conditions were equivalent, and both inferior to the black character condition, it can be inferred that the results were due to the enhanced effect of a racial self schemata. Since the results showed that recall under the animal character condition was equivalent to the black character condition and that both were superior to the condition with the white characters, support is garnered for the position that the effect is due to suppressed recall under conditions incompatible with racial self schemata. The ability to pose such a directional explanation represents one of the virtues of the experimental method.

Sewell and Walker, (1982) examined the issue of how different work conditions affect performance and also illuminates the social dynamics of experimentation. In this research, the performance of low income 5th and 6th grade black children was examined under four conditions designed to manipulate the type of incentive provided for successful performance. In the Social Reward condition the experimenter responded with "unrestrained enthusiasm" to task efforts and accomplishments of the children. The experimenter would thus respond with comments like "fantastic," "you're doing great," "excellent." In the Ethnic Consciousness condition the experimenter attempted to appeal to students' racial pride and identity for incentive purposes. While holding up a poster containing pictures of renowned African American persons from diverse occupational fields, the experimenter said "The opportunities for blacks who have done well in school to succeed are present in every occupation. These individuals (pointing to poster) are examples that blacks are talented, bright and beautiful and can learn well. If you really believe that, please show me by doing well -your very best on these tasks I am about to ask you to do." A third condition involved a Monetary Reward. Here, children could earn up to one dollar on the basis of their performance on the tasks. Finally, there was a Control condition. Subjects in this condition received only the instructions for working the tasks and thus no incentive was provided. Each subject completed two different tasks: a paired associate learning task in which they had to learn to put words into pairs according to the experimenter's specifications and the Ravens Progressive Matrices Test, for which they had to choose the next logical geometrical pattern that would follow a sequence of patterns. Performance was highest under the ethnic consciousness condition for both task types, while the control condition produced the lowest performance. Obviously, the ethnic consciousness condition was construed in light of the experiential reality of African American children, and it produced the most favorable results. The performance differences are linked to the social dynamic differences among the conditions and as such the different incentive conditions represent different social *contexts*. Thus, it seems fair to say that a contextual variable is being manipulated in this experiment rather than a stimulus variable per se. In each instance, subjects had to work on the exact same tasks, but they worked on them under different (social) contexts.

An investigation by Moore and Retish (1974) also speaks to the social dynamics of experimentation. These researchers examined the Wechsler Preschool and Primary Scale of Intelligence performance of a group of black preschool children. As the name implies, this scale is seen as an index of intelligence and provides an I.Q. score for each child. Each child was tested twice; once by a black examiner and once by a white examiner. The testing or placement of subjects in all conditions of a relevant variable (i.e., testing by a white or black examiner)

represents a variant of the random assignment scheme. Since every subject is exposed to all levels or experimental conditions, differences that
occur as a function of condition can be seen as due to the different
attributes of the (deliberately manipulated) conditions employed and
particularly not because of subject idiosyncrasies. This technique is referred to as repeated measures and the design is referred to as a within
subject design. The point here is that this is functionally equivalent to
random assignment of each subject to but one condition or level of the
independent variable. This latter technique is classically referred to as a
between group or independent design and it represents the types of
designs of the examples prior to the Moore and Retish one.

Six different experimenters were used in the Moore and Retish
study (three black and three white adult females). All experimenters
went through an extensive 13-hour training program to insure that the
intelligence test was administered in a uniform fashion, thus standard-
izing the test administration as much as possible. Results revealed that
children scored higher on the overall I.Q. scale and on the verbal and
performance subscales when tested by black experimenters. In spite of
serious efforts to standardize the testing situation, apparently the test
was not responded to in equivalent terms regardless of race of the tester.
While one can do no more than speculate as to the factors which actually account for the performance difference, it seems plausible that issues centering around racial perception—especially as it relates to
differential communication receptiveness—likely plays a part. At any
rate, experiments like these clearly show limitations in perception of
the subject as a passive entity in the research setting and highlight the
importance of pursuing the social psychology of experimentation in its
own right. The experiment also gets away from the conception of the
experimental setting as a necessarily constricted or contrived one. Indeed, these children were tested for "IQ" under real testing conditions
such that the scores produced could have qualified as officially measured levels of intelligence. Yet the "official" scores differed "simply"
based on the race of the person administering the test.

Sutherland and Harrell, (1987) focused on race within an experimental paradigm, but their work has aimed at capturing certain outcomes arising from experiences with racism. Indeed, this work has
explicitly attempted to discern, in a laboratory setting, various physiological responses brought on through racist encounters. In essence it
has developed an experimental psychological analog to racism and its
physiological consequences. In this rather unique approach to the
study of racism, 62 African American college women were exposed to
three distinct scenarios or "image scenes." In each case the subject is to
imagine that she is experiencing the activity in the scene. One scene
was labelled "fearful." Here a script was presented to the subjects via

audio tape which described a nurse preparing a syringe to draw blood from the individual. A second scene was labelled "neutral." Here the script described the individual taking a pleasant walk through a park. The third scene was termed "racially noxious." This scenario described the individual as being unjustly accused of shoplifting by a group of whites in a suburban shopping mall. Further, the whites were shouting that there should be a law against black people being allowed in the mall. The procedure involved repeated measures. Once hearing a given scenario, subjects were instructed to spend thirty seconds imagining themselves going through the experience depicted.

Measures of physiological reactions were taken during a rest period before presentation of a given scenario, during scene presentation, during the imagining period, and during a second rest period or a recovery period. Of particular interest was the recording of facial muscle activity, specifically corrugator (associated with frowning) and zygomatic (associated with smiling) muscle response and of heart rate activity. Corrugator response was found to increase significantly during the imagining period with the racially noxious and fearful scenes. Virtually no changes in corrugator activity occurred during the neutral scene. Moreover, corrugator activity during the imagining period was not different for the fearful and racially noxious conditions. No significant changes in zygomatic activity occurred with respect to the racially noxious and fearful scenes across periods. However, there was a significant increase in such activity from scene presentation to imagine period with respect to the neutral scene. Increased heart rate activity was more pronounced in the fearful and racially noxious conditions than in the neutral condition. In all, the fact that responses to the racially noxious condition paralleled those for the fearful condition suggested to these authors that racism can indeed be stressful, and over long periods of time they posit that such encounters can take a physical toll on black people. It would seem this would be especially the case for black persons who dwell on such racial encounters. Being able to capture such racial experiences in a controlled experimental procedure allows for the rather precise specification of factors and outcomes operative in such encounters. This is one advantage of experimental methodology. Moreover, in this case as in others, a particular construction of experimental conditions was obviously inspired by consideration of certain African American experiences. Further, the conditions constructed were not artificial, but instead were conceived to mirror real world occurrences. In fact, they led to reactions that could not have been discerned in the absence of sophisticated quantification procedures and laboratory instrumentation.

Tuck and Boykin (1989) set out to counter certain claims about the relationship of African American home environmental factors and academic/task performance. Overstimulating home environments of African-American children, being too active and too noisy, have been hypothesized to have deleterious effects on African American children's cognitive functioning and correspondingly to lead the children to respond as though they were perceptually deaf or, at least inattentive under "normal" circumstances (Marans and Lourie, 1967). Elsewhere, *Boykin (1982)* has argued, to the contrary, that the presence of relatively high physical stimulation levels found in many African American homes leads often to black children living under such conditions to have increased receptiveness to heightened variability and intensity of stimulation. Further, such greater receptiveness, or increased "psychological verve," would lead to increased performance under task conditions that are high in physical stimulation. Tuck and Boykin tested this formulation. Sixty African American and sixty white elementary school children (fourth and sixth graders) from low income backgrounds were given tasks to perform under both more varied and less varied format conditions. In the less varied format, tasks of four different types were presented in a blocked sequential pattern, i.e., all of one type first, then all of another, etc. In the varied format, the tasks were presented in a random sequential pattern, regardless of type. Assessments were made of the subjects' perceived home stimulation level and preference for stimulation variability. Academic measures were also obtained.

The results were complicated, but most germane to the formulation presented was that when aggregated across the four task types, performance was higher under the more varied than under the less varied format, for both African American and white children. However, the increase was substantially greater for the African American children. White children did significantly better than African American children under the less varied format, but there was no difference between the groups under the more varied format. Further, when examining other factors, African American children—as contrasted with the white subjects—perceived greater physical stimulation in their homes. African American children also expressed preference for greater levels of stimulus variability than their white counterparts. Yet, African American children scored lower on a standardized achievement test and were rated lower in classroom motivation and performance by their teachers than were the white children. Home stimulation perception was positively correlated with the level of stimulus variability preferred for both African American and white children. However, for African American children, home stimulation perception was negatively related to the three academic measures but positively related to performance under the more varied format condition. That is, black children who reported high home stimulation levels were rated by their teachers as lower in motivation, academic standing, and performance on standardized achievement tests. However, the greater their perceived home stimulation, the greater their performance when task conditions provide more variability.

Tuck and Boykin employed both African American and white children and thus were able to demonstrate the interaction of context and racial group. The fact that the performance profiles for the African American and white children were different as a function of task performance context suggests that caution be exercised before making sweeping nomothetic claims about context independent performance effects. The fact that the different performance profiles are linked to home environmental factors gives credence to the notion that the differences may be culturally linked, thus giving acceptability to the notion that culture and context must be simultaneously considered in the specification of cognitive outcomes in empirical research. The study examined performance across four types of problem solving tasks that tapped into distinctly different cognitive operations (e.g., listening skills, visual discrimination, high speed scanning, and spatial memory). The results thus cast a wide swath of generalizability across intellectual processes.

The issue of prescriptive pedagogy is also implicated in this project. It is clear that more refined research should be done before actual classroom procedures are recommended. However, in discerning performance contexts and conditions that are particularly facilitating for African American children, the study provides beacons for how actual pedagogical procedures can be altered to more greatly optimize the academic performance of African American children. Finally, and perhaps most important, this investigation demonstrates how proactive assumptions from an African American perspective can lead to different kinds of research questions, different behavioral codifications, different operationalizations of variables, and results that provide avenues for the meaningful incorporation of the prevailing experiences of African Americans into academic/cognitive situations that can lead to positive effects on cognitive outcomes for African American children.

Allen and Boykin (1990) took issue with the characterization of African American children as hyperactive and in need of interventions to reduce their hyperactivity in order to optimize their cognitive functioning. The researchers reasoned, instead, that what is often misconstrued as hyperactivity is indeed the manifestation of a culturally distinct inclination to exhibit a rhythmic movement expressive orientation. They further reasoned that such movement expressiveness could be capitalized upon in academic or task settings to enhance African American children's performance. In the spirit of this conceptual scenario, Allen and Boykin examined 40 African American and 32 white low income grade school children for their learning to associate item pairs. Level of learning was ascertained for all children under two distinct conditions. In one condition,children remained stationary and rehearsed the pairs of items to be learned in essentially a rote fashion (low movement expressiveness). In a second condition (high movement expressiveness), children were presented the item pairs to the beat of rhythmic-percussive music, and were encouraged to move to the beat of the music while engaging in rehearsal. The number of items correctly paired served as the performance outcome measure. Since the "correct" pairing of two items was determined essentially on a random basis, no a priori knowledge of the correct answers was really possible. Consequently, the number of correctly paired items could readily be viewed as indicative of the level of learning as a function of the rehearsal (learning) conditions. For this investigation, children had to pair a given food picture item with a given animal picture item.

The findings revealed overall performance was greater when it followed the low movement expressive learning context than when it followed the high movement expressive context. We could have drawn the nomothetic conclusion from this (main effect) finding that learning is inferior when accompanied by a context which provided rhythmic music and opportunity for movement. Yet when we go beneath this "general" finding to examine the interaction of ethnic group and learning context a very different performance picture emerges. We found the white children indeed performed significantly better under the low movement expressive condition than they did under the high movement expressive condition, but the opposite trend emerged for the African American children. The decline in performance for white children under the high movement expressive condition was quite precipitous, largely explaining the "general" performance finding. Furthermore, while the white children's performance was significantly superior to that of the African American children under the low movement context, the African American children's performance was significantly superior to that of the white children under the high movement condition.

The study and its results were more complex than presented here. But enough is presented to reinforce several important points about experimental research. As already mentioned, the results point to the limitations that can arise from a predisposition to make nomothetic claims. Clearly, a rather distorted view of the results would have been given if no consideration of the interaction of ethnic group and learning context had been made. Indeed, the movement expressive context was generated with salient cultural experiences of African Americans in mind. Thus, the interplay of culture and context is illuminated quite straightforwardly. The investigation also serves to underscore the importance of perspective in the conduct of research. Rather than starting from a pejorative standpoint about the inclinations of African American children, this investigation started from an integrity standpoint.

Rather than, for example, attempting to devise interventions which directly attempt to alter the behavior of African American children to make it less negative in order to affect performance outcomes, the investigators devised an alternative learning context which could capitalize on the integrity of the behavioral grammar African American children brought to the learning situation. Rather than attempting to show ways for the African American children to alter their inclinations to better fit the "normal" or more standard low movement learning context so they could perform like white children, this investigation demonstrated there was a latent competency in African American children that was waiting to be expressed under the appropriate culturally facilitating conditions. These insights would have been virtually unavailable to an "objective" researcher working from a deficit or pejorative perspective. Clearly, conceiving the phenomenon of interest to be hyperactivity rather than as a rhythmic movement expressive orientation would lead to quite different empirical and methodological manifestations.

This empirical project can be categorized as another example of prescriptive pedagogy. Furthermore, by attempting to engineer a learning situation that qualitatively captured certain cultural features of the African American experience it, of necessity, created a situation for learning that had a qualitatively distinct patterning or character. This is quite a different tack from trying to isolate a specific stimulus element to activate specific response outcomes. Consequently, this investigation would seem to qualify as providing examples of contextual variables rather than stimulus variables, per se. The interwoven pattern of the music, percussive beat, rhythmic movement of the experimenter and the children is an amalgamation of factors that together form a cohesive cultural context, a context whose Afro-cultural character would be compromised to the extent that any of the separate elements of the full scenario were eliminated.

Allen and Boykin were also able to provide qualitative insights that conceivably undergirded the divergent performance profiles for the African American and white children under the two different learning contexts. The kind of anecdotal information this investigation was set up to acquire could easily be acquired in any experimental investigation. Even if unsystematic or informal, as was the present case, anecdotal information can contribute input that gives the systematic data explanatory texture. In this instance, the white children were observed to be more task involved and task focused than the African American children in the low movement expressive learning context. The African American children appeared to be more bored, uninterested and restless. In the high movement expressive learning condition the white children appeared to be distracted or even puzzled by the presence of the music and disconcerted in their attempts to move to the music; several seemed to like the music and the chance to move, but were not adept at coordinating the music movement and rehearsal of the pairs. In both scenarios, rehearsal activity seemed to suffer. Yet, in the high movement expressive condition, most of the African American children displayed considerable task engagement and task interest and were readily able to coordinate the music movement and rehearsal activity with virtually no prodding.

Summary

This paper has addressed many concerns. It has examined the character, scope and nature of experimental psychology in a constructively critical fashion. It has attempted to balance this domain's limitations with its redeeming qualities. It has provided several concrete examples of experimental psychological research done in recent years that, in fact, represent a merger with a proactive African American perspective. Hopefully, the research examples provided give students of black psychology directions to pursue, and provide encouragement to others to undertake research using experimental methods and content. Utilization of principles of experimental psychology in the service of black psychology is not beyond the reach of all but "a chosen few." It does not represent a pipe dream to be fulfilled by subsequent cohorts of scholars. Solid, proactive and potentially beneficial exemplars are already available. To be sure, such work has not been without flaws and limitations. But the lesson here is that when judiciously and self-consciously applied, the domain of experimental psychology can merge with the objectives and perspectives of black psychology in order to help illuminate and enhance the psychological texture of the African American experience. Surely more can be done in this regard. Hopefully, more will be done.

References

Adair, J. (1973). *The human subject: The social psychology of the psychological experiment*. Boston: Little Brown and Company.

Akbar, N. (1985). Our destiny: Authors of a scientific revolution. In H. McAdoo, & J. McAdoo (Eds.), *Black children*. Beverly Hills: Sage Publications.

Allen, W. (1978). The search for applicable theories of black family life. *Journal of Marriage and Family, 40*, 117-129.

Allen, B. & Boykin, A.W. (1990). The influence of contextual factors on black and white children's performance: Effects of movement opportunity and music. Submitted for publication.

Altman, I. (1987). Centripetal and centrifugal trends in psychology. *American Psychologist, 42*, 1058-1069.

Banks, W. (1982). Deconstructive falsification: Foundations of critical method in black psychology. In E. Jones, & S. Korchin (Eds.), *Minority mental health*. New York: Praeger.

Boring, E. (1950). *A history of experimental psychology*. New York: Appleton-Century.

Boykin, A.W. (1977). Experimental psychology from a black perspective: Issues and examples. *Journal of Black Psychology, 3*, 29-49.

Boykin, A.W., Franklin A.J., & Yates, J.F. (1979). Worknotes on empirical research in black psychology. In A.W. Boykin, A.J. Franklin, & J.F. Yates (Eds.), *Research directions of black psychologists*. New York: Russell Sage.

Boykin, A.W. (1982). Task variability and the performance of black and white schoolchildren: Vervistic explorations. *Journal of Black Studies, 12*, 469-85.

Boykin, A.W., & Toms, F. (1985). Black child socialization: A conceptual framework. In H. McAdoo, & J. McAdoo (Eds.), *Black children*. Beverly Hills, CA.: Sage Publications.

Brofenbrenner, U. (1979). *The ecology of human development: Experiments by nature and design*. Cambridge, MA: Harvard University Press.

Christensen, L. (1988). *Experimental methodology*. 4th ed. Boston: Allyn and Bacon.

Clark, C. [Sayed Khatib] (1972). Black studies or the study of black people. In R. Jones (Ed.), *Black psychology*. 1st ed. New York: Harper and Row.

Clark, X. C. [Sayed Khatib], McGee, D., Nobles, W., & Akbar, N. (1976). Voodoo or IQ: An introduction to African psychology. Chicago: Institute of Positive Education Black Pages.

Danzinger, K. (1985). The origins of the psychology experiment as a social institution. *American Psychologist, 40*, 133-40.

Dewey, J. (1931). *Philosophy and civilization*. New York: Minton, Balch and Company.

Ericsson, K., & Simon, H. (1980). Verbal reports as data. *Psychological Review, 87*, 215-251.

Ericsson, K., & Simon, H. (1984). *Protocol analysis: Verbal reports as data*. Cambridge, MA: MIT Press.

Estes, W. (1979). Experimental psychology: An overview. In E. Hearst (Ed.), *The first century of experimental psychology*. Hillsdale, NJ: Erlbaum.

Gergen, K. (1978). Toward generative theory. *Journal of Personality and Social Psychology, 36,* 1344-1360.

Gordon, T. (1973). Notes on white and black psychology. In *The white researcher in black society.* C. Clark [Sayed Khatib] (Ed.), *Journal of Social Issues, 29,* 87-95.

Hanson, N. (1958). *Patterns of discovery.* London: Cambridge University Press.

Hearst, E. (1979). One hundred years: Themes and perspectives. In E. Hearst (Ed.), *The first century of experimental psychology.* Hillsdale, NJ: Erlbaum.

Jones, J. (1979). Conceptual and strategic issues in the relationship of black psychology to American social science. In A.W. Boykin, A.J. Franklin, & J.F. Yates (Eds.), *Research directions of black psychologists.* New York: Russell Sage.

Jones, J. (1986). The concept of race in social psychology: From color to culture. In L. Wheeler, & P. Shaver (Eds.), *Review of personality and social psychology.* Vol. 4. Beverly Hills: Sage Publications.

Koch, S. (1985). Wundt's creature at age zero -and a centenarian. In S. Koch, & D. Leary (Eds.), *A century of psychology as a science.* New York: McGraw-Hill.

Marans, A., & Lourie, R. (1967). Hypotheses regarding the effects of child rearing patterns on the disadvantaged child. In U. Hellmuth (Ed.), *Disadvantaged child.* Seattle, Wash.: Special Child Publications.

McGuire, W. (1983). A contextualist theory of knowledge: Its implications for innovation and reform in psychological research. In L. Berkowitz (Ed.), *Advances in experimental social psychology.* New York: Academic Press.

McLoyd, V., & Randolph, S. (1984). The conduct and publication of research on Afro-American children. *Human Development, 27,* 65-75.

Mischel, T. (1975). Psychological explanations and their vicissitudes. In *Nebraska symposium on motivation.* Lincoln: University of Nebraska Press.

Moore, C., & Retish, C. (1974). Effects of the examiner's race on black children's Wechsler Preschool and Primary Scale of Intelligence IQ. *Developmental Psychology, 10,* 672-676.

Neisser, U. (Ed.). (1982). *Memory observed.* San Francisco: W. Freeman.

Neisser, U. (Ed.), (1986). *The school achievement of minority children.* Hillsdale, NJ: Erlbaum.

Rogoff, B. (1982). Integrating context and cognitive development. In M. Lamb, & A. Brown (Eds.), *Advances in developmental psychology (Vol. 2).* Hillsdale, NJ: Erlbaum.

Sampson, E. (1978). Scientific paradigms and social values: Wanted—a scientific revolution. *Journal of Personality and Social Psychology, 36,* 1332-42.

Scarr, S. (1985). Constructing psychology: Making facts and fables for our times. *American Psychologist, 40,* 499-512.

Sewell, T., & Walker, D. (1982). The effects of material and symbolic incentives on the learning ability of low SES black children. *Journal of General Psychology, 106,* 93-99.

Sherwood, J., & Nataupsky, M. (1968). Predicting the conclusions of black-white intelligence research from biographical characteristics of the investigator. *Journal of Personality and Social Psychology, 8,* 53-58.

Simmons, W. (1985). Social class and ethnic differences in cognition: A cultural practice perspective. In S. Chipman, J. Segal, & R. Glaser (Eds.), *Thinking and learning skills*, Vol. 2. Hillsdale, NJ: Erlbaum.

Smith, R., & Lewis, R. (1984). Race as self schema affecting recall in black children. *Journal of Black Psychology, 12*, 15-29.

Snodgrass, J., Levy-Berger, G., & Haydon, M. (1985). *Human experimental psychology*. New York: Oxford University Press.

Spence, J. (1985). Achievement American style: The rewards and costs of individualism. *American Psychologist, 40*, 499-512.

Staats, A. (1983). *Psychology's crisis of disunity*. New York: Praeger.

Stevens, S. (Ed.). (1951). *Handbook on experimental psychology*. New York: Wiley.

Sutherland, M., & Harrell, J. (1987). Individual differences in physiological responses to fearful, racially noxious and neutral imagery. *Imagination, Cognition and Personality, 6*, 133-150.

Thomas, C. (1970). Psychologists, psychology and the black community. In I. Korten, S. Cook, & J. Lacey (Eds.), *Psychology and the problems of society*. Washington, DC: American Psychological Association.

Tuck, K., & Boykin, A.W. (1989). Task performance and receptiveness to variability in black and white low-income children. In A. Harrison (Ed.), *The eleventh conference on empirical research in black psychology*. Washington, DC: NIMH Publications.

Weiner, B. (1986). *An attributional theory of motivation and emotion*. New York: Springer-Verlag.

Woodworth, R., & Schlosberg, H. (1954). *Experimental psychology*, 2nd ed. New York: Holt and Company.

Organizational Psychology: African American Perspectives

Phillip J. Bowman

Introduction

Organizational psychology has become an increasingly important area in the expanding field of American psychology (Dunnette, 1983; Katz & Kahn, 1978; Tuttle, 1983; Schultz & Schultz, 1986). As we approach the 21st century, psychologists are being called upon to explain human behavior in complex organizations, and to utilize their knowledge to solve organizational problems. Organizational psychologists conduct basic and applied research on social psychological processes involved in organizational functioning and/or utilize knowledge from such studies to help organizations run more effectively and efficiently. Despite the focus in this chapter on African Americans, the critical issues highlighted have relevance for all organizations faced with the challenge of incorporating members of diverse racial, ethnic and class groups. Demographic trends make this a special challenge for organizations in the United States where African Americans, Latinos, and Asians will make up an increasing portion of a shrinking workforce well into the 21st century. During the 20th century, organizational psychologists helped managers increase the effectiveness of organizations through a better understanding of areas such as individual differences, man-machine systems, groups dynamics, and leadership. The 21st century may well require psychologists who can also help insure that the unique cultural heritage of diverse race and ethnic group members becomes assets to organizations. It would indeed be an irony of history if African American culture, once blamed as a major barrier to effective role performance, becomes an essential source of organizational diversity, creativity, vitality and productivity.

To be sure, effective and efficient organizations in all sectors of society have been hallmarks of great nations—from ancient Egypt to Timbuktu to the United States. Shein (1970) in a widely read book on *Organizational Psychology* noted:

"The effective utilization of people in organized human effort has always been a pressing problem. The pharaoh building a pyramid faced problems fundamentally similar to those faced by the corporation executive or university president of today. Each must figure out (1) how to organize work and allocate it to workers; (2) how to recruit, train, and effectively manage the people available to do the work; (3) how to create work conditions and reward and punishment systems which will enable workers to maintain high effectiveness and sufficient morale to remain effective over long periods of time, (4) how to adjust their organization to changing environmental conditions and technological innovations, and (5) how to cope with competition or harassment from other organizations or groups within their own organizations (pp. 1-2)."

Indeed, such questions lie at the heart of "organization," and have had to be faced and resolved by managers and their advisors throughout history. However, new problems confront organizational psychologists today as the world shrinks into an interlocking global economy, as industrialized nations transform into post-industrial societies, and as people in all nations increasingly move to culturally heterogeneous urban communities, and work in multicultural organizational settings (Ficker & Graves, 1978; Koehn, 1983; Starbuck, 1983; Onibokun, 1973). Within various cultural contexts, such changes will continue to pose complex challenges for psychologists interested in the effective functioning of private sector, government and other formal organizations.

Over the past 30 years, what is typically referred to as Industrial/Organizational (I/O) psychology has become the major area for American psychologists specializing in organizational behavior (i.e., Cascio, 1984; Dunnette, 1983; Schultz & Schultz, 1986; Thayer, 1983). Traditionally, I/O psychology has concentrated on military, industrial, and business organizations, despite the broader goal of understanding human behavior in all types of organizations. There has also been some attention to cross-national organizational psychology issues, but has focused less attention on multicultural challenges within nations (Barrett & Bass, 1983; Triandis, 1984). Existing literature has yet to adequately address critical issues confronting African Americans, Latinos or Asians in organizational settings within the United States. Traditional studies of African Americans have been based largely on white/black comparisons of ability, work attitudes and other characteristics with a black deficit model often used to interpret findings (i.e., Dugan, 1966; Forginne & Peters, 1982; Grant & Bray, 1970; Miller & Miner, 1983; Schul & Anthony, 1978; Slocum & Strawser, 1972; Weaver, 1978). Emphasis is much less often placed on either organizational barriers to explain problems, or on ethnic and cultural strengths to explain adaptive organizational behaviors (Bowman, 1977; Illgen & Youtz, 1984; Pettigrew, 1987).

In the remainder of this chapter, the expanding field of I/O psychology will be briefly highlighted, followed by a discussion of critical issues that must be addressed to better understand the experience of African Americans in organizational settings.

During early periods of civilization, pharaohs including Cheop, Chepheren and Mycerinus effectively managed large scale organizations to build magnificent pyramids along the Nile river in Africa. History also reveals that pharaohs effectively managed complex hierarchies of leadership in governmental, commercial, educational and religious organizations within great cities. These early managers appeared to be more dedicated to spiritual than profit motives, but they faced the same age old challenge of effectively utilizing human resources, organizing effective social-technical systems and solving pressing organizational problems.

Traditional Perspectives: I/O Psychology

Scope

In recent years, I/O psychology has expanded so much in breadth and diversity that only a brief outline is within the scope of this section. In contrast to earlier periods where emphasis was on professional practice, I/O psychology has now become an academic discipline with a comprehensive blend of research, theory and practice (Guion, 1965; Staw, 1984; Thayer, 1983).

One way to conceptualize the scope of I/O psychology is to review chapters included in the *Handbook of Industrial and Organizational Psychology* (Dunnette, 1983). As outlined in Table 1, the 37 chapters in the Handbook are organized into three groups with two sections each. Within the three broad groups, chapters focus on (1) theoretical and methodological foundations of I/O psychology, (2) individual and job measurement with a focus on management of individual behavior in organizations, and (3) description and measurement of organizations as well as behavioral processes in organizations. The first group includes four chapters on conceptual foundations and six chapters on methodological foundations of I/O psychology. The second group incorporates four chapters on basic attributes of individuals in relation to behavior in organizations and ten chapters on the practice of I/O psychology. The final group includes five chapters on attributes of organizations and their effects on members as well as eight chapters on behavioral processes in organizations.

Table 1
Scope of the Handbook of I/O Psychology (1983)

A. Theoretical and Methodological Foundations of I/O Psychology
   I. Conceptual Foundations of I/O Psychology
      1. Theory Building in Applied Areas
      2. General Systems Approach to Organizations
      3. Motivation Theory in I/O Psychology
      4. Human Learning
   II. Methodological Foundations of I/O Psychology
      5. Problems and New Directions for Industrial Psychology
      6. Psychometric Theory
      7. Design and Conduct of Quasi-Experiments and
         True Experiments in Field Settings
      8. Multivariate Procedures
      9. Field Research Methods
      10. Laboratory Experimentation
B. Individual and Job Measurement and Management of
   Individual Behavior in Organizations
   III. Basic Attributes of Individuals in Relation to Behavior in
      Organizations
      11. Aptitudes, Abilities and Skills
      12. Vocational Preferences
      13. Personality and Personality Assessment
      14. Background Data
   IV. The Practice of I/O Psychology
      15. Job and Task Analysis
      16. Engineering Psychology
      17. Behaviors, Results, and Organizational Effectiveness
      18. Recruitment, Selection, and Job Placement
      19. Personal Training
      20. Managerial Assessment Centers
      21. Conflict and Conflict Management
      22. Technology of Organizational Development
      23. Management of Ineffective Performance
      24. Consumer and Industrial Psychology
C. Description and Measurement of Organizations and of Behavioral
   Processes in Organizations
   V. Attributes of Organizations and their Effects on Members
      25. Organizations and their Environments
      26. Organizational Structure and Climate
      27. Structure and Dynamics of Behavior in Organizational
         Boundary Roles
      28. Role-Making Processes Within Complex Organizations
      29. Control Systems in Organizations
   VI. Behavioral Processes in Organizations
      30. Nature and Causes of Job Satisfaction
      31. Stress and Behavior in Organizations
      32. Decision Making and Problem Solving
      33. Group Influences on Individuals
      34. Leadership
      35. Communication in Organizations
      36. Change Processes in Organizations
      37. Cross-Cultural Issues in I/O Psychology

When compared to the content of introductory I/O textbooks, the Handbook covers methodological and theoretical issues in much greater detail:

"Research methodology and strategies for research are given much deeper attention and greatly increased breadth of coverage in the Handbook. Various theories are covered in greater detail, and many of the authors are presenting new conceptualizations for the first time" (Dunnette, 1983, p. 8).

In contrast, introductory level I/O texts are less technical, focus more on practical issues and are more student-relevant. For example, Schultz & Schultz (1986) note in their popular text:

"Our purpose in this book is not to train people to become industrial psychologists but rather to acquaint students—most of whom will work for some kind of organization—with the principles, problems, and occasional pretenses of I/O psychology. In addition, we believe that it is important to show students how psychology will aid them in their careers, and how the findings of industrial psychologists will directly influence their lives as job applicants, employees, managers and consumers" (p. vii).

It is also interesting to note that, although the Handbook included one chapter on cross-cultural issues, there is no topical focus on African Americans, Latinos, or Asians. In reference to this omission, the editor notes that a major gap occurs in the lack of topical coverage given to special "groups such as women, minorities, the disadvantaged, or to particular occupational subgroups." This omission occurs despite the fact that existing research has found that African Americans and other "special groups" often have both some unique characteristics and some distinct organizational experiences (i.e., Forginne & Peters, 1982; Illgen & Youtz, 1984; Pettigrew, & Martin, 1987).

Trends

As an area of American psychology, I/O psychology can be traced to the early years of the 20th century (Dunnette, 1983). In 1913, Hugo Munsterberg, a German psychologist teaching at Harvard University, published a book titled the *Psychology of Industrial Efficiency*. However, the major forces which have shaped modern I/O psychology include: (1) the use of psychologists by the U.S. Army during World War I for the systematic screening, classification, selection and placement of recruits, (2) the series of studies commenced in 1924 at the Hawthorne, Illinois plant of Western Electric Company which provided new insight into complex human relations, morale and motivational problems in organizations, (3) the use of over 2,000 psychologists during World War II to identify individuals for complex weapon system training and to improve advanced man-machine systems, and (4) the recognition that psychologists can help increasingly complex organizations in business, government and other sectors become more efficient and effective (Dunnette, 1983; Katzell & Guzzo, 1983; Tuttle, 1983).

Spurred by the foregoing historical forces, I/O psychology has become a major subfield in American psychology (Schultz & Schultz, 1986; Thayer, 1983). For example, there are over 2,000 members of the Society for Industrial and Organizational Psychology, Division 42 of the American Psychological Association. The stated purpose of Division 42 is to "promote human welfare through the various applications of psychology to all types of organizations providing goods or services, such as manufacturing concerns, commercial enterprises, labor unions or trade associations, and public agencies (Schultz & Schultz, 1986)." Most I/O psychologists still work in industrial or business organizations, but increasing numbers are employed by government, educational and other formal organizations. They also work for consulting firms offering services to a wide range of organizations: or as faculty members in universities, often serving as part-time consultants to various organizations. As an indication of demand, I/O psychologists currently have higher salaries than any other group of psychologists including clinical psychologists. Given the career opportunities and financial rewards, it should not be surprising that the number of I/O psychologists has more than doubled since 1970 and related courses are among the most popular at both the graduate and undergraduate levels (Thayer, 1983; Tuttle, 1983).

African American Perspectives: Critical Considerations

Despite its many virtues, I/O psychology has yet to adequately address critical organizational issues facing African Americans, Latinos, or other underrepresented racial and ethnic groups. In this section, some of the unique problems and related challenges confronting African Americans in formal organizations will be systematically considered. As suggested earlier, traditional perspectives tend to view the unique organizational problems of African Americans as either of marginal significance, or according to a deficit model. We need to better understand the social psychology of chronic role strains faced by African Americans in various organizations, how such role strains are exacerbated by cultural conflicts and complicated further by imperatives for collective modes of coping with racial inequality.

I/O psychology has yet to adequately clarify the nature and consequences of discouraging barriers that persistently frustrate achievement strivings of African Americans in valued organizational roles. Nor have the cultural conflicts which make it difficult for African Americans and other people of color to function in mainstream organizations been carefully examined. Furthermore, organizational complexities which occur when individuals choose collective modes of coping with racial inequalities have seldom been considered. Therefore, systematic barriers to equal representation, respectful cross-ethnic relations and meaningful participation in major organizational roles all remain unresolved issues. Drawing on work by Boykin (1983) and others, the triple quandary framework, can help delineate these issues for future organizational research and action. The triple quandary paradigm is first highlighted, followed by a discussion of related directions for I/O psychologists who want to go beyond traditional deficit perspectives in work with African Americans.

Triple Quandary

A triple quandary framework has evolved over the past 20 years as a basis to conceptualize the unique problems of African Americans in all sectors of society (Bowman, 1977; Boykin, 1983; 1985; Boykin & Toms, 1985; Cole, 1970; Young, 1970). According to this conceptual framework, African Americans must simultaneously negotiate through three distinctively different realms of experience—*mainstream, culture* and *minority*. Each of these realms of experience raises critical organizational issues for African Americans which have not been examined adequately by I/O psychology.

Mainstream quandary. The lives of African Americans are significantly shaped by mainstream American society, despite important cross-ethnic differences and growing subethnic diversity. As noted by Young (1970), African American survival as well as achievement require effective participation "in work systems, judicial systems, in consumption systems, in bureaucratic organizations as both clients and employees." Moreover, black families, schools, the mass media and other socialization agencies transmit values to African Americans regarding the desirability of success in mainstream organizational roles (Boykin & Toms, 1985). Therefore, it is not surprising that African Americans' hopes for achievement in family, educational, work, and civic organizations are similar to those of other ethnic groups in America and the world community. However, despite the common hopes, the achievement strivings of African Americans in major organizational roles are much more often frustrated by persistent failure (Astin, 1980; Farley & Allen, 1987; Illgen & Youtz, 1984). Therefore, in their strivings for access and success in valued organizational roles, African Americans often must find ways to cope with the discouragement of frequent rejections, and poor performance ratings (Bowman, 1977; 1984; 1989; Bowman & Howard, 1985; Bowman, et al., 1982; Green, 1982; Greenhaus & Galvin, 1972). The more ambitious or cherished the mainstream organizational strivings, the more potentially devastating the motivations, emotional and psychosocial consequences of failure (Bowman, 1990a; 1990b).

Despite recent discussion about a declining significance of race, the increasing numbers of African Americans who gain access to non-traditional organizational roles face serious difficulties in efforts to survive and advance (i.e., Blackwell, 1981; Bass, 1984). However, before a person can be concerned about a job promotion, he or she must first obtain a job. Hence, current trends make access to adequate education and joblessness more basic issues (Astin, 1980; Bowman, 1989). Joblessness among African Americans, especially males, has risen at an alarming rate since the 1950s; the differential vulnerability of black workers is spurred by post-industrial automation and deindustrialization which continue to displace unskilled and semi-skilled jobs (Bowman, 1984; 1988; Wook, 1980). By the year 2,000, industrial robots will perform as many as four million factory jobs and those jobs that employ most black males are being hardest hit ("Retraining displaced workers," 1982; Wexley, 1984). Currently, a growing third of African Americans who are employable are either unemployed, employed irregularly, or too discouraged to seek employment. Another growing one-third hold low-level jobs without decent wages and little opportunity for advancement. A decreasing number hold jobs which pay sufficiently to keep themselves or their families out of poverty.

Most predominantly white universities and private business organizations are at best cautious about the idea of recruiting chronically jobless African Americans, especially from urban areas. When they have attempted, many problems have occurred as noted in the following comments about an innovative effort by a high-technology firm to recruit, hire and train black workers labeled as the "hardcore unemployed":

> Many problems never before encountered by trainers were discovered when the program began. There were serious problems in communications, not just in communicating ideas or concepts, but the more basic problem of understanding spoken words. If the trainers were white, there was hostility and fear on

the part of the trainees. Many trainees had mannerisms, habits, and dress styles that trainers found unorthodox and offensive. A rapport had to be established before the actual job training could begin. The trainees needed to be convinced that the program was genuine and that the training was geared directly to a job and to correcting their deficient abilities. Only in this way did the trainees develop any real motivation to learn" (Schultz & Schultz, 1986, p. 237).

Culture quandary The organizational quandary among African Americans created by mainstream goals and restricted opportunities may be further exacerbated by cultural conflicts. Guided by Afro-centric models, a growing number of scholars lend support to the notion that African Americans are carriers of a unique and virtuous cultural tradition which has been retained across the generations (Ashante, 1980; Akbar, 1976; Baldwin, 1981; Jackson 1976; Karenga, 1980; Nobles, 1991). Afro-centric scholars have acknowledged the eroding effects of racial oppression on material and explicit aspects of African culture in the United States (Baldwin, 1991; Berry & Blassingame, 1982; Dubois, 1903; Hale, 1982; Herskovits, 1935; Nobles, 1988; Sudarkasa, 1988). However, several aspects of subjective African American culture appear to have been successfully transmitted from one generation to the next. For example, Boykin (1983) specifies nine cultural motifs which currently find expression among African Americans—spirituality, harmony, movement, verve, affect, communalism, expressive individualism, orality and social time orientation. While these motifs are considered to be essentially African, other scholars have focused more on African American cultural strengths which have been reinforced by racial oppression in America such as a strong work ethic, achievement orientation, extended family, para-kinship and religion (i.e., Hill, 1971).

The retention of African American cultural strengths may empower individuals with an adaptive "bi-culturality" to effectively negotiate the gap between a unique African heritage and mainstream organization expectations (i.e., Bowman, 1985; 1989a; 1989b; 1991a; DuBois, 1903). However, Boykin & Toms (1985) suggest that for African Americans the "attendant negotiational demands are inherently problematic" because their indigenous cultural heritage is "antithetical to mainstream American cultural self-understanding." They suggest that intractable cultural conflicts create serious problems for African Americans in mainstream organizations:

> Suffice it for now that it is difficult to put spirituality, communalism, a rhythmic-movement orientation, expressive-individualism, an affective orientation and the likes in the service of mainstream institutional strivings. Likewise, Euro-Americans

find it easy from their dominant cultural-definitional view-point to view spirituality negatively as "voodoo" and "superstition," communalism as dependency, a movement rhythmic orientation as hyperactivity, expressive individualism as being unsystematic or showing off, or to see an affective orientation as immature, irrational and too emotional (p. 43).

Thus, cultural conflicts may occur when American organizations refuse to extend the principle of cultural pluralism to African Americans, despite the fact that this principle is usually extended to other ethnic groups. Boykin suggests that this selective racism is caused by the very nature of African and European cultures. However, others blame such racism on economic imperatives of slavery and subsequent systems of racial hegemony in America. Hence a shrinking multicultural labor force in post-industrial America may motivate a greater appreciation of a strong work ethic, achievement orientation, para-kin relations, religious ethics and other African American cultural traditions as assets to organizational effectiveness in the 21st century.

Minority quandary Because of intergroup inequalities, racial-ethnic minority group members often participate in organizational activities to promote both individual survival and collective social change. In addition to the double quandary of mainstream discouragement and cultural conflict, African Americans are also faced with collective political imperatives (Blackwell, 1985; Harding, 1981; Morris, 1984; Yetman & Steele, 1974). Hence, beyond mainstream and cultural imperatives, minority status may compel African Americans toward organizational activities in behalf of the group; such activities enable individuals to cope with more pervasive race and class inequities. To some degree, such minority group inequities challenge African Americans to look beyond individual mobility to organizational roles that facilitate collective social change.

Organizational involvement instigated by minority group imperatives is often functional rather than intrinsic, active rather than passive and collectivistic rather than individualistic. For African Americans, special difficulty may occur within organizations that discourage social change commitments, expect passive rather than activist styles, and reward individual rather than collective modes of coping with inequality. The serious role conflicts that result may further add to chronic role strains among African Americans produced by restricted organizational access and cultural insensitivity.

Organization Issues: Strategic Responses

Building on what Dubois (1903) called "double consciousness," the challenge to I/O psychology is to clarify the manner in which a "triple consciousness" effects African Americans in organizational settings. The triple quandary framework suggests that African Americans often (1) confront repeated failure in valued life roles when discouraging barriers restrict significant involvement in mainstream organizations, (2) face stressful cultural conflicts when African-based motifs are not included within the range of accepted ethnic styles in major societal organizations, and (3) experience multiple role complications when progressive, active and collective minority coping orientations fail to conform to intrinsic, passive and individualistic expectations within traditional organizations. Hence, organizational psychology must seek to better understand and develop strategies to eliminate the unique role disjunctures, role conflicts, and role complexities which increase organizational problems among African Americans. Guided by the triple jeopardy paradigm, researchers can be beyond traditional deficit perspectives to address the critical issues of *significant involvement, cultural sensitivity* and *functional relevance.*

Significant Involvement

I/O psychologists must conduct careful studies on the issue of significant involvement to provide needed insight into the problems of restricted opportunity and mainstream discouragement among African Americans. This research must clarify the nature and consequences of discouraging barriers which restrict the achievement of valued goals among African Americans in mainstream organizations. Effective organizational strategies for increasing their meaningful participation and leadership in all sectors of society need to be driven by such research.

Illgen & Youtz (1984) and others emphasize the need for I/O psychologists to distinguish between two related problem areas—access and treatment. Consideration should be given to organizational and personal characteristics that impede African American access to important entry level roles, and those that adversely affect their treatment in these roles and other organizational roles across one's career:

> Access discrimination refers to limitations unrelated to actual or potential performance placed on minority group members at the time the job is filled such as rejection of applicants, lower starting salaries, limited advertising of position openings, or failure to send recruiters to locations where minority members are more likely to be available. Treatment discrimination occurs

once the minority group members have gained access into the organization. Some examples are slower rates of promotion, assignment to less desirable jobs, lower and/or less frequent raises, or fewer opportunities for training (Illgen & Youtz, p. 3).

Studies have emphasized the serious difficulties African Americans experience in access to higher educational organizations (Astin, 1982; Thomas, 1981), to unskilled jobs in industrial organizations (Bowman, 1989; Wilson, 1987) and to high level professional and technical jobs in all sectors (Farley & Allen, 1987; Blackwell, 1981). Research also documents serious treatment problems among African Americans who receive lower performance ratings (Landy & Farr, 1980), are often alienated within organizations (Pettigrew & Martin, 1987), and are less often promoted (Bass, 1984). I/O psychologists need to be beyond deficit models of individual differences in ability, to better clarify the range of barriers that impede equal access and treatment of African Americans in mainstream organizations. Existing literature suggests that we investigate the nature and effects of race specific barriers including various forms of racism (i.e., Bielby, 1987; Feagin, 1987), non-race specific barriers such as technological innovations in post-industrial organizations (i.e., Bowman, 1988; 1989a), and internal group-based factors that restrict career choices (i.e., Lee, 1983; Smith, 1980; Stanley & Russell, 1987). We also need to further clarify pivotal social psychological factors that impede and promote adaptive modes of coping with various barriers to effective organizational performance (Bowman, 1984; 1985; 1989b; 1991a; Bowman & Howard, 1985; Bowman et al., 1982).

When I/O psychologists have considered the issue of significant involvement, far more attention has been placed on access than on treatment discrimination (Illgen & Youtz, 1984). However, Pettigrew & Martin (1987) and others have noted that both remain serious problems. Guided by a triple jeopardy model, their review emphasizes the need to consider problems in the recruitment, entry, and promotion of African Americans in predominantly white organizations. They note that significant involvement of African Americans is often restricted by (a) stereotypes which hinder access and treatment, (b) the solo role— when the person is the only one in their workgroup, and (c) the token role—when African American recruits are viewed by white organizational members as incompetent simply because affirmative action was involved in their selection. I/O psychologists should also go beyond a problem orientation and seek to identify exemplary organizations and organizational practices that successfully increase access to advancement prospects for African Americans. A systematic focus on the foregoing issues should provide a better basis to increase the significant involvement of African Americans in mainstream organizations. Indeed, related research and action may help increase the significant involvement of African Americans in the burgeoning field of I/O psychology.

Cultural Sensitivity

Because of demographic trends toward multicultural diversity, I/O psychology must provide additional insight into the manner in which cultural insensitivity and conflict restrict organizational effectiveness. Despite growing attention to cross-national issues, the nature and consequences of cultural conflicts which impede African Americans and other racial-ethnic group members in organizational settings are less well understood (Barrett & Bass, 1983; Pettigrew & Martin, 1987). Berry (1980) and other cross-cultural psychologists have distinguished between *etic* elements which are common across more than one culture, and *emic* elements which are unique to a particular cultural group. While most American ethnic groups are viewed as carriers of virtuous cultural traditions, social scientists have been less ready to extend this emic view to African Americans:

> To them, Black people are only Americans, without values and culture of their own to guard and protect, and without an opportunity to view themselves as other ethnic groups do. Thus, they would be less likely to organize themselves to take care of their own social problems (Hannerz, 1969, p. 195).

As suggested by the triple quandary paradigm, we need to explore the notion that Euro-centric ethnocentrism, racial hatred and cultural hegemony work more adversely against African Americans than other American ethnic groups in organizational settings.

I/O psychologists have yet to adequately address the *sources* and *consequences* of cultural insensitivity that impede equitable access and treatment of African Americans in major organizational roles (Pettigrew & Martin, 1987; Triandis, 1984). Existing social psychological evidence suggests that anti-black stereotypes combine with related attitudes as well as motivational, informational and affirmative action processes at the organizational level to reinforce discriminatory treatment of African Americans (Cook, 1987; Fiske, 1987; Nacoste, 1987). Research on whites has also shown that perceived self interest and stratification beliefs, in addition to racial prejudice, reinforce discriminatory practices and resistance to culturally sensitive organizational changes (Feagin, 1987; Kluegel, 1990; Kluegel & Smith, 1982). Moreover, sociologists remind us of the broader institutional sources of Euro-centric cultural insensitivity and discriminatory practices in business organizations (Smith, 1987; Braddock & McPartland, 1987). They note that cultural conflicts which impede African Americans within business organizations merely reflect similar patterns within educational organizations and other sectors of society.

In addition to the multiple sources of cultural insensitivity, I/O psychology must also provide a greater understanding of its consequences within organizational settings. In efforts to understand how cultural insensitivity impedes organizational effectiveness, psychologists have provided rather careful examinations of cultural bias in selection testing (Drasgow, 1982; Hulin, Drasgow & Parsons, 1983). However, they have not been as diligent in efforts to clarify effects of cultural insensitivity in other areas of organizational life (Bass, 1984; Illgen & Youtz, 1984; Triandis, 1984).

With a focus on racial stereotypes, Pettigrew & Martin (1987) speculate that cultural insensitivity toward African Americans often result in biased and stressful recruitment practices, assumed dissimilarities and exaggerated expectations on entry, and later polarized, biased evaluation of performance. Thus, cultural insensitivity may produce role strains among African Americans in mainstream organizations characterized by role conflicts, ambiguity and discouragement. A classic set of laboratory studies documented adverse effects of minority status, threat, and anxiety on the performance of African Americans in predominantly white workgroups (Katz, 1970; Katz & Benjamin, 1960; Katz, Epps & Axelson, 1964; Katz & Greenbaum 1963). More recently, despite finding many similarities in black-white subjective culture, Triandis (1984) also found evidence that intergroup hostility and other "cultural gaps" create special difficulties in the access and treatment of the chronically unemployed.

A more practical challenge to I/O psychology is to build on additional knowledge to develop effective strategies to reduce dysfunctional cultural conflicts in organizations. Some have emphasized the adaptive value of indigenous African American cultural strengths in promoting successful coping in major organizational roles (i.e., Bowman, 1989a; Bowman & Howard, 1985; Hayles, 1982; Hill, 1971). Others caution against multicultural trends and suggest that advancement in mainstream organizations is better served by assimilation and Anglo-conformity (Glazer & Moynihan, 1975; Yetman & Steele, 1978). An Afro-centric approach would require organizations to better accommodate distinct cultural patterns of African American members. On the other hand, a more Euro-centric approach would require African Americans to completely divest themselves of indigenous ethnic patterns in favor of European-American standards despite racist elements. Therefore, while some caution that too much accommodation to African American culture would impede organizational effectiveness, a growing number of psychologists emphasize the organizational benefits of incorporating diverse cultures (Hayles, 1982; Triandis, 1984).

Functional Relevance

I/O psychologists can provide valuable insight into organizational problems that occur as African Americans strive to cope with minority group inequalities in America. The Swedish sociologist, Gunnar Myrdal (1944), noted in his classic work *An American Dilemma* that America has had great difficulty bridging the gap between the *facts* of racial oppression and the *ideals* of freedom, justice and equality. This historical dilemma remains as much a challenge today as in the past, largely because of the disturbing increase in the number of chronically jobless African Americans in isolated urban communities (Bowman, 1989; Farley & Allen, 1987; Jaynes, 1989; Wilson, 1987).

History also reminds us that past successes in reducing racial inequalities have depended more on collective struggles of African Americans than on a moral initiatives to voluntarily extend American democratic privileges to oppressed racial minorities (Berry & Blassingame, 1982; Harding, 1981; Morris, 1984). It remains critical for researchers to examine organizational issues facing African Americans who participate in collective action to reduce racial inequalities and promote social change. Among African Americans, involvement in a wide range of voluntary organizational activities may be partially driven by the perceived relevance of this involvement to the collective struggle against racial inequality. Their organizational involvement has functional relevance for promoting social change in the interest of the group; thus, functional relevance becomes an important principle for understanding the instrumental, active and collective aspects of African American involvement in formal organizations.

I/O psychology should seek to further clarify how functional relevance among African Americans operates (1) to produce unique difficulties within mainstream organizations when collective commitments conflict with traditional role expectations, and (2) to increase participation in predominantly black organizations which work to improve the conditions of the African American population. We need to better understand the role conflicts, role overload and other difficulties that may occur when progressive, active and collective commitments interfere with expected modes of behavior in mainstream organizations (Gilkes, 1982; Gurin & Epps, 1974; Hall & Allen, 1982). For example, participation in "black caucuses" within mainstream organizations or in "black political activism" outside the organization may be viewed by more conservative members as inappropriate or even threatening. Moreover, collective commitments and activism may sometimes interfere with expected organizational duties, create multiple role strain and add to role discouragement. In addition to understanding these issues, another challenge would be to develop innovative strategies that reduce such role strains without impeding either collective commitments or the effectiveness of mainstream organizations.

The functional relevance imperative may not only influence role enactment among African Americans, but also their choice of organizational roles. For example, the vocational choice literature suggests that collective commitments may contribute to African American's persistent preferences for service-related jobs and careers (Stanley & Russell, 1987; Smith, 1980). Functional relevance may also be an important variable in African Americans extremely active participation in black organizations, although structural barriers and cultural conflicts within white organizations may indeed be major factors. African Americans have been found to be highly involved in black business organizations (Brandt, 1977), educational organizations (Sizemore, 1985), neighborhood organizations (Milburn & Bowman, 1991), political organizations (Baker & McCorry), and the black church (Nelsen, Yokley & Nelsen, 1971).

Going beyond the current emphasis on predominantly white business enterprises, I/O psychology must better clarify critical issues facing African Americans within the wide range of predominantly black organizations (Blackwell, 1985; Giamartino & Wandersman, 1983; Morris, 1984; Yearwood, 1980). What distinguishes successful black business organizations from the many that fail? How do leadership, performance appraisal and other organizational variables differentiate effective schools from the majority of ineffective schools in urban black communities? Do the structure, recruitment strategies and membership interaction patterns in effective inner city neighborhood organizations differ from those which are less effective? What is the relative importance of structural and subjective cultural variables in the effectiveness of black political organizations? Do Afro-centric values and related motivational dynamics differentiate active from less active members in professional organizations such as the Association of Black Psychologists? Is the effectiveness of complex community organizations such as the black church based more on community-based recruitment, "indigenous" quality-control circles, quasi-formal training, human resource development programs or strong leadership that manage the delivery of diverse community services?

Summary and Conclusion

The necessity to deal with behavioral problems in large work organizations are at least as old as ancient Egypt, where over 4,000 years ago massive workgroups constructed some of the most impressive and complex structures the world has ever known. However, the scientific field of I/O psychology emerged in the United States during the early 1900s to help solve increasingly complex behavioral problems in work, school, government and other organizations. Presently, this expanding subfield of American psychology has evolved into one of the most important areas of research, theory and practice. Unfortunately, I/O psychology currently leaves much to be desired in addressing the unique organizational experience of African Americans, Latinos, or Asian Americans. Despite its accomplishments, I/O psychology has provided little understanding of multicultural factors that influence organizational effectiveness. The triple jeopardy paradigm was discussed as a useful conceptual framework to guide future research on significant involvement, cultural sensitivity and functional relevance which represent major challenges for I/O psychology.

As we approach the 21st century, national demographic trends toward greater cultural diversity make the issues of significant involvement and cultural sensitivity important to both mainstream organizations and the African American community. Moreover, prospects for constructive solutions to the persistent American dilemma (democratic ideals versus racial oppression) continue to depend largely on functionally relevant organizational activities of African Americans. The traditional paradigm in I/O psychology should shift in at least three ways to address the triple jeopardy faced by African Americans in organizational settings. First, emphasis on deficit approaches to problems of access and treatment (i.e., individual differences) must shift to a more open systems approach which views organizational behavior within the context of a dynamic social system and diverse cultural ecologies (i.e., Katz & Kahn, 1980; Ogbu, 1978). Second, a narrow Euro-centric approach to black-white ethnic conflicts in organizations must shift. Hence, more Afro-centric approaches may better clarify organizational barriers and the adaptive virtues of cultural resources in organizational effectiveness (i.e., Bowman, 1989; Boykin, 1985). Third, the primary focus on industrial organizations must shift to a broader array of organizations, including those critical to the survival of African Americans in a complex post-industrial society (i.e., Bowman, 1988; Bowman & Milburn, forthcoming). The foregoing paradigm expansion would not only make I/O psychology more relevant to African Americans but also to an increasingly interlocking, culturally diverse and urban world community (Barrett & Bass, 1983; Starbuck, 1983).

More definitive research on this expanded paradigm can go beyond traditional studies in I/O psychology and add to our basic knowledge about human behavior in a broader range of complex organizations. In addition to its theoretical significance, such research can also help resolve some controversial practical questions. For example, should mainstream organizations continue to restrict cultural diversity because external pressures for multicultural changes threaten organizational effectiveness? Or must mainstream organizations rapidly diversify to accommodate African Americans and other racial-ethnic groups in response to demographic trends? Or should African Americans place their primary emphasis on building effective black organizations because restricted opportunities in mainstream organizations are so intractable? Or can African Americans finally follow European immigrants and assimilate into mainstream organizations with minimal ethnic distinction? Or, in line with what Triandis (1984) calls the principle of additive pluralism, can cultural gaps in organizations be best bridged by intercultural training where both groups add new dimensions to their experience without feeling less identified with their own culture? Each of these questions point to complexities in African American double consciousness, dual identity or bi-culturality in organizations. Along with other issues discussed in this chapter, these questions also await the attention of a new generation of I/O psychologists.

References

Allen, W. (1982). Race consciousness and achievement: Two issues in the study of graduate/professional students. *Integrated Education, 20*, 56-61.

Allen, W.R., & Farley, R. (1985). The shifting social and economic tides of Black America, 1950-1980. In R.H. Turner & J.F. Short (Eds.) *Annual review of sociology*. Palo Alto, CA: Annual Reviews, Inc.

Ash, P. (1972). Job satisfaction differences among women of different ethnic groups. *Journal of Vocational Behavior, 2*, 495-507.

Ashante, M.K. (1987). *The afrocentric idea*. Philadelphia, PA: Temple University Press.

Baker, L.J., & McCorry, J.J. (1976). *Black Americans in the political system*. Cambridge, MA: Winthrop.

Baldwin, J. (1990). Notes on an afrocentric theory of Black personality. *Western Journal of Black studies, 5*, 172-179.

Baldwin, J. (1991). African psychology: issues and synthesis. In R.L. Jones (Ed.), *Black psychology*. Berkeley, CA: Cobb & Henry.

Barrett, G.V., & Bass, B.M. (1983). Cross-cultural issues in industrial and organizational psychology. In M.D. Dunnette (Ed.), *Handbook on industrial and organizational psychology* (pp. 1639-1686). Chicago: Rand McNally.

Bass, B. (1984). The black minority in high-technology organizations: Interpersonal relationships, management and supervision. *Symposium on minorities in high technology organizations* (Paper). Pensacola, FL: Office of Naval Research.

Beehr, T.A., & Newman, J.E. (1978). Job stress, employee health, and organizational effectiveness: A facet analysis, model, and literature review. *Personnel Psychology, 31,* 665-99.

Berndt, H.E. (1977). *New rulers in the ghetto: The community development corporation and urban poverty.* Westport, CT: Greenwood.

Berry, J.W. (1980). Introduction to methodology. In A.C. Triandis & J.W. Berry (Eds.), *Handbook on cross-cultural psychology* (Vol. 2). Boston, MA: Allyn & Bacon.

Berry, M.F., & Blassingame, J.W. (1982). *Long memory: The black experience in America.* New York: Academic Press.

Bielby, W.T. (1987). Modern prejudice and institutional barriers to equal employment for minorities. *Journal of Social Issues, 43,* 79-84.

Bloom, R., & Barry, J.R. (1967). Determinants of work attitudes among Negroes. *Journal of Applied Psychology, 51,* 291-94.

Bowman, P.J. (1977). *Motivational dynamics and achievement of urban black students: A situational relevant-path goal expectancy approach.* Unpublished dissertation, University of Michigan.

Bowman, P.J. (1984a). A discouragement-centered approach to studying unemployment among black youth: Hopelessness, attributions and psychological distress. *International Journal of Mental Health, 13,* 68-91.

Bowman, P.J. (1984b). A path-goal approach to minority success in organizations: Implications for entry into high-technology roles. *Symposium on minorities in high technology organizations* (Paper). Pensacola, FL: Office of Naval Research.

Bowman, P.J. (1985). Black fathers and the provider role: Role strain, informal coping resources and life hapiness. In A.W. Boykin (Ed.), *Empirical research in Black psychology,* (pp. 9-19). Washington, DC: National Institute for Mental Health.

Bowman, P.J. (1988). Post-industrial displacement and family role strains: Challenges to the black family. In P. Voydanof, & L.C. Majka (Eds.), *Families and economic distress.* Newbury Park, CA: Sage.

Bowman, P.J. (1989a). Research perspectives on black men: Role strain and adaptation across the adult life cycle. In R.L. Jones (Ed.), *Black adult development and aging* (pp. 117-150). Berkeley, CA: Cobb & Henry.

Bowman, P.J. (1989b). Marginality, ethnicity and family life quality: National study of black husband-fathers. In H.P. McAdoo (Ed.), *Family ethnicity and diversity.* Newbury Park, CA: Sage.

Bowman, P.J. (1991a). Toward a cognitive adaptation theory of role strain: Relevance of research on black fathers. In R.L. Jones (Ed.), *Advances in black psychology.* Berkeley, CA: Cobb & Henry.

Bowman, P.J. (1991b). Psychological expectancy: Theory and measurement of black populations. In R.L. Jones (Ed.) *Handbook of tests and measurements for black populations.* Berkeley, CA: Cobb & Henry.

Bowman, P.J., & Howard, C.S. (1985). Race-related socialization, motivation and academic achievement: A study of black youth in three-generation families. *Journal of Academy of Child Psychiatry, 24,* 134-41.

Bowman, P.J., & Jackson, J.S., Hatchett, S.J., & Gurin, G. (1982). Joblessness and discouragement among black Americans. *Economic Outlook U.S.A.,* 85-88.

Boykin, A.W. (1983). The academic performance of African-American children. In J. Spence (Ed.), *Achievement and achievement motives*. San Francisco, CA: Freeman.

Boykin, A.W., & Toms, F.D. (1985). Black child socialization: A conceptual framework (pp. 33-51). In H.P. McAdoo & J.L. McAdoo (Eds.), *Black children: Social, educational and parental environments*. Newbury Park, CA: Sage.

Braddock, J., & McPartland, J.M. (1987). Social science evidence and affirmative action policies. *Journal of Social Issues, 43*, 133-43.

Cascio, W.F. (1984). Contributions of I/O psychologists to the bottom line. *The Industrial Organizational Psychologist, 31*, 21-24.

Cole, J. (1970). Black culture: Negro, black and nigger . . . *Black Scholar, 1*, 40-43.

Cook, S.W. (1987). Behavior-change implications of low involvement in an issue. *Journal of Social Issues, 43*, 105- 12.

Drasgow, F. (1984). Biased test items and differential validity. *Psychological Bulletin, 92*, 526-31,

DuBois, W.E.B. (1903). *The souls of black folk*. Greenwich, CT: Fawcett (republished 1961).

Dunnette, M.D. (1983) *Handbook of industrial and organizational psychology*. Chicago: Rand McNally.

Farley, R., & Allen, W.R. (1987) *The color line and the quality of black American life*. New York: Sage Foundation.

Feagin, J.R. (1987). Changing black Americans to fit a racist system. *Journal of Social Issues, 43*, 85-89.

Ficker, V.B., & Graves, H.S. (1978). *Social science and the urban crisis*. New York: Macmillan.

Fiske, S.T. (1987). On the road: Comment on the cognitive stereotyping literature on Pettigrew and Martin. *Journal of Social Issues, 42*, 113-118.

French, J.R.P., Jr., Caplan, R.D., & Van Harison, R. (1982). *The mechanism of job stress and strain*. Chichester, England: Wiley.

Giamartino, G.A., & Wandersman, A. (1983). Organizational climate correlates of viable urban black organizations. *American Journal of Community Psychology, 5*, 525-41.

Gilkes, C.T. (1982). Successful rebellion professionals: The Black women's professional identity and community commitment. *Psychology of Women Quarterly, 6*, 289-311.

Glazer, N. & Moyniham, D.P. (1975) *Ethnicity: Theory and experience*. Cambridge: Harvard University Press.

Grant, D.L., & Bray, D.W. (1970). Validation of employment tests for telephone company installation and repair occupations. *Journal of Applied Psychology, 54*, 7-14.

Green, L.A. (1982). A learned helplessness analysis of problems confronting the black community. In S. Turner, & R. Jones (Eds.), *Behavioral modification in black populations: Psychosocial issues and empirical findings* (73-93). New York: Plenum.

Gurin, P., & Epps, E. (1974). *Black consciousness, identity and achievement*. New York: John Wiley & Sons.

Hale, J. (1982). *Black children: Their roots, culture and learning styles*. Provo, UT: Brigham Young University Press.

Harding, V. (1981) *There is a river: The struggle for freedom in America.* New York: Harcourt-Brace-Jonavich.

Herskovits, M.J. (1935). Social history of the Negro. In C. Murchinson (Ed.), *A handbook of social psychology,* (207-267). Worchester, MA: Clark University Press.

Hill, R. (1971). *The strengths of black families.* New York: Emerson Hall.

House, J.S. (1981). *Work stress and support.* Reading, MA: Addison-Wesley.

Hulin, C.L., & Drasgow, F., & Parsons, C.K. (1983). *Item response theory: Applications to psychological measurement.* Homewood, IL: Dow Jones-Irwin.

Ilgen, D.R., & Yontz, M. (1974). Factors affecting the evaluation and development of minorities in organizations. *Symposium on minorities in high technology organizations* (Paper). Pensacola, FL: Office of Naval Research.

Jackson, G. (1976). The African genesis of a black perspective in helping. *Professional psychology, 7,* 292-308.

Jaynes, G.F., & Williams, R.M (1989). *A common destiny: Blacks and American society.* Washington, DC: National Academy Press.

Kahn, R.L., Wolfe, D.M., Quinn, R.P., Snock, J.D., & Rosenthal, R.A. (1964). *Organizational stress: Studies in role conflict and ambiguity.* New York: Wiley.

Katz, I. (1970). Experimental studies of Negro-white relationships. In L. Berkowitz (Ed.), *Advances in experimental social psychology* (Vol. 5.). New York: Academic Press.

Katz, I., & Benjamin, L. (1969). Effects of white authoritarianism in biracial work groups. *Journal of Abnormal and Social Psychology, 61,* 448-56.

Katz, I., Epps, E., & Axelton, L.J. (1964). Effects upon Negro digit-symbol performance of anticipated comparison with whites and with other Negroes. *Journal of Abnormal and Social Psychology, 69,* 77-83.

Katz, I., Greenbaum, G. (1963). Effects of anxiety, threat, and racial environment on task performance of Negro college students. *Journal of Abornmal and Social Psychology, 66,* 562-567.

Katzell, R.A., & Guzzo, R. (1983). Psychological approaches to productivity improvement. *American Psychologists, 38,* 468-72.

Karenga, M. (1982). *Introduction to black studies.* Los Angeles, CA: University of Sankore Press.

Kluegel, J.R., & Smith, E.R. (1982). Attitudes toward affirmative action: Effects of self-interest, racial affect and stratification beliefs on whites views. *Social Forces, 61,* 797—823.

Koehn, H.E. (1983). The post-industrial worker. *Personnel Management Journal, 12,* 244-48.

Landy, F.J., & Farr, J.L. (1980). Performance rating. *Psychological Bulletin, 87,* 72-107.

Lee, C.C. (1983). An investigation of athletic career expectations of high school student athletes. *Personnel and Guidance Journal, 61,* 544-47.

McGrath, J.E. (1983). Stress and behavior in organizations. In M.D. Dunnette (Ed.), *Handbook of industrial and organizational psychology* (pp. 1351-1396). Chicago: Rand McNally.

Milburn, N., & Bowman, P.J. (1990). Neighborhood involvement: Demographic and community embedment factors. In J.S. Jackson et al. (Eds.), *Black American life: Findings from a national survey*. Newbury Park, CA: Sage.

Miles, R.H., & Perreault, W.D. (1976). Organizational role conflict: Its antecedents and consequences. *Organizational Behavior and Human Performance, 17*, 19-44.

Millner, N. (1987). Hazards in the translation of research into remedial interventions. *Journal of Social Issues, 43*, 119-126.

Miner, J.B., & Brewer, J.F. (1983) The management of ineffective performance. In M.D. (Ed.), *Handbook of industrial and organizational psychology* (pp. 995-1030). Chicago: Rand McNally.

Morris, A. (1984). *Origins of the civil rights movement: Black communities organizing for change*. New York: Free Press.

Myrdal, G. (1944). *An American dilemma*. New York: McGraw-Hill (first edition 1944, Harper & Row).

Nacoste, R.W. (1987). Social psychology of affirmative action: The importance of process in policy analysis. *Journal of Social Issues, 43*, 127-32.

Nelsen, H.M., Yikley, Y.L., & Nelsen, A.K. (1971), *The black church in America*. New York: Basic Books.

Nobles, W. (1988). African-American family life: An instrument of culture. In H.P. McAdoo (Ed.), *Black families* (pp. 44-53). Newbury Park, CA: Sage.

Nobles, W. (1991). African philosophy: Foundations of black psychology, In R.L. Jones (Ed.), *Black psychology*. Berkeley, CA: Cobb & Henry

Parker, D.F., & DeCotiis, T.A. (1983). Organizational determinants of job stress. *Organizational Behavior and Human Performance, 32*, 160-77.

Ogbu, J.U. (1988). Black education: A cultural ecological perspective. In H.P. McAdoo (Ed.), *Black families* (pp. 169-184). Newbury Park, CA: Sage.

Onibokun, A.G. (1973). Urbanization in the emerging nations: A challenge for pragmatic comprehensive planning. *Planning Outlook, 13*, 52-66.

Pettigrew, T.F., & Martin J. (1987). Shaping the organizational context for black Americans. *Journal of Social Issues, 43*, 41-78.

Retraining displaced workers: Too little too late (1982). *Business Week*, July, 178-185.

Sailer, H.R., Schlacter, J., & Edwards, M.R. (1982). Stress: Causes, consequences, and coping strategies. *Personnel, 59*, 35-48.

Schul, F., & Anthony, W.P. (1978). Do black and white supervisory problem solving styles differ? *Personnel Psychology, 31*, 761-82.

Schultz, D.P., Schultz, S.E. (1986). *Psychology and industry today: An introduction to industrial and organizational psychology*. New York: Macmillan.

Sizemore, B.A. (1985). Pitfalls and promises of effective school research. *Journal of Negro Education, 54*, 269-88.

Slocum, J.W., & Strawser, R.H. (1972). Racial differences in job attitudes. *Journal of Applied Psychology, 56*, 28-32.

Smith, A.W. (1987). Racial trends and countertrends in American organizational behavior. *Journal of Social Issues, 43*, 91-94.

Smith, E.J. (1980). Profile of the black individual in the vocational literature. In R. Jones (Ed.), *Black psychology* (2nd ed). NY: Harper & Row.

Stanley, R.B., & Russell, J.E. (1987). Perspectives on vocational behavior 1986: A review. *Journal of Vocational Behavior, 31*, 111-173.

Staw, B.M. (1984). Organizational behavior: A review and reformulation of the field's outcome variables. *Annual review of psychology, 35*, 627-666.

Starbuck, W.H. (1983). Organizations and their environments. In M.D. Dunnette (Ed.), *Handbook of industrial and organizational psychology* (pp. 1069-1124). Chicago: Rand McNally.

Sudarkasa, N. (1988). Interpreting the African heritage in Afro-American family organizations. In H.P. McAdoo (Ed.), *Black families*, 27-43. Newbury Park, CA: Sage.

Summers, L.S. (1983). Stress management in business organizations. Part II: Research. *The industrial-organizational psychologist, 20*(3), 29-33.

Thayer, P.W. (1983). Industrial/organizational psychology: Science and application. In C.J. Scheirer, & A.M. Rogers (Eds.), *The G. Stanley Hall lecture series* (Vol. 3). Washington, D.C.: American Psychological Association.

Triandis, H.C. (1984). Notes on recruitment, selection, and retention of minorities in organizations. *Symposium on minorities in high technology organizations*. Pensacola, FL: Office of Naval Research.

Tuttle, T.C. (1983). Organizational productivity: A challenge for psychologists. *American Psychologist, 38*, 479-486.

Wilson W.J. (1987). The truly disadvantaged: The inner city, underclass, and public policy. Chicago: University of Chicago Press.

Weaver, C.N. (1978). Black-white correlates of job satisfaction. *Journal of Applied Psychology, 63*, 255-58.

Wexley, K.N. (1984). Personnel training. *Annual review of psychology, 35*, 519-51.

Yearwood, L. (1980). *Black organizations: Issues and survival techniques*. Lanham, MD: University Press of America.

Yetman, N.R., & Steele, C.H. (1975). *Majority and minority: The dynamics of racial and ethnic relations*. Boston, MA: Allyn & Bacon.

Young, V. (1974). A black American socialization pattern. *American Ethnologist, 1*, 405-413.

The African Genesis of the Black Perspective in Helping

Gerald G. Jackson

This article suggests that African Americans can be understood best from a design that recognizes a cultural connection to Africa, and it shows, through the illustration of specific strategies, that the more advantageous treatment of black clients would be based on an Africentric perspective.

A problem for many African American people in America is not that they are without a culture and ancestry, but rather that their culture and African cultural heritage is rejected by the dominant cultural group (C. Thomas, 1973), who by their rejection imply that those unlike them are inferior, deprived, and/or culturally disadvantaged (Vontress, 1969). A more exemplary perspective, from the standpoint of African Americans, would be to recognize that they are not disadvantaged per se but are often placed in situations in which they are at a disadvantage (Simpkins, Gunnings, & Kearney, 1973), and therefore to appreciate their differences (Wittmer, 1971). One barrier, it is hypothesized, to the realization of the goal of multiculturalism, is the exclusive use of what is termed the Eurocentric cultural perspective. A second-order problem for mental health professionals who may have sensed a problem is, until lately, the absence of another cultural framework that would serve to place the problem in relief. The emergence of idiosyncratic systems of mental health in African countries will be used to serve as a link to the solution of certain problems in contemporary America. As a means, therefore, of assisting a range of professionals, this article presents the salient aspects of the two alleged cultural perspectives, and assesses the relative merits of each in addressing the needs of African American clients.

Basic Features of the European Perspective

The cornerstone of the European perspective is the drive to dichotomize. This predisposition emanates from Western culture (N. Smith, 1974) and is reinforced by a dichotomous interpretation of body functions which, in turn, introduces this drive into mental functions

This article is a revised version of an earlier publication.

(Pinderhughes, 1971). For example, Plato divided the human soul into two parts, the rational and the irrational (Nathan & Harris, 1975). To the rational soul, he ascribed leadership, immortality, and divinity and gave as its province the brain. Conversely, he attributed to the body the irrational soul and gave as its characteristics mortality and the base emotions of men. Centuries later, but in the same mold, Descartes postulated a sharp division between the mind and the physical world (Ruch, 1967). Descartes viewed human beings as uniquely different from other animals, a difference he attributed to their possession of a mind and a body, whereas, other animals, accordingly, only have bodies (Kendler, 1968). The upshot of dichotomism is a cultural approach that is cognitive, is a person-to-object orientation, and is individually focused (Nichols, 1974), or summarily speaking, one in which events are best understood when they can be counted and measured in quantifiable terms (Nichols, 1974b).

Another cultural attribute that facilitates the continuation of the problem of African Americans in receiving adequate services and camouflages the deleterious effects of the adoption of a dichotomous method of reasoning by Americans in general (e.g., Cleaver, 1968; Goodman, 1970), is fadism (Howe, 1973-1974). To elaborate, Kozol (1972) observed in the 1970s after the civil rights movement of the 1960s that the plight of the African American person is no longer regarded as pertinent or as crucial as such new fads as women's liberation or white ethnic groups, and he articulated how the shift in attention is characteristic of Americans. What is meant by this claim is not that women or white ethnic groups are not without legitimate grievances or special needs that have been blocked but that the needs of one group are shifted to another. Rather than expanding the total range of concerns and the allocation of resources, groups that are deemed deviant by society are placed in a competitive situation. A major problem evolving from this cultural propensity is that in many cases the basic problems of each group go unsatisfied.

Since the publication of the *Black perspective of Counseling* (Jackson, 1976a) this writer has learned that there are several Eurocentric beliefs and assumptions that have obviated the adoption of a black perspective. These beliefs are that humankind consists of well-defined races, as opposed to cultural enclaves; that some races are superior to others; that superior races should rule over the inferior ones; and that attempts should be made to insure that racial-superiority beliefs are put into practice. The corollary of these beliefs are the following assumptions: (1) The world dominance of Europeans is the consequence of the evolution of the most fit to lead (social Darwinism). (2) Africans were an uncivilized group before Europeans enlightened them (colonialism). (3) The behaviors, beliefs, and attitudes of African Americans are solely the consequence of an Euro-American cultural and philosophical tradition (dichotomism). (4) African culture and philosophy had no redeeming qualities upon which to base the solution of contemporary problems (ignominious past hypothesis). (5) The Western tradition of Cartesian logic is the only rational means for interpreting reality; therefore, it is the only basis upon which a system can be devised for counseling African Americans.

Consistent with the preceding assumptions, the black perspective of counseling confined its analysis to Anglo-American history and focused its criticisms and recommendations on problems of immediate importance to African Americans. Many African American writers alleged that the source of the problem of counseling African Americans was the basic orientation of counselors to focus on the individual, to the exclusion of environmental factors, and to rest their practices on racist beliefs about African Americans. As a consequence, it was proposed that an environmentally focused model be used with African Americans. Similarly, counselors and counselor-educators were instructed to change their culturally deprived definition of African Americans, system-maintenance concept of counseling goals and objectives, Anglo-American way of interacting with African Americans, and middle-class expectations and beliefs about intelligence, language, family, personality development, community, and American society.

Exponents of a black perspective of counseling reacted to the implicit assumption in the Eurocentric outlook of white racial superiority and countered that they were superior to other racial groups in providing counseling and training for African Americans, had a subculture upon which to predicate counseling theories and practices, and should, as a result of these sui generis factors, be in positions of authority.

Despite the claims made by a number of African American writers, no encompassing theory or orientation emerged from their works to explain behavioral and cognitive differences among African Americans and Euro-Americans, Hispanic-Americans, and African and Caribbean immigrants. The trend has been to be either eclectic in the advocacy of counseling theories and techniques or, in the case of African American behavior therapists, to endorse overtly the theory and techniques of behavior therapy and suggest covertly that the user employ an African American cultural referent.

The overall failure of a black perspective to devise a counseling system that included the African American social experience and subculture was not a manifestation of deficient analytical skills but the result of the temporal framework used and the consequent tendency to be reactive instead of proactive in thrust. In short, the Eurocentric approach and its black perspective derivative both lacked a system that would allow for an appreciation of group differences, the centrifugal force in counseling African Americans.

As an alternative, in this chapter an attempt will be made to illustrate how an Africentric framework facilitates an appreciation of group differences. Its assumptions are that cross-cultural counseling has not occurred with African Americans, because Euro-Americans and a sizable proportion of African American counselors are unaware of the cross-cultural aspects of the process of counseling African Americans; that even when they are conscious of behavioral differences between African Americans and Euro-Americans, their racial socialization and academic training constrains them to perceive the physical attributes and cognitive style of African Americans in a negative, unefficacious, or romantic way; that there is an African American cognitive style, and it is based, in part, on the continuation of an African ethos that must be recognized as legitimate; and that there is no traditional Euro-American school of counseling or psychotherapy that can be applied uniformly to all African Americans.

In general, an Africentric way of thinking went beyond the crystallization of a black perspective of counseling (Jackson, 1976a). It opened the door to an Africentric psychology (Jackson, 1976b), upon which to sustain a theory of counseling and psychotherapy (Jackson, 1976b), and provided a framework to assess extant systems and approaches (Jackson, 1976b, 1979b). Correlatively, it provided new interpretations and definitions of black self-concept, personality, family, mental health research, psychopathology (Jackson, 1976b, 1982), and furnished alternative explanations for the success of certain approaches and techniques with African Americans (Jackson, 1972a, 1972b). Most central to the underlying issue of racial difference in counseling, it provided a framework for interpreting clashes between African American and Euro-American professionals along cultural rather than racial lines (Jackson, 1979c).

As a backdrop, several Africentric theorists have made the following observations of differences between African Americans and Euro-Americans. They noted that African Americans tended to perceive events as a whole visual picture (symbolic imagery) whereas Euro-Americans tended to perceive reality through a theoretical statement that broke down things and people into parts (discursive reasoning). African Americans tended to prefer inferential reasoning, based upon contextual, interpersonal, and historical factors; and Euro-Americans preferred either inductive or deductive reasoning, based upon a belief in the permanency of the stimuli. African Americans preferred to approximate space, numbers, and time, based upon an affectively based dialectical system, which was in contrast to Euro-Americans, who tended to prefer precision, based upon a concept of one-dimensional time and objective space between individuals. African Americans preferred to focus on people and their activities, based upon a nature-centric orientation and human nature norm, as opposed to Euro-Americans, who showed a propensity toward things, based upon a Eurocentric orientation and middle-class, male, Caucasian norms. African Americans, based upon an axiology of cooperation, preservation of life, affiliation, and collective responsibility, had a comparatively keener sense of justice and were quicker to analyze it and perceive injustice than were Euro-Americans, based upon their valuation of competition, conflict, control of life, ownership, and individual rights. African Americans were viewed as relatively more altruistic and concerned about the next person, based upon an ontology of spiritual essence, collectivism, interdependence, and oneness of being, than were Euro-Americans, based upon their belief in material essence, individualism, independence, and control of nature. African Americans, based upon an epistemology of affect, immersion in experience, flexibility, and complementarity of differences, preferred novelty, freedom, and personal distinctiveness to a greater degree than did Euro-Americans, based upon their belief in object-measure, observation of experience, rigidity, and duality of differences. Finally, African Americans, based upon a multimodal definition of the communication process, were more proficient in nonverbal communications and were less word dependent than were Euro-Americans (ebonics versus standard English).

The genesis of the preceding group differences is revealed in C. Diop's (1974) "Two Cradle Theory" of cultural differences between Aryans and Africans. He theorized that each group had distinguishable cultural differences based upon climatic and physical environment factors. Aryans evolved a patriarchal system that consisted of the suppression of women, materialistic religion, sin and guilt, xenophobia, the tragic drama, city-state, individualism, pessimism, and a propensity for war. In contrast, Africans had a less harsh climate, and it fostered a matriarchal system that consisted of the freedom of women, religious idealism, the tale as a literary form, no concept of sin, xenophilia, the territorial state, social collectivism, optimism, and a desire for peace.

Rather than accept the cultural differences, J. Kovel's (1970) research revealed that Europeans rejected African culture and the physical characteristics of Africans. J. Hodge, D. Struckmann, and L. Trost (1975) took the notion of white racism a step further and showed how it was the consequence of a Western philosophical system. Mental health theoreticians and practitioners, as the work by C. Willie, B. Kramer, and B. Brown (1973) documents, endorsed, supported, and advanced the supposition that African Americans had no culture other than that which they gained from exposure to Europeans. The field of counseling, the black backlash in mental health, and the emergence of a black perspective of counseling illustrate and attest to the extension of the non-European cultural-antecedent hypothesis to their theories, perceptions, and practices with African Americans (Jackson, 1977, 1979a).

Expression in Mental Health

Consistent with the cultural attributes noted above, the doctrine of color-blindness suggests that we should avoid the use of skin color differences in our work as mental health professionals (Fibush, 1965; Siegel,1970; Trueblood, 1960); however, the obvious signs of a racial schism among mental health professions suggest that this concept, along with the Eurocentric perspective of mental health, may have out-lived its usefulness (G.G. Jackson, 1979). To illustrate, Comer (1970) in a discussion of the stimuli of the black backlash in mental health, inad-vertently disclosed the range of concerns that can be said to characterize the white backlash. He revealed, for instance, that some researchers viewed the charges against white researchers in the black community as unjust (e.g., Lightfoot & Foster, 1970; Sue & Sue, 1972; C. Thomas, 1974; R. Williams, 1974b) and as part of a ploy on the part of certain blacks to gain control of research and intervention program money. Others, he summarized, viewed the negative attitude toward testing (e.g., G.D. Jackson, 1975) and research (e.g., Taylor, 1973; Nobles, Note 3) as an understandable but excessive and self-defeating reaction to the histori-cal black-white relationship. Finally, some felt the reaction was healthy, and in some cases just, but one which would pass in time as African American people gained more success in all phases of American life (cf. Carpenter, 1975). Cobbs (1970) termed the white backlash the "climate of retaliation" and suggested that psychiatrists and other professionals deny their culpability in the existence of white racism by assuming that they are exempt. In his opinion though, it is precisely because so many people assume they are excused that the climate of retaliation is present in the United States today. Furthermore, for those who may not be cognizant of the split, commencing in the 1970s were distinct associa-tions of African American psychiatrists (C. Pierce, 1970), social workers (Sanders, 1970), psychologists (R. Williams, 1974a), and counselors (Daley, 1972), and there were a number of publications advocating a black psychology (Mosby, 1972; White, 1970) or African psychology (Cedric X, McGee, Nobles, & Luther X, 1975; Nobles, 1972, 1973, 1974a, 1974b; Luther X, 1974) as well as journals that highlight the African American experience in mental health (e.g., including their inaugural dates, *Black Books Bulletin*, Fall 1971; *Black Scholar*, November 1969; *Jour-nal of Afro-American Issues*, November 1972; *Journal of Black Psychology*,

August 1974; *Journal of Black Studies*, September 1970; *Journal of Non-White Concerns*, October 1972).

Cultural Differences as the Antecedent

One major obstacle in the struggle to cement differences is the presumption that African American people in America are without a cultural antecedent to the "Black" experience (cf. Clark, 1970; Sanders, 1971) in the United States (e.g., Brody, 1966; Glazer & Moynihan, 1963; Myrdal, 1944). This cultural bias has served generally to obviate the possibility that the problems associated with providing mental health services to them may be grounded in differing cultural perspectives. One cultural perspective, for example, that was not destroyed through the machination of American slavery (cf. Blassingame, 1972; Hersovits, 1968), and is therefore rooted in traditional West African culture, portrayed a positive image of African Americans (Nobles, 1974b) that is unlike the Eurocentric perspective in which blackness was associated with negative factors (Jordan, 1968; Kovel, 1970; Schwartz & Disch, 1970). Reinforcing the presumption alluded to, and the faulty inferences made from the premise that African American people are without cultural links to Africa, is the absence of an African counterpart to the mental health movement in the United States. Fortunately, the emergence of an African American mental health movement in many West African nations today opens up this dormant area of inquiry and heuristically suggests a new conceptual framework for assessing a number of perennial concerns.

The African Basis of the Africentric Approach

What is frequently eclipsed from Westerner's designed purview is the alternative reality that not all people construe external events in dichotomous terms (cf. N. Smith, 1974). Lienhardt (1961) found, for example, that in Africa the Dinka tribe had no concept of "mind"; that is, they did not compartmentalize or posture a mediating agent between the individual and his external world (N. Smith, 1974). Interpreted from a Eurocentric perspective, this approach was dismissed by associating it with "primitive" people (e.g., Bellah, 1964). In contrast, what is illustrative of the diunital aspect of the Africentric approach (Dixon & Foster, 1971) in focusing on human behavior and external events is partially revealed in the assertion by Lichtenstein (1971) that neither the behavioral view of external causation of behavior nor the phenomenological view of the psychological event contained within the person would be fathomable to such a man. The other part of this cultural perspective is revealed in the criticism by Nobles (1973) of the approaches used to explain the formation of black self-concepts. In addition to the traditional view of self-concept development, he criticized both the behavioral and phenomenological approaches as a means of explaining the development of a black self-concept and postulated a view based on an African philosophical frame of reference.

In the ensuing discussion, it can be seen that, in addition to maintaining a perception of the universe in which opposites are united, the Africentric approach has been consonant with the African view of the primacy of the group, authoritarianism, and a number of ramifications of these basic cultural attributes. Of immediate concern is the depiction of the African perspective and how the emerging definition of mental health is an outgrowth of the culture.

Philosophical Base of an African Perspective

One paradox that adherents of the Eurocentric perspective may detect is the diunital interpretation of guidance in an African milieu. Guidance in Africa, according to Esen (1972), involves helping people to consolidate their roots in the traditions that give them their identity and concomitantly involves helping them move without guilt and excessive conflict toward new perceptions of themselves and their role in a rapidly changing society or one in which the transition has resulted in a number of sociopsychological problems (Lambo, 1966). It is viewed in general then as neither the total acceptance of one way of life or another, but as a composite. Similarly, Hunt (1974) pointed out that the black perspective entails neither the elevation of the cognitive nor the affective domain but the recognition and acceptance of the strengths of both. In operation, it allows one or the other domain to take primacy depending on the situation. Philosophically speaking, Esen noted that the guidance movement in the United States was influenced substantially by neorealism, which posits that there is an objective outer world, filled with the common objects of experience that are there whether we are aware of them or not. In this scheme, according to Esen, we are capable of experiencing these objects through the senses and may alter the situation as we like through the kinds of decisions we make or the method of action we choose to take. Ultimately, the nature and outcome of our intervention is dependent on the types of choices and actions brought to bear on the real situation. In Esen's estimation, it is this philosophical viewpoint that has resulted in the belief among guidance people that the significance and central facet of objective reality is the person. Therefore, to effect change in this reality, the person must first become aware of self (cognition) and then do things (decision and action), which is the reason why in Western thought the individual is the focus of guidance endeavors. Furthermore, in Esen's assessment, this orientation explains why the task of the counselor is to stimulate the process of cognition and to facilitate meaningful decisions and actions.

In contrast, in African society the group, which may include the family or clan, is the reality (e.g., Nobles, 1972, 1974b). Within this framework, the individual exists so that the group might survive and his or her individualism is realized via the prosperity of the group (Nobles, 1973). Asserting the interest of the individual above those of the group would be deviant or undesirable behavior in this context.

Last, self-actualization is the accrual of authority to the group's accredited spokesman, who is regarded as the conscience of the people. Authority then, rather than reason or free choice, becomes the guiding principle of the individual's life. This deemphasis of rationalism, individual rights, and roles should not be construed as abrasive though, because in contrast to the impersonal or person-to-object norm of behavior in the United States (Slater, 1970), the African perspective is balanced by a form of interaction called the "care syndrome" (Esen, 1973). Thus, child rearing, for example, is marked by a comparatively high degree of physical contact, and the responsibility for raising children is shared between the biological parents and other members of the family (Elam, 1968; Esen, 1973).

Role of the Helper

The role of the helper is one example of the African cultural perspective in practice. As a guideline to the African's actions, it has been noted that he or she is more likely to have passed through an authoritarian, other-directed upbringing, and consequently will probably see professionals as authority figures. Similarly, caring is interpreted as including the judicious manipulation of the environment, which may entail botanical and pharmacological empiricism as well as practices akin to family therapy or community mental health (Edgeron, 1971; Laosebikan, 1973). Furthermore, it is presumed that the frequent involvement in the counseling process of the significant others in the client's life is essential, because to proceed otherwise, it is felt, would be to encourage a client to make self-centered decisions without regard for the feelings of his or her family. As a result of this belief, it is stressed that the professional's mission is to encourage the client to take into account the significant others in his or her life during the process of decision making. In fact, the success of the "witch doctor" (Lambo, 1964) has been related to the patient's familiarity with the treatment environment, the presence of another member of the family, and an open-door policy (Laosebikan, 1973).

Approach to Helping

To engage an African in counseling, in contrast to the Eurocentric perspective of mental health in the United States, it has been suggested that a professional will need to go out and bring in for counseling those who may have problems but are either unaware that they do or are for some reason unwilling to refer themselves (Esen, 1973). Contacted in this manner, it is asserted, Africans are far less likely to resent this as an interference in their private affairs because situations corresponding to this are an everyday occurrence in African family life. The professional, according to reports, will also find the initial stage of counseling relatively easy because of the care syndrome or the desire to want to care for others and the reciprocal expectation that others will want to care for you.

In terms of techniques, group approaches are advocated over dyadic methods because they coincide more with a group orientation, but the latter is not ruled out as a possibility and this flexibility reflects the overriding presence of the Africentric approach. When dyads are used, a directive approach is viewed as more appropriate (Olaoye, 1974). The "do-it-yourself" aspect of the nondirective approach is generally seen as threatening to the client and may result in the client's withdrawal. More specifically, psychoanalysis as a form of treatment and personality theory are not viewed as suitable in an African setting (Laosebikan, 1973). First of all, and in contrast to the Eurocentric approach, the ascription of causes to elements beyond the African person's control, it has been asserted, encourages him or her to see as useless the implicit demand of psychoanalysis to be introspective and soul searching (Prince, 1960). Second, this approach has been faulted for being inconsistent with the traditional role organization of African societies (Laosebikan, 1973). On the other side of the therapeutic continuum, even the behavior therapy approach is viewed as needing extensive modification in an African cultural milieu; however, unlike psychodynamic systems, it is seen as having a number of distinct advantages (Laosebikan, 1973).

Parallels Between the Afro and African Perspectives

Although the black perspective in mental health is still in an embryonic stage of development (e.g., G.G. Jackson, 1977), its derivation from an African framework is lucid. One conspicuous manifestation of the transmittal of the "care syndrome" is Paul Smith's (1974) assertion that counseling was a part of black heritage and his citation of such figures as David Walker, Henry Garnet, Denmark Vessey, and Harriet Tubman as examples of persons who participated in the counseling process by attempting to assist people to think, feel, and do things directed toward their problem-solving goals. Clearly then, the ego ideal from the Africentric perspective is preferably black (e.g., W. Cross, 1971), whereas from a Eurocentric perspective it is white (e.g., Kennedy, 1952; Shane, 1960). Less discernible, possibly, is the parallel ascription of power to the group. Another is a recognition and appreciation of strengths possessed by African American people and their cultural mode of expression. For example, strengths have been reported in the black family (Fibush, 1965; Hays & Mindel, 1973; Hill, 1971; Nobles, 1974a), client (R. Brown, 1973; G.G. Jackson, 1972a; Phillips, 1961; Stikes, 1972), and professionals that had been heretofore neglected because they were not found to a high degree among whites. In addition, these strengths, emanate from West African culture and explain, to a degree, why African American people could endure the atrocities of the slave system and survive their double bind in America. As a corollary, the delivery of mental health services has been defined in terms of this Africentric ideal (A. Cross, 1974; Denmark & Trachtman, 1973; Howley, 1972; G.G. Jackson, 1974; Jenkins, 1969; Kerr, 1972; W. Pierce, 1972; C. Thomas, 1972; Whitaker, 1972). Thus, one view of service delivery pictures the ideal professional as an African American person who embraces the Africentric perspective in the use of techniques and in charting treatment goals (W. Banks, 1972; Taylor, 1973). A second view advocates groups modeled on African American culture (Toldson, 1973) and asserts a comparative advantage to all-African American therapy groups (Brayboy, 1971; Brayboy & Marks, 1968; Carter & Dunston, 1973; Davis, Sharfstein, and Owens, 1974; O. Smith and Gundlach, 1974; Suggs, 1975). Similarly, another view of service delivery incorporates the African American aesthetic (e.g., Cedric X, McGree, Nobles, & Luther X, 1975) into dyadic and group treatments (Toldson & Pasteur, 1972; 1975).

Another way of demonstrating the connection between West African society and the development of an Africentric perspective in mental health in the United States is to highlight a definition by exponents of a Africentric perspective of the role of the helper and the recommended approach to helping.

Role of the Helper

Mindful of the synthesis of hereditary and environmental factors in the mental health of the individual and the central importance of the group, professionals have been charged with providing successful experiences for African American clients, because only by repeated success, increasing competence, and group-built self-esteem, will they be equipped to reach the point at which they are able to ignore minor slights (C.T. Williams, 1949). In the same vein, it has been deemed essential for African American clients to be centrally involved in counseling programs (Cassel, 1969), and consequently it is recommended to professionals that they perceive their African American clients as people with emerging power and influence (Charnofsky, 1971). For example, Record (1961) suggested that in order to develop counseling programs that are consistent with the underlying values of a democratic society, minority pupils must become effective participants in, as well as critics of, that school, community, and society throughout which they encounter repeated instances of prejudices and discrimination. This view of reality, he felt, should be the guiding principle from which specific programs are developed.

Illustrative of the cultural rather than racial bent of this perspective, to accomplish the above objectives it has been suggested that: (a) African American professionals become involved in the African American community as a means of desensitizing the African American client to the role of the professional (Jones & Jones, 1970); (b) the racial understanding in white clients (Anderson & Love, 1973; Barham, Price, Esham, and Spradlin, 1974; Stern & MacLennan, 1974) and professionals (Bryson, Renzaglia, & Danish, 1974; A. Hilliard, 1974; Sedlacek & Brooks, 1973b) be increased; (c) models be used that focus on society and not the individual as the locus of the blame (Gilbert, 1974; E. Gordon, 1970; Gunnings & Simplins, 1972; Pinderhughes, 1966; R. Tucker & Gunnings, 1974). Furthermore, strategies for amending institutional racism (Sedlacek & Brooks, 1973a, 1973b) and the racism in the legal system (Hilliard, Dent, Hayes, Pierce, & Poussaint, 1974), which includes prisons (Johnson, 1974; Jones & Jones, 1972), have been advanced. This focus on the acceptance of African American culture as an antecedent to effective treatment includes, it will be seen, one's approach to helping as well.

Approach to Helping

As a prerequisite to working with African American clients, proponents of the Africentric perspective contend that professionals must abandon the doctrine of color blindness, the medical model, and psychoanalysis and include African American culture and the African American experience as treatment variables in the developed paradigms (L. Brown, 1951; Calnek, 1972; E. Gorson, 1970; Harper, 1973; G.G. Jackson, 1972b; G.G. Jackson & Kirschner, 1973; Shannon, 1970, 1973; Stikes, 1972; Toldson & Pasteur, 1972).

Comparable to the African perspective, the concept of client selection has been broadened to include seeking him or her out in their natural environment (J. Clarke, 1972; J. Gordon, 1965; Haeltenschwiller, 1971; P. Smith, 1971; C.G. Williams, 1974). It has also been suggested that the criterion of establishing appointments and the typical approach to structuring that calls for verbalization of the parameters of the interview (Overall & Aronson, 1963) be dropped (J. Gordon, 1965; Roghenberg, 1970; Vontress, Note 4). Once treatment has started, it has been recommended that the effects of discrimination be considered immediately (see Gochros, 1966) and that the client be assisted in gaining the fortitude to deal with the mechanisms of discrimination in the United States (Grier and Cobbs, 1971; Stikes, 1972; C.G. Williams, 1974); and to accomplish this goal it has been espoused (Toldson & Pasteur, 1972) that professionals must give instruction in African American ideology and cultural identity, which entails the social and political realities of existing symbiotically with the larger culture. Any other posture, it has been asserted, is merely another means of perpetuating the slavery of both blacks and whites—blacks to their victimized status and whites to their illusions of superiority (E. Barnes, 1972). Therefore, for many, a good prognosis for an African American client has been interpreted as the ability to bring change in the American system (Grier & Cobbs, 1971; Stikes, 1972; C.G. Williams, 1974), and so construed, success for the professional is measured against the reduction of racism in the larger system (Siegel, 1970). Last, one's professional mission becomes that of helping clients realize themselves through social involvement (M. Jackson & DePuydt, 1974). More popular exclusionary variables, which evolved from the primary one cited, are differences in language, values, education, income, housing, and culture in general. It is these secondary exclusionary factors that the visceral racist gives as excuses for conforming to the practices established to exclude African American people (Thalberg, 1973-1974) or to reinforce racial stereotypes. Aiding in the perpetuation of the inferior status of African American people is the Eurocentric cultural propensity to assess a person's worth, value, and dignity on the basis of his or her material wealth (Weber, 1930) and the kindred notion of the primacy of the individual, which can be seen in the idea of "rugged individualism" or "do-your-own thing" (cf. Luther X, 1974). In other words, things determine a person's worth and inferentially are interchangeable with human life (cf. Slater, 1970). In fact, Kovel (1970) observed that without the mystique of property, the entire system of dichotomizing and its concomitant freedom from moral restraints would all break down. Of greater importance in understanding the plight of African American people because of their skin color is Kovel's assertion that property in the modern Western matrix is "filthified" matter to be controlled and enjoyed without conscious guilt; therefore, the further the African American was subjected to the force of the economic market, the further the white could proceed in a quest for the guilt-free realization of his or her illimitable desires. Today, technology has supplanted the usefulness of African Americans as economic property (Yette, 1971), however, general acknowledgement of this possibility exists in a more disguised form. For example, Kohlberg (1968) indicated that a willful blindness to the abuse of African Americans in America is a powerful national trait, and Killens (1970) added that white Americans pretend that black Americans are invisible because the existence of them contradicts the protestations by Americans of freedom and human brotherhood.

The White Backlash in Helping

One implication of the adherence of a large proportion of African Americans to the Africentric approach to life and as a means of conveying dissatisfaction with the methods of allocating creature comforts was the emergence of a white backlash among mental health professions. In an earlier article on the subject Jackson (1979a) pointed out how this backlash aimed to perpetuate the belief in the inferiority of African Americans by: (a) attacking any virtues attributed to blackness of skin; (b) conducting studies whose conclusions found African Americans to be inferior to whites in terms of intellect, morality, or professionalism; (c) advancing Eurocentric cultural norms as the only means of determining normality, and (d) using methods of inquiry that resulted in negative conclusions about African Americans. In effect and as a consequence of therapists having views of African Americans that conform to the stereotypes held by Americans in general (e.g., Bloombaum, Yamamoto, and James, 1968), they have either translated these views into their practices or theories (Sanders, 1972; A. Thomas & Sillen, 1972; Willie, Kramer, & Brown, 1973) or cited secondary exclusionary variables as the cause of problems.

With specific reference to techniques and apparently in line with the African view of authority and the care syndrome, a directive approach, which mirrors these cultural factors, has been advocated over a nondirective one (Eltzroth, 1973; Harper & Stone, 1974; P. Smith, 1968; Stikes, 1972; S. Tucker, 1973; Vontress, 1968; C.G. Williams, 1974) and the use of peer relationships or of significant others in the process of treatment (R. Brown, 1973; G.G.Jackson, 1972a; Sue, 1983; Vontress, 1968). Techniques such as behavior modification have either been disclaimed (Cobb, 1984) in terms of how they have been used in the past on African American clients, or recommended for use only when under the control of African Americans (Bardo, Bryson, & Cody, 1974). In short, even though behavior modification techniques have been seen as progressive in comparison to psychodynamic ones (F. Harper, 1973; Hayes & Banks, 1972), professionals have been cautioned about using them if they are not familiar with African American culture (W. Banks, 1972; Calhoun & Wilson, 1974).

The preceding account, while giving some evidence of the need to introduce the Africentric approach into our thinking, did not delineate the cultural contingencies maintaining the practice of disregarding African American culture as a positive remedy to the mental health needs of African American clients. Without ferreting out these factors, American history reveals, the concerns raised will be superficially examined and remain perennial. Starting with a biological definition of races, in the ensuing account the process governing the failure of mental health professionals to appreciate the significance of the African American experience is delineated. Similarly, to allay fears that the advocacy of pro-African American endeavors are inferentially anti-white, two examples in which Africentricity was cast in a positive light are presented.

Mechanisms Perpetuating an Impasse

Within the species of homo sapiens, races are not divisible merely by skin color, but by urine, blood type, ability to taste certain substances, and fingerprints, and even when these factors are apprised, they apply only to breeding populations and not to individuals (Goldsby, 1971). There is no scientific evidence, therefore, to support an inference that whiteness of skin, which is caused by the inability to produce melanin (Welsing, 1974), invests such persons with innately superior abilities. Yet in the United States, skin color does connote differences in ability and behavior (J. Williams, 1964, 1966; Williams, Tucker, & Dunham, 1971), and these differences in perception reflect dichotomous thinking. For example, research discloses that the general view of African Americans in America is that they are genetically inferior, superstitious, lazy, emotional, musical, ignorant, very religious, physically dirty, criminal, sexually promiscuous, and sensitive (J. Banks, 1972; Bayton, 1941; Bayton, Austin, & Burke, 1965; Ogawa, 1971), or the opposite of whites, who are pictured as more intelligent, more virtuous, more sexually controlled by the mere fact of being white (Clark, 1970). The methods, however, by which Americans in general and mental health professions in particular act on these stereotypes are subtle. Because it is illegal to exclude persons because of their skin color or slave heritage, the primary exlusionary variable such as race have been attributed to the ascendancy of Freudian psychology (Goldstein, 1973), a lack of skill in dealing with such a factor (Meier, 1959), and economics (Bernard, 1953; Shane, 1960). In contrast, this heuristic article suggests that it may be more constructive to explore other cultural systems as a means of establishing a baseline to the problems discussed and to appreciate cultural differences when considering the behavior of African American people in the United States. In keeping with this aim, the following examples are intended as graphic proof of the existence of the Africentric approach in the field of mental health in which fadism, dichotomism and individualism are not its major ingredients. The article by Rutherford Stevens (1947) not only establishes one baseline of the problems in administering mental health services to African American clients but is also a precursor of many of the positions advocated by professionals embracing the Africentric approach today. First, Stevens noted, in contrast to the view that the skin color of a African American professional imposed an additional liability in therapy (Curry, 1963, 1964; Grier, 1967; Harrison & Butts, 1970; Layne, 1949), that being African American was an advantage in dealing with African American soldiers because he did not have to overcome those defenses which the European-American psychiatrist was constrained to evaluate more or less blindly in arriving at his conclusions (cf. W. Banks, 1972; J.J. Jackson, 1972; Vontress, 1973). Second, he observed that the problems experienced by European-American military psychiatrists in assisting African American soldiers with their emotional problems was the result of their socialization or the acceptance of many false concepts of African American people. Third, he cited psychosocial factors in the etiology of the emotional problems exhibited by African American soldiers. Fourth, he acknowledged that errors were being committed in diagnosing African Americans, and he attributed this failure to a lack of understanding of the peculiar life circumstances of African Americans by medical personnel (cf. Chess, Clark, & Thomas, 1953). Fifth, he indicated that a more favorable treatment outcome would occur if the therapist conveyed to the client that he understands the racial as well as the other aspects of his problems. In fact, an understanding and discussion of racial factors, Stevens suggested, had therapeutic value in itself, and he added that positive therapeutic results could be achieved in many instances by simply reeducating the patient to the nature of his complaints, increasing his self-esteem, and appealing to his self-pride and race pride. Sixth, he called on psychiatrists to study, understand, and aid in the prevention of racial problems by furthering the practice of the principles of a real democracy (cf. Green, 1974; Lide, 1973; Shannon, 1970).

Relatedly, Carter and Dunston (1973) reported that in developing a treatment model for African American college drug addicts, two important factors that had to be considered were being African American and being addicted to drugs. In the same vein, they noted that the poor success that psychiatrists have generally had with African American patients in the past was probably the result of a failure to recognize sociocultural issues as significant and the reference group for such individuals (cf. G.G. Jackson & Kirschner, 1973); therefore, in evaluating their client's drug abuse, Carter and Dunston gave consideration to these factors. They pointed out that while their clients could be distinguished from drug abusers in the ghetto, they shared with them, in contrast to European-American drug abusers of similar economic class, membership in a minority group and common experiences. Furthermore, according to Carter and Dunston, the addicts resented being compared to the European-American drug abuser because in their view, the alienation experienced by the European-American drug abuser was a "cop-out." According to the report, the most important characteristic of the therapy regimen was that the group leaders tried to help the African American addicts deal with the identity problems of being African American while functioning in a predominantly European-American society. It was also noted that the African American professionals served as role models, and the evidence cited for this claim was the observation that clients began to modify their forms of speech and style of dress and became involved in black social groups. These professionals, it was indicated, were able to convey the idea that although they, too, were minority members, they had refused to let this impede them from coping with the problems of race and reality. Finally, in a manner illustrative of the Africentric approach to treatment, the authors added that addicts fell into the same general psychiatric diagnostic categories as their white counterparts and presented similar diagnostic pictures.

Implications

The primary purpose of this chapter was to explore a new conceptual framework for interpreting the behavior of African American clients and professionals and consequently abate the racial schism between professionals on this matter. On a secondary level, it suggested that in order to appreciate the demand for more African American professionals (Boxley, Wagner, 1971; Boxley, Padilla, and Wagner, 1973; C. Pierce, 1968; Sager, Brayboy, & Waxenberg, 1972; Washington & Anderson,

1974), mental health models that include the strength of African American people and take into account the racism prevalent in the United States as an etiological factor, and an Africentric approach to life would have to be considered. Serious consideration of the tenets of this approach, it is proposed, would conceivably overcome the deficiencies inherent in a system whose models depict life as fundamentally a cognitive transaction (i.e., testing exaltation of the experimental design, "blank screen" professional, social aloofness) — as envisioned, professionalism would no longer be defined as emotional detachment in therapy, avoidance of social issues such as racism (e.g., Green, 1974), or the use of assessment instruments whose fundamental merit are that their results can be counted and measured. More profoundly, the new perspective would ameliorate the propensity to think in oppositional terms that have fostered problems in therapy for children, women, lower-class whites, and African American people, and in terms of conflicts among mental health professions, therapy camps, and between the public and the profession. The African approach is by definition a synthesis, and consequently it comes closest to the reality true professionals embrace but are frequently prevented from affirming by their encapsulation in professional jurisdictional lines, training, or financial considerations. The African approach suggests that the merits of professionals are not restricted to their skin color but include the ability to appreciate cultural differences, the use of culturally specific techniques, and the performance of a professional role that is in concert with this culture. Consequently, it is within the pale of white professionals to augment their understanding by reading journals that focus primarily on African American clients, taking part in interracial group encounters, and finally, possibly admitting to ignorance and doing an internship in a predominantly African American environment. Blackness of skin, on the other hand, is no immunity to ignorance; and consequently, African American professionals should not feel that there is a perfect correlation between being an African American and understanding African American clients. There is a tremendous difference between cognitively noting certain behavioral differences and successfully treating a person with skills based on another cultural perspective; and as this article suggests, the latter is a synthesis that is just emerging.

References

Anderson, N., & Love, B. (1973). Psychological education for racial awareness. *Personnel and Guidance Journal, 51,* 666-670.

Banks, J. (1972). Racial prejudice and the black self-concept. In J. Banks, & J. Grambs (Eds.), *Black self-concept: Implications for education and social science.* New York: McGraw-Hill.

Banks, W. (1972). The black client and the helping professional. In R. Jones (Ed.) *Black psychology* (1st ed). New York: Harper & Row.

Bardo, H., Bryson, S., & Cody, J. (1974). Black concern with behavior modification. *Personnel and Guidance Journal, 53,* 20-25.

Barham, C., Price, M., Esham, Y., & Spradlin, F. (1974). Implementation of a simulation of change model for elementary students. *Journal of Non-White Concerns, 2* 71-78.

Barnes, E. (1972). Counseling and the black student: The need for a new view. In R. Jones (Ed.), *Black psychology* (1st ed). New York: Harper & Row.

Bayton, J. (1941). The racial stereotypes of Negro college students. *Journal of Abnormal and Social Psychology, 36,* 97-102.

Bayton, J., Austin, L., & Burke, K. (1965). Negro perception of Negro and white personality traits. *Journal of Personality and Social Psychology, 1,* 250-253.

Bellah, R. (1964). Religious evolution. *American Sociological Review, 29,* 358-374.

Bernard, V. (1953). Psychoanalysis and members of minority groups. *Journal of American Psychoanalytic Association, 1,* 256-267.

Blassingame, J. (1972). *The slave community: Plantation life in the antebellum South.* New York: Oxford University Press.

Bloombaum, M., Yamamoto, J., & James Q. (1968). Cultural stereotyping among psychotherapists. *Journal of Consulting and Clinical Psychology, 32,* 99.

Boxley, R., Padilla, E., & Wagner, N. (1973). The desegregation of clinical psychology training. *Professional Psychology, 4,* 259-264.

Boxley, R., & Wagner, N. (1971). Clinical psychology training programs and minority groups: A survey. *Professional Psychology, 2,* 75-81.

Brayboy, T. (1971). The black patient in group therapy. *International Journal of Group Psychotherapy, 21,* 288-293.

Brayboy, T., & Marks, M. (1968). Transference variations evoked by racial differences. *American Journal of Psychotherapy, 22,* 474-480.

Brody, E. (1966). Psychiatry and prejudice. In S. Arieti (Ed.), *American handbook of psychiatry.* New York: Basic Books.

Brown, L. (1951). Psychoanalysis vs. the Negro people. *Masses and Mainstream, 4* 16-24.

Brown, R. (1973). Counseling blacks: Abstractions and reality. In C. Warnath (Ed.), *New directions for college counselors.* San Francisco: Jossey-Bass.

Bryson, R., Renzaglia, G., & Danish, S. (1974). Counseling black youth: A quest for legitimacy. *Journal of Non-white Concerns, 2,* 218-223.

Calhoun, J., & Wilson, W. (1974). Behavior therapy and the minority client. *Behavior Therapy, 5,* 299-302.

Calnek, M. (1972). Readers' comments. *Social Casework, 54,* 503.

Carpenter, J. (1975). Black actions and reactions to white racism in American education. *Journal of Black Psychology, 1,* 65-83.

Carter, J., & Dunston, J. (1973). Treating the black college drug abuser. *Journal of the National Medical Association, 65,* 127-131.

Cassel, R. (1969). Counseling the disadvantaged. *Education, 90,* 107.

Cedric X, McGee, P., Nobles, W., & Luther X. (1975). Voodoo or IQ: An introduction to African psychology. *Journal of Black Psychology, 2,* 9-29.

Charnofsky, S. (1971). Counseling for power. *Personnel and Guidance Journal, 49,* 351-357.

Chess, S., Clark, K., & Thomas, A. (1953). The importance of cultural evaluation in psychiatric diagnosis and treatment. *Psychiatric Quarterly, 27,* 102-114.

Clark, K. (1970). Black and white: The ghetto inside. In R. Guthrie (Ed.), *Being black.* San Francisco: Canfield Press.

Clarke, J. (1972). Student personnel work and minority groups. In T. O'Banion, & A. Thurston (Eds.), *Student development programs in the community junior college.* Princeton, N.J.: Prentice-Hall.

Cleaver, E. (1968). *Soul on ice.* New York: Delta Books.

Cobb, C. (1974). Behavior modification in the prison system. *Black Scholar, 5,* 41-44.

Cobbs, P. (1970). White mis-education of the black experience. *Counseling Psychologist, 2,* 22-27.

Comer, J. (1970). Research and the black backlash. *American Journal of Orthopsychiatry, 40* 8-11.

Cross, A. (1974). The black experience: Its importance in the treatment of black clients. *Child Welfare, 52,* 158-166.

Cross, W. (1971). The Negro-to-black conversion experience. *Black World, 7,* 13-27.

Curry, A. (1963). Some comments on transference when the group therapist is Negro. *International Journal of Group Psychotherapy, 23,* 363-365.

Curry A. (1964). The Negro worker and the white client. *Social Casework, 45,* 131-136.

Daley, T. (1972). Life ain't been no crystal stair. *Personnel and Guidance Journal, 50,* 491-496.

Davis, M., Sharfstein, S., & Owens, M. (1974). Separate and together: All-black therapy group in the white hospital. *American Journal of Orthopsychiatry, 44,* 19-25.

Denmark, F., & Trachtman, J. (1973). The psychologist as counselor in college 'high risk' programs. *Counseling Psychologist, 4,* 87-92.

Dixon, V., & Foster, B. (1971). *Beyond black or white.* Boston: Little Brown.

Edgerton, R. (1971). A traditional African psychiatrist. *Southwestern Journal of Anthropology, 27,* 259-278.

Elam, H. (1968). Psycho-social development of the African child. *Journal of the National Medical Association, 60,* 104-109.

Eltzroth, M. (1973). Vocational counseling for ghetto women with prostitution and domestic service backgrounds. *Vocational Guidance Quarterly, 22,* 32-39.

Esen, A. (1972). A view of guidance from Africa. *Personnel and Guidance Journal, 50,* 792-298.

Esen, A. (1973). The care syndrome: A resource for counseling in Africa. *Journal of Negro Education, 42,* 205-212.

Fibush, E. (1965). The white worker and the Negro client. *Social Casework, 36,* 271-277.

Gilbert, G. (1974). The role of social work in black liberation. *Black Scholar, 6,* 16-23.

Glazer, N., & Moynihan, D. (1963). *Beyond the melting pot.* Cambridge, Mass.: M.I.T. Press.

Gochros, J. (1966). Recognition and use of anger in Negro clients. *Social Work, 11,* 28-34.

Goldsby, R. (1971). *Race and races.* New York: Macmillan.

Goldstein, H. (1973). *Social work practice: A unitary approach.* Columbia, S.C.: University of South Carolina Press.

Goodman, P. (1970). *New reformation.* New York: Random House.

Gordon, E. (1970). Perspectives on counseling and other approaches to guided behavioral change. *Counseling Psychologist, 2,* 105-114.

Gordon, J. (1965). Project cause, the federal anti-poverty program, and some implementations of subprofessional training. *American Psychologist, 20,* 334-343.

Green, R. (1974). The social responsibility of psychology. *Journal of Black Psychology, 1,* 25-29.

Grier, W. (1967). When the therapist is Negro: Some effects on the treatment process. *American Journal of Psychiatry, 123,* 1587-1591.

Grier, W., & Cobbs, P. (1972). *Jesus bag.* New York: McGraw-Hill.

Gunnings, T., & Simpkins, G. (1972). A systemic approach to counseling disadvantaged youth. *Journal of Non-White Concerns, 1,* 4-8.

Haeltenschwiller, D. (1971). Counseling college students in special programs. *Personnel and Guidance Journal, 50,* 29-35.

Harper, F. (1973). What counselors must know about the social sciences of black Americans. *Journal of Negro Education, 42,* 109-116.

Harper, F., & Stone, W. (1974). Toward a theory of transcendent counseling with blacks. *Journal of Non-White Concerns, 2,* 191-196.

Harrison, P., & Butts, H. (1970). White psychiatrists' racism in referral practices to black psychiatrists. *Journal of National Medical Association, 62,* 278-282.

Hayes, W., & Banks, W. (1972). The nigger box or a redefinition of the counselor's role. In R. Jones (Ed.), *Black psychology* (1st ed). New York: Harper & Row.

Hayes, W., & Mindel, C. (1973). Extended kinship relations in black and white families. *Journal of Marriage and the Family, 35,* 51-57.

Herskovits, M. (1968). *The myth of the Negro past.* Boston: Beacon Press.

Hill, R. (1971). *The strength of black families.* New York: Emerson Hall.

Hilliard, A. (1974). A helping experience in African education: Implications for cross-cultural work. *Journal of Non-White Concerns, 2,* 133-144.

Hilliard, T., Dent, H., Hayes, W., Pierce W., & Poussaint, A. (1974). The Angela Davis trial: Role of black psychologists in jury selection and court consultations. *Journal of Black psychology, 1,* 56-60.

Howe, I. (1974). Living with kamp and schlaff literary tradition and mass education. *American Scholar, 43,* 107-112.

Howley, J. (1972). An agency's preparation for internal advocacy. *Social Casework, 53,* 204-208.

Hunt, D. (1974). Reflections on racial perspectives. *Journal of Afro-American Issues, 2,* 361-370.

Jackson, G.G. (1975). On the report on the Ad Hoc Committee on Educational uses of Tests with Disadvantaged Students: Another psychological view from the Association of Black Psychologists. *American Psychologist, 30,* 88-93.

Jackson, G.G. (1972). Black youth as peer counselors. *Personnel and Guidance Journal, 51,* 280-285(a).

Jackson, G.G. (1972). The use of roleplaying job interviews with job corps females. *Journal of Employment Counseling, 9,* 130-139(b).

Jackson, G.G. (1974). Project d.e.e.p.—An innovative adult educational program. *Adult Student Personnel Journal, 6,* 10-15.

Jackson, G.G. (1975). *Cultural context of the racial backlash in helping.* Manuscript submitted for publication.

Jackson, G.G. (In Press). The emergence of a black perspective in counseling. *Journal of Negro Education.*

Jackson, G.G., & Kirschner, S. (1973). Racial self-designation and preference for a counselor. *Journal of Counseling Psychology, 20,* 560-564.

Jackson, J.J. (1972). Face to face, mind to mind, it sho' nuff ain't no zombie jamboree. *Journal of the National Medical Association, 64,* 145-150.

Jackson, M., & DePuydt, D. (1974). Community service: An adjustment motif for minority students. *Journal of Non-White Concerns, 2,* 94-97.

Jenkins, S. (1969). The impact of the black identity crisis on community psychiatry. *Journal of the National Medical Association, 61,* 422-429.

Johnson, R. (1974). A counselor education outreach program: Serving the black inmate. *Journal of Non-White concerns, 2,* 80-93.

Jones, M., & Jones, M. (1970). The neglected client. *Black Scholar,1,* 35-42.

Jones, M., & Jones, M. (1972). Counselor, community and the black prisoner. *Black Scholar, 4(2),* 46-55.

Jordan, W. (1968). *White over black: American attitudes toward the Negro 1550-1812.* Baltimore, Md: Penguin Books.

Kendler, H. (1968). *Basic psychology.* New York: Appelton-Century-Crofts.

Kennedy, J. (1952). Problems posed in the analysis of Negro patients. *Psychiatry, 15,* 313-327.

Kerr, N. (1972). The black community's challenge to psychology. In R. Pugh (Ed.), *Psychology and the black experience.* Monterey, Calif.: Brooks, Cole.

Killens, J. (1970). The black psyche. In R. Guthrie (Ed.), *Being black.* San Francisco: Canfield Press.

Kohlberg, L. (1968). Early education: A cognitive-developmental view. *Child Development, 39,* 1013-1062.

Kovel, J. (1970). *White racism: A psychohistory.* New York: Vintage Books.

Kozol, J. (1972). Moving on-to nowhere. *Saturday Review,* Dec. 9, pp. 10-14.

Lambo, S. (1964). The village of Aro. *Lancet, 11,* 513-514.

Lambo, S. (1966). Socio-economic change, population explosion and changing phases of mental health programs in developing countries. *american Journal of Orthopsychiatry, 36,* 77-83.

Laosebikan, S. (1973). Mental health in Nigeria. *Journal of Black Studies, 4,* 221-228.

Layne, E. (1949). Experience of a Negro psychiatric social worker in a Veterans Administration mental hygiene clinic. *Journal of Psychiatric Social Work, 19* 102-105.

Lichenstein, P. (1971). A behavioral approach to 'phenomenological' data. *Psychological Record, 21*, 1-16.

Lide, P. (1973). The National Conference on Social Welfare and the Black Historical Perspective. *Social Service Review, 47*, 171-203.

Lienhardt, G. (1961). *Divinity and experience London: Oxford University Press.*

Lightfoot, O., & Foster, D. (1970). Black studies, black identity formation and some implications for community psychiatry. *American Journal of Orthopsychiatry, 40*, 751-755.

Meier, E. (1959). Social and cultural factors in casework diagnosis. *Social Work, 4*, 15-26.

Mosby, D. (1972). Toward a new specialty of black psychology. In R. Jones (Ed.), *Black psychology.* New York: Harper & Row.

Myrdal, G. (1944). *An American dilemma: The Negro problem and democracy* (2 vols.). New York: Harper.

Nathan, P., & Harris, S. (1975). *Psychopathology and society* New York: McGraw-Hill.

Nichols, E. (1974). Culture affects thought process. *Guidepost*, Feb. 22, p. 7.

Nichols, E. (1974). *Philosophical aspects of cultural differences: A human ecological view.* Discussion held at the First National Symposium on Mental Health in the Black Community, Philadelphia, PA.

Nobles, W. W. (1972). African philosophy: Foundations for black psychology. In R. Jones (Ed.), *Black psychology.* New York: Harper & Row.

Nobles, W. W. (1973). Psychological research and the black self-concept: A critical review. *Journal of Social Issues, 29*, 11-31.

Nobles, W. W. (1974a). African root and American fruit: The black family. *Journal of Social and Behavioral Sciences, 20*, 66-77.

Nobles, W. W. (1974b). Africanity: Its role in black families. *Black Scholar, 5(9)*, 10-17(b).

Nobles, W. W. (1974). *Extended-self: Rethinking the so-called Negro self-concept issue.* Paper presented at the meeting of the National Association of Black Psychologists, Nashville, TN.

Nobels, W. W. (1980). Extended self: Rethinking the so-called Negro self-concept. In R.L. Jones (Ed.), Black psychology (2nd ed.). New York: Harper & Row.

Ogawa, D. (1971). Small-group communication stereotypes of black Americans. *Journal of Black Studies, 1*, 273-281.

Olaoye, E. (1974). From Nigeria. *Personnel and Guidance Journal, 53*, 51.

Overall, B., & Aronson, H. (1963). Expectations of psychotherapy in patients of lower socio-economic class. *American Journal of Orthopsychiatry, 33*, 421-430.

Phillips, W. (1961). Notes from readers. *Harvard Educational Review, 31*, 324-326.

Pierce, C. (1968). Manpower: The need for Negro psychiatrists. *Journal of the National Medical Association, 60*, 30-33.

Pierce, W. (1972). The comprehensive community mental health programs and the black community. In R. Jones (Ed.), *Black psychology.* New York: Harper & Row.

Pinderhughes, C. (1966). Pathogenic social structure: A prime target for preventive psychiatric intervention. *Journal of the National Medical Association, 58*, 424-429.

Pinderhughes, C. (1971). Psychological and physiological origins of racism and other social discrimination. *Journal of the National Medical Association, 63*, 25-29.

Prince, R. (1960). The 'brain fag' syndrome in Nigerian students. *Journal of Mental Science, 106*, 559-607.

Record, W. (1961). Counseling and communication. *Journal of Negro Education, 30*, 451.

Rothenberg, L. (1970). Relevance is a many-splendored thing. *School Counselor, 17*, 367-369.

Ruch, F. (1967). *Psychology and life*. Glenview, Ill.: Scott, Foresman.

Sager, C., Brayboy, T., & Waxenberg, B. (1972). Black patient-white therapist. *American Journal of Orthopsychiatry, 42*, 415-423.

Sanders, C. (1970). Growth of the association of black social workers. *Social Casework, 51*, 27-284.

Sanders, C. (1971). Reflections on the black experience. *Black World, 20*, 75-79.

Sanders, C. (1972). *Black professionals' perceptions of institutional racism in health and welfare organizations*. Fair Lawn, N.J.: R. Burdick.

Schwartz, G., & Disch, R. (1970). *White racism: Its history, pathology and practice*. New York: Dell, 1970.

Sedlacek, W., & Brooks, G. (1973). Racism and research: using data to initiate change. *Personnel and Guidance Journal, 52*, 184-188. (a)

Sedlacek, W., & Brooks, G. (1973b). Racism in the public schools: A model for change. *Journal of Non-White Concerns, 1*, 133-143.

Shane, M. (1960). Some subcultural considerations in the psychotherapy of a Negro patient. *Psychiatric Quarterly, 34*, 9-27.

Shannon, B. (1970). Implications of white racism for social work practice. *Social Casework, 51*, 277-284.

Shannon, B. (1973). The impact of racism on personality development. *Social Casework, 54*, 519-525.

Siegel, B. (1970). Counseling the color-conscious. *School Counselor, 17*, 168-170.

Simpkins, G., Gunnings, T., & Kearney, A. (1973). The black six-hour retarded child. *Journal of Non-White Concerns, 2* 29-34.

Slater, P. (1970). *The pursuit of loneliness*. Boston: Beacon Press.

Smith, N. (1974). The ancient background to Greek psychology and some implications for today. *The Psychological Record, 24*, 309-324.

Smith, O., & Gundlach, R. (1974). Group therapy for blacks in a therapeutic community. *American Journal of Orthopsychiatry, 44*, 26-36.

Smith, P. (1968). Counselors for ghetto youth. *Personnel and Guidance Journal, 47*, 279, 281.

Smith, P. (1971). The role of the guidance counselor in the desegregation process. *Journal of Negro Education, 11*, 347-351.

Smith, P. (1974). Counseling from the past and present with blacks. *Journal of Negro Education, 43*, 489-493.

Stern, E., & MacLennan, B. (1974). Integrating minority and majority youth: A socio-drama group as a human relations model. *Journal of Non-White Concerns, 2*, 146-155.

Stikes, C. (1972). Culturally specific counseling: The black client. *Journal of Non-White Concerns, 1*, 15-23.

Sue, D., & Sue, S. (1972). Ethnic minorities: Resistance to being researched. *Professional Psychology, 3*, 11-17.

Sue, S. (1973). Training of 'third world' students to function as counselors. *Journal of Counseling Psychology, 20*, 73-78.

Suggs, R. (1975). An identity group experience: Changing priorities. *Journal of Non-White Concerns, 2*, 75-81.

Taylor, P. (1973). Research for liberation: Shaping a new black identity in America. *Black World*, May, pp. 4-14, 65-72.

Thalberg, I. (1974). Visceral racism. *Equal Opportunity*, Winter, pp. 66-68; 70; 72-74.

Thomas, A., & Sillen, S. (1972). *Racism and psychiatry*. New York: Brunner & Mazel.

Thomas, C. (1972). Psychologists, psychology, and the black community. In R. Jones (Ed.), *Black psychology*. New York: Harper & Row.

Thomas, C. (1973). The system—maintenance role of the white psychologist. *Journal of Social Issues, 29*, 57-65.

Thomas, C. (1974). The significance of the e(thnocentrism) factor in mental health. *Journal of Social Issues, 2*, 60-69.

Toldson, E. (1973). The human potential movement and black unity: Counseling blacks in groups. *Journal of Non-White Concerns, 1* 69-76.

Toldson, I., & Pasteur, A. (1972). Soul music: Techniques for therapeutic intervention. *Journal of Non-White Concerns, 1*, 31-39.

Toldson, I., & Pasteur, A. (1975). Developmental stages of black self-discovery: Implications for using black art forms in group interaction. *Journal of Negro Education, 44*, 130-138.

Trueblood, D. (1960). The role of the counselor in the guidance of Negro students. *Harvard Educational Review, 30*, 324-426.

Tucker, R., & Gunnings, T. (1974). Counseling black youth: A quest for legitimacy. *Journal of Non-White Concerns, 2*, 208-216.

Tucker, S. (1973). Action counseling: An accountability procedure for counseling the oppressed. *Journal of Non-White Concerns, 2*, 35-41.

Vontress, C. (1968). Counseling Negro students for college. *Journal of Negro Education, 37*, 37-44.

Vontress, C. (1969). Cultural differences: Implications for counseling. *Journal of Negro Education, 37*, 266-275.

Vontress, C. (1973). Counseling the racial and ethnic minorities. *Focus on Guidance, 5(6)*, 1-12.

Vontress, C. (1974). *Cross-Cultural counseling in perspective*. Presented at the Annual Meeting of the American Personnel and Guidance Association, New Orleans.

Vontress, C. (1974). *Cross-cultural counseling in perspective*. Papers presented at the meeting of the American Personnel and Guidance Association, New Orleans, LA.

Washington, K., & Anderson, N. (1974). Scarcity of black counselors: A crisis in urban education. *Journal of Non-White Concerns, 2*, 99-105.

Weber, M. (1930). *The protestant ethic and the spirit of capitalism*. London: Allen R. Unwin.

Welsing, F. (1974). The cress theory of color-confrontation. *Black Scholar, 5*, 32-40.

Whitaker, L. (1972). Community mental health wars and black ownership. *Professional psychology, 3*, 307-310.

White, J. (1970). Toward a black psychology. *Ebony*, September, pp. 44; 45; 48-50; 52.

Williams, C.G. (1974). A model for counseling 'high promise minority freshmen.' *Journal of Non-White Concerns, 2* 87-93.

Williams, C.T. (1949). Special considerations in counseling. *Journal of Educational Sociology, 22,* 608-613.

Williams, J. (1964). Connotations of color names among Negroes and Caucasians. *Perceptual and Motor Skills, 18,* 721-731.

Williams, J. (1966). Connotations of racial concepts and color names. *Journal of Personality and Social Psychology, 3,* 531-540.

Williams, J., Tucker, R., & Dunham, F. (1963-69). Changes in the connotations of color names among Negroes and Caucasians. *Journal of Personality and Social Psychology,* (1971), *19,* 222-228.

Williams, R. (1974a). A history of the Association of Black Psychologists: Early formation and development. *Journal of Black Psychology, 1,* 9-24.

Williams, R. (1974b) The death of white researchers in the black community. *Journal of Non-White Concerns, 2,* 116-132.

Willie, C., Kramer, B., & Brown, B. (Eds.), (1973). *Racism and mental health.* Pittsburgh: University of Pittsburgh Press.

Wittmer. J. (1971). Effective counseling of children of several American subcultures. *School Counselor, 19,* 49-52.

X, Luther, (1974). Awareness: The key to black mental health. *Journal of Black Psychology, 1,* 30-37.

Yette, S. (1971). *The choice. The issue of black survival in America.* New York: Berkeley Medalion.

Counseling African Americans: From Theory to Practice

Courtland C. Lee

This chapter deals with the issue of counseling African Americans in the present and future American society. The last several decades have seen black people make considerable social and economic advances. Indeed, gains made by blacks have initiated movements for social justice and equality by groups as diverse as women, the elderly and the physically disabled. Despite advances however, the traditions of oppression and racism that have characterized much of the African American experience still exert profound negative pressure on the lives of many black people. Demographic data for example, on poverty, unemployment and educational underattainment for African Americans (U.S. Bureau of the Census, 1985, 1986; U.S. Department of Labor, 1986) point to a serious stifling of human potential. Likewise, disturbing statistics and reports on phenomena such as adolescent pregnancy (Children's Defense Fund, 1988), the manhood plight (Cordes, 1985), and the increase of single parent families (Cordes, 1984) in the black community underscore the fact that there are serious challenges to human growth and development and bring into question just how pervasive recent social gains for African Americans have actually been. These challenges which confront black people are linked in an extricable fashion. There is no doubt that continued economic disadvantage and social discrimination are the ultimate source of the psychosocial challenges facing African Americans. Significantly, on the threshold of a new century, many blacks still find themselves in the backwaters of career, educational and social progress.

Contemporary counseling professionals whose mission is to promote human development, therefore, are confronted with important challenges in their attempts to successfully intervene in the lives of black clients. Counseling blacks requires not only an understanding of the theoretical and practical traditions of the counseling profession, but an appreciation of the dynamics of black culture and the societal forces which impinge upon black mental health and well-being.

A Historical Perspective

The idea that counseling blacks requires awareness, knowledge and skills that differ from the traditions of the profession is still relatively new. Jackson (1977), in tracing the emergence of a black perspective in counseling, suggests that although rudimentary notions on differential therapeutic approaches for black people appeared in the 1940's, the bulk of the knowledge base was developed in the 1960's and 1970's. These decades, a period of social and political ferment in America, saw the rise of a generation of black scholars who made major contributions to the profession. Many of these thinkers (Banks, 1972; Harper, 1973; Nobles, 1972; Vontress, 1970), African American counterparts to Carl Rogers, Albert Ellis and Fritz Perls, stated that black culture with its African origins was qualitatively different from European-based white culture. Therefore, the validity of theories and techniques grounded in European and European American cultural traditions had to be questioned when applied to counseling interactions with African Americans. These pioneering scholars established new theoretical and practical directions for counseling blacks.

The 1970's also saw black and white scholars initiate attempts to empirically validate new theoretical notions on and models for counseling black people. A body of research evidence began to emerge that aimed at providing answers to questions on race as a variable in the counseling process (Harrison, 1975; Sattler, 1977). While this research often yielded confusing and conflicting results, it served the purpose of stimulating thinking and continued investigation of the dynamics of counseling black clients.

With the advent of the 1980's, the knowledge base developed by black scholars in the 1960's and 1970's contributed to an important professional trend in counseling. Because of the contributions black scholarship has made, the total profession has come to recognize the importance of considering cultural diversity in the counseling process. This has led to a profusion of counseling professionals from diverse cultural and ethnic backgrounds advancing the notion of *multicultural counseling*. Multicultural counseling places the emphasis for counseling theory and practice equally on the cultural impressions of both the counselor and the client (Axelson, 1985). Counseling professionals must consider differences in language, social class and culture variables between helper and client to be potential impediments to effective intervention and work to overcome the barriers such variables might produce in the counseling process (Sue, 1981).

There is, however, an inherent danger in the growing acceptance of multicultural counseling. Looking to the future, as other ethnically and culturally diverse groups gain prominence in American society and their concerns exert influence on the counseling profession, the unique needs of black people, which served as the original source of multicultural counseling notions, are in jeopardy of becoming lost in the amalgam of this new discipline.

The challenge then is to use the short but stimulating African American scholarly legacy to chart future directions in which the academic, career and personal-social issues of black people continue to be uniquely addressed in counseling practice.

Prelude to Practice

Before examining counseling practice for black clients, it is important to consider several issues that must be understood if effective therapeutic intervention is to take place.

The Pitfalls of a Monolithic Perspective

In discussing the whole concept of counseling blacks, there is a danger of assuming that all black people are the same and that one methodological approach is universally applicable in any counseling intervention with them. Indeed, if one reviews much of the psychological or counseling literature related to black issues, he or she might be left with the impression that there is an all-encompassing black reality and that all black people act, feel and think in a homogeneous fashion. Such an impression invariably leads to a monolithic perspective on the black experience in America as well as stereotypic thinking in which African Americans are considered indistinguishable from one another in attitudes, behaviors and values. Counseling professionals possessing such a perspective run the risk of approaching black clients not as distinctive human beings with individual experiences, but rather in stereotypical fashion.

African American people, as do all people, differ from one another in experiences. Each black person is a unique individual who is the sum total of his or her common human experiences, specific cultural experiences and personal life experiences. Indeed, it has been asserted that attempting to identify common experiences among black people is a precarious enterprise, because blacks are not a homogeneous group (Dillard, 1983). Blackwell (1975) suggests the black community is a complex entity whose strength emanates from its diverse nature. The counseling process with black individuals, therefore, must incorporate the notion that there is a high degree of intragroup variability among blacks and that interventions must be client and situation-specific.

Significantly, within the body of theoretical knowledge on black psychology and mental health can be found important ideas which suggest significant intragroup variability among African American people. This knowledge base focuses on the concept of black identity formation and the possibility that blacks go through a series of stages in their efforts to establish stable personalities within American society (see chapter by Cross, et al, in present volume).

This notion of stages in black identity formation has led to the emergence of a body of empirical evidence which suggests that variation in black attitudes toward racial identity may have an effect on counseling process and outcome (Helms, 1986; Parham & Helms, 1981; Pomales, Claiborn & La Fromboise, 1986; Ponterotto, Anderson & Grieger, 1986). If such variation has been suggested, it is incumbent upon counseling professionals to approach intervention with black clients in an individualistic as opposed to a monolithic manner.

The Promise of a Proactive Perspective

Far too often, counseling intervention with African American clients is designed to counteract the negative effects of extreme environmental press on intra- and interpersonal functioning. Counseling is generally a reactionary process that focuses on the remediation of educational, economic, or social deficiencies which are the result of negative transactions between black people and their environments. Counseling outcomes for African American people, therefore, are in many cases reconstructive in nature. The goal of counseling black people traditionally has been rehabilitation as opposed to prevention.

However, if counseling is to be a comprehensive and effective discipline for helping black people, the scope of services offered should be proactive in nature. Counseling practices must move beyond merely assisting black clients react to negative environmental forces to a point where the goal of intervention is helping them develop mastery skills. Helping African American clients develop environmental mastery skills enables them to confront challenges in a competent and proactive manner.

Central to the development of a proactive approach to counseling blacks is the emergence of a life-span developmental perspective among mental health professionals. Life-span development is an orientation concerned with the optimization of the developmental processes in the course of human life from birth to death (Baltes, Reese & Lipsitt, 1980). Danish (1980) suggests that when a non-developmental framework is adopted by counselors, interventions are directed at remediation. Crises and problems are to be coped with or adapted to, whereas with a life-span human development approach, counseling practice is aimed at enhancement or optimal development. In counseling African Americans, such a perspective would emphasize facilitating normal human development, from conception to death, in a black cultural context. Adopting the proactive stance inherent in a life-span human development approach, would help counseling professionals promote mastery and competence in their interventions with black clients.

Directions for Counseling Practice

According to Gladding (1988), counseling is a relatively short-term interpersonal, theory-based professional activity guided by ethical and legal standards that focus on helping basically psychologically healthy persons to resolve situational and developmental problems. These problems center around educational, career and personal-social matters. Counseling is a process in which clients learn how to make decisions and formulate new ways of behaving, feeling and thinking (Smaby & Tamminen, 1978). Thus, counseling involves both choice and change, evolving through distinct stages as exploration, goal setting and action (Egan, 1986).

Counseling professionals working with African American clients, therefore, must facilitate this process of client choice and change within an African American cultural context. What follows are counseling practices for promoting black educational, career and personal-social development and insuring African American psychological health. These practices evolve out of an understanding of and appreciation for the unique history and cultural experiences of black people.

Promoting Educational Development and Achievement

Education has been a major concern for African Americans since the days of slavery. Blacks have always placed a great value on educational development, often risking their lives simply to learn to read and write. Indeed, the social and economic progress that blacks have made in America has been, to a degree, proportional to the educational opportunities available to them. Despite advances, African Americans have faced formidable challenges to their educational development. Both historical and contemporary data (Woodson, 1972; U.S. Bureau of the Census, 1985) attest to a serious stifling of educational achievement, aspiration and pride on the part of many black people. The complexities of racism have often served to make blacks the victims of lowered expectations from representatives of the educational system, making failure an integral part of the African American educational experience (Kozol, 1967; Jerrems, 1970). Frustration, underachievement or ultimate failure often comprise the educational reality for scores of blacks and have been the justifications for erroneous claims of limited learning potential among African Americans (Jencks, 1972; Jensen, 1969).

Educational counseling for black people must be considered in a life-span developmental perspective that starts with early education and continues through post-secondary learning experiences. Counseling professionals working from a developmental perspective must promote the development of attitudes, behaviors and skills on the part of blacks that are necessary to meet the challenges of an inherently racist educational system (Washington & Lee, 1981).

All educational counseling interventions for blacks must be delivered within the context of and with an appreciation for African American history and culture. The knowledge base for the black perspective in counseling makes evident that promoting black educational development can only be accomplished when the African American worldview is made an integral part of the intervention process (Cross, 1974; Stikes, 1972; Toldson & Pasteur, 1982).

For African American youth, the task of promoting educational development primarily entails the work of the school counseling professional. From kindergarten through high school, school counselors must adopt roles and functions that emphasize the development of black youth and their potential as opposed to the remediation of their supposed deficiencies (Lee, 1982a).

Working with black students, school counseling professionals must promote the development of positive self-identity, positive interpersonal relations, and responsible behavior. It has been suggested that culture-specific curriculum materials and African American aesthetic dimensions (i.e. music, poetry, graphic expression and expressive movement) be incorporated into traditional individual and group counseling interactions with students to facilitate such personal and social growth (Lee & Lindsey, 1985; Lee, 1987; Toldson & Pasteur, 1972).

In addition to student intervention, counselors must be prepared to intervene into the educational system to effect institutional change for the benefit of black students (Gunnings & Simpkins, 1972). Counselors should be ready to assume the role of student advocate (Lee, 1982b) and intervene in the educational system, when necessary, on behalf of students in ways designed to eradicate inherent problems and insensitivities that block constructive learning. Beyond high school, counseling professionals must address the inherent challenges in the person-environment interaction that occurs between black students and institutions of higher education. This is particularly pertinent for the ever-growing number of black students entering white bastions of higher education with limited traditions of diversity. As Fleming (1984) suggests, the power of racism is prevalent in black students' transactions with these institutions. Significantly, in many instances it is not academic pressure at these schools, but rather the quality of non-academic life experiences, that is the cause of stress for black students. Counseling professionals whose focus is college student development must work to improve both the quality of education and the total educational environment for African American students.

One aspect of such improvement is to insure that a supportive atmosphere exists for black students in the higher educational setting. Several facilitative roles would be important in promoting such an atmosphere. First, in keeping with the communal nature of black culture (Nobles, 1972), counselors working in higher education should initiate support groups for black students. Such groups should have as their goal providing students with a mutually supportive setting in which they can share perceptions and feelings associated with being black on a predominately white campus. In such a group setting it is anticipated that participants can develop personal insights and skills to cope more effectively with academic and social concerns (Lee, 1982c). Second, it is important that counseling professionals support student involvement in black cultural activities in the higher educational setting. Such activities promote a sense of cultural connectedness and can enhance the quality of life for black students in the college environment. Third, as with school counselors, college student development professionals must serve as advocates for black students in their transactions with institutional agents.

In order to continue the social and economic progress blacks have made in recent decades, educational development must be promoted at all levels. The forces which serve to impede black educational achievement must be confronted and eradicated. Counseling for black educational development therefore, implies that helping professionals must assume proactive roles. Counseling practice must focus not on remediating educational failure among blacks, but rather on promoting educational achievement across the life-span.

Promoting Career Development

The world of work for black people has often been landscaped with unfulfilled dreams, wasted potential, dashed hopes and economic struggle. Despite recent economic gains, labor force participation data from the 1980's present a bleak picture of black occupational involvement. For example, the unemployment rate for black high school graduates is generally three times the rate for whites (American Council on Education, 1988); twenty-five percent of all young adult black males have never held a job (National Alliance of Business, 1987); and blacks are overrepresented in the slow-growing or declining occupations but underrepresented in the fastest growing occupations (Kutscher, 1987).

Data such as these lend further credence to Smith's (1975) analysis of the status of the African American in vocational literature, which portrays the black individual as a vocationally handicapped person. If, as the vocational literature and labor force statistics would suggest, black career potential is often not realized, then a great deal must be done to insure maximum African American labor force participation in the emerging post-industrial work world.

Contemporary career development is conceptualized as a lifelong developmental process by which an individual attempts to express a self-concept within the complex and dynamic world of work (Super, 1957). Given this, the goal of career counseling is helping people integrate and apply an understanding of self and the environment to make appropriate career decisions and changes (Sears, 1982). Although promoting career development through the counseling process can be a complex task for all people, its challenges are often compounded for many blacks, given the traditions of socioeconomic disadvantage that may serve to impede their life progress. Promoting the career development of blacks from a lifespan developmental perspective, therefore, is a process in which counseling professionals must help African Americans understand and deal with the multiple factors which may influence and ultimately hinder the dynamics of their career choices.

Children   The process of promoting African American career development must begin with career education in childhood. At the elementary school level, counseling professionals need to provide comprehensive programs of career education and guidance that insure that black children start to develop both self-awareness and aspects of career awareness. Since self-concept is considered to be a major aspect in career development, programmatic efforts should be made to insure that black children develop a positive self-identity as African Americans. Counselors should employ culture specific counseling techniques to cultivate self-pride from a black perspective in young children (Lee & Lindsey, 1985). In preparing to ultimately enter the world of work, black children must learn from an early age that positive validation of their personhood will not often come from environmental sources. Therefore, they must develop pride-in-self which is the hallmark of a positive self-concept.

It is also important that black children become aware of as wide a range of career opportunities as possible. Through field trips and *Career Days*, where a variety of black occupational role models are providing forums to share their experience in the world of work, school counselors can assist young black children in starting to understand the scope of career options available to them.

Adolescents. To meet the career needs of adolescents, the American School Counselors Association (1985) developed a statement on the role of school counselors in career guidance. The statement emphasizes that counselors should enlist the aid of people from both inside and outside the school setting in addressing the career development needs of adolescents. To meet the needs of black adolescents, career education should take the form of comprehensive life-planning (Lee & Simmons, 1988). Adolescent black youth may find long-range educational or career planning difficult, particularly when social or economic disadvantage make meeting basic needs on a short-term basis a constant challenge.

Any life-planning counseling intervention for African American adolescents should provide comprehensive experiences that promote long-range career goal setting, including the development of occupational, educational and marriage and family plans. Such an intervention should include components that provide for guidance, counseling, consultation, and coordination activities on the part of counseling professionals.

The guidance component of such an intervention should help adolescents develop an awareness of life planning issues and crucial decisions that must be made regarding work and related issues. The guidance experiences should make black youth aware of the possibility of change in their lives and the necessity to plan for it as well as have them gain an awareness of different lifestyles.

The counseling component should promote life-planning in four important ways: (1) by promoting self-awareness of abilities, interests and values; (2) by promoting an expansion of educational and occupational options; (3) by encouraging educational and occupational decision making based on knowledge and experience; and (4) by encouraging youth to anticipate future events. Both individual and group counseling experiences should help adolescents improve their self-concept and provide them with information to begin making sound educational and career choices.

The purpose of any consultation component in a life-planning intervention should be to promote the participation of black parents in the adolescent decision-making process. Parental influence has been found to be an important variable in goal setting among black adolescents (Lee, 1984; McNair & Brown, 1983). Counselors need to consult with black parents to assist them in developing effective decision making and communication skills so that they can impact positively on the educational, occupational and marriage and family planning of their adolescent children.

Finally, counseling coordinators should coordinate black educational, community and business resources with the life-planning processes of adolescents. Through a school-community-business network, counselors can have positive black community role models from both traditional and nontraditional occupational fields develop mentor relationships with young people. Through such relationships young people would be exposed to significant others who represent occupational success in a variety of fields and who have made crucial life decisions.

The four components of such an intervention serve to provide a supportive and relevant context within which black adolescents can develop the attitudes and skills needed to make tentative life and career choices. They also incorporate significant others who are important sources of guidance from the black family and community into the adolescent career planning process.

A comprehensive intervention strategy such as this would increase the career expectations and visions of African American youth. Such a strategy would promote African American adolescent career development and challenge the obstacles often associated with social and economic disadvantage for black youth.

Adults Promoting the career development of black adults must be based on a knowledge of African American adult developmental issues. At present however, little is actually known about the dynamics of normal black adult developmental processes. Counselors engaged in adult career interventions, therefore, must initiate comprehensive investigative efforts to learn more about normal black adult development.

Career counseling for black adults has several important aspects. First, when necessary it is important to help black adults find ways to meet their basic needs. Career exploration cannot take place when an individual's attention is focused on meeting basic needs on a day-to-day basis. Second, black adults may need help in raising their personal expectations about opportunities and success in the world of work. This may be important when a black adult has a narrow view of the range of job options, limited educational background, or lack of job training. Raising personal expectations can be accomplished through counseling strategies that focus on helping black adult clients identify and reinforce self-perceptions of unique abilities and resources, develop positive attitudes toward the workplace through interaction with role models, learn self-assertion skills, and acquire relevant career information.

Third, counselors may need to help black adults clarify the meaning of their work in terms of both mental and physical health. Counseling interventions should include methods to help African American adults improve the quality of their working lives. Such interventions may include helping clients develop personal strategies to reduce stress and improve factors that may negatively influence their interactions with the workplace.

Fourth, it is important that career counselors direct their attention toward social conditions in the workplace itself when working with African American adults. In so doing, a counselor would be assuming the role of career development advocate (Lee, 1989). A career development advocate channels energy and skill into helping black adults break down institutional and social barriers that impede full workforce participation. When necessary, such a professional must be willing to act on behalf of disenfranchised black adults and actively challenge discriminatory traditions and preconceived racist notions that stand in the way of equity in the workplace. Likewise, a career counselor in this role can push for continuing legislation that abolishes discriminatory employment practices. Career development advocates, through efforts both with and for their clients, can help black adults empower themselves to seize new occupational opportunities in a post-industrial American society.

Career development is a life-long process of occupational exploration and decision-making. This process can be fraught with peril for many African Americans. Career counseling practice for blacks then must be a process of planning and action to maximize occupational opportunities in an ever-changing work world.

Promoting Personal and Social Development

Personal-social development is the ultimate goal of any type of counseling intervention. According to Axelson (1985), the terms *personal* and *social* communicate the idea that human development involves both relations with oneself and those with others and society. Personal and social counseling therefore, must take into consideration an individual in interaction with his or her environment. The personal-social counseling process entails helping people learn environmental adaptation behaviors that lead to psychological well-being.

Environmental adaptation and psychological well-being have been problematic for African American people due to the social forces that have impacted negatively upon their personal and social development in America. African Americans, by and large, have experienced considerable frustration in their person-environment transactions with American society. The historic challenges inherent in the restricted and often extreme conditions facing large segments of the black community have undermined self-esteem, disrupted social relationships, caused frustration and promoted high levels of stress. Such frustration and stress have generally led to the development of maladaptive behavior patterns among blacks. The psychological effects of such maladaptive behavior have often been devastating, many times leading to a sense of intra- and interpersonal inadequacy among blacks.

Recently, a call has gone forth to the mental health professions to promote personal and social development in the black community (Gary & Jones, 1978; King, 1980; Pierce, 1981; Thomas & Comer, 1973). The main thrust of this call has been the idea that promoting personal and social development among black people rests on their ability to use resources to effectively combat the debilitating effects of negative environmental forces (Myers, 1973). The goal of counseling professionals then, involves helping black people develop functional environmental coping behaviors that lead to personal adjustment and optimal mental health. The operational therapeutic objective is to assist black clients in achieving personal empowerment for environmental mastery and competence. Majors and Nikelly (1983) have suggested that counselors take new directions in their efforts to help African American clients empower themselves. These new directions include modalities that incorporate elements of the immediate environment, raise consciousness and focus on group solidarity to promote active change. Modalities such as these should focus on enhancing positive African American lifestyles and behaviors.

When counseling professionals seek to incorporate elements of the immediate environment into the black empowerment process, they must facilitate the development of family and community therapeutic resources. Importantly, Nobles (1972) has stressed the importance of the African philosophical notion of kinship or collective unity as an important foundation for African American mental health intervention. Undoubtedly, the black family is the most important resource that helping professionals can tap into to promote personal-social counseling effectiveness. In spite of all the challenges to its integrity, the family is the bedrock of African American psychosocial well-being (Billingsley, 1968; Hill, 1971). Family intervention therefore, should be a major therapeutic modality for fostering personal empowerment.

Programmed family intervention must provide for the inclusion of relatives and the inherent strength of kinship social support processes as an integral part of proactive developmental counseling. In helping black clients become proactive, as opposed to reactive in their environmental interactions, counseling should be conducted within the context of the family unit. Whenever possible, counseling services should be offered in a supportive family group format where members can draw on each others strengths for problem resolution and proactive strategy formation.

In addition to the family, the black community offers other institutions that provide a network of social support that can be incorporated into the counseling process. The black church, for example, has long been a bastion of group solidarity and an institution devoted to raising levels of black consciousness. Indeed, the black church has been the traditional source looked to for psychological well-being for many African Americans (Gordon & Jones, 1978); developmental counseling methodology should incorporate aspects of the multifaceted black religious experience in remediating the effects of negative environmental press as well as preventing the formation of maladaptive behavior patterns.

Likewise, other social support entities within the black community can be called into counseling service. Counselors should find ways to coordinate paraprofessional development programs to involve selected community people in counseling service delivery. These paraprofessionals should be sensitive caring individuals who share the unique worldviews of clients. Such individuals can form a constructive part of the social network in the black community and can be vital cogs in the psychoeducational helping process.

Counseling practice for promoting personal-social development among African Americans must draw its strength from the collective unity of the black community. Helping professionals working to promote environmental mastery skills in black clients must cultivate the supportive social network inherent in the black family and community. Proactive developmental counseling interventions aimed at advancing personal adjustment and optimal mental health can be helpful if conceptualized as a collective African American enterprise.

Implications for Counselor Training and Research

Given the legacies of the past, realities of the present and challenges of the future, new directions in the training of counselors who can effectively address the mental health needs of African Americans are needed. Implementing proactive life-span developmental academic, career and personal-social counseling practices for blacks implies that new emphases are required in counselor training programs.

Future counseling professionals will need new knowledge and skills if they are to successfully intervene into the lives of black people.

First, training experiences for counselors should include an opportunity for developing self-awareness. Counselors must develop an awareness of their own cultural heritage and its relationship to the realities and dynamics of African American cultural life. It is important that counseling professionals have an understanding of differences as well as similarities in their cultural backgrounds and those of their African American clients. Such an understanding has the potential for increasing empathic effectiveness. In addition, counselor training should provide the opportunity for self-analysis of prejudicial assumptions and biases about African American people. It is important during the course of training that counseling professionals have forums for critically examining themselves and their own potential for intervening successfully into the lives of black clients, given their cultural background and preconceived notions about African American attitudes, behaviors and values.

Second, counselors should be provided with a thorough review of the history, experiences and cultural dynamics of African Americans. Counseling professionals must have an understanding of the nuances of black culture and their crucial importance in the helping relationship. Specifically, training direction should be given on developing an understanding of the black frame of reference and ways to incorporate inherent black cultural strengths into the helping process.

Third, along with self-awareness and an understanding of black history and culture, it is essential that newly emerging counseling professionals have an understanding of human development across the life-span. Such knowledge would provide a solid conceptual base for appreciating the developmental dynamics of African American behavior and personality. It is important that future counseling practice be guided by concepts of normal development across an African American life-span. Such concepts will help counseling professionals enhance primary prevention, as opposed to rehabilitation, service delivery modalities.

Fourth, it is crucial that new counseling professionals have knowledge of traditional, as well as recently developed black, theoretical notions of counseling theory and methodology. A blending of such notions into a well-defined skill base will insure programmed intervention into the lives of black clients that is characterized by the highest levels of empathy and effectiveness.

Finally, counselors must learn skills for social action. Many of the psychological and social challenges facing blacks are environmentally induced. Therefore, full human potential can only be realized when environmental barriers to optimal black development are removed.

Counselors need to change agent and client advocacy skills for effective environmental intervention to eradicate systematic barriers to black development.

New training implies new research directions. As theoretical and methodological notions about counseling African American people continue to evolve, so too do new research questions. The primary goal of future research must be the empirical validation of evolving notions about African American counseling and development. There are several directions that are important for future research on counseling African Americans. To begin with, new counseling process and outcome studies must be designed and conducted. These studies are necessary to answer questions about theoretical notions on black divergence from therapeutic traditions in counseling methodology and its impact on client outcomes. Empirical evidence is needed to support ideas about the effectiveness of culture-specific counseling interventions in changing attitudes, values and behaviors among African American clients. These investigations must provide answers to the fundamental question: *Are culture-specific models and methods more effective with black clients than traditional (i.e., white) counseling interventions?* Importantly, evaluation of innovative counseling methodologies for African American clients, in terms of their outcomes, should be made an integral part of all service delivery.

Research is also needed in the area of normal development across the life-span for black people. Specific investigations that assess mental health outcomes by attempting to delineate the developmental processes of the person-environment interaction among African Americans need to be conducted. This is particularly important, as was stated previously, in the area of normal black adult development. New studies need to investigate the coping styles and mastery skills of African American adults. An empirically validated knowledge base concerning normal African American development is crucial for proactive counseling interventions that focus on prevention as opposed to remediation.

New research efforts must also be initiated in the area of black career development. Smith (1975) laid out a research agenda that called for experimental efforts to support theoretical ideas about variables related to African American career development. This agenda called for research to investigate the relationships among black family influences, self-concept, gender differences and career development. Importantly, any such research should be conducted from a life-span perspective, with a major emphasis placed on the variables which seem to influence the career development of African American adults.

Empirical investigation should be initiated to produce new inventories that assess significant developmental aspects of African Americans. A crucial aspect of this process must be studies that produce valid and reliable information for instruments that assess African American personality and behavioral dynamics. Until such empirical data are provided, instruments will remain *experimental* in nature and of little practical use in providing valid and reliable information to enhance counseling practice with African American clients.

Finally, all research efforts should be structured to investigate intragroup differences among African Americans. The majority of research evidence concerning the dynamics of counseling African Americans has been gathered in a comparative context with whites. Such evidence lends credence to the concept that the African American experience is a monolithic entity and that there is no within-group variability among black people. All future research efforts on counseling process and outcome, therefore, should continue to investigate within-group differences among blacks.

Conclusion

As counseling African Americans moves from theory to practice, a dramatic shift in the focus of mental health intervention is needed. The profession must cease engaging in interventions that view black people as helpless victims of negative environmental press who must be rehabilitated. Instead, counseling services must be delivered in the belief that African Americans are psychologically healthy, undergo normal developmental experiences and have the resources to competently deal with problems and challenges. Counseling practice, therefore, must be undertaken from an African American life-span developmental perspective that is aimed at promoting optimal mental health and well-being. The major focus of future counseling practice must be prevention of the problems that lead to African American maladaptive attitudes and behavior rather than the remediation of the consequences of such attitudes and behaviors. Counselors must facilitate the development of black environmental mastery skills.

Finally, training and research efforts must coincide with the implementation of new innovations in practice. The dawn of a new century must see the rise of a new counseling professional, one who is armed with a solid knowledge base to meet the challenges of counseling black people. The continued survival of African Americans demands no less.

References

Banks, W.M. (1972). The black client and the helping professional. In R.L. Jones (Ed.), *Black psychology*. New York: Harper and Row.

Billingsley, A. (1968). *Black families in white America*. Englewood Cliffs, NJ: Prentice Hall.

Blackwell, J.E. (1975). *The black community: Diversity and unity*. New York: Dodd, Mead.

Children's Defense Fund. (1988). *The health of America's black children*. Washington, DC: The Children's Defense Fund.

Cordes, C. (1984, August). The rise of one-parent black families. *APA Monitor*, pp. 16-18.

Cordes, C. (1985). Black males face high odds in a hostile society. *APA Monitor*, pp. 9-11, 27.

Cross, A. (1974). The black experience: Its importance in the treatment of black clients. *Child Welfare, 52*, 158-166.

Gary, L.E., & Jones, D.J. (1978). Mental health: A conceptual overview. In L.E. Gary (Ed.), *Mental health: A challenge to the black community*. Philadelphia: Dorrance & Co.

Gordon, T.A., & Jones, N.L. (1978). Functions of the social network in the black community. In L.E. Gary (Ed.), *Mental health: A challenge to the black community*. Philadelphia: Dorrance and Co.

Harper, F. (1973). What counselors must know about the social sciences of black Americans. *Journal of Negro Education, 42*, 109-116.

Hill, R. (1971). *The strengths of black families*. New York: Emerson Hall.

Jackson, G.G. (1977). The emergence of a black perspective in counseling. *Journal of Negro Education, 46*, 230-253.

Lee, C.C. (1982a). The school counselor and the black child: Critical roles and functions. *Journal of Non-White Concerns in Personnel and Guidance, 10*, 94-101.

Lee, C.C. (1982c). Black support group: Outreach to the alienated black college student. *Journal of College Student Personnel, 23*, 271-273.

Lee, C.C. (1984). Predicting the career choice attitudes of rural black, white, and Native American high school students. *Vocational Guidance Quarterly, 32*, 177-184.

Lee, C.C., & Lindsey, C.R. (1985). Black consciousness development: A group counseling model for black elementary school students. *Elementary School Guidance & Counseling, 19*, 228-236.

Lee, C.C. (1987). Black manhood training: Group counseling for male blacks in grades 7-12. *The Journal for Specialists in Group Work, 12*, 18-25.

Lee, C.C., & Simmons, S. (1988). A comprehensive life-planning model for black adolescents. *The School Counselor, 36*, 5-10.

Majors, R., & Nikelly, A. (1983). Serving the black minority: A new direction for psychotherapy. *Journal of Non-White Concerns in Personnel and Guidance, 11*, 142-151.

McNair, D., & Brown, D. (1983). Predicting the occupational aspirations, occupational expectations, and career maturity of black, white, male and female tenth graders. *Vocational Guidance Quarterly, 32*, 29-36.

Myers, E.R. (1973). Implications of the emerging discipline of community psychology for black social workers. In *Nation building time: Proceedings of the 5th annual conference of NABSW*.

National Alliance of Business (September 30, 1987). A critical message for every American who plans to work or do business in the 21st century. New York: *New York Times Magazine*.

Nobles, W. (1972). African philosophy: Foundations for black psychology. In R.L. Jones (Ed.), *Black psychology*. New York: Harper & Row.

Parham, T.A., & Helms, J.E. (1981). The influence of black students' racial identity attitudes on preferences for counselor's race. *Journal of Counseling Psychology, 28*, 250-257.

Pierce, W.D. (1981). The comprehensive community mental health programs and the black community. In R.L. Jones (Ed.), *Black psychology* (Second edition). New York: Harper & Row.

Pomales, J., Claiborn, C.D., & La Fromboise, T.D. (1986). Effects of black students' racial identity on perceptions of white counselors varying in cultural sensitivity. *Journal of Counseling Psychology, 33*, 57-61.

Smith, E.J. (1975). Profile of the black individual in vocational literature. *Journal of Vocational Behavior, 6*, 41-59.

Stikes, C. (1972). Culturally specific counseling—The black client. *Journal of Non-White Concerns in Personnel and Guidance, 1*, 15-23.

Washington, V., & Lee, C.C. (1981). Teaching and counseling the black child: A systemic analysis for the 1980's. *Journal of Non-White Concerns in Personnel and Guidance, 9*, 60-67.

White, J.L. (1970). Toward a black psychology. *Ebony, 25*, 44-45, 48-50, 52.

Psychological Functioning In African Americans: A Conceptual Guide For Use in Psychotherapy

Arthur C. Jones

Over the past two decades, clincians and clinical researchers have outlined a number of salient factors in the conduct of psychotherapy with black Americans. The issues considered have included transference and countertransference problems (Jones & Seagull, 1977; Schacter & Butts, 1968), interracial therapist-patient dynamics (Block, 1968; Gardner, 1971; Jackson, 1973; Jones & Seagull, 1977; Sue, 1981; Waite, 1968), the impact of social class (Acosta et al., 1982; Brill & Storrow, 1969; Carkhuff & Pierce, 1967; Jones, 1974; Mayo, 1974; Sue, 1981; Yamamoto & Goin, 1965), the general problem of racial bias in mental delivery systems (Acosta et al., 1982; Anderson et al., 1977; Cole & Pilisuk, 1976; Gibbs, 1975; Jackson et al., 1974; Sue, 1977; Warren et al., 1973), and the use of appropriate techniques with black patients (Banks, 1975; Cheek, 1976; Harper & Stone, 1974; Shipp, 1983; Sue, 1981; Tounsel & Jones, 1980; Wilson & Calhoun, 1974; Wyatt et al., 1976). While the size of the literature attests to the increased awareness among mental health professionals that race is an important factor in psychotherapy with black patients, there has yet been little attempt to develop a comprehensive conceptual framework for viewing mental health functioning in blacks from varying social, economic, and subcultural backgrounds. Such a framework would provide a guide for the selection of appropriately diversified psychotherapy interventions for patients from different backgrounds and with different types of presenting problems, thus avoiding the trap of attempting to construct a profile of "the" black patient.

Conceptualizations of Black Psychopathology

There has been relatively little written about the unique aspects of psychopathology in blacks. Prior to the 1970s, the most widely cited scholarly efforts were those by Kardiner and Ovesey (1951) and Grier and Cobbs (1968). Both works stressed the negative impact of racial oppression on the psychological development of African Americans. While this was an important contribution, neither of these works specified the conditions under which successful adaptation can occur. Rather, they appeared to suggest that status as an African American automatically carries with it a high risk for the development of serious psychopathology.

Recently, several black theoreticians have highlighted the healthy potential of African American psychological adaptation. Nobles (1976, 1980a, b), for example, has emphasized the concept of strong group identification, or "we-ness," as a positive African American trait. Similarly, Akbar (Luther X, 1974), Cook and Kono (1977), and White (1980) have focused on the growth-promoting aspects of black culture and consciousness. These theoreticians' writings have provided a refreshing contrast to the kind of deficit-model thinking evident in works such as that by Kardiner and Ovesey (1951). However, there is still an absence of a practical clinical guide regarding conceptualization and intervention with patients who function at varying levels of black consciousness. Moreover, there has been little written concerning what effects, positive as well as negative, American acculturation might have on individual patients' lives. That is, the issue of cultural heterogeneity in African Americans has still received only minimal attention.

A Working Framework for Viewing African American Psychological Adaptation

A useful way to conceptualize adaptation in African Americans is first to describe the psychological tasks which face all blacks, regardless of background, and then to develop a model for viewing individual differences. This approach leads to the selection of flexible, individualized psychotherapy interventions. The proposed model employs this approach.

Four classes of variables comprise the structure for the model. These are: 1) reactions to racial oppression; 2) influence of the majority culture; 3) influence of traditional African American culture; and 4) individual and family experiences and endowments. A description of each of these classes of variables follows, including illustrations of their use as a basis for conceptualizing psychotherapy approaches. Finally, an overview of the interactive aspects of the model is provided.

Reactions to Racial Oppression

One task facing virtually all African Americans is the development of ways to cope with experiences of racial prejudice and discrimination (Comer, 1980). This is an experience that is shared with members of other oppressed ethnic minority groups. However, both the high visibility of blacks (because of color), and the negative cultural meanings attached to the colors black and brown (Kovel, 1970), serve to intensify the experience of racism for black people. In addition, the existence of color as the distinguishing feature of group identity renders it extremely difficult for blacks to assimilate into the larger society by voluntarily relinquishing psychological ties with the "mother" culture.

Historically, blacks have adopted a variety of strategies for dealing with personal experiences of racial oppression. To a large extent, the strategies adopted have been determined by particular environmental exigencies. During slavery, for example it was adaptive for blacks to blunt the overt expression of affect and to employ covert channels for resistance to oppression (Adams, 1976). At the other extreme, the period of the late 1960s and 1970s favored the free expression of affect, particularly anger, and fostered positive black identity and pride (Adams, 1976; Cross, 1980; Hall et al., 1972; Tounsel & Jones, 1980). At other points in history, such various tactics as "Uncle Tomming," developing a "common bond" with white Americans, and "redefinition" of self have proved adaptive (Adams, 1976; Tounsel and Jones, 1980). At times, particular coping strategies have been necessary for physical survival as well as for successful psychological adaptation. But especially important is the fact that because blacks have used different strategies at different points in history, numerous variants of these have been transmitted from one generation to the next. When individual differences are added, the possible variations increase tremendously. A given individual may employ any combination of approaches, some unconscious and some conscious.

In psychotherapy, it frequently becomes important for the therapist to help patients identify consciously those daily modes of dealing with racial difficulties which they have selected. The therapeutic task then becomes one of comparing these strategies with the range of available options, enabling the patient to make more active, conscious choices. Poor adaptation is likely to occur when the patient has chosen to react in a particular way for unconscious reasons when a more effective, consciously selected approach may be available. Maladjustment also occurs when cognitive rigidity prevents the patient from viewing realistically the range of behavioral options.

Case Example

A recent divorced, 25-year-old black male medical student entered psychotherapy because he was having frequent migraine headaches which, upon thorough medical examination, appeared to have no organic basis. The patient attributed the headaches to the "racist" medical school environment. In the past month, he had decided to confront this problem head-on by telling one of his basic science professors that he knew that he (the professor) was a racist and that he was not going to "stand for" mistreatment (biased grading, singling out for questions in class) anymore. In exploring the circumstances surrounding the perceived mistreatment, it became clear to the therapist that the patient's complaints were founded in fact. However, it was also clear that the patient's behavior, if continued, would undoubtedly lead to his dismissal from medical school. After some work in therapy, it surfaced that the patient's recent divorce, though described initially to the therapist as "smooth," was accompanied by a significant amount of underlying anger. This made the patient particularly vulnerable to mistreatment by others and, inadvertently, was partially responsible for his choice of coping strategy in response to his experiences of racial discrimination. As the patient became aware of this, he was able to maintain an appropriate level of anger at his professor but, in addition, was able to consider a wider range of choices in dealing with the situation. He finally decided to enlist the aid of a minority liaison officer in filing a formal grievance. This led to increased tension between the student and the professor, but he was able to pass all of his courses for the quarter and the frequency of his migraine headaches decreased considerably. While he remained anxious about his ability to confront racial problems at school, he also experienced feelings of relief and increased confidence in his ability to negotiate "the system." He perceived this as good preparation for his future career as a black physician.

The critical factor in the choice of ways for dealing with instances of racial oppression is the ability of the patient to survey the options available and make conscious, deliberate choices which are compatible with his or her values, goals, and psychological makeup. In this context, there is no one type of "right" behavior. For example, a maintenance man working for a bigoted, narcissistic employer might well decide that "Uncle Tomming" is preferable to being "assertive" and losing both his job and his ability to support his family. Just as blacks as a group have favored different types of strategies during different historical periods, individuals may choose tactics which maximize their ability to achieve particular life goals within particular environments.

Influence of the Majority Culture

African Americans as a group have adopted, to a significant extent, the values, mores, and orientations of majority American culture. In fact, some observers have argued that certain segments of African American subculture reflect an exaggerated mimicry of majority culture behaviors and values (Frazier, 1962). While this claim may be disputed, it is a truism that blacks have been influenced significantly by Anglo traditions (Billingsley, 1968).

A common stereotypic notion is that being black is synonymous with being "lower class," and that black values and behaviors are radically different from those of the white middle-class mainstream. By implication, the therapist working with black clients must learn to be "hip," to understand what it means to be poor, and must be prepared to work with people who lack "psychological-mindedness." As Billingsley (1968) points out, such notions are inconsistent with the basic sociological facts of African American life. For example, Billingsley maintains that at least half of the black population in the United States can be considered "middle class" or above with respect to social status and additional factors such as educational achievement within the black community. Moreover, those classified as "lower class" share with those of the middle class many of the same values with respect to education, family pride, and financial aspirations. Thus, although African Americans experience significant *economic* disadvantages when compared with Anglos, their aspirations and values often match those of Anglos to a significant degree.

Again, the task for the psychotherapist is to assist patients in making clear, conscious choices. One difficulty in this regard is that much of black behavior historically has been motivated by unconscious internalization of the majority culture's pejorative view of blacks (Cross, 1980; Hall et al., 1972; Thomas, 1971). Concomitantly, many blacks' assimilation of majority cultural values may be viewed as an unconscious attempt to avoid black identification. This is likely one reason why the social movements of the 1960s and early 70s were accompanied by a heightened interest among blacks in exclusively black-oriented readings, activities, and personal associations. It appeared that an important stage in overcoming negative internalized feelings about blackness was a total immersion in a black-oriented lifestyle (Cross, 1980; Hall et al., 1972; Thomas, 1971). However, patients who are able to come to comfortable terms with their blackness may also be in a position to make flexible choices with regard to majority culture interests and values. This sometimes involves discarding the notion that activities can be classified on an *a priori* basis with respect to their acceptability as "black" behaviors.

Case Example

A popular 13-year-old black girl attending a predominantly black public school and living in a predominantly black neighborhood was referred to a psychologist by a pediatrician to whom her mother had brought her because of a recent increase in abdominal pains. A physical examination and laboratory tests failed to uncover a medical basis for the symptoms. A psychological evaluation revealed that the patient appeared to be reacting to her parents' recent divorce. In addition, the girl, normally very popular with her peers, had begun playing the violin in the school orchestra and had received excellent feedback from her teachers about her musical abilities. As a consequence she had begun to develop an active interest in European classical music and had begun listening to a regular late-afternoon classical music radio program. Some of her friends had begun to ridicule her for her interest in "white" music and she became dismayed at her fantasy that her interests might result in a loss of her popular status in her peer group. This fear exacerbated the reactive symptoms associated with her parents' divorce.

Psychotherapy was focused on helping this patient work through her feelings about her parents' divorce. In addition, considerable time in therapy was spent on her fear of losing her favored status in her peer group. As the patient became comfortable with the compatibility between her blackness and her classical music interest, she was able to adopt a low-key public approach to the music which resulted in much less alienation from her friends. At the same time, she was able to continue her interest and feel comfortable with the pursuit of an activity which was unique within her peer group. Eventually some of her friends expressed an interest in joining her intermittently to listen to the classical music program.

Black psychotherapy patients demonstrate a wide range of variability with regard to their adoption of majority culture interests and values, with varying degrees of associated internal conflict. Psychological evaluation of this area also includes an assessment of the degree to which the patient has internalized pejorative cultural images of blackness. The therapist aims for the goal of helping the patient make choices which are compatible temperamentally and which can be integrated with a positive black identity.

Influence of Traditional African American Culture

The work of several black theoreticians has been helpful in elucidating factors within African and African American cultural traditions which function as a source of positive psychological adaptation for many blacks. Nobles' (1976, 1980a, b) work is perhaps best known. Nobles maintains that a common thread runnning through all African cultures and their African American derivatives is the notion of group identification, or "we-ness," as a source of orientation for individuals within the culture. Hence, the African notion that "I am because we are; and because we are, therefore, I am" (Nobles, 1980a, p. 29) is seen as an important factor to be taken into account in understanding African American psychological functioning. This community orientation contrasts with the individual, or "I do my thing, you do yours" focus of the majority culture. A concrete expression of this community orientation is reflected in the ubiquitously strong extended black family (Billingsley, 1968; White, 1980). Other aspects of black culture which may serve as sources of adaptation include a strong emphasis on spirituality (Nobles, 1980a; White, 1980), a flexible concept of time (Nobles, 1980), a well-developed ability to use affect (Thomas, 1971), and a general sensitivity to others (White, 1980).

As with majority culture influences, blacks vary considerably in their adoption of interests, values, and behaviors derived from African American traditions. However, a therapist with knowledge of the culture can help patients learn to use aspects of these traditions to deal with internal conflicts and to facilitate personal growth. Again, the extent to which this can be done varies as a function of the individual life circumstances of the patient.

Case Example

L, a 31-year-old black man who worked as a paraprofessional in a black community service agency of a small midwestern city experienced an acute paranoid schizophrenic episode one night which was expressed behaviorally in his roaming his neighborhood, shouting, "You niggers are not going to control my life anymore," and making threats on the lives of eight separate neighbors whom he had decided were involved in a conspiracy to poison him and his children. One of the neighbors phoned a black psychologist who knew both L and the community. The psychologist suggested that a close friend of L's attempt to "talk him down," and that several relatives be called to help. The friend was successful in getting L to come into his home for a cup of coffee. Meanwhile, the psychologist and several of L's relatives arrived and a spontaneous "party" began. One of L's cousins established an extended dialogue with L, expressing his caring for L and encouraging others at the party to follow suit. After two hours, L's agitation diminished considerably, and he agreed to an appointment with the psychologist the next day.

He was able to make an active commitment to treatment, including a referral for antipsychotic medication and long-term individual psychotherapy, supplemented by family therapy sessions, which included several members of L's extended family. Following a leave of absence of several months, L was able to return to his job and was promoted to a supervisory position. His relatives joked affectionately with him about the night in which he had turned into a "crazy nigger."

The use of traditional African American values and culture to facilitate effective treatment is potentially an exciting development. Recently, Jackson (1983) has outlined ways in which this area of the black experience can be expanded to provide the basis for comprehensive treatment planning in certain black patients.

Individual and Family Experiences and Endowments

The three classes of variables described above all operate in the context of a set of personal and family experiences and endowments for each patient, resulting in a unique level of psychological adaptation. For example, individual traumatic experiences (e.g., survival of an airplane crash), disturbance in family relationships, and the presence of physical handicaps are all factors contributing to various patients' decisions to seek psychotherapy. These factors may sometimes have little to do with the patient's status as a black person.

Case Example

A 25-year-old, single black woman sought psychotherapy for her nine-year-old son because of behavior problems at school, including frequent fights with classmates, "hyperactivity," and destruction of school property. The therapist quickly discovered that the mother and son had a pathologically close relationship. The son's attempt to separate psychologically from his mother appeared to be at the basis of much of his problematic behavior. The mother had been deprived and abused as a child, and appeared to be attempting to meet many of her frustrated emotional needs through her relationship with her son. Individual psychotherapy with mother and son separately was aimed at helping the two learn to function apart from each other. Attention to racial and cultural factors played a minimal role in the treatment regimen.

The author has found that central therapeutic issues which are relatively independent of race can frequently be missed by therapists in their treatment of black patients.

An Interactive Model

In summary, the model outlined consists of four classes of variables to be considered in understanding psychological functioning in any given black psychotherapy patient: 1) reactions to racial oppression; 2) influence of the majority culture; 3) influence of traditional African American culture; and 4) individual and family experiences and endowments. In reality, it is difficult to separate the influence of each of the classes of variables, since they overlap to a significant degree. Figure 1 illustrates this point. The overlapping circles reflect the fact that each set of factors may be viewed as having both a separate influence on psychological functioning and an influence on the operation of the other factors. The specific content of each set of factors is derived from a clinical assessment of the individual patient.

It is also important to note that within this framwork there are substantial individual differences with respect to the relative degrees of influence of each of the four factors. A person raised in a bigoted section of the south, for example, and whose parents were killed by members of

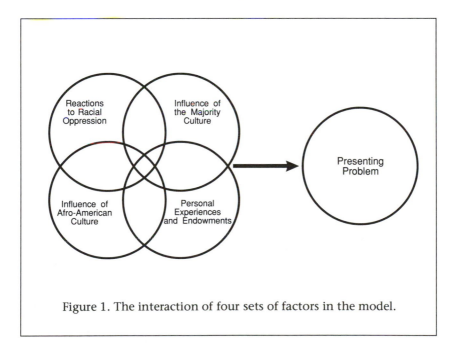

Figure 1. The interaction of four sets of factors in the model.

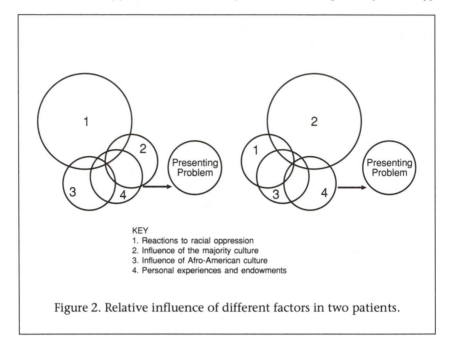

KEY
1. Reactions to racial oppression
2. Influence of the majority culture
3. Influence of Afro-American culture
4. Personal experiences and endowments

Figure 2. Relative influence of different factors in two patients.

the Ku Klux Klan, may well live a life so dominated by experiences of racial tension that the development of a way of coping with racism may overshadow other aspects of psychological functioning. In contrast, a person raised in an aristocratic black family in New England may be guided disproportionately by influences derived from the majority culture. Figure 2 illustrates the application of this model to represent these two cases. Obviously, the variety of possible combinations, both with respect to content and relative influence of each of the four factors, is infinite. In addition, judgments concerning psychopathology do not stem from the model directly, but rather from the assessment of the clinician using the model.

Conducting Psychotherapy

The principal advantage of this model as a framework for psychotherapy is that it forces the therapist to conceptualize different patients' psychological difficulties as deriving from uniquely different sets of influences. The theoretical orientation of a given therapist, of course, will determine to a large extent the specific way in which the model is employed. Issues of transference and countertransference (Jones &

Seagull, 1977) as well as the variable of the race of the therapist (Jackson, 1973; Jones & Seagull, 1977) are also important factors in determining how the model will be applied.

It should be noted that the value orientation of the therapist may also provide an important guide in the use of the model. The author, for example, has been particularly interested in the development of clinical interventions which focus on the use of traditional African American cultural experiences as a source of personal growth (Tounsel & Jones, 1980). Other black clinicians have expressed similar interests (Jackson, 1980; Jackson, 1983; Shipp, 1983). The proposed model can be utilized to assist in understanding the *context* of traditional black experiences in a given person's life and provide a basis for the design of interventions which have the potential to be effective. Therapists with other values and/or orientations may find this contextual framework equally useful.

While this framework was developed as a way of conceptualizing mental health problems in black therapy patients, the general approach might well be employed as a way of viewing psychological functioning in other ethnic minority patients as well. In doing so, the types of material forming the content of the various categories would vary somewhat among different ethnic minority groups.

References

Acosta, F.X., Yamamoto, J., & Evans, L.A. (1982). *Effective psychotherapy for low income and minority patients.* New York: Plenum Press.

Adams, H. (1976). *The use of Gestalt therapy as an alternative treatment approach used with the black client.* Paper presented at the First Annual Symposium for Delivery of Mental Health Services to the Black Consumer, Milwaukee, Wisc., April.

Anderson, G., Bass, B.A., Mumford, P.R., & Wyatt, G.E. (1977). A seminar on the assessment and treatment of black patients. *Professional Psychology, 8,* 340-348.

Banks, H.C. (1975). The black person as client and therapist. *Professional Psychology, 6,* 470-474.

Billingsley, A. (1968). *Black families in white America.* Englewood Cliffs, NJ: Prentice-Hall.

Block, J.B. (1968). The white worker and the Negro client in psychotherapy. *Social Work, 13,* 36-42.

Brill, N., & Shoorow, H. (1960). Social class and psychiatric treatment. *Archives of General Psychiatry, 3,* 340-344.

Carkhuff, R., & Pierce, R. (1967). Differential effects of therapist race and social class upon patient depth of self-exploration in the initial clinical interview. *Journal of Consulting Psychology, 31*, 632-634.

Cheek, D.K. (1976). *Assertive black . . . puzzled white.* San Luis Obispo, CA: Impact.

Cole, J., & Pilisuk, M. (1976). Differences in the provision of mental health services by race. *American Journal of Orthopsychiatry, 46*, 410-425.

Comer, J.P. (1980). White racism: Its root form, and function. In R.L. Jones (Ed.), *Black psychology*, 2nd ed. New York: Harper & Row.

Cook, N.D., & Kono, S. (1977). Black psychology: The third great tradition. *Journal of Black Psychology, 3*, 18-28.

Cross, W.E. (1980). Models of psychological nigrescence: A literature review. In R.L. Jones (Ed.), *Black psychology*, 2nd ed. New York: Harper & Row.

Frazier, E.F. (1962). *Black bourgeoisie.* New York: Collier. Gardner, L.H. (1971). Psychotherapy under varying conditions of race. *Psychotherapy: Theory, Research and Practice, 8*, 78-87.

Gibbs, J.T. (1975). Use of mental health services by black students at a predominately white university: A three-year study. *American Journal of Orthopsychiatry, 45(3)*, 430-445.

Grier, W. H., & Cobbs, P. M. (1968). *Black rage.*, New York: Basic Books.

Hall, W. S., Cross, W. E., & Freedle, R. (1972). Stages in the development of black awareness: An exploratory investigation. In R. L. Jones (Ed.), *Black psychology*, 1st ed. New York: Harper & Row.

Harper, F. D., & Stone, W. D. (1974). Toward a theory of transcendent counseling with blacks. *Journal of Nonwhite Concerns in Personnel and Guidance, 2*, 191-196.

Jackson, A. M. (1973). Psychotherapy: Theory, Research and Practice, *10*, 273-277.

Jackson, A. M. (1983). A theoretical model for the practice of psychotherapy with black populations. *Journal of Black Psychology, 10*, 19-27.

Jackson, A. M., Berkowitz, H., & Farley, G. K. (1974). Race as a variable affecting the treatment involvement of children. *Journal of the American Academy of Child Psychiatry, 13(1)*, 20-31.

Jackson, G. G. (1980). The African genesis of the Black perspective in helping. In R. L. Jones (Ed.), *Black psychology*, 2nd ed. New York: Harper & Row.

Jones, A., & Seagull, A.A. (1977). Dimensions of the relationship between the black client and the white therapist: A theoretical overview. *American Psychologist, 32*, 850-855.

Jones, E.E. (1974). Social class and psychotherapy: A critical review of the research. *Psychiatry, 37*, 307-320.

Kardiner, A., & Ovesey (1951). *The mark of oppression: Explorations in the personality of the American Negro.* New York: W. W. Norton.

Kovel, J. (1971). *White racism: A psychohistory.* New York: Viking.

Luther X (Weems). (1974). Awareness: The key to black mental health. *Journal of Black Psychology, 2(1)*, 30-37.

Mayo, J.A. (1974). The significance of sociocultural variables in the psychiatric treatment of black outpatients. *Comprehensive Psychiatry, 15*, 471-482.

Nobles, W.W. (1976). Black people in white insanity: An issue for black community mental health. *Journal of Afro-American Issues, 4(1)*, 21-27.

Nobles, W.W. (1980a). African philosophy: Foundations for black psychology. In R.L. Jones (Ed.), *Black psychology*, 2nd ed. New York: Harper & Row.

Nobles, W.W. (1980b). Extended self: Rethinking the so-called Negro self concept. In R.L. Jones (Ed.), *Black psychology*, 2nd ed. New York: Harper & Row.

Schacter, J.S., & Butts, H.F. (1968). Transference and countertransference in interracial analysis. *Journal of the American Psychoanalytic Association, 16*, 792-808.

Shipp, P.L. (1983). Counseling blacks: A group approach. *The Personnel and Guidance Journal, 62*, 108-110.

Sue, D.W. (1981). *Counseling the culturally different: Theory and practice.* New York: John Wiley

Sue, S. (1977). Community mental health services to minority groups: Some optimism, some pessimism. *American Psychologist, 32*, 616-624.

Thomas, C.W. (1971). *Boys no more.* Beverly Hills: Glencoe Press.

Tounsel, P.L., & Jones, A.C. (1980). Theoretical considerations for psychotherapy with black clients. In R.L. Jones (Ed.), *Black psychology*, 2nd ed. New York: Harper & Row.

Waite, R. (1968). The Negro patient and clinical theory. *Journal of Clinical and Consulting Psychology, 32*, 427-433.

Warren, R.C., Jackson, A.M., Nugaris, J., & Farley, G.K. (1973). Differential attitudes of black and white patients towards treatment in a child guidance clinic. *American Journal of Orthopsychiatry, 43(3)*, 384-393.

White, J.L. (1980). Toward a black psychology. In R.L. Jones (Ed.), *Black psychology*, 2nd ed. New York: Harper & Row.

Wilson, W., & Calhoun, J. F. (1974). Behavior therapy and the minority client. *Psychotherapy: Theory, Research and Practice, 11(4)*, 317-325.

Wyatt, G., Strayer, R., & Lobitz, C. (1976). Issues in the treatment of sexually dysfunctioning couples of Afro-American descent. *Psychotherapy: Theory, Research and Practice, 13*, 44-49.

Yamamoto, J., & Goin, M. K. (1965). On the treatment of the poor. *American Journal of Psychiatry, 122*, 267-271.

White Racism:
Its Root, Form, and Function

James P. Comer

After the *Report of the National Advisory Commission on Civil Disorders* implicated white racism as the major cause of black and white conflict and violent civil disorders, responses ranged from angry rejection of the notion to serious calls for corrective action. One of the weaknesses of the report was that it failed to demonstrate the psychological roots, forms, and functions of racism and their direct relationship to interracial conflict and violence.

Racism is a low-level defense and adjustment mechanism utilized by groups to deal with psychological and social insecurities similar to the manner in which individuals utilize psychic defenses and adjustment mechanisms to deal with anxiety.

In fact, the potential for a racist adjustment is rooted in personal anxiety and insecurity. A given society may promote and reward racism to enable members of the group in control to obtain a sense of personal adequacy and security at the expense of the group with less control. Racism is manifest in at least four major forms and in a racist society is transmitted from generation to generation as a positive social value similar to patriotism, religion, and good manners.

Racism cannot be explained on a here-and-now basis, nor can it be understood as a function of any single social condition of the past such as slavery. As evidence, Caribbean, Central, and South American countries with a history of slavery are less overtly racist today than most of the United States. Racism has a history peculiar to the specific social context in which it occurs. White racism in America grows out of the social conditions of sixteenth-century Europe and Africa and was shaped by forces specific to the formation, religious and political ferment, geography, and economics of this country.

The Reformation and the Justification of Slavery

Prior to the Protestant Reformation, which took root in sixteenth-century Europe, the exploitation of one group by another group to achieve economic, social, and psychological security did not have to be justified. Every race of man was subject to slavery, and the enslavement of women for sexual exploitation is as old as the institution of slavery itself. William Graham Sumner, a political and social scientist, wrote of Roman slavery:

The free men [Romans] who discussed contemporary civilization groaned over the effects of slavery on the family and private interest, but they did not see any chance of otherwise getting the work done.

The Protestant Reformation spawned the belief in man's direct accountability to God, implying personal dignity and rights unrecognized before. From that point on, particularly so because the Reformation was characterized by fanaticism and extremism, it was necessary to demonstrate that the slave was a different kind of man-indeed, less than a man. That same Reformation served as a stimulus to the rise of capitalism and European expansion.

With the discovery of the new and rich land overseas, hands and bodies were needed to exploit it. But because of religious percepts that were deeply ingrained by the seventeenth, eighteenth, and nineteenth centuries, it was necessary to de-value the man who would be used to exploit the new land. No less than Her Majesty Queen Elizabeth was burdened with the awesome decision between religious values and personal greed. She said of the activities of the capricious slaver Captain John Hawkins, "It is detestable and will call down vengeance from Heaven upon the undertakers." English historian Daniel P. Mannix pointed out that Hawkins showed Her Majesty his profit sheet; she not only forgave him but became a shareholder in his second slaving voyage.

The highly religious early American handled the conflict with equal aplomb. Historian Basil Davidson wrote, "If European attitudes toward Africans in these early times [fourteenth and fifteenth centuries] displayed a wide range of contrasts, they were generally uniform in one important respect. They supposed no natural inferiority in Africans, no inherent failure to develop and mature." But when necessary it was relatively easy to reduce the black African—different in culture, appearance, and religious practice-to the picture of a savage beast suitable for enslavement.

Because of the revolutionary ferment, with much rhetoric about freedom, rights and representation, it was particularly necessary to show the black man as an "unfit." A determined and prolonged propaganda campaign was waged in the press, by the politician, from the pulpit, and among the populace. It established the notion that slavery was not only just but beneficial. The slaver and slave-holder viewed themselves as agents of God bringing religion, light, and civilization to black heathens. These rationalizations "poisoned" the social atmosphere of American toward blacks and firmly established the notion of white superiority and black inferiority.

Patterns to Adjustment to Slavery

The effect of slavery on the slave served to reinforce the rationalization for the institution. Most of the stabilizing aspects of African culture were destroyed. Families and kinsmen were often separated. The African kinship system, economic system, government system, work, recreation, and religious systems were not permitted. Only those elements of the culture like music, the dance, and other nonthreatening features were permitted. Far from home, easily identified, socially disorganized, and despised throughout the populace, it was fairly easy to force the black African into a subservient, powerless position of forced dependency, exploitation, rejection, and/or abuse relative to an all-powerful white master and in a degraded position relative to the entire white population.

A range of adjustments to varied conditions of slavery was made by blacks with varying consequences. Identification with the master and aggressor was a frequent adjustment mode. Imitation, emulation, and acceptance of the master's values and style were a frequent consequence of this adjustment pattern. When the master was extremely paternalistic, severe dependency and infantilization frequently occurred through this mechanism. Many slaves utilized religion and personal skills to develop a relatively positive self-concept and lifestyle independent of the master, in spite of the conditions of slavery. At the opposite pole was the slave who rejected and/or rebelled against the master and his values and style.

While many, using this pattern, made satisfactory adjustments through other mechanisms, it often led to an unstable existence. There was no longer an African culture that cherished and reinforced values and relationships leading to a delay of gratification and the development of attitudes of respect for the self and responsibility toward other people. The culture of slavery, with no real opportunity for manhood or adequacy, independent of the church and the master, often fostered the immediate gratification of sexual and aggressive impulses. It was to this group of slaves, reacting as could be predicted, that the apologists and rationalizers pointed to justify the slave system. All circumstances of slavery-from house to field, from a relatively humane to an animal-like existence-resulted in consequences that ranged from severe, disabling psychic, emotional, and social trauma to moderate impairment such as low self and group esteem.

Economic exploitation was only one benefit of slavery to whites. (There was economic advantage in slavery for poor whites in that it kept blacks off the better job market.) J.D.B. DeBow, editor of the most influential pre-Civil War periodical in the South, *DeBow's Review*, pointed up another benefit. He wrote:

The poor white laborer at the North is at the bottom of the social ladder, whilst his brother here has ascended several steps and can look down upon those who are beneath him [black slaves], at an infinite remove . . . . No white man in the South serves another as a body servant, to clean his boots, wait on his table, and perform the menial services of his household.

Social distance or higher status over blacks was a way in which poor whites, often living under difficult circumstances and coping with life's tasks quite poorly, could view themselves as relatively adequate.

But the psychological benefits for whites were even more extreme. Prior to the middle of the twentieth century, America was a land of rigid religious doctrine coupled with the laxity that rapid expansion, wealth, and an individualistic frontier spirit fosters. Thus man sinned, but he could not see it. It had to be denied or seen in others. Nobody was more vulnerable to the "projection of evil" or psychological exploitation than the black man.

Projection of *Bad Impulses*

Until relatively recently, the wish or expression of normal sexuality and normal forms of aggression have been viewed as bad . . . sinful . . . wrong. To reduce guilt and anxiety, the wish or desire for expression of these impulses was often projected onto blacks. Louis Jolyon West, a psychiatrist wrote, "In spite of the historical fact that for more than 250 years in North America whites were often raped, enslaved, and slain by Indians while the Negro was the white man's helper, it is still the Negro who appears in the white Oklahoma maiden's dream as the ominous rapist, and the sight of a Negro boy dancing with a white girl still moves Oklahomans to feelings and acts of violence (15, p. 647). Charles Pinderhughes, a psychoanalyst, gives a likely explanation. He points out that if a group is different in appearance, culture, and behavior—particularly when a low value is given the specific differences—the group can be associated with low things—the bottom, buttocks, genitals, and sexuality.

The apologists for slavery had made their case well and such an association was quite possible. The average white American, until recently, knew little of the black kingdoms of Ghana, Mali, and Songhay or the highly ordered societies of the Yoruba, Ashanti, or Ibo. The myth was that the African was a naked, lustful savage running loose in the jungle before he was rescued by the white man. The Indian, while different, was an enemy to be destroyed, not to be exploited—a noble savage. Thus rationalization and debasement did not have to be carried as far in that case.

A United States Congressman from South Carolina presented the viewpoint of many in a poem written in 1837; it is short of being a classic but revealing nonetheless. He wrote:

> In this new home, what'er the Negro's fate-More bless'd his life than in his native state! Instructed . . . in the only school Barbarians ever know—a Master's rule, The Negro learns each civilizing art that softens and subdues the savage heart, Assumes the tone of those with whom he lives, Acquires the habit that refinement gives, And slowly learns, but surely while a slave, The lesson that his country never gave.

This picture, combined with the fact that slavery left many without a purpose or opportunity beyond the gratification of basic human drives-sexual, aggressive, survival—rendered blacks as a group vulnerable to the projections of "bad impulses." The fact that the black man could not defend himself against physical, social, or psychological abuse without fear of extreme repression did not help the situation.

Skin color differences in the racist American milieu had an impact that they did not and do not have in other places. This characteristic, perhaps more than any other, facilitated the projection of "evil" sexual and aggressive impulses onto blacks. Psychoanalysts have repeatedly found among their patients a psychic association of blackness with darkness, fear, evil, danger, sexuality, and aggression. West wrote:

> For man, daytime is a good time, the safe time, the healthy time, when he can see what is going on and make his way in the world. The daydream is aspiration; but the nightmare is consummate terror . . . Night is the time of secret, mystery, magic, danger, evil; and the man of the night is black (15, pp. 646-647).

References

Botkin, B.A. (1945). *Lay my burden down.* Chicago: University of Chicago.

Comer, J.P. (1968). Individual development and black rebellion: Some parallels. *Midway, 9(1)*, 40-46.

Davidson, B. (1959). *The lost cities of Africa.* Boston: Atlantic-Little, Brown.

Davidson, B. (1961). *Black mother.* Boston: AtlanticLittle, Brown.

DeBow, J.D.P. (1963). The interest in slavery of the southern non-slave holder. In E.L. McKitrick (Ed.), *Slavery defended: The views of the Old South.* Englewood, Cliffs, N.J.: Prentice-Hall.

Gibbs, Jr., J.L. (Ed.) (1966). *Peoples of Africa.* New York: Holt, Rinehart & Winston.

Grayson, W.J. (1856). *The hireling and the slave, chicora and other poems.* Charleston, S.C.: McCord & Co.

Jordan, W.D. (1968). *White over black.* Chapel Hill: University of North Carolina Press.

Mannix, D.P., and Cowley, M. (1965). *Black cargoes.* New York: Viking.

National Advisory Commission on Civil Disorder (1968). *Report of the National Advisory Commission on civil Disorders.* New York: Bantam.

Newby, I.A. (1965). *Jim Crow's defense.* Baton Rouge: Louisiana State University Press.

Pinderhughes, C.A. (1969). Understanding black power: Processes and proposals. *American Journal of Psychiatry, 125,* 15521557.

Sumner, W.G. (1959). *Folkways.* New York: Dover.

West, L.J. (1967). The psychobiology of racial violence.*Archives of General Psychiatry, 16,* 645-651.

X, Malcolm (1966). *The autobiography of Malcolm X* (with the assistance of Alex Haley). New York: Grove Press.

The Other Bodies in the River

Lloyd T. Delany

The murky Mississippi River flows slowly through the state of Mississippi. And the Pearl River winds a snake's course into the main stream. In 1964, when an honest search began for three missing civil rights workers, it was natural to drag the rivers.

James Chaney, Andrew Goodman, and Michael Schwerner were found. Shot, and then buried in a pit. But there were other bodies in the rivers. Two were found in the Mississippi, and a couple more in the Pearl before the graves of the murdered civil rights workers were uncovered. Then the dragging of the rivers ceased. There was no investigation into those other deaths. No one really knows why the bodies were in the river, or really who they were, or how many more remain in the mud. Kipling wrote of "the great, grey, green, greasy Limpopo River." It is a terrible temptation, when speaking of the Mississippi, to add the word *deadly*.

As a nation, we do well what Freud termed *the work of mourning*, a task he described as necessary to assuage feelings of loss and guilt after facing a death. We have mourned the death of Martin Luther King, Jr., very well, indeed.

White America is shocked frequently by such violence. There is mourning in varying degrees—depending on how well-known the victim is. And we float down the River Styx while as a nation we drown the memory of violence over and over again.

For there is a sickness in our society. White racism. It is classic pathology with the usual destructive behavior: acting out, denial of reality, projection, transference of blame, disassociation, justification. The sickness of racism runs deep in the history of this nation, and no institution in society is immune.

Acting Out

The National Advisory Commission on Civil Disorders released its report after a lengthy study, and the report traces the history of violent acting out through many yesterdays:

Cincinnati Riot of 1829: "White residents invaded Cincinnati's

'Little Africa,' killed Negroes, burned their property and ultimately drove half of the colored population from the city."

New York Riot, 1863: "The crowd refused to permit firemen in the area, and the whole block was gutted. Then the mob spilled into the Negro area, where many were slain and thousands forced to flee town."

New Orleans Riot, 1870 (quoting General Sheridan): "At least nine-tenths of the casualties were perpetuated by the police and citizens by stabbing and smashing in the heads of many who had already been wounded or killed by policemen . . . It was not just a riot, but an absolute massacre by the police."

The Commission report documents scores of such examples in decade after decade. Pathological acting out of hate also can be found in lynching statistics. The authoritative *Documentary History of the Negro People in the United States*, edited by Herbert Aptheker (Citadel Press) proves that 3,426 blacks are known to have been lynched between 1882 and 1947. The National Association for the Advancement of Colored People found that between 1892 and 1918, a black man, woman, or child was lynched every three and one-half days somewhere in this country.

As the President's Commission on Civil Disorders traces the patterns of racial conflict, it becomes apparent that up to and including World War II acting out involved white racists physically attacking, destroying, and burning blacks and black property. Following World War II, and to some extent during it, the patterns of racial conflict shifted. Black violence emerged, almost entirely in attacks on property *within* the black community. Few whites were physically attacked in these disorders.

This is crucial in the context of today. For whites cringing at the prospect of black violence, it should be comforting to note that the Commission finds that all of the 1967 disorders, including those listed as the eight major areas—Buffalo, Cincinnati, Detroit, Milwaukee, Minneapolis, Newark, Plainfield (N.J.), and Tampa—involved primarily destruction of ghetto property. Almost all the serious injuries and deaths involved blacks killed by law enforcement agents.

Violence, black violence, has meant burning their own black neighborhoods, looting local stores, destroying property within the ghetto areas. These are attacks on the *symbols* of ghetto oppression.

Recent pathology involving law enforcement agents is familiar: State troopers with tear gas to halt the march to Jackson, Mississippi, in 1966 following the shooting of James Meredith; the National Guardsmen who shot into Newark riot area stores which had remained untouched because they bore signs indicating black ownership.

No one has made this pathology as clear as Dick Gregory, the actor

and active civil rights worker, in an interview in the Long Island newspaper, *Newsday*. Here is part of what he said:

> *You ought to try to integrate those schools like we did in Greenwood,*
> *Mississippi. Spent a whole summer talking to colored folk, trying to*
> *get them to commit their kids. Had to lie to them, tell them the*
> *government was going to protect them, but we knew damn good and*
> *well we were all going to get killed. And you finally get 12 black kids*
> *committed, but the morning school is open, you only get eight.*
> *Maybe you've got to feel what its like to be walking down the street*
> *with that little black kid's hand in your hand. And your hand is*
> *soaking from your sweat, because you know what's going to happen.*
> *But the kid don't. And so you approach those steps to that school, not*
> *only are you attacked by the white mob, but also by the sheriff and*
> *the police . . .*
>
> *The next thing you know, you're knocked down in the gutter with*
> *that cracker's foot on your chest and a double-barrelled shotgun on*
> *your throat. And he's saying 'move, nigger, and I'll blow your brains*
> *out.' Which is interesting because that's the only time that cracker*
> *admits we got brains . . .*
>
> *Maybe you have to lay in that gutter, knowing it's your time now,*
> *Baby, and then look across the street . . . laying down in that gutter,*
> *from that gutter position and see the FBI standing across the street*
> *taking pictures . . .*
>
> *And then as you lay there in that gutter, man, it finally dawns on*
> *you that that little five-year-old kid's hand is not in the palm of your*
> *hand anymore. And that really scares you . . .*
>
> *And you look around trying to find the kid. And you find him just in*
> *time to see a brick hit him in the mouth.*
>
> *Man, you wouldn't believe it until you see a brick hit a five-year-old*
> *kid in the mouth.*

Denial

California's former State Superintendent of Public Instruction,
Max Rafferty, spoke against the new Civil Rights Bill by evading the
issue. The *San Diego Union* article about his speech in that city reported:

> *Rafferty said the Bill is "superfluous and redundant" and would have*
> *a wicked result raising false expectations. "There are four things*
> *causing American sickness," Max Rafferty told the group, "and I*
> *think that everyone will agree there is a sickness." Rafferty listed*
> *them as violence, pornography, law breakers, and tolerance for drug*

users and addicts. Rafferty said he would have voted against the
Civil Rights Bill "because it will not do any good."

The Jackson, Mississippi, *Clarion-Ledger* used both denial and dis-association in a 1964 editorial before the bodies of the murdered civil rights workers were found.

If they were murdered, it is by no means the first case of such dispo-
sition by Communists or their dupes to insure their silence. However,
the careful absence of clues makes it seem likely that they are quar-
tered in Cuba or another Communist area awaiting their next task.
There is no reason to believe them harmed by citizens of the most
law-abiding state of the Union.

After the assassination of Martin Luther King, Jr., Georgia's Gover-nor Lester G. Maddox, reported by United Press International, demon-strated both denial and what, as a clinician, I can only call *thought disorder*. Maddox said:

Could it be the Communists had decided that he, Dr. King, had lost
his effectiveness, and this was a way to revitalize their efforts? Or
was this only to pass the Bill (Civil Rights Bill) . . . I believe they
done him in, and I will continue to believe that until they apprehend
the killer or prove otherwise. I hope I am wrong, and the guilty person
is apprehended.

This Communist-connected form of denial is particularly danger-ous, for it denies not only white citizen responsibility, but it takes the race problem right out of this country. Should this projection of the race problem onto Communists continue, it could discredit both whites and blacks who are working together to end a national shame. In addition, it will further disillusion and alienate American youths of both races, young people who seek a better future.

Denial must end, because it will take all the cooperation citizens of this country can summon to cure the sickening results of racism. Black nationalists certainly are guilty of denial, but they are hardly a threat. Everyone knows that they are playing games with their dreams of sepa-rate communities. Before his murder, Malcolm X gave up the whole business of separatism and shifted toward working with both white and black elements of the community.

Martin Luther King moved from being a black civil rights worker into working for a total civil peace. He rose through the ethnocentric viewpoint to the broader vision of economics and peace.

What a symbol it is: King went into Memphis over a strike of *garbage* collectors. A strike by the lowest paid men in our society.

Certainly a shocking example of denial is the persistent rumor that Martin Luther King arranged for his own martyrdom, that he was somehow involved with his assassin. Obviously, he knew he was in danger when he went to Memphis. He lived with danger.

It should not have been necessary for Martin Luther King to stage marches in Montgomery, Birmingham, Selma, or to go to jail 30 times trying to achieve for his people those rights which people of lighter hue are entitled to simply by being born.

The Commission on Civil Disorders clarifies the pathology of denial: "What white Americans have never fully understood, but what the Negro can never forget, is that white society is deeply implicated in the ghetto. White institutions created it. White institutions maintain it, and white society condones it."

This sickness, which the Commission has once more diagnosed, has been explained many times and many ways. Two black men, commenting 74 years apart, spoke typically and similarly about the pathology of denial. Frederick Douglass, the leading Negro abolitionist from the early 1840s until his death, wrote in 1892:

Where rests the responsibility for the lynch law . . . not entirely with the ignorant mob . . . they are simply the hangmen, not the court, judge, or jury. They simply obey the public sentiment . . . the sentiment created by wealth and respectability, by press and pulpit.

The late Dr. Benjamin Mays, then retired president of Morehouse College, said in his eulogy to Dr. Martin Luther King, Jr.:

Make no mistake, the American people are in part responsible for Martin Luther King's death. The assassin heard enough condemnation of King and of Negroes to know that he had public support. He knew that there were millions of people in the United States who wished that King were dead. He had support.

The roots of denial are as old as the nation itself. They go deep into our foundations. Thomas Jefferson, author of the Declaration of Independence, wrote the words: "All men are created equal, . . . endowed by their Creator with certain unalienable Rights, that among these are Life, Liberty and the pursuit of Happiness." Jefferson held in bondage 106 men, women, and children—slaves. On August 26, 1814, in a letter to a friend, Edward Coles, he wrote:

Nothing is more certainly written in the book of Fate than that these people are to be free. Nor is it less certain that the two races, equally free, cannot live in the same government. Nature, habit, opinion, have drawn indelible lines of distinction between them.

Too little of our denial in thought and emotion has changed with time. White society has suffered from a long illness.

Disassociation

The process of disassociation is far more sweeping than that of denial, for in disassociation, large segments of one's actions are treated as though they never existed. Reasonable Americans now realize they disassociated when they forgot about those three murdered civil rights workers. And it is becoming politically popular to point to our disassociation with the misery of the American Indian.

But few Americans remember the internment in the United States in virtual concentration camps of 72,000 American citizens during World War II—Japanese American citizens. Except for the weaker parallel of Indian removal in President Jackson's day, there was no precedent in American annals for a mass internment without evidence of disloyalty, and with race as the sole determining factor. More than 30,000 families were imprisoned.

There had been a long history of strong racism directed at Japanese residents on the West Coast. As early as 1906 students of oriental background were segregated in San Francisco schools. Japanese immigrants fared exceedingly well as farmers and, beginning in 1913, land ownership laws were passed specifically to limit Japanese land holdings in California. Limits on Japanese immigration to this country became more and more stringent over the years.

The late Earl Warren, who was Chief Justice of the U.S. Supreme Court, was California's Attorney General at the beginning of World War II. That very different man led the movement to send Japanese, citizens and aliens alike, to internment camps.

War is an emotional time, but color counts. German American citizens kept their homes and their jobs. The racial composition of Hawaii differs from that of California. There was no such internment in Hawaii. In a speech to a convention of California district attorneys and sheriffs shortly after Pearl Harbor, Warren explained the total absence of fifth column and sabotage activities on the part of Japanese Americans was a "studied effort to hold off until zero hour." There are no recorded cases of Japanese American spy activity during World War II.

The scholarly book, *California*, by John W. Caughey (Prentice-Hall) describes clearly what happened after President Roosevelt signed executive order 9066, giving the War Department authority to act on *enemy aliens*.

> General J.L. DeWitt then ordered *"voluntary departure"* of Japanese
> from designated coastal areas, an 8 P.M. to 6 A.M. curfew . . . and
> on March 27, 1942, evacuation of all Japanese—citizens and aliens
> alike. Some 110,000 persons were subject to this order, two thirds of
> them American citizens. Japanese Americans of western Washington

and Oregon and southern Arizona were included, but the main body to be evacuated was from California.

The evacuees were transferred to more distant relocation centers, two of them on the eastern margin of California, the other eight scattered as far east as Arkansas. These were called Relocation *rather than* Concentration *camps. Barbed wire fences and armed guards gave the opposite impression.*

Some youths were released from the centers through enlistments or the draft, many of the young men went off to the battlefields in Europe and later in the Pacific, where they performed with extraordinary valor. A few were released to go to guaranteed jobs outside General DeWitt's prescribed area. Late in the war, a few were permitted to come back to California. Most were kept in camps until after V-J Day, and the Centers were not closed until January 1, 1946.

Transference of Blame

Racism, among other things, is a chronic blaming process, a process which requires self-fulfillment. The person who needs to blame the ghetto man for living in squalor, who claims that the Negro is incapable of being educated, or that the Negro doesn't really want to work, must, by the nature of the blaming process, perpetuate that which he deplores. Less than one week after the assassination of Martin Luther King, Jr., then Congressman George Bush(R) Texas, submitted a bill under which persons convicted of breaking the law during civil disorders would be prevented from either keeping or getting federal jobs. The National Commission on Civil Disorders carefully explains that the dearth of jobs is a basic cause for disorders in the ghetto.

Transference is a defense mechanism by which an individual evades responsibility for his own acts by placing blame elsewhere. Perhaps no characteristic of racism is more common in this nation.

Negroes are getting tired of being blamed for living in substandard housing, for being unemployed and underemployed, and for "not taking advantage of" educational opportunities.

The Commission on Civil Disorder says:

Pervasive unemployment and underemployment are the most persistent and serious grievances in minority areas. They are inextricably linked to the problem of civil disorder . . . Despite growing federal expenditures for manpower, development, and training programs, and sustained general economic prosperity and increasing demands for skilled workers, about two million—white and nonwhite—are permanently unemployed. About 10 million are underemployed, of whom six and a half million work full time for wages below the poverty line.

About housing, the Commission reported that

. . . nearly six million substandard housing units remain occupied in the United States. The housing problem is particularly acute in minority ghettos . . . many ghetto residents simply cannot pay the rent necessary to support decent housing. In Detroit, for example, over 40 percent of the nonwhite occupied units require rent of over 35 and one-half per cent of the tenant's income.

Second, discrimination prevents access to many nonslum areas, particularly in the good suburbs where good housing exists . . . The Federal programs have been able to do comparatively little to provide housing for the disadvantaged. In the 31-year history of subsidized federal housing, only about 800,000 units have been constructed . . . By a comparison of a period of only three years longer, FHA insurance guarantees have made possible the construction of over 10 million middle and upper income units.

About education, the Commission stated that

. . . education in a democratic society must equip the children of a nation to realize their potential . . . For the community at large, the schools have discharged this responsibility well, but for many minorities, and particularly for the children of the racial ghetto, the schools have failed to provide the educational experience which could help overcome the effects of discrimination and deprivation.

Projection and Justification

The Negro in our society is the victim of one of the most commonly employed devices used by individuals to avoid dealing with deep-seated conflicts. Projection lets a man attribute to others characteristics of his own which he knows or fears are unacceptable to others. James Baldwin, in *The Fire Next Time*, comments on how well white racists use this device:

If one examines the myths which proliferate in this country concerning the Negro, one discovers beneath these myths a kind of sleeping terror of some condition which we refuse to imagine. In a way, if the Negro were not here, we might be forced to deal within ourselves and our own personalities with all those vices, all those conundrums, and all those mysteries with which we infest the Negro race . . . The Negro is thus penalized for the guilty imagination of the white people who invest him with their hates and longings, and the Negro is the principal target for their sexual paranoia . . .

We would never allow Negroes to starve, to grow bitter and to die in ghettos all over the country if we were not driven by some nameless fear that has nothing to do with Negroes. We would never victimize, as we do, children whose only crime is color. We wouldn't drive Negroes mad as we do by accepting them in ball parks and on concert stages, but not in our homes, not in our neighborhoods, not in our churches.

Justification is fairly obvious. It is racist. And it is sick. Like a letter to the editor published in *Newsday* in May, 1968:

I am a white middle-class American who along with tens of millions of other middle-class Americans, both black and white, has been roundly criticized and condemned as a "racist" by the President's Commission on Civil Disorders.

I am a white middle-class American who served his country in World War II, who managed via 22 years of hard work and initiative to pull himself and his family out of the slums of Manhattan to life in a middle-class community in a house which will require 19 more years of labor to pay for.

I am tired of hearing Whitey blamed for all the plights and ills of the Negro in Harlem and elsewhere, and I am sick and tired of the "get Whitey" slogans of the black extremists who would rather take what Whitey possesses rather than working for it like this Whitey has.

Yes, I am a white middle-class American, tired but proud of the community in which I now reside . . . . If this be labeled racist by the learned gentlemen of the President's panel, I shall wear this label with pride. (Editor's note: The letter was signed, we withhold the name here.

A reprint by the group for the Advancement of Psychiatry describes the adverse psychiatric effects of attitudes in whites in which:

. . . a feeling of superior worth may be gained merely from the existence of a down-graded group. This leads to an unrealistic and unadapted kind of self-appraisal based on invidious comparison, rather than on solid personal growth and achievement . . . And even encourages the expression of hostile or aggressive feelings against whole groups of people.

It forces a distortion of reality and provides a target in the lower status group for the projection of painful feelings from one's self or from the significant people in the immediate environment onto members of the segregated group. Anxiety springing from unrelated personal problems may thus be combatted by inappropriate displacement of the constrictual feelings to the area of race relations.

Such displacement impedes direct and mature facing and dealing with the actual anxiety-arousing conflicts.

There should be pride of race in every man. The white man who justifies his prejudice refuses to accept reasons for blacks' pride. And the Negro in our culture suffers from lack of both white and black acceptance of black dignity and honor in our history. Take a few examples: that black men were with Columbus—one of them a ship's pilot; that Estevanico, a black man, discovered and explored the Southwest; and the Negro, Du Sable, founded Chicago.

Since the man who wrote to *Newsday* fought in World War II, his life may have been saved by a Negro. Dr. Charles Drew established the method for preserving blood plasma. After Dr. Drew developed this method, blood plasma was given according to race, contrary to all scientific fact that there is no difference. This irrational practice since has been discontinued.

Men like the letter writer forget that the first man to die for this nation's independence was Crispus Attucks, that 5,000 other black men fought in the American Revolution. Blacks fought with Jackson in the War of 1812; 186,000 of them in the Civil War; blacks rode with Teddy Roosevelt's Rough Riders in the Spanish American War; black units in World War I won special commendations for gallantry. Black men fought German racism in a *segregated* army in World War II, and black men died in higher proportion than whites in Viet Nam.

Certainly racism and bigotry are not limited to the United States. They are universal. In the Sudan, the Muslim North commits genocide on the African South. In India, the Hindu is directed against the Dravidian of the South. The Hottentots regard themselves as the Khoikhoin—the chosen people. The Chinese culture is highly racist; the Chinese look down on everybody else.

But our own racism is our own pathology. And we must face it. The recent rash of civil rights laws often is cited as an example of our progress. Yet these laws actually contain little that the Civil Rights Act of 1875 does not contain.

A critical question about the kind of society we are is answered by Dr. Kenneth Clark. Called to testify before the President's Commission on Civil Disorders, he said:

I read the report of the 1919 riot in Chicago, and it is as if I were reading the report of the investigating committee of the Harlem Riot of 1935, the report of the investigating committee on the Harlem Riot of 1943, the report of the McCone Commission on the Watts Riot.

"I must say in candor to you members of this commission—it is kind of Alice in Wonderland, with the same moving pictures shown over and over again. The same analysis. And the same inaction."

References

Clark, K. (1965). *Dark ghetto*. New York: Harper & Row.
Du Bois, W.E.B., Smith, P. (1966). *The souls of black folks*. New York: Fawcett.
Fanon, F. (1963). *The wretched of the earth*. New York: Grove Press.
Parsons, T., & Clark, K. (1966). *The Negro American*. Boston: Houghton Mifflin.
X, Malcolm (1965). *The autobiography of Malcolm X*. New York: Grove Press.

Racism: A Cultural Analysis of the Problem

James M. Jones

Introduction

This chapter takes the view that despite the fact that pollsters report that racial attitudes of white Americans are becoming more tolerant, racism continues to be a problem in America. Racism continues to be a problem because there continue to be major disparities between African American and white citizens which reflect the fact that historical biases have not been ameliorated; there are substantially lower participation rates for African Americans in major sectors of American commerce, education, political and legal activities which suggest that African Americans are still not participating as full citizens in this society; there is evidence that the more positive racial attitudes reported by pollsters do not reflect the ongoing white antipathies toward African Americans demonstrated by ingroup preference and self-interest.

A review of current statistics on racial disparities in health, education and welfare and related life circumstances reveals the substantial black-white gaps that over the past several decades have not diminished in spite of absolute gains for blacks. Consideration of aspects of African American culture will suggest that while discrimination on the basis of race (skin color) has been legislatively extirpated, continued biases associated with cultural aspects of black life abound.

Given the fact of a multicultural population, group differences are a reality with potential to be a major source of strength to the fabric of this society. However, for this to happen, we need to find ways to make people in power appreciate this potential and utilize and/or share their power in ways that insure broader contributions and participation of racial and ethnic minority segments of the population.

This chapter is organized to explore the above observations and arguments. Using the black-white relationship as a model of the problem, I will consider ways of understanding the problem as a matter of causation (the systemic bias versus individual inadequacy) and the differential remedies these causes imply, and examine an approach to African American culture which emphasizes its multidimensionality as well as its evolutionary character. Aspects of black culture offered as guides to this discussion are organized around the acronym *TRIOS*, standing, respectively, for *T*ime, *R*hythm, *I*mprovisation, *O*ral Expression, and *S*pirituality. The next section considers the relative effects of skin color and culture as the basis of contemporary "racial" disadvantage. The role of power in maintaining racial disadvantage is also discussed. Finally, I suggest that the amelioration of racial bias requires a more inclusive multidimensional view of psychosocial characteristics and their corresponding cultural determinants, and the dynamics of inter-group relations that follow from perceived ingroup similarity and outgroup differences.

A Look at the Problem

There is factual, as well as presumptive, evidence that race, gender, age, and ethnicity all influence behavioral outcomes in this society. The central concern is with ways which outcomes are *negatively* influenced by these factors. These negatively influencing factors are:

Prejudice:

the prior negative judgment of the members of a race or religion or the occupants of another significant social role, held in disregard of the facts that contradict it . . . an affective, categorical mode of mental functioning involving rigid prejudgment and misjudgment of human groups (Jones, 1972, p. 61).

Discrimination:

those systematically differential behavioral outcomes associated with social categories. It is seen as following from the prior negative judgments characteristic of prejudice.

Racism:

results from the transformation of race prejudice and/or ethnocentrism through the exercise of power against a racial group defined as inferior, by individuals and institutions with the intentional or unintentional support of the entire culture (Jones, 1972, p. 172).

While each of these negatively influencing factors creates problems of opportunity for groups in this society, the remedies implied by each vary. For example, it is usually considered that prejudice, being a *prior judgment*, only requires one to bring the prejudiced person in contact with the victim to learn about the group characteristics, to reduce stereotypes, and to rely on more individuating information in making judgments about a specific member of that group (Deutsch & Collins, 1951; Lockesley, Ortiz, & Hepburn, 1980). Discrimination, on the other hand, is the behavioral consequence of such negative judgments and its remedy is often quota-based programs of equal opportunity and affirmative action. Racism, too, has several different characteristics, one of which is *institutional racism*, which does not require proof of intention to discriminate and may be remedied by affirmative action programs. The most intractable, yet possibly most critical, is *cultural racism*, which requires a new look at cultural assumptions and their manifestations in social organization.

In the following pages, I will summarize some of the evidence for the negative consequences of being African American in this country. I will consider a number of explanations of these disparities in a later section. Although concerned with racial bias here, it is obvious that in many cases, the disparities now are wholly independent of economic considerations. In this light, I agree with Wilson (1978) that economic class is a powerful determinant of outcomes for all citizens of this country. I will not, however, argue that economic condition is more or less important than race, but will suggest that the race/culture intersection defines a critical dimension of racism in contemporary society.

Ways of Understanding the Problem

Historically, psychology, particularly social psychology, has focused its attention on PREJUDICE: a faulty generalization from a group characterization (stereotype) to an individual member of the group, irrespective of either a) the accuracy of the group stereotype, or b) the applicability of the group characterization to the individual in question. This prevailing approach clearly emphasizes individual characteristics of judgment and information-processing tendencies and capabilities. The resultant attitudinal biases have historically been associated with both a negative motivation to harm dissimilar others or a positive motivation to help similar others.

A significant body of persuasive evidence has accumulated in the past few years suggesting that prejudice has a general cognitive information-processing basis which is exploited by the realities of interracial dynamics in this society. The illusory correlation idea (Hamilton & Gifford, 1976) offers a basis for associating negative traits with African Americans; the cognitive complexity idea (Linville & Jones, 1980) sets conditions for both the negative bias against African Americans as well as potential for positive bias based on interracial contact and group boundaries; Brewer (1979) has presented strong evidence for the inclusionary dimension of prejudice (in-group favoritism).

Additional evidence has shown that actual perceptual and behavioral bias against blacks continues to be widespread in spite of attitudinal surveys suggesting that racial attitudes are becoming more positive. Crosby, Bromley & Saxe (1980) have presented persuasive evidence for bias against blacks in helping, aggression and non-verbal indicators of hostility. Gaertner and Dovidio (1981) argue persuasively for the continued biases of whites who are well intentioned. McConahay and Hough (1976) makes a similar argument citing the displacement of conventional negativity to contemporary symbols of racial disaffection (busing, affirmative action, etc.)

The notion of prejudice is concerned with individual cognitive judgments and the affective tone attached to them. Statistics on well being are clearly aggregated for African Americans as a group. Can one reconstruct these group outcomes on the basis of individual antipathies? We believe not. The wide range of differences in disparate outcomes across regions of the country, age groups, economic, political and educational strata and so on are more parsimoniously explained by a patterning of systemic responses to African Americans. The first idea we should consider is *discrimination*.

Discrimination refers simply to differential treatment of individuals on the basis of their social category by people or the institutional policies they create and enforce. As I noted earlier, discrimination may be thought of as the behavioral consequences of prejudice. In this regard, it was institutional racism (the institutionalized form of racial discrimination) that led President Lyndon Johnson to issue Executive Order 2301 establishing affirmative action as a remedy for discrimination. Because President Johnson viewed racial discrimination as an institutional problem, the remedy was not required to meet an *intentionality* criterion. That is, evidence of racial disparities, was *ipso facto* evidence of discrimination and institutional culpability and affirmative action was seen as both a necessary and appropriate remedy.

President Johnson was persuaded by the report of the Kerner Commission (National Advisory Commission on Civil Disorders, 1968) that the problem of African Americans was caused by white racism. Further, that white racism was found in institutional practices and was responsible for the pages of statistics showing the disadvantaged plight of African Americans. While the fact of negative disparities for African Americans was persuasive for President Johnson, former President Reagan's administration took an opposite view.

The Reagan administration's approach to affirmative action, led by the Head of the Division of Civil Rights in the Justice Department,

Bradford Reynolds, rested on two major points. Before a remedy for alleged institutional discrimination can be considered, according to this view, the aggrieved party must prove:

1. the discrimination was intentional, and
2. the accuser was him or herself *personally* discriminated against.

The first point significantly reduces the scope of remedies of racial discrimination since only in those cases where intent can be proven is any remedy required. The second point further restricts the domain of discrimination remedies since only if a specific case of discrimination can be documented is any remedy required, *and only for the documented case!* Therefore, the aggregate basis for determining the existence of discrimination with corresponding widespread group remediation (i.e., quota-based affirmative action) would no longer serve to eliminate restrictive practices. Therefore, one could characterize President Johnson's policies as consistent with the traditional liberal view that povery and dependency reside in causes external to the victims; whereas, President Reagan's rings a more conservative theme suggesting that a person's disadvantage is not caused by differential treatment, but by the victim's personal inadequacies.

There is a body of data which reveals racial disparities on several meaningful indices of life in America. However, just as the philosophies of the administrations of Presidents Reagan and Johnson clearly illustrate, our understanding of and reaction to these disparities depend

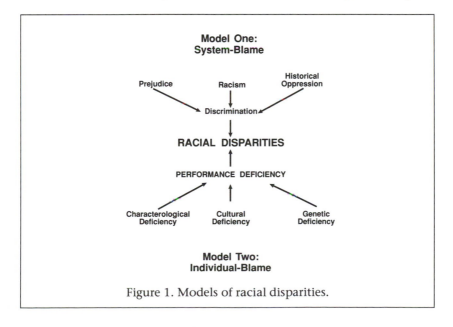

Figure 1. Models of racial disparities.

largely on where we see the locus of causality. Figure 1 depicts these two contrasting viewpoints or models for understanding the source of these racial disparities.

The critical starting point is the fact of racial disparities, found in the middle of the models. Moving from here to the top, we have Model One which presumes that racial disparities result from systemic or structural features of the nation's institutions (and the persons who run them). These systemic features may be the result of individuals who act in prejudicial ways, the historical legacy of denial, oppression and legislative, judicial, educational and economic arrangements which thwarted and suppressed African Americans (often by design). This "System-Blame" point of view is associated with Allport's (1954) telescopic model of prejudice occurring at increasingly macro-systemic levels of society and Jones' (1972) analysis of institutional and cultural racism. Although the "system-blame" approach is generally at a molar level of social analysis, it does not preclude the more molecular approaches of traditional social psychological analyses which focus on individuals and attitudes and behaviors because it also recognizes the *prejudice-discrimination* link.

Moving to the bottom of Figure 1 we arrive at another perception of causes of racial disparities. In this view, there is an implicit assumption that the system (both structure and function) is an opportunity based meritocracy. Failure to benefit from or be successful in the system can only be attributed to inadequacies in the individual. This "Individual Blame" point of view accepts the idea that African Americans are worse off than whites as a group, but attribute this disparity to inferior performance of blacks, which is in turn attributed to their inferior character, culture or genes. When a society espouses meritocractic bases of outcome predicated on a belief in equity (outcomes proportional to inputs) then such disparities can be fully justified on the basis of presumed deficiencies.

A possible midway position between Models One and Two acknowledges past discrimination but not contemporary bias. This view is expressed in two forms:1) there is no contemporary inequality of treatment, therefore, no needed remediation; and 2) contemporary inequality is only due to historical inequities and discrimination against whites is inappropriate since it attempts to remedy a past wrong with a contemporary one.

Most distressing for our analysis is the evidence that the general tendency among white Americans is to view racial disparities from the perspective of Model Two. Kluegel and Smith (1985) have presented substantial and convincing data that show white Americans believe racial disparities in SES are due primarily to lack of motivation among African Americans, that there are no "structural" impediments to SES advancement for African Americans and that the "system" is an opportunity structure for *anyone* with the individual characteristics to get ahead.

Based on white respondents' answers to questions about causes of SES differences between African Americans and whites, the following profile emerged: In the age range 40-60, where we might presume the highest concentration of people with power and influence to occur, only 33% believe discrimination is a cause of SES differences between African Americans and whites, while nearly 70% believe motivational factors are responsible. While the profile improves significantly for younger white Americans, they too feel motivation is a more prevalent cause than discrimination for black-white SES disparities. This blame-the-victim approach (cf. Caplan and Nelson, 1973; Ryan, 1971) is consistent with a general tendency to make dispositional attributions for the behavior of others and to commit the "fundamental attributional error" (Pettigrew, 1978; Ross, 1977) by discounting environmental influences on behavior.

Obviously the remedy to African American-white disparities will vary depending on whether one believes Model One or Model Two gives the best accounting. However, the two approaches are not mutually exclusive. That is, historically, the systems of discrimination and oppression (systematic banking and real estate practices of red-lining, the separate but equal doctrine legalized by the *Plessy v. Ferguson* decision of 1896, and employment discrimination) not only created the conditions of racial disparities but also contributed substantially to the creation of a ghetto environment in which basic opportunities were not available.

Being in a restricted, disadvantaged environment, and unpredictable, offers minimal advantage to institutionalized education, offers little employment, and maintains a reward structure that encourages certain forms of lawlessness and family disintegration, the more successfully one adapts to this environment and its requirements for "success," the less likely one is to develop attributes that are functional in the broader society. Thus, the intersection of Models One and Two can be conceived as a sinister *double-bind*, such that short-term adaptation may lead to long term disadvantage. This problem is further exacerbated by the prevailing notion that the circumstances of disadvantage and truncated opportunity are actually *caused* by those who are victimized by it.

There is ample evidence that Americans' belief in the principle of equity translates further to a belief that this is a *just* society (Lerner, 1980). This leads to a general individual-blame orientation as we have already seen from the Kluegel and Smith (1985) data. But it also further underscores the double-bind. African Americans have less of nearly every tangible evidence of socioeconomic/education success than whites. These are the differential outcomes of living in this society. To maintain one's belief in equity (and justice) the differential outcomes *must* be balanced by perception of differential *inputs*. The lesser inputs of African Americans are inferred by whites to be lower motivation, and deficiencies of character and ability (see Model Two). Thus, whites are in positions of power which enable them to define what shall constitute acceptable inputs, and further, are and have been in positions to structure African Americans environments such that adaptation to them decreases the likelihood of developing those characteristics rewarded by the supposed meritrocracy within the broader society.

The above double-bind for African Americans, fueled by a power differential and sustained by whites' self-interest is the heart of the notion of *cultural racism*. In this view, the maintenance and functioning of opportunity structures (i.e., formal institution of education and training, employment and informal associations that facilitate access to opportunity) in this country is predicated on certain values of individuality, future-orientation, written and material approaches to accomplishment which define appropriate inputs. If a person does not or cannot operate within this framework, he or she is either obliged to operate within another opportunity strucutre (usually at variance with the prevailing societal one), or is at a disadvantage within the majority context. If a group has evolved from a cultural legacy and tradition at a variance with this framework, it too is at a collective disadvantage or must develop a group opportunity structure. That is, the group must find ways to use the cultural legacy instrumentally in giving the opportunity for development, growth and accomplishment in this society. In the following section, we will discuss one approach to racial disparities that is based upon the above view of cultural racism.

African American Culture: The Trios Approach

Racism as an explanation for racial disparities is associated with the system-blame approach. Individual racists are presumed to develop and maintain racially biased systems, while institutions operate in such a fashion that African Americans receive less of the positive outcomes they dispense, and more of the negative sanctions. The authorizing, enabling and guiding force behind both individual and institutional forms of bias is the cultural context with its assumptions of value, opportunity, accomplishment and merit.

African American motivational and ability deficiencies are offered as explanations for racial disparities by individual blame proponents based in part on the notion that African Americans have inherent (genetic or cultural) tendencies and/or capacities that put them at a disadvantage in a competitive meritocracy. The cultural perspective on black-white disparities suggests that negative adaptations to slavery and oppression have left blacks with behavioral, cognitive and attitudinal characteristics that run counter to the norms of this society.

The cultural approach taken here is conceived to have two principle components:

A. *Reactionary Component.* This approach suggests that African Americans lost whatever culture they may have had in Africa and that such as there is any African American culture at all, it consists in the collective adaptations blacks have made to a racist and oppressive society. Since many of these so-called adaptations are considered maladaptive in the larger society, a "culture of poverty" or "cultural disadvantage" perspective describes this conception.

B. *Evolutionary Component.* This view suggests that African American culture represents the unfolding of a cultural core laid on an African past, and characterized in function, if not form, across the cultures of the African diaspora.

The comprehensive system-blame point of view to be expressed here is that the system of government that unfolded from the cultural legacy of British colonial racism and imperialism accomplished the intricate patterns of racist control by:

1. Oppressing and dehumanizing blacks in ways that created a hostile, pernicious and largely untenable environment to which they as a group had to adapt to which adaptation now is characterized within the "reactionary" perspective of African American culture (see Note 1).
2. Establishing a cultural context in which certain attributes and values (among them white skin) were held up as the standard of conduct and competence against which all alternatives were judged deficient. Beginning with skin color, the African American presence and cultural style were viewed as a persistent and deficient alternative.

If one believes that African American culture has a significant evolutionary component deriving from an African legacy just as African American color clearly derives from that same legacy, then African Americans are disadvantaged not only by the color of their skin, but by the content of their character. This, in my view, is the problem of cultural racism.

There is one other perspective that needs to be considered. Cole (1970) suggested that black culture consists of three parts:

A. *Mainstream experience.* African Americans, as with all citizens of this country, participate in the American Way. Differences exist, to be sure, but we all "die and pay taxes," although some die sooner and some pay proportionally more in taxes!

B. *Minority Experience.* The sense of being a numerical political or power minority is shared with other groups such as, at varying times, ethnic groups, poor people, women, older people, etc. When one is in such a situation, the concerns with powerlessness, discrimination and disadvantage lead to common experiences.

C. *Black experience.* Those experiences peculiar to being black in this society comprised of both reactionary and evolutionary components describe aspects of African American culture that do not include features common to others. Cole (1970) suggests these features include SOUL (defined by long suffering) and STYLE (described as the individual patterns of expressions).

Thus, black culture and African American personality that derives from that culture are multifaceted over both time and modality. That is, the reactionary-evolutionary distinction implies that elements of black culture have emerged and been elaborated over different historical eras and circumstances, and the three-tiered dimensions of Mainstream, Minority and Black cultural components combine in differing ways across people and groups. These multidimensional bases of black cultural experiences can be construed within the overall requirement of living in and adjusting to a multiracial society, and the facets of individual and collective adaptation both drive behavior and respond to it. That is, individual and collective behavioral styles both express the preferences of blacks and inform the mode and nature of adapation to the environmental realities.

The challenge for an African American person is, in this view, to determine how to integrate the necessities of adapting to an often oppressive and discriminatory system, and the desire to be expressive of those values, beliefs and preferences that are the legacy of centuries of cultural evolution. The notion of *bi-culturality* is a way of identifying the dynamic of this integrative process, with the challenge of rationalizing the demands of functional instrumentality and preferred expressiveness. That they often conflict makes the problems all the more difficult.

In the following section, I will review the *TRIOS* concept as one approach to bi-cultural integration. The concept attempts to specify dimensions of human experience upon which there may be evolutionary cultural differnces between an African and European tradition, and for which adjustments and accommodations to the instrumentality-expressiveness issues must be made. The long view of TRIOS should be as a balancing of human attributes that follow from cultural function and structure evolving over time. The patterning of these attributes within people and across groups will describe new ways of perceiving and evaluating inputs to a meritocractic society.

TRIOS

TRIOS is an acronym standing for five dimensions of human experience, Time, Rhythm, Improvisation, Oral Expression and Spirituality. The concepts emerged from my analysis of racial differences in sports performance (Jones and Hochner, 1973), African religion and philosophy (Jones, 1972; Mbiti, 1970), Trinidadian culture (Jones and Liverpool, 1976), and psychotherapy with black clients (Jones and Block, 1984). For a detailed review of the development of the TRIOS ideas see Jones (1979).

These five dimensions reflect basic ways in which individuals and cultures orient themselves to living. They refer to how we experience and organize life, make decisions, arrive at beliefs, and derive meaning. TRIOS is important because on these dimensions of human experience we will find divergences between the Euro-American and African American perspective. The culture in which we live has evolved from the Euro-American perspective, but both have interacted and necessarily share in the fabric of contemporary culture.

TIME

The cornerstone of TRIOS is Time. Figure 2 depicts time at the apex of the TRIOS configuration because time is integral to all of life, to being. To paraphrase Descartes, *tempis fugit, ergo sum.* Time is an important concept for understanding racism for several reasons.

1. Cultures differ significantly in how they organize, perceive and value time. One of the enduring findings in psychology is the relationship between Future Time Perspective (FTP) and achievement attitudes and behavior. Future Time Perspective is defined as the length of the future time span that is conceptualized (Wallace, 1956). De Volder and Lens (1982) found that among a group of high school boys, grade point average and study persistence were associated with more positive regard for goals in the distant future and that studying hard was perceived as instrumental to reaching these distant future goals. LeShan (1957) found that the stories told by middle class adolescents described action that took place over a longer period of time (e.g., four months) than the action in stories told by lower class adolescents (e.g., thirty minutes). The literature on delay of gratification (Mischel, 1958; 1977) concerns the temporal span within which certain levels of inducement retain their reward value. It was proposed in the original studies conducted in Trinidad, that Trinidadians of African descent had a shorter temporal span for reward than Trinidadians of East Indian descent. This finding has now been generally extrapolated to other race and class differences

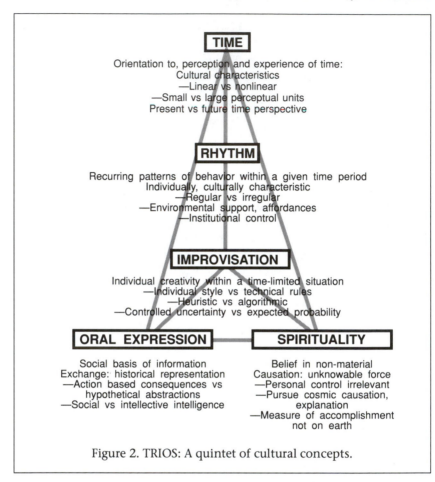

Figure 2. TRIOS: A quintet of cultural concepts.

corresponding to Black/lower class "deficiencies" in delay behavior (see chapter by Ward, et al, in the present volume that critically reviews this literature).

While ample evidence accumulates to suggest that failing to conceptualize goals, behaviors and rewards along an ever increasing future time dimension puts one "at risk" for successful achievement, there is also evidence that FTP is a particularly westernized cultural manifestation. For example, Levine, West and Reis (1980) examined a variety of differences between Brazilian and American (Californian) attitudes toward time and found consistent differences such that Brazilians could be described as less interested in and responsive to temporal accuracy (as measured by public clocks and an individual's watch), less concerned with timeliness in interpersonal behavior (as measured by concern with being on time or late), and more impressed with people who were *not* punctual (indicated by ratings of success of people who always came late).

In African philosophy, temporal perspective is decidedly not future oriented, and in fact, Swahili language does not even have a word for future (Mbiti, 1970). Rather, time is reckoned from the present, Sasa, to the past, Zamani, with meaning reserved only for events that take place in the present or the relatively near future.

2. The basis for FTP is a linear view of the movement of time. The linear assumption makes the future the inevitable point towards which the present moves. The present becomes a way station, a context for the development of strategies to move toward the future and to influence the nature and content of future outcomes. By contrast, a non-linear perspective concentrates on what Ornstein (1977) calls the "extended present." Events happening now are valued for their intrinsic worth, not for their value in instrumentalities toward a future goal, as with the Devolder and Lens (1982) findings.

Zimbardo, Marshall and Maslach (1971) actually tested differences between people with hypnotically induced "extended present" and those who were normally time-oriented. They found that in addition to using fewer future-tense verbs, these present-people were less responsive to social constraints (for example, experimenter directions) and less able to draw upon idealized or abstract representations of forms necessary to execute drawings. While roleplaying "extended present" subjects were able to replicate the verb-tense pattern, they were not able to mimic hypnotically induced subjects in these other ways.

The epitome of the non-linear perspective is given by a popular expression in Trinidad, Any Time is Trinidad Time! One might describe the approach to time in Trinidad as cyclical moving forward each year to the point of Carnival at which time culture returns to a common beginning advanced only slightly from the previous year. There is forward movement, but it is slow and maintains a powerful air of sameness.

3. One might describe the future/linear temporal approach as a structural one, and contrast it with the present-oriented/non-linear approach which is functional. A "second in time" is officially measured by 1,192,631,700 cycles of the frequency associated with the transition between two energy levels of the isotope cesium 133. This precise temporal structure defines the context within which behavior is played out. Thus an appointment is defined by the time for which it was set, and failure to respond to that time makes one LATE. A functional approach to time reckons time as a consequence of behavioral enactments. So a party that "begins" at 9:00 p.m. only does so within a structural frame of temporal reference. Within a behavioral or functional frame, it begins when people arrive.

The point of this is simple. When people whose values and experiences appear to place them at opposite ends of the FTP spectrum attempt to interact or communicate, it is very likely that they will behave differently, bring different expectations and assumptions to the interaction, derive differential meaning from certain events, and evaluate the other differently as a result of the interactions. If one of the interactants has a power advantage over the other, it is quite likely that such differences will have a negative effect on others' outcomes. In this society, linear perspective is normative and valued and deviations often put one "at risk."

Rhythm

Rhythm refers to a recurring pattern of behavior within a given time frame. Rhythm is associated with a flow of energy which drives behavior. When things seem to "click" we say we're "on a roll." In sports, momentum describes a steady acceleration of competence and execution. Building energy or rhythm requires that effort or behavior is synchronized with environmental forces through which it must operate. Thus synergy is a positive state associated with movement and flow between person and environment.

When preferred or natural rhythms of people are blocked repeatedly, performance, and often mental health, suffers. For example, sports teams that play "not to lose" usually do not win (Atkinson, 1972). People who are unable to relate their own behavioral patterns to outcomes (particularly success outcomes) often become disengaged from activities around them and depressed (Seligman, 1975). Boykin (1983, 1985) has shown more specifically that performance tasks in traditional school settings require a cognitive and behavioral approach that may be at variance with the rhythmic proclivities of urban lower income black (and, to a lesser extent, white) children.

Any source of regularity produces a rhythm. Thus we are not rehashing the old stereotype that blacks have rhythm and whites do not. Rather, all people and groups have preferred behavioral patterns and these are influenced by level of stimulation, and related environmental "affordances" (McArthur and Baron, 1983). To the extent that institutions are conceived from the perspectives of white middle-class rhythms and associated affordances, blacks and other groups are likely to be at risk in attempting to interact constructively with the institution.

Improvisation

Webster's Third International Dictionary (1968) defines improvisation as:

1. composing, reciting or singing on the spur of the moment;
2. making, inventing or arranging off-hand.

The first definition implies a kind of expressiveness, while the latter emphasizes inventiveness or creativity. Both definitions implicate immediacy or time pressure. Thus, we might define improvisation as expressive creativity under pressure of immediacy. The expressiveness aspect gives improvisation its personal mark or character, while the inventiveness must itself be goal-direct, or problem-solving. Thus, improvisation includes both expressive and instrumental features—that form of individual expressiveness that characterizes improvisation we might consider *style*.

Inventiveness under time pressures is the *instrumental* manifestation of improvisation. Given the sudden imposition of a needed or desired goal, how does one achieve it without prior planning? To achieve goals in such situations, one must have available a repertoire of relevant skills and the presence of mind to organize and implement them effectively. In fast paced athletic events where uncertainty and surprise are essential strategies, one is continually faced with situations calling for improvisation (Note 2).

Improvisation is by no means limited to music and sports. Viewed as a means toward achievement, traditional achievement goals must be viewed in relation to the systematic, predictable routes available to reach those goals. For African Americans, these routes have not been generally available and improvisation is often the adaptive and necessary alternate approach. For example, one of the most successful African American businessmen in this country, John Johnson, owner and publisher of *Ebony* magazine, among many other ventures, tells of the early days of his business in Chicago. As his magazines grew and his need for corporate office space grew, he faced the problem that real estate agents would not sell good space to a black man. Fully aware of this reality, Mr. Johnson represented himself as an assistant to a powerful white businessman for purposes of evaluating potential properties, and finally selected an appropriate one for his business. Finding alternate routes to common goals in this society is a legacy of racial bias and one driving force behind skill at uncertainty management.

Improvisation, then, is an achievement behavior. Its context is usually a moment in time, and its character includes both characteristic expressiveness of the performer (style) and creative use of available structures, resources, ideas, and so on. This characterization of improvisation can be expressed more formally as follows: Goal attainment = f(Performance Capacity + Individual Attunement + Situational Affordances/Demands)

Performance capacity refers to the level of skill or ability possessed by the performer, and the appropriateness of those skills to the goal at hand. Individual attunement refers to those sensibilities or predilections that characterize a person and his or her preferred mode of expression. Attunements are based, in part, on experience and ecological adaptation. Situational affordance/demands influence which skills and individual characteristics will likely be selected and/or effective.

Traditional achievement behavior seeks to control the situational affordances/demands such that they are in line with and draw upon those performance capacities most highly developed in the person. Thus control of the environment and situation are critical to achievement in the traditional view. Improvisational achievement, on the other hand, accepts (indeed *seeks*) the challenge of performing skillfully in an environment whose demands and affordances are not necessarily known in advance. These, then, represent two *styles* of achievement, *both* of which require skills for success. The former tries to anticipate and control the future and prepare the skills presumed to be most effective for those anticipated future situations. The latter develops skills through ongoing performance and rehearsal, thus building a repertoire available to be called upon instantaneously when an unpredictable situation demands.

In the lexicon of achievement and the contexts in which it is discussed, planful, future directed behavior is developed, prescribed and trained. Improvisational achievement is rarely mentioned and, when it is, usually carries pejorative connotations. "Playground basketball" is seen as undisciplined; jazz is seen as emotional expression a cut below classical western music; reflexive problem solving is seen as superior to impulsive style (Kagan, 1968). Traditional achievement is accomplished through practice, hard work and discipline while improvisational achievement is perceived to be raw ability or worse, luck. This culture values work, effort, and discipline even more than ability (Weiner, Frieze, Kukla, Reed, Rest and Rosenbaum, 1972). Stylish behavior is often called hot dogging, and improvisation is relegated to present-based behavior often described as an "inability" to plan or maintain future-oriented directions.

The point to be made here is that improvisation is an historical legacy of African American culture following in part from a present-oriented cultural style, in part from a context of oppression in which the future was unreliable, unpredictable and not guaranteed to occur at all, much less to occur with certain predictable features. Thus an improvisational style for black people is both preferred (by many) and demanded as a consequence of survival. It represents, in other words, both evolutionary and reactionary ingredients of black culture.

Oral Expression

Oral expression is the social basis of information exchange. If important information is communicated orally between people and over time, then interpersonal relationships will be important as will social knowledge and judgment. The broad implication of this view is that all forms of performance, judgment, and accomplishment will evolve from a basic social foundation.

In the midst of a literate culture in which written expressions of intelligence, opinion, ability and accomplishment tend to define the meritocracy, *oral traditions often put one at a disadvantage*. If this disadvantage is not taken into account, egregious errors in evaluation occur and products of oral traditions are at risk. For example, Cole, Glick, Gay, 1971, attempted to demonstrate similarities in memory capacities between Africans (Kpelle in Liberia) and Americans. Assuming categorization to be a general mnemonic strategy, they found that Africans were systematically and invariably less successful at memorizing certain information, no matter what structural mnemonic aids were given. However, when the context in which memory operates in Africa was considered, and the to-be-remembered words were embedded in a folkstory, African-American differences disappeared. If the educational system fails to recognize the contextual basis of memory and the oral style of information exchange, some children will be at risk in assessments of their functional intelligence. Another consequence of oral traditions is that language plays a critical role in information exchange and social relations. Because of its centrality, all features of language are important including linguistic, para-linguistic and non-verbal. All context-based language features of communication and expression imply a social reality. Formal systems and institutions are notable for their lack of social context. Further, the approach to language and communication is more often literal. Hence, opportunities for the effective use of non-verbal and paralinguistic aspects are reduced.

Yet the oral tradition is more than mere verbal interchagne. According to Jahn (1961), the Word, or "NOMMO" (in Nommo), is life itself. The "Nommo," is the life force, the spiritual-physical fluidity that gives life to everything. A newborn child does not have being until he/she is given a name by the father and that name is *pronounced*! The word embellishes and completes creation. It accompanies acts and gives them meaning. The fabrications of a goldsmith are not a creative suc-

cess without the verbal incantations that accompany the work as Leo-
pold Senghor, the late president of Senegal notes:

> The prayer, or rather the poem that the goldsmith recites, the
> hymn of praise sung by the sorcerer while the goldsmith is
> working for gold, the dance of this myth at the close of the
> operation, it is all —poem, song, dance —which, in addition to
> the movement of the artisan, completes the work and makes it
> a masterpiece (L'esprit de la civilisation ou les lois de la culture
> negro-africaine. *Presence africaine*, VIII-X, Paris, 1956).

With this profound significance of the word, of speaking meaning
into action and its products, it is important to trace the form and function of such origins in the evolution of a culture. The intersection of
African American culture surely must contain elements of each. Our
failure to recognize this near certainty, and to develop strategies for
understanding the resultant dynamics in performance, preference, belief and collective action is a major omission in our efforts to come to
terms with racial/cultural bias.

Spirituality

We define spirituality as a belief in non-material causation. According to Jahn (1961), African philosophy contains four primary categories within which all being is subsumed. They are:

I. *Muntu* —human being
II. *Kintu* —thing
III. *Hantu* —place and time
IV. *Kuntu* —modality

Everything there is belongs to one of these four categories and
must be conceived not as substance but as a force! NTU is the universal
force to which prefixes accord specific manifestations. Thus spirituality
is merely the force that resides in all beings, things, places/times and
modalities. While we tend to reserve force for *origins* in western
thought, it is present in all categories of being in traditional African
thought.

Not only is Muntu but one force in the world, but Muntu includes
the dead as well as the living, orishas, loas and ancestors. If the force in
all being is capable of exerting influence, then the material (Kintu) is
but one source of causation, living and dead, place and time and modality all contain force. This is the essence of a spiritual orientation as here
conceived.

If force is related to causation and causation to control, then one of the clear consequences of spirituality is a lessened sense of personal control. Apart from the mystical and religious practices and beliefs we associate with the concept of spirituality, the more practical and pervasive implication is for direct personal control of self-relevant events. Literature in psychology attests to the role personal control plays in performance, sense of well being and achievement in this society. The locus of control construct (Rotter, 1966) establishes the principle that being a cause is critical to self worth and accomplishment. DeCharms (1966) is even more explicit with his theory of personal causation in which one is either an origin or a pawn. The field-independence construct of Witkin (1957) is yet another approach with the same theme.

To the above constructs of causation we can add the compelling findings of Langer and her colleagues (See Langer, 1983) which show the lengths to which people will go to maintain belief in the value of being in control. For example, bingo cards that one selects are judged to be more valuable than those that are arbitrarily provided. Langer and Rodin (1976) made the more profound observation that elderly nursing home patients who were given some control over their lives (as simple as having plants to water and care for) were happier and lived longer than patients who were not offered this small control over their lives.

If by tradition, philosophy, and religious practice a people believes that causation and control are at best shared with other forces in the universe, then personal worth will be less highly associated with control. Perhaps it is a belief in and value placed on personal control that lies behind the capacity to engage in such controlling activities as the exploitation of slavery, colonialism and continuing more, subtle forms of racism, discrimination, and prejudice.

Thus, to understand the dynamic implications of spirituality is to understand the operation of psychological control and the philosophical context within which it resides. There are positives and negatives in every systematic position especially as it unfolds in behavior sanctioned by culture. We have, it seems, accepted and taken for granted the notion that we are, can be and should be in control of ourselves and the world around us. This belief has obvious positive consequences, but may have negative consequences as well. One of them, as alluded to above, may be the problem this volume addresses.

Conclusion

Multidimensional Approach to Cultural Diversity

On the basis of the preceding discussions, the "problem" of racism can be summarized:

Blacks are collectively living in a worse environment and benefitting less from the wealth and opportunity that this country offers than are whites. One of the problems is the extent of class differences among African Americans and the extent to which racism and class-based disadvantage are a singular problem. This is the essential view advanced by Wilson (1978). While it is true that significant class differences exist among African Americans, the disparities between African Americans and whites do not diminish very much as one moves up the economic spectrum. For example, the SAT score differences between African Amerian and white high school students continue to show differences in favor of whites even when white students from low income families (less than $6,000) are compared with African American students from high income families (over $50,000).

Whites believe there are very few, if any, *structural* barriers to African American opportunity, and, therefore, disparities are due mainly to motivational or ability deficiencies among African Americans. This perception leads to a further negative evaluation of African Americans which systematic research in social psychology (e.g., Crosby, et al., 1980; Gaertner and Dovidio, 1981; Gaertner and McLaughlin, 1983; McConahay and Hough, 1976) has shown to be manifested in a variety of more subtle ways than attitude surveys typically discern.

There is a strong ethnocentric bias in this country which generally accepts unquestioningly the superiority of traditional values of Euro-American origin. To the extent that those adaptive and evolutionary values of African Americans are at variance with the majority view, blacks will be in a difficult position. When this "home court advantage" is further supported by the power to define the inputs or instrumentalities comprising a meritocractic equity-based system of rewards, then blacks and all other groups are required to develop strategies that will confer efficacy on preferred patterns of behavior and developed abilities.

Blacks are in a double-bind in that those behaviors that may be adaptive to negative circumstances (such as those associated with economically depressed urban life exacerbated by systematic racism and oppression) present modest short-term gains but long-term losses in the inability to negotiate the success parameters of the larger society. There are enough exceptions to this generalization that we may, at the same time, look for those positive consequences of adaptation to the local environment for successful functioning in the larger context.

The power to define which instrumentalities (inputs) will be useful in realizing the meritocratic opportunities in this society rests with people who often believe that African Americans are not only different but also deficient and that those differences constitute a legitimate basis for differential outcomes.

How might one conceptualize the problem in such a way that potential solutions are conceivable? I would see the problem from two perspectives:

A. From a system-blame perspective, it is necessary to reduce barriers to opportunity that emanate from the operation of systematic disadvantage associated with discrimination. Thus the first approach to the problem is to reduce discrimination against African Americans. This is hardly a novel idea, but one for which there is important and exciting work being done that lends substantial weight of social and behavioral science findings to the effort. The basic discrimination problem can be conceived as follows: Human tendencies toward social categorization lead to in-group preference which lead to out-group discrimination. Thus discrimination against African Americans is the indirect result of social categorization. There are two general methods for reducing the categorization effects:

1. Reduce the salience of group boundaries which leads to a wider conception of ingroup and a smaller conception, correspondingly of out-group.
2. Increase the salience of individual variability by demonstrating the individuating information about people rather than category-based information.

The former approach emphasizes ways in which people are similar and draws upon human categorization tendencies to strengthen intergroup relations by using the resultant in-group biasing effects across a wider selection of categorical groups. Recent work by Gaertner and Dovidio has followed this course with promising results.

The latter approach, on the other hand, emphasizes the difference between people and by so doing highlights the fact that we are all different and therefore, it is more diagnostic to learn about a given person than to assume the categorical informaiton is applicable and appropriate. Work by Lockesley and her colleagues (Lockesley, Hepburn & Ortiz, 1982; Lockesley, Ortiz & Hepburn, 1980) and, more recently, analyses by Miller and Brewer have developed this idea into a concetpion that promises to reduce group boundaries by increasing perceived variability within and across groups.

B. A second approach is to acknowledge the possibilities of group differences and rather than perceive any and all differences as problematic, try to discern ways in which differences make a positive contribution to the aggregate set of capacities in the total social and cultural fabric of a multicultural society. To do this we clearly need to think differently about human diversity than we do now. We readily accept in principle the notion that diversity is good. Yet when it comes to practicality, the question always becomes what value or instrumentality does such a difference have for important goals in this society?

First of all, when one experiences multiple cultural components in his or her own daily life, tolerance for diversity and respect for difference tend to follow. The result is potentially a society in which diversity is itself a virtue and accepted as commonplace. One societal advantage is the notion that evolution of a species is made better by the variability of adaptation incident to diversity of population. There are several models in social psychology that suggest diversity of opinion, for example, improves group decision making (Janis and Mann, 1977). Latane and Wolf (1981) also suggest that minority influence may be critical to reverse the tendency for majorities to stagnate with their self-contained positions. Nemeth (1979) goes further by suggesting that the mere presence of a minority in a group task process will often serve to introduce more creative thinking among the majority members.

Second, one consequence of the individualistic, time urgent perspective is higher risk of coronary disease. However, even though pace of life was shown to be greater in Japan, coronary risk did not increase (Levine and Bartlett, 1984). Thus, collective action and cultural norms of functional inclusiveness (working together toward common goals) may well be an antidote to the negative consequences of individualistic competitiveness. The model of cultural diversity and bi-cultural adaptation with the emphasis on the cultural evolution of a group value system that downplays individualism and control and emphasizes non-material control and human comparability is one approach.

The emphasis on the written word in our culture permits a certain abstraction of human experience. Shall we send a memo or stop by and chat with an employee or colleague or have an all-hands meeting? Increasingly, good management is seen as including personal and social skills perhaps associated with an oral approach to interpersonal relationships. The aloof and powerful manager is giving way to the sensitive and accessible colleague.

The approaches to living envisioned by the TRIOS model represent not simply a basis for describing racial/cultural differences between black and white Americans. Rather, it is an attempt to systematically review aspects of racial difference in which the orienting premise does not put blacks at a deficient starting point, and further, elaborate the range of human behaviors deemed important in this society. In fact, I argue, the dimensions of TRIOS are important to any functioning society. Bi-culturality, thus, is a two-way street. While blacks have and must necessarily develop the same skills that whites must and do in this society, whites should recognize the salience of the flip side of traditional cultural truisms. It would be a worthwhile exercise to make a list of positive and negative expressions of characteristics assumed to be traditional in the Euro-American and African American adaptations of living in the United States. Also, we can learn from the experiences of people who are socializaed and forced to adapt to fundamentally different environmental circumstances. How does a person, born and raised in an urban ghetto of the northeast, or a rural barrio of the southwest or an Appalachian mountain village of West Virginia, convert an ecological/economic disadvantage to an occasion for growth and development? Do we have any understanding and how might we advance our own appreciation of differences by learning of what they consist? It has been shown that increased tolerance for others often accompanies the experience of intolerance at the hands of others. Learning therefore to understand and truly appreciate cultural diversity and the variety of circumstances from which individuals and groups evolve in this society is a backdrop for both the means of reducing social categorization and its corresponding discriminatory efforts.

TRIOS is offered as a set of ideas that may have currency for such an expanded appreciation of cultural diversity. It is not meant as a simple portrayal of black people as African people, but rather as a look at dimensions of human experience that are real, evolutionary and valid as legitimate human responses to survival in an oppressive environment and the inexorable processes of evolution.

Elsewhere (Jones, 1983) I have suggested that culture, not color, is the better way to approach matters of race in this society. The color approach emphasizes differences that are clear and undeniable. However, the important differences (those associated with culture and character) are not addressed by the focus on skin color. Thus, when we talk about blacks, for example, or whites, what are we saying? Perhaps little more than that skin color has been the organizing principle or schema for much of race relations in the United States for over three centuries.

The culture approach, by contrast, emphasizes the content of experience and its historical antecedents as a basis for coming together, sharing cultures, and recognizing the contributions different cultural groups make to our national culture. In this view, culture represents a way of bringing people and groups together, of both acknowledging boundaries (of ethnicity and culture) and transcending them by embedding them in the broader cultural concept.

As a problem, the fusion of color (perceived to be negative and often tied to presumptions of genetic inferiority in blacks) with culture as an inadequate expression and/or adjustment of blacks to contemporary modern society produces a context for the expressions of prejudice, discrimination and racism. However, the approach here advocated would eliminate this negative association and offer in its place a positive multidimensional view of incorporation and inclusion. I hope that some of the ideas presented here will, in the long run, prove positive and effective in making this a better and stronger society for all of our citizens.

Notes

1. It should be noted that reaction to such oppressive circumstances also has been a source of strength and resilience for black people.
2. Worthy and Markle (1970) called such activities "reactive" and hypothesized that blacks would excel at them. Data from Jones and Hochner (1973) supported the notion of black superiority at improvisational performance by showing blacks to be better hitters in baseball, relatively better shooters from the field in basketball. It was also shown that white professional basketball players shot free throws with greater accuracy than blacks. This reliable finding was interpreted to suggest that the conspicuous absence of improvisational opportunity may have a dampening effect on black performance.

References

Allport, G.W. (1954). *The nature of prejudice*. Reading, MA: Addison-Wesley Publishers.
Atkinson, J.W. (1974). The mainstream of achievement-oriented activity. In J.W. Atkinson, & J.O., Raynor (Eds.), Motivation and achievement. Washington, D.C.: Hemisphere.
Boykin, A.W. (1983). Performance of black children. In J. Spence (Ed.), *Motivation and achievement in children*, pp. 323-371. San Francisco: W.H. Freeman and Company.

Boykin, A.W. (1985). *Developing a paradigm to examine culture heuristically.* Invited address at the Annual Meeting of the Eastern Psychological Association Convention, Boston, March.

Brewer, M.B. (1979). In-group bias in the minimal intergroup situation: A cognitive-motivational analysis. *Psychological Bulletin, 86,* 307-324.

Caplan, N., & Nelson, S.D. (1973). On being useful: The nature of consequences of psychological research on social problems. *American Psychologist, 28,* 199-211.

Cole, J.B. (1970). Culture: Negro, black and nigger. *Black Scholar, 1,* 40-44.

Cole, M., Glick, J., Gay (1971). *The cultural context of learning and thinking.* New York: Basic Books.

College Entrance Examination Board. (1985). *Equality and excellence: The educational status of black Americans.* New York: Author.

Crosby, F., Bromley, S., & Saxe, L. (1980). Recent unobtrusive studies of black and white discrimination and prejudice: A literature review. *Psychological Bulletin, 87,* 546-563.

DeCharms, R.E. (1966). *Personal causation.* New York: Wiley.

Deutsch, M., & Collins, M.E. (1951). *Interracial housing: A psychological evaluation of a social experiment.* Minneapolis: University of Minnesota Press.

De Volder, M.L., & Lens, W. (1982). Academic achievement and future time perspective as a cognitive-motivational concept. *Journal of Personality and Social Psychology. 42,* 566-571.

Gaertner, S.L., & Dovidio, J.F. (1981). Racism among the well-intentioned. In J. Bermingham, & E. Clausen (Eds.), *Racism, pluralism, and public policy: A search for equality,* (pp. 208-222). Boston: G.K. Hall.

Gaertner, S.L., & McLaughlin, J.P. (1983). Racial stereotypes: Associations and ascriptions of positive and negative characteristics. *Social Psychology Quarterly, 46,* 23-30.

Hamilton, D.L., & Gifford, R.K. (1976). Illusory correlation in interpersonal perception: A cognitive bias of stereotypic judgments. *Journal of Experimental Social Psychology, 12,* 392-407.

Jahn, J. (1961). *Muntu: An outline of the new African culture.* New York: Grove Press.

Janis, I.L., & Mann, L. (1977). *Decision making.* New York: The Free Press.

Jones, J.M. (1979). Conceptual and strategic issues in the relationship of black psychology to American social science. In A.W. Boykin, A.J. Franklin, & J.F. Yates (Eds.), *Research directions in black psychology* (pp. 390-432). New York: Russell Sage Foundation.

Jones, J.M. (1983). The concept of race in social psychology: From color to culture. In L. Wheeler, & P. Shaver (Eds.), *Review of personality and social psychology,* (Vol. 4) (pp. 117-149). Beverly Hills, CA: Sage Publications.

Jones, J.M., & Block, C.B. (1984). Black cultural perspectives. *Clinical Psychologist, 37,* 58-62.

Jones, J.M., & Hochner, A. (1973). Racial differences in sports activities: A look at the self-paced versus reactive hypothesis. *Journal of Personality and Social Psychology, 27,* 86-95.

Jones, J.M., & Liverpool, H. (1976). Calypso humour in Trinidad. In A. Chapman, & H. Foot (Eds.), *Humour: Theory and Research* (pp. 259-286). London: John Wiley, Ltd.

Kleugel, J.R., & Smith, E.R. (1986). *Beliefs about inequality: American's views of what is and what ought to be.* Chicago: Aldine Publishing Company.

Langer, E.J. (1983). *The psychology of control.* Beverly Hills, CA: Sage.

Langer, E.J., & Rodin, J. (1976). The effects of choice and enhanced personal responsibility for the aged: A field experiment in an institutional setting. *Journal of Personality and Social Psychology, 34,* 191-198.

Latane, B., & Wolf, S. (1981). The social impact of majorities and minorities. *Psychological Review, 88,* 438-453.

Lerner, M.J. (1980). *The belief in a just world: A fundamental delusion.* New York: Plenum.

Leshan, L.L. (1952). Time orientation and social class. *Journal of Abnormal and Social Psychology, 47,* 589-592.

Levine, R.V., & Bartlett, K. (1984). Pace of life, punctuality, and coronary heart disease in six countries. *Journal of Cross-Cultural Psychology, 15,* 233-255.

Levine, R.V., West, L., & Reis, H. (1980). Perceptions of time and punctuality in the United States and Brazil. *Journal of Personality and Social Psychology, 38,* 541-550.

Linville, P.W., & Jones, E.E. (1980). Polarized appraisals of out-group members. *Journal of Personality and Social Psychology, 38,* 689-703.

Lockesley, A., Borgida, E., Brekke, N., & Hepburn, C. (1980). Sex stereotypes and social judgment. *Journal of Personality and Social Psychology, 39,* 821-831.

Lockesley, A., Hepburn, C., & Ortiz, V. (1982). Social stereotypes and judgments of individuals: An instance of the base-rate fallacy. *Journal of Experimental Social Psychology, 18,* 23-42.

Lockesley, A., Ortiz, V., & Hepburn, C. (1980). Social categorization and discrimination behavior: Extinguishing the minimal intergroup discrimination effect. *Journal of Personality and Social Psychology, 39,* 773-783.

Mbiti, J.S. (1970). *African religions and philosophy.* New York: Doubleday.

McArthur, L.Z., & Baron, R.M. (1983). Ecological theory of perception. *Psychological Review, 90,* 215-238.

McConahay, J.B., & Hough, J.C. (1976). Symbolic racism. *Journal of Social Issues, 32,* 23-45.

Mischel, W. (1958). Preference for delayed reinforcement: An experimental study of a cultural observation. *Journal of Abnormal and Social Psychology, 56,* 57-61.

Mischel, W. (1961). Preference for delayed gratification and social responsibility. *Journal of Abnormal and Social Psychology, 62,* 1-7.

National Advisory Commission on Civil Disorders. (1968). Report of the National Advisory Commission on Civil Disorders. New York: Bantam Books.

Nemeth, C. (1979). The role of an active minority in intergroup relations. In W.G. Austin, & S. Worschel (Eds.), *The social psychology of intergroup relations,* (pp. 225-236). Monterey, CA: Brooks/Cole.

Ornstein, R.E. (1977). *The psychology of consciousness.* New York: Harcourt, Brace & Janovitch.

Pettigrew, T.F. (1979). The ultimate attribution error: Extending Allport's cognitive analysis of prejudice. *Personality and Social Psychology Bulletin, 5,* 461-476.

Ross, L. (1977). The intuitive psychologist and his shortcomings: Distortions in the attribution process. In L. Berkowitz (Ed.), *Advances in experimental social psychology, 10*, (pp. 173-220). New York: Academic Press.

Rotter, J.B. (1966). Generalized expectancies for internal versus external control of reinforcement. *Psychological Monographs*, 80 (1, Whole No. 609).

Ryan, W. (1971). *Blaming the victim.* New York: Pantheon.

Senghor, L. (1956). L'esprit de la civilisation ou les lois de la culture negro-africaine. *Presence Africaine*, VIII-X, Paris.

Seligman, M.E.P. (1975). *Helplessness: On depression, development and death.* San Francisco: W.H. Freeman.

U.S. Department of Commerce, Bureau of the Census. (1984).

Statistical Abstract of the United States, 104th Edition. Washington, DC: U.S. Government Printing Office. U.S. Department of Labor. (1965). The Negro family: The case for national action. Washington, DC: U.S. Government Printing Office.

Wallace, M. (1956). Future time perspective in schizophrenia. *Journal of Abnormal and Social Psychology, 52*, 240-245.

Webster's Seventh New Collegiate Dictionary. (1965). Springfield, MA: G&C Merriam Company.

Weiner, B., Frieze, I., Kukla, A., Reed, L., Rest, S., & Rosenbaum, R.M. (1972). In E.E. Jones, D.E. Kanouse, H.H. Kelley, R.E. Nisbett, S. Valins, & B. Weiner (Eds.), *Attribution: Perceiving the causes of behavior* (pp. 95-120). Morristown, NJ: General Learning Press.

Wilson, W.J. (1978). *The declining significance of race.* Chicago: University of Chicago Press.

Witkin, H.A., Dyk, R.B., Faterson, H.F., Goodenough, D.R. & Karp, S.A. (1962). *Psychological differentiation.* New York: John Wiley Publishers.

Worthy, M., & Markle, A. (1970). Racial differences in reactive versus self-paced sports activities. *Journal of Personality and Social Psychology, 10*, 439-443.

Zimbardo, P.G., Marshall, G., & Maslach, C. (1971). Liberating behavior from time-bound control: Expanding the present through hypnosis. *Journal of Applied Social Psychology, 1*, 305-323.

Dimensionalizations of Racialism

Jerome Taylor

Over the past several years, we have engaged the task of identifying variables that have much to do with the growth and survival of the black community. We have moved from rhetorical concerns about white racialism toward serious theorizing and empirical research on this matter.

Dimensionalization of Racialism

Racialism is a term that is used differently, explained differently, and deployed differently to account for a heterogeneous range of social phenomena. Not uncommonly, assumptions are made that racialism is a unitary rather than a differentiated process, that its determinants are simplistically rather than complexly organized, and that its expression has uni-form rather than multi-form parameters. The present discussion offers an alternative to these assumptions by offering a conceptual taxonomy that generates 144 types of racialism. Assuming that not all varieties of racialism are equally vulnerable to change and that a single change strategy is not equally effective with all varieties of racialism, it is expected that the present taxonomy and its empirical translation will have implications for differentially effective approaches to remediating racialistic orientations.

Conceptual Dimensions of Racialism

Two Racialistic Contents. An analysis of the meaning content of racialism begins with a prior analysis of the broader concept of prejudice. Allport (1958) defines prejudice as " . . . an antipathy based upon a faulty and inflexible generalization. It may be felt or expressed. It may be directed toward a group as a whole, or toward an individual because he is a member of that group" (p. 10). Allport calls attention to the social objects of prejudice, an individual or a group, to the mode of its expression, covert or overt, to the process which partially organizes it, faulty generalization, and to the affective tone which accompanies it, antipathy. To the last, the writer would include unusual fear or anxiety as significant effects which augment or act independently of antipathy. The writer would offer one further suggestion: The individual does not have to experience antipathy for his/her behavior or attitudes to have antipathetic consequences. In essence, the intent of the behavior or attitude is less important than its consequence.

When prejudice, as discussed above, is developed along racial or color lines, it seems useful to refer to it as *racialism*, a term which distinguishes it from other forms of social prejudice. Racialistic contents may be *racist* or *nonracist*. Racist contents reflect stereotypically organized beliefs that race is a primary determinant of human characteristics and that one race is inherently inferior or superior to another with respect to these characteristics. Nonracist contents are the residual category of racialistic orientations not covered by the racist definition. This two-fold classification suggests that while all instances of racism are simultaneously examples of racialism, not all racialism is racistically organized. For example, a white individual may experience antipathetic feelings toward a black person because he/she feels the latter is undermining his job security, not because he feels primarily that the black is inferior to him. This distinction between racist and nonracist racialistic contents may be important, since nonracist contents may be more amenable to change than racist contents.

Twelve Racialistic Incident Categories. Racialistic Incidents classified by either of the Racialistic Content categories may vary importantly with respect to: 1) The Setting of Occurrence; 2) The Mode of Expression; and 3) Manifestation. Each of these three characteristics has important defining attributes which should be considered conjunctively with Racialistic Content categories.

1. Setting refers to whether an *individual* or an *institution* is the carrier of the racialistic orientation. While the meaning of 'individual' is straightforward, the complementary term 'institution' requires some discussion. Institution is considered from a sociological perspective, referring not only to associations developed by a society but also to its normative way of viewing, doing, or thinking about things. A society that associates, for example, the color black with meanings that are sinister and unhappy predisposes its members toward a type of institutional racialism. Where such associated meanings are assimilated by blacks, the writer refers to this process as nadanolitization, a problem which has been addressed by Milliones (1970).
2. Mode of Expression has reference to whether the incident is *overtly* or *covertly* mediated. In a previous paper (Taylor, 1971a), the author referred to incidents overtly mediated as being obvious, undisguised, ingenuous, and open to public view.

Moreover, it was suggested that the individual was well aware of his racialistic orientation. Covertly mediated incidents, by contrast, were described as disguised, disingenuous, and not readily open to public view. In addition, it was suggested that the individual or institution may not be aware of its racialistic orientation.

3. Manifestation of racialism may be *attitudinal* or *behavioral* or some combination of both. Attitude is considered to refer to an affective and/or cognitive predisposition. Behavior refers to actual and identifiable action on the part of individuals and to formal and informal rules, policies, and conformance guidelines in the case of institutions. While the defining attributes of behavior for individuals and institutions might appear conceptually disjunctive, it is argued that the action impact of an institution's formal and informal rules and policies does affect an individual just as the specific and identifiable actions of one individual affects the life of another.

If one considers the logical combinations given by the two types of Settings, the two types of Modes, and the two types of Manifestations, eight varieties of Racialistic Incident Categories are defined: 1) Covert x Individual x Attitudinal; 2) Covert x Institutional x Attitudinal; 3) Overt x Individual x Attitudinal; 4) Overt x Institutional x Attitudinal; 5) Covert x Individual x Behavioral; 6) Covert x Institutional x Behavioral; 7) Overt x Individual x Behavioral; and 8) Overt x Institutional x Behavioral. If one combines the Attitudinal and Behavioral attributes of the Modes of Expression dimension, four additional types of Incident Categories are given: 9) Attitudinal-Behavioral x Institutional x Covert; 10) Attitudinal-Behavioral x Institutional x Overt; 11) Attitudinal-Behavioral x Individual x Covert; and 12) Attitudinal-Behavioral x Individual x Overt. Additional combinations are possible, but the writer is of the opinion that their merit, as well as the merit of those presented, can only be determined by subsequent research.

In another paper (Taylor, 1971a), the author has presented examples of each of the first eight Racialistic Incident categories. Perhaps a summarization of some illustrations presented in that paper will serve to anchor the use of these Incident categories. Consider a Type I category (Covert x Individual x Attitudinal) Incident: A first grade teacher introduced the subject of color symbolism by equating the color black with unhappy and sad moods and with evil intentions. This example was considered *covert* because the teacher did not realize the implications of her lesson, *attitudinal* because it reflected a racialistic predisposition (black is unhappy, sad, and evil), and *individual* because only the teacher was involved. A Type 2 (Covert x Institutional x Attitudinal) example would be the widespread use of phrases like 'black ball,' 'washing sins white as snow,' 'black sheep,' etc. This example is considered *institutional* because it reflects the society's customary way of viewing things, *covert* because there is not often an awareness of the racialistic meanings of these phrases, and *attitudinal* because it predisposes the racialistic association of black with attributes generally considered undesirable. Examples in which differing Modes, Manifestations, and settings are reflected can be generated for each of the twelve Incident categories.

Six Sociogenic Variables. Given the allocation of racialistic orientations by Incident and Content Categories, a third dimension to consider is defined by attention to those factors which have shaped the racialistic orientation. Such factors are referred to here as Sociogenic Variables. These six variables, discussed previously (Taylor, 1971a), will be enumerated with major defining attributes.

1. Social Effect. Following Kelman (1958), it is believed that some attitudes are acquired through social compliance: " . . . an individual accepts influence because he/she hopes to achieve a favorable reaction from another person or group. He/she adopts the induced behavior—not because he/she believes its content—but because he expects to gain specific rewards or approval and avoid specific punishment or disapproval by conforming" (p. 53). Thus, a person may come to adopt a racialistic position not because he/she believed deeply in it, but because its momentary endorsement brings social approval or averts social reproval.

2. Internalization. In contrast to racialistic positions which are momentarily adapted for social effect, there are others which are adapted because they are intrinsically rewarding (cf. Kelman, 1958). Racialistic orientations of this type are congruent with the individual's value system. An individual might feel blacks are bad or dirty not because this brings extrinsic social reward, but because such thoughts are intrinsically rewarding and congruent with his value system. To this writer, racialistic behaviors and attitudes of this type are learned and well ingrained.

3. Identification. This process refers to the individual's accepting influence because " . . . he wants to establish or maintain a satisfying self-defining relationship which he adopts through identification, but their specific content is more or less irrelevant. He adopts the induced behavior because it is associated with the desired relationship" (p. 53). Related to this position is that of Smith, Bruner, and White (1956), who suggest that opinions can play the role of " . . . facilitating, describing or

simply maintaining an individual's relations with other individuals" (p. 41). In contrast to racialistic attitudes or behaviors organized for social effect, identificatory orientations are organized to fulfill needs for more sustained and socially meaningful relationships.

4. Utilitarianism or Instrumentalism. Katz (1960) has suggested that attitudes toward social objects are shaped by the manner in which they are associated with the fulfillment or frustration of needs. If certain social objects, for example, blacks, are seen as undermining one's job security or endangering the value of one's property, they are effectively devaluated. The important defining characteristic of utilitarian processes is given by the hypothesis that the attitudinal valence associated with social objects depends upon whether the latter are instrumental in facilitating or frustrating the fulfillment of social, personal or socioeconomic needs.

5. Frustration-Aggression-Displacement. Dollard, Doob, Miller, Mower, and Sears (1939) formulated the frustration-aggression hypothesis which postulates a predictable relationship between frustrating circumstances and aggressive response. The aggression, however, is displaced from the source which arouses it to another having little to do with it. Within this context, the social objects of racialism are not the true objects of the aggression. They are scapegoats only.

6. Ego Defense. This view assumes that racialistic expressions issue from personal insecurities and are basically efforts to solve internal conflicts (Katz, 1960). Displacement takes place as in frustration-aggression reactions, but here the wellspring of the displacement is some internal source and in frustration-aggression it is some external circumstance. Moreover, one might anticipate that the range of social objects affected by ego defense processes is wider than in frustration-aggression-displacement reactions. In another paper (Taylor, 1971b) the psychotherapy of an adolescent white male is presented and his racialistic behavior and attitude are traced to his genetic past. That paper summarizes also how the patient acted out racialistic orientations which importantly sprang from internal conflicts (cf Taylor, 1973).

It is recognized that a given Incident of racialism may be multiply determined and that more than one of the Sociogenic Variables may be operative simultaneously. It is suggested, however, that having a knowledge of the various Sociogenic Variables may lead one to consider differential intervention strategies. For example, a strategy effective in remediating racialistic orientations mediated by the social effect variable may not be equally effective with those mediated by the ego defense variable.

A Conceptual Taxonomy of Racialism

Definition. Classification of racialistic orientations within this taxonomy requires attention to the three previously discussed dimensions which centrally define it. First, one must decide which of two broad *Racialistic Contents* the orientation or events represents. Second, one must determine how to appropriate a given racialistic event or orientation into one of twelve *Racialistic Incident* categories. Third, one much decide which of six *Sociogenic Variables* importantly shapes the racialistic orientation. If one considers the Cartesian product of these possibilities (twelve Racialistic Incidents x two Racialistic Contents x six Sociogenic Variables), a conceptual matrix of 144 varieties of racialism is logically given. These 144 types are listed in the Appendix of this article. A central assumption to the conceptualizing work thus far is that we must take a more fine-grained approach to the study of racialism, examining each instance in terms of its conjunctive location across the three dimensions discussed.

Implications. It is suggested that allocation of racialistic orientations on each of the three dimensions alone and all three dimensions conjunctively offers promise of providing important information regarding differential *vulnerability to change, direction and expected extent of change*, and *strategy for change.* When one considers each of the dimensions alone, the following kinds of questions can be raised: Is a person who adopts a racialistic instance because of its association with social rewards or approval (the social effect Sociogenic Variable) easier to change than a person who adopts a similar instance to solve some internal conflict (the ego defense Sociogenic Variable)? Might there be differences in vulnerability to change among those holding racist and nonracist attitudes (Racialistic contents)? Might the individual adopting a racialistic position shaped by internalization processes be expected to change as much and in the same direction as another person adopting a similar position shaped by utilitarian-instrumental processes? Is a given change strategy, such as encounter sessions, equally effective with the individual manifesting racist attitudes as with nonracist attitudes? and so on.

When one considers all three dimensions conjunctively, the following kinds of questions may be raised: Are there fundamental differences in terms of vulnerability to change between an instance of racialism considered Racist x (Overt x Individual x Behavioral) x Ego Defense and another considered Nonracist x (Covert x Individual x

Attitudinal) x Social Effect? Given the same conjunctive type, one can raise the questions: Would there be anticipated differences in terms of expected change and direction of change a function of intervention? Would the same change strategy have equal effect with respect to both racialistic types? These and the many other questions generated by the proposed conceptual taxonomy can only be answered by empirical research.

Empirical Dimensions of Racialism

In this section is summarized our effort to map the conceptual achievements of the previous section into empirical strategies.

Two Racialistic Contents. Taylor, Dobbins, and Wilson (1972) developed a trial set of 60 items, 30 mapping the Racist and 30 the Nonracist Racialistic domains. These items, each rated on a seven-point scale, were administered to 150 white undergraduate college students. Item selection strategies were used to ensure that (a) Each item was significantly correlated with the domain for which it was written; (b) Each item was more correlated with the domain for which it was written than with the domain for which it was not written; (c) Each item was more highly correlated with its domain subscore than it was with a measure of social desirability; and (d) Each item significantly discriminated the upper and lower quartiles of the domain for which it was written. Application of these strategies resulted in the loss of 5 items for the Racist domain and 9 items for the Nonracist domain, leaving a final pool of 25 items for the former and 21 items for the latter. We now summarize five studies which bear upon the validity of these scales.

Dobbins (1974) reported a positive association between Ego Defensiveness and Racialism, both racist and nonracist varieties. More specifically subjects who agreed with such statements as "Since police have a very difficult job, I feel they should do anything necessary to maintain law and order" or "I believe that something should be done about white liberals who are political agitators," both items being taken from an Ego Defensiveness Scale developed by Taylor, Dobbins, and Wilson (1972), were more likely to be racialistically inclined. In a study conducted by Allen and Taylor (in preparation), it was found that negative attitudes toward school desegregation were directly related to level of the subject's racialism, both racist and nonracist varieties. Said differently, the higher the subject's level of racialism, the more negative the subject's attitude toward school desegregation.

While the two studies just reviewed were conducted on white subjects, a study by Barrett (1974) explored the effects of racialism and locus of control on black and white subjects' tendency to attribute more or less responsibility to a black or white stimulus person. He drew a sample of 158 high school students, 70 black and 88 white, to whom he administered the Racialism Contents Scale, The Rotter Locus of Control measure, and an attribution task. Among the many interesting findings of this study, Barrett found that black and white subjects who endorsed fewer racialistic stereotypes about blacks were similar in their perception of the severity of outcome. Not insignificant also was the finding that blacks are significantly less racialistic (mean = 130) than were whites (mean = 149). While the 19-point spread between blacks and whites achieved statistical significance, this difference brings no psychological comfort to this writer. The mean of 130 for blacks would suggest an appreciable amount of internalization of white stereotypes by blacks. There have been, however, two studies suggesting approaches to reducing this problem of nadanolitization.

Based upon a four-stage developmental view of Black Consciousness, Milliones (1973) found an inverse relationship between stage of Black Consciousness attainment and internalized racialistic dispositions among 150 black college students. Said differently, he found a progressive extrusion of internalized stereotypes as higher levels of Black Consciousness were attained. Similarly, Terrell (1974), who developed a measure estimating the degree of one's identification with a Black Nationalist's philosophy, found an inverse relationship between strength of identification and internalized stereotypes.

Eight (of Twelve) Racialistic Incidents. Allen (1974) developed a trial set of 222 items mapping each of the first eight Incident Categories previously described. For each category, 24 to 32 items were written to tap the subject's sensitivity to or awareness of racialistic vignettes identified as belonging to that category. All items forming the initial version of the Racialistic Incidents Inventory had been examined by one professor and two graduate students in clinical psychology to ensure each item's unique classifiability as a racialistic incident, as well as its location relative to one of six facets: Physical, Psychological; Economic; Political; Educational, and Social. To attenuate the effects of acquiescence, one-half of the items for each category were keyed negative and the remaining half positive. Each item was rated on a 7-point scale, and the entire RII was administered to 131 white college students. After eliminating items which were relatively nondiscriminating, relatively nonhomogeneous with its category subtotal, and relatively oversaturated with social desirability, 156 items remained, 14 to 26 for each category. We now examine some findings associated with the RII.

Allen (1974), Officer (1974), and Craig (1974), each sampling from rather different white populations, have found in general that subjects are least aware of Type 3 Category Incidents (Overt x Individual x Attitudinal), this finding being more clearly interpretable in Allen's study than in the remaining two. Closely behind Type 2 are Type 7 Incidents (Overt x Institutional x Behavioral). While there are variations in the prorated means across the Allen, Officer, and Craig studies, the results reported for Type 3 and 7 are consistent across the samples used.

In addition to examining peaks and valleys across RII Types, we also have examined the relationship between the Racialistic Contents Inventory and the RII. Since the writer has assumed that dimensions of the taxonomy are relatively independent, he would hope that Racialistic Contents and Racialistic Incidents are not strongly correlated; otherwise, he would need to speak of the one dimension rather than the two. These same comments would also obtain if we were to include Sociogenic Variables as the third dimension. This assumption has been examined in three studies, two of which are reported here. Allen (1974) administered both the RII and the Racialistic Contents Inventory. It will be recalled that the Contents Inventory contains two components, Racist and Nonracist. The 131 college subjects were divided at the median into two groups on each of these components, following which Hotelling's T^2 procedure was utilized to examine if the two groups on each component of the Contents measure would significantly differentiate the corresponding centroids estimated from the eight subscores on the RII. No statistical significance was obtained by this procedure for either the Racist or Nonracist component. Examining the correlation matrix involving all subscales of the RII and Contents Inventory, it was clear that there was more covariation within the RII (.26-.84) than between the RII and Contents (-.06 to .30). Univariate F-tests on the difference between the two groups on each RII subscale revealed that subjects either high in Racist or Nonracist varieties or racialism are less aware of Type 3 (Overt x Individual x Attitudinal) and Type 4 (Overt x Institutional x Attitudinal) Incidents from subjects low in Racist or Nonracist varieties of racialism. Additionally, subjects high in Racist Content were found to be less aware of Type 2 (Covert x Institutional x Attitudinal) Incidents than subjects low in Racist Content. That similar results were obtained by Allen and Taylor (in preparation) would suggest that the level of racialism, racist and nonracist, can make a difference in one's sensitivity to racialistic incidents. But the difference still is a relative one, that is, it is not possible to predict a person's level of sensitivity or awareness knowing only the person's level of racialism. These data are consistent with the notion of relative independence between the Contents and Incidents dimension of the taxonomy, but the data just reviewed also suggests where this assumption is most vulnerable.

Sociogenic Variables. The Ego Defensiveness Sociogenic Variable is the only one which has been developed and tested. We have previously reported that both varieties of racialism are significantly associated with Ego Defensiveness (Dobbins, 1974), a relation which also bears upon the assumption of relative independence among dimensions of the taxonomy, in this instance between Contents and Sociogenic Variables. A tentative pool of items has been written for the remaining Sociogenic Variables (Taylor, Dobbins, and Wilson, 1972) and will be revised further and tested in the near future. Completion of this dimension will permit full testing of the model and its assumptions that more fine-grained diagnosis of racialism will more effectively guide interventions directed toward its remediation.

References

Allen, J.G. (1974). *The development of a racialistic incidents inventory.* Unpublished doctoral dissertation. University of Pittsburgh.

Allen, J.G., & Taylor, J. (In press). Effects of racialistic orientation upon attitudes toward school desegregation.

Allport, G.W. (1958). *Nature of prejudice.* New York: Doubleday.

Barrett, R.K. (1974). *A study of the attribution of responsibility as a function of internal-external locus of control and interracial person perception.* Unpublished masters thesis. University of Pittsburgh.

Carter, G.R. (1974). An attributional analysis of black self-perception. Unpublished doctoral dissertation. University of Pittsburgh.

Coleman, L.G. (1975). *Toward the development of an instrument to measure identification with the heroic bad nigger social type.* Unpublished doctoral dissertation. University of Pittsburgh.

Craig, S.D. (1974). The effects of a workshop using simulations to assess the attitudinal awareness of educators toward low socioeconomic groups. Unpublished doctoral dissertation. University of Pittsburgh.

Cross, W. (1971). The negro-to-black conversion. *Black World* (pp. 13-27).

Dobbins, J.E. (1974). *A construct validational study of ego-defensiveness.* Unpublished masters thesis. University of Pittsburgh.

Dollard, J. et al. (1939). *Frustration and aggression* New Haven, Yale University Press.

Erikson, E.H. (1950). *Childhood and society.* New York: W.W. Norton and Company.

Katz, D. (1960). The functional approach to the study of attitudes. *Public Opinion Quarterly, 24,* 163-204.

Kelman, H.C. (1958). Compliance, identification, and internalization: Three processes of attitude change. *Journal of Conflict Resolution, 2,* 51-60.

Milliones, J. (1970). Identity and black children. *Notre Dame Journal of Education, 11,* 118-121.

Milliones, J. (1973). Construction of the developmental inventory of black consciousness. Unpublished doctoral dissertation. University of Pittsburgh.

Murdock, L.J. (1974). *Utilizing Smith's inventory to investigate black male and female differences in identity structure.* Unpublished doctoral dissertation. University of Pittsburgh.

Officer, A.D. (1974). *The development of a rationale to determine a need for a culture conflict training program designed to facilitate positive racial attitudes in college ROTC cadets.* Unpublished doctoral dissertation. University of Pittsburgh.

Penick, B. (1973) cited in Milliones, J. *Construction of the developmental inventory of black consciousness.* Unpublished doctoral dissertation. University of Pittsburgh.

Smith, M.B., (1956). *Opinions of personality.* New York: Wiley.

Smith, P.M. (1973). *Construction of an identity measurement.* Unpublished doctoral dissertation. University of Pittsburgh.

Taylor, J. (1971a). Proposal for a taxonomy of racialism. *Bulletin of the Menninger Clinic, 35,* 421-428.

Taylor, J. (1971b). The interface between racism and psychopathology: An approach through psychotherapy. *Psychotherapy: Theory, research, and practice, 8,* 73-77.

Taylor, J. (1973). The phenomena of acting in, out, through, up and without: Implications for treatment. *Psychotherapy: Theory, research, and practice, 10,* 78-82.

Taylor, J., Dobbins, J., & Wilson, M. (1972). *Racialistic Scales.* Unpublished inventory. University of Pittsburgh.

Terrell, F. (1974). *A sequential system for the development of a black nationalistic ideology scale.* Unpublished doctoral dissertation. University of Pittsburgh.

Table 1. Enumeration of 144 Conceptual Varities of Racialsm

Ref. No.	Incident Category		Sociogenic Variable		Racialistic Content
1.	Type 1*	x	Social Effect	x	Racist
2.	Type 1	x	Social Effect	x	Nonracist
3.	Type 1	x	Internalization	x	Racist
4.	Type 1	x	Internalization	x	Nonracist
5.	Type 1	x	Identification	x	Racist
6.	Type 1	x	Identification	x	Nonracist
7.	Type 1	x	Utilitarian	x	Racist
8.	Type 1	x	Utilitarian	x	Nonracist
9.	Type 1	x	Frust., Agg., Displ.	x	Racist
10.	Type 1	x	Frust., Agg., Displ.	x	Nonracist
11.	Type 1	x	Ego Defense	x	Racist
12.	Type 1	x	Ego Defense	x	Nonracist

*Type 1: Covert x Individual x Attitudinal

Ref. No.	Incident Category		Sociogenic Variable		Racialistic Content
13.	Type 2*	x	Social Effect	x	Racist
14.	Type 2	x	Social Effect	x	Nonracist
15.	Type 2	x	Internalization	x	Racist
16.	Type 2	x	Internalization	x	Nonracist
17.	Type 2	x	Identificaiton	x	Racist
18.	Type 2	x	Identification	x	Nonracist
19.	Type 2	x	Utilitarian	x	Racist
20.	Type 2	x	Utilitarian	x	Nonracist
21.	Type 2	x	Frust., Agg., Displ.	x	Racist
22.	Type 2	x	Frust., Agg., Displ.	x	Nonracist
23.	Type 2	x	Ego Defense	x	Racist
24.	Type 2	x	Ego Defense	x	Nonracist

*Type 2: Covert x Institutional x Attitudinal

Ref. No.	Incident Category		Sociogenic Variable		Racialistic Content
25.	Type 3*	x	Social Effect	x	Racist
26.	Type 3	x	Social Effect	x	Nonracist
27.	Type 3	x	Internalization	x	Racist
28.	Type 3	x	Internalization	x	Nonracist
29.	Type 3	x	Identification	x	Racist
30.	Type 3	x	Identification	x	Nonracist
31.	Type 3	x	Utilitarian	x	Racist
32.	Type 3	x	Utilitarian	x	Nonracist
33.	Type 3	x	Frust., Agg., Displ.	x	Racist
34.	Type 3	x	Frust., Agg., Displ.	x	Nonracist
35.	Type 3	x	Ego Defense	x	Racist
36.	Type 3	x	Ego Denfese	x	Nonracist

*Type 3: Overt x Individual x Attitudinal

Ref. No.	Incident Category		Sociogenic Variable		Racialistic Content
37.	Type 4*	x	Social Effect	x	Racist
38.	Type 4	x	Social Effect	x	Nonracist
39.	Type 4	x	Internalization	x	Racist
40.	Type 4	x	Internalization	x	Nonracist
41.	Type 4	x	Identification	x	Racist
42.	Type 4	x	Identification	x	Nonracist
43.	Type 4	x	Utilitarian	x	Racist
44.	Type 4	x	Utulitarian	x	Nonracist
45.	Type 4	x	Frust., Agg., Displ.	x	Racist
46.	Type 4	x	Frust., Agg., Displ.	x	Nonracist
47.	Type 4	x	Ego Defense	x	Racist
48.	Type 4	x	Ego Defense	x	Nonracist

*Type 4: Overt x Institutional x Additudinal

Ref. No.	Incident Category		Sociogenic Variable		Racialistic Content
49.	Type 5*	x	Social Effect	x	Racist
50.	Type 5	x	Social Effect	x	Nonracist
51.	Type 5	x	Internalization	x	Racist
52.	Type 5	x	Internalization	x	Nonracist
53.	Type 5	x	Identification	x	Racist
54.	Type 5	x	Identification	x	Nonracist
55.	Type 5	x	Utilitarian	x	Racist
56.	Type 5	x	Utilitarian	x	Nonracist
57.	Type 5	x	Frust., Agg., Displ.	x	Racist
58.	Type 5	x	Frust., Agg., Displ.	x	Nonracist
59.	Type 5	x	Ego Defense	x	Racist
60.	Type 5	x	Ego Defense	x	Nonracist

*Type 5: Covert x Individual x Behavior

Ref. No.	Incident Category		Sociogenic Variable		Racialistic Content
61.	Type 6*	x	Social Effect	x	Racist
62.	Type 6	x	Social Effect	x	Nonracist
63.	Type 6	x	Internalization	x	Racist
64.	Type 6	x	Internalization	x	Nonracist
65.	Type 6	x	Identification	x	Racist
66.	Type 6	x	Identification	x	Nonracist
67.	Type 6	x	Utilitarian	x	Racist
68.	Type 6	x	Utilitarian	x	Nonracist
69.	Type 6	x	Frust., Agg., Displ.	x	Racist
70.	Type 6	x	Frust., Agg., Displ.	x	Nonracist
71.	Type 6	x	Ego Defense	x	Racist
72.	Type 6	x	Ego Defense	x	Nonracist

*Type 6: Covert x Institutional x Behavior

Ref. No.	Incident Category		Sociogenic Variable		Racialistic Content
73.	Type 7*	x	Social Effect	x	Racist
74.	Type 7	x	Social Effect	x	Nonracist
75.	Type 7	x	Internalization	x	Racist
76.	Type 7	x	Internalization	x	Nonracist
77.	Type 7	x	Identificaiton	x	Racist
78.	Type 7	x	Identification	x	Nonracist
79.	Type 7	x	Utilitarian	x	Racist
80.	Type 7	x	Utilitarian	x	Nonracist
81.	Type 7	x	Frust., Agg., Displ.	x	Racist
82.	Type 7	x	Frust., Agg., Displ.	x	Nonracist
83.	Type 7	x	Ego Defense	x	Racist
84.	Type 7	x	Ego Defense	x	Nonracist

*Type 7: Overt x Individual x Behavioral

Ref. No.	Incident Category		Sociogenic Variable		Racialistic Content
85.	Type 8*	x	Social Effect	x	Racist
86.	Type 8	x	Social Effect	x	Nonracist
87.	Type 8	x	Internalization	x	Racist
88.	Type 8	x	Internalization	x	Nonracist
89.	Type 8	x	Identification	x	Racist
90.	Type 8	x	Identificaiton	x	Nonracist
91.	Type 8	x	Utilitarian	x	Racist
92.	Type 8	x	Utilitarian	x	Nonracist
93.	Type 8	x	Frust., Agg., Displ.	x	Racist
94.	Type 8	x	Frust., Agg., Displ.	x	Nonracist
95.	Type 8	x	Ego Defense	x	Racist
96.	Type 8	x	Ego Defense	x	Nonracist

*Type 8: Overt x Institutional x Behavioral

Ref. No.	Incident Category		Sociogenic Variable		Racialistic Content
97.	Type 9*	x	Social Effect	x	Racist
98.	Type 9	x	Social Effect	x	Nonracist
99.	Type 9	x	Internalization	x	Racist
100.	Type 9	x	Internalization	x	Nonracist
101.	Type 9	x	Identification	x	Racist
102.	Type 9	x	Identificaiton	x	Nonracist
103.	Type 9	x	Utilitarian	x	Racist
104.	Type 9	x	Utilitarian	x	Nonracist
105.	Type 9	x	Frust., Agg., Displ.	x	Racist
106.	Type 9	x	Frust., Agg., Displ.	x	Nonracist
107.	Type 9	x	Ego Defense	x	Racist
108.	Type 9	x	Ego Defense	x	Nonracist

*Type 9: Attitudinal-Behavioral x Institutional x Covert

Ref. No.	Incident Category		Sociogenic Variable		Racialistic Content
109.	Type 10*	x	Social Effect	x	Racist
110.	Type 10	x	Social Effect	x	Nonracist
111.	Type 10	x	Internalization	x	Racist
112.	Type 10	x	Internalization	x	Nonracist
113.	Type 10	x	Identification	x	Racist
114.	Type 10	x	Identificaiton	x	Nonracist
115.	Type 10	x	Utilitarian	x	Racist
116.	Type 10	x	Utilitarian	x	Nonracist
117.	Type 10	x	Frust., Agg., Displ.	x	Racist
118.	Type 10	x	Frust., Agg., Displ.	x	Nonracist
119.	Type 10	x	Ego Defense	x	Racist
120.	Type 10	x	Ego Defense	x	Nonracist

*Type 10: Attitudinal-Behavioral x Institutional x Overt

Ref. No.	Incident Category		Sociogenic Variable		Racialistic Content
121.	Type 11*	x	Social Effect	x	Racist
122.	Type 11	x	Social Effect	x	Nonracist
123.	Type 11	x	Internalization	X	Racist
124.	Type 11	x	Internalization	x	Nonracist
125.	Type 11	x	Identification	x	Racist
126.	Type 11	x	Identification	x	Nonracist
127.	Type 11	x	Utilitarian	x	Racist
128.	Type 11	x	Utilitarian	x	Nonracist
129.	Type 11	x	Frust., Agg., Displ.	x	Racist
130.	Type 11	x	Frust., Agg., Displ.	x	Nonracist
131.	Type 11	x	Ego Defense	x	Racist
132.	Type 11	x	Ego Defense	x	Nonracist

*Type 11: Attitudinal-Behavioral x Individual x Covert

Ref. No.	Incident Category		Sociogenic Variable		Racialistic Content
133.	Type 12*	x	Social Effect	x	Racist
134.	Type 12	x	Social Effect	x	Nonracist
135.	Type 12	x	Internalization	x	Racist
136.	Type 12	x	Internalization	x	Nonracist
137.	Type 12	x	Identification	x	Racist
138.	Type 12	x	Identification	x	Nonracist
139.	Type 12	x	Utilitarian	x	Racist
140.	Type 12	x	Utilitarian	x	Nonracist
141.	Type 12	x	Frust., Agg., Displ.	x	Racist
142.	Type 12	x	Frust., Agg., Displ.	x	Nonracist
143.	Type 12	x	Ego Defense	x	Racist
144.	Type 12	x	Ego Defense	x	Nonracist

*Type 12: Attitudinal-Behavioral x Individual x Overt

The African American Psychologist As Consultant and Therapist

Ferdinand Jones

Since the growth of race pride in African American communities in the 1960s, black clinical psychologists have been increasingly called upon to perform services with the expectation that their blackness makes their services special—a valid expectation according to many African American clinicians. An examination of some of the elements of that specialness is the intent of this discussion.

The rise in black awareness and the accompanying realization of the inevitable limitations of traditional social science because of white dominated theoretical positions account in part for the urgency to employ the black psychologist. During this time there has also been an emphasis on the development of community based and community controlled mental health programs. These kinds of programs have stimulated experimentation with innovative ideas. They have also challenged the traditional concepts of what mental health is and what treatment of "mental illness" is. One of the questions resulting from these critical perspectives is what qualifies one to deliver what services. The black psychologist, because he or she is a part of a broad challenging, reevaluative force in the culture, emerges as a sought-after professional person.

The black psychotherapist is frequently referred to African American individuals with psychological problems who will not consult anyone white. These individuals who seek help exhibit the entire range of traditionally described diagnostic pictures. They also collectively display all of the effects of being victims of white racism, that complicates whatever interpersonal and emotional struggles they are having (Grier and Cobbs, 1968, pp. 154-180). The clients tell the therapist that they could not feel comfortable talking to a white person about their problems; they do not feel that a white therapist will understand them; they cannot be convinced of the white therapist's interest in them; they feel too angry with whites to be able to focus on anything else in their presence.

Black clinicians in so much demand and legitimately needed by so many people and organizations must examine themselves. The exigencies of a changing field of practice require they reevaluate much of their training and thinking about psychology and African American people. They do this in the same spirit of racial awareness that involves all blacks. Critical introspection is not easy, particularly for the ambitious, achievement-inspired person who becomes a psychologist. It involves a challenge to both what she or he often struggled to attain and the understandable commitment to that which she or he has learned. What is demanded in this personal reevaluation is particularly difficult because it includes many self-image dimensions. This necessary process is also paradoxical. On one hand, black clinicians are in the business of promoting self-examination and therefore are well equipped to use it themselves. On the other hand, this very kind of inner-viewing is part of what is often criticized by many in the African American community as an avoidance of dealing with exploitative social and economic realities. It is perceived as a luxury we cannot afford. But African American clinicians are unquestionably in need of such review within themselves. They know what effects internal conflicts can have on behavior; and they inevitably have conflicts. They are oppressed like blacks everywhere, but they often enjoy enough environmental comforts to be able to think that they are escaping the full effects of oppression some of the time. Their effectiveness with community agencies and black clients depends on how successful they are in dealing with these conflicts. They have to establish fundamental goals for themselves in the light of which clearer perceptions and decisions can occur. Black clinicians must see that the society in which their professional success was achieved exists simultaneously in a context that can be also personally destructive. Their identification with all blacks' political struggle should be obvious. Fortunately, the nature of clinical work fosters this process of self evaluation. The black clients and community groups they work with and the climate of the times for all blacks stimulate the personal questioning and review required to perform their tasks. At least two elements of black psychologists' specialness have been implied in the discussion so far. They have the capacity for providing services in innovative community mental health situations. This capacity exists because they have reason to be as devoted to the overall challenge of the usual ways of thinking and doing things as are the communities they serve. They are also engaged in the inner personal struggles with their own blackness just like the individuals they are helping, and they can help them more comprehensively by being familiar with this. What else is special? At this point it might be better to discuss consultation and psychotherapy separately because of the psychologist's different skills, procedures, and roles in the different contexts.

The Black Consultant

One of the major reasons the African American psychological consultant is uniquely valuable to black community-based agencies and programs is that he or she knows the setting. Not merely because they are likely to be either a product of similar neighborhoods or at least have some kind of direct personal experiences with them, but also because they can understand the essentials of black life wherever it is in most of the country. This is not to imply any mysterious qualities to blackness; but there are certain common cultural perspectives we all understand and are better able to appreciate. The main point is that the black consultant cannot easily maintain the kind of uninformed-vision of black life which has dominated much of social science. As Billingsley asserts, "The best studies of blacks are by black scholars" (Billingsley, 1970, p. 138). Similarly, the black consultant is less apt to have the psychological need to distort the reality of black life, as is the unfortunate condition of many unenlightened white professionals. It is to the average white person's most basic, intimately personal advantage not to truly understand the black person's condition, and sadly, the white psychologist is generally no exception. Efforts on the part of whites to change this fact for themselves are understandably difficult. Kovel (1970), Delaney (1970), Billingsley (1970), Butts (1969), and others write convincingly of the vital dependence of whites upon a definition of blacks which requires that blacks remain "the problem." It seems to be possible for white psychologists to gain some understanding of this psychological phenomenon in personal terms only if they are unusually motivated and if they are unusually sensitive individuals. The black psychologist, however, has every motivation to maintain clear senses in this regard and is, therefore, definitely at an advantage.

> The writer, some years ago, was a consultant to a storefront mental health unit in a poverty area of New York City which employed community residents as community mental health workers. He participated one day with a worker in interviewing a desperate mother. She had come in because of a "housing problem." She was living with her eight children in a three-room apartment. She had never been married. She was about to be evicted for not paying the rent. She was also scheduled to go into the hospital the coming week to have a hysterectomy. The writer went through a personal inner process which involved an effort to achieve "professional" detachment from this emotionally painful material and to offer "objective" advice. He also could identify with the woman and her problems and felt her despair, anger, and hopelessness. Another part of him wanted to be angry with her and see her as the irresponsible, promiscuous stereotype of the hardhearted black woman. The

community worker, who was an expert at dealing with the reality problems the woman presented, began to handle them. He set about trying to find someone to watch over her children while she was in the hospital. He investigated better housing possibilities, etc. The consultant, aware of the mixture of reactions in himself, could eventually gain enough perspective to contribute an understanding based from on his training of that part of the woman's problems which involved her concept of herself as a person and as a woman. He could help to connect these aspects of the situation with the others. The situation itself helped him to resist the tendency to become professionally detached. The worker expected that the consultant would be helpful. There was no mistrust of motives or commitments because of a sharing of many common experiences: growing up in similar neighborhoods, an interest in black cultural expression, involvement in political struggles in the community and political struggles in the program itself. The client, although initially guarded with both worker and consultant, seemed nevertheless to expect an understanding of her situation. She showed this by her openness and frankness. The positiveness of all involved parties served to help the situation to become constructive. For the consultant it propelled his working through an unquestionably complicated psychological dilemma. He was free to offer what understanding he could on the basis of his expertise as well as his knowledge of the social and reality forces which produced the problems he was assisting to solve. The major point, however, is that the context for the black consultant was positive in the direction of achieving undistorted perception and therefore for freeing him to be optimally helpful; while for most whites it would not be as predictably constructive.

It is the experience of many African American psychological consultants to spend a great portion of their time listening to and talking with staff members in the programs they are consultants to. The consultant is very valuable in this respect. These on-the-spot sessions can be about anything, such as relationships among staff members, hiring and firing issues and family and personal subjects. This kind of service is not exclusive to the black consultant to community agencies, but in many instances the dimension of black-white is a significant aspect of it.

The black director of one program felt perplexed about her decision to fire an incompetent black staff member. A very excellent white staff member was the logical replacement. It was useful to go over some of the implications of her dilemma—both in personal terms and in terms of the needs of the program. The black consultant could readily understand the kind of struggle she was undergoing. He had similar questions himself in many instances. He also understood the realities of the program's setting and its goals in the context of the community it served. He could be of immeasurable help to her. The director finally decided to hire the white replacement and felt secure in her decision after having reviewed the problem with the consultant.

Black consultants can sometimes gain entry into situations closed to whites. Their actual acceptance requires more than their common racial membership, however. If it is clear to them and to their clients that they are as committed, as they are, to the necessary changes for African Americans, they can do much toward supporting feelings of unity together with whatever else they do. Because they often have been both educated in white graduate programs and "schooled" about whites, they know how to relate to white institutions and can often be a help in facilitating communication with whites when this is necessary.

> Some years ago a neighborhood association in Harlem waged a campaign to get the city to provide them more health services. It was necessary to educate the residents about the urgency of the situation and the need for their political action. Large numbers of individuals had to be organized to apply pressure on the city government. The black consultant helped to interest a Madison Avenue advertising agency in donating materials and staff for one aspect of the campaign. This meant working with the advertising agency to ensure that it provided what was needed without their trying to exercise any authority over how the campaign was being conducted. He also helped the community group to understand that the advertising agency could be controlled and could be useful in this particular project.

Black consultants can apply their understanding of psychological processes toward the development of pride in African American culture with individuals and agencies they serve. Again, if they have gained in their own internal struggles, they can be effective in aiding others. The ways this can be accomplished are numerous.

> A light skinned black social worker in a community mental health program was accused by some of her colleagues of being an "Aunt Tomasina." The black consultant had many talks with her about her despair over this. Her rightful membership in the black community was stressed and her own positive feelings about that identification emphasized. She was an extremely competent worker. With her strengthened sense of herself and her blackness, she could be freer to use her good skills and sensitivity to cope with the many aspects of her dilemma.

Is the patient sick or is it that their seeming suspiciousness and paranoia are justified reactions to white racism? This kind of question is often put to the black consultant. Here the limitations of some white clinicians are obvious. Their handicap is represented in their difficulties in communicating adequately with African American patients in making a diagnostic appraisal and is often further illustrated in a lack of understanding of the African American condition. It is progress however when there is enough awareness for the question to be raised. The black consultant can answer the question. He or she can also do some teaching about racism and its effects on its victims and its beneficiaries.

Black consultants cannot be peripheral to the forces for change in the communities in which they work. They have to get involved both psychologically and physically. At times their contribution may seem to have little to do with their skills as a psychologist. Their usefulness depends on their ability to be thoughtful and to have as broad a perspective on the issues with which they are confronted as possible. Then, they draw on their training, their experience, their knowledge of African American culture, and their commitment to change to come up with methods, ideas, and interpretations that can be employed by those to whom they consult.

The tensions that are inevitable between black and white staff members in some community programs are also often the focus of black psychological consultants, both formally and in their informal contacts. They must avoid being seen as the persons who can sweep problems under the rug. They know that the tensions have understandable origins. Realities of professional competence, basic decency in individuals, and the fact of legal rights in such situations need to be illuminated. These conditions require their sensitivity to the climate, mood, timing, and history of the setting. They can help to interpret and to focus on the important goals and to help others do so as well. The white staff members are often in need of guidance in understanding their black colleagues' hostility. The implications of this lack of understanding are enormous, of course. Ridding already hired whites of deeply ingrained distortions regarding blacks and themselves is not realistic or appropriate for most programs. Some efforts, however, can be made to at least acquaint them with the superficial aspects of their position. In some instances profound changes can be brought about; but these are not typical, unless there is a program set up that is aimed at profound change (See for example Jones and Harris, 1971). The black staff also often need help to deal effectively with realistic boundaries of expectation. And the white staff needs to be helped to deliver what they can deliver at the same time that their black colleagues are demonstrating leadership in terms of goals and tasks. The black consultant can be a resource for both groups.

> In one community mental health program in which the writer worked, the small group of blacks in professional positions

formed a black Professionals' Committee. When this group was mentioned in a general staff meeting, an angry black staff member, who was not professionally trained shouted, "What's this professional shit?"

Professionalism in the sense of a kind of elite status, represents so much of what is destructive in our attempts to be unified in the struggles for black definition and direction. It emphasizes intransigent differences; and the black consultant is very occupied in most community-based programs working with the tensions among the staff because of various frictions. It implies reverence for standards blacks have not participated in setting up. These standards also stress a social and economic hierarchy which depends on the maintenance of the status quo when what is so urgently needed is an overhauling and rethinking of what is best for delivering services to people. This becomes another area of conflict black consultants have to deal with in themselves. Again, it involves a challenge and sometimes a threat to what may be very basic to the consultants' images of themselves and to what they have tried to accomplish in their lives. It can include one's standard of living both in a financial sense and in terms of one's personal style and manner. Much distance can be felt between people if such matters get to mean too much. Avoiding this gulf is possible if the consultants can get their priorities structured in accord with the values that truly define humanity. This means an acceptance of the fact that one's own comfort and personal advancement is ultimately secondary to the progress and advancement of the masses of black people. This does not necessarily mean the acceptance of less than the common compensation for services or that one need move into a slum neighborhood. It refers, rather, to a considered ordering of one's personal convictions. This examination of the role of the black consultant has implied that the psychologist has a clinical background. However, it merely represents the experiences of this writer. Consultants with other kinds of professional backgrounds may draw other conclusions from their work. The issues of inner conflict regarding blackness and status, and the issue of a challenging perspective on the nature of psychological problems, plus the broader implications of both of these sets of factors are probably to be found in most situations in which black consultants are involved. What is to be stressed is an attitude, a perspective, an identification, and a direction in which the consultant and those who employ her or his services concur. The African American consultant who is effective is a participant and a facilitator in a process of enormous significance for black people. He or she can aid that process with the appropriate use of his or her skills and understanding as a psychologist. In defining their own the stance black consultants must personally and professionally parallel the forward movement of the people and the programs they serve.

The Black Therapist

The following discussion will not deal with many issues which appropriately belong—for example, referral patterns and problems, or the many factors involved in interracial therapy. The focus will be on what unique qualities characterize treatment of black individuals by black therapists. This is still an enormous subject which could be approached from many directions. Here the writer, based on his experiences, will attempt to merely highlight what appear to be factors common to the experience of other black therapists. This is a discussion about psychotherapy wherever it takes place—private offices, clinics, and in-patient settings.

As mentioned earlier, it is certainly true that a growing number of black individuals are deliberately seeking black therapists. We must perforce think about what it is we have to offer that cannot or not easily be found in the treatment of white therapists. This raises the first very crucial question: Is it really true that there is something in the black treatment situation which cannot be duplicated in the interracial one? The answer is certainly affirmative. The next questions then are "What is that quality?" "Is it necessary to the goals of treatment?"

Individuals seeking a therapist's help are in trouble. They want the earliest possible alleviation of the distress. During the course of treatment, other goals are sometimes agreed upon. These generally involve changing situations or a way of behaving which has been established over a long period of time. In terms then, of short-and long-range goals, the dimension of blackness can vary in the attention it receives in therapy. It also varies in individual clients. And the differences among therapists and how they have come to consider racial effects will certainly influence the handling of the black dimension. This is obviously a most complex subject, further complicated by all of the hazards of subjectivity common to most discussions of psychotherapy.

Most clinicians agree that effective treatment begins with the best possible assessment of the presenting problems. Black therapists with their inevitable familiarity with black life are in an informed position to evaluate these problems. They should be, therefore, significantly superior to their white counterparts with comparable clinical skills in this critical phase of the therapy process. They have another advantage in assessing the black individual's problems in the more likely readiness of the help-seeker to inform them about themselves. Anxiety about communication will be lowered and misunderstandings based on language and style will be minimized. There are certainly class and regional factors involved here too; but the black therapist is nevertheless more prepared to understand them than the non-black therapist starting from the position of the outsider.

In the initial contact, the black therapist can usually readily assess the meaning of the problems presented in the context of a life with which he or she is familiar. The client's way of expressing him or herself is less likely to be misunderstood. The usual kinds of self-protective guises commonly present in beginning interracial relationships are more likely to be absent. The black therapist is therefore in the position to make a quicker, more comprehensive diagnosis than his or her white counterpart. This advantage is important in terms of the speed of distress relief that is dependent on the development of a cooperative therapeutic relationship.

> A very intelligent black professional woman sought help because of extreme anxiety and depression. She related how miserable she was most of the time and how she had no satisfying relationships with people. She focused on her strong anger towards white people. The black therapist could see that her isolation from people was in general comprehensive. He could also appreciate, however, what was realistic in her feelings toward white people and not dismiss their importance as merely part of her psychopathology. The woman had been in treatment with white therapists and had not been helped. Her work with the black therapist went very well. He could accept her in the way she needed to be accepted, provide an identification for her, and particularly convey his understanding of the meaning of her mistrust for whites based on the facts of her history. The therapeutic relationship which is of such importance in therapy can certainly be fostered when both therapist and client are black, as we have begun to document. There are also instances, however, in which blackness can be an obstacle. Because of the pervasiveness of the myth of white supremacy in this society, there are, of course, many African Americans who feel that a white professional is likely to be a better trained, more competent person. Black therapists working with this handicap in their clients' thinking have to be sensitive to it, and to be secure enough in themselves to be able to help the client see it for what it is. This master-slave remnant rears up in many ways, and the black clients may often be unaware of the ambivalent contempt they may harbor toward their own folk. Their abuse of the therapist in the form of non-cooperation or criticism can often bring this to the surface. Their conflicts about race can then be interpreted and worked on.

The advantages of the black dyadinal treatment relationship are greater than such hindrances however. Indeed, the working out of conflicts about one's racial identity is of the utmost importance, and references to conflicts about blackness are to be seen in many facets of all black clients' lives; their emergence in therapy is therefore to be encouraged and welcomed. It is rewarding to achieve the feeling of kinship in therapy. For both parties the establishment of that foundation depends very much on the effective handling of the inner struggle regarding racial identity by the therapist. Conflicts about being black in a white dominated society are almost impossible for the white therapist to deal with sufficiently, yet this is a pivotal area in most black clients' psychological lives.

> A black man sought help from a prominent white therapist for problems regarding his marriage and other personal dilemmas. He was initially very depressed. The therapist expertly guided his client towards the resolution of the acute problems. The client's depression lifted and he felt healthy again. When attention was drawn to the personality factors which set the stage for a lot of his acute difficulties, the issue of his blackness and conflictual feelings about it loomed very large. The therapist could recognize how important these issues were for his client, but he couldn't really understand them enough to aid in their resolution (He could fortunately admit this.) The client found it impossible to get into this area with the therapist even though he had been genuinely helped with his initial symptoms and felt positively toward the therapist. They both agreed that he should see a black therapist to work on the personality issues.

The pervasiveness and complex depth of white racism is still not appreciated by establishment psychology or the mental health field in general. Consequently, white therapists often do not learn to be vigilant of racist tendencies in themselves and in the rest of the American society. They are therefore limited in their handling of the blackness dimension in their therapy with black clients even with the best intentions and the most proficient skills. Motivated white therapists can become knowledgeable about racism and its effects. They are unusual if they are, but when they do work on these issues, they begin to see the limitations of their own capacities to deal with the questions surrounding blackness in black clients, and they can therefore appropriately determine what they can and cannot do with this subject.

The black therapist is capable (if she or he is developmentally ready) to guide their black clients toward the resolution of their conflicts about blackness. This is not to minimize the importance of other psychological conflicts, dilemmas brought to therapy, but rather to stress that the subject of being an African American is a powerful dynamic much neglected in considerations of the personality development of black clients. We need to know conceptually infinitely more than we do about black identity development and black family life. We do know that most of the traditional literature in psychology contains the unspecific views of whites in this regard who were unable to know that their scholarship is as biased as it is.

"What does being black mean?"

"How black is black?"

"What do I have in me that's white?"

"Should I be ashamed of my white friends?"

"Should I be against interracial marriage, or against interracial adoption?"

"Do I have more in common with the whites on my job than the blacks who are doing different tasks?"

"Do I really want a different political system?"

"Should I teach my child to distrust whites?"

"Are my personal style of manners and my tastes consistent with being a proud black person?"

Time will probably tell us that the essential meaning of "being an African American" is unspoiled humanness and the tenacious ability to express it in spite of our oppression. In very general terms, therapy should be directed toward the emphasis on the return to humanness in all individuals. For black individuals in psychological trouble, self-concept improvement and the resolution of conflicts about what is important in one's life are goals one has in common with most other individuals. The difference for black clients is that a pivotal portion of an image of ourselves has been interfered with by the institutionalization of the white supremacy myth; and we have had to contend with the reality of how that threatens our self-esteem as well as with the specifics of our personal situations. Further, many of those standards of life which the American society defines as desirable are contaminated with antihuman qualities such as greed, unscrupulousness, and selfishness. The African American individual's behavior, when viewed against the backdrop of diseased standards, can be distortedly perceived as abnormal. For these reasons, the many stereotypes about African Americans flourish. African Americans' laziness, passivity, stupidity, childishness, supersexuality have meaning only in a setting characterized by ruthless competition, an overemphasis on form and quantity, too much of a premium placed on control and superficiality, and a denial of natural impulses and feelings. The therapist who is African American is capable of an undistorted view of her or his black clients' behaviors in this regard. She or he is in the position to help them not only to see themselves more realistically, but also to see the society in a clear light. This can be a health-producing experience in the most real sense. This also invariably involves questions of political activity and other actions toward altering that which is so destructive to people. The African American therapist logically encourages these actions.

In some instances, black therapists might suggest that their black patients involve themselves in appropriate political movements. Such direct guidance and other deviations from passive psychotherapy practices illustrate the natural inclination for the black therapist to expand the boundaries of treatment. What actually helps people in psychotherapy is one of the most debated issues in clinical psychology. This writer seeks all kinds of techniques to employ to help people who come to him and is frustrated because he is not more creative about it. The verbally centered insight aimed psychotherapies sometimes seem too limited—especially with lots of black people.

> It seemed to make sense to have therapy sessions in the home of one black family where the parents' severe marital disputes took place. The children could participate in the therapy sessions and the family in their own living room provided a natural setting for observing and interpreting the interaction between various family members.

> A psychotic, alcoholic African American mother, separated from her husband and trying to raise three children on public assistance, required a great deal of active intervention, in addition to office visits. The therapist kept close touch with the workers from several agencies who were involved with the family while he also built a relationship with the mother.

> A young black youth was in a destructively dependent relationship with a good but possessive mother which resulted in his trying to commit suicide. The therapist in the hospital actively assisted him in getting into a college where he could use his excellent intellect, be away from home in an acceptable way, and continue his treatment.

> The black mother was the primary patient, but the black therapist found it appropriate to see her children for varying lengths of time to discuss the kinds of difficulties the husbandless mother could not deal with. The benefits for the whole family were tremendous.

Black therapists need to have broad interpretations of what such terms as healthy, or well-adjusted, or normal, mean. They need to be particularly critical of the medical model as the only way of understanding an individual's attempts to cope with life. Clearly the interaction of black persons with their environment involves the very real fact of inconsistencies in America values, laws and customs and how they affect their functioning and feelings. Clinical judgments about black clients have to include this very significant phenomenon.

> A talented black teacher sought help for a phobia which handicapped her movements. She was a highly respected, churchgoing member of her community. As therapy progressed and the many conflicts she was trying to resolve with herself became apparent, she became more conscious of that part of her she had been taught to hold in public check, but which she would identify as her black cultural identity. Her style, and her priorities began to change. She found herself less liked by some of the people who previously admired her. Her own parents deplored her "militancy." But she was happier with herself and felt that she had more parts of her personality together. She ended treatment with the phobia having diminished in intensity and significance. She had made huge changes in her personality and in her pride in herself as a black woman.

Conclusion

The black clinical psychologist should be in the forefront of expanding and refining definitions of psychological problems and psychological treatment. This involves many dimensions of these complicated issues but seems to begin with an attitude which challenges much of what has been inaccurately attributed to the black condition by the dominant society and therefore reflected in graduate school curricula. This is the same spirit with which all African Americans are beginning to view their world and themselves. The specifics of what changes in the psychological help for individuals, families, groups or agencies will be made in the future cannot be concluded yet. The main objective of the black psychologist at this time is keeping open in our understanding of the situations our black brothers and sisters in trouble bring to us, to give proper weight to hazards of living in a complex, always potentially destructive world, and to be as creative as possible in offering our skills as psychologists.

References

Billingsley, A. (1970). Black families and white social science. *Journal of Social Issues*, *26*(3), 127-142.

Butts, H. F. (1969). White racism: Its origins, institutions, and the implications for professional practice in mental health. *International Journal of Psychiatry*, *8*(6), 914-928.

Delaney, L. T. (1970). The white American psyche-exploration of racism. In B. Schwartz, & R. Disch (Eds.), *White racism: Its history, pathology and practice*. New York: Dell.

Grier, W. H., & Cobbs, P. M. (1968). *Black rage*. New York: Basic Books.

Jones, F., & Harris, M. W. (1971). The development of interracial awareness in small groups. In L. Blank, G. Gottesgen, & M. Gottesgen (Eds.), *Encounter: Confrontations in self and interpersonal awareness*. New York: Macmillan.

Kovel, L. (1970). *White racism: A pschohistory*. New York: Pantheon Books.

The Black Community as the Source of Positive Self-Concept for Black Children: A Theoretical Perspective

Edward J. Barnes

A black graduate student asked the writer a question which served as the catalyst for this paper: "How does one rear a black child to have a positive self-concept or high self-esteem in this society?" This led to a reflection on the body of literature concerning personality development and functioning of the black child. As the writer pondered different works by various writers (mostly white), it became quite clear that those of us who are black cannot think of our children without thinking about our families. We cannot think about black children and black families without thinking about black communities. We cannot think about black children, black families, and black communities without, at the same time, realizing that this entire configuration of blackness is surrounded by a white racist society.

Two additional realizations occurred with great impact as the writer reviewed the literature: the essentially negative nature of the research, and the extent to which black children are separated from families even conceptually, and the further separation of black children and black families from the black community. But the most glaring factor concerns the separation of the black community from the surrounding white community. It is obvious that we who are concerned about black children must think about them in relation to black families and the black community, never forgetting that this entire configuration is embedded in a society which devalues everything black.

In the past decades significant events have occurred in the lives of African Americans. The civil rights movement of the early 1960s gave birth to a new breed of black youth. As the civil rights movement gave way to the forceful thrust of the rise of black consciousness, with its demands for liberation and self-determination, still another kind of young black was born. During this period a large literature concerning black identity emerged. The bulk of this literature does not reflect significant changes in psychological attributes of blacks. It would seem that such changes would be a necessary concomitant of the new stance being assumed by blacks vis-a-vis the white society. This seeming contradiction may be explained by reference to theoretical and methodological shortcomings to be ad-dressed later in this paper.

If the behavioral changes occurring in blacks, especially young blacks, during the past decade represent a positive change in self-con-cept, self-identity, and other areas, what factors made such change pos-sible? In other words, is it possible for a black individual to develop a positive self-concept in this society, and if so, what are the contributing factors?

The quest for self-identity is a search for answers to the questions: Who am I? What am I like as a person? Where do I fit in the world? The answers the individual arrives at are inextricably intertwined with how others see and interact with him. Leading authorities in this area (Mead, 1934; Cooley, 1956; Sullivan, 1953; Erikson, 1968; Essien-Udom, 1962) agree that the self-concept arises through the individual's interaction with other members of the society; parents, peers, teachers, and other representatives of society's institutions. According to Mead (1934), through identification and as a necessary means of communication the child learns to assume the roles and attitudes of others with whom he interacts, a posture having significance not only for how he responds to others, but also for how he reacts to himself. The continuity of the self derives from the collective attitudes of the society, or "generalized other," as Mead calls it; that is, the individual's sense of self is developed, molded, and controlled by his assuming the attitudes and definitions of others toward him. Thus, the extent to which an individual is a member of this society, its values, goals, attitudes, and norms are his. Even though each self has its unique characteristics, it is structured in terms of these societal attributes, and is, thus, also an individual reflection of the social process. (See Note 1) Cooley (1956) articulated this idea by invoking the image of the "looking glass"—namely, that the self is a looking glass mirroring the three primary components of the self-con-cept: "the imagination of our appearance to the other person; the imag-ination of his judgment of that appearance; and some sort of self feeling, such as pride or mortification" (p. 184). Sullivan (1953) articulates a similar conception in his proposition that the self-dynamism of the child is a function of the reflections of significant others. The "good me" represents the approving reflections; the "bad me" represents the disap-proving reflections.

Erikson's (1968) analysis of the concept gives rise to three different identities: ego, personal, and group identity. Ego identity concerns the quality of one's existence or an awareness of the fact that there is a continuity to the ego's synthesizing methods: "the style of one's indi-viduality and that this style coincides with sameness and continuity of one's meaning for significant others in the immediate community" (Er-ickson, 1968). Personal identity is the perception of the continuity of one's existence in time and space and the perception of the fact that others recognize one's sameness and continuity. Group identity is the group's basic way of organizing experience which is transmitted through child training "to the infant's early bodily experiences, and through them to the beginning of his ego" (Erickson, 1968, p. 47).

Thus, regardless of whether the concept is considered from a socio-psychology or from a dynamic psychology frame of reference, the nature of the child's social context is of primary significance for the development of the self-concept. What do these theoretical perspectives project concerning the possibilities of a black child's developing a positive self-concept in this society? A simple, direct deduction from these theories would suggest that such possibilities are nil. For example, for the black child, both the "generalized other" attitudes he (sic) theoretically assumes and the "looking glass" into which he gazes transmit the same message: He is an inferior human being, and because of this he is relegated to the lowest stratum of a color caste system. By accepting the values and attitudes contained in society's messages, his self-concept naturally is negative, nurtured through his contact with institutionalized symbols of caste inferiority on every hand. For example, when he looks around him, except in the spheres of athletics and entertainment, he sees very few Americans with his skin color who hold important (power) positions in the society. The mass media—especially, television—presents few black heroes. When they are portrayed, typically, they are cast in low-status roles, and until quite recently, were presented as amusingly ignorant (to whites). Observation of brutal, dehumanizing treatment of blacks at the hands of police and other law enforcement officials is commonplace. All of these communicate to the black child the lack of positive value and the negative value the society places on him. In addition to these direct negative indicators, there are indirect negative indicators such as the reactions of the child's own family who have been socialized to believe they are substandard human beings (Poussaint and Atkinson, 1970). The looking glass of the wider society reflects the undesirability of the black child's skin color and hair texture. In fact, these attributes belong to one of three categories of stigma outlined by Goffman (1963). In order to gain the esteem of the "generalized other," the child realizes that he must approximate the white ideal as nearly as possible. This means, among other things, rejecting himself and others like him.

Essien-Udom (1962) comments concerning the effects on blacks of assuming the attitudes, norms, and roles of the wider society:

> The tragedy of the Negro in America is that he has rejected his origins—the essentially human meaning implicit in the heritage of slavery, prolonged suffering, and social rejection. By rejecting his unique group experience and favoring assimilation

and even biological amalgamation, he thus denies himself the creative possibilities inherent in it and in his folk culture. This dilemma is fundamental; it severely limits his ability to evolve a new identity or meaningful synthesis, capable of endowing his life with meaning and purpose. (p. 9)

He learns that existence for him demands adhering to the role outlined by the white society. To challenge the definition assigned to him carries the risk and probability of his destruction. The Hollywood film *The Liberation of L.B. Jones* speaks eloquently to the consequences for blacks of challenging the society's definition of blacks. Dr. Martin Luther King, Jr., and Malcolm X are living testimonials to this fact. (Note 2)

Now that we have outlined some of the expected theoretical predictions, what does empirical observation reveal? Empirical findings coincide with expected findings based on theoretical projections. Findings from a variety of sources converge to indicate the black child's incomplete self-image (Rainwater, 1967; Gordon, 1965; Coles, 1965; Ausubel and Ausubel, 1963); his negative self-image and preference for things "white" (Proshansky and Newton, 1968; Rainwater, 1967; Stevenson, 1953; Goodman, 1952; Clark and Clark, 1947, Stevenson and Stewart, 1958; Radke and Trager, 1950; Morland, 1962; Landreth and Johnson, 1953); his rejection of and expressed hostility toward his own group (Goodman, 1952; Stevenson and Stewart, 1958; Clark and Clark, 1947).

If the black person feels disdain or hatred for his group, therefore for himself, and experiences himself as incomplete, as indicated above, then we can expect such factors to have negative effects on his behavior and experience. Data brought forth in support of this hypothesis can be subsumed under two categories: "cognitive and affective status" and "achievement orientation." The black is characterized by high anxiety level (Feld and Lewis, 1967; Hill and Sarason, 1966; Sarason et al., 1960; Palermo, 1959; Caldwell, 1959); a high level of maladjustment (Rainwater, 1967; Boykin, 1957), neuroticism (Hammer, 1953), and rejection of other blacks (Yarrow, 1958); inability to delay gratification (Mischel 1966, 1961b), reportedly a critical factor in immature, criminal, and neurotic behavior (Mowrer and Ullman, 1945); low-level orientation toward achievement (Mischel, 1961c); proneness toward delinquency (Mischel, 1961b); confusion of sexual identity or sex role adoption (Burton, 1961; Hokanson and Calden, 1960; Cott and Cott, 1963; Sclare, 1953); a sense of little personal control over his environment (Crandall et al., 1965); intellectual functioning typically at the low average to borderline range (Barnes, 1969), accompanied by poor ability for critical thinking—analytical and synthetical. (Note 3) Information from the achievement orientation domain shows black youngsters as low in achievement motivation (Rosen, 1959; Mussen, 1953; Deutsch, 1960; McClelland, 1961), or as unrealistically high in aspiration levels (Katz, 1968; Ausubel and Ausubel, 1958; Deutsch, 1960, Johnson, 1941). (Note 4)

Generally the literature paints a rather dismal picture of the black youngster from the standpoint of self-concept. Placing the black youngster within the context of the black family generates the following image. The "Negro" family is portrayed as having a life-style distinct from that of all other segments of the society. More often than not the father has deserted the family; the mother, frustrated because of her own unfulfilled needs and wishes, reacts harshly and rejects the children. Her frustration generally is a "causal" factor in her having more "illegitimate" children. The children, in turn, react to this hostile atmosphere by becoming aggressive, nontrusting, and uneducable. They experience unusual difficulty in differentiating between male and female roles, and cross-role adoptions are the rule. By age three or four the black child is aware of racial differences, including a knowledge of the usual associated stereotypes, but is slow to make racial distinctions, and parents (mother) are not able to help him with questions and anxiety around black-white issues and concerns. He frequently chooses white dolls and white friends and often identifies himself as white, or shows a pained reluctance to "admitting" he is "Negro." While much of the direct manifestation of "self-hate" disappears by age seven or eight, definite indications of it still exist later—for example, "shooting" dope to escape the image, or "pimping" and having illegitimate children to deny it. (Note 5)

Both theoretical perspectives and empirical findings project little hope for the development of positive self-images on the part of blacks in this society. But do the foregoing configurations of findings and projections tell the whole story? The writer thinks not. Theory can be questioned on the grounds of its failure to account for the full spectrum of findings in the various empirical studies; for example, what about that 33 to 77% in Clark's (1949) studies, the 87% in Greenwald and Oppenheim's study (1968), and the 46 to 68% in Morland's (1962, 1966) studies who did not select white dolls as being "like themselves"? How does one account for Boyd's (1952) findings of higher aspiration when groups are matched for age, IQ, and socioeconomic status? Lott and Lott's study (1963) suggests that blacks can have high and realistic levels of occupational aspirations. It is of interest to note that when empirical results are in the unexpected direction, usually they are interpreted to be inconsistent with theoretical expectations. The concept of "unrealistic (high) aspiration level" seems to serve that purpose. Because the validity of a theory or conceptual system rests upon its ability to explain and predict, one has to wonder about theory-conserving operations.

The history of this country is replete with instances of the creation of theories to demonstrate the inferiority of blacks—theories that can provide justification for the oppression of blacks, self-serving theories directed to maintaining the oppressor's convictions of his own superiority. Historically, biological or genetic factors have been invoked as explanatory modes to account for the status of blacks; today the vogue is to call forth environmental factors. However, as the writer has noted elsewhere (Barnes, 1969), it is of small benefit to blacks whether an environmental hypothesis is chosen over a genetic hypothesis, "if explanation remains at the level of the black individual or family and does not begin to deal with forces in the larger society responsible for creating these conditions" (p. 36). Where this observation is valid, contemporary social deprivation theories may be viewed as substituting environmental unchangeabilty for biologically determined immutability.

Theory, as explicitly stated and as implicitly interpreted and applied in empirical studies, gives little or no emphasis to the black community as a variable in development and functioning of the self-concept. Little emphasis is given to the black community as a processor of information and messages coming from the wider society. An implicit theoretical assumption is that the black family and child are recipients of direct impingements (messages) from the white society. Likewise, the "generalized other" in theory appears to be synonymous with "white society." This position or interpretation of theory gives no recognition to the possibility that the black community may serve as the child's social referent, thereby asserting influence as the "generalized other."

There is no place in theory or its empirical application for making a distinction between behavior emanating from role playing, on the one hand, and behavior stemming from enduring personality characteristics, on the other. This distinction is a crucial one because it is obviously important whether a given complex of behavior reflects an acting out of role behaviors, or whether it reflects enduring personality characteristics. The ability to distinguish between oneself and the role one plays may be a critical operation for blacks. Consider the lyrics that go with an old black folk song; "got one mind for white folk to see, 'nother for what I know is me" (Ames, 1950, p. 194). This is a succinct statement of the role-person distinction.

Maintaining this distinction is a task confronting each individual. The failure to distinguish between role and self, whether role is that of servility or superior being leads to trouble. Jung introduced the concept of the "persona" to describe this duality.

> The word "persona" is really a very suitable expression for it, since persona originally meant the mask worn by an actor to signify his role . . . . It is a *compromise between the individual and the society* as to

the kind of semblance to adopt, what a man should "appear to be." He takes a name, earns a title, represents an office, and belongs to this or that . . . . Society expects, and indeed must expect, that every individual should play the role assigned to him as completely as possible. Accordingly, a man who is a pastor, must not only carry out his professional functions objectively, but at all times and seasons he must play the role of pastor in a flawless manner. Society demands this as a kind of security . . . . It is therefore not surprising that everyone who wants to be successful has to take these expectations into account.

 The construction of a collectively suitable *persona* means a very great concession to the outer world. It is a real self-sacrifice which directly forces the ego into an identification with the *persona*, so that there are people who actually believe themselves to be what they present to the public view . . . . These identifications with the social role are a very fruitful source of neuroses. *A man cannot get rid of himself in favor of an artificial personality without punishment.* The mere attempt to do so releases, in all the ordinary cases, unconscious reactions in the form of moods, affects, fears, compulsive ideas, feelings, vices, etc. (White, 1948, p. 166; my emphasis)

Undoubtedly, there is a significant difference in the dynamics of the individual who seeks to be his role, and the individual who is thrust in his role against his wishes. In the latter case, the threat of or actual punishment keeps the individual in his role; in the former case, different incentives are involved. (Note 6) Where behavior is an acting out of role definitions, it is enough for the situation to change (change in statuses and role expectation) for behavior to change. A crucial issue regards the extent to which human behavior is generated by the social contexts in which it occurs and the extent to which individuals create a "portable" reality which determines their behavior irrespective of the situation.

 The theoretical position(s) and empirical studies cited do not view the black community as the highly complex, highly structured system that it is. For example, is it the case that middle-class urban blacks, living in a northeast metropolitan area, respond to messages (white racism) from the larger society in a manner identical to and with the same consequences for self-image as the nonworking lower class in the same area? We know, for example, that there are (and have been) blacks in this society who have solid, positive concepts and a strong sense of group belongingness. How can this be explained? Without modification and extension of current self theory, it cannot. Ralph Ellison (1967) placed this issue in perspective when asked by a group of young black writers to comment on how they might more accurately portray the complexity of the human condition, using the black experience as a theme.

Ellison, among other things, stated that the black writer would never see his subject as long as he accepted the black family as a broken one and a matriarchy, or of Harlem as "piss on the wall and blood on the stairs." Such stereotypes, as all stereotypes, have some grain of truth in them, but they do not come close to reflecting the complexity of the black condition, denying "that something else which makes for our strength, which makes for our endurance and promise" (p. 87). The concentration of the literature is on the lowest income, most oppressed black families and individuals. The findings from this group are used as an index to "understanding" and "explaining" blacks (Billingsley, 1968). The studies producing them grow out of present theory, and they feed back into theory. But obviously, to utilize information from this narrow segment of the black population as a basis for describing, explaining, and predicting for blacks is to err grossly. The practice possibly explains some of the contradictions and paradoxes in the literature regarding blacks.

We are fully aware of the many limitations in the operationalized definitions (measures) of self-concept and related dependent variables alluded to in the foregoing. The validity of the findings cited above could be questioned on these grounds; however, an examination of these considerations is beyond the scope of this paper. For present purposes we are accepting the measures of the variables at face value.

At this point we can refer to the question posed at the beginning of this paper regarding the possibilities of a black child's developing a positive self-concept in this society. That question can be translated as follows: Is it possible that the black community can and does serve as a mediator between the black child and the pernicious impingements of the white society, such that the child can develop a self-concept that is enhancing of himself and of his group, a self-concept that enables him to distinguish between who he is, his worth and value, on the one hand, and what the white society says about him on the other? An approach to answering this question requires a modification and extension of theoretical perspective—a perspective that considers the child in relation to the family, the child and family in relation to the black community, and the community, family, and child in relation to the wider society, and finally one that considers black people or the black community as a complex social system. This perspective emphasizes the interdependence of the black child and family with other levels of society and the great heterogeneity characterizing black people, as a group. It postulated the black community as social referent for the child, and as mediator between child and family and the wider society in the process of development of the self-concept. Further, this orientation shifts the focus from the behavior of individuals to recurrent interchanges between people, and may properly be called a *systems conception*.

Systems Approach to Development of the Self-Concept in Black Children

It is our intention to focus upon the social system, or the context in which social behavior takes place. We see social systems as a subclass of systems in general. As such they are subject to the principles of general systems theory (GST). According to Bertalanffy (1966), "general systems theory contends that there are principles of systems in general or in defined subclasses of systems irrespective of the nature of systems of their components, or of the relations of forces between them" (p. 708). Thus, GST is general in that it attempts to examine all types of systems. A system is an organization of elements united in a form of regular interaction and interdependence. General systems theory as an approach to organizing and looking at phenomena is, thus, applicable to the cell (biological system), to the individual (psychological system), and to groups or society (social systems). The focus of this paper is at the level of psychological and social systems.

The concept of a social system has been treated comprehensively by Talcott Parsons (1951, 1955). A social system is an aggregation of social roles or persons bound together by a pattern of mutual interaction and interdependence. It has boundaries which enable us to distinguish the internal from the external environment, and typically it is both a system for social units smaller than itself, and a subsystem for social units larger than itself.

The black family as a social system has been diagrammed by Billingsley (1968), as indicated—and grossly oversimplified—in Figure 1. As depicted the family is embedded in a network of mutually interdependent relationships with the black community and wider society. Just as the family is a subsystem of the black community, so are various patterns of interactions (*dyads*: father-son, mother-daughter, brother-sister; *triads*: grandmother-mother-daughter, etc.) subsystems of the family, which for them is a social system. The individuals in these various patterns, in turn, are subsystems to the larger interactive patterns (dyad, triad, etc.) within the family.

A key consideration in all of this concerns the mutually interdependent relations existing between the family and its members, on the one hand, and the family and the black community, on the other. It may be that, among other things, the nature of the relationship of the family to the black community is a key factor in development of the child's self image.

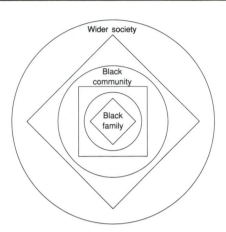

Figure 1. The black family as a social system.
The family is embedded in a matrix of mutually interdependent relationships with the black community and the wider society. And there are subsystems within the family: husband-wife; mother-son; father-daughter; grandmother-mother-daughter, and so forth.

The black community includes schools, churches, lodges, social clubs, funeral societies, organized systems of hustling and other institutions.

The wider society consists of major institutions: value, political, economic, health, welfare, and communication subsystems. (Adapted from A. Billingsley, *Black Families in White America*, Englewood Cliffs, N.J.: Prentice-Hall, 1968.)

Primary among the subsystems of the larger society having a direct impact on the black community, and through it, the family and family members are the communications, political, economic, educational, and values subsystems. Blacks have been systematically excluded from participation in these subsystems, while being gravely influenced by them. It is our contention that the nature and intensity of this influence varies differentially as a function of community characteristics and relation of families to the community. A second major feature of this theoretical orientation concerns the conception of blacks as the highly complex heterogeneous, diverse people that they are. Even though, in this country, black people are viewed as a group apart from other people, and as showing common intragroup attributes, behaviors, and conditions, great variations are also obvious. Billingsley (1968) offers the concept "ethnic subsociety" as a means of capturing this duality. This concept was taken from Milton Gordon's theoretical work *Assimilation in American Life* (1964). An ethnic group is a relatively large configuration of people with a "shared feeling of peoplehood." In this society such groups are organized around race, religion, national origin, or some combination of these. Gordon (1964) states that, common to the ethnic group:

is the social-psychological element of a special sense of both ancestral and future-oriented identification with the group. These are the "people" of my ancestors, therefore, they are my people, and will be the people of my children and their children. With members of other groups I may share political participation, occupational relationships, common civic enterprise, perhaps even an occasional warm friendship, but in a very special way, which history has decreed, I share a sense of indissoluble and intimate identity with this group and not *that* group within the larger society and the world. (p. 29)

This conception seems to reflect the reality of the existence of black people. It also reflects the growing black consciousness or awareness of our peoplehood, which is evolving at a rapid rate in black communities throughout the country. While we are one, as members of a color caste system, and by virtue of our common peoplehood, we are not a homogeneous mass. Billingsley (1968) has depicted the black community as an ethnic subsociety, as indicated in Figure 2.

Billingsley's conceptual model makes use of three dimensions in describing the black community as an ethnic subsociety. They are social dimensions on which members within an ethnic group vary—namely, social class, rural or urban residence, and region of the country lived in. For our purposes then, black groups not only are blacks to be compared or contrasted with whites, they also may be upper class, middle class, or lower class, with northern, southern, or western residence, with urban or rural backgrounds, and significantly they may be meaningfully compared and contrasted with each other.

As indicated by Billingsley (1968), the significance of social class is not to be able to make statements such as "middle-class whites and blacks have more in common than do middle- and lower-class blacks. Such a formulation obscures more than it reveals, and fails to make a distinction between the different types of identities people share. Gordon (1964) conceptualizes two types of identities people share: historical and participational. The ethnic group is the locus of a sense of historical identification. The intersection of ethnicity and social class is the locus of participational identification.

> With a person of the same social class but of a different ethnic group, one shares behavioral similarities but not a sense of peoplehood. With those of the same ethnic group but different social class one shares the sense of peoplehood but not behavioral similarities. The only group which meet both these criteria are people of the same ethnic group and social class (Gordon, 1964, p. 53)

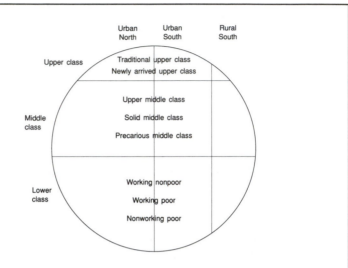

Figure 2. The black community as an ethnic subsociety.
This figure is conceptual and does not reflect the exact social and geographic distribution of the black population. In 1966, about 50 percent of all black families lived in the urban North, 25 percent in the urban South, and 25 percent in the rural South.

If income is used as an index of social class, about 50 percent of all black families fall into the lower class, about 40 percent in the middle class, and about 10 percent in the upper class. (Adapted from A. Billingsley, *Black Families in White America*, Englewood Cliffs, N.J.: Prentice-Hall, 1968.)

As Billingsley (1968) suggests, even though social class lines among blacks are less rigid than among other groups, social class distinctions within the black community do provide a distinct basis of differentiation which helps to condition the lives of blacks. Hence, we would expect differential responses to white impingements by people located at different positions in the structure, differential responses that have implications for black children's developmental status.

Developing Black Consciousness or Sense of Peoplehood

Considering the mutual interdependence of the black family and the black community, it is of critical importance to assess the status of black people in terms of extent of group unity, identification, sense of peoplehood, or what you will. Changes in the community have implications for changes in the family and in the units of which it is comprised. A growing pride, sense of peoplehood in the one, should be accompanied by a similar change in the other, along with the implications such changes carry for development of a positive self-concept in the child.

Carmichael and Hamilton (1967) argue for the development of a black norm by means of which black people must redefine themselves, set forth new values and goals, and organize around them. Barbara Sizemore (1969) and Barnes (1970) mount similar arguments, pointing out that for the black man to support the norms and values of the larger society means to support his own inferiority. It seems clear that the definition of what is "good" and "desirable" and what is "bad" and "undesirable" for a society is primarily in terms of the interests of those who hold the power in that society. The most cursory examination of the current status of blacks today and historically in this country reveals conclusively that the value structure and normative patterns of the society work in the interest of its whites and against the interests of blacks. In a word, the white society imposes a racist authoritarian ethic upon blacks. The black community must define what is "good" and desirable and what is "bad" and undesirable from the standpoint of its own interests and conditions of existence. Sizemore (1969) points out the undesirable implications of supporting the norms and values of the larger society. The support of this norm by a black person means to support his classification as a stigmatized being. For the stigmatized individual who cannot *pass,* he must decide to assume responsibility for the sin, thus shifting the burden from society to the victim, or to alienate himself from the community of the sinner. Obviously, a stigmatized status cannot provide a basis for development of a positive self-concept. The latter alternative of alienation (regroupment) allows for developing those conditions for self-determination.

Talcott Parsons (1965) observes the need for collective and mutual support on the part of the black people, particularly at the level of the family and local community, and suggests that the healthiest line of development for the black man would be toward group solidarity and cohesion and the sense that being a black man has positive value.

Erikson (1968) argues that self-determination is an integral part of ego identity:

> For the American, group identity supports an individual's ego identity as long as he can preserve a certain element of deliberate tentativeness, as long as he can convince himself that the next step is up to him and that no matter where he is staying or going he always has the choice of leaving or turning in the opposite direction. (p. 67)

He also states that a strong ego, secured in its identity by a strong society, does not need artificial inflation, for it tends to test what feels real, to master what works, to understand what proves necessary, to overcome the morbid and to transmit its purpose to the next generation for the creation of a strong mutual reinforcement with others in the group.

What is the status of black people with respect to the various imperatives outlined above? While blacks have always been aware of connections with other blacks in this country and others, they have not felt free to act on them. It was not until after World War II that blacks again embraced the theme put forth by Marcus Garvey and others, that blacks have a common history, a common position vis-a-vis the white world, and a common destiny. Developments over the last decade indicate a sharp rise in the number of black people who recognize the need for blacks to assert their own definitions, to reclaim their history and culture, and to create their own sense of community and togetherness. Throughout the country, middle- and upper-class blacks are turning to explicit recognition of a common destiny shared by blacks (Billingsley, 1968). There is no civil rights or protest activity that does not have privileged blacks in leadership positions. The ghetto uprisings of 1965, 1966, and 1967 in more than 100 cities had substantial support from middle-class blacks.

In many ways the group identification process shows itself—for example, growing resistance to school desegregation and to breakup of black communities through urban renewal, blacks quietly moving back into the ghetto and others refusing to move out, organization of black student groups at secondary and postsecondary levels, discussion groups focusing dialogue around the blacks' common destiny and potential for change.

Salient examples of group solidarity occurred around the election of black mayors in Cleveland, Gary, and Newark, feats made possible by blacks voting in large proportions and in a bloc for the black rather than the white candidate. Further moves toward self-determination and definition are reflected in rejecting the term *Negro* and replacing it with *Afro-American*, *African American*, and *black*, and the development of black aesthetic norms, as reflected in the natural hair style and "dress." All of these recent behavioral manifestations of a participational identification indicate an increase in magnitude of those dimensions of ethnic similarity.

Carmichael and Hamilton (1967) comment on the end significance of this process:

> When we begin to define our own image, the stereotypes—lies that the oppressor has developed—will begin in the white community and end there. The black community will have a positive image of itself it has created. (p. 37)

This view suggests that the black community, through a process of group solidarity, self-determination, and definition (development of black norms), can serve as a filter to sort out or attenuate the pernicious impingements from the larger (white) society, a process which should have a facilitating or enhancing effect on the development of the self-concept in black children.

The black Muslim organization is instructive regarding one approach to developing a black norm. In doing so, the founder, Mr. Muhammad, deals with negative identities: social definitions or the definition of Negro, ego identity, quality of one's existence in the face of significant others, and personal identity, individual name, or identity peg. The new social identity is born out of the community of Islam, an international brotherhood of Asiatics (Africa is a part of Asia). A new name, given by Allah, is substituted for the slave name, giving the individual a new identity peg. The quality of one's existence is enhanced by certain teachings. Arabic is taught in the school, as well as the civilization and religion of the black man. Members of the organization are encouraged to obey rules and regulations surpassing the Protestant Ethic in stringency. However, Mr. Muhammad does not expect his followers to accept the blame for their victimized status at the hands of society. He places the blame directly on society and further charges that such a society must be one of beasts and devils. This is his black norm. It serves not only as a source of positive identification for his followers, but also as a mode for delegitimizing (Note 7) messages from the white society.

Hence, in response to the question posed at the beginning of this paper, we can postulate that it is possible for a black child to have or develop a positive, actualizing self-concept in this society, under certain conditions. These conditions are that the black community containing the child and family be characterized by a sense of peoplehood, group identification, or black consciousness, or pride, and that the family be identified with or experience a sense of belonging to the community. It is postulated that when these conditions prevail, the black community, interposed between the family and white community, serves as a filter against the harmful inputs from the latter. In social system terms, the black community either rejects such messages as input or in its transformations of them renders them innocuous. Or to paraphrase Carmichael and Hamilton (1967), the stereotypes and lies of the oppressor will begin within the white community and die at its borders.

The theoretical perspective advanced here can also begin to explain some of the contradictions and paradoxes in the literature. Consider the complexity of the ethnic subsociety composed of the following classes: the lower class, which can be divided into nonworking poor, working poor, working nonpoor; the middle class, which can be divided into the precarious middle class, solid middle class, upper middle class;

and the upper class, which can be divided into recently-arrived upper class, and old families or traditional upper class. It would be unimaginable to think that individuals and families in such diverse life circumstances would respond uniformly to certain kinds of experiences, such as white racism. No doubt, the sense of peoplehood experienced with reference to blacks differs with different life experiences; children are differentially shielded from the ravages of such diseases as racism. The cases in the various studies cited that do not fall in the categories predicted by theory may be explainable with an adequate description of the populations from which the samples came, rather than merely being described as "Negro." The excess of negative findings, among other things, may be explainable on the basis of the location of the subjects, for those studies, in the ethnic subsociety. The generation of adequately defined samples of blacks would also make possible comparisons between blacks, probably the most crucial comparison anyway, if understanding, explaining and programming are primary goals of studies.

A social systems orientation assumes an interactive process among elements of the system: consequently, the relationship between black community, family group, and child is not conceptualized as reactive in nature. The child does not merely respond to the larger family group and the family group to the community. The relationship is one of interaction, which means that the input into each subsystem is transformed into output which is accepted as input by another system, and both become subsystems of a more general system. Thus, the nature of the relationships established between systems may be related to characteristics of the subsystems or systems. Consideration of some of them lead to certain propositions which can be subjected to empirical test: (a) The degree of identification of the family with the black community (ethnic subsociety) is a factor in its capacity to serve as a filter against harmful impingements from the white society; (b) the degree to which a black community can develop its own norms is contingent upon the degree to which its members perceive of themselves as sharing a common "peoplehood"; (c) families that perceive themselves as more centrally located (greater sense of belonging with respect to the ethnic subsociety) are more effective filters against racism; (d) families at different levels in the ethnic subsociety differ in degrees of identification with the subsociety; and therefore differ in their effectiveness as social filters; (e) input from family members is accepted as such by the children to a greater extent in those cases where the relationship defined by the parent-child subsystem is stable and consistent.

Some Observations on Methodology

Implicit in the foregoing discussion is the concept of communication process. As indicated in the postulate regarding a social system, the units are bound together in a pattern of mutual interaction and interdependence. Hence, the study of the self-image in the black child, or more properly of the processes by which white racism is absorbed, deflected, denied, combatted, succumbed to, and overcome by blacks, requires a methodological approach appropriate to the analysis of communication. Communication as a process can be divided into three levels: (a) action, (b) transaction, and (c) interaction (Note 8). Analysis of the communication process at the action level focuses on the content of the message and the occurrence of events in a regular fashion. This level of analysis is exemplified in a study of self-concept where one of its components is conceptualized as independence or autonomy, operationalized as problem-solving behavior (putting a puzzle together), carried out independently of an adult present in the child's setting. The investigator might count the number of times the child directs verbalization to the adult and classify (categorize) the content as *help seeking* or *other*. The important factor here is that no attempt is made to establish causal connections. The method is observation and categorization of actions. The appropriate statistical approach to handling data involves simple counting operations.

The communication process at the transaction level involves a unidirectional channel of communication between two systems. For example, A's output is accepted as input by B, but B's output is not accepted by A or any other system as input. The focus at this level is on the isolation of cause and effect or antecedent and consequent sequences. Most of the investigation of the self-concept are at this level.

The following section reports the findings of a study carried out by the writer, which illustrates this methodological approach. It also represents an initial step in the explanation of some of the implications of the theoretical perspective propounded in this paper.

Illustrative and Exploratory Investigation

The question posed concerned the relation between black consciousness (group identification, or sense of peoplehood), on the part of parents, and self-image, or self-concept, on the part of their children. Casual observations of friends, students, acquaintances, and their children suggested such a relationship. At the time this information was obtained, the writer was directing an evaluation of a year-long inservice training program for school personnel in the Dayton, Ohio, Model Cities schools. Eight elementary and two high schools were involved in the inservice training program.

The two variables studied, group identification and self-concept, are considered as states of the individual (hypothetical constructs), and as such give rise to observable behavior, such behavior being accessible to observation by techniques designed for that purpose. Group identification and self-concept are defined as indicated in the body of this paper.

From the total population of eight Model Cities elementary schools, four were chosen with the intent of maximizing socioeconomic differences, two schools in the most economically depressed areas and two in the least economically depressed Model City area. From the total population of kindergarten and first-grade classes in each school, a more or less random sample of 50 students was drawn. Samples of 50 subjects for kindergarten and first grade, respectively, were chosen randomly within limits of cooperation from a parochial Catholic school. This school was not located in and did not draw youngsters from the Model Cities area. All subjects in both groups were black. Samples within grades within schools were stratified by sex. For each group of 50 children at each class level, parents of 30 children, randomly selected from their group of 50, were tested. The majority of parents tested were female. Our children sample consisted of 250 males and females, and the adult sample consisted of 300 parents or caretakers, with a sex distribution of 100 fathers and 200 mothers. Average socioeconomic status for children attending school in the badly depressed areas was slightly lower than those attending school in less depressed areas, and both of the latter were lower than the Catholic school sample.

The questions investigated concerned the relationship between aspects of children's self-concept and achievement-test scores (reading readiness and reading), and parents' sense of *group belongingness* (identification), individual-system blame, racial militancy-race ideology, sense of personal control, and individual-collective action.

The instrument utilized with the children was labeled Ethnic Pictures Test (EPT). The subject's task was to choose pictures in response to verbally presented questions designed to tap friendship preferences, social valuation, and color preference or racial identification. Parents (both when present in the household) were tested after the children were tested, but before analysis of the latter's responses was undertaken. Parents responded to self-report techniques (opinions, knowledge, self-ratings, and self-definitions). Parents also responded to a data form providing for information on income, educational level, occupation, organizational memberships, names of neighbors, and frequency of social contacts with them, father's occupation at time respondent was 25 years of age, father's educational level, political affiliation, and last time voted.

A full analysis of the observations made is not presented here. Instead, I report only some of the more salient findings bearing upon the parent's perception of their relationship and orientation to the black ethnic subsociety and children's self-attitudes.

Preliminary data analysis reveals a significant relationship between SES level, using income and education as indices, and level of political activity; conception of term *black power* in political or militant terms; feeling strongly that black history and an African language should be taught in the early grades. Higher SES parents responded in the directions indicated to a greater extent than lower SES parents. Lower SES groups had more frequent contacts with and named a greater number of people as neighbors. When the overall group was classified on level of political activity, conception of "black power," and social contact with neighbors, significant differences in children's responses to EPT emerged. Regardless of SES, the EPT scores of children whose parents indicated a high level of political activity (attending and participating Model Cities Citizens Meetings, voting in the last national and local elections, voting for black candidates for city council and school board) indicated greater ethnic identification, as indicated by positive social valuation of group, friendship choices, and racial or color identification. The same held for the degree to which "black power" was conceptualized in political and militant terms, as well as for social contacts with neighbors, with a frequency of four or more times a month. And finally a positive relationship was found between parent measures on individual-system blame, individual-collective action, race ideology and children's EPT scores, when analysis was based on a dichotomous socioeconomic classification.

The relationships for higher SES groups were stronger. Given this fact, the child whose parents tended to blame the system for the conditions of blacks as a group and to endorse collective and militant action as an approach to the solution of the problems of blacks tended to score more favorably on the EPT. In this investigation, measures of group identity or black consciousness are provided by the instruments tapping the following dimensions: conception of "black power," political activity (voting for black candidates for local, state, and federal offices, etc.), racial militancy, individual-system blame; and individual-collective action (Note 9).

These findings support the notion that parental involvement in the black community and specific beliefs, attitudes, and orientations toward the conditions of one's group, defined as indices of black consciousness, or sense of peoplehood, is associated positively with more positive self-concepts in children. They also support the importance of recognizing the complexity of the black ethnic subsociety in designing studies.

Conclusion

Blacks are threatened with the specter of white racism from the cradle to the grave. Yet many escape the worst features of oppression, and many have shown an incredible capacity to survive, achieve, and conform in the face of impossible odds. Nevertheless, all blacks are members of a color caste system in this society and are subjected to ruthless oppression. We need to know more about the oppressor—his self-concept, factors in its development and maintenance, and the like. Surprisingly little is known to date. We need to know more about the dynamics of racism. We need to trace its dynamics and learn how it is transmitted. Thus, we need to study white families. We also need to study black families, but for a different set of reasons and from a different perspective. We need to study them as subsystems of the larger white society. Black children are at the center of our reasons for suggesting this study of black families. We need to study the process by which racism is absorbed, deflected, denied, combatted, succumbed to, and overcome by particular black families and individuals.

This paper represents a modest attempt to articulate a beginning perspective consistent with these objectives and concerns. However we realize that more important than papers and studies, we need strategies of action to combat the insidious limitation on the ability of blacks to care for their children. Perhaps if we can delineate the process whereby societal racism is transformed into personal terms, we will be in a more propitious position to structure those strategies necessary to save the children.

We have concluded with a hypothesis in need of immediate testing, namely, that a primary factor in developing strategies to save black children is the power to define and determine one's group, roles, and values. He who has power to define is the master of the situation.

Lewis Carroll (1947) understood this:

> "When I use a word," Humpty Dumpty said in a rather scornful tone, "it means just what I choose it to mean—neither more or less."

> "The question is," said Alice, "whether you *can* make words mean so many different things."

> "The question is," said Humpty Dumpty, "which is to be master—that's all." (p. 196)

Notes

1. As indicated by H. Cantril [(1963). *The psychology of social movements*. (New York: John Wiley), pp. 11-14], individuals, families, and communities do not adopt norms of the society without modification. Each of these units acts as a selective or transforming agent vis-a-vis behavioral and expectancy norms of the society. Such transformations or interpretations are influenced by a variety of factors both psychological and sociological. Consequently, it is not enough to be knowledgeable of the value structure, norms, etc., presented to a community or group to be able to know about what is interiorized. One must also have knowledge of community and group characteristics, and one must guard against oversimplification of this process. A shortcoming of self theory concerns its failure to isolate specific social referents involved in the development of self-concept. For example, does the community of a black child play a role in his self-concept and its development?

2. For a lucid treatment of the relationship between status and role, and the social process involved in forcing and maintaining role enactments for ascribed and achieved status, see T.R. Sarbin, (1970), A role-theory perspective for community psychology: The structure of social identity. In D. Adelson & B.L. Kalis (Eds.), *Community psychology and mental health* (San Francisco: Chandler), pp. 88-113.

3. E. Barnes [(1969). *Cultural retardation or shortcomings of assessment techniques, Selected convention papers* (Washington, DC: CEC), criticizes recent relevant literature in this domain from the standpoint, among others, of the status of the black community, family, and individual within society. The criticisms brought to bear in this article are relevant to other dimensions of functioning covered in the current paper.

4. Conceptualizations by B.C. Rosen [(1959) Race, ethnicity, and the achievement of syndrome, *American Sociological Review*, 24, 47-60; and E. Epps (1969), Correlates of academic achievement among northern and southern urban Negro students, *Journal of Social Issues*, 25, 55-70] point out the weaknesses of conceptualization in the areas of achievement motivation and aspiration levels. Epps's concepts of "hope for success" and "perceived probability of success" make for greater precision in studies of achievement motivation and provide a basis for a clearer distinction between this concept and that of aspiration level. Rosen's conceptualization advances the concept of achievement motivation by specifying the factors upon which achievement motivation depends in this society. These three factors he labels collectively as "achievement syndrome." The factors are (a) McClelland's "achievement motive," a personality characteristic; (b) achievement-value orientation, which involves a concern with social mobility and behavior

patterns instrumental in pursuing long-term goals; and (c) educational and vocational aspiration, which concerns the levels of academic and occupational achievements desired by parents for their children and by the children themselves.

5. For a representative article providing a general picture based on research findings of development and functioning of blacks, individual and family, see Lee Rainwater, (1967), Crucible of identity: The Negro lower-class family, in T. Parsons and K.B. Clark (Eds.), *The Negro American* (Boston: Beacon Press), pp. 160-204.

6. For a detailed and systematic treatment of this process, see Sarbin, *op cit.*, pp. 101-110.

7. C. Clark (1971), in Social change and the communication of legitimacy: The case for dispute settlement (*Journal of the Developing Areas*, 5, 577-588), defines and analyzes this concept, its operations, and application from the standpoint of relations between black and white groups.

8. C. Clark (1971), in General systems theory and black studies: Some points of convergences, in C. Thomas (Ed.), *Boys no more: A black psychologist's view of community* (Beverly Hills, CA: Glencoe Press), provides a systematic analysis of the communication process and types of communication.

9. It is assumed theoretically that black consciousness, or sense of peoplehood, or group identification, conceived as a complex psychological state, is reflected in certain attitudes, feelings, and behaviors which are amenable to observation by means of appropriate techniques. The techniques are given the names of the behavior, attitudes, and feelings which, theoretically, reflect black consciousness, or sense of peoplehood. These instruments are (a) conception of *black power,* (b) political activity scale, (c) racial militancy scale, (d) individual-system blame scale, and (e) individual-collective action scale. The racial militancy, individual-collective blame, and individual-collective action scales are specially constructed internal-external control scales. For an account of how they were constructed, and examples of items, see Patricia Gurin et al., (1969), Internal-external control in the motivation dynamics of Negro youth (*Journal of Social Issues*, 1969, 75, 29-54). The race militancy factor "poses alternative forms of collective action for the respondent to choose. One is preference for protest and pressure activities; the other is a preference for less militant approaches such as relying on conversations and negotiations of Negro and white leaders on biracial councils (Gurin et al., p. 45)." The individual-collective action factor contrasts individual effort and mobility with group action as the best way to overcome discrimination (Gurin et al., p. 45). The individual-system blame factor refers to the individual's explanation for the plight of

the black's condition—political, economic, social, and cultural—in this society.

The political activity scale taps the respondent's report regarding actual behavior in voting for issues, candidates, etc., having significance for black people, as well as participation in neighborhood and local political actions—e.g., attending Model Cities meetings, serving on citizens committees, attending open school board meetings, etc.

The "black power" factor refers to the extent to which the concept is viewed favorably and the extent to which it is defined in militant and political terms. D. Auerbach and L. Walker, in a study carried out in Detroit, found that southern-born blacks were less likely to interpret the term in militant terms and were less likely to have a positive attitude toward it. See their Meaning of black power: A comparison of white and black interpretations of a political slogan. Paper presented at the meeting of the American Political Science Association, Washington, DC, 1968.

See Nathan Caplan, The new ghetto man: A review of recent empirical studies (*Journal of Social Issues*, 1970, *26*, 59-74), for psychological characteristics of the young black militant. The characteristics outlined are polar to those traditionally associated with a negative self-concept and weak group identification, as reflected in black individuals. Outstanding are his changed conception of himself vis-a-vis the world around him, the acceptance of blame for the victimized status of the group, increased social insight into social barriers to realization of potential and aspirations, and a heightened sense of personal effectiveness.

References

Ames, R. (1950). Protest and irony in Negro folksong. *Social Science, 14*, 193-213.

Ausubel, D., & Ausubel, P. (1963). Ego development among segregated Negro children. In A.H. Passow (Ed.), *Education in depressed areas*. New York: Bureau of Publications, Teachers College, Columbia University, 1963, pp. 109-131.

Barnes, E.J. (1969). Cultural retardation or shortcomings of assessment techniques. In *Selected convention papers*. Forty-seventh Annual International Convention, Denver, Colorado, April, 1969. Washington, DC: The Council for Exceptional Children. pp. 35-43.

Barnes, E.J. *Counseling the black student: The need for a new view.* Pittsburgh: University of Pittsburgh Press, 1970.

Bertalanffy, L. Von. (1966). General system theory and psychiatry. In S. Arieti (Ed.), *American handbook of psychiatry* (Vol. 3). New York: Basic Books. pp. 705-721.

Billingsley, A. (1968). *Black families in white America.* Englewood Cliffs, NJ: Prentice-Hall.

Boykin, L.L. (1957). The adjustment of 2,078 Negro students. *Journal of Negro Education, 26,* 75-79.

Burton, R.J., & Whiting, J.W.M. (1961). The absent father and cross-sex identity. *Merrill-Palmer Quarterly, 7,* 85-95.

Caldwell, M.G. (1959). Personality trends in the youthful male offender. *Journal of Criminal Law, Criminology and Police Science, 49,* 405-416.

Carmichael, S., & Hamilton, C.V. (1967). *Black power: The politics of liberation in America.* New York: Vintage Books.

Carroll, L. (1947) *Through the looking glass.* New York: Doubleday.

Clark, C. (1971). General systems theory and black studies: Some points of convergence. In C. Thomas (Ed.), *Boys no more: A black psychologist's view of community.* Beverly Hills, CA: Glencoe Press.

Clark, K.B., & Clark, M. (1947). Racial identification and preferences in Negro children. In T.M. Newcomb, & E.L. Hartley (Eds.), *Readings in social psychology.* New York: Holt, Rinehart & Winston, pp. 169-178.

Coles, R. (1967). It's the same but it's different. In T. Parsons, & K.B. Clark (Eds.), *The Negro American.* Boston: Beacon Press. pp. 254-279.

Cooley, C.H. (1956). *Human nature and the social order.* New York: Free Press.

Crandall, V.C., Katkovsky, W., & Crandall, J.J. (1965). Children's beliefs in their own control of reinforcement in intellectual academic achievement situations. *Child Development, 36,* 91-109.

Crayton, H.R. (1951). The psychology of the Negro under discrimination. In A. Rose (Ed.), *Race prejudice and discrimination.* New York: Knopf. pp. 276-290.

Deutsch, M. (1960). *Minority group and class status as related to social and personality factors in scholastic achievement.* Monograph No. 2. Ithaca, NY: The Society for Applied Anthropology, Cornell University Press.

Ellison, R. (1967, March). A very stern discipline. *Harper Magazine,* 76-95.

Erikson, E.H. (1968). *Identity, youth, and crisis.* New York: Norton.

Essien-Udom, E.U. (1962). *Black nationalism.* New York: Dell.

Feld, S., & Lewis, J. (1967). *The assessment of achievement anxieties in children.* Unpublished manuscript, Mental Health Study Center, National Institute of Mental Health.

Goffman, E. (1963). *Stigma.* Englewood Cliffs, NJ: Prentice-Hall.

Goodman, M.E. (1952). *Race awareness in young children.* Cambridge, MA: Harper.

Gordon, J. (1965). *The poor of Harlem: Social functioning in the underclass.* Report to the Welfare Administration. Washington, DC: U.S. Government Printing Office, July 31, 1965.

Gordon, M. (1964). *Assimilation in American life.* New York: Oxford University Press.

Greenwald, H.J., & Oppenheim, D.B. (1968). Reported magnitude of self-misidentification among Negro children-Artifact? *Journal of Personality and Social Psychology, 8*, 49-52.

Hammer, E.F. (1953). Negro and white children's personality adjustment as revealed by a comparison of their drawings (H-T-P). *Journal of Clinical Psychology, 9*, 7-10.

Hill, K.T., & Sarason, S.B. (1966). The relation of test anxiety and defensiveness to test and school performance in the elementary school years: A further longitudinal study. *Monographs of the Society for Research in Child Development, 31*, (whole no. 2).

Hofanson, J.E., & Calden, G. (1960). Negro-white differences on the MMPI. *Journal of Clinical Psychology, 16*, 32-33.

Johnson, C.S. (1967). *Growing up in the black belt.* New York: Schocken.

Katz, I. (1968). Academic motivation and equal educational opportunity. *Harvard Educational Review. 38*, 57-66.

Landreth, C., & Johnson, B.C. (1953). Young children's responses to a picture and interest designed to reveal reactions to persons of different skin color. *Child Development, 24*, 63-79.

Lott, A.J., & Lott, B. (1963). *Negro and white youth: A psychological study in a border-state community.* New York: Holt, Rinehart & Winston.

Mead, G.H. (1934). *Mind, self, and society.* Chicago: University of Chicago Press.

McClelland, D.C. (1961). *The achieving society.* New York: Van Nostrand Reinhold.

McLuhan, M. (1966). *Understanding media: The extensions of man.* New York: New American Library.

Mills, C.W. (1963). Methodological consequences of the sociology of knowledge. In I.L. Horonitz (Ed.), *Power, politics and people: The collected essays of C. Wright Mills.* New York: Ballantine. pp. 453-468.

Mischel, W. (1961a). Delay of gratification, need for achievement and acquiescence in another culture. *Journal of Abnormal and Social Psychology,. 62*, 543-552.

Mischel, W. (1961b). Father-absence and delay of gratification: Cross-cultural comparisons. *Journal of Abnormal and Social Psychology,. 63*, 116-124.

Mischel, W. (1961c). Preference for delayed reinforcement and social responsibility. *Journal of Abnormal and Social Psychology,. 62*, 1-7.

Mischel, W. (1966). Theory and research on the antecedents of self-imposed delay of reward. In B. Maher (Ed.), *Progress in experimental personality research* (Vol. 3). New York: Academic Press.

Morland, J.K. (1962). Racial acceptance and preference of nursery school children in a southern city. *Merrill-Palmer Quarterly, 8*, 271-280.

Morland, J.K. (1966). A comparison of race awareness in northern and southern children. *American Journal of Orthopsychiatry, 36*, 22-31.

Mowrer, O.H., & Ullman, A.D. (1945). Time as a determinant in integrative learning. *Psychological Review, 4*, 187-201.

Mussen, P.H. (1953). Differences between the TAT responses of Negro and white boys. *Journal of Consulting Psychology, 17*, 373-376.

Palerno, D.S. (1959). Racial comparisons and additional normative data on children's Manifest Anxiety Scale. *Child Development, 30*, 53-57.

Parsons, T. (1951). *The social system.* New York: Free Press.

Parsons, T. (1965). Full citizenship for the Negro American? In T. Parsons, & K.B. Clark (Eds.), *The Negro American*. Boston: Houghton Mifflin.

Parsons, T., & Bales, R.F. (1955). *Family socialization and interaction process*. New York: Free Press.

Poussaint, A., & Atkinson, C. (1970). Black youth and motivation. *Black Scholar*, *1*, 43-51.

Radke, M., & Trager, H.G. (1950). Children's perceptions of the social roles of Negroes and whites. *Journal of Psychology*, *29*, 3-33.

Rainwater, L. (1967). Crucible of Identity: The Negro lower-class family. In T. Parsons, & K.B. Clark (Eds.), *The Negro American* pp. 160-204. Boston: Beacon Press.

Rosen, B.C. (1959). Race, ethnicity, and the achievement syndrome. *American Sociological Review*, *24*, 47-60.

Sarason, S.B., Davidson, K.S., Lighthall, F.F., Waite, R.R., & Ruebush, B.K. (1960). *Anxiety in elementary school children*. New York: John Wiley.

Sclare, A. (1953). Cultural determinants in the neurotic Negro. *British Journal of Medical Psychology*, *26*, 278-288.

Sizemore, B.A. (1969). Separatism: A reality approach to inclusion? In R.L. Green (Ed.), *Racial crises in American education*. Chicago: Follett Educational Corporation.

Stevenson, H.W., & Stewart, E.C. (1958). A developmental study of racial awareness in young children. *Child Development*, *29*, 399-410.

Sullivan, H.S. (1953). *The interpersonal theory of psychiatry*. New York: Norton.

White, R.W. (1948). *The abnormal personality: A textbook*. New York: Ronald Press.

Yarrow, M.R. (1958). Interpersonal dynamics in a desegregation process. *Journal of Social Issues*, *14*, 3-63.

Applications of Psychology and the Criminal Justice System: A Black Perspective

Thomas O. Hilliard

> Traditionally law has functioned as the handmaiden of the propertied class in our society. So it was to be expected that lawyers in the legislative halls, lawyers on the bench and lawyers in the executive branch of government would combine their talents to perpetuate by law this particularly American doctrine of racism predicated upon a claimed color inferiority.
>
> Judge George W. Crockett, Jr.

Since the inception of the Association of Black Psychologists in 1968, and its mission of politicizing black psychology and increasing the relevance of psychology to black people, a major productive direction has been the applications of psychology to the legal system. This direction of the professional energies of black psychologists is consistent with the staggering problems encountered by large numbers of blacks with the legal system and coincides with the burst of activity in the area of forensic psychology generally.

While there is increased interest in the broad applications of psychology and the law, there is a particular need to focus on the unique relationship of these disciplines to the black community. First, the relevance of such an emphasis is suggested by the numbers of black people having day-to-day interactions with the legal system. Also, black people, typically having limited financial resources, often have been denied specialized expertise in their legal cases. Further, there are severe problems and limitations in theories, methodologies, and research conclusions of psychology as they pertain to black people. More specifically, the discipline of psychology's relationship to the black community is characterized by racism, insensitivity, gross distortion and inappropriate methodologies. For instance, Robert Guthrie's *Even The Rat Was White*, and Alexander Thomas' and Samuel Sillen's *Racism and Psychiatry* provide extensive documentation of the historic and contemporary manifestation of racism in the disciplines of psychology and psychiatry, respectively. Thus, even when psychological resources are utilized in the interest of black clients, they are likely to be inappropriately utilized, and ineffective. Finally, there is a rapid emergence of the field of black psychology as a discipline, aimed at the systematic study of black people, which reformulates the black experience.

During the decades since the formation of the Association of Black Psychologists, innovative and substantive applications of psychology and the law to the black community ranged from the use of psychologists in the jury selection of major criminal trials, and intelligence testing litigation in California to employment testing discrimination and penal reform. Efforts have been expanded to the legislative area. While the applications of psychology and law in the black community embrace both civil and criminal law, the present paper will restrict its focus to issues related to blacks in relationship to the criminal justice system. Necessarily omitted, then, are substantive areas such as personal injury, child custody, workmen's compensation, involuntary hospitalization, racial discrimination in psychological testing, etc. (Hilliard, T., 1976) (See Note 1).

Psychology and the Criminal Justice System

The applications of psychology and the criminal law have the longest history and most extensive utilization within the legal field, particularly around the issue of criminal responsibility. This broad area includes the utilization of the behavioral sciences in preventive and rehabilitative efforts such as jury selection, socio-psychological determinants of criminal behavior, mental impairment and criminal conduct, psychological evaluation and treatment of juvenile offenders, and finally, penal reform. The relevance of work in criminal law is underscored by the well-documented fact that a disproportionately large number of black males comprise the population of prison and correctional facilities in this country.

While much of the contemporary work in the applications of psychology to the criminal justice system is innovative and more well publicized, there are historical precedents for such collaboration in the work of the early black psychologists. For instance, Dr. Francis Sumner, acknowledged as the first black psychologist in the United States, conducted empirical studies on attitudes of blacks toward the criminal justice system in the 1930's and 1940's, and Frederick Watts did clinical research on delinquency among black males (Guthrie, 1976). Similarly, black sociologist Henry Bullock (1961) conducted systematic studies on the relationship of prison sentences to race. Thus, the contemporary efforts by black psychologists in relationship to the criminal justice system represents a continuing involvement in an abiding area of concern to black behavioral scientists.

Jury Selection

There is considerable historical and contemporary evidence to demonstrate that blacks are consistently tried before all-white juries or juries in which blacks are seriously underrepresented (Bell, 1973; Ginger, 1969; Hilliard, 1974; Hayes, 1975). The significance of the predominance of whites on juries is highlighted by the voluminous historical and social science data which provide meticulous documentation of the widespread and pervasive nature of white racism toward blacks in America (Delaney, 1975; Franklin, 1969; Howard, 1972; National Advisory Commission on Civil Disorders, 1968; Myrdal, 1944; Jordan, 1968). Further, there is a substantial literature on perceptual processes that shows that social attitudes, values, needs, perceptual "set" or expectancy influence perceptions, and may cause marked perceptual distortions (Postman, Bruner, & McGinnes, 1948; Postman & Crutchfield, 1952; Epstein & Rock, 1960). In fact, there are social psychological data which support the conception that jury decision-making is subjective and based on factors other than "objective" and rational evaluation of the evidence. For example, Richard Kulka and Joan Kessler (1973) presented a paper, "Is Justice Really Blind?—The Influence of Physical Attractiveness on Decisions of Simulated Jurors," which reports preliminary data on their study of the relationship of physical attractiveness of the litigants to trial outcome. Specifically, the research was designed as a "mock" civil trial to determine the effect of the rated physical attractiveness of plaintiff and defendants on the verdict and size of damages awarded in a negligence case. The negligence trial was presented in an identical manner to all participants, except that the slides depicting the plaintiff and the defendants were systematically varied for different degrees of physical attractiveness. The research results indicated that when the plaintiff was rated as physically attractive, and the defendant was unattractive, the jury decision was in favor of the plaintiff. Also, the attractive plaintiff tended to get higher amounts of money awarded for damages. Kulka and Kessler also interpret their results as supporting previous studies of jury decision-making which show jurors' perceptions of the severity of accidents vary with the attractiveness of the victim or plaintiff (Landy & Aronson, 1969; Walster, 1966). These results, then, are consistent with the socio-psychological literature on the influence of personal attractiveness on variables such as likability (Byrne, London, & Reeves, 1968; Walster, Aronson, Abramson and Rotman, 1966) and evaluation of anti-social behavior (Dion, 1972). Personal attractiveness is also associated with the traits of credibility, honesty or likability (Dion, 1972; Dion, Berscheid & Walster, 1972; Kalven & Zeisel, 1966). This small but suggestive body of studies demonstrates the potency of subjective and non-evidentiary variables on jury decisions, and suggests the difficulties of blacks receiving a fair and impartial trial in either civil or criminal cases in which they are judged by white jurors.

The typical situation for black defendants in the criminal justice system, then, is to be tried before a predominantly or exclusively white jury, quite probably with racist attitudes which affect their overall participation in court proceedings. These internalized attitudes, values, beliefs, and norms will color the juror's attitude toward the litigants, determine what information or evidence is seen or fails to be seen, the perceptions and emotional reactions to witnesses, including expert witnesses, interpretations of events and facts, and conceptions of how a "reasonable man" would approach a given situation. Daniel Swett (1972), in an article titled "Cultural Bias in the American Legal System," points to the inherent racism and middle-class bias that permeates the courtroom setting and, in fact, the entire legal process. He further identifies several factors which penalize blacks and other ethnic minorities in the trial process:

> the value system of the legal profession, the procedures by which juries are selected, the value system of the jurors, the lack of articulation in communication between the culturally different, and the professionals composing the court, and the negative stereotype of cultural minorities held by professionals.

Louis Knowles and Kenneth Prewitt (1972) reach similar conclusions:

> Black people living in ghettos isolated from white society have developed styles of grooming and dress, a vocabulary, and a set of traditions that are strange and incomprehensible to most whites. A white jury called upon to evaluate the evidence surrounding an incident involving black people in their own community faces a very difficult task because of this cultural barrier.

They further state that:

> The influence of other factors such as hair style, dress, and bearing of black witnesses is more difficult to ascertain. But undoubtedly, most white jurors react unfavorably to proud, aloof youth with tight pants and "naturals," which they associate with Black Power and rebellious violence. Whites subconsciously view such assertions of cultural differences as a threat to the established order.

Another study which was conducted to determine the problems associated with blacks and jury service points out poignantly the racism of white jurors (Broedor, 1972). The author conducted interviews with jurors following several trials and pinpointed some of the blatant racist attitudes. He states:

> At least two such jurors were themselves strongly prejudicial

against Negroes. Both readily admitted prejudice when interviewed; and, one, who almost hung the jury, sought to justify
his prejudice, and said that he saw nothing wrong with convict-
ing a defendant because of his race, even if the evidence were
not particularly strong.

The juror summed up his views in this manner:

Niggers have to be taught to behave. I felt that if he hadn't
done that, he'd done something else probably even worse, and
that he should be put out of the way for a good long while.

The cumulative effect of the deep-seated nature of racism in white
America, cultural differences between whites and blacks, and the effect
of personal biases on perceptions and beliefs underscore the formidable
problems that blacks face in courts, without a "jury of peers."

While the composition of juries has always been a concern of
lawyers, it has been only recently that psychologists have been used to
augment the skills of lawyers in jury selection, particularly in political
trials. The rationale for such collaboration is based on the purported
expertise of the behavioral sciences in attitude assessment and measurement, clinical skills in personality assessment, using verbal and nonverbal cues, and knowledge of group processes. One of the initial attempts
at the utilization of behavioral science expertise in jury selection was the
criminal trial of Huey P. Newton in 1967 in Oakland, California. Attorney Charles Garry, spurred by the realization that the defendant, Huey
P. Newton, would not be afforded a "jury of peers" under the system
utilized in Alameda County, employed the skills of an array of social
scientists in tasks ranging from the filing of Amicus Curiae briefs to
providing expert testimony and consultation to counsel. The behavioral
scientists were utilized to challenge methods of selection of jury panels,
racism of white jurors, use of pre-emptory challenges against all blacks,
socio-political implications of a "death qualified jury," and limitations
of the *voir dire* in eliminating racist jurors (Ginger, 1969). Further, Attorney Garry employed the services of a sociologist to provide the scientific
perspective of sociology to supplement the more intuitive assessment of
lawyers in determining the attitudes of jurors toward blacks, militancy,
capital punishment, etc. The acquittal of Huey P. Newton provides some
support to the value of behavioral scientists.

A similar case was the criminal trial of Angela Davis in Santa Clara
County in 1972. A significant dynamic in the case was the transfer of
the "change of venue" to Santa Clara County, a county in which only
1% of the population was black and, according to a number of so-
cial/psychological indicators (i.e., attitudes toward open housing), politically conservative and racist. Thus, Attorneys Leo Branton and
Howard Moore, aware of the difficulties of achieving a fair and impartial

jury, enlisted the support of a team of black psychologists from the Bay Area Association of Black Psychologists to assist in the selection of the jury. They were all clinical psychologists with the exception of one who was an experimental psychologist. This combination of specialties was chosen to maximize clinical assessment skills and to provide experimental rigor for a still unrefined technique. Specifically, Howard Dent, William Hayes, Thomas O. Hilliard, William Pierce and Ann Ashmore Poussaint were requested initially to assist counsel by the assessment of socio-political attitudes of the jurors, particularly attitudes toward communism, blacks, militancy and women. However, the team of black psychologists enlarged the scope of its work to include the assessment of personality variables, and prediction of group dynamics in jury deliberations. Thus, personality variables such as cognitive style, ego strength, suggestibility, and dependence were examined. Cognitive style, for instance, was chosen, for there is evidence that different personality types perceive, attend to, and experience the world quite differently. They also have different capacities for employing cognitive functions such as attention and concentration which are quite directly related to their ability to listen objectively and weigh evidence (Shapiro, 1965). Further, personality characteristics such as assertiveness, emotional dependence, persuasibility, were useful in prediction of the group dynamics likely to occur in jury deliberations, consistent with empirical data on the emergence of leadership patterns in groups and the effect of group norms and pressures on individuals in small group situations, (Cartwright, D. Zander, A., 1960). According to the defense lawyers, and interestingly, the prosecutor, the late Albert Harris, Jr., the use of behavioral scientists significantly affected the case in favor of the defense. William Hayes (1975) presented a paper "Sociological and Psychological Principles of Jury Selection" in which he reviewed the use of behavioral scientists in jury selection, appraiseed their value, responded to criticism of their methodologies and extracted the unifying sociological and psychological principles in the different trials. He concluded that while further study of the effectiveness of behavioral scientists in jury selection should be undertaken, the success of those legal cases in which scientific jury selection has been utilized suggests its utility.

Criminal Responsibility

The role of psychological and psychiatric impairment and criminal conduct is the most controversial area within the field of forensic psychology and has, also, generated the most professional activity. That is, the law has presumably made specific provisions for those individuals who engage in behaviors that would otherwise fall within the criminal code, but who are seen as not responsible for their behavior because of "mental disease" or severe psychiatric impairment. Specifically, the criminal law provides that, in addition to the punishable behavior (i.e., homicide, theft, assault), an appropriate "mental state" or "mens rea" (guilty mind) is a necessary element in the definition of a criminal offense. Thus, theoretically, if a defendant in a criminal proceeding is able to demonstrate for the court sufficient mental retardation or psychiatric disturbance, their criminal conduct may be "excused," and they may be treated by a mental health institution, rather than the criminal justice system.

The most typical and widely utilized form of the issue of criminal responsibility is the issue of "legal insanity" as a defense for a crime. The definition of legal insanity has been a troublesome and problematic area for the law, particularly around the standard or criteria for insanity and varies between jurisdiction from the McNaghten rule, the Durham rule, and the American Law Institute standard. In fact, there is growing disenchantment with the "insanity defense," and many judges and legal scholars are now advocating the abolishment of the insanity defense. Another form of the issue of criminal responsibility is embodied in the legal concept of "diminished capacity" in a few jurisdictions such as California and Colorado. "Diminished capacity" refers to the absence of the proper "mental state" or "specific intent" required for the crime alleged, though not as extreme as "legal insanity." For example, first degree murder may require "malice aforethought" or "deliberation" to accompany the homicidal act. Yet, according to section 1016 of the Penal Code of the State of California, evidence that the defendant suffered from a mental illness, mental defect or from the effects of intoxication from alcohol or any other substance is admissible to raise a reasonable doubt as to the existence of a required mental state. Therefore, the well acknowledged and documented high use of drugs and alcohol in the black community, and the number of crimes committed by blacks while intoxicated, would suggest the possible application of diminished capacity in judicial proceedings.

Psychological evaluations, then, are utilized in a variety of court situations including the determination of criminal responsibility, competency to stand trial, and during the post-trial phase around dispositional goals or sentencing. There are, however, special problems associated with the psychiatric and psychological examination of black defendants, who constitute the bulk of the population of prisons and correctional facilities. First, if the black defendant is able to obtain psychiatric or psychological testimony at all, his low income status will necessitate his examination by a court appointed professional or by a staff member of a court psychiatric clinic. I have observed that while the defendant population is predominantly black, the psychiatric and psychological evaluations are conducted by clinicians who are almost exclusively white. For instance, an American Psychology and Law Society Newsletter (1977) reports the results of a Manpower Data Survey of American Psychological Association members whose primary employment was related to the criminal justice system, found that 98.4% of the respondents were white. Thus, black defendants are vulnerable to the widespread misassessment by white clinicians, and the proclivity of clinicians to evaluate blacks from the frame of reference of white society. Consistent with my observations are research data that show socio-economic biases of examiners influence prediagnostic impressions, diagnostic scores, and prognosis (Jones, E., 1974). In my judgment, few white clinicians are aware of the different values, modus operandi, communication styles and system of reference of blacks, which William Grier and Price Cobbs in *Black Rage* termed the "Black Norm." Thus, it is not surprising that black defendants, juvenile and adult, are often seen as "anti-social," "sociopathic," "psychopathic" and thereby have a poor prognosis for rehabilitation or treatment. Also, these white clinicians, psychiatrists and psychologists often have no supervised experience with black clients and are unaware of the social and cultural dimensions of clinical work. Often they are completely unfamiliar with literature which is *routine* reading for black psychologists, psychiatrists, psychiatric social workers and even students, such as *Black Rage*, by William Grier and Price Cobbs, Reginald Jones' *Black Psychology*, *Black Families in White America* by Andrew Billingsley, Nathan Hare's *Black Anglo-Saxons*, and unaware of any of the black professional journals like the *Journal of Black Psychology* and the *Black Scholar*. Further, these psychologists rely heavily for their diagnostic formulations on the traditional psychological tests, the M.M.P.I., Rorschach, W.A.I.S., and Bender Gestalt, which abound in cultural biases and limited empirical validity. It has been my experience that most white psychologists are not aware of the severe problems and limitations of traditional psychological instruments concerning standardization, validity and reliability with blacks, cultural and language biases, and problems in their administration, scoring and interpretation. Nor are they aware of the empirical research or clinical data that indicate that the race of the examiner may affect the examinee's responses, and for many blacks, negatively (Hilliard, A. 1975). Finally, these psychologists often are not community oriented and are totally unaware of community mental health and other resources that may be enlisted to support community alternatives to incarceration.

These severe limitations in clinical training and coursework in black psychology, awareness of current thinking and literature in black psychology and mental health raise serious questions as to whether many white clinicians should even be qualified as "expert witnesses" in court cases pertaining to black defendants. Their qualifications to effectively evaluate black clients should be the subject of lengthy cross examinations. In fact, the American Psychological Association's National Conference on "Levels and Patterns of Professional Training" (Korman, 1975) suggests that many white professionals may be in violation of acceptable ethical standards for their professional conduct with ethnic minorities.

A related problem associated with the psychiatric and psychological examination of black defendants is the allegiance of the examiner. Often, the primary identification and allegiance of mental health professionals in court clinics or forensic clinics is to the court which provides the financial resources for their existence, and retains administrative and supervisory authority for their activities. The issue of the allegiance of the psychological examiner is critical, for it accentuates the mistrust and "cultural paranoia" harbored by many low-income black defendants for white middle class professionals. Further, court appointed psychologists, or psychiatrists or mental health professionals who conduct psychological evaluations for forensic clinics attached to the courts waive rights to client confidentiality, and privileged communications. In contrast, middle and upper-income clients utilize the expertise of private mental health professionals who are selected by their attorneys. Thus, the psychologist or psychiatrist whose report or testimony is damaging to his client is not typically requested to either submit a report or to provide testimony to the court. In fact, attorneys for affluent clients often have the freedom and financial resources to "shop around" for experts favorable to their defense. Dr. Bernard Diamond, forensic psychiatrist, in an article entitled "The Fallacy of the Impartial Expert" points to the selection bias inherent in the choice of court appointed experts. Dr. Diamond (1975) concludes:

> The selection of court appointed psychiatrists is seldom made from the random universe of the psychiatric population. Certain psychiatrists tend to be appointed over and over again.

He further states:

> In many communities, the District Attorney has an undue influence over the courts in the selection of the panel from which the court-appointed expert is drawn. Psychiatrists who have more liberal views which have been revealed through their testimony in previous cases may be systematically excluded from appointment by the court. It is only natural for the District Attorney to recommend a panel of psychiatrists who are known to be reliable in expressing extremely conservative opinions, and who follow the strictest possible interpretation of the McNaghten rules. (Granted, the defense psychiatrist is chosen by counsel just because he is more liberal and more advanced in

his views). And probably, those psychiatrists who do a great deal of defense work are apt to be unconsciously identified with the defendant, to be overly sympathetic and motivated to be an advocate for the underdog. But I assert that those psychiatrists who seek out and tend to receive appointment by the court as so-called impartial experts have an equal probability of being overly identified with authority, of being a sort of watchdog of the public morals, and motivated toward seeing that no criminal "gets away with anything."

The preceding discussion describes the unique problems associated with the current utilization of psychological evaluations with low income black defendants. In summary, the problems identified clustered into the following broad areas:

1. Lack of availability and accessibility of forensic psychology services to low income black defendants.
2. The professional incompetence of white professionals with black populations which causes inappropriate assessments and recommendations.
3. The lack of allegiance of psychological examiners to the black defendant, and consequent problems in establishing adequate rapport.
4. Biases inherent in the selection of court appointed experts.

Penal Reform

A variety of actions have been initiated to use the legal system to ameliorate abuses of psychosurgery and behavior modification, to limit dangerous experimentation, and to protect civil rights of prison inmates (Slovenko, 1973).

A major attempt to address the issue of prison reform was initiated in *Spain v. Procunier* at San Quentin Prison in California. The "San Quentin Six" inmates of the "Adjustment Center" at San Quentin initiated a class action suit in which they challenged the conditions of their confinement and the nature of the physical and psychological conditions of the Adjustment Center. Specifically, they charged that the conditions of their confinement to the Adjustment Center constituted "cruel and unusual punishment," and a denial of their eighth amendment constitutional rights. In addition to the wealth of data and documentation of the prison conditions, Attorney Mark Merin, counsel for the plaintiffs, enlisted the professional expertise of a team of psychiatric experts to conduct independent investigations of the conditions and assess their psychological impact on the inmates. Thus, each behavioral scientist toured and inspected the Adjustment Center and conducted diagnostic interviews with the inmates. These examinations of the inmates, Johnny Spain, Fleeta Drumgo, David Johnson, Luis Talamentez, Hugo Pinel and Willie Tate, centered on the impact of prolonged confinement, excessive chains and shackles, isolation from normal human contact, lack of physical exercise, the absence of rehabilitative efforts, and the indeterminate sentence. Following the examinations, the behavioral scientists were to serve as expert witnesses in court proceedings. Although each behavioral scientist conducted an independent assessment of the Adjustment Center and its effects on the inmates, there was unanimity as to the severity and deleterious nature of the conditions. For instance, Dr. Lee Coleman concluded:

> Their frustration finally leads to a profound helplessness, and hopelessness which is the foundation of human destruction.

Similarly, Dr. Phillip Zimbardo, social psychologist, (1974) in reference to the Adjustment Center conditions noted:

> I cannot recall being in a situation which conveyed such a total atmosphere of intimidation, fear, control, domination, anonymity and absence of human values . . . I must conclude: that this set of conditions are such as to offend the sensibility of any decent person, to be without sufficient justification, to be for the convenience of the institution and contrary to the mandate of society, and alien to the development of the individual's potential, to predispose inmates to pathological influences and internal derangements making rehabilitation less—rather than more likely.

Dr. Zimbardo's conclusion was consistent with an earlier experimental study of simulated prison conditions and their effect on college students who served as the subjects (Haney, Banks and Zimbardo, 1973). This experimental study attempted to recreate a "mock" prison environment by creating situations of confinement, powerlessness, frustration, arbitrariness of authority, emasculation, etc. The subjects showed marked loss of personal identity, passivity, dependency, and helplessness. In fact, according to the authors:

> The most dramatic evidence of the impact of this situation upon the participants was seen in the gross reactions of five prisoners who had to be released because of extreme emotional depression, crying, rage and acute anxiety. The pattern of symptoms was quite similar in four of the subjects and began as early as the second day of imprisonment.

While the "mock" prison setting was considerably less stressful than the Adjustment Center conditions, the results corroborated the evaluations and testimonies of the behavioral scientists as to the devastating and pathological nature of the prison conditions. Interestingly, Dr. Zimbardo found, after an extensive computer search of the American Psychological Association's abstract research service (PASAR), a range of psychological variables that were directly applicable to the impact of the prison conditions. The variables included: "crowding," "loss of privacy," "invasions of personal space," "sensory deprivation," "social isolation," "boredom," "sensory overload," "confinement," "power," "decision-making," "interpersonal reciprocity," "noise," "helplessness," "apathy," etc.

These extreme conditions, according to Dr. Bernard Diamond's testimony, lead to the politicization of prison inmates. Although this politicization enhances the inmates' ability to survive psychologically, it also causes severe reactions from prison guards. As Dr. Diamond (1974) states:

> I think the politicization of the Adjustment Center inmate has been an important factor in, perhaps, delaying or even minimizing the disintegration that takes place. The significance and meaning of politicization, which has been quite marked in recent years, of the kind of new role for the prisoner of the hero, the martyr . . . I think it's very much to their credit that they're able to achieve this despite the overwhelming circumstances. And I think it does play some part in contributing to what could be called ego strength and avoiding the more obvious manifestation of deterioration of the kind which is even more malignant with an apathetic withdrawal.

The role of political activism in the psychological functioning of inmates concurs with my own observations and is corroborated with empirical data which show that psychological health is associated with political activism among blacks (Hilliard, T., 1972).

Finally, after an inspection of the Adjustment Center, and interviews with the "San Quentin Six" (Hilliard, T., 1974), my own conclusions concerning the conditions of the Adjustment Center were:

> Overall, it is my professional opinion that despite the benevolent and therapeutic sound of the title "Adjustment Center," its physical environment and psychological climate is overwhelmingly negative and antagonistic to effective rehabilitation. In fact, I would submit that the conditions of the Adjustment Center are both hostile and provocative. That is, that the normal and typical experiences in the Adjustment Center stimulate, and indeed provoke hostility, resentment, and resistance to this type of treatment. Essentially, inmates are treated as animals or sub-humans. They are constantly in chains, experience the crudest of living conditions, endure prolonged confinement and isolation from normal human contact, and are severely limited in physical activity and recreation. There is no apparent positive reinforcement. This overwhelmingly negative

environment leads to hostility, bitterness, frustration, and despair. Ideally, penal and correctional institutions purport to develop the inmate's sense of empathy, identification, and respect for society and its institutions, however, the prison system breeds an acute awareness of injustice and insensitivity and engenders a basic contempt for society.

I therefore affirm that it is my professional opinion that the physical and psychological conditions connected with life in the Adjustment Center are cruel and unusual punishment and clearly inconsistent with positive mental health.

Subsequently, Judge Alfonso Zirpoli ruled that the conditions of the Adjustment Center indeed constituted "cruel and unusual punishment" in violation of the Eighth and Fourteenth Amendments to the Constitution of the United States.

Summary

The present paper was directed to the identification of substantive application of psychology and the criminal justice system to the black community. A review of key areas of the interface of psychology and law focused on jury selection, criminal responsibility and prison reform. Clinical case data, psychological theory and empirical data were employed to demonstrate both useful action models and techniques, and existing psychological literature that may assist in addressing problems of blacks involved with the criminal justice system. Racism associated with the discipline of psychology and its practice on a community level was described in terms of how it serves as an impediment to the effective delivery of services.

Notes

1. The present paper is adapted from a more extensive monograph by the author, *Psychology, Law, and the Black Community* prepared for the conference on "Mental Health and the Black Community." Howard University, Washington, DC. April, 1976.

References

Allen, R.C., Ferster, E.Z., & Rubin, J.C. (1975). *Readings in law and psychiatry* (2nd ed.). Baltimore: John Hopkins Press.

American Psychology Law Secrets Newsletter. (1977). 9(2).

Argyle, M., & McHenry, R. (1971). Do spectacles really affect judgments of intelligence? British *Journal of Social and Clinical Psychology, 10,* 27-29.

Arnold, W.R. (1971). Race and ethnicity relative to other factors in juvenile court dispositions. *American Journal of Sociology, 77,* 211-227.

Bell, D. (1973). *Race, racism and American law.* Boston: Little Brown.

Billingsley, A. (1968). *Black families in white America.* Englewood Cliffs, NJ: Prentice-Hall.

Broeder, D.W. (1972). The Negro in court. In C. Reasons, & J. Kuykendall (Eds.), *Race, crime and justice.* Pacific Palisades, CA: Goodyear Publishing Company.

Broeder, D.W. (1965). Plaintiff's family status as affecting jurors behavior. *Journal of Public Law, 14,* 131-143.

Bryan, W. (1970). *The chosen ones: The psychology of jury selection.* New York: Vantage Press.

Bullock, H. (1961). Significance of the racial factor in the length of prison sentences. *Journal of Criminal Law, 14,* 131-143.

Burns, H. (1973). Black people and the tyranny of American law. *The Annals of the American Academy of Political and Social Science, 407,* 156-166.

Cartwright, D, & Zander, H. (1960). *Group dynamics: Research and theory* (2nd ed.). Evanston, IL: Row, Peterson.

Coleman, L. (1974). Testimony prepared for Spain v. Procunier. San Francisco.

Crockett, G. (1972). Racism in the law. In C. Reasons, & J. Kuykendall (Eds.), *Race, crime and justice.* Pacific Palisades, CA: Goodyear Publishing Company.

Delaney, L. (1972). The other bodies in the river. In R.L. Jones (Ed.), *Black psychology.* New York: Harper & Row.

Diamond, B. (1975). The fallacy of the impartial expert. In R. Allen, E. Ferster, & J. Rubin (Eds.), *Readings in psychiatry and law* (2nd ed.). Baltimore: John Hopkins Press.

Diamond, B. (1974). Testimony prepared for *Spain v. Procunier.* San Francisco.

Dion, K. (1972). Physical attractiveness and evaluation of children's transgression. *Journal of Personality and Social Psychology, 24,* 207-213.

Dion, K., Berscheid, E., & Walster, E. (1972). What is beautiful is good. *Journal of Personality and Social Psychology, 24,* 3, 285-290.

Drew, J. (1973). Judicial discretion and the sentencing process. *Howard Law Journal, 17,* 858-864.

Efran, M.G. (1974). The effect of physical appearance on the judgment of guilt, interpersonal attraction, and severity of recommended punishment in a simulated jury task. *Journal of Research in Personality, 8,* 45-54.

Epstein, W., & Rock, I. (1960). Perceptual set as an artifact of recency. *American Journal of Psychology, 73,* 214-28.

Franklin, J. (1969). *From slavery to freedom* (rev. ed.). New York: Vintage.

Ginger, F. (1969). *Minimizing racism in jury trials.* Berkeley: The National Lawyers Guild.

Grier, W., & Cobbs, P. (1968). *Black rage.* New York: Bantam.

Guthrie, R.V. (1976). *Even the rat was white.* New York: Harper & Row.

Haney, C., Banks, C., & Zimbardo, P. (1973). Interpersonal dynamics in a simulated prison. *International Journal of Criminology and Penology, 1,* 69-97.

Hayes, W. (1975). *Sociological and psychological principles of jury selection.* Unpublished paper.

Hare, N. (1965). *Black Anglo-Saxons.* New York: Mongani & Mansell.

Harris, P. (1976). *Black rage: Political psychiatric defenses.* Unpublished paper, San Francisco Community Law Collective.

Higgenbotham, A.L. (1973). Racism and the American legal process 1619-1896. *The Annals of the American Academy of Political and Social Science, 407,* 1-17.

Hilliard, A. (1975). The strength and weakness of cognitive tests for young children. In J.D. Andrew (Ed.), *One child indivisible,* pp. 17-34. Washington, DC: National Association for the Education of Young People.

Hilliard, T. (1972). Personality characteristics of black student activists and non-activists. In R.L. Jones (Ed.), *Black psychology.* New York: Harper & Row.

Hilliard, T. (1974). The Angela Davis trial: Role of black psychologists in jury selection and court consultation. *Journal of Black Psychology, 1,* 56-60.

Hilliard, T. (1976). A psychological evaluation of the Adjustment Center in San Quentin Prison. *The Journal of Black Psychology, 2,* 75-82.

Hilliard, T. (1976, April). *Psychology, law and the black community.* Prepared for the conference "Mental Health and the Black Community," Howard University, Washington DC.

Howard, J. (1972). Toward a social psychology of colonialism. In R.L. Jones (Ed.), *Black psychology.* New York: Harper & Row.

Jones, E. (1974). Social class and psychotherapy: A critical review of research. *Psychiatry, 37,* 307-320.

Jones, R. (Ed.). (1972). *Black psychology.* New York: Harper & Row.

Jordan, W.D. (1968). *White over black.* Chapel Hill: North Carolina Press.

Kalven, H., & Zeisel, H. (1966). *The American jury.* Boston: Little Brown.

Katz, J., Goldstein, J., & Dershowitz, A.M. (Eds.). (1967). *Psychoanalysis, psychiatry and law.* New York: Free Press.

Kessler, J.B. (1973). An empirical study of six and twelve member jury decision-making processes. *University of Michigan Journal of Law Reform, 6,* 712-735.

Knowles, L., & Prewitt, K. (1972). Racism in the administration of justice. In C. Reasons, & J. Kuykendall (Eds.), *Race, crime and justice.* Pacific Palisades, CA: Goodyear Publishing Company.

Korman, M. (1976). *Levels and patterns of professional training in psychology.* Washington, DC: American Psychological Association.

Kulka, R., & Kessler, J. (1973). Is justice really blind—the influence of physical attractiveness on decisions of simulated jurors. Unpublished paper presented at the Speech Communication Association, New York.

Landy, D., & Aronson, E. (1969). The influence of the character of the criminal and his victim on the decisions of simulated jurors. *Journal of Experimental Social Psychology, 5,* 141-152.

Lerner, M. (1965). Evaluation of performance as a function of performance, reward and attractiveness. *Journal of Personality and Social Psychology, 1,* 355-360.

Myrdal, G. (1944). *An American dilemma* (Vols. I & II). New York: Harper & Row.

National Advisory Commission on Civil Disorders. (1968). *Report of the National Advisory Commission of Civil Disorders.* New York: Bantam.

Postman, L., & Crutchfield, R. (1952). The interaction of need, set, and stimulus structure in a cognitive task. *American Journal of Psychology, 65,* 196-217.

Sage, W. (1973). Psychology and the Angela Davis jury. *Human Behavior.* 56-61.

Shapiro, D. (1965). *Neurotic styles.* New York: Basic Books.

Sigall, H., & Ostrove, T. (1975). Beautiful but dangerous: Effects of offender attractiveness and nature of the crime on juridic judgment. *Journal of Social Psychology, 31,* 410-414.

Slovenko, D. (1973). *Psychiatry and law.* Boston: Little, Brown.

Stone, A. (1975) *Mental health and law.* National Institutes of Mental Health Monograph. Bethesda, MD.

Swett, D. (1972). Cultural bias in the American legal system. In C. Reasons, & J. Kuykendall (Eds.), *Race, crime and justice.* Pacific Palisades, CA: Goodyear Publishing Co.

Thornberry, T.P. (1973). Race, socio-economic status and sentencing in the juvenile justice system. *Journal of Criminal Law and Criminology, 64,* 90-98.

Walster, E. (1966). Assignment of responsibility for an accident. *Journal of Personality and Social Psychology, 3,* 73-79.

Wolfgang, M.E., & Riedel, M. (1973). Race, judicial discretion, and the death penalty. *The Annals of the American Academy of Political and Social Science, 407,* 119-133.

Zimbardo, P. (1974, July). Affidavit prepared for *Spain v. Procunier.*

Ziskin, J. (1975). *Coping with psychiatric and psychological testimony* (2nd ed.). Beverly Hills, CA: Law and Psychology Press.

Paradigms of African American Research

Na'im Akbar

There has been a growing awareness over the last twenty years that science is not sacrosanct. The recognition that science is *a* method and not *the* method of observation has increasingly been suggested in the writings of philosophers of science, scientists and scholars in a wide variety of disciplines. Scientific paradigms themselves are unstable and are subject to frequent transitions. Paradigms, as discussed by Thomas Kuhn (1970), are a set of implicit assumptions held by members of a particular scientific community, be they physicists, mathematicians, psychologists or others. The paradigm is the shared conception of what is possible, the boundaries of acceptable inquiry, the limiting cases. Within science a paradigm allows a certain stability in models, methods, and modalities of knowledge, but at the price of a certain insensitivity to new input. African American scholars, particularly those in the social sciences have been most vocal and critical of the scientific paradigms which exist in Euro-American social science (Akbar, 1981; Baldwin, 1981; Clark, 1972; Dixon, 1976; Ladner, 1973; Nobles, 1978 and Richards, 1981.) According to these scholars, traditional scientific paradigms have served the function of perpetuating oppression and erroneously depicting the reality of the victims of oppression.

The assumption guiding the traditional paradigms often couched in esoteric and obscure scientific jargon has essentially been: normative reality is that reality characterizing the observations, behaviors or aspirations of middle class, Caucasian males of European descent. Concepts, models, methods and modalities which reaffirm the normality, superiority and legitimacy of this group are the models, methods and modalities with axiomatic legitimacy within the Western scientific arena.

Webster defines research as "investigation or experimentation aimed at the discovery and interpretation of facts, revision of accepted theories or laws in the light of new facts, or practical application of such new or revised theories or laws." Unfortunately, "research" is not like the "searches" which characterized the Ancient African scholars who devoted their scientific endeavors to the pursuit of "Truth." Research does, however, involve a careful, systematic, patient study and investigation undertaken to establish facts or principles. African

American scientists must devote themselves to gain knowledge of the facts of ourselves, of our condition and establishing principles for the restitution of ourselves and the amelioration of our condition. Research is an instrument and as with any instrument, its benefit or its danger rests upon its usage. There is neither implicit benefit nor danger in the instrument of research, but the research must be guided by a set of principles which insure the ultimate utility of that research. The principle which must guide African American research must be an objective of self knowledge and collective liberation. Research is actually a product of certain presumed paradigms or particular models, methods and modalities. The paradigms dictate the parameters of certain models, the validity of certain methods and the appropriateness of certain modalities for investigation. The paradigm dictates what to look for, how to look as well as how to use what is found. The models constitute the definition of what to look for. In sociology, the model is the underlying theory of society; in educational and psychological research, it is the underlying theory of man or mind. The model determines the answers of your research in that it predetermines what will be seen when the investigation begins. The questions predetermine the answers (Clark, et al.s, 1976). The method determines how to look. The method, predetermined by the model dictates how the questions are going to be answered. The method is selected as an instrument of the pre-established model. Contrary to the usually more objective view of research methodology the emphasis here is that the model precedes the search determined by the qualities pursued and it is selected to identify those qualities to the exclusion of other sets of qualities. Scientific methodology is only one such instrument of pursuit. The modality determines the expression or implementation of what the method has identified. Structured by a model, guided by a method, the modality becomes the particular form or matter of expression determined by the research findings.

Given this progression both the questions and answers of the research investigation are actually predetermined by the paradigm.

This discussion will first of all look at some examples of research based on the traditional paradigms for investigations of the African American community. It will demonstrate how the models, methods and modalities of this traditional research have been counteractive to the needs of African Americans and how they have perpetuated the racist and destructive motives of the exploiters of those communities. The second part of the discussion will suggest an alternative paradigm and some models, methods and modalities which are consistent with the survival, growth and perpetuation of African American communities.

The Traditional Paradigm and Models

Kuhn (1970) asserts that "for a time paradigms provide model problems and solutions to the community of (scientific) practitioners." The paradigm which has operated throughout much of the Euro-American history of social science has been the affirmation of the normality of the male Caucasian of European descent and his relative superiority to other peoples.

This paradigm delimits the array of questions which may be raised in investigating the human being in his varied forms and sundry environments. Whether the investigation is anthropological, sociological or psychological, the normative model is the male Caucasian of European descent. Even the U.S. Census statistics have been broken down into the categories of "whites" and "non-whites," which implies a racial identity only relative to the "norm."

The model dictated by this paradigm is one which has been identified as a "Eurocentric model" (Baldwin, 1976, 1980). The more one approximates this model in appearance, values and behavior, the more "normative" or "normal" a person is considered to be. The problem created for African American communities by such a model is the implicit assumption of deviance on the part of anyone who varies from this model. As early as 1840, medical researcher, Dr. Samuel Morton (Stanton, 1960) concluded from his craniometric research that the brain of various races of man became successively smaller as one descended from the Caucasian to the Ethiopian. Dr. Morton continued: "The brain differential accounted for those primeval attributes of mind, which, for wise purposes have given our race a decided and unquestionable superiority over all nations of the earth."

A brief look at the models of prominent figures of Euro-American psychology reveals the prominence of the paradigm of white supremacy. G. Stanley Hall, founder of the *American Journal of Psychology* and first president of the American Psychological Association states in his classic 1904 textbook entitled *Adolescence* that:

> Certain primitive races are in a state of immature development and must be treated gently and understandingly by more developed peoples. Africans, Indians and Chinese are members of adolescent races in a stage of incomplete development. Carl Jung (1935, 1968) in a similar implication of "primitiveness" stated "he (the Negro) has probably a whole historical layer less (in the collective unconscious) than you (Caucasians). The different strata of the mind correspond to the history of the races."

A perusal of the traditional social science literature reveals unquestionably that an essential characteristic of this research model is its assumption of white supremacy. Almost without exception, the research that has been conducted on black bodies, minds and groups within the model of traditional western science shows blacks to be categorically inferior to whites. The mere fact that blacks are only studied in comparison with whites reveals that the underlying model is whiteness. McGhee and Clark (1973) appropriately observe that:

> Where there is equality between things, there are no differences and therefore no psychological research. The way a person frames a question determines the limits within which his answer can possibly fall.

White supremacy is not the only characteristic of the traditional Western model. The model is also primarily individualistic. It assumes that the person is best understood as separate from others and characteristics suggestive of interdependence are viewed as deviant. In the psychological literature, dependence has been identified as fundamental in a broad array of mental abnormalities from depression to schizophrenia. As a result, the general motif of the culture is one of individualism and a defiant independence. The idea of internal fate control pervades the literature as a preferred personality characteristic. Concepts of internal fate control and independence as desirable personality traits are essentially camouflaged descriptions of the rugged individualistic immigrant from Europe who conquered and settled those shores of North America. It is a desirable quality to view nature as an enemy and to subdue it at all cost. The idea of subjecting environmental obstacles to the control of the powerful is implicit in such conceptualizations of human personality and motivation. It is only incidental if those obstacles happen to be other people such as Native Americans, African or Aboriginal Hispanics. They are all dispensable if they stand in the way of European fate control.

Predictably, the literature shows African Americans to be consistently in the pathological or abnormal direction along these individualistic dimensions. Blacks show higher tendencies of interdependence, dependence and internal fate control. The mutual reliance (which has a natural ecological parallel in all dimensions of nature) is viewed as pathological dependence when African Americans are (invariably) compared with Euro-Americans. The consistently high faith in a Supreme Being and belief in a systematic and orderly universe by African people throughout the diaspora is viewed as "low internal fate control" by the psychologists, "superstitious behavior" by anthropologists and a variety of other pejorative descriptions by other social scientists. In point of fact, these data merely confirms another characteristic of the Eurocentric model which maintains that the Western worldview is the normative worldview. It also structures the observation so that those characteristics are the ones which are investigated.

Another assumption of the Eurocentric model of human being is that mentally healthy and effectively functioning people are competitive. Human beings are axiomatically assumed to be in conflict and human accomplishment is realized through the triumph over conflict. David McClelland (1965) writes in the *Harvard Business Review* that "the need for achievement is an essential ingredient for entrepreneurial success." Of course, he concludes that "South Americans, East Indians, poor people from other countries and Black Americans lack this (achievement) drive." The assumption of course is that the drive for power, control and authority which characterizes high need achievers is desirable. McClelland and other psychologists who have lauded the benefits of high need achievement have failed to consider the marked correlation between the manifestation of this drive and the authoritarian personality. They are both characterized by a rigidity of thought process, a tendency to manipulate people as objects and an excessive sense of ones own moral rightness as reflected in the high achievement orientation as well as the characteristics of the racist. This characteristic of the model adds to white supremacy, the features of masculine desirability and achievement/authoritarian orientations. Another assumption of the traditional Western model or conceptualization of the ideal which guides research activity is the idea that what is real or knowable is material, quantifiable and directly observable. As observed by McGhee and Clark (1973), Clark, et als (1976), and many others, Western man has all but lost sense of spiritual and non-material reality. In the light of this epistemology, it becomes clear why Western thinkers consistently equate material affluence and technological opulence with social and cultural development. Chief Fela Sowande (1971) observes:

> But, of course when an individual has grown so insensitive to the non-material world that he can no longer look at things of the flesh through the eyes, but sees instead the things of the spirit through the eyes of the flesh, then he has indeed become a witting or an unwitting victim for the forces of destruction.

This emphasis on the material, the observable and the quantifiable is the hallmark of scientific method and it reveals the critical role played by models in determining "what to look for." Our suggestion is that the characteristics of white supremacy, individualism, competitiveness, authoritarianism, sexism and materialism characterize the traditional Western models for research. Therefore, any research which operates from this paradigmatic position utilizing models of Western science would observe the African American community from this particular point of reference. Non-whiteness, communalism, cooperation, femininity would all be in someway viewed as deviant or at best, non-normative.

Methods of Traditional Research

As we have discussed above, methodology follows from the model and determines *how* to look. Based upon the assumptions of the model, it dictates how the researcher should proceed in affirming his model within the guidelines of his paradigm. The methodology or how to do the research is determined by the model. In the words of Dr. D. Philip McGhee (1974):

> Because the empirical foundations of Western science find their generic antecedents in the philosophical assumptions of the oppressor, we can easily understand why their primary premise becomes: 'that which is like me is good while that which is different from me is bad, or white is good, black is bad.'

The traditional researcher, then, on the basis of the aforementioned model can safely establish his behavior, his group, his culture as a norm and seek to assess predictable deviations from that norm. An example of the consequence of such methodology is the frequent deficit model of research. The poor and black are identified as "culturally deprived," "socially handicapped" and "disadvantaged." These states of being are ascribed to them on the basis of their deviation from affluent and white groups along several observable, material dimensions. In other words, according to Thomas and Sillen (1972) "the behavior, language and thought of the poor represent deficits that are not present in the middle class." One would similarly expect that good research methodology would require comparisons with "appropriate normative" groups and those normative groups to which blacks are compared are invariably similar to the white supremacy model.

Another characteristic of the traditional methodology is its approach to sampling. Those African Americans identified for sampling are those who typify the expectation of deviance from the model. Disproportionate numbers of studies on African Americans look at prison inmates, delinquents, academic non-achievers, poor, welfare recipients, single parents, etc. The focus on this population becomes a methodological self-fulfilling prophecy of the characteristics already implied in the model. Much research has focused on clinical case histories as a model of black personality. Notorious among these are the studies of Grier and Cobbs (1968), Kardiner and Ovesey (1955) and Karon (1958). These writers operate within the tradition of the model by assuming personality deficiency by overgeneralizing the crippling impact of oppression. The methodology focuses on a sampling approach which assumes African Americans to be disfigured victims of oppression or in some way deviant when the behavior observed is actually realistic and normally adaptive within the social context. Another aspect of the methodology has to do with the guidelines for observation. What of reality is attended to and what is ignored is determined by methodology. For example, objectivity is assumed to be the greatest virtue of the scientific methodology (which is the method of choice in traditional Western research). Several writers have questioned the valuelessness of objectivity (Akbar, 1981; Carruthers, 1972 and Clark, et al., 1976). This writer (Akbar, 1981) has argued elsewhere that one fact often denied is that the use of an "objective" approach *is* a value. When an observer chooses to suspend from his observations certain levels of reaction, then a value judgment *is* made. This is, in fact, a very important value because implicit in this decision is the choice to ignore certain sources of information which could critically alter ones observations. Particularly, the social scientists create an unreal situation by assuming that the observer is not a participant in his observations and that the observer or his surrogate (in the form of observational instruments) does not generate a reaction to the characteristics of her/himself.

As noted above, the surrogate of the observer is the instrument for his observation. The usual instrument in traditional research is testing. No particular test has been any more destructive in its conclusions about African Americans than the IQ test.

The IQ test is utilized as a very common research and assessment instrument. It assumes that conditions surrounding the test behavior are constant and differences in scores reflect "real" differences in the subjects. Consequently, it is not unusual to find statements such as the following by Dr. Carl Brigham (1932):

> ... the army tests *proved* [italics mine] the superiority of the Nordic type over the Alpine, Mediterranean and Negro groups . . . as racial admixture increases, American intelligence would decline at an accelerating rate owing to the presence here of the Negro.

Comparative performance on an instrument constructed on the basis of certain restricted learning experiences is used to affirm the basic difference between groups who primarily differ in precisely those experiences under consideration. The test given rather readily assumes, however, that differences in scores on such a fabricated instrument reflect differences in factors which have undefined origins and nature. It is not unusual that we err along the lines described by Guilford (1967):

> In comparing two social groups on the basis of scores from a

particular test, it would be important to know that test measures the same ability or abilities in both groups. If it does not,
the use of the scores would be like comparing the weight of one
group with the metabolic rate of the other.

What is true of the IQ test is equally or more true of most tests
used in traditional research. They all reflect the perspective of the
model being utilized. The structure, the content and the behaviors that
are sampled are all reflections of the model described above. The tests of
personality, motivation and other characteristics are all directive in determining what will be observed. The compelling conclusion is that the
models perpetuate the model in that the types of instruments, the identification of subjects and the samples of behavior to be observed are all
predetermined by the paradigm shaping the researchers observations.

Modalities of Traditional Research

The method confirms the model, then the model is perpetuated
in the modalities of implementing the research findings. The modalities are the ways in which the research findings are implemented. Based
upon a firm adherence to the methodology described above whereby
one systematically chooses the behaviors, the subjects and the instruments predicated on a particular model of community and man, the
results of the investigation are then interpreted in the light of the pre-
established model from which one began. The cycle is almost complete,
except for the perpetuation of the model by research-based programmatic interventions. With the legitimization of science, the policymakers are equipped with the kinds of conclusions which continue to
establish the conditions which maintain the assumptions of their
model. Of course, in the instance of traditional social science research,
these policies perpetuate the white supremacy paradigm.

An example of such conclusions, bolstered by research is one by
Shockley (1966) based upon his studies intended to demonstrate the
intellectual inferiority of blacks:

> Can it be that our humanitarian welfare programs have already
> selectively emphasized high and irresponsible rates of repro-
> duction to produce a socially relatively unadaptable human
> strain?

Once his studies have demonstrated the "unadaptibility" of that
human strain (i.e., African Americans) he is only a step away from suggesting controlled growth of that "inferior strain." The policy was implemented by accelerated efforts to develop birth control policies and
family planning for this "human strain." The justification for such pol-

icies is never connected with the potentially genocidal implication, instead the argument is made that such policies improve ones economic well-being because "the poverty of black communities is perpetuated by their tendency to have such large families." Of course, no mention is made of the fact that the infant mortality rate is three times higher among those same families.

Conclusions such as the one above by Shockley and the one below by Jensen have had disastrous effects in terms of public policy for African Americans. Jensen (1968) observed that:

> Attempts to provide compensatory education for disadvantaged children have failed because they are based on the assumption that blacks could attain the same level and quality of intelligence as whites.

The willingness of the government during conservative political times to eliminate support for effective education of all citizens is a direct outgrowth of such research-based" conclusions. One might, of course, question whether blacks *should* "attain the same level and quality of intelligence as whites." Since intelligence is a non-specific factor determining a person's effective adaptation to *his* environment and realizing the critical distinction between white and black environments in the American context, then it could be potentially self-destructive for a black person to have the same level and quality of intelligence as whites.

Unfortunately, the modalities chosen for the implementation of traditional research findings are ones that encourage blacks to become more in accord with the original paradigm of masculine Caucasian behaviors. As Glazer and Moynihan (1963) conclude: "The Negro is only an American and nothing else. He has no values and culture to guard and protect." But, such a conclusion is utterly dehumanizing as is suggested by Andrew Billingsley (1968), when he observes:

> To say that a people have no culture is to say that they have no common history which has shaped and taught them. And to deny the history of a people is to deny their humanity.

The Paradigm and Model of African American Research

The paradigm which must emerge to structure our models must be one which facilitates the best of human development. It must be a "natural" or generally human paradigm (Akbar, 1980) rather than the narrow ethnocentric paradigm which describes a particular human.

The new paradigm should offer a balance between the extremely material and esoteric perspective represented in the traditional Eurocentric paradigm and the extremely spiritual and esoteric perspective of the Oriental paradigm. This paradigm which emerges from an African worldview does not presume that the only form of the human being is African. The paradigm suggests that the human being should be viewed as being consistent with and harmonious in his relationship with nature. It adopts the basic ontological position of the Africentric worldview of "I am because we are" (Mbiti, 1970; Nobles, 1980). It also views spirituality as being endemic to the human make-up, therefore, behavioral observations are at best approximations to visualizing the true nature of the human being.

The model which emerges from this paradigm has several characteristics. It assumes that all human beings should be (1) free to grow and realize their highest human potential; (2) free from oppressive and humanly demeaning environments; (3) free to live cooperatively with human beings; (4) free to develop knowledge of oneself and or ones historically and culturally determined identity; (5) free to defend oneself against the dehumanizing influences of anti-human forces and (6) free to achieve human dignity. This model is intended to structure the nature of research conducted on black people from the vantage point of a perspective which fosters black survival and development. The model intentionally and appropriately biases our observations of black people and black communities. As the traditional model described above is designed to perpetuate the oppression of blacks and affirm the superiority of whites, this model is consistent with the needs of our communities (and of any civilized human community, for that matter.) At the same time it does not assume a contrasting inferior/superior relationship to other human beings in order to affirm its parameters.

The traditional model of research implies the characteristics of the researcher by assuming that certain scientific research skills have been acquired namely by way of educational legitimization such as a Ph.D or some similar research training. We suggest, consistent with Chief Fela Sowande's (1971) criteria for meaningful research, that researchers should meet certain criteria. These criteria are:

> Relationship index (which is) the extent to which the researcher identifies with the culture within which the subject of research is found. . . . the individual conducting the research, by which his personal 'Worldview,' his concept of 'Nature,' etc., indicate what possibilities there might be that research results may be unwittingly filtered through unsuspected or unacknowledged prejudices.

Methods of African American Research

Two issues must be addressed in a discussion of methods of African American research. One issue should be how the aims of the foregoing model will be investigated and pursued. The other issue is the types of research and instruments which should be used in these investigations. In the light of the first issue, Dr.Dubois McGhee (1973) makes a relevant observation:

> Racial ascription is the common denominator that is systematically woven through the international fabric of human life on this planet. Thus, understanding the depth, height and width of our experiences as a collectively common one, makes our study of black self imperative to our survival and advancement as well as critical to a more comprehensive understanding of the nature of universal man.

This quote addresses two components of the methodological question. The first component that is delineated is that the subjects for investigation will be black people. Unlike the traditional research models which almost invariably focus on black/white comparisons, the African American research model views blacks as normative for blacks. The diverse occurrence of black people in a wide variety of social, economic, political and even cultural environments produces a broad base for identifying meaningful variables of similarity among black people.

The second component identified in Dr. McGhee's quote is the need for "study of the black self." This self study will generate theory from an appreciation of the culture and history of black people and will supply new concepts and instruments for observation. Both the content and instruments for black research should emerge from the fertile cultural ground of the African and African American (African West Indian or other appropriate groups') experiences. For example, rather than asking "How should blacks be involved in mental health centers?" we should ask "What kinds of mental health structures do blacks have and use?" Rather than test children's knowledge of alien environmental artifacts to determine intelligence, they could be tested on their knowledge of indigenous cultural artifacts. Rather than study ways of teaching black mothers, middle class non-black techniques of child-rearing, researchers might look at "successful" black children and determine by what techniques were they raised.

The African American model in its holistic approach encouraged methodologies which look at people in a non-fragmented way. McGee and Clark (1973) observe:

> The Western inability to synthesize body (material) and mind (spiritual) has led some respected scientists to make the absurd comment that black people in America are "good" in athletics,

but poor in thinking. Such scientists fail to recognize that to have a good body means that one has a good mind and vice versa; one cannot exist without the other. If the body is poor, the mind is also, and vice versa.

The second issue of methodology is the "how" or types of research procedures which appropriately address the model. There are four (4) general types of research which are most relevant to an African American paradigm: (1) theoretical, (2) critique or falsification research, (3) ethnographic and (4) heuristic research.

Theoretical research is for the purpose of generating questions. Theory development grows from self-reflective observation and the introspective analysis of ones experience. No data beyond ones subjective and affective appraisal of his experience are necessary. This is not unlike the procedure for the ground-breaking and paradigm-setting work of Freud, Jung, William James, Skinner and the vast array of luminaries in all fields of social science research who never produced a control group while laying the cornerstone for Western thought. Once a logically coherent and systematic theory is in place, then one extension may be to raise questions which may require empirical answers. The empirical question is neither necessary nor sufficient as evidence for the validity of theory. Considering the conspicuous absence of introspection and self-study within the context of the appropriate worldview for African people, then it would seem that empirical questions would be premature in the absence of a theoretical base from which to generate such questions.

Curtis Banks (1980) has identified "deconstructive" or falsification research as another type of research. Such research is concerned with an analysis of the constructive validity of traditional research. The falsification researcher is concerned with demonstrating the fallacy of the inferences and the methodological distortions of that traditional research. This is a process of undoing the kinds of destructive inferences about African Americans which we have described above as emanating from traditional research. Falsification research involved both theoretical dismantling as well as empirical rebuttal.

Ethnographic research is probably the only authentic form of empirical research that is appropriate for this point in our development. This approach permits the researcher, having passed the "Relationship Index," (Sowande, 1971) to observe black people where they are and to take on the responsibility of defining what's observed. The researcher fulfilling the criteria of a worker within the African paradigm can begin to identify those characteristics of black people which are most fruitful in the light of our research model. Rather than cataloging deficiencies of black people, the ethnographic researcher can identify those strengths and self-affirmative patterns which have facilitated our growth.

Finally, heuristic research offers the bridge to our discussion of modalities. This research follows from the ethnographic research in that it begins to articulate culturally adaptive styles and begins to demonstrate the benefits which come from adapting that style. The objective of this research is to fortify those structures and styles which can be demonstrated to be beneficial to the survival and advancement of black people. Heuristic research might serve as a device by which appropriate instruments for measuring the black experience might be identified. If tests are to be used, what kinds of tests would be most appropriate in identifying those qualities which have emerged as valuable for survival from the ethnographic research?

Modalities of African American Research

The enactment or implementation of the research findings from above is an inseparable part of African American research. Policy and institutional application may or may not follow directly from traditional research. If vital institutions which maintain your model are already in existence, then concerns about implementation are not as urgent. In the case of African Americans with few, if any, vital institutions, the modalities of implementation are urgent. This becomes the process of liberation and institution-building for an historically oppressed people. The interpretation and implementation of our research must not fail as Carter G. Woodson (1931) described the higher education of the African American which:

> . . . has been largely meaningless imitation. When the Negro finishes his course in one of our schools he knows what others have done, but he has not been inspired to do much for himself.

The programs which emerge from our research must have immediate relevance in correcting our oppressed condition and advancing us in the light of the model described above.

One modality which should be considered is that our research should be problem-oriented. Heuristic research must affirm benefit and not function as research for research's sake as is the case for some traditional research. The objective should always be to apply directly research findings to some problem or goal which would enhance the development of our communities. Even in the case of the destructive or falsification research which we discussed above, the ultimate objective should be to define an alternative and constructive direction.

An example of the problem-orientation modality can be seen in research on hypertension. Most of our communities are plagued by deaths related to hypertension. We should combine the efforts of the physicians, social scientists and affected groups to understand the inter-relationship of nutrition, stress, racism, and social organization on hypertension. The specific goal of the research should be a reduction of the death rate from hypertension. As is implied in this example, we must focus on interdisciplinary approaches to research. Our efforts must not be restricted by narrow, traditional disciplinary lines.

Another modality of our research is an out-growth of the holistic model of man which requires us to transcend the conventional perimeters of research. We must be willing to recognize the metaphysical dimension of human experience. We must begin to investigate systematically arenas of nature and human experience which have been traditionally viewed as "unresearchable." Certainly, the spiritual dimension is a critical component of the black experience and research which ignores this dimension ignores the assets of an important aspect of the total human experience. Psychic research must be included in our investigations because psychic phenomena are an important aspect of the African experience throughout the diaspora. We must understand how faith, prayer and meditation work since so much of our history has been guided by such forces. It is critical to understand if consciousness is a continuous state and what consequences ensue from altered states.

The final modality of our research must be directed towards the development of institutions. Institutions are the forces which maintain and perpetuate the paradigm or model of man. If the model which we have articulated is necessary for the liberation and advancement of African people, then it is critical to establish institutions which will accomplish that end. As we identify the adaptive strategies and characteristics for our advancement from our research methods, then those strategies must serve as the guidelines for structuring our institutions. Educational institutions must offer content with advance self-knowledge as well as offering instruction through the demonstrated modalities which build on our strengths. Economic institutions must be built which address our critical survival needs while being consistent with our model of man and community. Our religious institutions must be critiqued and developed along lines which foster our spirituality and enhance our collective development. All of these modalities provide the ultimate objective of augmenting and institutionalizing the African American paradigm.

Conclusion

Traditional research in black communities has been based upon a model which fosters the advancement of Euro-Americans at the expense of African Americans. This research has emanated from a set of paradigmatic assumptions which assumes that normative reality is defined by those characteristics of male Caucasians of European descent. The human being is assumed to be at his best when *he* is *white, materially* accomplished, achieved through *competitive, independent* assertiveness. *She* who is *black, poor* and *submissive* is by definition inferior, abnormal and/or unintelligent, according to this model. The methods of traditional social science research have been selected in order to identify precisely those qualities which the model has identified as acceptable. The "how" of the research simply reaffirms what the model or paradigm has defined as should be the "what" of the research. The modalities of traditional research become the policy implementation which confirms, sustains, and perpetuates the original model.

An African American paradigm is proposed which is essentially humanistic and holistic. It establishes a model of man which stipulates freedom for complete human development and self-knowledge. The methodology fosters this development and four (4) types of research are proposed which would advance this model for African Americans. Finally, the modalities of problem-resolution, metaphysical qualities and institution building are suggested as the essential path for implementing the research. The urgency of human liberation and development is advanced as the major determinant of effective implementation of our research and the model of the African American paradigm.

In conclusion, we must carefully evaluate the approach to research which has emerged from traditional Euro-American social science research. We must understand that methodology is not free of bias and in fact, methodology is a form of systematic bias. The application of that method must be consistent with our paradigm or the outcome will only confirm the paradigm that gave rise to the methodology. This means that the persisting effort to investigate the African American experience from the Euro-American framework will only perpetuate the notion of deficient blacks. If the research in our communities is to foster the growth and development of those communities, then we must be clear about the goals of that research. If our research is to be in the universal tradition of the great scientists of ancient times, then we must expand our vision to greater horizons for study.

References

Akbar, N. (1980). *The evolution of human psychology for African Americans.* Unpublished manuscript presented to SREB Student Conference, Atlanta.

Akbar, N. (1981). Our destiny: Authors of a scientific revolution. *The Fifth Conference on Empirical Research in Black Psychology*, Washington: NIMH.

Baldwin, J. (1976). Black psychology and black personality. *Black Books Bulletin, 4*(3), 6-11.

Baldwin, J. (1980). The psychology of oppression. In M. Asante, & A. Vandi (Eds.), *Contemporary black thought.* Beverly Hills: Sage Publishers.

Banks, W.C. (1980). *Theory in black psychology.* Paper presented at the *Thirteenth Annual National Convention of the Association of Black Psychologists*, Cherry Hill, NJ.

Bridgman, C. (1923). *A study of American intelligence.* Princeton: Princeton University Press.

Carruthers, J. (1972). *Science and oppression.* Chicago: Northeastern Illinois University's Center for Inner City Studies.

(Clark) X, C. (1975). Voodoo or IQ: An introduction to African psychology. *Journal of Black Psychology, 1*(2), 9-29.

Dixon, V. (1976). Worldviews and research methodology. In L. King, et al. (Eds.), *African philosophy: Assumptions and paradigms for research on black persons.* Los Angeles: Fanon Center.

Glazer, N., & Moynihan, D. (1963). *Beyond the melting pot.* Cambridge: M.I.T. Press.

Grier, W., & Cobbs, P. (1968). *Black Rage.* New York: Basic Books.

Jensen, A. (1969). How much can we boost IQ and scholastic achievement? *Harvard Educational Review, 39*, 1-123.

Jung, C. (1968). *Analytical psychology: Its theory and practice.* New York: Vintage Books.

Kardiner, A., & Ovesey, J. (1951). *The mark of oppression.* New York: Norton.

Karon, B. (1958). *The Negro personality: A rigorous investigation of the effects of culture.* New York: Springer.

Kuhn, T. (1970). The structure of scientific revolutions. *International Encyclopedia of Unified Science, 2*(2). Chicago: University of Chicago Press.

Ladner, J. (Ed.), (1973). *The death of white sociology.* New York: Vintage Books.

Mbiti, J.S. (1970). *African religions and philosophy.* New York: Anchor Books.

McClelland, D. (1965). Achievement motivation can be developed. *Harvard Business Review, 43*(6), 6-18.

McGhee, D. (1974). Critical elements of black mental health. *Journal of Black Health Perspectives, 1*(4), 52-58.

McGhee, D., & X (Clark), C. (1973). *Genetic research and black intelligence.* Los Gatos, CA: Nefertiti Publishers.

Moynihan, D. (1965). Employment income and the ordeal of the Negro family. *Daedulus, 94*, 745-770.

Nobles, W.W. (1980). African philosophy: Foundations for black psychology. In R. Jones (Ed.), *Black psychology,* (2nd ed.). New York: Harper and Row.

Richards, D. (1980). European mythology: The ideology of progress. In M. Asante, & A. Vandi (Eds.), *Contemporary black thought.* Beverly Hills: Sage Publishers.

Shockley, W. (1972). Possible transfer of metallurgical and astronomical approaches to the problem of environment versus ethnic heredity. Quoted by Thomas, A., & Sillen, S. in *Racism and psychiatry*. Secaucus, NJ: Citadel.

Stanton, W. (1960). *The leopard's spots: Scientific attitudes toward race in America, 1815-1819*. Chicago: University of Chicago Press.

Thomas, A., & Sillen, S. (1972). *Racism and psychiatry*. New York: Brunner/Mazel.

Woodson, C.G. (1933). *The miseducation of the Negro*. Washington, D.C.: Associated Publishers.

Mental Health of African Americans: Research Trends and Directions

Lawrence E. Gary

In 1978, the Subpanel on the Mental Health of Black Americans underscored the need for an increase in mental health research which reflects the cultural, social, political, economic and physical realities of black people (Report to the President's Commission on Mental Health, 1978). The Subpanel suggested that the paradigm for this research include the effects of racism and its accompanying discriminatory practices on the mental health of blacks. In addition, it was suggested that a cultural relativity frame of reference be used to guide this research and that such views or practices as the following be rejected: a) the assumption that black Americans are a homogeneous group; b) the tendency to use white, middle-class norms as the standard by which to evaluate minority ethnic populations; c) the tendency to focus on low-income and institutionalized blacks; and d) the tendency to employ victim-blaming and deficit frames of reference when studying black behavior. Central to examining the mental health status of blacks, as underlined by the Subpanel, is the development of mental health definitions and classification and assessment methods from the perspectives of the black community. Since the publication of this landmark report, much has been written on the mental health of black people. Many social and behavioral scientists have attempted to correct major shortcomings of past research, thereby generating a new body of knowledge. It is now necessary to critically assess the present state of knowledge in the mental health field and to determine whether or not recent research has indeed responded to the numerous criticisms cited in the literature (see, e.g., Adebimpe, 1981; Billingsley, 1968; Gary, 1978; Jackson, Tucker, & Bowman, 1982; Jones & Korchin, 1982; Thomas & Sillen, 1972; Willie, Kramer, & Brown, 1973). Thus, the major objectives of this chapter are: 1) to document the fact that research is a significant industry; 2) to review the relatively recent research on black mental health; and 3) to offer suggestions for future research.

The Research Industry

In the United States, research and development (R&D) represent a major business enterprise. For example, in 1985, R&D expenditures were approximately $107 billion for the four principal economic sectors—federal government, industry, universities, colleges, and other nonprofit institutions (U.S. Bureau of the Census, 1985, p. 576). These expenditures represented 2.7 percent of the Gross National Product in 1985 (p. 577). Furthermore, the R&D industry, in 1984, employed an estimated 744,000 full-time scientists, engineers, and technicians (p. 581). At least 14 percent of these R&D scientists and engineers were employed at institutions of higher education (103,000), while 74 percent were in private industry (548,300). In addition, while private industry was a major funding source and a receiver of funds in 1985, universities and colleges received approximately 9 percent of the $107 billion (p. 577). The R&D industry as a viable business enterprise is quite evident when one examines the patterns of funding in the past ten years. In 1975, $35.2 billion were devoted to R&D funding, which increased nearly three times as much by 1985.

Funding for basic and applied research, although percentage wise the federal government as a funding source is declining, comprised 47.3 percent of all R&D monies in 1985. In 1970, 60.1 percent of total research was funded by the federal government. Most of this federal support, unfortunately, was in the area of national defense $34.3 billion, compared to $5.4 billion for health, $293 million for psychology, and $463 million for social sciences (p. 579). In fact, areas such as education, training, employment and community development funding declined during the past ten years, while federal funding for national defense R&D activities increased steadily.

Mental health research has been primarily supported by the federal government through the National Institute of Mental Health (NIMH). In a recent NIMH report (1986), it was revealed that the R&D budget for 1985 was approximately $133.2 million and that 1,111 grants were awarded (NIMH, 1985). However, the report noted that R&D funding has declined steadily since 1966, although there has been a slight upward trend beginning in 1981. While it is evident that funding for R&D activities in some areas has been declining, the research industry for the most part has continued to increase and to remain a major business enterprise.

In view of the large sum of monies contributed to mental health research, an important question becomes: What percentage of these funds has black researchers received to conduct R&D activities? According to the NIMH report (1986), the number of paid grants to minority researchers has been significantly low since 1970. In 1985, 144 grants relevant to minorities were awarded. Ninety (8% of the total number of awards grants) grants were relevant to blacks. It must be noted, however, that only 34 grants relevant to minorities were of major focus on one of the five major U.S. ethnic/racial groups. In addition, Robinson (1971) conducted a survey of 552 minority research projects funded by the federal government. The results of his study revealed that only 18 of these research projects were granted to traditionally black universities and colleges. His findings demonstrate that the progress in acquiring research funding has been insignificant. In 1972, the Center for Minority Group Mental Health Programs awarded only $1.10 for research on minority groups while NIMH's R&D budget for extramural activities equaled $82.5 million (Research in the Service of Mental Health, 1975, p. 31). These data suggest that black and other minority researchers continue to receive a very limited proportion of the designated mental health research funds and, thus, play a minor role in the mental health research business enterprise. As noted by Sue, Ito and Bradshaw (1982), funding can have "a profound impact in the direction, quality, and quantity of research" (p. 55). They also noted that issues and problems related to health, alcohol and drug use, and racism are urgent ones for minority groups and have been inadequately addressed, due to insufficient research funds.

Black Mental Health

In this section, the current state of knowledge on the epidemiology of mental health and illness in the black population and those factors believed to influence mental health status will be reviewed. This involves reviewing the literature on treatment rate studies, epidemiologic community surveys and small-scale community surveys, and assessing the present status of conceptual and methodological concerns. First, it is important to highlight the major limitations of past research.

Major Theoretical and Methodological Problems

Several social and behavioral scientists have identified numerous deficiencies in much of the theoretical and empirical research on black Americans (see, e.g., Banks, 1976; Billingsley, 1968; Gary, 1978; Jones & Korchin, 1982; Thomas & Sillen, 1972; Williams, 1974; Willie, Kramer, & Brown, 1973 for detailed reviews). As a consequence, much of what is known about black mental health must be regarded with caution. Some underlying factors which, to a large extent, set the stage for flawed research include: 1) the pervasiveness of racism and prejudice in America; 2) the shortage of black social scientists in decision-making positions, particularly with regard to funding; and 3) the needs and concerns of black people have low priority in this country.

Given these underlying factors, it becomes evident why many conceptual and methodological problems exist in the study of blacks. Some of the more persistent problems are: 1) the lack of a general theory to delineate the effects of racism on mental health; 2) the lack of a general theory to delineate normal and abnormal functioning in black communities; 3) theoretical assumptions that blacks are a homogeneous group with no distinctive values, beliefs, and expectations; 4) few attempts to examine the applicability of concepts across groups; 5) the application of majority group-derived measures to blacks; 6) a tendency to generalize to the larger black population on the basis of studies with small samples; 7) a tendency to study the lowest income group and captive groups such as prisoners, college students, and mental patients; 8) a great emphasis on racial comparative paradigms 9) denial of the importance of intraracial comparative paradigms and the need for research on large, representative samples of blacks; 10) a tendency to focus on pathology rather than strengths; and 11) a failure to recognize the effects of the researcher's race, biases, and training on the entire research process. The byproducts of these problems are simplified and erroneous interpretations of research findings on black Americans and invalid evaluations of the adequacy of studies that do not use the racial comparative paradigm.

Treatment Studies

One method of determining the incidence and prevalence of mental illness in the general population is by examining admission records of mental institutions and hospitals. This method of assessing psychiatric morbidity, however, has inherent problems. For example, Neighbors (1984) outlines three major problems. First, there is an implied assumption that hospital admission rates represent true estimates of the prevalence of mental illness. Such an assumption suggests that persons who are not in psychiatric facilities must be mentally healthy. Secondly, he notes that treatment studies often fail to control for social and environmental factors. Thirdly, some treatment studies fail to compute utilization rates for both public and private institutions. In view of these problems, Neighbors concludes that the treatment rates approach is an adequate operational indicator of mental disorder. Moreover,

treatment studies involving blacks warrant critical examination because of the use of biased assessment techniques and measures, sociocultural disparities between the clinician and the patient, and the
negative stereotypes of blacks. Such factors are believed to increase the
likelihood of misdiagnosis among blacks (Adebimpe, 1981; Cannon &
Locke, 1977; Gynther, 1972; Snowden & Todman, 1982).

In spite of these drawbacks, treatment data can be a useful source
for examining the mental health status of blacks who are in-patient or
out-patient care. This data source is valuable in that it documents the
types of institutions to which blacks are admitted, the types of diagnoses they are likely to receive, a comparison of blacks to other groups,
and the background characteristics of blacks who are receiving psychiatric care. Therefore, it will prove beneficial to provide an overview of a
national survey of mental disorders based on the treatment rate approach. A national survey conducted in 1975 by the National Institute
of Mental Health (NIMH) (1981) of selected mental health facilities
revealed that whites and members of "all other races" experience significant differences in primary diagnosis at the time of admission. Another
major finding was that schizophrenia and depressive disorders were the
two most frequently assigned diagnoses. Across selected mental health
facilities, schizophrenia was more prominent among members of "all
other races" than among whites (24% vs. 15%). Depressive disorders
were more commonly found among whites than among members of
"all other races" (19% vs. 11%). It is important to note that schizophrenia was also most common among males from "all other races", 25
percent, as contrasted with 13-23 percent of the remaining sex-race
groups. Depressive disorders, on the other hand, were least likely to be
found among nonwhite males (5% vs. 13%-24% for other sex-race
groups). It is particularly interesting to note that a high proportion of
males of "all other races" (14%) were classified as having no mental
disorder, in comparison to other groups (7% for white males, 9% for
white females; 9% for females of "all other races"). Overall, these statistics demonstrate that a disproportionate number of "all other races"
admissions are assigned more severe diagnoses than their white counterparts. In another statistical report from NIMH (Series CN No. 3,
1980) comparing Hispanics, blacks and whites, it was reported that,
regardless of the type of facility, a high distribution of Hispanics and
blacks received more serious diagnoses. The percentage of admissions
with schizophrenia in outpatient facilities was highest among Hispanics and blacks than among whites (16.7%, 14.2% vs. 9%, respectively).
In contrast, depressive disorders, a less serious set of mental disorders,
were more prominent among whites than among Hispanics and blacks
(13.5% vs. 9.5%, 9%, respectively). Whites were also more frequently

diagnosed with personality disorders, in comparison to black and Hispanic admissions (11.2% vs. 4.3%, 6.3%, respectively).

These findings demonstrate the significant differences in distributions of schizophrenia and depressive disorders between whites and minorities. Furthermore, both surveys clearly show that blacks consistently received the more severe diagnoses, despite the type of facility. This, however, was not the case with Hispanic admissions. The largest percentage of white admissions, on the other hand, were more likely to receive a less serious diagnosis of depressive disorder. These findings, therefore, provide some support for the argument that minorities,particularly blacks, are more likely to be assigned diagnoses of psychotic disorders, rather than affective disorders. In fact, these data support the assertion that minorities are apt to be overdiagnosed in some categories and underdiagnosed in others (Adebimpe, 1981). Given that diagnostic differences exist between minority ethnic groups and whites and the fact that larger percentages of minorities are assigned the more serious diagnoses, many scientists assert that these differences reflect inaccurate psychiatric assessments and diagnoses and not "true prevalence" of psychopathology (Adebimpe, 1981; Carter, 1974; Gullattee, 1969). Psychiatric misdiagnosis is a serious problem, because diagnosis serves as the basis for treatment, referral, and subsequent discharge (Baskin, Bluestone, & Nelson, 1981). The relationship between type of diagnosis, type of treatment, and ethnicity of patient has been documented in the literature (Cox, 1979; Flaherty & Meagher, 1980). For example, Cox compared the diagnoses and treatment modalities of black and white mental health consumers. The author found that black clients were assigned less autonomous treatment more often than whites. He also found that blacks, in comparison to whites, were more often labeled schizophrenic which frequently occurred at an earlier age. Furthermore, individual, group, and family therapy were often provided to whites, while black clients tended to receive institutional care. It was concluded that these instances reflect biases held by middle class whites that whites are "good treatment" cases, while black clients are not. Data collected by Flaherty and Meagher (1980) was similar to that of Cox. They studied the charts of black and white patients, all diagnosed as schizophrenic. Race was found to be a significant factor in the number of days spent in the hospital (29.09 for blacks; 48.60 for whites), the number of days on medication (6.71 for blacks; 3.58 for whites). the number of times in seclusion and restraint (78% of the time for blacks; 46% for whites), and the privilege level (2.64 for blacks; 3.08 for whites). The ordering of recreational therapy (47% for blacks; 78% for whites) and occupational therapy was also significantly influenced by race of patient. The authors concluded that the discrepancy in the treatment of mental patients with identical diagnoses was due to discriminatory stereotypes.

The two studies presented here indicate a need for further systematic research of this issue. In general, it appears that blacks are unlikely candidates for individual treatment of any kind of noninstitutionalized treatment and are more likely to be terminated from care prematurely. It also appears that regardless of the psychiatric diagnosis, blacks receive harsher treatment (e.g., drug therapy, seclusion and restraint) than their white counterparts. The disparate distribution of diagnostic categories between whites and non-whites (e.g., schizophrenia, paranoia, depression) begs the question of whether or not black hospital admissions have been properly identified, classified, and treated. Researchers and clinicians call for more studies to establish cultural and behavioral norms for minority groups, to test within-group comparisons, to investigate the effects of communication and language barriers, and to construct new assessment measurements that are culturally sensitive. Suggestions for new definitions of mental health and illness reflecting a multi-cultural perspective are proposed as a possible solution to reducing diagnostic errors. Diagnostic errors attributed to test bias, the lack of sufficient minority clinicians, the lack of understanding about minority behavior patterns from its own frame of reference, the lack of research interest in minority mental health problems, and racism have been outlined as some of the major concerns cited in the literature.

Epidemiologic Community Surveys

In the early 1960s, the epidemiologic community survey was introduced as a technique that would provide a better estimate of the "true prevalence" of mental illness in the general population and eliminate many of the problems inherent in treatment data (Gurin, Veroff, & Feld, 1960; Leighton, Harding, Macken, MacMillan, & Leighton, 1963; Srole, Langner, Michael, Opler & Rennie, 1962). Through these field studies, researchers interviewed large numbers of persons in their homes, relying primarily on short screening psychiatric symptom and dysfunction scales. While this approach proved to be expedient, inexpensive to administer, and valuable in eliminating value judgments by clinicians, it has not been free from problems. Researchers primarily criticized the short screening measures as lacking the sensitivity to diagnose discrete mental disorders (Dohrenwend, 1975; Weissman & Klerman, 1978). In essence, these measures were no more than gross estimates of rates of mental disorders. Furthermore, the epidemiological approach has been fraught with conceptual and methodological problems, specifically when used in black communities. Essentially, these earlier epidemiological surveys revealed conflicting mental illness rates for blacks and whites. Dohrenwend and Dohrenwend (1969) reanalyzed the data from of eight community studies on the prevalence of mental illness. Their analysis showed that in four studies blacks had higher rates of mental illness and in the other four studies whites had higher rates of mental illness. Dohrenwend and Dohrenwend attributed these conflicting results to contrasting conceptions and measures of mental illness, different sampling designs, and simplistic analytic procedures. Consequently, it was concluded that "true" prevalence of mental illness for various racial groups has yet to be determined.

In addition, Dohrenwend (1975) in a later critical review, pointed to other problems that were inherent in the eight epidemiologic community studies which preclude making conclusive statements about mental illness prevalence. One was the problem of sampling the different class and racial groups without confounding the two groups. He suggested that this might be resolved by either employing stratified samples with optimal numbers in each class/racial category or employing large random samples from each racial group with representative numbers of advantaged and disadvantaged persons. A second problem was developing measures of various mental disorders that permit valid class and race comparisons. For instance, Dohrenwend compared two techniques of assessing the mental health status of five ethnic groups. Psychiatrists interviewed all subjects using a short symptoms checklist and a more traditional clinical interview with open-ended questions and probes. In short, the results showed that: 1) when using the short-screening measure, Puerto Ricans exhibited the highest psychiatric impairment among the five ethnic groups, while the Irish exhibited the lowest impairment; and 2) when using the clinical interview, blacks exhibited the highest impairment while Puerto Ricans exhibited the lowest psychiatric impairment. His results then showed that the effects of using different interview procedures were strongest for the ethnic minorities. Dohrenwend suggested that these differences reflect inadequate assumptions regarding the nature of mental illness. This explanation, however, does not really address the race differences. Although,it will be necessary to examine the relationship between short screening measures and mental disorders. Thus, in view of this fact, the goal of early community studies to obtain "true" prevalence of mental illness in the general population, particularly for ethnic minorities had not at all been achieved; such short screening measures "hardly cover the full range of psychiatric disorders" (Dohrenwend, 1975,p. 376).

In an attempt to avoid pitfalls which emerged in the 1950s and

1960s community surveys, epidemiologists in the 1970s modified their overall goal, employed sophisticated sampling and statistical procedures, increased the size of minority samples, and more importantly, developed reliable measures of assessing mental health status (e.g., Antunes, Gordon, Gaitz, & Scott, 1974; Comstock & Helsing, 1976; Ilfeld, 1978; Kessler, 1979; Warheit, Holzer, & Arey, 1975; Warheit, Holzer, & Schwab, 1973). The goal of these epidemiological surveys was to obtain the prevalence of mental health via global assessments within the general population. The approach, however, continued to be the short symptom checklists of non-specific diseases. Thus, the later researchers did not purport to determine the actual prevalence of specific mental disorders. The sophisticated sampling procedures entailed randomly selecting city blocks, households, and individuals within those households. This sampling method ensures each an equal probability of being selected. And, in some surveys, a patient control group is included for validation purposes. Analytic procedures included the use of multivariate statistics which allow simultaneous control of a number of variables (Warheit et al., 1975). Multivariate analyses were particularly useful in interpreting data on racial and class comparisons. The number of minorities in community surveys increased, but there continued to be an inadequate representation of black people and black men in particular (Williams, 1986). Finally, the attempt to develop reliable measures consisted of test-retest changes in scores of treated and untreated groups and demonstrated consistency of results across various samples. But once again, the validity and reliability of mental health measures were tested with small samples of blacks.

As scientists searched for the ultimate valid and reliable mental health measure, a number of terminologies (e.g., subjective well-being, psychological distress, and depressive symptoms) and different types of measures were employed in mental health research. The measures typically tapped two distinct states: affective states and psychosomatic states. In view of these methodological changes, what have we learned about the mental health of blacks in the general population? In brief, we learned that blacks exhibit higher levels of psychological distress than whites (Neighbors, 1984). However, when social class is controlled, blacks either exhibit lower levels of distress than whites or exhibit distress levels equal to that of whites (for indepth reviews, see Neighbors, 1984 and Williams, 1986). As concluded by Neighbors, community surveys demonstrate in large, that race is not a significant factor in mental health. He further concludes that this finding is intriguing, considering that blacks are more often exposed to negative stressors than are whites. Unfortunately, the community surveys of the 1970s, like their predecessors, were subject to methodological limitations. For example, the community surveys were regional in scope, used a wide variety of measures, and relatively small black samples (Neighbors, 1984). Consequently, these shortcomings limited the generalizability of the findings and did not permit adequate socioeconomic breakdowns within black samples. The more recent studies on the issue of race and mental health corroborate the findings of research conducted in the 1970s (Kessler, 1979; Kessler & Neighbors, 1985; Neff, 1984). While these studies have reanalyzed previous data, the questions posed by researchers are different. For example, Kessler and Neighbors (1985) examined data from eight epidemiologic surveys in an attempt to test for an interactive effect of race and class. Essentially, their reanalysis demonstrated that: 1) blacks had significantly higher gross distress scores than whites; 2) once social class is introduced into the equation, race differences disappear; and 3) when examined further for an interactive effect, lower-income blacks report more distress than lower-income whites. In other words, the latter finding showed that racial differences in psychological distress were more pronounced among people in the lower classes. Kessler and Neighbors suggested that a failure to recognize interactive effects of this sort can lead to the effect of race being underestimated while the effect of social class being overestimated. They concluded by suggesting that future researchers investigate determinants of race differences in distress, other than social class. Moreover, Kessler and Neighbors' finding demonstrates the importance of intra-racial variations in mental health. The fact that middle-to-upper-income blacks exhibited lower levels of psychological distress than their lower-income counterparts implies that some blacks are more at risk for mental disorders than others. Moreover, as Neighbors (1984) notes, even among low-income blacks, levels of distress may vary when factors such as age, education, and access to support networks are examined. To date, epidemiologic community surveys have primarily focused on social class and racial comparisons. In particular, attempts to demonstrate the extent to which blacks and whites respond to social and environmental stresses often result in a unidimensional portrayal of blacks and inaccurate interpretations about correlates of mental health important for this group (Neighbors, 1984). National epidemiologic studies are needed to examine variations in mental health and illness among blacks (Williams, 1986). Key to conducting such studies is the development of sampling strategies that ensure adequate representation of both noninstitutionalized and institutionalized black people (Jackson, Neighbors, & Gurin, 1986; Williams, 1986).

Intra-Racial Comparisons of Mental Health

Much of the present knowledge on black mental health and illness stems from racial comparative paradigms. This method, however, does not address the issue of heterogeneity in the black population. The possibility that variations due to ethnicity, geographical location, education, religion, economic status, family structure, and gender has yet to be systematically tested on large, representative samples of blacks. Factors such as these have proven to be significant correlates of mental health and illness for the white population. The National Survey of Black Americans (NSBA) is one such attempt to address the need for intra-racial comparisons of black mental health (Jackson, et al., 1986). This cross-sectional study examined the mental health status, major and daily stresses, and coping strategies of 2,107 adults. In brief, their multivariate analysis demonstrated that education, employment status, and gender were significantly related to mental health. Men, employed persons, and persons with high education reported low psychological distress in comparison to their female, unemployed and low education counterparts. Jackson, et al. (1986) also found that older, never married persons were more likely to report psychological distress than were younger, never married persons. Finally, unlike most studies, this study did not report income as a significant correlate for global distress. A further analysis showed that income was negatively related to distress only for individuals who reported having economic problems. While only one national community survey on black mental health functioning exists, many local community surveys on relatively large samples have been conducted (e.g., 'Dressler, 1985; Dressler & Badger, 1985; Gary, 1985, 1986; McAdoo, 1983; Nobles, 1979).

The Institute for Urban Affairs and Research (IUAR) at Howard University has conducted five major surveys on mental health and related phenomena: Pathways: A Study of Black Informal Support Networks (Gary, Brown, Milburn, Thomas, & Lockley, 1984), Stable Black Families (Gary, Beatty, Berry, & Price, 1983), Community Participation (Wilson, 1981), Help-Seeking Behavior Among Black Males (Gary, Leashore, Howard, & Buckner-Dowell, 1983), and Conceptions of Mental Health (Gary, 1985). IUAR's research has been concentrated in the mid-Atlantic region of the country—Maryland, Virginia, and Washington—where there are large numbers of blacks. The major findings of each study will be highlighted to further our knowledge of subgroup variations within the black population regarding global mental health.

Pathways. In this study, the social support networks and their relationship to stress and mental health were examined in a sample of 451 adults residing in Richmond, Virginia. Depressive symptoms served as the mental health index. Significant independent relationships to depressive symptoms existed for sex, marital status, age, income, employment status, and education. Depressive symptoms were lowest for men, married individuals, middle-to old-aged persons, employed persons, individuals with a college background, and persons with a household income of $25,000 or more. Community participation was significantly related to depressive symptoms. Individuals with no community participation reported greater depressive symptoms than did those with some community participation. Finally, the majority of this sample reported that they were not aware of mental health facilities in their communities. In terms of the utilization of such facilities, only a small percentage of the respondents had used a mental health center within the past year.

Stable Black Families. The primary purpose of this study of 26 husband-wife and 24 single mother families residing in Washington, D.C. was to determine the critical factors and conditions that contribute to strong black family life. While this study's focus was on stability and strengths, it also identified the families' major concerns and problems. Considering that these families were viewed as stable and strong families by their community members (*note*: families were selected on the basis of nominations from various organizations), it was particularly interesting to assess their mental well-being. Using depressive symptoms as an index of mental health, the typical relationships were found. Men had lower depressive symptoms than women, married women had lower depressive symptoms than single women, and individuals with incomes above $25,000 had lower depressive symptoms than those with incomes less than $25,000.

Community Participation. One major objective of the community participation study was to systematically study intra-group differences in psychological well-being. In addition to the examination of the relationship of demographic factors to mental health, the study examined the influences of community participation, racial consciousness, and religious involvement on mental health. The sample consisted of 204 adults from two Virginia suburbs in the Washington, D.C. metropolitan area. Psychological well-being was measured by the psychopathology scale, self-rating of mental health, and the affect-balance scale. In general, an overwhelming majority of the sample reported positive affects, few symptoms, and rated their emotional health over the past year as good to excellent. Surprisingly, no significant demographic differences in psychological well-being were found. This was also the case for the sociocultural variables—community participation, religious involvement, and racial consciousness. One possible explanation for the absence of intra-group variation was that so few individuals perceived themselves as having poor psychological well-being.

Help-Seeking Behavior Among Black Males. This was a survey of 142 black men from the Washington, D.C. metropolitan area to examine life events, problems, psychological distress, and help-seeking behavior. Depressive symptoms represented the distress index. The major findings were that men who were 45 years or older, had family incomes above $20,000, experienced low conflict with mates, lived in households of three to four persons, and were employed reported the lowest levels of depressive symptoms. Sociocultural factors such as religious involvement, racial consciousness and community were not significantly related to depressive symptoms.

Conceptions of Mental Health. This was a survey of 411 Baltimore, Maryland residents' attitudes toward mental health centers. The Community Behavioral Inventory, based on 68 vignettes portraying blacks in a variety of situations, was used to tap attitudes and behaviors related to utilization of mental health centers, community involvement, church involvement, tolerance, of substance use, and racial consciousness. The analyses revealed that most of the respondents had neutral attitudes toward mental health centers, while at least a third of the sample held positive attitudes and a fifth held negative attitudes. Women and married persons were more likely to have positive attitudes than were men and unmarried respondents. Racial consciousness was the only sociocultural variable related to attitudes toward mental health centers. Individuals who scored high on the racial consciousness measure tended to have higher positive attitudes than did those who scored low.

In summary, the findings from the various IUAR studies strongly support the existence of intra-group differences in mental health on the basis of sociodemographic characteristics. These characteristics included income, sex, marital status, and age. Intra-group variations due to sociocultural characteristics were not consistently found, except for community participation and racial consciousness. This area, however, has not received further analysis because of the initial objectives of the studies. Much of the data is still being analyzed, using multivariate statistical techniques. Relationships between social support, stress and mental health are under investigation using the Pathways data. For example, preliminary analyses revealed that individuals who were unemployed were more likely to exhibit positive mental health when they were involved in support networks that were perceived as helpful rather than not helpful (Gary, Brown, Lockley, & Weaver, 1984). A finding such as this one illustrates the importance of examining subgroup variations. Information on the relationships between mental health and sociocultural characteristics is forthcoming.

Directions For Future Research

When one peruses the mental health literature, one immediately recognizes the need for more empirical research in all areas of mental health and illness. Tantamount to the need for more research are the need for more funds from public and private sources and the need for more black scientists on research review boards and in policy-making positions. Furthermore, in tandem with these needs is the need for the researchers to strengthen their relationships with practitioners(or social service agencies) and the lay community (Sue, et al.,1982). Collaboration with the lay community and practitioners in all aspects of the research process reduces conflict among the three groups, promotes the value and relevance of research, expedites data collection, and creates a pool of advocates for black mental health research. Sue, et al. suggest that an initial research priority should be to obtain systematic and accurate information on minorities. Research on minorities are for the most part at the elementary stages of development—the needs assessment stage. They note that basic demographic information, such as knowing how many Asians and Hispanics are in this country, is still lacking. This is also true for Afro Americans, particularly in reference to African American males. Basic knowledge about the prevalence of mental disorders within the black population is also lacking. Although there is some general knowledge about the number of blacks who are in treatment and the types of diagnoses they receive, little is known about their experiential history. More systematic research is needed on these individuals' family backgrounds, environmental conditions, psychosocial stresses, developmental and genetic histories, and socio-demographic characteristics. Systematic investigation of these factors provides scientists with the opportunity to identify individuals who are at particular risk for mental illness, the genetic and sociocultural precursors to mental illness, and intra-group variations in the prevalence, incidence, and types of mental illnesses. More research is needed to identify individuals who are mentally ill and remain in the community. Epidemiologic community surveys have attempted to determine the distribution of mental illness within the general population, but they have been hampered by the nonspecificity of short screening measures. These measures only permit one to estimate rates of global mental health or distress, rather than discrete psychiatric disorders. Consequently, it will be necessary to develop measures capable of classifying individuals according to various clinical categories. Indeed, these instruments must be relevant to the experiences of black people. It will be particularly important to discover how these individuals manage to remain in the community without receiving formal treatment. An examination of their major and minor stresses, adaptive capacities, and social networks may prove to be key factors in this regard. Other mental illness-related issues needing further research are the appropriateness of diagnostic and assessment measures and treatment methods to black people. Numerous studies document that blacks receive more severe diagnoses and tend to score higher on, for example, the MMPI paranoia and schizophrenia scales in comparison to their white counterparts (Gynther, 1972). In essence, blacks tend to have hallucinations, delusions, somatization, and hostility. These symptoms can be attributed to affective disorders or schizophrenia. But, in the case of blacks and Hispanics, these symptoms are usually diagnosed as schizophrenia. Research thus implies that clinicians' attitudes toward minority group members must be changed and that more structured diagnostic instruments are needed. Lawson (1986) suggests that biological measures be employed as assessment tools and in treatment. But, he also notes the need for more systematic research on inter-and intra-racial differences in response to psychotropic medications for different racial and ethnic patients, and the role of psychosocial factors in prescribing psychotropic medication. Not surprisingly black mental patients often receive higher dosages of medication than do whites, because blacks are typically perceived as more violent than whites. Although much has been learned about mental health and its correlates, there is room for expansion in this area. While it is now established that the mental health status of blacks is not significantly lower than the mental health of whites, little is known about subgroup differences among blacks. Moreover, little systematic attention is devoted to causal factors in positive mental health and the conceptions of mental health in the black community. Indicators of mental health such as self-esteem, racial consciousness, mastery, achievement, and happiness should be examined using national samples that consist of a true cross-section of black America. But before such large-scale studies can be conducted, the relevance and appropriateness of research concepts and instruments to blacks should receive systematic examination. Finally, theoretical models must be developed to permit meaningful analyses of black mental health and illness. Specific attention should be devoted to the influence of social and political structures on the mental health status of black people (Myers, 1982).

Summary

In this chapter, the importance of the research industry was discussed. Research and development expenditures were reviewed in terms of federal and private support, the percentage of funds received by universities and colleges, and the percentage of funds granted for various research areas. While it is clear that only a small number of black researchers receive grants, we lack systematic information on the reasons for such low involvement of blacks in this industry. A major segment of this chapter was devoted to an overview of the present state of the knowledge on black mental health and illness and the various limitations inherent in this knowledge base. Beginning with a discussion of the major conceptual and methodological problems, we proceeded to examine the literature on treatment rates and epidemiologic community surveys of mental health and illness. We concluded this section by reviewing the findings of mental health research conducted at the Institute for Urban Affairs and Research at Howard University. In the final section several suggestions were made concerning directions for future research. Primary among these suggestions was a need for more funding from public and private sources. Specific research areas in which scientists should give greater emphasis were outlined: a) a closer examination of discrete psychiatric disorders among blacks; b) the expansion of mental health research using national samples; c) a concentration on intra-racial comparisons of mental health and illness; and d) the development of culturally relevant theoretical models, concepts of mental health and illness, and research instruments.Until these suggestions are implemented in a comprehensive manner, the present state of knowledge on black mental health must be interpreted with some caution.

References

Adebimpe, V., (1981). Overview: White norms and psychiatric diagnosis of black patients. *American Journal of Psychiatry, 138,* 279-285.

Antunes, G., Gordon, C., Gaitz, C., & Scott, J., (1974). Ethnicity, socioeconomic status and the etiology of psychological distress. *Sociology and Social Research, 54,* 361-368.

Banks, W. C., (1976). White preference in blacks: A paradigm in search of a phenomenon. *Psychological Bulletin, 83,* 1179-1186.

Baskin, D., Bluestone, H., & Nelson, M., (1981). Ethnicity and psychiatric diagnosis. *Journal of Clinical Psychology, 37,* 529-537.

Billinglsey, A., (1968). *Black families in White America.* Englewood Cliffs, N. J.: Prentice-Hall.

Cannon, M. S. & Locke, B. Z., (1977). Being black is detrimental to one's mental health: Myth or reality? *Phylon, 38,* 408-428.

Carter, J. H., (1974). Recognizing psychiatric symptoms in black Americans. *Geriatrics, 29,* 95-99.

Comstock, G. & Helsing, K., (1976). Symptoms of depression in two communities. *Psychology of Medicine, 6,* 551-563.

Cox, A., (1979). A black-white comparison of differential diagnoses and treatment modalities in a community mental health center over time. *NABSW Black Caucus Journal, 10,* 3-8.

Dohrenwend, B. P., (1975). Sociocultural and social-psychological factors in the genesis of mental disorders. *Journal of Health and Social Behavior, 16,* 365-392.

Dohrenwend, B. P. & Dohrenwend, B. S., (1969). *Social status and psychological disorder: A causal inquiry.* New York: Wiley-Interscience.

Dressler, W. W., (1985). Extended family relationships, social support, and mental health in a southern black community. *Journal of Health and Social Behavior, 26,* 39-48.

Dressler, W. W. & Badger, L. W., (1985). Epidemiology of depressive symptoms in black communities: A comparative analysis. *Journal of Nervous and Mental Disease, 173,* 212-220.

Gary, L. E., (1986). Predicting interpersonal conflict between men and women. *American Behavioral Scientist, 29,* 635-646.

Gary, L. E., (1985). Attitudes toward human service organizations: Perspectives from an urban black community. *Journal of Applied Behavioral Science, 21,* 445-458.

Gary, L. E. (Ed.), (1978). *Mental health: A challenge to the black community.* Philadelphia, PA.: Dorrance.

Gary, L. E., Beatty, L., Berry, G., & Price, M., (1983). *Stable black families.* Washington, D. C.: Institute for Urban Affairs and Research, Howard University.

Gary, L. E., Brown, D. R., Lockley, D. S., & Weaver, G. D., (1984). The mental health consequences of unemployment. Paper presented at Congressional Black Caucus Health Braintrust, Washington, D. C.

Gary, L. E., Brown, D. R., Milburn, N., Thomas, V. G., & Lockley, D. S., (1984). *Pathways: A study of black informal support networks.* Washington, D. C.: Institute for Urban Affairs and Research, Howard University.

Gary, L. E., Leashore, B., Howard, C., & Buckner-Dowell, R., (1983). *Help-seeking behavior among black males.* Washington, D. C.: Institute for Urban Affairs and Research, Howard University.

Gullattee, A. C., (1969). The Negro psyche: Fact, fiction and fantasy. *Journal of the National Medical Association, 61,* 119-29.

Gurin, G., Veroff, J., & Feld, S., (1960). *Americans view their mental health.* New York: Basic Books.

Gynther, M. D., (1972). White norms and black MMPI's: A prescription for discrimination? *Psychological Bulletin 78,* 386-402.

Ilfeld, F., (1978). Psychological status of community resident along major demographic dimensions. *Archives of General Psychiatry, 35,* 716-724.

Jackson, J. S., Neighbors, H. W., & Gurin, G., (1986). Findings from a national survey of black mental health: Implications for practice and training. In M. R. Miranda & H. H. L. Kitano (Eds.), *Mental health research and practice in minority communities.* Rockville, MD.: National Institute of Mental Health, DHHS.

Jackson, J., Tucker, B., & Bowman, P., (1982). Conceptual and methodological problems in survey research on black Americans. In W. Liu (Ed.), *Methodological problems in minority research*. Chicago, Il.: Pacific/Asian American Mental Health Research Center.

Jones, E. E. & Korchin, S. J. (Eds.), (1982). *Minority mental health*. New York: Praeger.

Kessler, R. C., (1979). Stress, social status, and psychological distress. *Journal of Health and Social Behavior, 20,* 259-272.

Kessler, R. C. & Neighbors, H. W., (1985). A new perspective on relationships among race, social class and psychological distress. An Arbor, MI.: ISR, Survey Research Center, University of Michigan.

Lawson, W. B., (1986). Racial and ethnic factors in psychiatric research. *Hospital and Community Psychiatry, 37,* 50-54.

Leighton, D., Harding, J., Macklen, D., MacMillen, A., & Leighton, A., (1963). *The character of danger: Psychiatric symptoms in selected communities.* New York: Basic Books.

McAdoo, H. P., (1983). *Extended family support of single black mothers.* Columbia, MD.: Columbia Research Systems.

Meyers, H. F., (1982). Stress, ethnicity, and social class: A model for research with black populations. In E. E. Jones & S. J. Korchin (Eds.), *Minority mental health*. New York: Praeger.

National Institutes of Mental Health, (1986). *Research information source book, fiscal year 1985.* Rockville, MD.: Division of Biometry and Applied Sciences, NIMH.

National Institutes of Mental Health, (1981). *Characteristics of admissions to selected mental health facilities, 1975: An annotated book of charts and tables,* Series CN No. Rockville, MD.: U.S. Department of Health and Human Services.

National Institute of Mental Health, (1980). *Hispanic Americans and mental health services: A comparison of Hispanic, black, and white admissions to selected mental health facilities, 1975,* Series CN No. 3. Rockville, MD.: U.S. Department of Health and Human Services.

National Institute of Mental Health, (1975). *Report of the research task force.* Washington, D.C.: U.S. Government Printing Office.

Neff, J., (1984). Race differences and psychological distress: The effects of SES, urbancity and measurement strategy. *American Journal of Community Psychology, 12,* 337-351.

Neighbors, H. W., (1984). The distribution of psychiatric morbidity in black Americans: A review and suggestions for research. *Community Mental Health Journal, 20,* 169.

Nobles, W. W, (1979). *Mental health support systems in black families.* Washington, D.C.: U.S. Department of Health, Education, and Welfare.

President's Commission on Mental Health, (1978). *Report to the President* (Reports of Special Populations Subpanel on Mental Health of black Americans, Vol. III). Washington, D.C.: U.S. Government Printing Office.

Robinson, T. N., (1971). Minority research studies. Unpublished Mimeograph.

Snowden, L. & Todman, P., (1982). The psychological assessment of blacks: New and needed developments. In E. E. Jones & S. J. Korchin (Eds.), *Minority mental health*. New York: Praeger.

Srole, L., Langner, T., Michael, S., Opler, M., & Rennie, T., (1962). *Mental health in the metropolis: The mid-town Manhattan study* (Vol. I). New York: McGraw-Hill.

Sue, S., Ito, J., & Bradshaw, C., (1982). Ethnic minority research: Trends and directions. In E. E. Jones & S. J. Korchin (Eds.), *Minority mental health.* New York: Praeger.

Thomas, A., & Sillen, S. (Eds.), (1972). *Racism and psychiatry.* New York: Bruner/Mazel.

U.S. Bureau of the Census, (1985). *Statistical abstract of the United States 1986* (106th Edition). Washington, D.C.: U.S. Department of Commerce.

Warheit, G., Holzer, C., & Arey, S., (1975). Race and mental illness: An epidemiological update. *Journal of Health and Social Behavior, 16,* 243-256.

Warheit, G., Holzer, C., & Schwab, J., (1973). An analysis of social class and race differences in depressive symptomatology. *Journal of Health and Social Behavior, 14,* 291-299.

Weissman, M. & Klerman, G., (1978). Epidemiology of mental disorders: Emerging trends in the United States. *Archives of General Psychiatry, 35,* 705-712.

Williams, D., (1986). The epidemiology of mental illness in Afro-Americans. *Hospital and Community Psychiatry, 37,* 42-49.

Williams, R. L., (1974). Scientific racism and IQ—The silent mugging of the black community. *Psychology Today, 7,* 32, 34, 37-38, 41, 101.

Willie, C. V., Kramer, M., & Brown, B. S. (Eds), (1973). *Racism and mental health.* Pittsburgh, Pa.: University of Pittsburgh Press.

Wilson, M. J., (1981). Evaluating mental health status in black adults. In J. McAdoo & W. E. Cross, Jr. (Eds.), *Fifth conference on empirical research in black psychology.* Washington, D.C.: National Institute for Mental Health.

Race, Class and Ethics in Research: Belmont Principles to Functional Relevance

Phillip J. Bowman

Introduction

As in any area of professional practice, ethics among scientific researchers involve principles that govern improper and proper modes of conduct. Although all researchers are concerned with ethics, various scientific disciplines which conduct research on human subjects have emphasized different ethical issues. Moreover, standards for proper research conduct has shifted radically over time and vary across national settings. Ethical issues have been especially controversial in biomedical studies, but questionable human subject practices in psychological and social research have also been hotly debated in recent years (Kidder & Judd, 1986; Shaughnessy & Zechmeister, 1985). Despite the use of multiple methods, psychologists' extensive use of experimental designs has resulted in a special concern with the issue of deception (American Psychological Association, 1982). In contrast, social psychologists' and sociologists' more frequent use of sample survey methods leads to a greater emphasis on the issue of confidentiality (American Sociological Association, 1971). The extensive use of archival records by sociologists, economists and political scientists also make confidentiality a special issue (e.g. American Political Science Association, 1968). Anthropologists' preference for more intensive and qualitative ethnographic methods may account for the emphasis by the American Anthropological Association (1973) on the protection of general communities being studied (i.e., often racial-ethnic groups or Third World cultures).

Although questionable practices may occur in research on any group, race and/or class inequalities create special human subject vulnerabilities. For example, the so-called medical experiments carried out on Jews by Nazi German researchers in concentration camps were systematically guided by racism, ethnic hatred and bigotry. As a result of the War Crime Trials following World War II, the Nuremberg code was drafted in 1947 as a set of standards for judging physicians and other scientists who conducted experiments on concentration camp prisoners. This early code of conduct has served as a prototype for later guide-lines in the United States which have been initiated in response to questionable practices in biomedical, psychological and social research on vulnerable groups. In addition to treatment of subjects, the value implications of their selection, the problem definition and utilization of findings are also often complicated by race and class divisions.

Critical Ethical Issues

We turn now to a broader discussion of ethical issues involved in research on vulnerable race and class groups, followed by a more specific focus on African Americans. Two specific studies on African Americans will be highlighted to further illuminate crucial ethical issues, principles and guidelines with relevance to research on groups made vulnerable by race and class inequalities.

Vulnerable Race and Class Groups

Generally, scientific research on human subjects is conducted in academic, governmental, or foundational settings with data collection forays into various communities. Psychologists and other research sci-entists therefore occupy positions which tend to align them with mid-dle class perspectives, values and interests (Blauner & Wellman, 1973; Honigan, 1969; Montero, 1977). From this vantage point, the specific problems selected for research have usually been cast in terms of phe-nomena deemed problematic for societal management, system mainte-nance and the control of deviance. Hence, research has often focused special attention on groups perceived by white middle class standards to be weak or deviant: racial-ethnic minorities, the poor and welfare recip-ients, juvenile delinquents and criminals, alcoholics and drug addicts, patients and prisoners, children and old people, college students and military personnel. As groups which are often viewed as problematic (i.e., dependent, deficient, deserving special treatment, etc.), they have been especially vulnerable to misuses and abuses of scientific research. Members of such groups are disproportionately subjected to ethically questionable research practices; they may be attractive human subjects for both theoretical and applied research because they are easy to iso-late, lack power, or knowledge, or the will to resist.

To be sure, race and class bias may result in questionable ethical practices even when research scientists are well intentioned (e.g., Montero & Levin, 1977; Couchman, 1973). Many well intentioned researchers are seeking to advance the state of their discipline while producing what they believe will be socially useful information. However, serious ethical questions are raised when (1) research subjects are systematically selected from vulnerable race and class groups for studies without ample safeguards for their health, emotional well-being or dignity, (2) research problems are selected and defined narrowly in terms of middle class values to support victim blame theories, and (3) research findings are systematically utilized to support policies or programs to permit the manipulation of a less privileged group by a more advantaged and powerful group. This prevailing race and class bias in scientific research poses both theoretical problems for various disciplines as well as practical problems in efforts to resolve social issues of high national priority.

In scientific terms, the problem of race, class and ethics in research seriously undermines the theoretical goals of various disciplines (e.g., Jackson, Tucker & Bowman, 1990; Moore, 1973). Specifically, theory-building is too often based on an inadequate database, the range of competing hypotheses considered are commonly restricted, and forums are seldom organized with sufficient diversity for thorough and enlightened discussions of research findings. Hence, a less biased scientific research agenda based on problems defined in terms of various race, ethnic and class viewpoints would promote a fuller understanding of human behavior and social life. In more practical terms, the prevailing bias in scientific research restricts the development of more general knowledge useful for a wide range of societal groups (e.g., Bengton, Grigsby, Corry & Hruby, 1977). For African Americans and others, new ethical standards must both eliminate their special risks for mistreatment as research subjects and insure knowledge development helpful in their efforts to overcome race and class barriers and to improve their own life chances.

Research on African Americans: Case Studies

To further illuminate the problem of race, class and ethics in research the remainder of this paper highlights critical issues involved in two landmark studies on African Americans. First, the Tuskegee Syphilis Experiment highlights the special vulnerability of African Americans to unethical research practices and illustrates the importance of standard policies and procedures to protect human participants in scientific studies (Jones, 1981). Second, the National Surveys of Black Americans involved ethical issues where there remain less consensus (Jackson & Gurin, 1987; Jackson et al., 1990). Here emphasis is placed on the importance of new, emerging principles to insure significant involvement and functional relevance in research on vulnerable race and class groups.

Tuskegee Syphilis Experiment

Experimental methods continue to be the most widely employed design in both biomedical and psychological research. The Tuskegee Syphilis Experiment, conducted on a sample of low income black males between 1929 and 1972, spurred a process of legislative and administrative changes which have greatly increased the protection of human participants in biomedical, psychological and social research. In 1973, a U.S. Senate committee held special hearings directly prompted by the revelation of the Tuskegee Experiment which was finally halted after over 40 years. The National Research Act of 1974 called for the creation of a National Commission for the Protection of Human Subjects in Biomedical and Behavioral Research. In 1978, this Commission issued a report on a broad set of ethical principles to provide a basis on which specific policies could be formulated, criticized and interpreted. This report, titled "The Belmont Report: Ethical Principles and Guidelines for the Protection of Human Subjects," remains the primary foundation for the specific policies that currently govern research on humans. The National Research Act also required the formation of Institutional Review Boards at all research institutions, such as colleges and universities, to establish policies in line with the Belmont principles to control human subjects violations.

Background of the experiment: A case study The current protections enjoyed by human participants in research can be traced in large measure to the Tuskegee Syphilis Experiment. In 1929, the U.S. Public Health Service and the private Rosenwald Fund supported a series of demonstration programs for the control of syphilis. The demonstration project at Macon County, Alabama, ended in 1931, but a research idea for an extended monitoring of the effects of untreated syphilis emerged. The project staff tried to think of a way to continue their involvement with this large, unsolved public health problem, since funds for the screening and treatment demonstration program were about to end. What resulted was the Tuskegee Experiment which has become a monumental symbol of race and class immorality in scientific research.

The three stated objectives of the extended monitoring were: (1) to study the untreated course of syphilis in black people for comparison with an earlier sample of the white population; (2) to raise the consciousness of the public to the problem of syphilis, and (3) to maintain the momentum of public health work in the area by sustaining cooperative arrangements among state, local, and Tuskegee Institute medical personnel. The experimental monitoring of untreated syphilitics, which began as a short-term demonstration, was extended decade after decade into the 1970s. The researchers were initially intrigued by an incredible 36% syphilis rate, much of it transmitted congenitally (from infected mother to her fetus), but an insignificant rate of treatment. Study procedures included periodic checks of the untreated syphilitics, which required the painful and sometimes dangerous lumbar puncture method for diagnosing neural syphilis.

Manipulation of treatment   Initially penicillin, the present treatment for syphilis, was not yet available. However, the most scientifically unjustifiable manipulation of all came when penicillin treatment was systematically withheld from subjects for years despite its proven effectiveness. By 1933, the research project had involved 412 syphilitics and 204 controls (all black males) and had become committed to following up untreated cases to autopsy. Investigators actively worked, often in collaboration with other health workers, to withhold effective treatment from the identified cases. The researchers argued that penicillin treatment would be ineffective in the late states of their subjects diseases and that scientific benefits of studying their elderly subjects justified continuation of the project. Unknown to the research participants, they had become subjects of a study dedicated to preserving their diseases until death. When the subjects died, families were offered burial stipends in exchange for permission to perform autopsies.

There has now been much debate about why the Tuskegee Experiment was condoned and managed to escape termination for four decades. Clearly, some of the reasons have to do with race and class of the victims—blacks, impoverished, diseased elderly in the rural south especially vulnerable to the local and federal white medical power structure. Subjects received, in exchange for their participation, noncurative medical and more frequent medical attention than they might have received otherwise. In additional to vulnerabilities of the victims, we must also focus on the culpability of the researchers. One troublesome aspect of the Tuskegee Experiment for the research establishment was that the investigators seemed to be well intentioned with little incentive other than proper scientific mission and altruism. They were friendly and even affectionate with their subjects, took pride in their work, published their findings in the scientific literature, and welcomed visiting scientists and medical workers. Early complaints were met with surprise, ignored or rejected as uninformed in informal peer reviews.

At any rate, the Tuskegee Experiment debate intensified the demand for more systematic policies, safeguards and formal reviews to prevent future abuses with human subjects. The study also raised clear race and class issues with the suspicion that the study would not have been undertaken with white or middle class research subjects. In fact, the National Medical Association has gone so far as to charge the study officials with genocide of poor and uneducated blacks. They point to the fact that many of the research subjects, who were systematically untreated, died or were severely incapacitated as a result of their syphilis. The Tuskegee Experiment, along with other abuses of research on vulnerable human subjects, resulted in the Belmont principles which now anchor the specific codes of conduct considered standard among researchers (Deiner & Crandall, 1978; Jones, 1981; Kamin, 1974). The special vulnerabilities of African Americans, and other groups facing race and class inequalities, make such guidelines for the protection of human subjects especially critical (e.g., Burt, 1972; Hearnshaw, 1979; Jones, 1971).

Belmont Principles: The Protection of Human Subjects

Ethical principles that have long guided scientific inquiry in various disciplines include the responsibility to seek knowledge, to conduct studies in a competent manner, to report findings accurately, to manage research resources honestly, to acknowledge fairly in scientific reports individuals who contributed to a study, to consider the consequences of a research effort for society, and to publicly speak out on societal concerns that are related to a scientific expertise (Deiner & Crandall, 1978). Going beyond these general ethical issues, the Belmont report focused specifically on three principles to guide policies and guidelines for the protection of human subjects — *personal respect, beneficence* and *justice*.

First, the principle of *personal respect* involves both the requirement to acknowledge the research subject's right to autonomy and the requirement to protect those with diminished autonomy. These principles require specific policies to insure that subjects participate in the study voluntarily and have adequate information about the research situation and possible consequences. These guidelines protect subjects from questionable practices such as involving people in studies without their knowledge or consent, coercing people to participate, withholding from subjects the true nature of the study, deceiving research subjects, violating the self-determination of subjects through behavioral control or character change, invading the privacy of research subjects and failing to treat them with fairness and consideration.

The principle of *beneficence* not only requires that research subjects not be harmed, but that the maximizing of possible benefits also occur.

This principle dictates specific safeguards to minimize risks that might occur to subjects, and to maximize benefits to subjects, researchers, scientific disciplines and the larger society. A special dilemma may arise in making decisions about when possible benefits justify certain risks, and when benefits should be foregone due to risks. Safeguards need to discourage studies which involve more than the minimal risks of everyday life, and eliminate questionable practices such as leading subjects to commit acts that diminish their self-esteem, exposing subjects to mental or physical stress, withholding benefits from subjects in the control groups, not removing harmful aftereffects, and failing to maintain pledges of anonymity or confidentiality.

The principle of *justice* demands that scientific research not unduly involve subjects unlikely to benefit from any application of study findings. Justice directly involves fairness in the distribution of who ought to bear the burden of research and who ought to receive its benefits. This principle calls for specific guidelines to eliminate injustice that occurs when burdens and benefits are distributed unfairly. Special safeguards need to insure that vulnerable race and class groups are not systematically selected because of their compromised position, their open vulnerability, or their manipulability. These guidelines seek to discourage ethical problems in the overselection of vulnerable subjects, misuse of research results, and underutilization of findings.

National Surveys of African Americans

Sample survey research is widely used technology for promoting the goals of social scientists and human service practitioners. The systematic collection and analysis of questionnaire data from probability samples have emerged as important enterprises for both theory building and effective service delivery. More and more, professionals in social welfare, public health, employment training, and other human resource programs are depending on survey data for assessments of needs, program evaluations, policy decisions, and long-range planning.

A major challenge to those responsible for producing such data is to overcome the cynicism toward research that is prevalent among high-risk minority populations with special human service needs. African Americans and other racial and ethnic minority groups experience more poverty and racial discrimination and are at a higher risk for a wide range of related social problems than others in this country. However, they have expressed widespread resistance to survey studies despite the role of such studies in the development and delivery of more responsive services. "Is this another . . . study by those . . . ?" "What good is it going to do us?" "I am not interested!" Such responses to researchers conducting survey studies in ethnic minority communities became commonplace during the last two decades and will probably remain a serious challenge throughout the 1990s. Why is there such cynicism and resistance to survey research among racial minorities? What are some of the emerging strategies being utilized to reduce such resistance?

The central thesis of this chapter is that future survey studies in racial minority communities are seriously threatened unless new norms of accountability are articulated, codified, and practiced. These new standards must respond to the specific grievances of study respondents regarding the ethics and validity of research that does not incorporate their interests. As Bengstson et al. noted, these criticisms raise serious

> . . . questions concerning the value of scholarly studies with no immediate payoff to groups from whom data are collected, and concerning the validity of studies designed and interpreted by white middle class researchers without roots in minority communities.

To offset such criticism, several survey researchers have responded with innovative practical, methodological, and theoretical approaches. Most of these efforts fall short of the most strident demands for "community control" and "relevance to community needs" advanced by research subjects and community advocates. Nevertheless, these strategies represent emerging standards of responsiveness among survey researchers toward racial and ethnic populations that are no longer readily accessible subject pools. In addition to conventional ethical and scientific considerations, research among racial minorities also must be guided by what may be referred to as the principles of *significant involvement* and *functional relevance*. In this context, *significant involvement* calls for members of the group under study to have a central role in the entire research process. *Functional relevance* dictates that studies should operate to promote the expressed needs and perspectives of the study population.

To help clarify these two principles, the author will briefly summarize related methods and strategies used by past survey researchers to adapt to resistance in high-risk minority populations. I will then critique these strategies in light of the concepts of significant involvement and functional relevance and describe how these principles were incorporated into all phases on an innovative national survey of African Americans conducted in 1979 and 1980. Although this illustration focuses primarily on the implications of these principles for research on African Americans, such standards of accountability also are relevant for studies conducted among Mexican Americans, Native Americans, and other high-risk groups who suffer from socially structured inequalities.

Adaptive Strategies

To salvage studies under increasing fire by minority communities, survey researchers responded with an array of innovations to conventional procedures. A review of the literature indicates that these innovations were centered on four main strategies: (1) using indigenous interviewers, (2) seeking assistance from indigenous consultants or advisory groups, (3) instituting trade-off and exchange arrangements, and (4) targeting research explicitly to the needs of the community.

Indigenous interviewers. Among the first and most widely adopted strategies was the utilization of indigenous interviewers matched by race and sometimes by social class background. In her research on survey studies of the poor conducted between 1967 and 1972, Weiss reported that three-quarters of the studies tried to match interviewers by race or ethnicity. The reasons given for matching interviewers by race focused on the effectiveness of this strategy for promoting rapport, access of interviewers to respondents, and communication; indigenous interviewers also reduce biased responses, locate hard-to-find respondents, and eliminate the difficulty of recruiting nonindigenous interviewers for roles with high security risk in unfamiliar communities.

Community consultants and groups. Another common practice is to make contacts with indigenous consultants or community groups. When consultants are employed, they usually are not research scientists, but, rather community liaisons. Caplan presented a classic example of this procedure in his discussion of the indigenous "anchorman's" role in ghetto research:

> Even though the most crucial role played by this person would be during the period of actual data collection, there are a variety of important social services he can provide prior to that time. He knows how to explain the purpose of the interview to the community. He can help train interviewers . . . He can provide important criticism of the language and phrasing of the interview items and can judge sensitivity to content. His knowledge of target areas can enable the sampling section to overcome the drawbacks of outdated census information and thereby help reduce sampling error . . . He knows how to find people in casual settings and how to ease the mind of respondents, many of whom may have learned from neighbors that a "strange man" (the interviewer) came around wanting to ask them some questions.

Caplan went on to say that the role of the ghetto anchorman also includes lending local "legitimacy" to the survey operation, providing emotional support to interviewers, and, once the fieldwork is complete and editing has begun, helping reduce ambiguities in the language used by respondents. When collaboration is sought with advisory committees or contact is made with the community groups rather than individuals, the assistance requested still has been largely restricted to the role of indigenous anchorman.

Trade-off and exchange arrangements. An ironic consequence of making contact with community members, especially in groups, is that it often has increased organized resistance to survey research because community groups have been the primary vehicles through which resistance is articulated as specific grievances and demands. To neutralize the charges of exploitation, racism, and elitism, survey researchers often have attempted to barter with a number of practical trade-off strategies.

After reviewing several studies that attempted to circumvent problems of community resistance, Cromwell, Vaughan, and Mindel concluded:

> A summary of this work suggests the importance of the exchange process in the form of a number of trade-offs between researcher and community residents in return for cooperation. These trade-offs might include hiring local persons to do the field work, paying protection money, reporting the results of the research to community residents, and providing technical assistance to the community upon request.

Other exchange strategies have included payments to research subjects for their time and such nontraditional practices as allowing community representatives to have collegial input into theoretical conceptualization and veto power over the uses that may be made of the research, including decisions about publication. Needless to say, the resistance of many traditional survey researchers to exchange strategies, especially the more radical ones, often has been as adamant as that of community advocates towards the proposed studies of the survey researchers.

Relevance to community needs. Particularly challenging to conventional white middle class researchers conducting studies in socially "distant" ethnic communities has been the demand to make studies relevant to community needs. As was just noted, the agreement to feed results back to community residents and to promote the utilization of findings have been frequent components of exchange strategies. In addition, survey researchers increasingly have found it necessary to gear their studies to theoretical issues that are relevant to pressing community problems and to avoid invidious victim-blaming perspectives in favor of more culturally sensitive approaches.

In some cases, community residents, in their demands for relevance have rejected scientific and academic surveys altogether. For example, Bengston et al. (1977) were surprised when representatives from the minority communities under study questioned the value of their scientific research goals, despite efforts to ensure cultural sensitivity and relevance to policy issues. To gain the support of community representatives, these researchers had to incorporate several exchange strategies and demonstrate that their findings were useful not only to academics and policymakers but to local minority communities. Even though assessments of needs and social program evaluations often are explicitly linked to pressing community problems, respondents may have to be convinced of their relevance. Despite their role in reducing resistance, strategies to improve relevance sometimes have been viewed as a compromise to the integrity of researchers' goals.

Critique of Adaptive Strategies

To be sure, the unconventional procedures of using indigenous interviewers, soliciting the support of community consultants and local groups, offering trade-offs, and explicitly designing studies relevant to a community's needs have tended to reduce subordinate group members' resistance to survey research. Yet, these strategies certainly have not dissolved friction and often fall far short of eliminating the sources of the grievances of community residents. This persistent opposition, in spite of innovative strategies, continues to challenge survey researchers. However, a closer look at the various strategies points up several limitations in relation to the principles of significant involvement and functional relevance that remain at the heart of community resistance.

Although adaptive strategies provide a measure of community involvement and relevance, minority groups have called for "more" control and commitment to relevance. Specifically, they have demanded that committed indigenous researchers be allowed to design studies that take into account the expressed needs of community representatives and to make explicit arrangements to promote analysis, dissemination, and utilization activities that will improve the lives of high-risk minority groups. These demands are the central challenge to survey research in minority communities and threaten to make future studies even more arduous than before. Stressing the difficulty of finding "qualified" indigenous study directors, most survey researchers question the scholarly integrity of studies when community representatives who are not trained as research scientists control key research decisions. Few researchers are willing to give up the prerogative of making decisions about the substance, design, or reporting of their findings, despite rhetoric calling for community involvement.

In an insightful study of the relationship of research organizations to the subordinate groups they study, Weiss noted a clear pattern of restricted community involvement and an unresponsiveness to the needs of community residents. The involvement of community representatives was essentially limited to interviewing, field logistics, and marginal advisory roles to reduce the practical problems of data collection. Weiss found that most often community members were contacted to promote acceptance of the study or to help recruit interviewers; they seldom were asked to contribute "to the formulation of research objectives or to the interpretation or dissemination of the findings." Noting that the past actions of research organizations have been taken primarily in the service of their studies, she concluded:

> It appears that the payoff to the low income or minority community will come, if at all, in the analysis of research data and the uses made of the findings. Therefore the main responsibility of researchers is to formulate research from the onset in ways that respect the concerns and rights of respondents . . . We can also try to be more sensitive to alternative perspectives in the formulations and design of research and interpretation of our data. There may even be some dignity enhancing contributions that we can make during field work that we seem so far to have missed.

National Survey: A Case Study

To illustrate further how emerging strategies can be extended to reflect more fully the principles of significant involvement and functional relevance, the author will highlight features of the National Survey of African Americans. The manner in which this survey was planned, designed, and conducted represents an impressive illustration of how a major research organization incorporates new standards of accountability to ensure the inclusion of these two principles. The methodological details of the survey are presented elsewhere. The discussion in this article is limited to the strategies used to ensure significant involvement and functional relevance at each phase of the research process: planning, conceptualization, development of the questionnaire, data collection, and analysis.

Sponsors and Purpose

The survey consists of three major components: (1) the Study of African American Life—a national cross-sectional study of 2,107 African American adults—sponsored by the National Institutes of Mental Health (NIMH), (2) the Three-Generational Family Study—a national study of over 1,000 three-generational African American families—sponsored by the National Institute on Aging, and (3) a postdoctoral training program in survey research sponsored by NIMH. The Ford Foundation provided supplementary funds to assist in the collection and analysis of data.

The two national studies involved interviews conducted during 1979 and 1980 with over 3,400 African Americans living in over seventy-six distinct areas in the continental United States. Because of the probability sampling method, the findings are accurately generalizable to (1) the entire black population of adults at least 18 years old and (2) three-generational black families of grandparents, parents, and grandchildren at least 14 years of age. The general purpose of both these massive studies was to generate a national data base for more penetrating analyses of factors that threaten and promote well-being among African Americans and to support the socially responsible utilization of findings.

The areas covered in the two-hour interviews included the sociodemographic and educational background of respondents and issues of underemployment-unemployment and economic status, mental and physical health status, life stress and utilization of resources, family and community support systems, and ethnic identity and political participation. Although data from the study of adults provide a basis for examining these theoretically and policy-relevant areas in heterogeneous subgroups of the black population, data from the study of three-generational families permit a unique analysis of sociocultural change and continuity across generations. The postdoctoral training program offers opportunities to promote analysis, dissemination, and utilization activities among researchers from the study population.

Planning

As noted earlier, most survey research in black communities has failed to involve the indigenous population in the planning and design of studies. Also, few studies have systematically focused on substantive issues identified as critical by members of the black community. Most of the Ph.D.–level staff members, including the principal investigator of this national survey, were black. These staff members assumed the primary responsibility for setting the goals and devising the general research strategy. To be sure, the black research scientists relied heavily on advice from various technical experts and colleagues. Consultation with nonblack sampling, field, and coding experts and senior program directors with extensive experience in large-scale survey research proved critical to the success of the project.

However, decision making and the formulation of objectives remained the primary responsibilities of the black research staff and an expanding number of other black experts. Particularly critical at the planning stage was input from an advisory board of African American scholars and human service experts who contributed to the rich interdisciplinary substantive focus of the study. The advisory board members helped delineate the overall plan for the study and were consulted at several other phases in the process.

Development of the Questionnaire

To broaden the involvement of the study population in the conceptualization and development of the questionnaire, the primary research staff used several strategies. First, members of the advisory board were consulted to help formulate specific objectives, concepts, and hypotheses that were particularly sensitive to the unique perspectives of the black population. Second, work groups, consisting of a primary researcher and black graduate students from various social science and professional disciplines, were organized in each major substantive area of interest. These work groups were charged with making an extensive, critical review of the literature as a basis for conceptualizing specific factors that bear on the quality of life of African Americans. They were encouraged to develop theoretical approaches and concepts that represent alternatives to those that guide traditional victim-blaming studies and policy orientations.

Third, grass-roots focus groups of four or five black adults from diverse backgrounds were organized to "reality test" further the hypotheses and concepts developed by the work groups. This approach, which adapted a procedure often utilized in market research, included a small-group discussion format to scrutinize further and refine the theoretical and conceptual perspectives. Together, input from advisory board, graduate students, and grass-roots focus groups broadened the involvement of community representatives and resulted in a substantive focus that better reflects their expressed concerns.

The principles of significant involvement and functional relevance also guided the process by which abstract study concepts were translated into specific items on the questionnaire. The senior staff-graduate student work groups evaluated existing measures from other studies. Their reviews resulted in the preliminary selection of some standard items, the modification of several others, and the development of new measures to operationalize innovative approaches or concepts for which no existing measures were appropriate. To go beyond standard procedures geared toward measurement equivalence, a modified back-translation procedure was adapted to ensure conceptual equivalence and cultural sensitivity. Back-translation is a procedure, often used in cross-cultural research, of successive translations to produce questions that have comparable meaning in two or more cultures. Although originally used to translate entire questionnaires from one language to another, the procedure has increasingly been used in small-group settings to develop more meaningful questions for special cultural or subcultural groups.

The focus-group discussions and the back-translation of preliminary questions resulted in final wordings of questions that had a shared meaning among the research staff and the various community groups with divergent backgrounds. Open-ended probes of many of these questions were included in two extensive pretests to develop further a set of questions in the final questionnaire that had greater meaning for and were more culturally sensitive and relevant to the study population. Thus, the senior staff-graduate student work groups, focus-back-translation groups, and extensive pretest samples in urban and rural areas in the North and South allowed input from expanding subgroups of the study population in the development of the questionnaire.

These procedures increased accountability by enabling numerous representatives of the black population to help specify concepts and question wordings that are better geared to the realities of their lives. For example, such input led to the inclusion of several questions on the role of religion as a major source of material, emotional, and community support. Moreover, innovative conceptual and measurement approaches to investigating such issues as discouragement in job searches, illness behavior, racial identity, and quality of life were developed through the various modes of involvement.

Data Collection

In line with the adaptive strategies discussed earlier, the survey's field procedures included extensive training and employment of indigenous interviewers, the use of local community leaders as regional field coordinators, and the development of contacts in various community organizations. Several other exchange strategies were utilized, including payment of subjects, security escorts for interviewers on request, and the

commitment to send respondents and community leaders a brief research report. The national data-collection operation was supervised by
senior staff members who not only had lived in predominantly black
communities, but had extensive experience in coordinating field logistics in such areas. This led to the development of more efficient sampling and interviewing procedures that were better geared to the reality
of black communities.

Equally important as data collection strategies in reducing resistance to the survey were public relations activities that emphasized its
relevance for advancing new theoretical perspectives and approaches to
solving problems of concern to black people. These activities were conducted after the extensive training of interviewers in community relations. Specific activities included active communication with field staff
and community leaders, persuasive doorstep techniques, follow-up letters to those who initially refused, and strategic use of media publicity.
To be sure, these strategies had a marked effect on the enthusiasm of
interviewers, respondents, community leaders, and study staff throughout the arduous field period. Such strategies not only enhanced the view
that indigenous community members were significantly involved in the
survey but they legitimated the purpose of the study as reflecting community interests. Public relations activities that projected an image of
significant involvement and functional relevance combined with other
adaptive field procedures to reduce resistance among respondents. The
overall response rate was about 70 percent, despite the large proportion
of the national probability sample that resides in urban areas where
household surveys are difficult to conduct.

Data Analysis and Reporting

As Weiss noted, the black community should receive the greatest
payoff from survey research from the way data are analyzed and in the
use made of the findings. Several arrangements have been implemented
and others planned to ensure that the analysis, interpretation, dissemination, and utilization of the data are consistent with the standards of
significant involvement and functional relevance. First, all study respondents received an initial report of the preliminary analysis and
have been placed on a mailing list to receive future information about
the study. Second, the overall objectives of the research effort—innovative conceptual approaches and a rich set of indicators—enhance the
utility of the data for analysis that is particularly relevant to the interests
of the community. Third, the analysis of data by the black senior research staff, graduate students, and national advisory board also should

promote specific analytic themes and an interpretation of findings that are particularly sensitive to unique aspects of the black experience.

The postdoctoral training program affords an increasing number of black researchers the opportunity to develop stronger research skills and to contribute to analysis, dissemination, and utilization goals of the research program. It makes the data available to new and established doctoral-level researchers for secondary analyses. This is the primary vehicle for providing systematic access to the national data on black adults and three-generational families.

Although more and more black doctorates are receiving research training in the behavioral sciences, only a few have the requisite skills or access to resources necessary to conduct penetrating analyses of the national survey data. The program has provided such opportunities to sixteen postdoctoral scholars since 1980. It is unique in that it builds on the internationally known resources of the University of Michigan's Institute for Social Research and provides postdoctoral fellows with technical assistance for data analysis, intensive summer research training in multivariate analysis, and special seminars and workshops. Collaborative research conducted among senior researchers, graduate students, and postdoctoral fellows has resulted in several papers that have been presented at professional meetings and in published articles. Moreover, several dissertations that analyze these data have been completed, and three major monographs are in progress that focus on themes, such as African American life at the threshold of the 1980s, coping with stress in black America, and the resources of older African Americans. The overall goal is to produce scholarly and policy-relevant data analyses that provide unique insight into African American life and to promote the dissemination and utilization of these findings for more responsive interventions, programs, and services that enhance the well-being of the black population.

Conclusion

Past abuses of human subjects in scientific research have led to a growing concern with related ethical issues and policies to prevent future violations. Because of race and class inequalities, African Americans and other groups continue to be especially vulnerable to questionable research practices. The Tuskegee Syphilis Experiment highlights these special vulnerabilities and also provided the impetus for the formulation of more stringent policies to protect human subjects in research. The Belmont principles of personal respect, beneficence and justice have led to guidelines and safeguards which should indeed help prevent future abuses. However, persistent inequalities make it important to monitor the ethics of research on vulnerable groups in low income communities, institutions and other settings. Also increased attention should also be given to other emerging ethical issues in high risk communities such as significant involvement and functional relevance.

The responsibility that survey researchers assume for incorporating new standards of accountability into the research process may determine the future of survey studies among blacks and other subordinate groups. The legitimacy of survey research is no longer judged solely on the grounds of the research design or on the contribution to scholarship, but also on the level of involvement by group representatives in the research process and the benefits accrued to the community under study. Although a challenge to past practice, these new rulings have given way to innovative practical, methodological, and theoretical approaches. These adaptive strategies, in turn, offer great potential for the advancement of the research goals of social science and human service organizations in high-risk minority populations. Future survey studies among other minority groups would do well to consider the various strategies and procedures utilized in the exemplary national study of African American life. The various principles and techniques highlighted in this article should be particularly helpful to human service agencies that look to survey research as a source of data for assessments of needs and program planning in local communities. Researchers may have to become more committed to design of responsive and relevant studies and more creative in communicating the purpose and results of their studies to community representatives. Research on subordinate racial and ethnic groups should not only have a role in advancing the paradigms of scholars or bureaucrats, but also consider and incorporate the perspectives and interests of the study population. The incorporation of these perspectives and interests would further advance the goals of scientific inquiry and problem-oriented research.

References

American Anthropological Association (AAA). (1973). *Professional ethics.* Washington, D.C.: American Anthropological Association.

American Political Science Association Committee on Professional Standards and Responsibilities (APSA). (1968). Ethical problems of academic political scientists. *P.S., Newsletter of the American Political Science Association,* pp. 1, 3.

American Psychological Association (APA). (1982). *Ethical principles in the conduct of research with human participants.* Washington, D.C.: American Psychological Association.

American Sociological Association (ASA). (1971). *Code of Ethics.* Washington, D.C.: American Sociological Association.

Bengston, V.L., Grigsby, E., Corry, E.M., & Hruby, M. (1977). Relating academic research to community concerns. *Journal of Social Issues, 33,* 75-92.

Blauner, R., & Wellman, D. (1973). Toward the decolonization of social research. In J. Ladner (Ed.), *The death of white sociology* (pp. 310-330). New York: Random House.

Burt, C. (1972). Inheritance of general intelligence. *American Psychologist, 27,* 175-190.

Caplan, N. (1969). The indigenous anchorman: A solution to some ghetto survey problems. *The Analyst, 1,* 20-34.

Couchman, I. (1973). Notes from a white researcher in black society. *Journal of Social Issues, 29,* 45-52.

Cromwell, R.E., Vaughn, E.C., & Mindel, C.H. (1975). Ethnic minority family research in an urban setting: A process of exchange. *American Sociologist, 10,* 141-150.

Diener, E., & Crandall, R. (1978). *Ethics in social and behavioral research.* Chicago: University of Chicago Press.

Fein, E. (1971). Inner city interviewing: Some perspectives. *Public Opinion Quarterly, 34,* 625-629.

Guttentag, M. (1973). Relevance and values in urban research. In commentary, *Human Organization, 30,* 205-208.

Hearnshaw, L.S. (1979). *Cyril Burt, Psychologist.* London: Hodder & Stoughton.

Hessler, R.M., & New, P.K. (1972). Research as a process of exchange. *American Sociologist, 7* 13-15.

Honigmann, J. (1969). Middle class values and cross-cultural understanding. In J. Finney (Ed.), *Culture change, mental health, and poverty.* New York: Simon & Schuster.

Jackson, J.S., & Gurin, G. (1987). *National survey of black Americans.* Ann Arbor, MI: Institute for Social Research.

Jackson, J.S., Tucker, B., & Bowman, P.J. (1990). Conceptual and methodological problems in survey research on black Americans. In R.L. Jones (Ed.), *Advances in black psychology.* Berkeley, CA: Cobb & Henry.

Jacobson, D. (1971). Comment on Guttentag. In commentary, *Human Organization, 30,* 208.

Josephson, E. (1970). Resistance to community surveys. *Social Problems, 18,* 117-129.

Jones, J.M. (1981). *Bad blood: The Tuskegee syphilis experiment.* New York: Free Press.

Jones, R.S. (1971, February). The sociology of knowledge: Proving blacks inferior, 1870-1930. *Black World*, 4-19.

Kamin, L.J. (1974). *The science and politics of IQ.* Hillsdale, NJ: Erlbaum.

Kidder, L.H., & Judd, C.M. (1986). *Research methods in social relations.* New York: Holt, Rinehart & Winston.

Lansing, J., Withey, S.B., & Wolf, A.C. (1971). Working papers on survey research in poverty areas. Ann Arbor, Mich.: Institute for Social Research.

Montero, D. (1977). Research among racial and cultural minorities: An overview. *Journal of Social Issues, 33,* 1-10.

Montero, D., & Levin, G.N. (Eds.) (1977). Research among racial and cultural minorities: Problems, prospects, and pitfalls. *Journal of Social Issues, 33,* 4.

Moore, J.W. (1967). Political and ethical problems in a large scale study of a minority population. In G. Sjoberg (Ed.), *Ethnics, politics, and social research.* Cambridge, Mass.: Schenkman.

Moore, J.W. (1973). Social constraints on sociological knowledge: Academics and research concerning minorities. *Social Problems, 21,* 65-77.

Myers, V. (1977). Survey methods for minority populations. *Journal of Social Issues, 33,* 11-19.

Schuman, H., & Converse, J.M. (1971). The effects of black and white interviewers on black responses in 1968. *Public Opinion Quarterly, 35,* 44-68.

Shaughnessy, J., & Zechmeister, E.B. (1985). *Research methods in psychology.* New York: Alfred A. Knopf.

Spiegel, H.B., & Alicea, V.G. (1969). The trade-off strategy in community research. *Social Science Quarterly, 50,* 593-603.

Voss, H.L. (1966). Pitfalls in social research: A case study. *American Sociologist, 3,* 136-140.

Weinberg, E. (1971). *Community surveys with local talent: A handbook.* Chicago: National Opinion Research Center.

Weiss, C. (1977). Survey researchers and minority communities. *Journal of Social Issues, 33,* 20-35.

Williams, J.A. (1964). Interviewer-respondent Interaction: A case study of bias in the information interview. *Sociometry, 27,* 338-352.

X (Clark), C. (1973). The white researcher in black society. *Journal of Social Issues, 29,* 1.

Indexes

Author Index

Subject Index